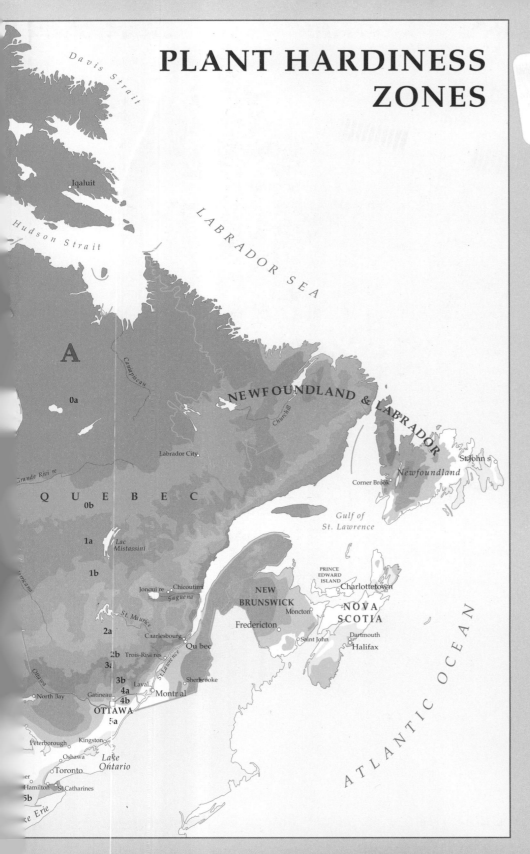

GARDEN PLANTS
AND FLOWERS

GARDEN PLANTS
AND FLOWERS

CANADIAN EDITION

IAN SPENCE

EDITOR **LORRAINE JOHNSON**

Editor, Canada	Julia Roles
Project Editor, Canada	Ian Whitelaw
Senior Editors	Annelise Evans, Jill Hamilton
Senior Art Editor	Alison Donovan
Project Art Editor	Murdo Culver
Designers	Gillian Andrews, Tai Blanche, Vanessa Hamilton, Rachael Smith
Editors	Louise Abbott Pamela Brown, Candida Frith-Macdonald, Letitia Luff, Mary Sutherland
Managing Editor	Anna Kruger
Managing Art Editor	Lee Griffiths
DTP Designers	Milos Orlovic, Louise Waller
Media Resources	Lucy Claxton, Richard Dabb
Picture Research	Samantha Nunn
Production Controller	Mandy Inness

First Canadian Edition, 2006

Copyright © 2003, 2006 Dorling Kindersley Limited
Text copyright © Ian Spence

Dorling Kindersley is represented in Canada by
Tourmaline Editions Inc.
662 King Street West, Suite 304
Toronto, Ontario M5V 1M7

Library and Archives Canada Cataloguing in Publication

Spence, Ian
Garden plants and flowers : A-Z guide to the best plants for your
garden / Ian Spence. -- 1st Canadian ed. / Lorraine Johnson.

Includes index.
ISBN-13: 978-1-55363-064-7
ISBN-10: 1-55363-064-5

1. Plants, Ornamental--Encyclopedias. I. Johnson, Lorraine, 1960-
II. Title.

SB404.9.S74 2006   635.9'03   C2005-905858-7

Color reproduction by Colourscan, Singapore
Printed and bound by Toppan Printing, Hong Kong

06 07 08 09 7 6 5 4 3 2 1

Discover more at
www.dk.com

Contents

6   Introduction

A–Z OF GARDEN PLANTS

8

Trees and shrubs

10

12   Using trees and shrubs

14   A–Z of trees and shrubs, including
special features on:

- *Camellia* • Cherry (*Prunus*) • Dogwood
(*Cornus*) • *Fuchsia* • Heather (*Erica*)
- *Hydrangea* • Maple (*Acer*) • *Rhododendron*
- *Rosa* • *Viburnum*

Climbing plants

130

132   Using climbers in the garden

134   A–Z of climbing plants, including special
features on:

- *Clematis* • *Rosa*

Flowering plants

156

158   Using flowering plants – perennials,
annuals and biennials, and bulbs

166   A–Z of flowering plants, including
special features on:

- *Aster* • *Chrysanthemum* • Daffodil (*Narcissus*)
- *Dahlia* • *Geranium* • *Hosta* • *Iris*
- *Lilium* • *Pelargonium* • Pinks (*Dianthus*)
- Primrose (*Primula*) • *Saxifraga* • *Tulipa*
- Waterlily (*Nymphaea*)

Bamboos and grasses

340

342   Using grasses in the garden

344   A–Z of bamboos, grasses, rushes,
and sedges

Ferns

356

358   Using ferns in the garden

360   A–Z of ferns

CARING FOR PLANTS

366

368   Planning your garden

371   Climate and location

374   Buying plants

376   Soils and compost

379   Planting basics

382   Pruning

385   Routine tasks

391   Raising your own

396   Avoiding problems

PLANT SELECTIONS

400

Lists of plants for specific sites
and purposes:

- *Exposed sites* • *Seaside gardens* • *Dry sun*
- *Damp shade* • *Dry shade* • *Deep shade*
- *Heavy soils* • *Acidic soils* • *Limy,
alkaline soil* • *Ornamental herbs* • *Rock-garden
plants* • *Fragrant plants* • *Bog-garden plants*
- *Sloping sites*

406   Index

419   Picture credits

Key to symbols used in the text

‡   Height of mature plant

↔   Spread of mature plant

Z   Hardiness zone of plant (see endpapers for the
Plant Hardiness Zones of Canada map)

T   Plant is tender and may be damaged by
temperatures below freezing. The minimum
temperature (min.) for cultivation appears after
the symbol.

introduction

Gardening has become one of the most popular leisure activities for Canadians. Whether in cities or small towns, in the suburbs or at the cottage, we are discovering the many pleasures of nurturing plants to create beautiful, lush landscapes.

For many of us, the obsession sneaks up slowly — a few annuals planted along the walkway, some herbs by the deck — and soon we're hooked, making regular trips to the nursery to find new plants and buy the latest cultivars. Our fellow enthusiasts, novice and experienced alike, are quick to share with us not only their knowledge but also their plants, passing along perennial divisions and seeds, and, most importantly, their encouragement to try something new. There are always new plants to discover, no matter how long you have been gardening. Every year, the horticultural industry in Canada expands the already wide-ranging variety of plants available, introducing new species and cultivars to tempt gardeners. Specialist plant societies and local horticultural groups add to the mix with seed exchanges and plant sales brimming with old favorites as well as hard-to-find offerings of unusual species.

Garden Plants and Flowers is likewise brimming with temptation. Accompanying the detailed information on more than 2,500 plants are luscious color photographs for every entry. The entries have been divided into chapters that cover trees, shrubs, flowering plants, grasses, ferns, and climbing plants. Within each chapter, entries are arranged alphabetically by botanical name, and common names, where they exist, are also provided.

In addition to basic information on each featured plant, there is practical advice on caring for plants — including propagation, water and nutrient requirements, and disease and pest control — as well as quick-reference lists of plants for different sites and uses in the garden. All is tailored to the needs of Canadian gardeners, with Canadian hardiness zone information included for each species. Dig in!

LORRAINE JOHNSON

A–Z of GARDEN PLANTS

In this plant catalog, more than 2,500 plants are illustrated, and information given on many more, to enable you to create your own collection of star plants for the garden. To make it easier to choose, the catalog is divided into chapters covering different groups of plants, from trees and shrubs to climbing plants, flowering plants, bamboos and grasses, and ferns. Within each chapter, plant entries are ordered alphabetically by their botanical names, so that you can quickly look up a particular plant. Familiar common names are included in each entry.

Trees and Shrubs

using trees and shrubs

Trees and shrubs are essential to the garden, providing a framework within which other, less permanent plants can be displayed. They also have a tremendous range of habits, shapes, flowers, and foliage. By wisely selecting different trees and shrubs, you can have flowers every month of the year as well as spectacular autumn color. Even after the leaves drop, many trees and shrubs have distinctive bark that looks stunning throughout the winter. Evergreen trees and shrubs also provide that vital element – year-round privacy – and a constant foil to the changing highlights of other plants.

How to place trees and shrubs in the garden

Trees and shrubs, once planted, will be in your garden for a long time and will form the main structure of the design, so choose them carefully and plant them before other types of plants such as bulbs and border perennials. Think about what role they are to play in the garden.

Many trees and shrubs are handsome enough to be grown on their own, as a focal point to draw the eye to a particular point in your garden or simply as a specimen to be admired in solitary splendor. Pick a tree or a shrub that will achieve a suitable size when mature: it must be large enough to be interesting, but not so huge that it will overshadow other plantings.

One of the best ways of using trees and shrubs is in mixed borders, when combined with more seasonal or showy plants. You can also use them to create microclimates within the border; for example, birches (*Betula*) give light, dappled shade that is ideal for woodland plants such as anemones.

Trees and shrubs can be grown as hedging, either as boundaries or to subdivide the garden. Hedges are much more pleasing than fencing and are invaluable for attracting wildlife and nesting birds, which then help to control pests without having to reach for the sprayer.

You can plant a living screen to hide unsightly views or objects like compost piles, and to provide privacy or shade. Trees and shrubs also make more effective windbreaks than solid barriers, because they diffuse wind without creating the turbulence found in the lee of a fence or wall. A delightful use of trees and shrubs is to frame a view of the surrounding landscape, creating a seamless transition from your garden to the countryside.

You can even grow dwarf trees and shrubs in containers, making it easier to enjoy them close up.

Variations on a theme This mixed border includes trees and shrubs and some perennials with a wide variety of forms, heights, and textures, yet the restrained palette of colors, in shades of green, white, and gold, pulls the planting together for a harmonious display.

Year-round interest

One of the great joys of gardening is watching trees and shrubs changing throughout the year. Many are very decorative in more than one season. Among the first signs of spring is the bursting of trees into bloom, and with a mix of plants, you can maintain a continuous display of flower from spring through summer. Some trees and shrubs also produce fruits that add a splash of vivid color and will entice birds into the garden.

Autumn is the time for foliage to impress with brilliant hues of gold, purple, and crimson. The new leaves of some trees and shrubs, including conifers, may also be tipped with color in spring. In winter, some trees and shrubs reveal attractively textured and colored bark or bright stems.

When choosing trees and shrubs, remember to consider these features and how they will complement other plantings through the seasons.

Spring blossoms Ornamental cherries, like this Fuji cherry (*Prunus incisa*), make lovely specimen trees.

Summer fruits Viburnums produce masses of berries – in blue, black, or scarlet (here 'Compactum').

Autumn leaves Some deciduous trees, such as this vine maple (*Acer circinatum*) glow with color at leaf fall.

Winter bark The spectacular bark of trees like this birch, *Betula papifera*, is best appreciated in winter.

Growth habits of trees and shrubs

Before selecting trees or shrubs for your garden, consider their ultimate shapes. There are many habits and forms available, such as prostrate, conical, pyramidal, and globular, as well as those shown (*see right*). The type you choose will depend on the amount of space in, and the style of, your garden. A columnar tree, for example, would be a better choice for a limited space than a tree with a broad, spreading canopy. Be aware also of the eventual height of the mature tree or shrub. A very large specimen tree could cast shade over most or all of the garden.

The growth habit of a tree or shrub also contributes to the style of your garden. Columnar trees, such as the Italian cypress (*Cupressus*), commonly evoke a formal atmosphere, while weeping trees, for example willows (*Salix*), look especially graceful when stirred by a breeze. Shrubs such as pyracanthas can be grown as a free-standing plant or trained up against a wall. The shape and size of a tree can be modified by pruning (*see below*).

Columnar tree This type of tree has a narrow, upright shape, with thin, upward branches from top to bottom. The main stem often forks into two or three higher up.

Standard tree These trees have a single clear trunk, or stem, and a rounded canopy, or head, of branches.

Mounding shrub These shrubs form a dense, rounded outline.

Weeping tree The branches of this type of tree cascade outward to form a mushroom shape or fall straight down toward the ground.

Multistemmed shrub These shrubs possess many dense and twiggy, upright, or arching stems.

What is the difference between trees and shrubs and other perennials?

Trees and shrubs are all woody, perennial plants and are much longer-lived than herbaceous perennials. Trees generally have one main stem or trunk with a head of branches above. A shrub has many branches arising near the base of the plant and lacks a central trunk. Some trees do however have a shrubby habit, naturally growing with more than one stem.

It is generally easy to distinguish a woody plant from a herbaceous one. Trees and many shrubs have rigid stems with a protective outer layer of

bark, which is quite distinct from the soft, green stems of herbaceous perennials (*see pp.160–161*). In some shrubs, called subshrubs, the stems may be more flexible and similar in appearance to herbaceous shoots – except for the stem bases, which in subshrubs are distinctly woody.

Woody stems heal over, or callus, when cut, so most trees and shrubs can be pruned (*see pp.382–384*). This can be done to keep the plant healthy, to train it into a different shape (*see right*), or to keep it to the desired size.

The power of pruning If left to its own devices, this form of the Monterey cypress, *Cupressus macrocarpa* 'Goldcrest', becomes a stately columnar tree of up to 15ft (5m) in height (*see left*). With regular pruning, however, it can assume a quite different character, such as a picturesque piece of topiary (*see right*), but this does require frequent clipping to keep a neat shape.

You could also try less radical degrees of pruning trees and shrubs, for example removing the lower branches of a shrub to make a clear trunk, or shaping several into a screen or hedge.

ABELIA

THESE DECIDUOUS AND EVERGREEN shrubs are grown for their profuse clusters of white, pink, or cerise flowers and glossy, rounded foliage. The flowers are borne on slender, arching stems during summer and autumn, and in some species, such as *Abelia chinensis* (Z7) and *A. schumannii*, they are scented. The size of different cultivars can vary dramatically, from 5ft (1.5m) to 15ft (5m) or more in height, and between 6ft (2m) and 12ft (4m) in width. Abelias are generally trouble free and ideal for sunny border sites. If you have room, they make attractive planting partners for lespedezas (*see p.81*) and hydrangeas (*see pp.72–73*). Where marginally hardy, grow against a warm, south- or west-facing wall.

Cultivation Grow in any fertile, well-drained soil in full sun and shelter from cold, drying winds. **Prune** deciduous species in late winter or early spring, removing misplaced or crossing shoots to maintain a good shape. For evergreen species, lightly trim back after flowering any flowered shoots that would spoil the symmetry. **Take** softwood cuttings in early summer, or semiripe cuttings in late summer (*see p.394*).

Abelia × grandiflora (Glossy Abelia)
Z5b ‡ 10ft (3m) ↔ 12ft (4m), semievergreen, fragrant flowers in midsummer to autumn

ABELIOPHYLLUM DISTICHUM
White forsythia

‡↔ 5ft (1.5m)

CLUSTERS OF FLOWERS borne on the bare wood of this deciduous shrub open from late winter to perfume the garden with a delicate scent. Matte green leaves follow, and turn purple before falling in autumn. This open, spreading shrub is related to the forsythia (*see p.58*) and just as versatile. You can grow it as a freestanding shrub in a sunny border, but train it against a sheltered, south- or west-facing wall and it will reward you by bursting into flower earlier and more profusely. It makes a fine companion for other early-flowering shrubs such as mahonias (*see p.87*), forsythias, and viburnums (*see pp.126–127*).

Cultivation Grow in fertile, well-drained soil in full sun. **Prune** after flowering; if freestanding, cut back flowered shoots to strong buds or shoots close to the base. If wall-trained, cut back all flowered shoots to within 2–4 buds of a permanent framework. **Take** semiripe cuttings, or layer low-growing shoots, in summer (*see pp.394–395*).

Abelia schumannii
Z7 ‡ 6ft (2m) ↔ 10ft (3m), deciduous, lightly scented flowers in late summer to autumn

Abelia floribunda
Z8 ‡ 10ft (3m) ↔ 12ft (4m), evergreen, flowers early summer, may spread farther when grown against a wall

Abeliophyllum distichum
Z5b ‡↔ 5ft (1.5m) White flowers sometimes tinged with pink

ABIES
Fir

LONG, SWEEPING BRANCHES are a typical feature of these stately, evergreen conifers. They make excellent specimen trees and can also be used to provide shelter from wind or as a screen. The needles usually range in color from mid-green to bluish green, with silvery undersides. In late spring and early summer, some plants produce decorative cones; erect, purplish blue ones on the upper branches will be female, while the pendent cones lower down are male, usually green maturing to brown or purplish blue. For small gardens there are several dwarf firs, such as *Abies balsamea* 'Nana', (Z2), which grows to just 3ft (1m), ideal for a rock garden. *A. grandis* (Z6) attains a majestic stature of up to 150ft (45m).

Cultivation Grow in any fertile, moist but well-drained, neutral to slightly acidic soil in sun, sheltered from cold winds. Most tolerate a little shade. Like most conifers, they need no pruning. **Sow** seed (*see pp.391–392*) in containers when ripe or in winter; expose seed to cold for three weeks before sowing. Firs are prone to infestation by adelgids, black aphidlike insects covered in a fluffy white secretion. They may cause foliage to yellow but can usually be tolerated.

Abies veitchii (Veitch fir)
Z4 ‡ 50–70ft (15–20m) ↔ 12–20ft (4–6m), fast-growing, with 2––3in (5–8cm) long female cones

Abies procera (Noble fir)
Z5 ‡ 80–150ft (25–45m) ↔ 20–28ft (6–9m), silvery gray bark, bears green or brown, 6–10in (15–25cm) long female cones

Abies lasiocarpa 'Compacta' (Subalpine fir)
Z2b ‡ 10–15ft (3–5m) ↔ 6–10ft (2–3m), small, slow-growing type of corkbark fir, with a neat conical shape

Abies koreana (Korean fir)
Z4 ‡ 30ft (10m) ↔ 20ft (6m), produces decorative female cones that are 2–3in (5–8cm) long, from a young age

Abies nordmanniana 'Golden Spreader'
Z6 ‡ 3ft (1m) ↔ 5ft (1.5m), slow-growing, shrubby dwarf conifer with spreading branches and greenish brown cones

ABUTILON

Flowering maple, Indian mallow

A LONG FLOWERING SEASON, often continuously from spring until fall, is a key attraction of these rather spindly stemmed shrubs, most of which benefit from some support. They flower in shades of red, orange, soft violet-blue, pink, and white; some even have bicolored flowers. There are also several that have variegated leaves. Where not hardy, grow in a greenhouse or as houseplants; train marginally hardy abutilons against a warm wall.

Cultivation Under cover, grow in any fertile, well-drained soil or soil-based potting mix in a container. Position in full sun; in frost-prone areas grow abutilons in pots in a sheltered site and bring the plants under cover during winter. **Prune** in late winter or early spring, cutting back flowered shoots to a permanent framework of main stems (*see p.383*), and taking out any misplaced or crossing shoots. **Sow** seed (*see pp.391–392*) in spring after all danger of frost has passed; take softwood cuttings in spring, or semiripe cuttings in summer (*see p.394*). If whiteflies or red spider mite infest plants under glass, biological controls may be effective (*see p.397*).

Abutilon x 'Souvenir de Bonn' (Chinese lanterns)
Z8 ‡ 10ft (to 3m) ↔ 6–10ft (2–3m), vigorous, erect evergreen, flowers from spring into early fall

WHITEFLIES ON LEAVES can be a problem, but usually only on the more tender abutilons that are grown under glass for all or part of the year.

Abutilon megapotamicum (Trailing abutilon)
Z8 ‡↔ 6ft (2m), semievergreen or evergreen, ideal against a wall; flowers borne from summer to fall

Abutilon 'Boule de Neige'
Z8 ‡ to 12ft (4m) ↔ to 10ft (3m), vigorous evergreen, erect to spreading habit, flowers from spring to fall

Abutilon vitifolium 'Veronica Tennant'
Z8 ‡ 15ft (5m) ↔ 8f (t2.5m), fast-growing, deciduous, upright – sometimes treelike shrub, flowers in early summer

ACACIA
Wattle

‡100ft (to 30m)
↔30ft (to 10m)

CLUSTERS OF TINY, often sweetly fragrant, bright yellow flowers clothe these fast-growing, deciduous and evergreen trees and shrubs in winter or spring. These tropical plants are tender and should be grown in a cool or cold greenhouse, or as a houseplant, though they may survive against a warm wall in parts of Zone 8.

Cultivation Grow in reasonably fertile, neutral to acidic soil. Position in full sun, out of cold winds. In colder areas, grow in pots of soil-based potting mix and bring under cover in winter. **Prune** (*see pp.382–383*) deciduous species in spring, removing any crossing or misshapen branches to maintain a good framework, and evergreens after flowering, lightly trimming shoots that spoil the shape of the tree. Cut flowered shoots on wall-trained shrubs to within two to four buds of the permanent framework in late winter or early spring. **Sow** seed (*see pp.391–393*) at 64°F (18°C) in spring after soaking in warm water until the seeds are swollen. Take semiripe cuttings (*see p.394*) in summer.

ACALPHYA

THESE TROPICAL SHRUBS make exotic bedding plants for summer in a cool climate, where they are also often cultivated as potted plants. Some, for example *Acalphya hispida* (T min. 55°F/13°C), the chenille plant or red-hot cat's tail, are grown for their long, catkinlike clusters of usually pinkish crimson or scarlet flowers. Others, such as *A. wilkesiana*, have inconspicuous flowers but ornamental foliage, which is mottled or variegated. Given the right conditions, they can grow very quickly and make fine accent plants, although they may not reach their full height in a single season.

Cultivation Outdoors, grow in fertile, well-drained soil in full sun or partial shade. If growing them in pots, use a soilless potting mix and position in full light. **Keep** plants in frost-free conditions throughout the winter; they are susceptible to damage at temperatures below 50–55°F (10–13°C). **Apply** a balanced fertilizer at monthly intervals in spring and summer, and water regularly during summer. **Lightly trim** shoots that spoil the shape of the plant. **Take** softwood cuttings in spring or semiripe cuttings in late summer (*see p.394*).

Abutilon vitifolium var *album*
Z8 ‡15ft (5m) ↔ 8ft (2.5m), fast-growing, deciduous shrub, sometimes treelike, flowering in early summer

Abutilon pictum 'Thompsonii'
Z8 ‡15ft (5m) ↔ 6–15ft (2–5m), evergreen, erect shrub or small tree, flowers from spring to fall

Acacia baileyana (Cootamundra wattle)
T min. 35–41°F (2–5°C) ‡15–25ft (5–8m) ↔ 10–20ft (3–6m), small tree or large shrub, evergreen flowers from winter to spring

Acalphya wilkesiana (Copperleaf)
T min. 50°F (10°C) ‡6ft (to 2m) ↔ 3–6ft (1–2m), spreading shrub, green- or copper-tinted flowers often hidden by blue, pink, or coppery

ACER
Maple

ACERS ARE PRIZED FOR THEIR DELICATE FOLIAGE, which is particularly fine and fernlike in some cultivars of Japanese maple (*Acer palmatum*, Z5b–6). There is enough variety in the group to provide interest at any time of the year. Some have brightly colored leaves in spring, others have variegated gray-green, white, or pink foliage, and many give a brilliant display of intense reds, yellows, and oranges in fall. Nearly all maples are deciduous. Several also have handsome bark, which helps to enliven the winter months; on *Acer griseum* (Z6) it peels attractively, while on *A. davidii* (Z6b) and *A. pensylvanicum* (Z2b) it is striped and streaked in green and white. The inconspicuous spring flowers are followed by winged fruits, joined in pairs. Maples include both trees and shrubs, with a type to suit most gardens. The largest trees make striking specimens if you have the space, while smaller trees and those of shrubby habit can be grown in gardens of any size. Many cultivars are excellent grown in containers; the restricted root space will keep them compact, and less hardy varieties can also be moved to a sheltered position close to the house during the coldest months. Maples run the range of Canadian hardiness zones from 2–8.

Cultivation   Maples prefer well-cultivated soil in sun or partial shade. **Plant** container-grown trees at any time of the year, but bare-root trees only when dormant, from late autumn to early spring. Water well before and after planting, and continue watering regularly during the first year. **Shelter** those with delicate foliage from cold winds and late frosts that can scorch the young leaves. **Stake** taller maples and those grown in exposed gardens. **Prune** young plants to form the basic framework for the tree or shrub; after this maples need minimal pruning. Remove badly placed and crossing shoots to maintain a well-balanced shape (*see p.382*), and cut out any dead or diseased wood from late autumn to midwinter, or in spring for plants in containers. **Sow** seed outside as soon as it is ripe (*see pp.391–392*), and take softwood cuttings of cultivars in early summer (*see p.394*). In some cultivars, mites may cause small growths called galls; although unsightly, they are harmless.

Looking after maples in containers

Maples grown in containers require more care than those planted in open ground, because the roots cannot grow deep down in search of water and nutrients. A thick mulch (*see p.388 and below*) will help retain moisture, but you will still need to water regularly – probably daily during dry spells. Top-dress the container annually (*see below*) in early spring to remove weeds and algal growths in the surface layer and provide the plant with the nutrients it needs for the growing season. Every three to five years, repot your maple, either back into the same container or into a slightly larger one. Remove the plant from its pot, then gently tease out the roots and cut back any large, coarse ones. Put the tree in the new container, then fill in with fresh soil mix so the root ball sits at the same level as before. Water in well and mulch.

1 Using a trowel or a small hand fork, scrape away the top 2in (5cm) of old soil mix and mulch, here bark chips, and discard.

2 Top up with fresh soil mix combined with some slow-release fertilizer. Water well and top with a fresh mulch to suppress weeds.

① *Acer cappadocicum* ↕70ft (20m) ↔ 50ft (15m) ② *circinatum* ↕15ft (5m) ↔ 20ft (6m) ③ *davidii* 'George Forrest' ↕↔ 50ft (15m), interesting bark ④ *griseum* ↕↔ 30ft (10m), attractive bark ⑤ *japonicum* 'Aconitifolium' ↕15ft (5m) ↔ 20ft (6m) ⑥ *negundo* 'Flamingo' ↕50ft (15m) ↔ 30ft (10m) ⑦ *negundo* 'Variegatum' ↕50ft (15m) ↔ 30ft (10m) ⑧ *palmatum* f. *atropurpureum* ↕25ft (8m) ↔ 30ft (10m) ⑨ *palmatum* 'Bloodgood' ↕↔ 15ft (5m)

⑩ *palmatum* 'Butterfly' ‡10ft (3m) ↔ 5ft (1.5m)   ⑪ *palmatum* 'Chitoseyama' ‡6ft (2m)
↔10ft (3m)   ⑫ *palmatum* 'Corallinum' ‡4ft (1.2m) ↔ 3ft (1m)   ⑬ *palmatum* Dissectum
Atropurpureum Group ‡6ft (2m) ↔ 10ft (3m)   ⑭ *palmatum* 'Garnet' ‡6ft (2m) ↔ 10ft (3m)
⑮ *palmatum* var. *heptalobum* ‡15ft (5m) ↔ 20ft (6m)   ⑯ *palmatum* 'Linearilobum' ‡15ft (5m)
↔12ft (4m)   ⑰ *palmatum* 'Red Pygmy' ‡↔5ft (1.5m)   ⑱ *palmatum* 'Sango-kaku'
‡20ft (6m) ↔ 15ft (5m)   ⑲ *platanoides* 'Crimson King' ‡80ft (25m) ↔ 50ft (15m)
⑳ *pseudoplatanus* 'Brilliantissimum' ‡20ft (6m) ↔ 25ft (8m)   ㉑ *rubrum* 'October
Glory' ‡70ft (20m) ↔ 30ft (10m)   ㉒ *rubrum* 'Schlesingeri' ‡70ft (20m) ↔ 30ft (10m)
㉓ *saccharinum* ‡80ft (25m) ↔ 50ft (15m)   ㉔ *shirasawanum* 'Aureum' ‡↔ 20ft (6m)

AEONIUM

PRIZED FOR THEIR EXOTIC FORMS, aeoniums bear tight rosettes of fleshy leaves in shades of light green to a striking black-purple. From spring to summer, they send up clusters of small starry flowers in pale to bright yellow, white, pink, or copper-red. With some species, the flowering stem dies back once the seed is set. Aeoniums look stunning in containers, especially grouped with other succulents, or with the dark leaves of cultivars such as 'Zwartkop' contrasted with silvery blue or gray foliage. Grow them in pots on a patio or in a well-drained border in sun or partial shade. Where not hardy, grow as houseplants or in a temperate greenhouse.

Cultivation Grow in fertile, well-drained soil or cactus soil mix, in sun or partial shade. **Keep** the plants fairly dry during their dormant period in winter. **Sow** seed (*see pp.391–392*) in heat in spring. **Take** cuttings (*see p.394*) in early summer, waiting until the cut surface of the cuttings calluses, or heals over, before inserting them in sandy soil mix. Place them in good light and keep warm and barely moist until rooted. Aeoniums are prone to attack by aphids (*see p.398*).

AESCULUS
Horse chestnut, Buckeye

HORSE CHESTNUTS ARE HANDSOME trees with fingered leaves that turn golden yellow or glowing orange in autumn. In spring and early summer, they are covered in large spikes or "candles" of white or pink flowers. In autumn, their smooth or prickly coated, rounded fruits split to reveal shiny, brown seeds or conkers; they are toxic if eaten. Because of their size – up to 80ft (25m) – most horse chestnuts can be grown only in large gardens. Their spreading branches and large leaves cast a deep shade under which little will grow. However, *Aesculus × mutabilis* 'Induta' (Z5) and *A. parviflora* are shrubby and smaller in size and look impressive in medium-sized gardens. They are best used as large specimens in lawns.

Cultivation Grow in any fertile soil in sun or partial shade. **Prune** young trees to remove misplaced or crossing shoots (*see p.382*) in late winter or early spring to maintain a healthy framework of branches and good symmetry. **Sow** seed (*see pp.391–393*) in a seedbed outdoors as soon as it is ripe. *A. parviflora* can be propagated by removing suckers – cut away a stem with its own roots at the base of the plant and replant it.

AUTUMN FOLIAGE

Aesculus parviflora
Z4b ↕ 10ft (3m) ↔ 15ft (5m), suckering shrub that will grow in all but very poorly drained soils, smooth-skinned fruits

Aeonium arboreum 'Zwartkop'
T min. 50°F (10°C) ↕↔ to 3ft (1m), pyramid-shaped spikes of yellow flowers develop from black-purple rosettes in late summer

Aesculus × neglecta 'Erythroblastos'
Z5 ↕ 30ft (10m) or more ↔ 25ft (8m), red stalks and leaves that unfold from cream to green by midsummer

Aesculus hippocastanum
Z5 ↕ 80ft (25m) ↔ 70ft (20m), vigorous tree with a rounded, spreading shape, bears the familiar, spiky-shelled conker

AGAVE

NATIVE TO DESERTS AND MOUNTAINS, these bold, structural succulents have fleshy, spiked leaves up to 6ft (2m) long, in wide-spreading rosettes. In summer, mature plants may produce funnel-shaped flowers on leafless stems that soar up to 25ft (8m). With most species, the main rosette dies after flowering and fruiting, but leaves a number of offsets – smaller rosettes that develop around it – to mature in later years. These can be split off to make new plants. Where not hardy, grow agaves in containers that can be moved into frost-free conditions over winter. The spiked leaves are very sharp, so avoid planting them close to seating and play areas.

Cultivation Grow in slightly acidic, fertile, very well-drained soil or cactus soil mix in full sun. **Sow** seed (*see pp.391–392*) in heat in early spring. **Remove offsets** in autumn or spring. **Insert** unrooted offsets in pots containing equal parts peat and sharp sand. Rooted offsets can be treated like mature plants.

ALNUS
Alder

‡ to 80ft (25m)
↔ to 30ft (10m)

FAST-GROWING AND TOLERANT of poor soils, alders are useful trees and shrubs. They are deciduous, and broadly conical in shape, with toothed leaves, and delicate catkins appearing in late winter to spring. The catkins, usually yellow, are followed by green fruits that turn brown in autumn and look like tiny pine cones. Alders, especially those with ornamental foliage such as *Alnus rubra, A. glutinosa,* and *A. incana,* make attractively light, slender specimen trees. They do not mind wet feet, so they are a sound choice for a damp site or by a stream or pond. Because they are quick-growing, they make ideal screens or windbreaks.

Cultivation Grow in fertile, moist, but well-drained soil in full sun; *A. cordata* and *A. incana* will tolerate dry soils. **Pruning** is rarely necessary: remove branches that cross or spoil the shape of the tree between the time of leaf-fall and midwinter to avoid sap bleeding. **Sow** seed (*see pp.391–393*) in a seedbed as soon as it is ripe. **Take** hardwood cuttings in winter (*see p.394*).

Alnus incana (Gray alder)
Z4 ‡ 70ft (20m) ↔ 30ft (10m), makes an excellent windbreak because it thrives in cold, exposed situations

Agave americana 'Mediopicta' Variegated Century Plant
T min. 41°F (5°C) ‡ 6ft (2m) ↔ 10ft (3m), flowers in summer on stems up to 25ft (8m) tall

Alnus cordata (Italian alder)
Z5 ‡ 80ft (25m) ↔ 20ft (6m), tolerates dry soil, catkins appear in late winter before the leaves

Alnus glutinosa 'Imperialis'
Z4 ‡ 80ft (25m) ↔ 30ft (10m), mid-green, deeply cut leaves to 4in (10cm) long, good as lawn specimen

AMELANCHIER

Juneberry, Shadbush, Serviceberry

A TREE FOR ALL SEASONS, the amelanchier is superb value in the garden. Spring to early summer is a high point, when these broad, shrubby trees bear masses of beautiful, star- or saucer-shaped, white flowers, just as the silver or bronze young leaves are opening. Add to this their richly colored autumnal foliage, succulent fruits, and light, airy growing habit, and you have a plant that has something of interest all year round. The small, maroon to purple-black fruits are very attractive to birds. Make the most of this fine tree by growing it as a specimen. Amelanchiers also make a substantial additions to shrub borders.

Cultivation Grow in acidic, fertile, well-drained soil in sun or partial shade. *A. alnifolia* is lime-tolerant. **Prune** out branches that cross or spoil the shape in late winter or early spring. **Remove** suckers (shoots growing up at ground level away from the main stem) in winter. **Sow** seed (*see pp.391–393*) outdoors as soon as it is ripe. **Take** greenwood or semiripe cuttings (*see p.394*) in summer. **Peg** low branches into the soil in autumn to root (*see layering, p.395*). If any branch appears "scorched" or blackened, as if held in the smoke of a bonfire (the sign of a disease called fireblight), it must be removed.

Amelanchier lamarckii
Z4 ‡30ft (10m) ↔ 40ft (12m), leaves emerge as bronze, then turn dark green, white flowers appear midspring

ANDROMEDA

Bog rosemary

‡to 16in (40cm)
↔ to 24in (60cm)

IMAGINE A HEATHER with long, narrow, green leaves, and you have the bog rosemary, a small, wiry-stemmed, evergreen shrub that enjoys the same conditions as ericas (*see pp.52–53*) and callunas (*see p.31*), being native to peat bogs in cool regions. *Andromeda polifolia* (Z2) is the most commonly grown species of bog rosemary; its cultivars vary in size, from 2in (5cm) to 16in (40cm) tall, and in flower color – either pink or white. Bog rosemaries thrive only in moist, acidic soils. If your soil is not suitable, a raised bed or container filled with acidic soil mix or compost will suffice. They are suitable for a woodland setting or a shady rock garden.

Cultivation Grow in moist, acid soil with plenty of well-rotted organic matter added to it, in sun or partial shade. If your soil is dry, spread a layer of leaf mold or garden compost around the plants each spring, ideally after heavy rain; this will help retain moisture and keep down weeds. **Take** softwood cuttings in summer (*see p.394*), or pot up rooted layers in autumn or spring (*see p.395*).

① *A. polifolia* 'Alba' Z2 ‡6in (15cm) ↔ 8in (20cm), semiprostrate, free-flowering ② *A. polifolia* 'Compacta' Z2 ‡12in (30cm) ↔ 8in (20cm), dense, twiggy habit

ARALIA

‡↔ to 30ft (10m)

THESE EXOTIC-LOOKING TREES grow mainly in mountainous woodland. Their large, handsome leaves are arranged in pairs; in some, they are covered in large bristles. *Aralia elata* is the largest species. In late summer and early autumn, they produce clusters or spikes of small, white or greenish white flowers (with no hint of pink), followed by black fruits. Aralias are suitable only for large gardens, in prominent positions where their striking leaves can be admired. They look good in shady borders, woodland plantings, and by streams.

Cultivation Grow in fertile soil with plenty of well-rotted organic matter added, in an open or part-shaded site, sheltered from strong winds that may damage the leaves. Trees in very fertile soil can produce soft growth prone to damage by frost. **Remove** badly placed branches or frost-damaged shoots in early spring, and remove suckers growing up around the tree when seen. If variegated forms produce shoots with all-green leaves, prune them out. **Sow** seed (*see pp.391–392*) in containers as soon as ripe; place in a cold frame. **Take** root cuttings (*see p.394*) in winter. Aphids may attack the soft flower stalks.

Aralia elata 'Variegata'
Z5 ‡↔ 30ft (10m) deciduous tree, flowers late summer to early autumn

ARAUCARIA ARAUCANA
Monkey puzzle

ONE OF THE MOST ANCIENT TREES, the monkey puzzle is so-called because its branches are clad in sharp, scalelike leaves that make them uncomfortable, if not impossible, to climb. Although hailing from the tropical rainforest, this araucaria is hardy in temperate zones, and has long been a garden favorite for its novelty value. Many, unfortunately, are planted in gardens that are far too small (especially since they are deceptively slow-growing when young), necessitating unsightly lopping that ruins their shape. They need plenty of room for their forms to develop – at first conical, then losing the lower branches to form a graceful, rounded head atop a tall, clear trunk. Male and female cones tend to be borne on different trees; female cones are more rounded than the male ones.

Cultivation Grow in any fertile, well-drained soil in an open site, but sheltered from cold winds. **Sow** seed (*see pp.391–393*) in a seedbed as soon as it is ripe. **Take** cuttings (*see p.394*) from vertical shoot tips in midsummer and root in a cold frame. Cuttings from horizontal branches never make upright trees.

ARBUTUS
Madrone, Strawberry tree

ARBUTUS ARE BROAD, sometimes bushy trees with attractive, peeling, red-brown bark and dark, glossy leaves. Clusters of tiny white or pink flowers are produced from autumn to spring. These are followed by bright orange to red, strawberry-like fruits (hence the common name), which are edible, if rather tasteless. Although they can reach up to 50ft (15m), they are slow-growing, and many will remain small shrubs for several years. Arbutus are excellent for a large shrub border or as specimens, where their handsome, colored barks can be admired.

Cultivation Grow in fertile soil, enriched with plenty of bulky, well-rotted organic matter, in a sheltered site in full sun with protection from cold winds, even when mature. Both *A. andrachnoides* and *A. unedo* will tolerate alkaline soils; other species, such as *A. menziesii*, need acidic soils. **Prune out** any misplaced shoots to maintain a good shape in winter or late spring when the tree is dormant, but keep pruning to a minimum. **Sow** seed (*see pp.391–392*) in containers as soon as it is ripe and place in a cold frame. **Take** semiripe (stem-tip) cuttings in summer (*see p.394*).

Arbutus × andrachnoides
Z8 ‡ ↔ 25ft (8m), white, sometimes pink-tinged, flowers in autumn to spring, grown for red bark, fruits are rare

Araucaria araucana
Z7 ‡ 50–80ft (15–25m) ↔ 22–30ft (7–10m), has tough, dark gray-brown bark with horizontal ridges

Arbutus unedo (Strawberry tree)
Z7 ‡ ↔ 25ft (8m), fruits appear with pendent flowers in autumn but take a year to ripen fully

Arbutus menziesii (Madrone)
Z7 ‡ ↔ 50ft (15m), spreading, shrubby habit, free-flowering, bears white flowers in 8in (20cm) spikes in early summer

ARCTOSTAPHYLOS
Bearberry

THESE MOSTLY EVERGREEN, low-maintenance shrubs originate from western North America, particularly California. They range in habit from mat-forming to upright; some bearberries eventually reach 20ft (6m) tall with a similar spread, while *Arctostaphylos alpina* (Z2) is just 2in (5cm) tall and 8in (20cm) across. All bear bunches of delicate, white to pink, urn-shaped flowers in winter or spring. Small berries, usually scarlet but sometimes brown, purple, or black, follow in autumn. Low-growing bearberries look excellent as groundcover in a shrub border or in a large rock garden. The larger, upright species look at home in an open, woodland garden.

Cultivation Grow in moist, fertile, well-drained, acidic soil in full sun or partial shade. Less hardy species need shelter. **Sow** seed (*see pp.391–392*) in containers in a cold frame in autumn, immersing the seeds in boiling water for about 20 seconds before sowing. This softens the hard seed coats. **Take** sem ripe cuttings (*see p.394*) in summer or layer in autumn (*see p.395*). Shoots growing along the soil surface often produce roots at the leaf joints, layering naturally. Lift, sever, and pot these up to make new young plants.

Arctostaphylos uva-ursi 'Wood's Red'
Z1 ‡ to 4in (10cm) ↔ to 20in (50cm), low-growing, densely branched, suitable for a rockery or the front of a shrub border

ARGYRANTHEMUM
Marguerite

ARGYRANTHEMUMS ARE HARD-WORKING shrubs that produce a succession of cheery, daisylike blooms from early summer through to autumn. There are single- and double-flowered types, in hues of white, soft yellow to apricot, and pale pink to deep cerise. Formerly classed as chrysanthemums, they have similar foliage: almost fernlike, and either green or grayish green. They are invaluable in pots, in summer bedding designs or in mixed borders where they inject a light and breezy feel. Some make elegant specimens or are trained as standards (in a "lollipop" shape with a single, bare stem and a bushy head).

Cultivation Grow in well-drained fertile soil in full sun. Most species will tolerate salt-laden winds in coastal areas. **Pinch out** the growing tips of young plants to encourage a bushy habit. **Prune back** flowered shoots to within 1in (2.5cm) of their base after flowering or in early spring. **Apply** a deep winter mulch if the temperature in your area falls below 23°F (–5°C) for long periods, taking cuttings in late summer as insurance against losses. Alternatively, lift the plants and overwinter in frost-free conditions. **Take** softwood cuttings in spring or semiripe cuttings in summer (*see p.394*).

Argyranthemum gracile 'Chelsea Girl'
T min. 35°F (2°C) ‡↔ 24in (60cm), compact plant with sparse flowers, grown for its filigree foliage, good as a specimen plant

Argyranthemum 'Vancouver'
T min. 35°F (2°C) ‡ 36in (90cm) ↔ 32in (80cm), compact plant with double flowers and gray-green leaves, good for a small garden

Argyranthemum 'Mary Wootton'
T min. 35°F (2°C) ‡3½ft (1m) ↔ 3ft (1m), open habit, gray-green leaves, flowers open pale pink but fade to white with age

Argyranthemum 'Jamaica Primrose'
T min. 35°F (2°C) ‡3½ft (1m) ↔ 3ft (1m), open habit with long branching stems, flowers are 2½in (6cm) across, good as a standard

ARTEMISIA

Mugwort, Sagebrush, Wormwood

see also p.189

‡2in–5ft (5cm–1.5m)
↔6in–5ft (15cm–1.5m)

ARTEMISIAS HAVE FERNY, aromatic, gray or silver foliage that gives year-round interest and acts as a contrast for flowering plants or those with bolder leaves. There are evergreen and deciduous types, all bearing tiny, unimpressive flowers – the leaves are the chief draw. Artemisias look good in herb gardens (French tarragon is a form of *Artemisia dracunculus*, Z4), rock gardens, and shrub or flower borders. They are often featured in drought-tolerant, Mediterranean-style gardens, although a few, notably *A. lactiflora* Z5, need moist soil.

Cultivation Grow in fertile, well-drained soil in a sunny position. In heavy clay soil, dig in plenty of sharp sand to improve drainage; plants can be short-lived in wet conditions. **Prune** plants that have grown overlarge and leggy to the ground, in autumn or spring, to encourage a compact habit. **Sow** seed (*see pp.391–392*) in containers in a cold frame in autumn or spring. **Take** heel cuttings in early summer (*see p.394*). **Prone** to mildew (*see p.398*) if damp.

① *A. abrotanum* Z4 ‡↔ 3ft (1m), semievergreen, flowers in late summer ② *A. arborescens* Z4 ‡3ft (1m) ↔ 5ft (1.5m), evergreen with silky leaves

AUCUBA

AUCUBAS ARE USEFUL, EVERGREEN SHRUBS grown for their bold, glossy foliage and large fruits. They hardly ever suffer from pests and diseases, and tolerate all sorts of difficult growing conditions, including full shade, dry soils, pollution, and salt winds. This makes them a popular choice for town gardens. Aucubas can be used as specimen plants in lawns, in mixed and shrub borders, or for informal hedging (if trimmed, they do not fruit as well). The variegated and spotted cultivars (such as 'Sulphurea Marginata' Z7) make a bright splash in a dark corner where little else will grow.

Cultivation Grow in any fertile soil except waterlogged conditions, in full sun or full shade; variegated species prefer partial shade. In areas with hot summers, grow in full shade. Use soil-based potting mix if growing in a container. Apply a liquid fertilizer once a month and water freely when in full growth, but sparingly in winter. **Trim** aucubas in spring to shape and cut back hard if they are growing too large. Prune wayward shoots by cutting them well back into the center of the bush. **Sow** seed (*see pp.391–392*) in containers in autumn. **Take** semiripe cuttings (*see p.394*) in summer.

Aucuba japonica (Spotted laurel)
Z7 ‡↔ 10ft (3m), female plants will produce bright red berries (*see inset*) if a male is grown nearby

25 TREES AND SHRUBS

TREES AND SHRUBS

AZARA

STRONGLY VANILLA-SCENTED FLOWERS are the main attraction of this group of evergreen shrubs and small trees. The flowers are produced in tight clusters or spikes carried on the undersides of the branches, with different species flowering at times ranging from midwinter to midsummer. The flowers have no petals, but showy stamens give them a decorative, fluffy appearance. Berries may follow after hot summers. These trouble-free shrubs need a sunny and sheltered position, ideally against a warm wall: they are often wall-trained. The green leaves vary in size and are sometimes in distinctive unequal pairs, with a small leaf opposite a much larger one.

Cultivation Grow in moist soil enriched with plenty of well-rotted organic matter. Site in sun or partial shade, sheltered from cold winds, which will scorch the leaves and cause them to drop. In colder areas, grow and train azaras against warm sunny walls or in a cool greenhouse. **Prune out** shoots that spoil the shape of the shrub after flowering; if wall-trained, prune back flowered shoots to two to four buds above the permanent framework of branches.

Azara microphylla (inset: *microphylla* 'Variegata')
T min. 35–41°F (2–5°C) ‡30ft (10m) ↔ 12f (t4m), hardiest of the species, will also tolerate full shade

BALLOTA

THESE EVERGREEN OR SEMIEVERGREEN PLANTS form mounds or mats of rounded, aromatic, yellow-green to gray-green leaves. Small, funnel-shaped flowers in shades of green, purple, white, or pink are produced from late spring until late summer, but the attractive foliage is the main reason for growing ballotas. They make an excellent foil for more colorful plants, such as brightly flowered border phloxes (*see pp.306–307*) daylilies (*Hemerocallis, see p.258*), and achilleas (*see pp.166–167*). For a more subtle effect, grow them alongside plants like helichrysums (*see p.256*) and lavender (*Lavandula, see p.80*) for contrasting foliage textures within the same color range.

Cultivation Grow in poor, dry soil that is free-draining. Position in full sun. **Trim back** all flowered shoots to within 1in (2.5cm) of old growth after flowering or in mid- to late spring; alternatively, trim back in spring to keep the plants compact. A thick, dry winter mulch helps protect plants in cold areas. **Divide** perennials (*see p.395*) in spring. **Take** softwood cuttings of shrubs in late spring or semiripe cuttings in early summer (*see p.394*).

① *B.* 'All Hallows Green' Z8 ‡24in (60cm) ↔ 30in (75cm)
② *B. pseudodictamnus* Z8 ‡18in (45cm) ↔ 24in (60cm)

BERBERIS
Barberry

BARBERRIES ARE GROWN FOR their ornamental foliage and their glowing, yellow to dark orange flowers. The flowers are produced in spring and summer, usually in small clusters, and are often followed by colorful fruits in autumn. There are evergreen and deciduous barberries, many of the latter showing fiery autumn colors. All have spiny stems, making an excellent choice for an impenetrable hedge, but with a wide range of species and cultivars to choose from, you can find a barberry for almost any exposure in the garden. They range from large specimens for hedging or borders to dwarf shrubs suitable for rock gardens.

Cultivation Grow in any moist but well-drained soil. Position in full sun or partial shade: autumn colors and fruiting are best in full sun. **Prune** after flowering: lightly trim or prune shoots that spoil the shape of evergreens, and cut back flowered shoots of deciduous types to strong buds or shoots. Trim hedges after flowering. **Take** semiripe cuttings of both types or softwood cuttings of deciduous types in summer (*see p.394*). Powdery mildew can be a problem (*see also p.398*); cut out badly affected parts.

Berberis darwinii (Darwin Barberry)
Z7 ‡↔ 10ft (3m), upright, evergreen, flowering in spring, sometimes again in autumn, with blue-black fruits in autumn

Berberis thunbergii 'Rose Glow'
Z4b (1m) occasionally more ↔ 8ft (2.5m), rounded and deciduous, with the first leaves of the season unvariegated

Berberis × stenophylla 'Corallina Compacta'
Z6b ↕↔ to 12in (30cm), evergreen, a dwarf cultivar of this normally large species, makes good edging

Berberis wilsoniae
Z6 ↕ 3ft (1m) ↔ 6ft (2m), mounding evergreen, with bright red-orange autumn leaf color

Berberis julianae (Wintergreen Barberry)
Z6 ↕↔ 10ft (3m), dense, upright evergreen, oblong blue-black fruits with a white bloom on them in autumn

Berberis thunbergii 'Dart's Red Lady'
Z4b ↕ 3ft (1m) occasionally more ↔ 8ft (2.5m), deciduous, deep red-purple leaves turning bright red (*see inset*) in autumn

Berberis 'Goldilocks'
Z6b ↕ 12ft (4m) ↔ 10ft (3m), evergreen, first upright, then spreading in shape, leaves to 2in (5cm) long

BETULA
Birch

THESE GRACEFUL, DECIDUOUS trees provide a display in every season: the textured bark, often peeling and silvery white or coppery brown, looks stunning in winter when there is little else to see; male and female flowers are borne in separate catkins on the same tree during spring, and the small, toothed, mid- to dark green leaves generally turn a soft yellow in autumn. This is a large group, with several species suitable for small gardens. The slender forms of many species look particularly attractive if room can be found for a small group of trees. The spreading *Betula medwedewii* and the popular weeping birches are among the most beautiful and elegant of specimen trees for a garden.

Cultivation Grow in reasonably fertile, well-drained soil. Site in sun or light, dappled shade; most will tolerate exposed positions. **Prune out** any misplaced or crossing branches during winter, when the trees are dormant, to maintain a healthy framework of branches. **Sow** seed (*see pp.391–393*) in a seedbed outdoors in autumn. **Take** softwood cuttings (*see p.394*) in summer. Mildew (*see p.398*) may appear, but mature trees should recover without spraying. Young trees could be treated if badly affected. Borers and gypsy moth larvae are common.

Betula papyrifera (Canoe birch, Paper birch)
Z2 ‡ 70ft (20m) ↔ 30ft (10m), new bark is pale orange-brown, paling with age, and autumn leaves are yellow to orange

Betula medwedewii (Transcaucasian birch)
Z5b ‡↔ 15ft (5m), growth is upright at first, becoming more spreading with age, male catkins to 4in (10cm) long (*see inset*)

Betula pendula 'Youngii' (Young's weeping birch)
Z2 ‡ 25ft (8m) ↔ 30ft (10m), a domed form of the usually upright silver birch, suitable for small gardens

Betula nigra (Black birch, River birch)
Z3 ‡ 60ft (18m) ↔ 40ft (12m), conical to spreading in habit, the bark fissured and gray-white or blackish on old trees

Betula utilis 'Silver Shadow'
Z3 ‡ 60ft (18m) ↔ 30ft (10m), with larger leaves than many other birches and particularly bright white bark

BRACHYGLOTTIS
Senecio

EVERGREEN SHRUBS WITH CLUSTERS of creamy white to deep yellow flowers in summer, these are ideal for exposed and coastal gardens. 'Sunshine', the most widely grown, belongs to a popular group of small cultivars called the Dunedin Hybrids. Usually about 30in (75cm) tall, these form mounds of oval, wavy-edged leaves, hairy at first, and produce clusters of bright yellow flower heads from summer until autumn. Other choices include *Brachyglottis repanda*, a spreading shrub to 10ft (3m) tall and wide with dark green leaves and creamy white flowers, and the compact *B. rotundifolia* (T min. 41°F/5°C) at 3ft (1m) more suitable for small gardens. Grow them in shrub borders; the foliage makes an effective contrast to narrow-leaved shrubs such as hebes (*see p.69*).

Cultivation Grow in well-drained soil in full sun. **Trim back** or lightly prune shoots that spoil the shape of the shrub after flowering. **Take** semiripe cuttings (*see p.394*) in summer.

BUDDLEJA
Butterfly bush

‡↔ to 15ft (5m)

THE FRAGRANT FLOWERS of buddlejas are wonderful for attracting hordes of butterflies. Most widely grown is the hardy *Buddleja davidii* (Z5b) and its cultivars, most growing to 8–10ft (2.5–3m) tall in a single season, with pink, purple, lilac, or white flowers in conical spikes on tall, arching shoots from late summer to early autumn. *B. globosa* (Z8), the orange ball tree, is a larger, rounded shrub, also hardy, that flowers in early summer. Buddlejas may be deciduous, semievergreen, or evergreen. They make an effective backdrop to other summer-flowering shrubs such as St. John's wort (*Hypericum, see p.74*) or potentillas (*see p.99*).

Cultivation Grow in fertile, well-drained soil in full sun; poorer soils are tolerated. **Prune** *B. davidii* and its cultivars by cutting old stems back to the base, in early spring (*see p.383*). Trim other buddlejas after flowering, only to keep them neat and within bounds. **Take** semiripe cuttings (*see p.394*) in summer or hardwood cuttings of *B. davidii* in autumn. If caterpillars are troublesome, pick them off by hand.

BUPLEURUM FRUTICOSUM
Shrubby hare's ear, Thorow-wax

EXCELLENT FOR COASTAL AREAS because it will withstand salt spray, this evergreen has a spreading habit, making it ideal for covering a wall or bank, or in a seaside garden. The small, starry, yellow flowers surrounded by leafy bracts are borne in rounded clusters from midsummer until autumn. This can grow to be a large and dense shrub, so it needs positioning near the back of a shrub or mixed border. Grow with other shrubs such as hawthorns (*Crataegus, see p.46*), St. John's wort (*Hypericum, see p.74*), and buddlejas (*see left*). Grow smaller speices in a rock garden.

Cultivation Will grow in any well-drained soil, preferring full sun in a warm, sheltered site. **Prune off** the fading flowers to prevent self-seeding. Trim back shoots that spoil the shape of the shrub in mid- or late spring: it will also tolerate hard pruning if it outgrows its space. **Sow** seed (*see pp.391–392*) in a container in a cold frame in spring. **Take** semiripe cuttings (*see p.394*) in summer.

Brachyglottis 'Sunshine'
T min. 35°F (2°C) ‡30in (75cm) ↔ 3ft (1m), tolerant of all but the shadiest, wettest locations, thrives in coastal gardens

① *B. davidii* 'Royal Red' ‡10ft (3m) ② *B. davidii* 'White Profusion' ‡10ft (3m) ③ *globosa* ‡↔ 15ft (5m) ④ *B.* 'Lochinch' ‡8ft (2.5m) ↔ 10ft (3m)

Bupleurum fruticosum (Shrubby hare's ear)
Z7b ‡6ft (2m) ↔ 8ft (2.5m)

BUXUS

Boxwood, Box

EVERGREEN BOXWOOD IS ONE OF the garden's most versatile plants. Although many varieties are naturally large and shrubby, all respond well to regular trimming. Tiny, yellow-green flowers appear in spring, but it is the neat, leathery foliage that steals the show. Used in hedges or screens, it furnishes a constant backdrop for seasonal action in the borders. You can clip boxwood into ornamental topiary shapes; simple forms need trimming only once or twice a year. Dwarf varieties were traditionally used to create knot gardens and parterres; they are also excellent for edging paths and borders, and as groundcover. Canadian hardiness zone for boxwoods included here is 6.

Cultivation Boxwood needs fertile, well-drained soil, ideally in partial shade; dry soil and full sun can cause dull or scorched foliage. **Trim** shrubs and hedges in summer; boxwood tolerates hard pruning in late spring if fertilized and well watered. **Take** semiripe cuttings in summer (*see p.394*). **Powdery mildew**, Pythium root rot, canker, dieback, and lead spots are common problems. Scale insects, leaf miners, psyllids, mites, and caterpillars can occur.

CALLICARPA

Beautyberry

‡3–10ft (1–3m)
↔ 3–8ft (1–2.5m)

APTLY NAMED, THE BEAUTYBERRY is valued for its vibrantly colored, bead-like, autumn berries. These remain on bare stems of deciduous species after the leaves fall, bringing color to a winter garden. Berries may be violet, lilac, white, or dusky purple and are most abundant after a long, hot summer. If you have space, plant groups of three or more to maximize fruiting. These shrubs are deciduous or evergreen with deep green or bronze leaves and varied habits. They bear clusters of small, white, red, purple, or pink flowers in summer. Other berrying shrubs and trees, such as cotoneasters (*see p.45*) and sorbus (*see p.118*), make good companions.

Cultivation Fertile, well-drained soil in full sun or light, dappled shade is suitable. **Cut back** the previous year's growth to the main stems in early spring (*see p.383*). If drastic pruning is required, cut back flowered shoots close to the base. **Sow** seed (*see pp.391–393*) in pots in a cold frame in autumn or spring. **Take** softwood cuttings in spring or semiripe cuttings in summer (*see p.394*).

CALLISTEMON

Bottlebrush

‡3–50ft (1–15m)
↔ 3–25ft (1–8m)

THE DISTINCTIVE, BRISTLY flower spikes that give these evergreen shrubs and trees their common name emerge in spring or summer. *Callistemon linearis* and *C. speciosus* (T min. 41°F/5°C) bloom into autumn. Bold hues of crimson, purple, pink, white, or gold flowers are set off by simple, leathery leaves. *C.* 'Firebrand' also has silvery pink shoots. Habits vary, but many have a spreading form. Tie them in loosely to trellises for an unusual wall covering. Natives of Australia, bottlebrushes thrive at the base of a warm wall in a shrub border, along with ceanothus (*see p.36*) and lavenders (*see p.80*). Grow tender species in containers and overwinter them in a cool greenhouse.

Cultivation Bottlebrushes like moist but well-drained, neutral to acid soil, in full sun. **Lightly trim** any shoots after flowering that spoil the shape of the shrub; the plants tolerate hard pruning if frost-damaged or grown out of their allotted space. **Sow** seed (*see pp.391–393*) on the surface of moist soil mix, in spring at 61–64°F (16–18°C). **Take** semiripe cuttings in late summer (*see p.394*).

B. sempervirens ① 'Elegantissima' ‡↔ 5ft (1.5m)
② 'Handsworthensis' ‡↔ 15ft (5m) ③ 'Latifolia Maculata'
‡8ft (2.5m) ↔ 6ft (2m) ④ 'Suffruticosa' ‡3ft (1m) ↔ 5ft (1.5m)

Callicarpa bodinieri var. *giraldii*
Z6b ‡10ft (3m) ↔ 8ft (2.5m), deciduous, upright bush, clusters of small pink flowers in midsummer

Callistemon pallidus (Lemon bottlebrush)
T min. 45°F (7°C) ‡↔ 6–12ft (2–4m), erect to spreading shrub, downy shoots, dark to gray-green leaves, 4in (10cm) flowers spring to midsummer

CALLUNA VULGARIS
Scots Heather

see also p.48
and pp.52–53

BELOVED BY BEES, THIS EVERGREEN SHRUB and its
cultivars have stems thickly encrusted with purple,
red, pink, or white bell-shaped flowers from
midsummer to late autumn. The flower spikes can
be up to 4in (10cm) long but become shorter as the
plants age. The foliage is usually dark green and
purple-tinged in winter; the linear leaves lie flat along
the stems. There are over five hundred, prostrate to
upright cultivars to choose from; all make excellent
groundcover, and some have striking foliage, like the
terracotta 'Firefly'. Grow in wildlife gardens, with
dwarf rhododendrons (*see pp.104–107*) and
conifers. All callunas mentioned here are in hardiness
Zone 4, although they may survive in Zone 3 with
winter protection.

Cultivation Callunas need an open site with well-drained, acidic
soil. **Cut back** flowered shoots to within 1in (2.5cm) of older growth
in early spring. **Mulch** with leaf mold or composted bark (*see p.388*)
in spring or autumn to encourage growth. **Take** semiripe cuttings 2in
(5cm) long in midsummer (*see p.394*). **Layer** shoots in spring as for
ericas (*see p.52*).

'Gold Haze'
‡4–24in (10–60cm) ↔ 18in (45cm), pale yellow foliage is retained
all year, white flower spikes are 2–4in (5–10cm) long

'Anthony Davis'
‡18in (45cm) ↔ to 30in (75cm), gray-green leaves, white flowers
over 4in (10cm) long, good for cutting

'Robert Chapman'
‡10in (25cm) ↔ 26in (65cm), gold foliage turns red and orange in
winter and spring, purple flower spikes are 2–4in (5–10cm) long

'Silver Knight'
‡16in (40cm) ↔ to 30in (75cm), downy gray foliage darkens to
purple-gray in winter, flower spikes are 2–4in (5–10cm) long

'Beoley Gold'
‡14in (35cm) ↔ to 30in (75cm), pure white flower spikes are
2–4in (5–10cm) long

‡3–70ft (1–20m)
↔2–25ft (60cm–8m)

THESE ELEGANT, EVERGREEN SHRUBS suit a range of uses from borders to woodland settings. They are also excellent container plants, and this is an ideal way of growing them if your soil is alkaline (high lime content), since camellias prefer a neutral to acidic soil. There are over 250 species, and the largest are very tall, but there are many smaller cultivars that are more suited to most gardens. The exquisite flowers in shades of pink, scarlet, and white appear in spring and last for several weeks. Borne singly or in clusters, they last well as cut flowers and some are slightly fragrant. Flowers may be single or double and vary considerably in size, the largest measuring 5in (13cm) or more across, but the average bloom is about half that size. The commonly grown camellias mentioned here are hardy in Zone 8; where not hardy, grow in a cool greenhouse. Dark green, glossy foliage guarantees that camellias stay beautiful all year.

Cultivation Grow in moist but well-drained, humus-rich, acidic soil (pH 5.5–5.6). **Shelter** from cold winds and position in partial shade, since early sun may damage the buds and flowers on frosty mornings. **Plant** with the top of the root ball just below the surface of the soil. Mulch in spring with 2–3in (5–8cm) leaf mold or shredded bark **Apply** a balanced fertilizer in mid-spring and again in early summer, and keep well watered during dry spells to prevent bud drop. **Protect** roots with a thatch of bracken or straw during prolonged cold spells. **Prune** lightly to shape in late spring or early summer after flowering, and deadhead. **Take** semiripe cuttings from late summer until early winter (*see p.394*). Viruses, bud and spider mites, canker, dieback, and weevils can be troublesome (*see p.398*).

Pruning young camellias

Young camellias develop a variety of habits. Careful pruning of young plants can help produce a well-balanced shape and encourage new, bushy growth. Reduce any thin, weak growth by cutting back to two or three buds or pruning it out entirely. Established plants require very little pruning. If plants have outgrown their space they can be cut back hard in early spring.

Shorten vigorous main shoots to balance shape

Remove badly placed dual leader

Pinch out tips to encourage branching at base

Tall central stem makes plant suitable for training against wall

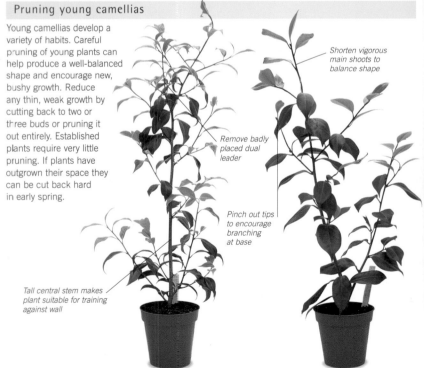

① *Camellia* 'Inspiration' ‡12ft (4m) ↔ 6ft (2m) ② *japonica* 'Adolphe Audusson' ‡10–20ft (3–6m) ↔ 3–10ft (1–3m) ③ *japonica* 'Alexander Hunter' ‡10–20ft (3–6m) ↔ 3–10ft (1–3m) ④ *japonica* 'Apollo' ‡10–20ft (3–6m) ↔ 3–10ft (1–3m) ⑤ *japonica* 'Ave Maria' ‡10–20ft (3–6m) ↔ 3–10ft (1–3m) ⑥ *japonica* 'Berenice Boddy' ‡10–20ft (3–6m) ↔ 3–10ft (1–3m) ⑦ *japonica* 'Betty Sheffield Supreme' ‡6–12ft (2–4m) ↔ 5–10ft (1.5–3m) ⑧ *japonica* 'Elegans' ‡10–20ft (3–6m) ↔ 3–10ft (1–3m)

⑨ *japonica* 'Gloire de Nantes' ‡10–20ft (3–6m) ↔ 3–10ft (1–3m) ⑩ *japonica* 'Guilio Nuccio' ‡10–20ft (3–6m) ↔ 3–10ft (1–3m) ⑪ *japonica* 'Hagoromo' ‡10–20ft (3–6m) ↔ 3–10ft (1–3m) ⑫ *japonica* 'Julia Drayton' ‡10–20ft (3–6m) ↔ 3–10ft (1–3m) ⑬ *japonica* 'Jupiter' ‡10–20ft (3–6m) ↔ 3–10ft (1–3m) ⑭ *japonica* 'Mrs D.W. Davis' ‡10–20ft (3–6m) ↔ 3–10ft (1–3m) ⑮ *japonica* 'R.L. Wheeler' ‡10–20ft (3–6m) ↔ 3–10ft (1–3m) ⑯ *japonica* 'Rubescens Major' ‡10–20ft (3–6m) ↔ 3–10ft

(1–3m) ⑰ *reticulata* 'Arch of Triumph' ‡10ft (3m) ↔ 15ft (5m) ⑱ *reticulata* 'William Hertrich' ‡↔ 20ft (6m) ⑲ *tsaii* ‡30 t (10m) ↔ 15ft (5m) ⑳ × *williamsii* 'Anticipation' (Z8–10) ‡12ft (4m) ↔ 6ft (2m) ㉑ × *williamsii* 'Bow Bells' ‡12ft (4m) ↔ 3–10ft (1–3m) ㉒ × *williamsii* 'Donation' ‡15ft (5m) ↔ 8ft (2.5m) ㉓ × *williamsii* 'J.C. Williams' ‡6–15ft (2–5m) ↔ 3–10ft (1–3m) ㉔ × *williamsii* 'Saint Ewe' ‡6–15ft (2–5m) ↔ 3–10ft (1–3m)

CARAGANA

Peashrub

THESE DECIDUOUS SHRUBS OR SMALL TREES thrive in
exposed sites with dry soils. They are found from
Eastern Europe to China, and their tolerance of
difficult conditions makes them very garden-worthy.
They have attractive leaves, and delicate, pealike
flowers in yellow, white, or pink, followed in autumn
by long, slender, brown pods. Caraganas are useful
as a windbreak or can be grown in a shrub or mixed
border with other trees and shrubs. *Caragana
arborescens* 'Pendula' is often sold grafted on top of a
straight, clear stem to form a small weeping standard.
The dwarf *C. arborescens* 'Nana' is slow-growing, to
30in (75cm) tall and wide, with twisted branches; it
makes an unusual rock-garden plant.

Cultivation Grow in well-drained, reasonably fertile soil in full sun.
Will also tolerate poor, dry soils in exposed places. **Prune** minimally,
only to remove any misplaced shoots, in late winter or early spring.
Sow seed in containers in a cold frame as soon as it is ripe (*see
pp.391–392*); or sow in spring, presoaking the seeds before sowing to
soften the seed coat. **Take** softwood cuttings in spring (*see p.394*).

CARPINUS

Hornbeam

THERE ARE 35–40 SPECIES of these deciduous,
woodland trees, several of which make good garden
trees and can also be grown as handsome hedges.
Grown as trees, they have an elegant habit, ranging
from columnar and pyramid-shaped – the flamelike
Carpinus betulus 'Fastigiata' is particularly popular –
to rounded and spreading. Their beechlike foliage is
mid- to dark green and often glossy; smooth, fluted
gray bark is another pleasing feature. In spring, they
produce yellow-green catkins, followed by drooping,
hoplike, green fruits, maturing to brown or yellow.
Autumn foliage color is striking, too, when the leaves
turn to gold and amber.

Cultivation Grow in reasonably fertile, well-drained soil in sun or
partial shade. **Prune** young trees to remove any misplaced or crossing
branches in late winter or early spring; trim hedges in mid- to late
summer. Hornbeams can withstand severe pruning if they outgrow
their space. **Sow** seed in a seedbed outdoors in autumn (*see
pp.391–393*). **Take** greenwood cuttings in early summer (*see p.394*).

CARYOPTERIS

SMALL, DAINTY SHRUBS with a mound-forming
habit, caryopteris bear masses of small, fluffy flowers
in shades of blue. The group includes both these
deciduous shrubs and some perennials, found in a
variety of habitats from dry, hot slopes to woodland.
They flower from late summer until autumn; most
have gray- or silvery green foliage, giving a cool look,
although 'Worcester Gold' has warm yellow foliage.
Caryopteris are elegant front-of-border shrubs,
especially planted in groups; they make a striking
contrast with yellow-flowered potentillas (*see p.99*)
or St. John's wort (*Hypericum, p.74*).

Cultivation Grow in light but moderately fertile soil, in full sun.
Plant against a warm wall in very cold areas, especially if summers are
also cool. **Prune** the previous year's flowered shoots in early spring,
cutting them back to only three or four good buds, so that a
permanent stubby framework of shoots develops. If necessary,
caryopteris can be cut down almost to soil level. **Sow** seed in autumn
in a cold frame (*see pp.391–392*). **Take** softwood cuttings in late
spring, or semiripe cuttings in early summer (*see p.394*).

Caragana arborescens (Siberian pea tree)
Z2 ‡20ft (6m) ↔ 12ft (4m), thorny shrub, light green leaves, pale
lemon flowers in late spring

Carpinus betulus
Z5 ‡80ft (25m) ↔ 70ft (20m), as a tree pyramid-shaped, rounded
when mature; retains brown leaves over winter

Caryopteris × clandonensis 'Kew Blue' (Bluebeard)
Z6 ‡3ft (1m) ↔ 5ft (1.5m), excellent on chalky soils, leaves silver-
gray underneath, attractive seedheads

CASSIOPE

ORIGINATING FROM WINDSWEPT ARCTIC and alpine regions, this is a small group of dwarf, evergreen shrubs with a ground-hugging habit. They have tiny, overlapping, almost scalelike leaves that clasp the short, slender stems. In late spring and early summer, they produce tiny, nodding, bell-shaped flowers that hang singly or in pairs. The flowers are white, sometimes tinged red. Cassiope do best in acidic soil and need plenty of moisture. They are so small that they are suitable only for the rock garden or alpine trough, or perhaps planted in drifts in open woodland. 'Edinburgh' is the easiest to grow, and looks good with dwarf rhododendrons and conifers in an open position.

Cultivation Best grown in a sheltered site in moist, acidic soil in partial shade or an open sunny site. *C. tetragona* tolerates some alkali. **Sow** seed in a container in a cold frame in autumn (*see pp.391–392*). **Take** semiripe cuttings in summer (*see p.394*), and layer shoots in autumn or early spring (*see p.395*).

CATALPA

CATALPAS ARE DECIDUOUS TREES with year-round appeal, with their showy, often beautifully colored foliage, large flowers, and distinctive seed pods. The bell-shaped flowers are borne in upright clusters in mid- and late summer. They are followed in autumn by beanlike seed pods, usually more than 1ft (30cm) long. Catalpas have a wide, spreading habit and are best admired when grown as specimen trees on a lawn. Several varieties can be pollarded (cutting the trunk to 3 ft (1m), then cutting stems back to this stubby head each year) to produce lollipop-shaped, foliage shrubs with very large, ornamental leaves. They will thrive in sheltered city gardens.

Cultivation Grow in fertile, moist but well-drained soil in full sun, with shelter from strong winds. **Protect** young plants from severe frosts with burlap. **Prune** in late winter or early spring, either to pollard (*see above*), or in trees, only if necessary to maintain a healthy branch framework. **Sow** seed in pots in autumn (*see pp.391–392*). **Take** softwood cuttings in late spring or summer (*p.394*).

Catalpa bignonioides (Indian bean tree)
Z5 ↕ ↔ 50ft (15m), broad heart-shaped leaves, fragrant flowers, pencil-thin seed pods to 16in (40cm) long (*see inset*)

Cassiope fastigiata 'Edinburgh'
Z3 ↕ ↔ to 10in (25cm), low-growing but with upright shoots, flowers produced at stem tips in late spring

Catalpa bignonioides 'Aurea' (Southern catalpa)
Z5 ↕ ↔ 30ft (10m), slow-growing, leaves bronze when young, unfold in early summer, good pollarded to form a shrub (*see inset*)

Catalpa speciosa (Indian cigar, Northern catalpa)
Z5 ↕ ↔ 50ft (15m), spreading habit, flowers larger and showier than most other catalpas, seed pods to 20in (50cm) long

CEANOTHUS
California lilac

VIGOROUS, SPREADING SHRUBS, California lilacs are grown for their masses of usually blue, but sometimes white or pink flowers. They flower abundantly, in small fluffy clusters at the tips of stems or on small sideshoots. Most of the evergreen ceanothus are best suited to growing against a wall or fence or in a sheltered spot. Prostrate or low-growing species make superb groundcover plants and are ideal for sloping banks. The deciduous types, generally hardier than the evergreens, make more compact plants, especially if pruned annually back to a stubby framework of stems, and are ideal in a border. California lilacs are not very long-lived and dislike being transplanted.

Cultivation Grow in any fertile soil in full sun, sheltered from strong, cold winds. **Tolerant** of alkaline soils but may develop yellow leaves (chlorosis) on shallow, limy soils. **Prune** in early spring, lightly trimming evergreens to maintain a good shape, and cutting deciduous types back to a permanent framework; treat all wall-trained plants as for deciduous species. **Take** greenwood cuttings of deciduous types in summer or semiripe cuttings of all types in late summer (*see p.394*).

CHECK AND LOOSEN TIES
If wall-training a ceanothus, check the ties regularly. If they become too tight, they can restrict and chafe the growing stems.

Ceanothus 'Cascade'
Z8 ↕↔ 12ft (4m), vigorous, arching evergreen, flowering from spring to early summer

Ceanothus 'Blue Mound'
Z8 ↕ 5ft (1.5m) ↔ 6ft (2m), prostrate, mound-forming evergreen, flowering in late spring

Ceanothus 'Blue Cushion'
Z8 ↕ 18–30in (45–75cm) ↔ 3–6ft (1–2m), spreading but dense and tidy evergreen, ideal as a groundcover plant, flowering profusely in summer

Ceanothus × *pallidus* 'Perle Rose' (California lilac)
Z8 ↕↔ 5ft (1.5m), bushy, deciduous type, flowering from midsummer to autumn

CEDRUS
Cedar

↕130ft (to 40m)
↔30ft (to 10m)

THESE LARGE, EVERGREEN conifers make impressive specimen trees, needing plenty of space if their stature is to be fully appreciated (although there are some dwarf cultivars). Conical when young, they later develop spreading, horizontal branches. Cedars are best grown on their own, or with other large trees where space allows; they are very long-lived. Their needles are arranged in clusters on short shoots; there are cedars with either bright golden or glaucous blue foliage, as well as plain green. Male cones are cylindrical and light brown; female cones are oblong or barrel-shaped, and green when they first appear, ripening and turning brown over two years.

Cultivation Grow in any reasonably fertile soil in an open, sunny position. **Prune** only if the trees happen to produce two leading shoots, cutting out the weaker shoot in autumn. **Sow** seed (*see pp.391–393*) in spring after keeping them moist and in a refrigerator at 32–41°F (0–5°C) for three weeks.

CERATOSTIGMA
Chinese plumbago

TRUE BLUE, LATE-SUMMER FLOWERS, from pale Wedgwood to deep indigo, distinguish these small shrubs, all growing to about 3ft (1m) tall. The group also includes the woody-based perennial *Ceratostigma plumbaginoides* (Z6), which is short and perfect for the front of a border. There are deciduous, evergreen, or semievergreen species, the leaves of all turning red in autumn to provide a brilliant foil for late flowers. Their coloring is particularly dramatic in a mixed or shrub border next to yellow daylilies (*Hemerocallis, see p.258*) or St. John's wort (*Hypericum, see p.74*). Growth often dies back in very cold winters but usually regrows in spring.

Cultivation Grow in light, reasonably fertile soil, in full sun. **Prune back** to within 1in (2.5cm) of a permanent framework after flowering or in early spring. **Remove** any growth that has been damaged during winter in spring; new shoots will appear from the base. **Take** softwood cuttings in spring or semiripe cuttings in summer (*see p.394*). Shoots can be layered (*see p.395*) in autumn. Susceptible to powdery mildew (*see also* Mildew, *p.398*); increase air circulation around plants.

CERCIDIPHYLLUM
Katsura tree

FIERY AUTUMN DISPLAYS OF yellow, orange, and red leaves that smell of burned sugar when crushed are the chief attraction of this tree. The mid-green, oval to rounded leaves are also bronze when young. The best autumn color is produced on acidic soils. All katsuras belong to one species, *Cercidiphyllum japonicum*. There is a weeping form and also a variety that is a smaller tree, despite being called *magnificum*. Planted as a specimen tree, the katsura can show off its form, pyramidal when young and becoming more rounded with age. Open woodland settings are also attractive if space allows.

Cultivation Grow in good, fertile soil enriched with plenty of well-rotted organic matter in sun or partial shade, sheltered from cold, drying winds. **Prune out** any crossing branches or those that spoil the shape of the tree in late winter or early spring. Plants often develop several main stems, but these can be reduced to one if desired, provided that the tree is still young. **Take** basal cuttings in late spring, semiripe cuttings in midsummer (*see p.394*).

Cedrus deodora 'Aurea' (Himalayan cedar)
Z7 ↕15ft (5m), a slow-growing cultivar with golden yellow spring foliage that becomes greener in summer

Ceratostigma willmottianum
Z7 ↕3ft (1m) ↔5ft (1.5m), bushy deciduous shrub with purple-edged leaves, turning red in autumn

Cercidiphyllum japonicum
Z5 ↕70ft (20m) ↔50ft (15m), eventual size is affected by climate; the tree tends to remain smaller in cooler areas

CERCIS
Redbud

↕↔ 30ft (to 10m)

DECIDUOUS TREES from woodland edges, these make excellent specimen plants in a yard or in a large shrub border. They are grown for their foliage and their clusters of pink or purple flowers, borne in profusion in spring before the leaves. The flowers of the Judas tree, *Cercis siliquastrum* (Z7), appear directly on the branches. This is the largest species; choose *C. chinensis* (Z6) or *C. canadensis* (Z5b) for a smaller yard; the latter can also be kept small by pollarding (cut the trunk to 3 ft (1 m), then cut the shoots that emerge back to this head each year). The leaves of all species are heart-shaped, and turn yellow in autumn.

Cultivation Grow in fertile, moist but well-drained soil in full sun or partial shade. Plant while the trees are young; older plants resent root disturbance. **Prune out** crossing branches in late winter or early spring to maintain a healthy, well-shaped framework. *C. canadensis* 'Forest Pansy' can be pollarded in early spring for larger, showier foliage. **Sow** seed (*see pp.391–392*) in containers in a cold frame in autumn. **Take** semiripe cuttings (*see p.394*) in summer.

CHAENOMELES
Flowering quince, Japanese quince, Japonica

↕ 8ft (to 2.5m)
↔ 15ft (to 5cm)

THESE VERSATILE SHRUBS, among the first to flower, are usually grown in shrub borders or trained against a wall but also make a useful groundcover or a shady, informal hedge. They are also tolerant of urban conditions. Deciduous and spiny-branched, they flower in shades of red and pink. The flowers, single or double, are borne all along the stems, appearing before and with the leaves. They are followed in autumn by applelike, yellow to green fruits, which are edible after being cooked; the true edible quince is a different tree, *Cydonia* (*see p.47*).

Cultivation Grow in reasonably fertile soil: avoid very alkaline soil, where the leaves may yellow. **Position** in full sun or partial shade. **Cut back** shoots after flowering: cut to strong buds lower down, or if wall-trained cut back to the permanent framework. **Sow** seed (*see pp.391–393*) in a cold frame or seedbed. **Take** semiripe cuttings (*see p.394*) in summer or layer shoots (*see p.395*) in autumn.

Chaenomeles × *superba* 'Crimson and Gold'
Z5b ↕ 3ft (1m) ↔ 6ft (2m), later flowering than others, into late spring, green fruit ripening to yellow in autumn

Cercis canadensis 'Forest Pansy' (Eastern redbud)
Z5b ↕↔ 15ft (5m), may not flower in all locations, but the purple foliage gives a reliable display

Chaenomeles speciosa 'Moerloosei'
Z5b ↕ 8ft (2.5m) ↔ 15ft (5m), particularly early-flowering, with fragrant fruits (*see inset*) in autumn

Chaenomeles × *californica* 'Enchantress'
Z6b ↕ 8ft (2.5m) ↔ 6ft (2m), the autumn fruits are large and golden yellow

CHAMAECYPARIS
False cypress

IDEAL FOR HEDGING, these evergreen, coniferous trees are not overly vigorous and tolerate some clipping; their attractive growth habit also makes many of them handsome specimen plants. Grow them with other conifers such as *Cupressus* (*see p.46*) or with large rhododendrons (*see pp.104–107*). There are also many dwarf or slow-growing cultivars, and these can be used in smaller borders or even in large rock gardens. The leaves are scalelike and flattened; contact with the foliage may aggravate some skin allergies. False cypresses bear round or oval male cones in spring, which are followed in summer by round or angular female cones that ripen in autumn. The Canadian hardiness zone ranges from 4–6.

Cultivation Grow in moist but well-drained, preferably neutral to acidic soil, although they will tolerate deep, alkaline soils. Position in full sun. **Trim** trees used for hedging from late spring to autumn, but do not cut into older wood. **Sow** seed (*see pp.391–393*) in a seedbed outdoors in spring or take semiripe cuttings (*see p.394*) in late summer.

① *lawsoniana* 'Pembury Blue' ↕50ft (15m) ② *nootkatensis* 'Pendula' ↕100ft (30m) ③ *obtusa* 'Nana Aurea' ↕6ft (2m) ④ *pisifera* 'Filifera Aurea' ↕40ft (12m)

CHIMONANTHUS PRAECOX
Wintersweet

POWERFULLY FRAGRANT, WAXY flowers hang from the bare shoots of *Chimonanthus praecox* throughout winter. This deciduous shrub has flowers that are pale sulfur yellow, stained brown or purple inside. Young plants take a few years to reach flowering age. Although the shrub is not unattractive in leaf, winter is its real season of interest, so plant it near a doorway or where you will come across it and its extraordinary scent on winter walks. It can also be trained against a sunny wall, and this may be advisable in cooler areas, because good, sunny summers are needed to ripen the wood in an open position.

Cultivation Grow in any fertile, well-drained soil in full sun. **Prune** only mature shrubs that flower regularly in late winter, when dormant, or in early spring. Cut out any crossing or misshapen branches to maintain a healthy framework and good shape; cut back the shoots of wall-trained plants to 2–4 buds above the permanent framework of branches. **Sow** seed (*see pp.391–392*) in containers in a cold frame as soon as it is ripe. **Take** softwood cuttings (*see p.394*) in summer.

Chimonanthus praecox 'Grandiflorus'
Z7 ↕12ft (4m) ↔ 10ft (3m), flowers that are both larger and a deeper yellow than the species

CHIONANTHUS
Fringe tree

LARGE, ATTRACTIVE SHRUBS, fringe trees are grown for their long, narrow leaves and their fragrant, white flowers, which are borne in clusters during summer. Two spreading, deciduous shrubs from this large and varied genus are grown in gardens: *Chionanthus retusus* (Z6) has upright flower clusters and peeling bark, while *C. virginicus* has hanging flower clusters and larger leaves that have bright, golden yellow autumn color. In autumn, the flowers of both shrubs are followed by blue-black fruits. Fringe trees make excellent specimen plants; they also work well grown in a shrub border along with plants such as abelias (*see p.14*), choisyas (*see p.40*), or camellias (*see pp.32–33*).

Cultivation Grow in reasonably fertile soil in full sun: *C. retusus* tolerates alkaline soil, but *C. virginicus* needs an acidic soil. Flowering and fruiting are best in climates with hot summers. **Prune out** crossing or badly placed branches in winter or early spring, to prevent growth becoming unhealthily crowded. **Sow** seed (*see pp.391–392*) in containers in a cold frame in autumn; germination may take as long as 18 months.

Chionanthus virginicus (White Fringe tree)
Z5 ↕10ft (3m) ↔ 10ft (3m) or more, the lower branches can be pruned back to the trunk to encourage a more treelike form

CHOISYA

Mexican orange blossom

THE GLOSSY, AROMATIC FOLIAGE of these evergreen shrubs guarantees a year-round appeal in any garden, quite apart from the fact that most give a superb, late summer and autumn show of abundant, starry, sweetly fragrant flowers. Of the commonly available Mexican orange blossoms, 'Aztec Pearl' and *Choisya ternata* are particularly good value, since they also produce an early flush of blooms in late spring before the main flowering toward the end of summer. Although *C. ternata* 'Sundance' rarely flowers, this is more than made up for by its spring foliage, which can light up the dullest border with a ray of sunshine.

Cultivation Choisyas prefer a fertile, well-drained soil in full sun but tolerate partial shade. Where not hardy, grow in a cool greenhouse. **Trim** any shoots that spoil the shape of the shrub after flowering. **Take** semiripe cuttings in summer (*see p.394*). Snails and slugs have a liking for these shrubs; while the plant is small and vulnerable, it is well worth discouraging them (*see p.260*).

CISTUS

Rock rose, Sun rose

↕↔ most to 3ft (1m),
some to 6ft (2m)

ROCK ROSES ARE EVERGREENS, grown for their profuse, saucer-shaped flowers in white to purplish pink. They appear from early to late summer; each bloom lasts only one day but is quickly replaced to keep the display going. Rock roses thrive in sunny spots in a shrub border, at the base of a wall or spilling over the side of a raised bed. They appreciate dry conditions and poor soil, and so grow very well as low-maintenance container plants and alongside such demanding plants as shrub roses that take a lot out of the soil. They can be short-lived; take cuttings to make replacement plants. Except where noted, those mentioned here are tender (T min. 41–45°F/ 5–7°C).

Cultivation Grow rock roses in full sun, in poor to reasonably fertile, well-drained soil, including alkaline soil. **Pinch out** the growing tips of young plants to encourage a bushy habit; lightly trim shoots that spoil the shape of the shrub in spring, or after flowering. Old, woody plants are best replaced. **Sow** seed (*see pp.391–392*) in a cold frame when it is ripe, or in spring. **Take** softwood cuttings in summer (*see p.394*).

CLERODENDRUM

THIS IS A LARGE GROUP OF TROPICAL and subtropical plants, although some of the elegant, shrubby species are robust enough to be grown outdoors in cooler, temperate climates. The hardy, deciduous shrubs include *Clerodendrum trichotomum* (Z6), a large shrub for a garden or woodland glade, and the glory flower (*C. bungei* Z8), smaller but still up to 6ft (2m) tall. Where not hardy, grow in a warm greenhouse. Both are valued for their large clusters of often fragrant flowers, usually produced from late summer to autumn.

Cultivation Grow in soil enriched with well-rotted organic matter to make sure it is fertile and moist but well-drained, in full sun. **Pruning** is rarely needed by *C. trichotomum*; wayward branches can be removed, or shoots trimmed, in late winter or early spring. *C. bungei* should be cut back to a low, permanent framework in early spring. **Sow** seed (*see pp.391–392*) at 55–64°F (13–18°C) in spring. **Take** semiripe cuttings in summer (*see p.394*), rooting them in a heated propagator. *C. bungei* tends to produce suckers (a new shoot growing from below ground) that can make new plants: scrape back the soil to find one that has developed some roots in autumn or spring; carefully cut it away from the parent plant; and pot it up.

Choisya ternata 'Sundance'
Z7b ↕↔ 8ft (2.5m), the buttery young foliage is best in bright sun, achieving only a greenish yellow in shade

① × *argenteus* 'Peggy Sammons' ↕↔ to 3ft (1m)
② × *dansereaui* 'Decumbens' ↕↔ 3ft (1m) ③ × *hybridus*
Z7b ↕↔ to 5ft (1.5m) ④ × *skanbergii* Z7b ↕↔ to 3ft (1m)

Clerodendrum trichotomum var. *fargesii*
Z6 ↕↔ 15–20ft (5–6m), dark clusters of fruits that follow the pinky white flowers in midsummer to late autumn

CLETHRA

Summersweet, Sweet pepper bush,

THESE EVERGREEN AND DECIDUOUS SHRUBS and trees
are grown for their handsome foliage and spikes of
white flowers. The blooms are very fragrant and are
borne from mid- to late summer; sited beneath the
canopy of a woodland garden, they will perfume the
still air wonderfully. Summersweets can also be grown
in a shady corner of a shrubbery, or close to a seating
area where their scent can be enjoyed. The lily-of-
the-valley tree (*Clethra arborea*) is not hardy, and in
temperate climates is best grown in a large tub so that
it can be moved under cover to a cool greenhouse for
the winter. This plant is not commonly grown in
North America.

Cultivation Grow in dappled shade in acidic, fertile, moist, well-
drained soil. In containers, use an acidic potting mix. **Prune out**
wayward branches in late winter, and for *C. alnifolia,* once mature, cut
back a few of the old stems to the base; this stimulates strong new
growth. *C. arborea* need only be deadheaded, although it can be
pruned to fit the available space. **Sow** seed (*see pp.391–392*) at 43-
–54°F (6–12°C) in spring or autumn. **Take** semiripe cuttings of
deciduous species in mid- or late summer (*see p.394*).

COLUTEA

Bladder senna

↕↔ 6–10ft (2–3m)

Decorative, greenish brown, inflated
seedpods give these deciduous shrubs
their common name. They are good all-
round plants with soft, pale or blue-
green foliage and, in summer, large,
yellow or brown, pealike flowers that are followed by
the fat pods. Bladder sennas are very resilient plants
and can be used in problematic sites such as exposed
and coastal areas, sloping, free-draining banks,
gardens affected by urban pollution, and sites with
poor, dry soils.

Cultivation Bladder sennas will tolerate most conditions although
they prefer reasonably fertile, well-drained soil in full sun. **Prune** them
according to the available space; either removing only wayward, dead
or damaged branches, or keeping the shrub small by cutting it down
to a low, permanent framework in late winter or early spring.
C. arborescens can also be trained as a standard. **Sow** seed (*see
pp.391–392*) in autumn or early spring and germinate with the
protection of a cold frame.

CORDYLINE

Cabbage palm, Cabbage tree

THE PALMLIKE CORDYLINES are architectural shrubs
that can bring a touch of the exotic to a temperate
garden. In warm areas use them as focal points; given
the time and space most species will become treelike
in stature. Where not hardy, grow them as houseplants and move them under cover in winter;
cordylines make handsome plants in a conservatory or
greenhouse. These plants are valued mainly for their
spiky, leathery leaves, often variegated or brightly
colored. An occasional bonus in summer are tall,
heavy stems of white, perfumed flowers, followed by
beadlike berries in white, red, purple, or blue.

Cultivation Grow in fertile, well-drained soil in full sun or semishade; the cultivars with colored foliage prefer some shade. In
containers, use any good potting mix with some added grit and top-
dress annually in spring (*see p.386*). **Sow** seed (*see pp.391–392*) in
spring at 61°F (16°C), or for an instant result cut well-rooted suckers
(small plantlets growing up around the central crown) away from the
parent plant in spring and pot them up individually.

Clethra arborea (Lily-of-the-valley tree)
T min. 45°F (7°C) ↕ 25ft (8m) ↔ 20ft (6m), young shoots are red,
the spikes of flowers may be up to 6in (15cm) long

Colutea arborescens
Z4 ↕↔ 10ft (3m), flowers over a very long period in summer, often
still in bloom as the first pods are developing

Cordyline australis 'Torbay Red'
T min. 50°F (10°C) ↕ 10–30ft (3–10m) ↔ 3–12ft (1–4m), the
eventual size is largely dependent on the prevailing climate

CORNUS
Dogwood

BEAUTIFUL FLOWER HEADS, DECORATIVE BARK, and vibrant autumn leaves make these outstanding garden plants. Dogwoods include deciduous shrubs, small trees, and woody-based perennials. Some, such as *Cornus alternifolia*, have an airy, tiered shape and make graceful specimen trees. Many of the shrubby types, such as *C. alba*, *C. sanguinea*, and *C. sericea* and their cultivars, are grown principally for their bright red, yellow, or green bark. These dogwoods are especially welcome in winter, when the thickets of stems seem to glow with color; the color is at its most intense if the plants are regularly coppiced. Creeping *C. canadensis* (Z2) can be used in woodland or as groundcover in a shrub border. The small, starry flowers are borne in clusters at the tips of the shoots, and in dogwoods grown for their flowering displays, for example *C. capitata*, *C. florida*, *C. kousa*, *C. nuttallii*, and many hybrids, they are surrounded by prominent petal-like bracts (modified leaves), which may be cream, white, or pink. In some plants, the berries or strawberry-like fruits that follow the flowers in autumn could cause mild stomach upset if they are eaten.

Cultivation Dogwoods can be grown in sun or partial shade. **Plant** flowering dogwoods (those with large bracts) in fertile, neutral to acid soil with plenty of well-rotted organic matter added to it. All other types tolerate a wide range of conditions. Those that are grown for their winter stem color are best positioned in full sun. **Prune** hard (coppice) those grown for stem color every spring to produce young shoots, which have the brightest color (*see below*). Other dogwoods require little pruning except to keep them within bounds or to maintain the shape of the shrub; cutting out one in four of the older shoots in late winter or early spring every year will restrict the spread of the shrub. **Renovate** neglected plants by cutting out old wood at the center of the shrub. **Sow** seed in a seedbed in autumn, or expose it to a period of cold weather and sow in spring (*see pp.391–393*). Take hardwood cuttings (*see p.394*) of dogwoods grown for stem color in autumn.

How to coppice dogwoods

Allow a full year after planting for the shrub to develop, then cut back hard before growth starts in spring. Afterwards apply a general organic fertilizer around the shrub to encourage strong new growth and mulch with a thick layer of well-rotted organic matter.

▷ **Pruning for colored stems** *In the first year after planting, cut back all the stems to 2–3in (5–8cm) from the base. After this the stems can be cut back each spring to just above two buds of the previous year's growth; this allows the plant to develop into a larger shrub.*

Old wood will be hidden by shrubs in front

Hardest pruned shrub remains smallest

◁ **Staggered pruning** *Where shrubby dogwoods are planted in a group, coppicing to varying levels creates a sloping effect rather than a dense mass of stems of uniform height. This is particularly useful for breaking up a border and making it look more interesting.*

① ***Cornus alba* 'Elegantissima'** Z2 ↕↔ 10ft (3m) ② *alba* 'Kesselringii' Z2 ↕↔ 10ft (3m) ③ *alba* 'Sibirica' Z2 ↕↔ 10ft (3m) ④ *alba* 'Spaethii' Z2 ↕↔ 10ft (3m) ⑤ *alternifolia* 'Argentea' Z4 ↕ 10ft (3m) ↔ 8ft (2.5m) ⑥ *capitata* Z8 ↕↔ 40ft (12m) ⑦ *controversa* 'Variegata' Z5 ↕↔ 25ft (8m) ⑧ **'Eddie's White Wonder'** Z7 ↕ 20ft (6m) ↔ 15ft (5m)

⑨ *florida* 'Cherokee Chief' Z5b ↕20ft (6m) ↔25ft (8m)   ⑩ *florida* 'Spring Song' Z5b ↕20ft (6m)
↔25ft (8m)   ⑪ *florida* 'Welchii' Z5b ↕20ft (6m) ↔25ft (8m)   ⑫ *kousa* var. *chinensis* Z6 ↕22f (t7m)
↔15ft (5m)   ⑬ *kousa* 'China Girl' Z6 ↕22ft (7m)   ↔15ft (5m)   ⑭ *kousa* 'Satomi' Z6 ↕22ft (7m)
↔15ft (5m)   ⑮ *macrophylla* Z7b ↕40ft (12m) ↔25ft (8m)   ⑯ *mas* Z4b ↕↔15ft (5m)

⑰ 'Norman Hadden' Z8 ↔25ft (8m)   ⑱ *nuttallii* Z7 ↕40ft (12m) ↔25ft (8m)
⑲ *nuttallii* 'Colrigo Giant' Z7 ↕40ft (12m) ↔25ft (8m)   ⑳ 'Porlock' Z6 ↕30ft (10m)
↔15ft (5m)   ㉑ *sanguinec* 'Winter Beauty' Z4 ↕10ft (3m) ↔8ft (2.5m)   ㉒ *sericea*
'Flaviramea' Z2 ↕6ft (2m) ↔12ft (4m)   ㉓ *sericea* 'Kelseyi' Z2 ↕30in (75cm) ↔5ft (1.5m)

CORYLOPSIS
Winter hazel

THE SLENDER, BARE SHOOTS of these small trees and shrubs bear fragile, pendent clusters of bell-shaped flowers in spring before the leaves emerge. The flower clusters are fragrant and are up to 6in (15cm) long. The leaves are broadly oval and pale to dark green. These are graceful shrubs with open, spreading habits and look handsome in partly shaded sites, such as in a woodland setting. Combine these trouble-free plants with other early flowering trees and shrubs, such as *Corylus avellana* 'Contorta' (*see right*), magnolias (*see p.86*), and small willows (*Salix, see p.114*).

Cultivation Corylopsis prefer reasonably fertile, acidic soil that is reliably moist but well-drained and in partial shade. **Prune out** misplaced or crossing shoots if necessary, to maintain a good shape and healthy framework of shoots, immediately after flowering. **Take** greenwood cuttings – from slightly more mature shoots than softwood – in summer (*see p.394*). Layer shoots in autumn (*see p.395*).

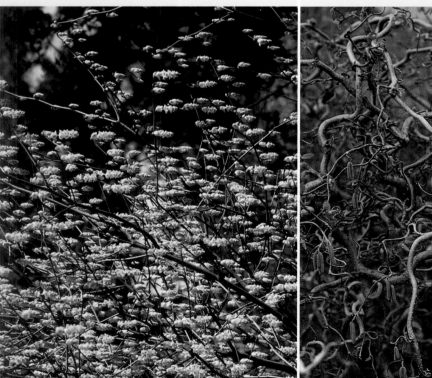

Corylopsis glabrescens
Z7 ‡ ↔ 15ft (5m), upright shrub, dark green leaves with blue-green undersides, flowers in midspring

CORYLUS
Filbert, Hazel

LONG CATKINS AND ATTRACTIVE FOLIAGE and habits make hazels worthy garden plants. These small to medium-sized, deciduous shrubs and trees begin the season in late winter or spring by producing yellow, occasionally purple, male catkins. Broadly heart-shaped, toothed leaves follow that may be colored. Some foliage displays autumnal tints. *Corylus avellana* 'Contorta' has strikingly twisted stems that enhance the winter garden and are favorites with flower arrangers. Edible hazelnuts and filberts are produced by *C. avellana* and *C. maxima* (Z5) in autumn. Larger hazels look good as specimens; use smaller species in a border with shrubs such as hamamelis (*see p.68*) or mahonias (*see p.87*).

Cultivation Hazels grow well in fertile, well-drained, preferably chalky or alkaline soil, in sun or partial shade. **Remove** suckers (strong, straight growths from the base of the plant) as soon as you see them. **Layer** shoots (*see p.395*) in autumn. **Prune** if needed only to keep them in shape, in winter or early spring (*see p.383*).

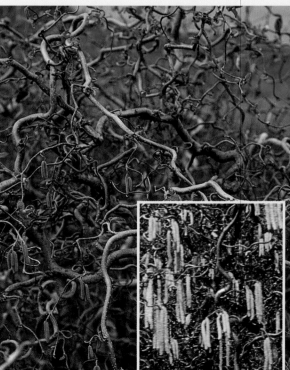

Corylus avellana 'Contorta' (Corkscrew hazel)
Z3 ‡ ↔ 15ft (5m), upright shrub with mid-green leaves, 2½in (6cm) catkins in late winter and early spring (*see inset*)

COTINUS
Smoke bush

‡ 5–30ft (15–10m)
↔ 15–25ft (5–8m)

THIS SMALL GROUP OF deciduous shrubs and small, bushy trees are prized for their ornamental, colorful foliage and unusual flowers. These are tiny, but mass in great plumes above the foliage in summer. These resemble puffs of smoke from a distance – hence the common name. The flowers are followed by tiny fruits lasting into autumn, when the foliage changes color. That of *Cotinus coggygria* 'Royal Purple' turns from dark red-purple to red; that of *C.* 'Grace' from purple to a bright, translucent scarlet. They look particularly good in autumn as specimens or planted in groups.

Cultivation Cotinus prefer reasonably fertile, well-drained soil, in sun or partial shade. Purple-leaved types have the best-colored foliage in full sun. **Cut out** misplaced or crossing shoots to maintain a well-shaped flowering shrub, in late winter or early spring (*see p.382*). For the best foliage display, keep 3–5 main stems to 24–36in (60–90cm) long and in early spring, cut all shoots to 2–3 buds above the main stems. **Take** softwood cuttings (*see p.394*) in summer or layer shoots (*see p.395*) in spring.

① *Cotinus coggygria* 'Royal Purple' Z4b ‡ ↔ 15ft (5m), flowers green, turning gray in autumn ② 'Grace' Z5 ‡ 20ft (6m) ↔ 15ft (5m), vigorous, flowers purple-pink

COTONEASTER

DENSE BUT DAINTY FOLIAGE, a variety of ornamental forms, and autumn berries ensure this plant a place in many gardens. There are many deciduous, semi-evergreen, and evergreen shrubs to choose from. Tiny, pink or white flowers in summer are followed by masses of berries in vivid reds and yellows – all much appreciated by birds. The wide range of growth habits makes cotoneasters suitable for many sites. They can be grown as freestanding shrubs, weeping standards, hedging, trained against walls, or as groundcover. Dwarf species are suitable for a rock garden.

Cultivation Reasonably fertile, well-drained soil in sun or partial shade is best, but most cotoneasters tolerate dry conditions. Larger shrubs need protection from cold, drying winds. Dwarf evergreens fruit better if they are sheltered. Most cotoneasters require little pruning but will tolerate hard renovation pruning (*see p.384*) if required. **Trim** formal hedges in mid- or late summer. **Take** greenwood cuttings of deciduous species in early summer and semiripe cuttings of evergreens in late summer (*see p.394*).

Cotoneaster divaricatus (Spreading cotoneaster)
Z5 ‡8ft (2.5m) ↔ 10ft (3m), erect, deciduous shrub, dense leaves turn red in autumn (*see inset*), pink-white flowers in summer

Cotoneaster atropurpureus 'Variegatus' Z4b ‡18in (45cm) ↔ 35in (90cm), deciduous, compact, prostrate or wall shrub, leaf edges pink and red in autumn, orange-red berries

Cotoneaster horizontalis (Rockspray)
Z5 ‡3ft (1m) ↔ 15ft (5m), deciduous shrub, red autumn leaves (*inset*), pink white flowers in late spring

Cotoneaster × *watereri* 'John Waterer'
Z6b ‡↔ 15ft (5m), vigorous, evergreen or semievergreen shrub or tree, clusters of white flowers in summer

CRATAEGUS

Hawthorn

THESE EXTREMELY HARDY TREES and shrubs are particularly valuable in exposed or coastal gardens. They are usually spiny, deciduous, and medium-sized, with a rounded or spreading habit. Their mid- to dark green foliage often has attractive tints in autumn. Hawthorns produce flat clusters of white or pink blossoms at the ends of the branches. Birds enjoy the berries that follow in autumn, which are mostly scarlet, but sometimes are colored black, orange, yellow, or blue-green. *Crataegus laevigata* and *C. monogyna* (z3) make good hedging plants. The berries may cause stomach upsets if eaten.

Cultivation Hawthorns will grow in any soil, except waterlogged ground, in full sun or partial shade. **Prune out** any crossing or misshapen branches in winter or early spring to maintain a good shape and healthy framework of branches. Trim hedges after flowering or in autumn. **Remove** seed from the berries as soon as they are ripe and sow in a seedbed or in containers (*see pp.391–393*). Germination may take up to eighteen months.

Craetaegus laevigata 'Paul's Scarlet' Z6 ‡↔ to 25ft (8m), thorny, deciduous tree, lobed leaves, abundant flower clusters in late spring occasionally followed by red berries

CRYPTOMERIA JAPONICA

Japanese cedar

THIS CONIFEROUS TREE FROM THE FORESTS of China and Japan is grown for its neat, conical or columnar habit and evergreen foliage. This is produced in cloudlike clumps of soft, glossy, dark green needles. Large, round, female cones are borne singly, and the smaller, male cones cluster at the shoot tips. The red-brown bark is rugged and fibrous. This is a large tree, reaching up to 80ft (25m), but there are also several smaller cultivars that have pleasingly tinted foliage. Japanese cedars make handsome specimen trees, and the smaller types also blend well in a border with rhododendrons and azaleas (*see pp.104–107*). Try dwarf forms in a large rock garden with heaths (*Erica, see pp.52–53*) and heathers (*Calluna, see p.31*).

Cultivation The Japanese cedar tolerates most well-drained soils, including alkaline soils, in full sun or partial shade. It grows best in deep, fertile, moist but well-drained soil that has been enriched with organic matter. **Provide** shelter from cold, drying winds. This shrub requires no formal pruning. **Cut back** stems to within 24–36in (60–90cm) of ground level in spring, to reshape ungainly specimens.

Cryptomeria japonica 'Elegans Compacta' Z6 ‡6–12ft (2–4m) ↔ 20ft (6m), conical shrub, leaves are dark green when new, turning bronze in autumn, as shown here

x CUPRESSOCYPARIS LEYLANDII

Leyland cypress

‡120ft (35m)
↔ 15ft (5m)

THIS WIDELY GROWN CONIFEROUS TREE is most often used as a hedging or screening plant. It has a tapering habit and smooth bark that becomes stringy as it ages. The dense sprays of scalelike foliage are dark green with gray tints. Its dark brown female cones are larger than its yellow male cones. Cultivars with tinted foliage are available, in tones of gold, gray-green, blue-gray, bronze, and lime green. The Leyland cypress is a very fast-growing tree – if well maintained from a young plant, it forms a fine hedge or specimen tree, but if neglected, it can become a monster. If it grows too big, it is better to take it out and start over: you cannot cut it back into old wood because it will not regrow.

Cultivation Any deep, fertile, well-drained soil in full sun or partial shade will suit this vigorous tree. When grown as a specimen, it needs no formal pruning. **Trim** hedging plants, two to three times a year (without cutting into the old wood), finishing in early autumn (*see p.384*). **Take** semiripe cuttings (*see p.394*) in late summer.

x *Cupressocyparis leylandii* Z7 Often grown as a hedge, which must be trimmed several times a year to keep it under control

CUPRESSUS
Cypress

FROM THE SLENDER SILHOUETTE of the Italian cypress (*Cupressus sempervirens* Z7b) to the more stately Monterey cypress (*C. macrocarpa*), these evergreen, coniferous trees have attractive columnar or conical habits. There are also a few weeping cypresses. Cypresses have scalelike, sometimes glaucous foliage in dark, gray- or blue-green. The bark sometimes peels; the smooth cypress (*C. arizonica* var. *glabra* Z7b) has reddish-purple bark. Female cones are small and round and remain for several years; male cones are green and found on the shoot tips. Large cypresses are excellent specimen trees; smaller ones can be grouped with other conifers or shrubs. *C. macrocarpa* is good as a hedge or screen, especially in coastal areas.

Cultivation Since they come from dry, hillside forests, cypresses tolerate dry soils and grow in any well-drained soil in full sun. Provide shelter from cold, drying winds. **Trim** hedges in late spring (*see p.384*), but do not cut back into old wood because it will not regrow. **Take** semiripe cuttings (*see p.394*) in late summer. **Canker** may cause bark to recede, killing twigs and then the tree; cut affected branches back to healthy wood to stop it from spreading.

CYTISUS
Broom

ABUNDANT, PEALIKE FLOWERS are produced by these deciduous to evergreen shrubs in spring and summer. The flowers are often fragrant and are borne singly or in clusters, in a variety of shades from white and crimson to yellow. Long, flat, often downy seedpods follow. The usually small, palmlike leaves are mostly mid-green, but the shrubs often become leafless as they mature. Brooms vary in habit from prostrate or spreading to upright, arching or bushy. Smaller species and cultivars suit a rock garden and larger species a shrub or mixed border. The splendid, treelike *Cytisus battandieri* (*see below*) can be trained against a south-facing wall or fence, where it benefits from the shelter and its silvery leaves reflect the sun.

Cultivation Grow brooms in reasonably fertile soil in full sun. Less hardy species need protection from cold, drying winds. Brooms thrive in poor, acidic soils, but some may become chlorotic (show yellowing leaves) on shallow, alkaline soils. **Plant** young container-grown shrubs because older plants resent root disturbance. **Prune** flowered shoots to 2–3 buds above the main stems, after flowering. Do not cut into old wood because they do not regrow readily.

Cytisus × *praecox* 'Warminster' (Warminster broom)
Z6 ‡ 4ft (1.2m) ↔ 5ft (1.5m), deciduous, compact shrub with arching stems, flowers in mid- to late summer

Cupressus macrocarpa 'Goldcrest'
Z7b ‡ to 15ft (5m) ↔ 8ft (2.5m), narrowly conical, shallowly ridged bark, dense foliage

Cytisus battandieri (Pineapple broom)
Z7 ‡ ↔ 15ft (5m), deciduous, upright shrub, silvery leaves, pineapple scented flowers from mid- to late summer, needs shelter

Cytisus scoparius (Scotch broom)
Z6 ‡ ↔ 5ft (1.5m), deciduous, upright shrub with arching stems, abundant flowers, highly invasive in British Columbia.

DABOECIA CANTABRICA

Cantabrican heath, Connemara heath

THIS EVERGREEN, HEATHERLIKE SHRUB has given rise to a large number of garden plants. They are grown for their spikes of urn-shaped flowers, appearing from early summer to mid-autumn, in white and purple-crimson, and are typically larger than those of other heaths and heathers. The leaves are small, thin, and dark green. The species has a height of 10–16in (25–40cm) and spreads to 26in (55cm), but the cultivars vary in size. These shrubs make useful groundcover plants, around taller heathers or other acid-loving shrubs such as rhododendrons (*see pp.104–107*). If your soil is alkaline, grow them in large pots or a raised bed, in acidic soil mix.

Cultivation These shrubs need well-drained, acidic soil in full sun; they will tolerate neutral soil in partial shade. Daboecias are susceptible to root rot, particularly on heavy, wet soils, so on clay soil dig in some coarse grit to improve drainage. **Prune back** flowered growth in early or midspring each year to keep the plant shapely; the easiest way to do this is by clipping it over with shears. **Take** semiripe cuttings (*see p.394*) in midsummer.

DAPHNE

DELICIOUSLY FRAGRANT FLOWERS are borne very early, or sometimes very late, in the year on these shrubs, so plant them where the wonderful scent can be fully appreciated. The flowers, in shades of red-purple, pink, white, and yellow, may be followed by round, white, pink, red, orange, or purple fruits. Mostly slow-growing, daphnes are generally compact enough for even small gardens. They may be upright, bushy, or prostrate in habit, and there are deciduous, semi-evergreen, and evergreen species, all with neat, usually dark but sometimes variegated leaves. All parts of these plants are toxic, and the sap may irritate skin.

Cultivation Grow in reasonably fertile soil that is well-drained but does not dry out, and is preferably neutral (neither acid nor alkaline). Position in sun or partial shade; all resent root disturbance, so choose the site carefully. **Mulch** annually with organic matter around the base (*see p.388*) to keep the roots cool and moist. **Prune** only if absolutely necessary, in late winter or early spring. **Sow** seed in a cold frame as soon as it is ripe (*see pp.391–392*). **Take** softwood cuttings in early and midsummer, and semiripe cuttings in late summer (*see p.394*).

Daphne cneorum (Garland flower)
Z3 ‡6in (15cm) or more ↔ to 6ft (2m), trailing evergreen with pink or occasionally white, very fragrant flowers in late spring

Daboecia cantabrica 'William Buchanan'
Z6 ‡14in (35cm) ↔ 22in (55cm)

Daphne bholua 'Jacqueline Postill'
T min. 35°F (2°C) ‡6–12ft (2–4m) ↔ 5ft (1.5m), upright evergreen, fragrant flowers in winter or early spring, black-purple fruits

Daphne mezereum 'Bowles' Variety'
Z5 ‡to 6ft (2m) ↔ 3ft (1m), vigorous, upright, deciduous shrub, flowers in late winter or early spring, followed by yellow fruits

DAVIDIA INVOLUCRATA

Dove tree, Ghost tree, Handkerchief tree

THIS EXTRAORDINARILY BEAUTIFUL tree is festooned with pure white bracts (modified leaves) along the branches in spring. Its unique appearance is reflected in the variety of common names. The leaves are up to 6in (15cm) long, oval in shape with heart-shaped bases and sharply pointed tips. Mid-green and strongly veined, they have reddish stalks and soft hairs underneath. The bracts surround small flower heads, which are followed by greenish brown fruits in autumn. Davidia is a large tree; it is related to the dogwoods (*Cornus, see pp.42–43*), which includes more compact, but less dramatic, species suited to smaller gardens.

Cultivation Grow in fertile, well-drained but moisture-retentive soil, in sun or partial shade. Position where there is shelter from strong, cold winds. **Trim out** any crossing or misplaced branches on young trees in late winter or early spring. **Sow** whole fruits in a container as soon as ripe (*see pp.391–392*): germination will take at least two winters outdoors. Seed-raised trees may take up to ten years to reach flowering size. **Take** hardwood cuttings in winter (*see p.394*).

DEUTZIA

to 10ft (3m)

CLUSTERS OF STARRY, white or pink flowers, fragrant on *Deutzia gracilis* and *D. scabra*, almost smother these deciduous shrubs from midspring to midsummer. Most have oval leaves, although some are attractively willowlike. All are are easy to grow. The larger ones make good specimen plants, often developing beautiful peeling bark as they mature. In colder regions it is best to grow the less hardy types among other trees and shrubs, or in the shelter of a warm wall. Try them alongside shrubs such as mock orange (*Philadelphus, see p.93*) and weigelas (*see p.128*) for a harmonious early-summer show.

Cultivation Grow in fertile soil that is not too dry, ideally in full sun; some tolerate partial shade. **Cut back** flowered stems to strong buds or young shoots lower down. Encourage new growth on mature plants by cutting one in three or four of the old branches to the base. **Sow** seed in containers in a cold frame in autumn (*see pp.391–392*). **Take** softwood cuttings in summer or hardwood cuttings in autumn (*see p.394*).

Daphne laureola subsp. *philippi*
Z7b ‡ 18in (45cm) ↔ 24in (60cm), low, spreading ever-green, lightly scented flowers in late winter and early spring, black fruits

Daphne mezereum (February daphne)
Z5 ‡ 4ft (1.2m) ↔ 3ft (1m), upright, deciduous, small garden classic, flowers in late winter or early spring, fleshy red fruits

Davidia involucrata
Z7 ‡ 50ft (15m) ↔ 30ft (10m), this tree needs plenty of space to develop its shape and be seen at its best

① *gracilis* Z5b ‡↔ 3ft (1m) ② × *hybrida* 'Mont Rose' Z6 ‡↔ 3–6ft (1–2m) ③ *ningpoensis* Z7 ‡↔ 6ft (2m) ④ *scabra* Z6 ‡ 10ft (3m) ↔ 6ft (2m)

THESE UPRIGHT OR ARCHING, deciduous shrubs bloom in late spring to early summer, bearing clusters of tubular flowers at the tips of the branches and where the leaf stems join the shoots. The white or pink flowers are fragrant and backed by two papery bracts (modified leaves) that stay on the plant as the fruits develop. Narrow, pointed, pale to mid-green leaves and pale brown, peeling bark add to the attraction. Suitable for a shrub border or as specimen plants, these Chinese natives complement lilacs (*Syringa, see p.121*) and flowering currants (*Ribes, p.109*). Dipeltas may be hard to find and can be tricky to propagate, but once off to a good start they are easy to grow, so the search is worthwhile.

Cultivation Grow in fertile, well-drained, and preferably alkaline soil, in sun or partial shade. **Prune back** flowered shoots to strong buds lower down after flowering. Once mature, encourage new growth by cutting about one in three or four of the old stems back to the base of the shrub. **Sow** seed (*see pp.391–393*) in a seedbed in autumn or spring. **Take** softwood cuttings (*see p.394*) in summer.

BRILLIANT AUTUMN HUES of yellow, orange, red, and purple, often all on display at the same time, are the main attraction of this rounded shrub. The round leaves are similar to those of cercis (*see p.38*), as the name suggests, but the two have very different flowers. In midautumn, disanthus produces small, slightly fragrant, spidery, bright rose-red flowers. This shrub is native to mountain and forest habitats, and is ideal as a specimen in a woodland setting. For a superb show of leaf color in contrasting shapes in autumn, combine it with acers (*see pp.18–19*).

Cultivation Grow in preferably well-drained, acidic soil that has been enriched with well-rotted organic matter. Position in sun or partial shade where it will be sheltered from strong, cold winds. **Prune** minimally after flowering, cutting out only any crossing stems and those that spoil the shape of the shrub (*see p.382*). **Sow** seed in a seedbed in autumn or spring (*see pp.391–393*). **Layer** low-growing shoots (*see p.395*) in autumn.

TOUGH, FAST-GROWING, and resistant to coastal winds, these are immensely useful shrubs. Evergreen or deciduous, they have ornamental, lance-shaped to oval leaves. These may be plain green or silvery, and there are also many with silver or gold variegation. Evergreen elaeagnus make good hedges, and the variegated types are great for brightening up a dull border when used as specimen plants. As a bonus, small clusters of bell-shaped, sometimes very fragrant flowers are borne in summer or autumn, and these are occasionally followed by small berries.

Cultivation Grow in fertile, well-drained soil; dry soils are tolerated, but the leaves may become yellow on shallow, alkaline soils. Position ideally in full sun; evergreens tolerate partial shade. **Prune** deciduous plants in late winter or early spring, evergreens in mid- or late spring, removing any crossing branches and those that spoil the shape (*see p.382*). **Trim** hedges in late summer. **Cut out** any shoots that revert to plain green leaves on variegated types. **Take** greenwood cuttings in late spring or early summer, or semiripe cuttings of deciduous species in late summer (*see p.394*).

Dipelta floribunda
Z7 ‡↔ 12ft (4m), upright shrub, flowers in late spring and early summer, tolerates poor soils

Disanthus cercidifolius
Z7 ‡↔ 10ft (3m), the leaves are a cloudy blue-green before they take on these vibrant autumn colors

Elaeagnus × ebbingei 'Gilt Edge' (Gilt Edge Silverberry)
Z7 ‡↔ 12ft (4m), dense, rounded to spreading evergreen, leaves silver-scaly beneath, creamy white flowers in autumn

Elaeagnus pungens 'Maculata'
Z7b ‡12ft (4m) ↔ 15ft (5m), dense, slightly spiny ever-green, silvery white flowers in autumn, brown berries ripening to red

EMBOTHRIUM COCCINEUM
Chilean firebush, Flame flower

SPECTACULAR WHEN IN FLOWER, this evergreen tree or shrub and its cultivars have an upright, but freely branching or suckering habit, and are capable of very rapid growth in mild conditions. The glowing scarlet flowers are carried in dense clusters in late spring and early summer. The narrowly lance-shaped leaves are up to 5in (13cm) long. In areas where frosts are light and infrequent, they make good specimen trees.

Cultivation Grow in fertile, neutral to acidic soil enriched with well-rotted organic matter, in full sun or partial shade. **Trim off** any crossing shoots and those that spoil the shape in late winter or early spring. **Sow** seed (*see pp.391–392*) at 55–61°F (13–16°C in spring. **Take** greenwood cuttings in early summer, or semiripe cuttings in mid- or late summer (*see p.394*). Take root cuttings, or dig up rooted shoots (suckers) growing up around the main plant, in winter.

Embothrium coccineum
T min. 35°F (2°C) ‡10m (30ft) ↔ 5m (15ft) or more

ENKIANTHUS

PENDENT FLOWER CLUSTERS and rich autumnal foliage colors give these plants two seasons of interest. A small group, they are for the most part deciduous shrubs, sometimes trees. The small, delicate flowers are borne at the branch tips from midspring to early summer. They are urn- to bell-shaped, in shades from cream or pure white to pink and deep purple-red, with contrasting veins. The autumn display is more distinctive and varies according to the species. *Enkianthus campanulatus* (Z5b) passes through every shade from yellow to red; *E. perulatus* turns brilliant scarlet; and *E. cernuus* f. *rubens* is flushed reddish purple. They make ideal specimens in a woodland garden.

Cultivation Grow in acidic, moist but well-drained soil enriched with well-rotted organic matter. Position in an open site in full sun or partial shade. **Prune** in late winter or early spring, only to remove misplaced or crossing branches. **Sow** seed at 64–70°F (18–21°C) in late winter or early spring (*see pp.391–393*). **Take** semiripe cuttings in summer (*see p.394*) or layer in autumn (*see p.395*).

① *campanulatus* Z5b ‡↔ 12–15ft (4–5m) ② *cernuus*
f. *rubens* Z6 ‡↔ 8ft (2.5m) ③ *deflexus* Z8 ‡8–12ft (2.5–4m)
↔ 10ft (3m) ④ *perulatus* Z7 ‡↔ to 6ft (2m)

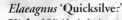

ERICA

Heath, Heather

HEATHS ARE EVERGREENS WITH MASSES of tiny, usually bell-shaped flowers ranging from shades of red and pink to white, with some bicolors. In some cultivars, the small, tightly curled leaves are tinted with red or gold, or color in cold weather, so the right choice of cultivars can provide interest throughout the year. Prostrate species make colorful groundcover, while the taller, upright types, such as *Erica arborea*, can make excellent specimen plants in borders. Heaths, which are related to heathers (*Calluna, see p.31*), will grow in a variety of conditions. Ericas shown here run the range of Canadian hardiness zones from 4–8a.

Cultivation Grow in well-drained, acid soil in an open site in full sun. A few winter- and spring-flowering types such as *E. carnea* and *E. × darleyensis*, will tolerate a slightly alkaline soil, as will summer-flowering *E. manipuliflora*, *E. terminalis*, and *E. vagans*. **Cut back** flowered shoots to within 1in (2.5cm) of the old growth after flowering. For taller, treelike cultivars cut back the stems to within two or three buds of the base, or to a permanent framework of shoots in early spring. **Layer** (*see below*) or take semiripe cuttings in mid- or late summer (*see p.394*). Heaths may be susceptible to fungal root rot and powdery mildew in warm and wet conditions: improve drainage to avoid these problems.

Using heaths in the garden

Heaths are valuable plants because they can provide color and interest throughout the year. They require very little attention beyond clipping once a year after flowering, making them ideal for a low-maintenance garden. Different colors can be grouped en masse in their own bed, but they are also effective growing with dwarf conifers such as junipers (see pp.76–77) and with rhododendrons (see pp.104–107). If you have alkaline soil, heaths can be grown in a raised bed filled with acidic soil mix or in large containers on the patio.

Easy ways to increase your plants

Layering Heaths and heathers root readily from the stems, so propagating them by layering is much easier than taking cuttings. From early to mid-autumn or in spring, make a shallow trench around the plant and refill with soil mixed with a little sharp sand and peat substitute, for example leaf mold, to provide a good rooting medium. Bend down healthy shoots and cover with some of the prepared soil. Peg down the shoots with wire staples or weigh down with a stone. The stems need not be cut. The next year, cut off the rooted stems; replant where they can grow into new plants.

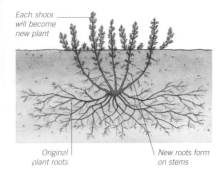

Each shoot will become new plant

Original plant roots

New roots form on stems

Dropping Lift a mature plant in spring. Dig a hole big enough to take not only the roots but two-thirds of the top-growth. Drop the plant into the hole and fill in around the roots with soil and a mixture of equal parts grit and acidic soil mix between the shoots. Arranging the shoots in rows or around the edge of the hole will make it easier to weed between them. Firm in gently and label. Keep well watered during dry spells. By autumn, the buried stems should have developed roots. Lift the plant and cut the rooted shoots from the parent. Pot up the young plants and grow on, or plant them in a sheltered spot.

① *Erica arborea* var. *alpina* ‡6ft (2m) ↔ 34in (85cm) ② *carnea* 'Ann Sparkes' ‡6in (15cm) ↔ 10in (25cm) ③ *carnea* 'December Red' ‡10in (15cm) ↔ 18in (45cm) ④ *carnea* 'Eileen Porter' ‡↔8in (20cm) ⑤ *carnea* 'Foxhollow' ‡6in (15cm) ↔ 16in (40cm) ⑥ *carnea* 'Springwood White' ‡6in (15cm) ↔ 18in (45cm) ⑦ *carnea* 'Vivellii' ‡6in (15cm) ↔ 14in (35cm) ⑧ *ciliaris* 'David McClintock' ‡16in (40cm) ↔ 18in (45cm) ⑨ *ciliaris* 'White Wings' ‡6in

(15cm) ↔ 18in (45cm) ⑩ *cinerea* 'C.D. Eason' ‡ 10in (25cm) ↔ 20in (50cm) ⑪ *cinerea* 'Eden Valley' ‡ 8in (20cm) ↔ 20in (50cm) ⑫ *cinerea* 'Fiddler's Gold' ‡ 10in (25cm) ↔ 18in (45cm) ⑬ *cinerea* 'Hoolstone White' ‡ 14in (35cm) ↔ 26in (65cm) ⑭ *cinerea* 'Purple Beauty' ‡ 1ft (30cm) ↔ 22in (55cm) ⑮ *cinerea* 'Windlebrooke' ‡ 6in (15cm) ↔ 18in (45cm) ⑯ × *darleyensis* 'Jenny Porter' ‡ 1ft (30cm) ↔ 2ft (60cm) ⑰ × *darleyensis* 'White Glow' ‡ 10in (25cm) ↔ 20in

(50cm) ⑱ *erigena* 'Golden Lady' ‡ 1ft (30cm) ↔ 16in (40cm) ⑲ *tetralix* 'Alba Mollis' ‡ 8in (20cm) ← 1ft (30cm) ⑳ *vagans* 'Birch Glow' ‡ 1ft (30cm) ↔ 50cm (20in) ㉑ *vagans* 'Lyonesse' ‡ 10in (25cm) ↔ 20in (50cm) ㉒ *vagans* 'Mrs D.F. Maxwell' ‡ 30cm (1ft) ↔ 45cm (18in) ㉓ *vagans* 'Valerie Proudley' ‡ 6in (15cm) ↔ 1ft (30cm) ㉔ × *williamsii* 'P.D. Williams' ‡ 1ft (30cm) ↔ 18in (45cm)

GLOSSY, EVERGREEN FOLIAGE and a profusion of flowers are the attractions of these excellent shrubs. Borne over a long period, mainly in summer, the flowers are tubular or saucer-shaped, in shades of white, pink, or red. Escallonias are undemanding plants, being fairly fast growing and drought tolerant. Widely grown as tough, wind-resistant hedges, they also make fine freestanding shrubs in a shrub or mixed border. They are particularly good in coastal areas, where the tough leaves stand up to salt-laden winds. Try them with other robust shrubs, such as cotinus (*see p.44*), lilacs (*Syringa, see p.121*), hypericums (*see p.74*), and potentillas (*see p.99*).

Cultivation Grow in fertile, well-drained soil. Position in full sun, with shelter from cold, drying winds. Many species and cultivars grow best with the protection of a sheltered wall. **Trim** back shoots that spoil the shape of the shrub lightly in mid- or late spring. **Clip** hedges after flowering. **Take** softwood cuttings in early summer or semiripe cuttings in late summer; or try hardwood cuttings from late autumn to winter (*see p.394*).

Escallonia 'Apple Blossom'
Z7b ‡↔8ft (2.5m), compact bush, slow-growing, flowers in early and midsummer, suitable for hedges

Escallonia 'Langleyensis'
Z7b ‡6ft (2m) ↔ 10ft (3m), arching, evergreen to semievergreen shrub, flowers in early and midsummer

Escallonia 'Pride of Donard'
Z7b ‡5ft (1.5m) ↔ 8ft (2.5m), compact, erect shrub (*see inset*), flowers are larger than most and borne in early to midsummer, suitable for hedging

Escallonia rubra 'Woodside'
Z7b ‡30in (75cm) ↔ 5ft (1.5m), dwarf form, flowers from summer to early autumn, cut out any vigorous shoots promptly

EUCALYPTUS

Gum, Ironbark

THESE DISTINCTIVE TREES and shrubs are grown for their handsome, often aromatic, evergreen foliage and their ornamental bark. The foliage is usually mid- or gray-green and leathery. The young, or juvenile, leaves are most attractive, and look rather like silvery blue pennies on *Eucalyptus gunnii*. They grow longer and droop as the plants mature. Small clusters of petalless flowers open in summer, and may be white, creamy yellow, or red. The bark is smooth and white in some species, flaking or striped in shades of green or tawny brown in others. As specimen trees they grow quickly and need quite a bit of space. However, with hard pruning (coppicing) each year, they may be grown as shrubs, which retain the appealing juvenile foliage.

Cultivation Grow in fertile, neutral to slightly acidic soil that does not easily dry out, in full sun, preferably with shelter from cold winds. **Prune** crossing or misplaced branches in late winter or early spring; to form a shrub, cut back stems to within two or three buds of the base, forming a stubby framework (*see below, left*). **Sow** seed at 55–64°F (13–18°C) in spring or summer (*see pp.391–392*).

Eucalyptus dalrympleana (Mountain gum)
Z8 ‡ 70ft (20m) ↔ 25ft (8m), vigorous tree, blue-green new leaves, flowers late summer to autumn, tolerates alkaline soil

EUCRYPHIA

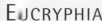

VALUED FOR THEIR late flowering, this is a small group of mostly evergreen, columnar trees and shrubs. Their beautiful, often fragrant flowers are white, occasionally pink or with pink edges to the petals, and have a fluffy mass of stamens at the center. They are borne from summer to early autumn, once the plants are a few years old. The leaves are leathery, usually oval, but sometimes made up of narrow leaflets along a central stalk. Eucryphias make glorious specimen plants or flowering hedges in a sheltered spot.

50ft (15m)
to 25ft (8m)

Cultivation Grow in fertile, moist but well-drained soil that is neutral to acidic. *E. x nymanensis* tolerates alkaline soil. Position with the roots in shade and the crown in full sun. Needs shelter from cold, drying winds in all but mild areas. **Remove** fading flowers if the plant is small enough to make this practical. **Prune out** any crossing or dead wood in late winter or early spring, or lightly trim shoots that spoil the shape in mid- or late spring (or for *E. lucida*, after flowering). Do not overprune, or you will lose the flowers. **Take** semiripe cuttings (*see p.394*) in summer, and overwinter new plants in frost-free conditions.

Eucalyptus gunnii (Cider gum)
Z7b ‡ 30–80ft (10–25m) ↔ 20–50ft (6–15m), flowers in summer or autumn (*see inset*), bark shed in late summer

COPPICING a gum tree, especially the snow and cider gums, is done by cutting back all stems to 2–3 buds every spring.

Eucalyptus pauciflora subsp. *niphophila* (Snow gum)
Z8 ‡ 20ft (6m) ↔ 20–50ft (6–15m), slow-growing, flowers late spring to summer, bark shed late summer to autumn

Eucryphia glutinosa T min. 35°F (2°C) ‡ 30ft (10m) ↔ 20ft (6m), deciduous or semievergreen tree or shrub, flowers in mid- to late summer, tolerates exposed sites

EUONYMUS
Spindle tree

COLORFUL FOLIAGE IS the main feature of this large group of shrubs and trees. Deciduous types have fiery autumn foliage and decorative lobed fruits, while most of the evergreens have bright variegation that brings color to the garden all year. The leaves are variable but usually broadly oval, and small clusters of purple-red or red-brown flowers appear in late spring or summer. The evergreens can be used as specimen shrubs in borders, or as hedging or groundcover. Some *Euonymus fortunei* types will climb if planted by a wall. Young plants are useful in winter windowboxes and containers. All parts may cause mild stomach upset if eaten.

Cultivation Grow in any well-drained soil deciduous species are more drought tolerant. Site in full sun (especially variegated types) or partial shade; in full sun they need moist soil. Shelter evergreens from cold, drying winds. **Prune** deciduous types in late winter or early spring if needed and evergreens if necessary after flowering (*see p.383*). **Sow** seed (*see pp.391–392*) in a container in a cold frame as soon as it is ripe. **Take** softwood cuttings of deciduous species, and semiripe cuttings of evergreens in summer (*see p.394*).

NONVARIEGATED SHOOTS should be removed as soon as they are seen to stop the plant from reverting. Green shoots in particular are vigorous and will take over the plant.

Euonymus fortunei 'Emerald 'n' Gold'
Z5 ‡24in (60cm) ↔ 36in (90cm) bushy, evergreen shrub, leaf edges turn pink in winter, white fruits and orange seeds

Euonymus fortunei 'Silver Queen'
Z5 ‡8ft (2.5m) ↔ 5ft (1.5m), upright, evergreen bush, pale green flowers and pink fruits, climbs if given support

Euonymus alatus (Burning bush)
Z3 ‡6ft (2m) ↔ 10ft (3m), dense, deciduous shrub, red-purple fruits with orange seeds, dark green leaves until autumn

Euonymus japonicus 'Ovatus Aureus'
Z5b ‡12ft (4m) ↔ 6ft (2m), slow-growing, evergreen bush or tree, good for hedging, rarely fruits, reverts to all-green shoots

Euonymus oxyphyllus
Z6b ‡8ft (2.5m) or more ↔ 8ft (2.5m), upright, slow-growing deciduous species, dull green leaves before autumn

EUPHORBIA
Milkweed, Spurge

see also
pp.242–243

IN THIS LARGE AND WIDELY VARIED group of plants, there are a few evergreen shrubs and trees. They are grown for their impressive foliage and distinctive flower heads. The leaves are mostly narrow and lance-shaped – in *Euphorbia characias* they are blue-green and very architectural. *E. × martini* (Z7b) has leaves that are flushed purple when young, on red-tinged stems; its flower heads are long-lasting and borne in spring and summer. The flowers are brown and honey-scented in *E. mellifera* (T min. 41°F/5°C), the honey spurge, and yellow-green with dark red nectar glands in *E. × martini* Spurges are suitable for coastal gardens. All parts of euphorbias can cause severe discomfort if eaten, and contact with the milky sap may irritate skin.

Cultivation Grow in well-drained soil in full sun. Dig in plenty of coarse grit on heavy clay soils to improve drainage. **Take** softwood cuttings (*see p.394*) in spring or early summer, wearing gloves, and dipping the ends in lukewarm water to prevent bleeding.

Euphorbia characias 'John Tomlinson'
Z7b ↕↔ 4ft (1.2m), upright shrub, huge and heavy flower heads from early spring to early summer, becoming almost round

EXOCHORDA
Pearlbush

↕↔ 6–12ft
(2–4m)

SHOWY, PURE WHITE flowers wreath the branches of these shrubs in spring to summer; no wonder the most popular variety is named 'The Bride'. All are deciduous, with an attractive, arching habit, and are equally impressive grown with other shrubs in a border or as isolated specimen plants. They flower at around the same time or a little later than the spring-flowering magnolias (*see p.86*), and their flowers are more resistant to frost, which makes them an excellent alternative for a blossom display in frost-prone areas where magnolia flowers might be spoiled.

Cultivation Grow in fertile, moist, but well-drained soil; these shrubs will tolerate all but the shallowest, alkaline soils, where the leaves may become yellow (chlorotic). Position in full sun or partial shade. **Cut back** flowered shoots to strong buds or young lower growths after flowering. Encourage fresh growth on mature plants by cutting one in three or four older branches back to the base every few years. **Take** softwood cuttings (*see p.394*) in summer.

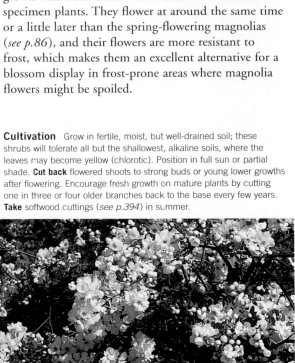

Exochorda × macrantha 'The Bride'
Z5 ↕ 6ft (2m) ↔ 10ft (3m), forms a compact, arching mound with fragrant flowers in late spring and early summer

FAGUS
Beech

THESE STATELY, DECIDUOUS TREES are grown for their fine forms and handsome foliage. They are large and spreading, with wavy edged or toothed, oval leaves. In most, these are pale green when they first open in spring, maturing to dark green and then taking on soft yellow or russet-brown tones in autumn, but there are several beeches with dramatic, dark, purple or coppery foliage. All make fine specimen trees in a large garden; the common beech, *Fagus sylvatica* (Z5b), is also popular as a hedge; when clipped, it retains its brown leaves all winter. For smaller gardens, look for narrow or compact forms, such as 'Purpurea Pendula', the weeping copper beech (Z5b), with branches that often trail to the ground.

Cultivation Grow in any well-drained soil; even chalk is tolerated. Position in sun or partial shade; purple-leaved types have the best foliage color in full sun. **Prune out** crossing branches and any that spoil the shape of the tree in late winter or early spring. **Trim** hedges of *F. sylvatica* in mid- to late summer. **Sow** seed in a seedbed in autumn or spring (*see pp.391–393*). Beeches are favorites of gray and red squirrels, which – although entertaining – can cause damage.

Fagus sylvatica 'Dawyck Purple'
Z5b ↕ 70ft (20m) ↔ 15ft (5m), particularly good purple-leaved type, also one of the narrowest columnar forms

FATSIA JAPONICA

Japanese aralia, Japanese fatsia

THE LARGE, GLOSSY GREEN LEAVES of these evergreen, spreading shrubs are ideal for creating a jungly garden and make a dramatic contrast to feathery foliage plants such as ferns (*see pp.356–365*). An excellent architectural plant for a shady border, it tolerates pollution and thrives in city gardens but is also a good choice for coastal areas, where the tough leaves will withstand salt-laden winds and sea spray. Broad, upright clusters of rounded, creamy white flower heads are produced in autumn, followed by small, round, inedible black berries. There are also some variegated cultivars, which need partial shade.

Cultivation This shrub will thrive in any fertile, moist but well-drained soil in full sun or partial shade, but needs shelter from cold, drying winds. **Trim** lightly or prune shoots that spoil the shape in mid- or late spring. **Remove** the fading flowers unless seed is wanted. **Sow** seed (*see pp.391–393*) at 59–70°F (15–21°C) in autumn or spring. **Take** greenwood cuttings (*see p.394*) in early or midsummer. Cold winds may cause blackening and die-back of shoots and leaves. Susceptible to spider mites and bacterial leaf spots.

Fatsia japonica
Z7b ↕↔ 5–12ft (1.5–4m), leaves are 6–16in (15–40cm) across

FICUS CARICA

Common fig

↕ 10ft (3m)
↔ 12ft (4m)

ONE OF THE OLDEST fruit trees in cultivation, figs thrive in regions with long, hot summers. *Ficus carica* can be grown as a free-standing tree but will quickly spread to cover a large area if trained against a wall. The handsome, deciduous foliage is its main attraction; it does produce edible figs, but these do not always mature in cooler climates. The fruits are green when young and mature after a long, hot summer into dark green, purple, or dark brown figs. The leaves can cause skin rashes in sunlight (photodermatitis).

Cultivation Figs prefer moist but well-drained soil, enriched with plenty of well-rotted compost, in full sun or partial shade, with shelter from cold, drying winds. **Restrict** the roots in a large pot or by a barrier in the soil for better fruiting. **Tie in** regularly new shoots of wall-trained plants. **Prune out** misplaced or crossing shoots that spoil the shape in late winter or early spring; prune wall-trained plants to fit available space. **Protect** trees from cold winds and frosts. Wasps attack ripe fruits.

Ficus carica (Edible fig)
Z6b The leathery leaves can reach 10in (24cm) across and are fairly tolerant of salty air

FORSYTHIA

THESE SUPERBLY RELIABLE, deciduous shrubs will be covered in flowers every spring and sometimes in late winter. The bright yellow flowers appear in profusion all along the length of the stems, singly or in small clusters, before the leaves open. Most forsythias are medium-sized, bushy or upright shrubs; a few are semievergreen. These versatile shrubs can be grown either freestanding or trained against a wall or a fence, and *Forsythia × intermedia* also makes a good hedging plant. A classic spring planting combination involves forsythias along with red-flowering currants (*Ribes, see p.109*).

Cultivation Reasonably fertile, moist but well-drained soil is needed. **Position** in full sun or partial shade. **Prune back** flowered shoots to strong shoots lower down after flowering. Cut about one-third to a quarter of old stems on mature plants to the base every 4–5 years: cut back hard neglected, leggy plants over two years to rejuvenate (*see p.384*). **Trim** hedges in summer. **Take** greenwood cuttings in early summer or semiripe cuttings in late summer (*see p.394*). **Birds** may eat some of the flower buds.

Forsythia suspensa (Weeping forsythia) Z5b ↕↔ 10ft (3m), upright or arching, leaves mid- to dark green, flowers in early and midspring, tolerates north- or east-facing wall

FOTHERGILLA

THERE ARE JUST TWO SPECIES of these deciduous, low-growing shrubs from woodlands and swamps. They are grown for their bottlebrush-like clusters of scented flowers, which are produced before the leaves unfold. Fothergillas have attractive, dark green foliage with toothed edges; they turn brilliant shades of red, orange, and golden yellow in autumn. The dwarf fothergilla (*Fothergilla gardenii* (Z5b) is the smaller of the two, forming a dense bush with a height and spread of 3ft (1m); it flowers in spring. The slow-growing *F. major* is an upright shrub and has more glossy leaves; its flowers are occasionally tinged with pink.

Cultivation Grow fothergillas in moist but well-drained, acidic soil that has been enriched with well-rotted organic matter. **Position** in full sun or partial shade; full sun encourages more flowers and better autumn color. **Prune off** crossing or misshapen shoots that spoil the shape of the shrub in late winter or early spring, only if necessary (*see p.382*). **Sow** seed (*see pp.391–393*) in a container in autumn or winter; it will take two years to germinate. **Take** softwood cuttings (*see p.394*).

FRAXINUS
Ash

THESE DECIDUOUS TREES ARE TOUGH as well as decorative. They tolerate pollution, wind, cold, and coastal conditions, and have fine foliage and sometimes colored winter bark. The leaves are made up of small leaflets along central stalks up to 20in (50cm) long. Ash trees are fast-growing and have attractive habits, ranging from narrow or columnar to round or spreading. Most ash trees have tiny flowers; those of *Fraxinus ornus* (Z7) and *F. sieboldiana* (Z7b) are ornamental. Most are suitable only for large gardens, growing 50–100ft (15–30m) tall: the weeping *F. excelsior* 'Pendula' (Z4b) is smaller than many. Ashes self-seed prolifically, so be vigilant in rooting out seedlings. They look good with trees such as birches (*Betula, see p.28*), beeches (*Fagus, see p.57*), and oaks (*Quercus, see p.103*).

Cultivation Grow in fertile, moist but well-drained neutral to acidic soil; *F. angustifolia* and *F. ornus* tolerate dry, acidic to alkaline soil. **Position** in full sun. **Sow** seed (*see pp.391–393*) in autumn or spring in an open frame; seeds need 2–3 months of cold before germination.

Fothergilla major
Z5b ↕8ft (2.5m) ↔ 6ft (2m), flowers in late spring and early summer, found naturally in dry woods and rocky riverbanks

Fraxinus excelsior 'Jaspidea'
Z4b ↕100ft (30m) ↔ 70ft (20m), yellow shoots/leaves in winter and spring, leaves dark green in summer, black buds in winter

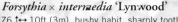

Forsythia × intermedia 'Lynwood'
Z6 ↕↔ 10ft (3m), bushy habit, sharply toothed leaves, flowers 1¼–1½in (2.5–3.5) across and borne in early and midspring

FUCHSIA

THE BRIGHTLY COLORED, PENDULOUS FLOWERS of fuchsias are unmistakable. They vary from elegant, single and semidouble forms to frilly, fully double blooms, and appear from summer until late autumn. Deciduous or evergreen shrubs, fuchsias are very versatile. They can be planted in mixed borders and as hedging, some can be trained against walls or grown as standards or pillars (*see below*), and cultivars with a trailing habit are ideal in raised containers, where the flowers spill over the edges to great effect. Where not hardy, grow fuchsias in a cool greenhouse, placing them outdoors in a protected area for the summer. Some fuchsias can be grown outdoors in the mildest parts of Zone 8, making showy plants either in borders or in containers underplanted with annuals. Except for *Fuchsia magellanica* (Z7, with extensive protection), fuchsias shown here are tender.

Cultivation Grow in fertile, moist but well-drained soil in full sun or partial shade, with shelter from cold, drying winds. **Plant** hardy fuchsias with the base of the stem 2in (5cm) below the soil surface, and protect them with a deep winter mulch of bark chips or similar material. Plant out tender cultivars in early summer, when the threat of frost has passed. **Water** well in summer and apply a balanced liquid fertilizer every two weeks. **Cut** the old stems of hardy fuchsias to the ground in spring. **Lift** tender cultivars in autumn, keeping them in a protected place during winter and spring, watering sufficiently to keep them just moist. **Take** softwood cuttings in spring (*see pp.394*). Fuchsias are prone to whiteflies, aphids, spider mites, and thrips. Black vine weevils sometimes cause damage, especially in pots where larvae may eat large areas of root (*see p.398*). Treat gray mold (botrytis) with fungicide, and rust (tiny orange spots) by removing affected leaves.

Pruning and training

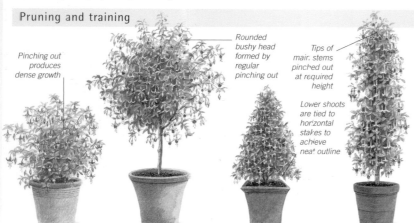

Bush When each shoot has made about three pairs of leaves, pinch out the tip. This encourages the plant to produce sideshoots. Continue to do this three or four times and then allow the plant to flower.

Pinching out produces dense growth

Standard This shape is achieved by training to an extendable stake, removing sideshoots. When the main stem reaches the required height, pinch out and treat the top as for a bush. Training takes 2–3 years.

Rounded bushy head formed by regular pinching out

Pyramid Allow the main stem to grow to 9in (23cm). Pinch out the tip, keeping one shoot to continue as a new leader. Pinch out all sideshoots at three pairs of leaves. Repeat until the right height and shape is reached.

Tips of main stems pinched out at required height

Lower shoots are tied to horizontal stakes to achieve neat outline

Column Allow two shoots to develop as central stems, and stop them at the desired height. Pinch the sideshoots regularly to create dense, bushy growth. As with a standard, this takes 2–3 years.

① *Fuchsia* 'Alice Hoffman' ↕↔ 18–24in (45–60cm) ② 'Andrew Hadfield' ↕ 8–18in (20–45cm) ↔ 8–12in (20–30cm) ③ 'Annabel' ↕↔ 12–24in (30–60cm) ④ *arborescens* ↕ 6ft (2m) ↔ 5½ft (1.7m) ⑤ 'Auntie Jinks' ↕ 6–8in (15–20cm) ↔ 8–16in (20–40cm) ⑥ 'Autumnale' ↕ 6–12in (15–30cm) ↔ 1–2ft (30–60cm) ⑦ × *bacillaris* ↕↔ 2–4ft (60–120cm) ⑧ 'Ballet Girl' ↕ 12–18in (30–45cm) ↔ 18–30in (45–75cm) ⑨ 'Bicentennial' ↕ 12–18in (30–45cm) ↔ 18–24in (45–60cm) ⑩ 'Billy

Green' ↕18–24in (45–60cm) ↔12–18in (30–45cm) ⑪ 'Bon Accorde' ↕18–24in (45–60cm) ↔18in (45cm) ⑫ 'Celia Smedley' ↕↔18–30in (45–75cm) ⑬ 'Checkerboard' ↕30–36in (75–90cm) ↔18–30in (45–75cm) ⑭ 'Coralle' ↕18–36in (45–90cm) ↔18–24in (45–60cm) ⑮ 'Dark Eyes' ↕18–24in (45–60cm) ↔24–30in (60–75cm) ⑯ 'Devonshire Dumpling' ↕↔to 3ft (1m) ⑰ 'Display' ↕24–30in (60–75cm) ↔18–24in (45–60cm) ⑱ 'Dollar Princess' ↕18in (45cm)

↔18–24in (45–60cm) ⑲ 'Flirtation Waltz' ↕18–24in (45–60cm) ↔12–18in (30–45cm) ⑳ fulgens ↕5ft (1.5m) ↔to 32in (80cm) ㉑ 'Garden News' ↕↔18–24in (45–60cm) ㉒ 'Genii' ↕↔75–90cm (30–36in) ㉓ 'Golden Marinka' ↕15–30cm (6–12in) ↔12–18in (30–45cm) ㉔ 'Gruss aus dem Bodethal' ↕12–18in (30–45cm) ↔18–24in (45–60cm)

㉕ *Fuchsia* 'Jack Shahan' ‡12–18in (30–45cm) ↔ 18–24in (45–60cm) ㉖ 'Joy Patmore'
‡12–18in (30–45cm) ↔ 18–24in (45–60cm) ㉗ 'La Campanella' ‡6–12in (15–30cm)
↔ 12–18in (30–45cm) ㉘ 'Lady Thumb' ‡6–12in (15–30cm) ↔ 12–18in (30–45cm)
㉙ 'Lena' ‡12–24in (30–60cm) ↔ 24–30in (60–75cm) ㉚ 'Leonora' ‡24–30in (60–75cm)
↔ 12–24in (30–60cm) ㉛ 'Love's Reward' ‡↔ 12–18in (30–45cm) ㉜ 'Lye's

Unique' ‡18–24in (45–60cm) ↔ 12–18in (30–45cm) ㉝ 'Machu Picchu' ‡↔ 12–24in (30–60cm)
㉞ *magellanica* ‡↔ 6–10ft (2–3m) ㉟ 'Margaret' ‡↔ to 4ft (1.2m) ㊱ 'Margaret
Brown' ‡↔ 24–36in (60–90cm) ㊲ 'Marinka' ‡6–12in (15–30cm) ↔ 18–24in (45–60cm)
㊳ 'Mary' ‡↔ 12–24in (30–60cm) ㊴ 'Micky Goult' ‡12–18in (30–45cm) ↔ 18–24in (45–60cm)
㊵ 'Mieke Meursing' ‡↔ 12–24in (30–60cm) ㊶ 'Mrs Lovell Swisher' ‡18–24in (45–60cm)

↔ 12–24in (30–60cm) ㊷ 'Mrs. Popple' ↕↔ 3–3½ft (1–1.1m) ㊸ 'Nellie Nuttall' ↕ 6–18in (15–45cm)
↔ 12–18in (30–45cm) ㊹ 'Other Fellow' ↕↔ 12–18in (30–45cm) ㊺ *paniculata* ↕↔ to 6ft (2m)
㊻ 'Peppermint Stick' ↕↔ 18–30in (45–75cm) ㊼ 'Phyllis' ↕ 3–5ft (1–1.5m) ↔ 30–36in (75–90cm)
㊽ *procumbens* ↕ 4–6in (10–15cm) ↔ 3–4ft (1–1.2m) ㊾ 'Red Spider' ↕ 6–12in (15–30cm) ↔ 12–24in
(30–60cm) ㊿ 'Riccartonii' ↕ 6–10ft (2–3m) ↔ 3–6ft (1–2m) ㉛ 'Royal Velvet' ↕ 18–30in (45–75cm)

↔ 12–24in (30–60cm) ㉜ 'Rufus' ↕ 18–30in (45–75cm) ↔ 30–60cm (12–24in)
㉝ 'Swingtime' ↕ 30–60cm (12–24in) ↔ 18–30in (45–75cm) ㉞ 'Thalia' ↕↔ 18–36in
(45–90cm) ㉟ 'Tom Thumb' ↕↔ 6–12in (15–30cm) ㊱ 'Winston Churchill' ↕↔ 18–30in
(45–75cm).

GARRYA

LONG CATKINS ADORN these tough, large, evergreen shrubs from mid- to late winter. Male and female flowers are borne on separate plants, the male catkins being more dramatic. The most widely grown is the silk-tassel bush, *Garrya elliptica* (Z7b), but *G.* × *issaquahensis* 'Pat Ballard,' with red-purple shoots, glossy leaves, and purple-tinged catkins, is also popular. Garryas are versatile: they can be grown in a border, trained against a wall, or even used as hedging. They tolerate urban pollution, and the leathery, wavy-edged leaves stand up to salt-laden winds and sea spray in coastal areas. Grow with other winter-flowering shrubs like *Jasminum nudiflorum* (*see p.76*) trained against a wall, mahonias (*see p.87*), and Christmas box (*Sarcococca, see p.116*).

Cultivation Grow in reasonably fertile, well-drained soil, in full sun or partial shade; shelter from cold winds where not fully hardy. **Prune** lightly after flowering, cutting out shoots that spoil the shape. Garryas tolerate hard renovation pruning (*see p.384*). **Take** semiripe cuttings (*see p.394*) in summer.

GAULTHERIA

Pernettya

COLORFUL AUTUMN FRUITS are the main attraction of these trouble-free, evergreen shrubs. They bear small flowers just ¼in (7mm) long, usually in small clusters, in spring or summer. These are followed in autumn by edible berries in dusky shades of red, purple, and pink to white. All other parts may cause stomach upsets if eaten. Small to medium-sized, these shrubs have neat, dark green, leathery leaves and varied habits. Gaultherias can be grown in shrub borders, rock gardens, or woodland settings, and they make excellent companions for rhododendrons (*see pp.104–107*). Some have been subject to name changes; they are often sold simply as pernettyas.

Cultivation Gaultherias need acidic to neutral, moist soil, ideally in partial shade, although they will tolerate full sun where the soil is permanently moist. **Prune** lightly after flowering, cutting back shoots that spoil the shape of the shrub. Restrict the spread of plants by removing suckering growths. **Sow** seed (*see pp.391–393*) in containers outdoors in a cold frame in autumn. **Take** semiripe cuttings (*see p.394*) in summer or remove rooted suckers in spring and replant.

Gaultheria tasmanica
T min. 41°F (5°C) ↕3in (8cm) ↔ to 10in (25cm), mat-forming, flowers in spring, sometimes white or yellow fruits borne freely even in shade

Garrya elliptica 'James Roof'
Z7b ↕↔ 12ft (4m), vigorous shrub, male plants noted for particularly long catkins up to 8in (20cm)

Gaultheria mucronata 'Mulberry Wine'
Z7 ↕↔ 4ft (1.2m), compact suckering shrub, berries profusely if a male is planted nearby

Gaultheria × *wisleyensis* 'Pink Pixie'
Z6b ↕to 12in (30cm) ↔ 18in (45m), vigorous, upright, spreads by suckers, pinkish summer flowers, dark purple-red fruit

GENISTA
Broom

THESE ELEGANT SHRUBS are grown for their pretty, pealike yellow flowers, borne in small clusters from spring to summer. They are related to the other brooms, cytisus (*see p.47*) and spartiums (*see p.118*). The leaves are small. Although some species are almost leafless and almost all are deciduous, the green stems give some color to a garden even in winter. Habits vary from upright to arching, treelike forms. Brooms contrast well with broader-leaved plants such as ceanothus (*see p.36*) and fatsias (*see p.58*). The Mount Etna broom makes a graceful specimen in a lawn or shrub border, while dwarf species, like the dense, spiny *Genista hispanica* (Z7b), suit rock gardens. Some have sharp spines, so be careful or wear gloves when handling.

Cultivation Genistas like light, poor to reasonably fertile, well-drained soil, in full sun. **Little pruning** is required apart from removing misplaced or crossing shoots that spoil the shape, in late winter or early spring. Avoid cutting into old wood, because it will not produce new shoots. **Sow** seed (*see pp.391–393*) in a cold frame in autumn or take semiripe cuttings (*see p.394*) in summer.

Genista lydia
Z3b ↕ to 24in (60cm) ↔ to 3ft (1m), domed shrub with spine-tipped, blue-green shoots, flowers in early summer

Genista aetnensis (Mount Etna broom)
Z7 ↕↔ 25ft (8m), weeping shrub or small tree, leaves produced only on the younger shoots, fragrant flowers borne in profusion at ends of shoots in mid- to late summer

GINKGO BILOBA
Maidenhair tree

PERHAPS THE MOST ANCIENT of all living trees, the ginkgo is an upright or columnar tree when young and becomes spreading as it ages. The deciduous foliage, which is similar to that of maidenhair ferns (*Adiantum, see p.360*) and gives the tree its common name, turns a soft, golden yellow in autumn. Catkin-like, yellow male flowers and tiny female flowers are produced on separate trees. Given warm summers, female flowers produce plumlike, yellow-green fruits in autumn that smell unpleasant but contain large nuts, which are edible. Trouble-free and easy to grow, ginkgos will tolerate atmospheric pollution and are excellent as landscape trees, as specimens, in borders, or even in containers.

Cultivation Any fertile, well-drained soil, in full sun will suit ginkgos. **Cut out** any crossing or misshapen branches that spoil the shape of the tree, in late winter or early spring, to maintain a healthy framework (*see p.382*). **Sow** seed (*see pp.391–393*) in a cold frame as soon as it is ripe. **Take** semiripe cuttings (*see p.394*) in summer.

Gingko biloba
Z4 ↕ to 100ft (30m) ↔ to 25ft (8m), extinct in the wild, the ginkgo makes an excellent urban and landscape tree

GLEDITSIA
Honey locust

DECORATIVE FOLIAGE AND SEED PODS, and an elegant, spreading habit, make these deciduous trees beautiful specimen plants. The glossy, fernlike leaves are divided into as many as 24 smaller, pale to dark green leaflets. In autumn, long, curved and twisted, pendent seed-pods and foliage in yellow tints give further interest. The widely grown *Gleditsia triacanthos* usually has spiny trunks and shoots. 'Elegantissima' is a much smaller and thornless form of this tree, while 'Rubylace' has dark bronze-red young leaves that turn to dark bronze-green by midsummer. To highlight the autumn foliage of these trees, grow them alongside dark-leaved shrubs like cotinus (*see p.44*). Honey locusts self-seed prolifically.

Cultivation Grow gleditsias in any fertile, well-drained soil, in sun. **Pruning** is rarely necessary **Sow** seed (*see pp.391–393*) in an open frame in autumn. Prepare the seed by chipping each seed coat with a knife or rubbing it with sandpaper to allow moisture in. **Gall midges** may cause swellings on the leaves.

GRISELINIA LITTORALIS
Broadleaf

‡ to 25ft (8m)
↔ to 15ft (5m)

THIS VIGOROUS, DENSE, EVERGREEN, upright shrub or small tree can make a superb windbreak hedge in an exposed garden. It is grown for its tough and handsome foliage. Tiny flowers are borne in late spring, with male and female blossoms on separate plants. They are followed by purple fruits in autumn if plants of both sexes are grown together. Although most often used as hedging, griselinias also make handsome specimen plants in a border. They are particularly good in coastal areas, where the leathery leaves can withstand salt-laden winds and sea spray.

Cultivation Light, fertile, well-drained soil in full sun, with shelter from cold, drying winds, is required. **Prune lightly** in mid- or late spring, cutting back shoots that spoil that shape of the shrub. **Trim** hedges once or twice a year. **Sow** seed (*see pp.391–393*) in spring at 55–64°F (13–18°C) or take semiripe cuttings (*see p.394*) in summer.

HALESIA
Silverbell, Snowdrop tree

BEAUTIFUL IN SPRING, this small group of deciduous, trouble-free shrubs and trees are grown for their pendent, bell-shaped, pure white flowers. These are generally borne in late spring, sometimes in early summer, and are followed in autumn by winged green fruits and golden foliage. The forms can vary from conical, as in *Halesia monticola*, to spreading, as in *H. carolina* (Z6) or *H. diptera* (Z5b). The more spreading types can be grown as trees or as shrubs in gardens of any size. Found naturally in woodland and woodland margins and near riverbanks, halesias make pleasing specimens as shrubs for the back of a border or as trees in a woodland setting.

Cultivation These plants prefer fertile, moist but well-drained, preferably neutral to acidic soil that is enriched with well-rotted compost. Position in sun or partial shade with shelter from cold winds. **Remove** misplaced or crossing shoots, in winter or late spring, to maintain a good shape. **Sow** seed (*see pp.391–393*) at 57–77°F (14–25°C) in autumn. **Take** softwood cuttings (*see p.394*) in summer, or layer low-growing shoots (*see p.395*) in spring.

Gleditsia triacanthos 'Sunburst'
Z4 ‡ 40ft (12m) ↔ 30ft (10m), fast-growing, fruitless, and thornless, light canopy can be underplanted, so suitable for gardens

Griselinia littoralis
Z8 There are variegated forms, but the bright, glossy apple green is best for hedging

Halesia monticola
Z6 ‡ 40ft (12m) ↔ 25ft (8m), usually conical, vigorous tree, flowers in late spring before or just as leaves unfold, fruits heavily

x HALIMIOCISTUS

CHARMING, FRAGILE FLOWERS are the main attraction of these small, evergreen shrubs. They are crosses between cistus (*see p.40*) and halimiums (*see right*). The flowers resemble rock roses (*Helianthemum, see p.70*) and are usually pure white or blotched with deep red at the bases of the petals. Several of these trouble-free, often spreading hybrids are grown in gardens, with flowering periods from late spring to late summer. Found where their parent species grow together in hot, dry, Mediterranean areas, they are happy in a rock garden or dry, sunny border alongside roses (*see pp.110–113*) and shrubs such as cistus and lavenders (*Lavandula, see p.80*).

Cultivation Plant these shrubs in very well-drained soil in full sun. **Provide** shelter from cold, drying winds. **Pruning** is rarely needed, but if necessary in mid- or late spring, lightly trim shoots that spoil the shape of the shrub. **Take** semiripe cuttings (*see p.394*) in late summer.

x *Halimiocistus sahucii*
T min. 35°F (2°C) ↕18in (45cm) ↔ 36in (90cm), compact, mounding or spreading, narrow-leaved, flowers in summer

x *Halimiocistus wintonensis* 'Merrist Wood Cream'
Z8 ↕24in (60cm) ↔ 36in (90cm), spreading shrub, white woolly leaves, flowers from late spring to early summer

HALIMIUM

UPRIGHT TO SPREADING, but almost all compact, these small, evergreen shrubs bear sprays of flowers from late spring to early summer. These are golden yellow, occasionally white, and their petals are sometimes blotched at the bases with maroon-purple. They will flower best in long, hot summers. Their leaves are generally small, light to gray-green, and sometimes silver-scaly or hairy. These trouble-free shrubs usually have an upright or spreading habit. Halimiums are naturally found in dry, rocky places and they thrive in rock gardens or at the front of a sunny border. You can also display them in pots on the patio, placed in the sunniest corner for the best show of flowers.

Cultivation Halimiums like moderately fertile, well-drained, sandy soil, in full sun, with shelter from cold, drying winds. Choose the planting site carefully, since plants resent disturbance or transplanting once they are established. **Trim lightly** or prune back shoots that spoil the shape after flowering; deadheading plants will help to prolong flowering. **Sow** seed (*see pp.391–393*) at 66–75°F (19–24°C) in spring. **Take** semiripe cuttings (*see p.394*) in late summer.

Halimium ocymoides 'Susan'
T min. 41°F (5°C) ↕18in (45cm) ↔ 24in (60cm), spreading shrub, flowers appear in summer and are often semidouble

HAMAMELIS

Witch hazel

FRAGRANT, SPIDERY BLOOMS and autumn color make these medium-sized to large, deciduous shrubs essential in the winter garden. The striking flowers, with four narrow, twisting, ribbonlike petals, cluster thickly on bare stems from autumn to early spring. The spider-shaped flowers are cold-resistant. The broad, oval leaves turn yellow in autumn. Try witch hazels as specimen plants in borders, or grow them in groups. Evergreen Christmas box (*Sarcococca confusa, see p.116*), which is also scented and winter-flowering, will show off the upright, open forms of witch hazels and fill the garden with delicious scent even in winter.

Cultivation Witch hazels prefer reasonably fertile, moist but well-drained, ideally neutral to acidic soil. They will also grow in deep, alkaline, humus-rich soil. Position them in sun or partial shade, in an open but not exposed spot. **Prune** any crossing shoots, in late winter or early spring, to maintain a good shape. **Named** witch hazels are grafted and are best bought from a nursery or garden center.

SUCKERS should be removed, otherwise they will spoil the shrub. Pull them off, or cut them off, at the base. Watch for buds sprouting and rub off.

Hamamelis mollis 'Brevipetala'
Z6b ↕↔ 12ft (4m), upright shrub, hairy, blue-green leaves turn rich yellow in autumn, fragrant flowers in mid- and late winter

HEBE

VARIED AND ATTRACTIVE, EVERGREEN FOLIAGE and pretty flowers, in a huge range of shrubs from low, sprawling plants to large domed bushes, means that there is a hebe for almost any situation. Hebes have neat, matte or glossy foliage in tones of gray-, blue-, or true green, sometimes with colored edges. Spikes up to 12in (30cm) long or clusters of small flowers are usually borne from early to midsummer. They vary in hue from white to pinks, blues, purples, or red. Hebes provide year-round interest in mixed or shrub border, rock gardens, gravel gardens, or in pots on the patio. In mild areas, particularly coastal ones, they can be used as hedging or as groundcover.

Cultivation Hebes grow in poor to reasonably fertile, moist but well-drained, preferably neutral to slightly alkaline soil. Sun or partial shade, with shelter from cold, drying winds, is best. **Remove** any misplaced growths that spoil the shape, in late winter or early spring, but little pruning is needed. **Take** semiripe cuttings (*see p.394*) in summer or autumn. **Downy mildew** may infect leaves in damp conditions: avoid watering from above and pick off spoiled leaves.

Hamamelis × *intermedia* 'Pallida'
Z6b ↕↔ 12ft (4m), vase-shaped habit, bright green leaves turn gold in autumn, large flowers in mid- to late winter

Hamamelis × *intermedia* 'Diane'
Z6b ↕↔ 12ft (4m), vase-shaped habit, leaves turn orange, yellow, or red in autumn (*see inset*), flowers mid- to late winter

Hebe albicans
Z8 ↕ 24in (60cm) ↔ 36in (90cm), dense, mound-forming or spreading shrub, flowers from early to midsummer

Hebe ochracea 'James Stirling'
T min. 35°F (2°C) ‡ 18in (45cm) ↔ 24in (60cm), dense, upright, then arching shrub with stiff shoots; foliage is golden yellow all year round, flowers are borne in late spring and early summer

HEDERA

Ivy

see also
pp.142–143

ALTHOUGH IT IS KNOWN AS A CLIMBING plant, there are a few named cultivars of the common ivy, *Hedera helix*, available that have an unusual, shrubby habit. Like the climbing ivies, they are evergreen and famously tough plants. *Hedera helix* 'Congesta' forms a neat, dense bush with erect, spirelike shoots. It is compact and would make a striking addition to a rock garden. *Hedera helix* 'Erecta' is more vigorous, with stiffly upright stems, and slow-growing. It is better suited to a shrub or mixed border, perhaps where its small leaves contrast with, for example, ferns (*see pp.358–365*) or broad-leaved plants such as bergenias (*see p.198*). The stems are brittle, so are best grown in a sheltered spot, or with the support of other shrubs or against a wall.

Cultivation Ivies grow in a variety of soils, but do best in fertile, moist but well-drained, preferably alkaline soil, in sun or partial shade, sheltered from wind. **Trim** to shape the shrubs at any time of the year. **Take** semiripe cuttings (*see p.394*) in summer.

CLIPPING HEBES with shears in mid- to late spring removes any frost-damaged growth, keeps a neat shape, and encourages new growth. You can also do this to deadhead hebes in late summer.

Hebe 'Great Orme'
T min. 41°F (5°C) ‡ ↔ 4ft (1.2m), open, rounded bush, flowers from midsummer through mid-autumn, fading to white as they age

Hebe pinguifolia 'Pagei'
Z7 ‡ 12in (30cm) ↔ 36in (90cm), erect, then semi-prostrate habit, purple stems, flowers late spring to early summer

① *helix* 'Congesta' Z5b ‡ ↔ 18in (45cm)
② *helix* 'Erecta' Z5 ‡ ↔ 3ft (1m)

HELIANTHEMUM

Rock rose, Sun rose

‡to 18in (45cm) ↔ 24in (60cm)

THE PRETTY, PAPERY, saucer-shaped flowers of these little evergreen shrubs have always been a firm favorite of gardeners. Most grow to only 6–12in (15–30cm) tall. A profusion of blooms, in a wide range of vivid and pale colors, are borne over a long period from late spring to midsummer against a background of silver to gray- or mid-green foliage. They love to bask in sunshine and, with their compact habit, thrive in dry conditions, such as a rock garden or a raised bed, or at the front of a border. A gravel mulch suits them very well, giving them a dry, warm, free-draining – and attractive – surface over which to spread.

Cultivation Rock roses enjoy well-drained, neutral to alkaline soil, in full sun. **Pruning** is very easy; after flowering use garden shears to trim the flowered shoots back to the old growth. **Take** softwood cuttings (*see p.394*) in late spring or early summer.

Helianthemum 'Rhodanthe Carneum'
Z6 ‡ 12in (30cm) ↔ 18in (45cm), sometimes sold as 'Wisley Pink', with a very long flowering season

HELIOTROPIUM

Heliotrope

‡ ↔ 24in (60cm)

HELIOTROPE IS A TREASURED garden plant, much loved for its dense, sweetly scented flower heads. Most heliotropes are related to *Heliotropium arborescens*, the only commonly grown species. Heliotropes are most often used as bedding or container plants for summer display. They can be overwintered under cover, but new plants grown over winter from cuttings taken from the parent often make more successful, bushier plants to set out the following year. The plant's wrinkled leaves are sometimes tinged purple, complementing the tiny blue or purple flowers borne in large clusters throughout summer. Heliotropes are attractive to butterflies.

Cultivation Grow heliotropes in any fertile, moist but well-drained soil, in full sun. In containers such as pots, tubs, and windowboxes, use any good-quality potting mix. **Sow** seed (*see pp.391–393*) at 61–64°F (16–18°C) in spring. **Take** softwood or semiripe cuttings (*see p.394*) in summer.

Helianthemum 'Fire Dragon'
Z6 ‡ 8–12in (20–30cm) ↔ 12in (30cm), a low, spreading, and compact plant, vivid orange-red flowers

Helianthemum lunulatum
Z6 ‡ 6in (15cm) ↔ 10in (25cm), small-flowered with a cascading habit, good for a sunny bank

Heliotropium arborescens 'Marine'
T min. 50°F (10°C) ‡ 18in (45cm) ↔ 12–18in (30–45cm), flower heads to 6in (15cm) across

HIBISCUS

FAMOUS FOR THEIR SPECTACULAR FLOWERS from spring until autumn, hibiscus are available in a rainbow of bright hues. The flowers are carried against glossy green, occasionally variegated foliage. Although the group includes many annuals and perennials as well as shrubs, the woody, deciduous *Hibiscus syriacus* and its cultivars are the most commonly grown in cool climates. Hibiscus are a welcome addition to a border and thrive in large pots. This is useful if you want to grow the Hawaiian hibiscus (*H. rosa-sinensis* T min. 50–55°F/10–13°C), because the container can be moved indoors over winter.

Cultivation Grow in moist, well-drained, preferably slightly alkaline soil, in full sun. The longer and hotter the summer, the more flowers are produced, so give hibiscus a warm, sheltered position in cooler areas, and apply a winter mulch (*see p.388*). Little pruning is needed other than to remove wayward branches and any dead or damaged wood. **Sow** seed (*see pp.391–392*) at 55–64°F (13–18°C) in spring. **Take** semiripe cuttings in summer (*see p.394*), or layer shoots (*see p.395*) in late spring.

Hibiscus syriacus 'Oiseau Bleu'
Z5b ↕ 10ft (3m) ↔ 6ft (2m), very popular for its novel color and frequently sold under the name 'Blue Bird'

Hibiscus syriacus 'Diana'
Z5b ↕ 10ft (3m) ↔ 6ft (2m), bears some of the largest flowers for this species, to 5in (13cm) across

Hibiscus syriacus 'Woodbridge'
Z5b ↕ 10ft (3m) ↔ 6ft (2m), with flatter, more mallowlike, but intensely colored blooms

HIPPOPHAE
Sea buckthorn

THESE TOUGH, DECIDUOUS shrubs or small trees are popular low-maintenance plants with a handsome, upright habit and narrow, silvery leaves. In autumn, abundant orange berries are borne if a male and a female are grown together; those of the willow-leaved sea buckthorn (*Hippophae salicifolia* Z4) are said to be the most nutritious fruits that can be grown in temperate climates. They have a sharp lemony taste and can be used in juice and preserves. The common sea buckthorn (*H. rhamnoides*) has spiny stems and is invaluable in areas buffeted by salt-laden winds and sea spray, where it can be used for hedges, windbreaks, and stabilizing sand dunes.

Cultivation Ideal conditions are full sun in moist but well-drained, slightly alkaline soil; in practice, these resilient plants will grow in most well-drained and sandy soils; will survive periods of drought, strong winds, and heavy rain. **Prune out** only those stems that are crossing or spoiling the shape of the shrub. **Sow** seed (*see pp.391–392*) in a cold frame as soon as it is ripe or in spring. **Take** semiripe cuttings in summer or hardwood cuttings in autumn (*see p.394*), or layer shoots (*see p.395*) in autumn.

Hippophae rhamnoides
Z2b ↕↔ 20ft (6m), bushy shrub or small tree, the berries persist on female plants through winter

HYDRANGEA

see also
p.143

‡↔ 3ft (1m) to
22ft (7m)

THESE SHRUBS HAVE LONG BEEN GARDEN favorites for their large, stately flower heads. These may be flat or domed and are made up of clusters of tiny, fertile flowers and larger, sterile flowers with petal-like sepals. The many cultivars of the most common species, *Hydrangea macrophylla*, include two types: hortensias have round "mopheads" of sterile flowers, whereas lacecaps have flat flower heads of fertile flowers edged with sterile ones. Flower color is affected by the acidity or alkalinity of the soil. Hydrangea blooms are blue on acid soils and pink on alkaline soils; on neutral soils the hues can be mixed, often being bluish pink. The white-flowered cultivars are not affected by pH. Most garden hydrangeas are deciduous. Some hydrangeas also have flaky, peeling bark and handsome foliage, which has good autumn color. These excellent plants can be used in many sites, especially as specimen plants or in borders. The flowers dry to parchment shades and are useful in arrangements.

Cultivation Hydrangeas thrive in moist, well-drained, fertile soil in sun or partial shade, if sheltered from cold, drying winds. **Pruning,** for most cultivars except those mentioned below, consists of cutting out misplaced or crossing shoots in late winter or early spring. **Sow** seed (*see pp.391–393*) in containers in spring. **Root** soft stem-tip cuttings in early summer or take hardwood cuttings in winter (*see p.394*). Hydrangea blooms may be spoiled by gray mold (botrytis) in very wet summers.

How to prune hydrangeas

Hard pruning (see left) of H. paniculata *in early spring – before it produces its flowering shoots – results in a much better show of flower. If not pruned, the plants, which normally put on a lot of growth, become very tall, and the flowers appear only at the tips where they are difficult to see.*

Hard pruning involves cutting off all the previous year's flowering wood to leave a base of woody stems, as low as 10in (25cm) in exposed gardens or 24in (60cm) at the back of a border. Cut each stem back to a pair of healthy buds at the required height. Neglected plants also respond well to this type of hard pruning.

Light pruning is advisable for hortensias *(also called mophead hydrangeas), all other* H. macrophylla *cultivars,* H. serrata *and its cultivars, and 'Preziosa" These hydrangeas all flower on stems formed in the previous year. On the whole, they manage this without much attention, but a little annual pruning enhances flowering and keeps the shrubs healthy.*

Leave old flower heads over winter to protect the new buds. Then, in late winter or early spring, prune the previous year's flowered shoots by up to 12in (30cm) to just above two strong buds (see inset). Cut out weak and thin shoots, and prune one or two of the oldest stems to the base.

① *Hydrangea arborescens* 'Annabelle' ‡↔ 8ft (2.5m) ② *arborescens* 'Grandiflora' ‡↔ 8ft (2.5m)
③ *aspera* Villosa Group (Z7b) ‡↔ 4–12ft (1–4m) ④ *involucrata* 'Hortensis' ‡ 3ft (1m) ↔ 6ft (2m)
⑤ *macrophylla* 'Ayesha' (hortensia) (Z6) 5ft (1.5m) ↔ 6ft (2m) ⑥ *macrophylla* 'Blue Bonnet'
(hortensia) ‡ 6ft (2m) ↔ 8ft (2.5m) ⑦ *macrophylla* 'Bouquet Rose' (hortensia) ‡ 6ft (2m) ↔ 8ft
(2.5m) ⑧ *macrophylla* 'Hamburg' (hortensia) ‡ 6ft (2m) ↔ 8ft (2.5m) ⑨ *macrophylla* 'Lanarth

White' (lacecap) (Z6) ‡↔ 5ft (1.5 m) ⑩ *macrophylla* 'Mariesii Perfecta' (lacecap) ‡6ft (2m) ↔ 8ft (2.5m) ⑪ *macrophylla* 'Veitchi' (lacecap) ‡6ft (2m) ↔ 8ft (2.5m) ⑫ *paniculata* 'Brussels Lace' ‡10–22ft (3–7m) ↔ 8ft (2.5m) ⑬ *paniculata* 'Floribunda' ‡10–22ft (3–7m) ↔ 8ft (2.5m)

⑭ *paniculata* 'Grandiflora' ‡10–22ft (3–7m) ↔ 8ft (2.5m) ⑮ *paniculata* 'Pink Diamond' ('Interhydia') ‡10–22ft (3–7m) ↔ 8ft (2.5m) ⑯ *paniculata* 'Praecox' ‡10–22ft (3–7m) ↔ 8ft (2.5m)

⑰ *paniculata* 'Unique' ‡10–22ft (3–7m) ↔ 8ft (2.5m) ⑱ 'Preziosa' ‡↔ 5ft (1.5m) ⑲ *quercifolia* ‡6ft (2m) ↔ 8ft (2.5m) ⑳ *quercifolia* 'Snow Queen' ('Flemygea') ‡6ft (2m) ↔ 8ft (2.5m) ㉑ *serrata* ‡↔ 4ft (1.2m) ㉒ *serrata* 'Bluebird' (lacecap) ‡↔ 4ft (1.2m) ㉓ *serrata* 'Rosalba' (lacecap) (Z6) ‡↔ 4ft (1.2m). H. arborescens Z3b H9–1; H. involucrata Z7b; H. macrophylla Z6; H. paniculata Z3b; H. quercifolia Z5b; H. serrata Z6.

HYPERICUM

St. John's wort

↔ 3–6ft (1–2m)

THIS DIVERSE GROUP ranges from large shrubs to small annuals and perennials, but in summer all bear similar, distinctive, bright yellow flowers with a central boss of golden stamens. Some are decorated with berries through autumn. The shrubs are most commonly cultivated, both evergreens and deciduous species that provide lovely autumn color. There is a hypericum for most situations: the larger species are good for a border, smaller ones for a rock garden. The spreading Rose of Sharon (*Hypericum calycinum*) makes ideal groundcover, although it can become invasive so is not recommended for borders.

Cultivation Larger shrubs prefer moist but well drained soil in sun or partial shade, the small rock-garden types full sun and good drainage. *H. androsaemum* and *H. calycinum* tolerate even deep shade. **Trim** in spring to keep them neat; larger deciduous species can be cut back hard to a permanent framework in early spring to keep them smaller. **Take** semiripe cuttings in summer (*see p.394*).

Hypericum androsaemum (Tutsan)
Z4 ‡ 30in (75cm) ↔ 36in (90m), bushy, deciduous shrub, flowers in midsummer, red berries ripen to black in autumn

ILEX

Holly

HOLLIES ARE BEST KNOWN for winter berries and stiff, prickly, evergreen foliage, but not all are spiny. Their glossy leaves may be plain dark or mid-green, or may be edged, splashed, or striped with silver or gold. The flowers are tiny, the berries usually red or black; they can cause a stomach upset if eaten. Female plants berry only if a male is nearby; hollies are often sold by sex so you can be sure of fruiting. Grow hollies in woodland, with winter-flowering shrubs like sarcococcas (*see p.116*) or mahonias (*see p.87*), or as specimens, so their dense, shapely forms and pale gray bark can be appreciated. *Ilex × altaclerensis* and *I. aquifolium* cultivars can be used as formal hedging, but frequent trimming can mean fewer berries.

Cultivation Best planted in early spring. Full sun encourages bright color in variegated hollies, but otherwise site in sun or shade in moist, well-drained soil. **Prune** free-standing specimens only if needed to maintain a well-balanced shape; trim hedges in late summer. Topiary may need an extra trim in spring. **Take** semiripe cuttings in late summer or autumn (*see p.394*).

PRUNING GROUNDCOVER
Encourage fresh growth by cutting *H. calycinum* back to the ground in spring, either with shears or a nylon-line trimmer.

Hypericum calycinum (Aaron's beard, Rose of Sharon)
Z5b ‡ 24in (60cm) ↔ indefinite, evergreen or semievergreen with creeping, rooting stems, flowers from summer to autumn

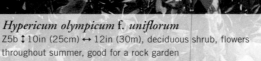

Hypericum olympicum* f. *uniflorum
Z5b ‡ 10in (25cm) ↔ 12in (30m), deciduous shrub, flowers throughout summer, good for a rock garden

***Ilex × altaclerensis* 'Golden King'**
Z6 ‡ 20ft (6m) ↔ 12ft (4m), compact, female shrub, good conical form (*see inset*), but berries can be sparse in some years

Ilex aquifolium 'J. C. van Tol'
Z7 ↕20ft (6m) ↔ 12ft (4m), broadly shaped, self-fertile female tree, berries are guaranteed every year without a male nearby

Ilex aquifolium 'Ferox Argentea' (Hedgehog holly)
Z7 ↕25ft (8m) ↔ 12ft (4m), slow-growing, upright, densely prickly male with spines both over and on the leaves

INDIGOFERA

↔ 6–10ft (2–3m)

THE EVERGREEN AND DECIDUOUS shrubby indigoferas are the most commonly cultivated in this large, varied group. They need space to grow and show off their elegant habits, for example in a shrub border, perhaps with euonymus (*see p.56*) and escallonias (*see p.54*), or trained against a sunny wall. Indigoferas bear masses of pealike flowers from early summer until early autumn, against a background of soft green leaves. *Indigofera amblyantha* and *I. heterantha* (Z7b) are the hardiest species and the best choice in temperate climates, unless you can provide a sheltered, south-facing wall. They respond well to annual pruning.

Cultivation Grow in moist but well-drained soil, in full sun. **Prune** hard in areas with severe winters only; in early spring, cut all stems down to within a few buds of their bases, leaving a low stubby framework (*see p.383*). For wall-trained shrubs, in late winter or early spring, remove or tie in branches growing too far outward, and trim sideshoots to within three or four buds of the main branches. **Take** semiripe cuttings in early or midsummer (*see p.394*).

Ilex aquifolium 'Amber'
Z7 ↕20ft (6m) ↔ 8ft (2.5m), compact, pyramid-shaped, female tree, bears abundant fruit when a male holly is close by

Ilex × altaclerensis 'Camelliifolia'
Z6 ↕46ft (14m) ↔ 40–50ft (12–15m), large, conical, female shrub with no spines, on leaves up to 5in (13cm) long

Indigofera amblyantha
Z7 ↕6ft (2m) ↔ 8ft (2.5m), deciduous shrub, particularly free-flowering

ITEA

↕ to 15ft (5m)

ONLY THE TWO species of itea illustrated here are very widely cultivated – for their tiny white flowers, borne in catkinlike clusters in summer. and also for their foliage, similar to that of holly. The leaves of the evergreen *Itea ilicifolia* are valuable for providing year-round greenery; those of the deciduous *I. virginica* give a spectacular autumn display of reds and purples before they fall.

Cultivation The less hardy evergreen iteas like fertile, moist, well-drained soil in a sunny, sheltered position; they thrive against a sunny, south-facing wall and with a thick winter mulch (*see p.388*), especially while young. Deciduous species prefer the shady, damp, slightly acid conditions of a woodland garden or dense shrub border. **Trim** evergreens only as necessary to keep them neat. Deciduous iteas can be kept shapely by cutting the flowered shoots back to strong, non-flowering sideshoots; once plants are mature, cut back one stem in four to the base each year to prevent congestion (*see p.383*). If wall-trained, cut back flowered shoots to a few buds from the framework branches. **Sow** seed when ripe (*see pp.391–393*). **Take** soft stem-tip cuttings in spring, or semiripe cuttings in summer (*see p.394*).

① ②

① *ilicifolia* Z7b ↕ 10–15ft (3–5m), flowers from midsummer to early autumn ② *virginica* (Sweetspire, Tassel-white) Z6 ↕ 5–10ft (1.5–3m), flowers in summer

JASMINUM NUDIFLORUM

Winter jasmine

see also p.144

↕ 10ft (3m)

MOST COMMONLY GROWN jasmines are climbers, but this one is a shrub, albeit a rather lanky one. The winter jasmine (*Jasminum nudiflorum*) may not be quite as intensely perfumed as its summer-flowering cousins, but is highly valued nevertheless for its golden flowers through the barest months of the year. This slender-stemmed, arching, often untidy plant is best wall-trained, perhaps with other winter favorites such as garryas (*see p.64*). Cut sprigs and bring them indoors while the buds are still closed; the warmth of a room should force them into flower early for a touch of winter cheer and delicate scent.

Cultivation Grow in fertile, well-drained soil in full sun or partial shade. **Prune** flowered shoots back to strong buds, and once plants are older, after flowering, remove up to one in four of the main stems at the base to encourage fresh growth (*see p.383*). **Take** semiripe cuttings in summer or autumn (*see p.394*); alternatively shoots can be layered (*see p.395*) in autumn.

Jasminum nudiflorum (Winter jasmine)
Z7 ↕ 10ft (3m), deciduous shrub with fragrant flowers in winter and early spring, leaves appear after flowering

JUNIPERUS

Juniper

THESE EVERGREEN, CONIFEROUS TREES and shrubs are grown for their sculptural habits and colorful foliage. They come in all shapes and sizes; large trees, dwarf cultivars, and spreading shrubs, and their leaves, or needles, can be dark green, golden yellow, or even blue. A fantastic tapestry of shapes, colors, and of textures can be built up by growing a collection of junipers together, or with other conifers. The females bear round, fleshy cones, rather like berries; these are used in cooking and also as one of the flavorings of gin. Junipers will tolerate a wide range of conditions: larger trees can be used as specimens, small shrubs in a rock garden with alpines, and prostrate cultivars as groundcover.

Cultivation Junipers are not fussy and will grow in any well-drained soil, in sun or partial shade. **Pruning** is generally unnecessary, although if prostrate species spread too far you can remove selected stems carefully to keep them within bounds. Propagation is tricky, and seed may take up to five years to germinate, so new plants are probably best bought from a nursery.

Juniperus squamata 'Blue Star'
Z5 ↕ 16in (40cm) ↔ to 3ft (1m), a compact, spreading bush forming wavelike, cascading shapes

***Juniperus scopulorum* 'Skyrocket'**
Z3 ‡20ft (6m) ↔ 20–24in (50–60cm), pencil-thin, columnar tree that provides a spectacular focal point

***Juniperus × pfitzeriana* 'Pfitzeriana Aurea'**
Z4 ‡36in (90cm) ↔ 6ft (2m), spreading shrub, the golden yellow needles become greenish yellow over winter

KALMIA

KALMIAS ARE ACID-LOVING, evergreen shrubs with clusters of pretty, pink, bowl-shaped flowers in mid-spring and early summer. Throughout the year, the branches are clothed with the glossy, leathery leaves. The slightly larger kalmias, such as *Kalmia latifolia* (Z5) and its cultivars, are spectacular in borders or among groves of trees. Small species, for example *K. microphylla* (Z4) can be used in a rock or woodland garden with heathers and dwarf rhododendrons, which require similar soil conditions.

Cultivation Grow in moist, acidic soil, preferably in partial shade unless the ground remains continually damp; a layer of leaf mold, pine needles, or mulch around the plants in spring will help retain moisture. If you live in an area with alkaline soil, grow kalmias in pots filled with acidic potting mix. **Prune** after flowering only if necessary to trim shoots that spoil the shape of the shrub. If you have a leggy specimen, renovate it over several seasons (*see p.384*) – except *K. angustifolia*, which can be cut back hard in a single year and will regrow well. **Take** semiripe cuttings in midsummer (*see p.394*), or layer low-growing shoots in late summer (*see p.395*).

***Juniperus chinensis* 'Pyramidalis'**
Z4 ‡6ft (2m) ↔ 24in (60cm), small cultivar with a neat, compact shape

***Juniperus communis* 'Compressa'**
Z3 ‡32in (80cm) ↔ 18in (45m), dwarf and slow-growing, suitable for combining with alpine plants in a trough or rock garden

***Kalmia angustifolia* (Lambkill, Sheep laurel)**
Z3 ‡24in (60cm) ↔ 5ft (1.5m), mound-forming shrub, flowers are occasionally white

KERRIA JAPONICA

Japanese Rose

↔ to 9ft (3m)

KERRIA AND ITS CULTIVARS are vigorous, suckering shrubs that are good value all year-round. In mid- and late spring, they bear single or double, golden yellow flowers. The deciduous foliage is bright green, gray-green, or variegated with creamy white. When the leaves fall, winter interest is then provided by the dense clumps of arching, light green stems. Grow kerrias in a border where they have room to spread out among other shrubs, or as part of a display of winter stems together with dogwoods (*Cornus, see pp.42–43*).

Cultivation Grow kerrias in fertile, well-drained soil in full sun or partial shade. **Prune** the stems when they have flowered to sideshoots or strong buds lower down on the shrub (*see p.383*). **Divide** the bush in autumn (*see p.395*), or propagate from suckers (stems growing up from the roots) in spring. Find a sucker and dig down to make sure it has developed some roots of its own. Cut it away from its parent, cut back its stem by a half, and replant it.

Kerria japonica 'Picta'
Z5 ‡ 5ft (1.5m) ↔ 6ft (2m)

Kerria japonica 'Golden Guinea'
Z5 ‡ 6ft (2m) ↔ 8ft (2.5m), very large single flowers up to 2½in (6cm) across

KOELREUTERIA

↔ 30ft (10m)

THESE MAKE FINE SPECIMEN trees throughout the year. They have a spreading shape, elegant, deciduous leaves, large clusters of yellow flowers in summer, and unusual, bladderlike fruits in the autumn. The golden rain tree (*Koelreuteria paniculata*) is the most widely available, and also perhaps the most impressive, of the three species. Its leaves emerge reddish pink in spring, mature to mid-green, and give a lovely show of butter yellow tints in autumn. In mid- and late summer, it bears sprays of small, golden flowers, up to 12in (30cm) long, followed by pink- or red-flushed fruit capsules. The flowers are more abundant in areas with long, hot summers.

Cultivation Grow in fertile, well-drained soil in full sun. **Prune** out any damaged or dead wood (*see p.382*) when dormant in winter, but no further pruning is necessary. **Sow** seed (*see pp.391–392*) in autumn, in a container, and place in a cold frame.

FRUIT CAPSULES

Koelreuteria paniculata (Golden rain tree, Pride of India)
Z7 ‡↔ 30ft (10m), leaves to 18in (45cm) long

KOLKWITZIA AMABILIS
Beautybush

‡10ft (3m)
↔ 12ft (4m)

IN FULL FLOWER, the beauty bush is an amazing sight. From late spring to early summer, the pale to deep pink blooms are borne in such numbers that they almost completely obscure the tapered, dark green leaves. This is a deciduous, suckering shrub with an elegant, arching habit. It makes an excellent border plant and is also wonderful grown as a specimen, so that its charms can be enjoyed to the full. Cultivars with brighter pink flowers or orange-yellow young foliage are available.

Cultivation This shrub prefers well-drained soil, preferably in full sun, although it will tolerate some shade. **Prune** shoots after they have flowered, to strong buds or shoots lower down on the plant. On mature plants, cut out about one-third to a quarter of old branches to the ground to encourage new growth (*see p.383*). **Propagate** the shrub from suckers (stems growing up from the roots) in spring. Find a sucker and dig down to see that it has developed some roots of its own. Cut it away from its parent, cut back its stems by half, and then replant it. Water well.

Kolkwitzia amabilis 'Pink Cloud'
Z5 ‡4ft (1.2m) ↔ 24in (60cm), widely available, bright, deep pink flowers

LABURNUM
Golden chain tree

‡↔ to 8m (25ft)

AS THE COMMON NAME SUGGESTS, these spreading trees are grown for their bright yellow, pealike flowers, which are produced in long pendent clusters in late spring and early summer. Any of this small group of compact trees is an excellent choice for a specimen tree in a small garden. Create a lovely arch, tunnel, or pergola – simply tie in the branches to a frame while they are young and supple. In this way, the pendent flowers can be enjoyed at their best. Plant purple flowers, such as alliums (*see p.174*), beneath them for a pleasing contrast. Weeping cultivars are available. All parts are highly toxic if ingested.

Cultivation Site laburnums in well-drained soil in full sun. **Train** by tying in shoots as they grow. In late summer, trim the sideshoots to two or three buds from the main stems to encourage branching. Remove any wayward shoots when they are still young, in late winter (*see p.382*). **Sow** seed of species (*see pp.392–392*) in a cold frame in autumn; plant seedlings quickly because they resent root disturbance.

Laburnum × *watereri* 'Vossii'
Z6 ‡↔ 25ft (8m), flower clusters up to 2ft (60cm) long

LAURUS NOBILIS
Bay laurel, Sweet bay

THE BAY LAUREL FORMS a large shrub or small, conical tree with evergreen, aromatic foliage that is used as a culinary flavoring. Cultivars with golden leaves are also available. Both male and female flowers are greenish yellow but are borne on separate plants in spring; if grown together, black berries may follow on the female. Bay is often clipped and looks elegant with other formal topiary, such as boxwood (*Buxus, see p.30*), or in a pot as an attractive patio plant. Neat bushes or standards in containers have the bonus of being easily moved under cover in winter, if needed. Bay can also be grown in its natural form as a specimen, in borders, or against a wall.

Cultivation Grow in moist, well-drained soil, in sun or partial shade, with some shelter. Remove wayward or crossing shoots of naturally shaped bay (*see p.382*). **Clip** topiary once or twice in summer to keep it neat. **Sow** seed (*see pp.392–392*) in pots in a cold frame in autumn; take semiripe cuttings (*see p.394*) in summer. Round, brown scale insects may be a problem on plants growing under cover; remove any shoots with mildew (*see p.398*).

Laurus nobilis
Z7 ‡40ft (12m) ↔ 30ft (10m), widely available, contact with foliage may aggravate skin allergies

LAVANDULA
Lavender

LAVENDERS ARE DESERVEDLY POPULAR PLANTS, grown for their evergreen, aromatic foliage, and scented flowers in mid- to late summer. There are many types, some more strongly perfumed than others, most with silvery foliage and nectar-rich flowers that are irresistible to pollinating bees. To dry the flowers so you can enjoy their summery aroma in winter, cut them before they are fully open and hang them upside down in bunches in a dry place. Lavenders can be used in borders and are classic partners for roses; they are wonderful grown as low edging for a bed, sending up great wafts of scent as you brush past. Where marginally hardy, grow in pots and overwinter in a cool greenhouse.

Cultivation Lavenders are undemanding, provided that they have well-drained soil in full sun. **Trim** in early or midspring: use shears to create a neat, rounded mound, taking off shoot tips but never cutting into old, bare wood. Trim lightly again to remove faded flower stalks (*see right*). **Sow** seed in a container in a cold frame in spring (*see pp.391–392*). **Take** semiripe cuttings in summer (*see p.394*) for quicker results.

Lavandula stoechas **subsp.** *pedunculata*
Z8 ↕↔ 24in (60cm), widely available subspecies of the vigorous French lavender, dark purple-red flowers

DEADHEADING LAVENDER
Tidy up lavender bushes when the flowers have faded, by trimming them over with a pair of garden shears, back to within 1in (2.5cm) of the old growth.

Lavandula angustifolia 'Munstead'
Z5 ↕ 18in (45cm) ↔ 24in (60cm), more compact than the species so better for border edging

Lavandula angustifolia 'Hidcote'
Z6 ↕ 24in (60cm) ↔ 30in (75cm), compact shrub whose vivid flowers contrast spectacularly with the silvery gray leaves

Lavandula angustifolia 'Nana Alba'
Z6 ↕↔ 12in (30cm), forms a very compact, neat bush, good for containers and edging, widely available

Lavandula 'Marshwood'
Z8 ↕↔ 24in (60cm), bushy plant with similar flowers to the French lavenders

LAVATERA
Tree Mallow

see also
p.270

‡↔ 6ft (2m)

THERE ARE LOTS OF MALLOWS; the shrubby ones need space to grow as they get quite large, but they respond well to hard pruning. They are valued for their profusion of ice-cream-colored flowers in summer and autumn. The foliage of both deciduous and evergreen types is soft green, with downy hairs, somewhat coarse in appearance, so these shrubs are best used to provide a substantial backdrop for smaller ornamental plants. Place them near the back of the border, preferably against a wall in areas with very cold winters. Mallows are ideal for coastal gardens, enjoying the sandy soil and often mild, frost-free conditions.

Cultivation Mallows prefer light, sandy soil in full sun, but tolerate heavier ground. In cold regions, the marginally hardy species may need shelter from cold, drying winds on a south-facing wall. **Prune** in early spring to keep the shrub compact, cutting stems back almost to the base. **Take** softwood cuttings (*see p.394*) in early summer; lavateras can be short-lived, and it is wise to grow replacements.

LESPEDEZA
Bush clover

‡ 6ft (2m)
↔ 10ft (3m)

THE BUSH CLOVERS are named for their blue-green leaves, borne in groups of three and looking like those of the common clover. There are annual and perennial species, but the most commonly available are the deciduous shrubs, which are grown mainly for their pealike flowers. They hang in long, dense clusters from the arching branches toward the end of summer and into autumn. This late flowering time makes lespedezas invaluable plants to team with rudbeckias (*see p.317*) and Michaelmas daisies (*Aster, see pp.192–193*) for a fabulous display of warm, glowing colors late in the season. Very cold winters may cut these plants down, but they will regrow.

Cultivation Grow in light, well-drained soil in full sun. **Prune** in early spring by cutting back all the stems to a low framework; if severe winters cause the top-growth to die back, then cut stems down to the base of the plant. **Sow** seed in containers outdoors in spring (*see pp.391–392*). *L. thunbergii* can be divided (*see p.395*), also in spring.

Lavandula angustifolia 'Loddon Pink'
Z6 ‡ 18in (45cm) ↔ 24in (60cm), more compact than the species and excellent for border edging

① × *clementii* 'Burgundy Wine' Z6 ‡↔ 6ft2 (m) vigorous, semievergreen ② × *clementii* 'Barnsley' Z5 ‡↔ 6ft (2m) vigorous, semievergreen, white flowers age to pink

Lespedeza thunbergii
Z5 ‡ 6ft (2m) ↔ 10ft (3m), flowers early autumn, may achieve full height only where the top-growth survives winter

LEUCOTHOE

THESE DECIDUOUS EVERGREEN and semievergreen shrubs resemble pieris (*see p.97*) in many ways, with an upright habit, arching branches, and attractive, bell-like, white flowers that appear in spring. The leaves of all are handsome, but novel foliage color is an added attraction in cultivars of *Leucothoe fontanesiana* such as 'Rainbow' and 'Scarletta' (Z6), which has dark red-purple young foliage that turns dark green in summer and then bronze in winter. Leucothoes grow best in a shady position, accompanying shrubs such as rhododendrons (*see pp.104–107*), ericas (*see pp.52–53*) and pieris, which all like similar soil conditions. Most are good choices for a woodland garden; the small *L. keiskei* (Z6) is suitable for a rock garden.

Cultivation Grow in partial or deep shade, in soil that is acidic and reliably moist; add plenty of well-rotted organic matter. **Prune** in late winter or early spring, only to take out any crossing or badly placed branches. **Sow** seed in containers in a cold frame in spring (*see pp.391–392*). **Take** semiripe cuttings (*see p.394*) in summer.

Leucothoe fontanesiana 'Rainbow'
Z6 ‡ 5ft (1.5m) ↔ 6ft (2m), clump-forming, makes good underplanting for a woodland garden, flowers in late spring

LEYCESTERIA FORMOSA

Himalayan honeysuckle

A FAST-GROWING SHRUB with hollow, bamboolike stems, this has unusual flowers appearing in summer, followed by small, round berries. The white flowers are covered by distinctive bracts (leaves growing at the flower base), forming drooping, pagoda-like clusters that made the plant a popular choice in Victorian shrubberies. These bracts persist to enclose purple-red berries. It is not widely grown today, even though it provides a long season of interest, from blue-green shoots in spring to good autumn color. Where not hardy, grow in a cool greenhouse.

Cultivation Grow in reasonably fertile, well-drained soil, in full sun or partial shade. **Protect** from cold, drying winds and protect with a thick mulch of organic matter around the base of the plant in winter where marginally hardy (*see p.388*). **Prune** after flowering by cutting back flowered shoots to young sideshoots or strong buds lower down – or, in spring, cut all the stems back hard (*see p.383*). **Sow** seed in containers in a cold frame in autumn (*see pp.391–392*). **Take** softwood cuttings in summer (*see p.394*).

Leycesteria formosa
T min. 41°F (5°C) ‡ ↔ 6ft (2m), upright, thicket-forming habit, suited to garden or shrub border, flowers from late summer to early autumn

LIGUSTRUM

Privet

MOST COMMONLY USED AS HEDGING, privets are evergreen or semievergreen shrubs found in many urban gardens, since they happily withstand shade and pollution. Easy to grow, they thrive in most garden soils and situations. White flowers with a musty scent appear in spring or summer, followed by black fruits. The dense, neat foliage is the main feature. The habit can be upright or conical, rounded or spreading. Some species, such as *Ligustrum japonicum* (Z7b), with large, glossy leaves, can be used as specimen shrubs or in a border. Others, such as the golden privet (*L. ovalifolium* 'Aureum' Z6), make the best hedges. All parts may cause severe discomfort if eaten.

Cultivation Grow in any well-drained soil in full sun or partial shade; variegated cultivars produce the best-colored foliage in full sun. **Prune** shrubs in late winter or early spring, cutting out overcrowded or crossing branches. **Clip** hedges at least twice a year. **Sow** seed in containers in a cold frame in autumn or spring (*see pp.391–392*). **Take** semiripe cuttings in summer, or hardwood cuttings in winter (*see p.394*). **Leaf miners** may attack privet, but they do no lasting damage.

Ligustrum lucidum 'Excelsum Superbum'
Z8 ‡ ↔ 30ft (10m), conical-shaped tree or shrub, evergreen leaves, flowers in late summer

LINUM ARBOREUM

Flax

see also
p.278

‡↔ 12in (30cm)

THIS TOUGH LITTLE SHRUB has flowers of deep yellow. Individual blooms are short-lived, but there are always plenty to take their place, borne from late spring through summer. As with many other types of flax, the flowers usually close in the afternoon. A dwarf evergreen, this flax originates in scrubby regions of Greece and western Turkey and is very suitable for sloping, free-draining banks, rock gardens, or the front of a sunny border. Create a Mediterranean atmosphere by growing it with other sun-loving, green and gold plants such as golden marjoram (*Origanum, see p.91*), helianthemum (*see p.70*), or gold-variegated elaeagnus (*see p.50*).

Cultivation Grow in light, reasonably fertile soil with added organic matter; dig in coarse grit for alpines and on heavy clay soils to improve drainage (*see p.377*). The plant must have a warm, sunny spot. Protect it from winter moisture. **Sow** seed in spring or autumn in containers in a cold frame (*see pp.391–392*). **Take** semiripe cuttings (*see p.394*) in summer.

Linum arboreum
Z6b ‡↔ 12in (30cm), thick, glaucous leaves often produced in rosettes

LIQUIDAMBAR

Sweetgum

‡ to 80ft (25m)
↔ to 40ft (12m)

THESE DECIDUOUS TREES BEAR maplelike leaves that turn stunning shades of purple, crimson, orange, and gold in autumn. In late spring tiny, yellow-green flowers are produced, followed by spiky, round fruit clusters. Liquidambars have an upright, open habit and look attractive either in a woodland setting or as specimens, isolated from other trees. The sweet gum (*Liquidambar styraciflua*) is an excellent choice as a street or garden tree, with its pyramid shape, glossy, dark green leaves, and gray, deeply grooved bark. Its leaves are a blaze of fiery color well into autumn. They are hardy to Zone 6.

Cultivation Grow in reasonably fertile, preferably acidic, moist but well-drained soil. The best autumn color is produced in full sun, but they will tolerate partial shade. **Prune** young trees to remove any crossing or misplaced branches, in late winter or early spring (*see p.382*). **Sow** seed in containers in a cold frame in autumn (*see pp.391–392*). **Take** soft stem-tip cuttings (*see p.394*) in summer.

① *styraciflua* 'Golden Treasure' ‡30ft (10m) ↔ 20ft (6m)
② *styraciflua* 'Worplesdon' ‡80ft (25m) ↔ 40ft (12m), in autumn, leaves turn orange and yellow with red-purple margins

LIRIODENDRON

Tulip tree

‡ to 70ft (20m)
↔ to 40ft (12m)

EXCELLENT AS A SPECIMEN, the tulip tree has distinctive leaves that turn from dark green to butter yellow in autumn. The trees are deciduous, with a stately, broadly columnar habit. In summer, mature trees produce interesting tulip-shaped, pale green flowers, which are inconspicuous from a distance. It is only in warm summers, when the wood has been well ripened, that the tree is likely to flower well. It is well worth growing for the foliage alone, but only if you have plenty of space. For a smaller garden, choose the more compact *Liriodendron tulipifera* 'Aureomarginatum' (Z5b).

Cultivation Grow in reasonably fertile soil that is moist but well-drained, and preferably slightly acidic. Will grow in full sun or partial shade. **Prune out** any crossing or misshapen branches while trees are young, in late winter or early spring, to create a healthy, well-shaped framework of branches (*see p.382*). **Sow** seed in containers in a cold frame in autumn (*see pp.391–392*). Leaf spot (*see p.399*) may affect trees but is generally worth treating only if they are young.

Liriodendron tulipifera
Z5b ‡100ft (30m) ↔ 50ft (15m), vigorous, broadly columnar to conical tree, leaves to 6in (15cm) long, flowers 2½in (6cm) long

LITHODORA

LITHODORAS ARE SMALL, spreading, evergreen shrubs grown for their profusion of funnel-shaped, blue or white flowers that appear mainly in the summer. Previously known as lithospermums, they can be upright or prostrate in habit, and have spear-shaped leaves that vary from dark green to gray-green. The leaves are hairy, which helps the plants conserve moisture. They originate from southern Europe and so enjoy free-draining, hot, dry conditions. They make good groundcover plants in a rock garden, at the front of a border, or in an alpine trough where they can cascade over the edge.

Cultivation Grow most lithodoras in well-drained, ideally alkaline soil, in full sun; however, *L. diffusa* 'Heavenly Blue' needs acidic soil with well-rotted organic matter added to it. If growing it in an alpine trough, use a potting mix of equal parts loam, leaf mold, and sharp sand. **Trim** shoots that spoil the shape after flowering, or to rejuvenate plants, shear over flowered shoots to within 1in (2.5cm) of the old growth in early spring. **Take** semiripe cuttings in summer (*see p.394*). Lithodoras can be troubled by aphids and spider mites (*see p.398*).

Lithodora oleifolia
Z7b ‡8in (20cm) ↔ 12in (30m), semiupright, loosely branched, pink-tinged buds turn sky blue when fully open

***Lithodora diffusa* 'Heavenly Blue'**
Z7 ‡6in (15cm) ↔ 24in (60cm) fast-growing, mat-forming shrub with many branches, popular rockery plant, leaves hairy on both sides flowers from late spring through summer

LONICERA
Honeysuckle

see also p.146

THESE HONEYSUCKLES ARE SHRUBS, not the more commonly grown climbers. There are two distinct types: deciduous species grown for their powerfully perfumed flowers (the most popular species, such as *Lonicera fragrantissima*, bearing these in winter and early spring), and small-leaved evergreens such as *L. nitida* and *L. pileata* (Z7), which have tiny flowers, purple berries, and a dense, neat habit are valuable for hedging and groundcover. All tolerate a wide range of conditions and need little maintenance. Their berries can cause mild stomach upset if eaten.

Cultivation Grow in any well-drained soil in full sun or partial shade. **Trim** deciduous shrubs after flowering if needed to restrict size, cutting back flowered shoots to strong sideshoots lower down. When plants grow old and growth is crowded, take out a main branch at the base. Evergreens can be trimmed as necessary. If *L. nitida* is grown as a hedge, it will need trimming at least twice, in summer. **Sow** seed (*see pp.391–392*) in a container when ripe, placing it in a cold frame. **Take** semiripe cuttings of evergreens in summer, and hardwood cuttings of deciduous types in autumn (*see p.394*). Aphids (*see p.398*) can be troublesome, particularly on plants in full sun.

***Lonicera × purpusii* 'Winter Beauty'**
Z5 ‡6ft (2m) ↔ 8ft (2.5m), twiggy habit, deciduous or semievergreen, heavily scented early spring flowers, berries rarely produced

LUMA

‡15–20ft (6–15m)
↔ 15–50ft (5–15m)

THESE SOUTH AMERICAN evergreen shrubs and small trees have aromatic, leathery leaves and cup-shaped, white flowers, blooming in summer and autumn. *Luma apiculata* is also prized for its striking peeling bark. The oval leaves are usually dark green, though *L. apiculata* 'Glanleam Gold' (T min. 41°F/5°C) has foliage with creamy yellow margins. The flowers are followed by purple or black berries. Grow lumas in small groups, or as a specimen in a lawn. In marginally hardy areas, they grow best against a warm wall. *L. apiculata* can also be used as a hedging plant.

Cultivation Grow in fertile soil, enriched with well-rotted compost, in full sun or partial shade. **Prune out** any crossing or misshapen branches (*see p.382*) in late winter or early spring to maintain a good shape and a healthy framework of branches and clip regularly to keep it neat. **Trim** hedges in spring. **Sow** seed in containers in a cold frame in spring (*see pp.391–392*); lumas may also self-seed in the garden. **Take** semiripe cuttings in late summer (*see p.394*).

MAACKIA

IF YOU ARE LOOKING FOR an unusual specimen tree for the garden, consider a maackia. Deciduous, it has fine leaves made up of several oval leaflets. In summer, it produces erect clusters of tiny, white, pea-like flowers, followed by long, flat seedpods. Native to woodland in East Asia, maackias are slow-growing trees. Although it may ultimately reach 50ft (15m), *Maackia amurensis* would be suitable for many years in smaller gardens. *M. chinensis* (Z6) is slightly smaller, at 30ft (10m) tall, with attractive, silvery gray–blue leaves. As well as specimen trees, maackias look good alongside other slender, delicate trees such as birches (*Betula, see p.42*) and mountain ash (*Sorbus, see p.118*).

Cultivation Maackias like reasonably fertile, well-drained soil that is neutral to acidic, in full sun. Little pruning is needed; remove any shoots that spoil the shape of young trees to encourage a good form (*see p.382*). **Sow** seed, after soaking, in containers or in a seedbed in autumn (*see pp.391–393*). **Take** stem-tip cuttings in early or midsummer (*see p.394*).

Lonicera nitida
‡6ft (2m) ↔ 4ft (1.2m), evergreen, good for hedging

Lonicera fragrantissima
Z7b ‡6ft (2m) ↔ 10ft (3m), arching, deciduous or semievergreen, fragrant spring flowers, dull red berries

Luma apiculata T min. 41°F (5°C) ‡↔ 30–50ft (10–15m), upright, vigorous, cinnamon-brown and cream bark, flowers from midsummer to midautumn, purple berries

Maackia amurensis (Amur Maackia)
Z3b ‡50ft (15m) ↔ 30ft (10m), open, spreading habit, flowers in mid- and late summer

MACLURA

THE MACLURAS GROWN IN GARDENS are large, deciduous shrubs or small trees, prized for their elegant foliage and unusual fruits. Both a male and a female need to be planted to obtain fruits, or you can buy a female plant with a male branch grafted on to it. They need long, hot summers to grow well and fruit. *Maclura pomifera* has a rounded habit and is thorny when young. It has tiny, cup-shaped, yellow-green flowers and dark green leaves that turn yellow in autumn, surrounding the fruits. *M. tricuspidata* (Z6b) is smaller and bushier, up to 20ft (6m) tall and wide, flowers in summer, and bears edible, orange-red fruits. Grow macluras among other shrubs or as specimens; *M. pomifera* can also be used for hedging.

Cultivation Grow in reasonably fertile soil in full sun. **Prune** young trees in late winter or early spring to remove any misplaced or crossing shoots; cut frost-damaged growth back to a strong bud. **Sow** ripe seed in pots in a sheltered spot outside (*see pp.391–392*). **Take** semiripe cuttings in summer, or take root cuttings in winter (*see p.394*).

MAGNOLIA

‡ to 70ft (20m)
↔ to 50ft (15m)

SPLENDID, SOLITARY, often fragrant, cup- or saucer-shaped flowers distinguish these stately, slow-growing, deciduous and evergreen trees and shrubs. A magnolia in full flower is a sight never to be forgotten. The range of flower colors includes pure white, pink, rich purple, and shades of creamy and greenish yellow. Most flower between early spring and early summer, many before the tough, but handsome leaves unfurl. Some produce conelike pods studded with red-coated seeds in autumn. Magnolias make fine specimens; some can be wall-trained.

Cultivation Grow in moist but well-drained, fertile soil in sun or partial shade. They prefer neutral to acidic soil, but some tolerate alkaline soil. **Prune** only if absolutely necessary, in late winter or early spring. **Take** softwood cuttings of deciduous species in early summer; take semiripe cuttings of evergreens in late summer or early autumn (*see p.394*). Magnolias are prone to coral spot, seen as orange pustules on dying stems; remove affected wood at once and burn it.

FROST PROTECTION When early-flowering magnolias are young, you can protect the flowers from cold with muslin.

Magnolia wilsonii
Z7b ‡↔ 20ft (6m), deciduous shrub or tree, red-purple shoots, leaves felted red-brown underneath, flowers in late spring

Maclura pomifera (Osage orange)
Z6 ‡ 50ft (15m) ↔ 40ft (12m), flowers in early summer, fruits (*see inset*) up to 5in (13cm) across

Magnolia × *soulangeana* (Saucer magnolia)
Z5b ‡↔ 20ft (6m), deciduous shrub or tree, may be wall-trained, flowers open in mid- and late spring, on bare branches

Magnolia 'Elizabeth'
Z5 ‡ 30ft (10m) ↔ 20ft (6m), deciduous tree, leaves bronze when young, then dark green, flowers mid- to late spring

Magnolia stellata (Star magnolia)
Z5 ‡ 10ft (3m) ↔ 12ft (4m), deciduous shrub, flowers in early to midspring before the leaves unfurl

MAHONIA

‡2–15ft (60cm–5m)
↔ 3–12ft (1–4m)

THESE EVERGREEN SHRUBS are valued for their honey-scented, winter or early spring flowers, and attractive foliage. The large, leathery leaves are divided into spiny leaflets. Most have either rounded clusters or star-burst spikes of yellow flowers that last for many weeks over winter, followed by purple to black berries. Although mahonias are mostly upright, some have a low-growing, spreading habit and make a good groundcover. Taller ones are ideal at the back of a border or as specimen plants. Use with other winter-interest plants such as holly (*see Ilex, pp.74–75*) and *Viburnum × bodnantense* (*see pp.126–127*).

Cultivation Mahonias prefer reasonably fertile soil enriched with well-rotted compost. Most prefer full or partial shade, but tolerate full sun where the soil is moist at all times. **Prune** after flowering, lightly cutting back shoots that spoil the shape. Mahonias regrow well from hard pruning if necessary (*see p.384*). **Take** semiripe cuttings (*see p.394*) from late summer until autumn.

Mahonia × media 'Charity'
T min 35°F (2°C) ‡ to 15ft (5m) ↔ to 12ft (4m), prominent flower clusters from late autumn to late winter

Magnolia 'Susan'
Z5b ‡ 12ft (4m) ↔ 10ft (3m), deciduous shrub, dark red-purple buds open in midspring (*see inset*), petals often twisted

Mahonia × wagneri 'Pinnacle' (California Holly Grape)
Z6 ‡ ↔ 5ft (1.5m), leaves bronze when young, maturing to bright green, flowers in spring

Mahonia aquifolium 'Apollo' (Oregon Grape Holly)
Z5 ‡ 24i (60cm) ↔ 3ft (1m), low-growing, with bright yellow flowers in spring, foliage turns rich purple in autumn

MALUS
Apple, Crabapple

AMONG THE MOST POPULAR flowering trees, especially since so many are ideally sized for the smaller garden, crabapples are famous for their fragrant, pink or white spring flowers. Red to purple-red fruits follow in the autumn; unpalatable raw, they can be made into wine and jellies. The fruits attract birds, and the autumn foliage color of these trees is often brilliant too, making them a real focus of interest late in the year. All crabapples are deciduous; some form a rounded crown, while others (such as *Malus floribunda*) have long, arching branches that are particularly graceful. They look equally good as specimens or with other small trees, such as hawthorns (*Crataegus, see p.46*), birches (*Betula, p.42*), and rowans (*Sorbus, p.118*).

Cultivation Grow in reasonably fertile soil that is moist but well-drained, in full sun; most tolerate partial shade. **Prune** young trees to remove any shoots that spoil a good branch framework in late winter or early spring (*see p.382*). **Sow** cleaned seed of *M. baccata* and *M. hupehensis* in autumn, in a seed bed (*see pp.391–393*); most others are grafted by nurserymen to control their size.

Malus hupehensis (Tea crabapple)
Z4b ↕↔ 40ft (12m), vigorous, spreading habit, large flower clusters in mid- to late spring (*see inset*), good autumn leaf color

MESPILUS GERMANICA
Medlar

↕ 20ft (6m)
↔ 25ft (8m)

THE MEDLAR IS A DECIDUOUS tree or large shrub that originates in mountainous regions of southern Europe and Asia. It makes an interesting specimen tree, with a pleasing, spreading habit, bowl-shaped, white (occasionally pink-tinged) flowers that appear from late spring to early summer, and round, fleshy fruits that follow in autumn. The fruits can be made into jelly. Raw fruits are an acquired taste; they are edible but only when well ripened or partly rotted ("bletted"). The medlar is lovely in autumn with other fruiting trees, such as hawthorns (*Crataegus, see p.46*) or crabapples (*Malus, see left*).

Cultivation Grow in reasonably fertile, moist but well-drained soil in full sun or partial shade. **Pruning** is unnecessary except to remove any shoots that are crossing, dead, or misshapen in late winter or early spring (*see p.382*). **Sow** seed in a seedbed in autumn (*see pp.391–393*).

Malus 'John Downie'
Z5 ↕ 30ft (10m) ↔ 20ft (6m), narrow habit, conical when mature, abundant fruit to 1¼in (3cm) long, good for jelly

Malus floribunda (Japanese crab apple)
Z5b ↕↔ 30ft (10m), dense, spreading habit, flowers in mid- and late spring, small, yellow fruits in autumn

Mespilus germanica
Z7 ↕ 20ft (6m) ↔ 25ft (8m) The foliage turns yellow-brown in autumn

METASEQUOIA GLYPTOSTROBOIDES
Dawn redwood

THIS PREHISTORIC TREE was once known only from fossils, and, following its rediscovery in the wild, it was reintroduced to the world by Harvard's Arnold Arboretum in 1944. It makes an outstanding specimen tree or on the edge of woodland. Native to the valley forests of central China, it is one of the few conifers that are deciduous. It has a narrow, conical shape, fibrous bark, and graceful branches. The soft, feathery leaves are a bright, fresh green; in autumn, they turn gold and then russet-brown. The female cones are light brown, on stalks; male cones are pendent. The dawn redwood should only be considered for very large gardens because it can reach a considerable height very quickly.

Cultivation Grow in moist but well-drained soil enriched with well-rotted compost, in full sun. In early years, growth is fast but will slow down once the tree starts to reach around 30ft (10m) tall. **Sow** seed in a seedbed (*see pp.391–393*) in autumn. **Take** hardwood cuttings in autumn or root semiripe cuttings in midsummer with bottom heat in a propagator (*see p.394*).

MORUS
Mulberry

THE BLACK, WHITE, AND RED MULBERRIES, native to China, Southwestern Asia, and the Americas respectively, were first cultivated to provide leaves for the silkworm industry. All have raspberry-shaped, edible fruits, first white or green, then ripening to dark purple, yellow, or red among attractive, rounded or heart-shaped leaves that turn yellow in autumn. Orange, scaly bark provides winter interest. Mulberries become beautifully shaped trees with age, so grow them as specimens – the small, weeping, white mulberry (*Morus alba* 'Pendula' Z3) is an excellent choice for small gardens. Do not site mulberries overhanging pavement: the fruits will stain it.

Cultivation Grow in reasonably fertile soil enriched with well-rotted compost, in full sun, with shelter from cold, drying winds. **Prune** only in late autumn or early winter, if necessary. If pruned at any other time, the cuts will "bleed" sap. Sow seed in containers in a cold frame in autumn (*see pp.391–392*). **Take** semiripe cuttings in summer, or hardwood cuttings in autumn (*see p.394*). Susceptible to powdery mildew (*see p.398*), which can be treated with a fungicide.

MYRTUS COMMUNIS
Common myrtle

↕ to 10ft (3m)

GROWN FOR ITS RICH, delicate scent, myrtle is a bushy, upright, evergreen shrub or tree with glossy, dark-green, aromatic leaves. It produces white, sweet-smelling, bowl-shaped flowers in abundance from spring to autumn. Both the flowers and the purple-black berries that follow in autumn are dependent on long, hot summers. Myrtles thrive only in a warm, sheltered position. They look well in shrub and mixed borders, or as an informal hedge. They can also be trained against a wall, or grown in containers on a patio where their scent can be best appreciated.

Cultivation Grow in reasonably fertile, moist but well-drained soil or soil-based potting mix, in full sun with shelter. **Lightly trim** or prune shoots that spoil the shape in mid- or late spring. If wall-trained, after flowering or in late winter or early spring, cut back flowered shoots to within 2–4 buds of the main stems. Trim hedges in spring (*see p.384*). **Sow** seed in containers in a cold frame in autumn (*see pp.391–392*). **Take** semiripe cuttings in late summer (*see p.394*).

Metasequoia glyptostroboides
Z5b ↕ 70–130ft (20–40m) ↔ 15ft (5m) or more, tolerates waterlogged sites, growth is slower on dry sites

Morus nigra (Black mulberry)
Z6 ↕ 40ft (12m) ↔ 50ft (15m), fruits pleasant, slightly acidic when eaten raw, good for jam and wine

Myrtus communis
Z8 ↕↔ 10ft (3m), branches arching with age, thrives in town and coastal gardens

NANDINA DOMESTICA
Heavenly bamboo

‡ to 6ft (2m)
↔ to 5ft (1.5m)

GROWING WILD in the mountain valleys of India, China, and Japan, heavenly bamboo is an elegant, upright shrub, grown for its flowers, fruits, and handsome foliage. The leaves are red to reddish purple when young, mature to green, and then turn vivid crimson again in late autumn. In midsummer, small clusters of star-shaped, white flowers with yellow centers are produced, followed, in warmer climates or after hot summers, by bright red fruits. Nandinas are evergreen or semi-evergreen, but may not survive very cold winters. Grow it with other shrubs that have good autumn leaf color. The low-growing *Nandina domestica* 'Firepower' (Z7) makes a good groundcover.

Cultivation Grow in moist but well-drained soil in full sun. **Prune back** hard after planting, then prune in midspring to keep the plant tidy and maintain a good shape (*see p.383*). **Sow** seed in containers in a cold frame as soon as it is ripe (*see pp.391–392*). **Take** semiripe cuttings in summer (*see p.394*).

Nandina domestica
Z7 ‡ 6ft (2m) ↔ 5ft (1.5m), can be invasive and "weedy" in hot climates, but behaves well in temperate gardens

NEILLIA

‡ ↔ 6ft (2m)

UNUSUAL SHRUBS with handsome foliage and flowers, neillias provide plenty of year-round interest. They are deciduous, originating from the Himalayas and East Asia, and are characterized by graceful, arching stems, dark glossy leaves, and, in late spring to early summer, masses of handsome, bell-shaped, pinkish white or rose pink flowers. Neillias have a thicket-forming habit, ideal for the back of a shrub or mixed border, or as a screen. If you have room for a single-season show, they look fantastic with other shrubs that flower at the same time, such as weigelas (*see p.128*) or mock oranges (*Philadelphus, see p.93*).

Cultivation Grow in fertile, well-drained soil in full sun or partial shade. **Prune back** flowered shoots after flowering to strong buds or shoots lower down on the stem. On mature plants, cut out an entire old branch every three or four years to encourage new growth from the base of the shrub (*see pp.382–383*). **Take** greenwood cuttings in early summer (*see p.394*), or dig up well-rooted, naturally layered stems from the edges of the plant (*see p.395*).

Neillia thibetica
Z7 ‡ ↔ 6ft (2m), suckering shrub with an upright then arching habit, tolerates most soils, blooms best in sun

NYSSA
Tupelo

THE TUPELO IS A DECIDUOUS TREE prized for its outstanding foliage, which is bronze when young, matures to dark green, then turns to brilliant hues of amber, ruby, and gold in autumn. It does produce tiny green flowers, followed by small, blue fruits, which are enjoyed many by birds. However, the autumn foliage colors are the main attraction. Tupelo makes an ideal specimen tree and looks effective planted near water (it thrives in wet, swampy areas). Try *Nyssa sinensis* with birches (*Betula, see p.28*) as the golden autumn foliage of the birch will contrast brilliantly with the tupelo's scarlet leaves.

Cultivation Grow in fertile, moist but well-drained, neutral to acidic soil, in sun or partial shade with shelter from cold, drying winds. **Choose** young, container-grown specimens, since they resent root disturbance more and more as they get older. **Trim** shoots that are crossing or misplaced in late winter or early spring to maintain a good shape and healthy framework (*see p.382*). **Sow** seed in a seedbed in autumn (*see pp.391–393*). **Take** greenwood cuttings in early summer, or semiripe cuttings in midsummer (*see p.394*).

Nyssa sinensis (Chinese tupelo)
Z7b ‡↔ 30ft (10m), broadly conical, often multistemmed, sweeping lower branches, green leaves turn fiery in autumn

OLEARIA
Daisy bush

THIS GROUP OF EVERGREEN SHRUBS is grown for its leathery leaves and and daisylike flowers borne singly or in clusters from spring to autumn. Flower colors are predominantly white, but include blue, mauve, pink, and yellow. *Olearia* × *haastii* is a dense, bushy shrub with fragrant flowers. It is tolerant of salty winds and can be grown as an informal hedge or windbreak. *O. macrodonta* is an upright shrub with hollylike, sharp-toothed foliage, white underneath. Its flowers are highly fragrant. *O. nummulariifolia* is a rounded, slow-growing shrub that does best planted against a warm, sunny wall where it is protected from drying winds. The dark green leaves look effective next to plants with bright leaves, such as elaeagnus (*see p.50*). *O. solandri* is a dense, heatherlike shrub with strongly scented flowers over a long period.

Cultivation Grow in fertile, well-drained soil in full sun, with shelter from cold, drying winds. **Prune** lightly in early spring, removing shoots that spoil the shape of the shrub. **Trim** hedges after flowering. They all tolerate hard pruning. **Take** semiripe cuttings in summer (*see p.394*).

ORIGANUM
Marjoram, Oregano

see also
p.295

AROMATIC PLANTS FROM the Mediterranean, marjorams may be shrubs, subshrubs (shrubs that are woody only at the base), or herbaceous perennials. All are very similar: small, with an upright to spreading habit and tiny, pink to mauve flowers borne through summer amid more conspicuous, often brightly colored bracts (modified leaves). The flowers are magnets for bees and other pollinating insects. Larger species are suited to a herb garden, raised bed, or in containers near the house, where the fragrant leaves can be rubbed to release their scent. They also look good as edging plants for borders or paths, where they will sprawl contentedly. Grow the tiniest species, such as *Origanum amanum* (Z6), in a rock garden, so they are not swamped by larger plants.

Cultivation Grow in full sun in poor to reasonably fertile soil. Very rich soil encourages leafy growth at the expense of flowers. Marjorams prefer a free-draining, alkaline soil. **Cut back** old flowered stems in early spring (*see p.383*). **Take** cuttings of new shoots growing from the base in late spring and treat as softwood cuttings (*see p.394*).

OSMANTHUS

USEFUL FOR A SHRUB BORDER or woodland garden, this group of evergreen shrubs is grown for its glossy, dark green foliage, and white, occasionally yellow or orange, jasmine-scented flowers. These are produced in early and midspring and are followed by round, blue-black fruits. *Osmanthus heterophyllus* (Z7) and *O.* × *fortunei* (T min. 41°F/5°C) have spiky, hollylike foliage. Osmanthus has a dense, neat habit and is an effective contrast to showier shrubs in the border. *O. delavayi* and *O. burkwoodii* are good for hedging, while *O. heterophyllus* 'Aureomarginatus' (Z7), commonly called false holly, will liven up a dull corner with its yellow-margined leaves.

Cultivation Grow in fertile, well-drained soil in sun or partial shade and shelter from cold, drying winds. **Trim** lightly or prune back shoots after flowering, taking out any that spoil the shape of the shrub (*see p.382*). Trim hedges in summer. All species tolerate hard pruning if necessary (*see p.384*). **Sow** seed in a container in a cold frame as soon as it is ripe (*see pp.391–392*). **Take** semiripe cuttings (*see p.394*) in summer and put in a propagator with bottom heat, or layer low-growing shoots in autumn or spring (*see p.395*).

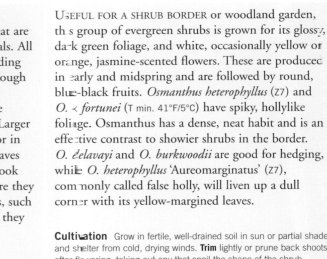

① × *haastii* T min. 35°F (2°C) ↕6ft (2m) ↔ 10ft (3m) ② *macrodonta* min. 41°F (5°C) ↕20ft (6m) ↔ 15ft (5m) ③ *nummulariifolia* Z7b ↕ 6ft (2m) ④ *solandri* T min. 35°F (2°C) ↕→ 6ft (2m), scented

Origanum 'Kent Beauty'
Z5 ↕4in (10cm) ↔ 8in (20cm), prostrate, with trailing stems, semi-evergreen, produces tubular, hoplike flowers

① × *burkwoodii* Z7 ↕↔ 10ft (3m), rounded habit, good for topiary ② *delavayi* Z7 ↕ 6–20ft (2–6m) ↔ 12ft (4m), rounded habit, can be wall-trained

OXYDENDRUM ARBOREUM
Sorrel tree, Sourwood

‡50ft (15m)
↔25ft (8m)

THE SORREL TREE is a deciduous tree or large shrub with a conical or columnar habit. It is a dual-season tree for interest, with white flowers in the summer and boldly colored foliage in the autumn. Its flowers, produced in late summer and early autumn, are tiny, about ¼in (6mm) long, but gain impact by being borne in large, airy plumes, up to 10in (25cm) long, at the ends of the shoots. The leaves are glossy, toothed, and dark green through summer, turning brilliant shades of red, yellow, and purple in autumn. Grow it as a specimen tree or in a woodland setting.

Cultivation Grow a sorrel tree in fertile, moist but well-drained soil, preferably acidic, avoiding exposed sites. **Prune** young trees in late winter or early spring to remove any crossing or misplaced branches. **Sow** seed in a container in a cold frame in autumn (see pp.391–392). **Take** semiripe cuttings in summer (see p.394).

Oxydendrum arboreum
Z6 ‡30–50ft (10–15m) ↔25ft (8m), urn-shaped flowers to ¼in (6mm) on panicles to 10in (25cm) long

PAEONIA
Tree Peony

see also p.298

‡↔to 7ft (2.2m)

SHRUBBY PEONIES, as opposed to the herbaceous kinds that die down each year, are commonly known as tree peonies. These peonies also have the characteristically voluptuous flowers in a wide range of color, occasionally scented, borne from late spring to early summer, with the bonus of permanent stature in a mixed planting. Flowers can be single or double, cup- or saucer-shaped, and up to 12in (30cm) across. The stamens in the center are often in a contrasting color. Leaves are usually mid- to dark green, often feathery. Grow these peonies in a shrub, mixed, or herbaceous border.

Cultivation Grow in deep, fertile soil enriched with well-rotted compost, in full sun or partial shade. Peonies prefer shelter from cold, drying winds. **Prune out** flowered shoots and, from time to time, old wood to encourage bushy growth (see p.382). **Take** semiripe cuttings in summer (see p.394).

PRUNING SPENT WOOD
Once shoots have flowered and set seed, they die back to new growth. Prune spent shoots back to a new leaf in autumn.

Paeonia delavayi
Z5b ‡6ft (2m) ↔ 4ft (1.2m), flowers 4in (10cm) across in early summer, leaves dark green and blue-green underneath

Paeonia suffruticosa 'Cardinal Vaughan' (Moutan)
Z5 ‡↔ to 7ft (2.2m), flowers 6–12in (15–30cm) across in late spring and early summer, dark green leaves blue-green beneath

Paeonia lutea var. *ludlowii* (Tibetan Peony)
Z6 ‡↔ 8ft (2.5m), flowers up to 5in (13cm) across in late spring, new leaves deep maroon (see inset), then bright green

PAULOWNIA

‡ to 40ft (12m)
↔ to 30ft (10m)

THESE VIGOROUS, DECIDUOUS trees
make striking additions to the garden.
They grow and flower best in areas with
long, hot summers. The fast-growing
Empress tree (*Paulownia tomentosa*) is
tolerant of air pollution. *P. fortunei*
(Z7) is smaller, to 25ft (8m) tall. Both bear their
fragrant flowers in late spring, often on near-
bare branches. Although they can make fine specimen
trees in a lawn, they are best coppiced (*see Cornus,
pp.56–57*), which will produce large ornamental
leaves, a good way to get the best from them in areas
where they do not flower reliably, or in small gardens.

Cultivation Grow in fertile, well-drained soil in full sun. Where not
hardy, shelter from cold, drying winds. **Prune** paulownias grown as
trees only if necessary. To obtain big leaves, cut back stems to within
2–3 buds of the main framework of shoots in early spring. **Sow** seed
in containers in a cold frame in spring or autumn (*see pp.391–392*).
Take root cuttings in winter (*see p.394*). Young plants benefit from
being grown on in pots and overwintered under cover.

PEROVSKIA
Russian sage

A GRACEFUL SHRUB, perovskia has tall, wandlike stems
of tiny, violet-blue flowers in late summer or early
autumn. Both stems and leaves are usually gray-white
or gray-green, and the foliage is aromatic, with a
pleasantly sharp, lemony scent. The stems can reach a
height of up to 4ft (1.2m) in a single season, bearing
their small flowers along about half their length.
Perovskias add height and a cloud of hazy blue in a
massed herbaceous planting, and like perennials, are
best cut back hard each spring, or they will become
leggy and bare. They also look striking against a gray
or white-painted wall.

Cultivation Grow in well-drained soil that is poor or reasonably
fertile in full sun. Perovskias will grow in dry, alkaline soils and in
coastal areas. **Prune hard** in spring, cutting back the previous season's
growth to within 2–4in (5–10cm); gradually, a permanent, stubby,
woody framework will develop (*see inset, below*). **Take** softwood
cuttings in late spring, or semiripe cuttings in summer (*see p.394*).

PHILADELPHUS
Mock orange

DELICIOUSLY FRAGRANT FLOWERS are a feature of this
group of mainly deciduous shrubs. The flowers are
cup or bowl-shaped, single, semidouble, and double,
and usually white, often with yellowish stamens. They
are produced either singly or in clusters. The leaves
are mid-green; *P. coronarius* (Z3) has white-variegated
and golden-leaved forms. You cannot miss a mock
orange in flower, because the scent drifts in the air for
a considerable distance. Grow them in a shrub border,
with other early and midsummer-flowering shrubs
like weigelas (*see p.128*), or as specimen plants. The
ones shown here have a Canadian hardiness zone
range of 3–5.

Cultivation Grow in any reasonably fertile, well-drained soil, in full
sun or partial shade. *P. microphyllus* needs full sun, but its golden-
leaved form 'Aureus' must have some shade. **Prune** after flowering,
cutting back flowered stems to strong buds or new shoots lower down.
On mature plants, cut one or two old branches to the base each year
to encourage new growth. **Take** softwood cuttings in summer, or
hardwood cuttings in autumn or winter (*see p.394*). Aphids may be
troublesome, as may powdery mildew (*see pp.398–399*), pick off
mildew-affected leaves and avoid overhead watering.

PRUNING PEROVSKIAS
Before new growth starts, cut
away old stubby parts of the
plant that did
not shoot the
previous year.

Paulownia tomentosa (Empress tree, Foxglove tree)
Z6b ‡40ft (12m) ↔ 30ft (10m), flowers well (*inset*) the year after a
hot summer; coppice plants for velvety leaves up to 20in (50cm)

Perovskia 'Blue Spire'
Z5 ‡4ft (1.2m) ↔ 3ft (1m), leaves slender and silver-gray, hugging
the stems, the flowers resemble those of lavender

① 'Belle Etoile' ‡4ft (1.2m) ↔ 8ft (2.5m) ② *coronarius*
'Aureus' ‡8ft (2.5m) ↔ 5ft (1.5m) ③ *microphyllus* ‡↔ 3ft (1m)
④ 'Virginal' ‡10ft (3m) or more ↔ 8ft (2.5m)

PHLOMIS

see also
p.306

THESE ATTRACTIVE AND UNDEMANDING evergreen shrubs are grown for their sagelike foliage and their unusual, often hooded, flowers. The leaves are variable in shape: narrow and lance-shaped to more oval. In color, they range from light green to gray-green, and are often hairy. The flowers are produced in early and midsummer in shades of golden yellow, lilac-pink, purple to pink, and occasionally white, and are borne in dense tiers, or clusters, on tall, erect stems. Then, ornamental seedheads extend the interest into winter. These small to medium-sized shrubs have an upright or rounded habit. Phlomis look particularly at home among herbs such as sage and lavender (*see p.80*), but they can also be grown in mixed or shrub borders. There are also some herbaceous phlomis.

Cultivation   Grow these shrubs in any fertile, well-drained soil in full sun. **Deadhead** for a longer flowering display and lightly trim any shoots that spoil the overall shape of the shrubs when flowering has finished. **Sow** seed (*see pp.391–393*) in spring, or take softwood cuttings (*see p.394*) in summer.

Phlomis fruticosa (Jerusalem sage)
Z8 ↕ 3ft (1m) ↔ 5ft (1.5m), mound-forming, evergreen shrub, gray-green leaves, dark golden flowers in early to midsummer

PHORMIUM
New Zealand flax

WITH STRIKING, SWORDLIKE FOLIAGE and exotic-looking flowers, these architectural plants develop into large, handsome clumps that can act as focal points in a border or gravel, by a building, or even as specimen plants in a lawn. Their versatility is enhanced by the range of leaf colors available, from bronze-green with rose pink margins to dark green with red, orange, or pink stripes. In summer, in milder areas, they produce tall, leafless spikes bearing abundant tubular flowers in erect clusters. They may not flower in colder areas. With their thick, tough leaves they are also ideal for coastal gardens where they often flower well. Plant a phormium in a large pot to add a touch of drama to a patio or terrace.

Cultivation   Grow phormiums in fertile, moist but free-draining soil where they receive full sun. These plants may survive winter temperatures as low as 10°F (-12°C) if they are given a deep, dry mulch (*see p.388*) around their roots. **Sow** seed (*see pp.391–393*) in spring. **Divide** the woody crowns of large, established clumps, also in spring, to increase stocks (*see p.395*); you may need a large knife to cut through the crown.

Phormium 'Bronze Baby'
Z8 ↕↔ 24–32in (60–80cm), dull red flower spikes are up to 12ft (4m) tall

Phormium 'Sundowner'
Z8 ↕↔ 6ft (2m), yellow-green flower spikes to 6ft (2m) tall

Phormium 'Dazzler'
Z8 ‡3ft (1m) ↔ 4ft (1.2m), flowers (*see inset*) are
2in (5cm) long

Phormium tenax
Z8 ‡12ft (4m) ↔ 6ft (2m), dull red flower spikes are up to 12ft
(4m) tall

PHOTINIA

THESE EVERGREEN OR DECIDUOUS SHRUBS and trees
are grown for their attractive foliage and varied habits.
Some are spreading trees, but many are upright or
rounded shrubs, ranging in height from 10ft (3m) to
40ft (12m). They produce small clusters of tiny, white
flowers in summer, although the deciduous species are
mainly prized for their autumn leaf colors and fruits.
Evergreen types often have striking, reddish new
leaves in spring before they turn glossy dark or mid-
green. Photinias look good in a shrub border or as
specimen plants. They can also be used as hedging
plants, where regular trimming encourages new,
colored foliage, or as standard plants in large pots.

Cultivation Grow in fertile, moist but well-drained soil, in full sun or
partial shade with protection from cold winds. **Trim** any crossing or
misshapen shoots in winter or early spring, to maintain a good shape
and a healthy framework of shoots. Trim hedges in summer when the
color of the young growth has faded. **Propagate** all types by semiripe
cuttings in summer; sow seed of deciduous types in autumn (*see
pp.391–393*). **Powdery mildew** may spoil the leaves (*see p.399*).

Photinia × fraseri 'Red Robin'
Z8 ‡↔ 15ft (5m) upright evergreen shrub or small tree, bronze to
scarlet young foliage, flowers in mid- to late spring

PHYGELIUS

‡ –1.2m (3–4ft)
↔ –1.5m (3–5ft)

HANGING CLUSTERS OF FLOWERS
produced over a long period in
summer, and often into autumn, are
the main reason for growing these
evergreen or semievergreen shrubs.
They have oval- to lance-shaped
leaves, and flowers in several shades of yellow, orange-
red, creamy yellow, and orange. Phygelia thrives in a
shrub border or at the base of a warm wall and
spreads by means of suckers. Where temperatures
often fall below freezing, treat them as herbaceous
perennials – although the top-growth may be killed
off, they should grow again in spring. The Canadian
hardiness zone ranges from 7b–8.

Cultivation Phygelius like fertile, moist, well-drained soil in full sun.
Deadhead to encourage more flowers. **Protect** the roots, where
marginally hardy, with a dry winter mulch of straw. Overwinter young
plants in frost-free conditions. **Cut back** the stems in spring of plants
being treated as herbaceous perennials; otherwise lightly trim any
shoots that spoil the shape. **Take** softwood cuttings (*see p.394*) in late
spring or remove rooted suckers for replanting in spring.

① *æqualis* 'Yellow Trumpet' ‡3ft (1m) ② × *rectus*
'African Queen' ‡3ft (1m) ③ × *rectus* 'Moonraker' ‡to 5ft
(1.5m) ④ × *rectus* 'Salmon Leap' ‡4ft (1.2m)

PICEA

Spruce

SPRUCES ARE EVERGREEN, coniferous trees grown mainly for their dense foliage and attractive shapes. The most familiar is the Norwegian spruce or "Christmas tree," *Picea abies* (Z2b). The needles vary in color from dark green to the silvery blue of *P. pungens* 'Koster' (Z2) and make a textural contrast to plants with bolder leaves. In summer and autumn, older trees produce green or red cones, which mature to purple or brown. The larger spruces are useful on their own, to show off their handsome forms, or in groups, especially to create shelter. Like all evergreen conifers, they provide a year-round backdrop and add structure to the garden. The dwarf or slow-growing spruces are suitable for small spaces and rock gardens. The Canadian hardiness zone ranges from 2–7b.

Cultivation Grow in any deep, moist, but well-drained soil, ideally neutral to acidic, in full sun. No pruning required. **Sow** seed in containers in a cold frame in spring (*see pp.391–392*). **Take** stem-tip cuttings (*see p.394*) of dwarf forms in late summer. May attract aphids (*see pp.398–399*); treat only badly affected young or dwarf plants.

① *abies* ‡to 130ft (40m) ↔ 20ft (6m) ② *glauca* 'Conica'
‡6–20ft (2–6m) ↔ 3–8ft (1–2.5m) ③ *mariana* 'Nana' ‡↔ to
20in (50cm) ④ *pungens* 'Koster' ‡ 50ft (15m) ↔ to 15ft (5m)

PICRASMA QUASSIOIDES

Quassia

THIS ELEGANT, UPRIGHT TREE is grown mainly for its attractive foliage, which fades to lovely shades of yellow, orange, and scarlet before the leaves drop in autumn. Oriental in origin, *Picrasma quassioides* bears a passing resemblance to the tree of heaven, *Ailanthus altissima*, to which it is related. Each glossy, mid-green leaf is divided into several leaflets. In early summer, minute, bowl-shaped green flowers are borne in clusters, but they have little ornamental value. Site this fine tree in an open position in a shrub border, or on the edge of a woodland setting with other trees and shrubs that also have good autumn color, such as *Disanthus cercidifolius* (*see p.50*) and *Nyssa sinensis* (*see p.90*).

Cultivation Grow in fertile, well-drained soil in full sun or partial shade. In cooler areas, choose a site that is not exposed to cold, drying winds. **Prune out** any crossing branches and those that spoil the shape of the tree in late winter or early spring. **Sow** seed in containers in a cold frame in autumn (*see pp.391–392*).

Picrasma quassioides
Z7 ‡↔ 25ft (8m), autumn foliage shown here

PIERIS

‡to 5m (15ft)
↔ to 12ft (4m)

THESE COLORFUL EVERGREEN shrubs are valued for their glossy, leathery foliage and delightful flowers. They are best placed in a shrub border or woodland garden, or in a container. Not all are large; 'Little Heath' and 'Purity' are popular for small gardens or pots. The young leaves are often brilliantly colored, and, in spring, clusters of small, white, or pink flowers almost cover the shrub. Rhododendrons and azaleas (*see pp.104–107*) and ericas (*see pp.52–53*) make good companions, as all require similar soil.

Cultivation Grow in reasonably fertile, moist but well-drained, acidic soil, or acidic soil mix, in full sun or partial shade. **Trim back** any shoots that spoil the shape after flowering, and remove faded flowers if the shrubs are not too large. **Sow** seed in containers in a cold frame in spring or autumn (*see pp.391–392*). **Take** softwood cuttings in early summer, or semiripe cuttings from mid- to late summer (*see p.394*).

Pieris japonica 'Blush' (Lily-of-the-valley bush)
Z5b ‡12ft (4m) ↔ 10ft (3m), compact and rounded shrub, pink-flushed, later all-white flowers in late winter and spring

Pieris japonica 'Flamingo'
Z6–8 H8–6 ‡12ft (4m) ↔ 10ft (3m), compact, rounded shrub, dark red buds, dark pink flowers in late winter and spring

PINUS
Pine

THE PINES COMPRISE A LARGE and varied group of evergreens, both trees and shrubs, with distinctive, needles, ornamental cones, and attractive, scaly bark. The larger species are tall trees with striking, sparsely branched silhouettes compared with other conifers. Habits vary, from slender giants such as the Scots pine (*Pinus sylvestris* Z2) to the umbrella-shaped stone pine (*P. pinea* T min. 41°F/5°C). In a spacious garden, they make grand specimen trees, either individually or in groups, and also excellent windbreaks; *P. radiata* (Z7b) and *P. nigra* tolerate coastal exposure. There are medium-sized and dwarf pines, often slow-growing, for the small garden and rock gardens, especially the cultivars of *P. sylvestris*, *P. densiflora* (Z5), and *P. mugo* (Z2b).

Cultivation Grow in any well-drained soil in full sun. Some species may be short-lived in shallow, alkaline soils; *P. nigra* and *P. mugo* both tolerate alkaline soil. No pruning required. **Sow** seed in a cold frame in spring (*see pp.391–393*). Pines may attract aphids (*see pp.398–399*) but rarely need treatment.

Pinus mugo 'Mops' (Dwarf mountain pine)
Z2b ‡to 11ft 3.5m) ↔ to 15ft (5m), often much smaller; dense, near-spherical bush, very resinous, scaly gray bark

Pieris formosa var. forrestii 'Wakehurst'
Z7 ‡to 15ft (5m) ↔ 12ft (4m), upright, suckering shrub, excellent new foliage, white flower clusters in late winter and spring

Pinus patula (Mexican weeping pine)
T min. 35°F (2°C) ‡50–70ft (15–20m) ↔ 20–30ft (6–10m), spreading or rounded tree, reddish-brown bark, thrives in mild areas

Pinus nigra (Austrian pine, European black pine)
Z4 ‡to 100ft (30m) ↔ 20–25ft (6–8m), domed tree, brown or black bark that becomes deeply fissured with age

PRUNUS
Ornamental cherry

THIS GROUP CONTAINS TWO VERY DIFFERENT types of plants: ornamental or flowering cherries that are deciduous, and evergreen laurels. In spring, ornamental cherries billow with flowers in shades of pink, white, and sometimes red. *Prunus × subhirtella* produces its delicate flurries of flowers in mild spells, sometimes in autumn but mostly in spring. Some, such as *P. maackii* and *P. serrula*, are also grown for their rich cinnamon-colored bark, and others, like *P. sargentii*, have leaves that color well in autumn. Laurels, on the other hand, are dense, bushy evergreens, such as *P. laurocerasus* and *P. lusitanica*, with much less showy flowers but handsome, glossy leaves. Prunus also includes many trees grown especially for fruit, including plum, peach, and cherry, but the fruits of laurels and most ornamental cherries can cause severe discomfort if eaten and should be left for the birds. Ornamental cherries are upright, rounded or spreading trees or shrubs; many are suitable for smaller gardens, and make excellent specimen plants. Laurels are classic and reliable hedging plants. Prunus run the range of Canadian hardiness zones from 1–7b.

Cultivation Grow in any moist, well-drained soil in full sun or partial shade. **Water** young trees well until they are properly established. **Prune** each of the types slightly differently. For most deciduous shrubs and trees, simply remove any misplaced shoots to maintain a good shape. This is best done in summer to avoid the fungal disease silver leaf, to which cherries are susceptible. For *P. glandulosa* and *P. triloba*, prune hard after flowering. **Trim** deciduous hedges after flowering and use pruners to cut back evergreens in early to midspring. **Sow** seed of species in containers outside in autumn (*see pp.391–392*), or propagate deciduous cultivars by greenwood cuttings, which are taken slightly later than softwood cuttings when the stem is a little firmer and darker (*see p.394*). Ornamental cherries are sometimes attacked by caterpillars, and birds occasionally strip the flower buds.

Using ornamental cherries in the garden

Wall of blossoms *Ornamental cherries can be trained against a wall to provide a generous display in even the smallest garden. Once the shrub has formed a framework, all that is needed is some routine tying in and pruning. Cut out older shoots that produce little growth and tie in younger shoots as replacements; new growth should be tied in while still young and pliable. Shorten weak shoots to encourage stronger growth, and prune back flowered shoots, while the plant is growing in late spring or summer. Check all ties when pruning, and replace any that are broken or restricting the stems.*

Ornamental hedging *Several ornamental cherries are suitable for growing as hedging. Evergreen shrubs such as P. laurocerasus and P. lusitanica make dense screens, whereas deciduous species, such as P. spinosa, P. cerasifera, and its cultivars like 'Nigra', will be more open. When planting, prepare the soil by adding plenty of well-rotted organic matter. Make sure the top of the root ball is just below soil level and firm in gently. The usual planting distance for hedging is 24–30in (60–75cm). Water well after planting and, in exposed situations, erect a wind barrier until the plants become established.*

① *Prunus* 'Accolade' ↕↔ 25ft (8m), early spring ② *avium* 'Plena' ↕↔ 40ft (12m), midspring ③ *cerasifera* 'Nigra' ↕↔ 30ft (10m), early spring, followed by edible fruit ④ × *cistena* ↕↔ 5ft (1.5m), late spring ⑤ *glandulosa* 'Alba Plena' ↕↔ 5ft (1.5m), late spring ⑥ 'Kanzan' ↕↔ 30ft (10m), mid- and late spring ⑦ 'Kiku-shidare-zakura' ↕↔ 10ft (3m), mid- and late spring ⑧ *laurocerasus* 'Otto Luyken' ↕ 3ft (1m) ↔ 5ft (1.5m), evergreen, spring and autumn ⑨ *lusitanica* subsp. *azorica* ↕↔ 70ft

(20m), evergreen, early summer ⑩ *maackii* ↕10m (30ft), ↔ 25ft (8m), midspring ⑪ 'Okame' ↕30ft (10m) ↔ 25ft (8m), early spring ⑫ *padus* 'Watereri' ↕50ft (15m) ↔ 30ft (10m), late spring ⑬ 'Pandora' ↕30ft (10m) ↔ 25ft (8m), early spring ⑭ 'Pink Perfection' ↕↔ 25ft (8m), late spring ⑮ *sargentii* ↕70ft (20m) ↔ 50ft (15m), midspring ⑯ *serrula* ↕↔ 30ft (10m), late spring ⑰ 'Shirofugen' ↕25ft (8m) ↔ 30ft (10m), late spring ⑱ 'Shôgetsu' ↕15ft (5m) ↔ 25ft (8m), late spring ⑲ *spinosa* ↕15ft (5m) ↔ 12ft (4m) early to midspring, followed by blue-black fruit (sloes) used to flavor alcohol ⑳ 'Spire' ↕30ft (10m) ↔ 20ft (6m), midspring ㉑ × *subhirtella* 'Autumnalis Rosea' ↕↔ 25ft (8m), autumn to spring ㉒ 'Taihaku' ↕25ft (8m) ↔ 30ft (10m), midspring ㉓ *triloba* ↕↔ 10ft (3m), early and midspring ㉔ 'Ukon' ↕25ft (8m) ↔ 30ft (10m), midspring

PYRACANTHA
Firethorn

EVERGREEN FOLIAGE, DAINTY WHITE FLOWERS, and bright autumn berries make these spiny shrubs both popular and useful. From late spring to midsummer, flat clusters of small, 5-petaled, open flowers, like those of the hawthorn, appear. Berries in vivid shades of orange, scarlet, and golden yellow follow and often persist through the winter – unless the birds eat them. Firethorns are spreading or upright in habit and can be grown as freestanding shrubs, as hedging, or, more commonly, trained against a wall or fence in a fan or espalier (several horizontal tiers) shape.

Cultivation Firethorns like fertile, well-drained soil in full sun or partial shade and tolerate north-facing walls. Where not hardy, provide shelter from cold winds. **Prune** freestanding shrubs in late winter or early spring by removing shoots that spoil the shape. In midsummer, prune each sideshoot of wall-trained shrubs to two or three buds from the base; tie in shoots regularly. Trim hedges in midsummer. **Sow** seed in containers in a cold frame in autumn (*see pp.391–393*) or root semiripe cuttings with bottom heat in summer (*see p.394*). **Scab**, a fungus, which causes dark scabby patches in damp weather, may affect berries and leaves; cut out affected shoots to healthy wood.

Pyracantha 'Soleil d'Or'
Z6 ↕10ft (3m) ↔ 8ft (2.5m), upright habit, flowers in early summer

Pyracantha 'Orange Glow'
Z7 ↕↔ 10ft (3m), upright, then spreading habit, flowers in late spring followed by dark orange to orange-red berries

Pyracantha 'Mohave'
Z6 ↕12ft (4m) ↔ 15ft (5m), vigorous, bushy habit, flowers in early summer followed by long-lasting berries

Pyracantha 'Golden Charmer'
Z7 ↕↔ 10ft (3m), vigorous, bushy habit with arching branches, flowers in early summer

PYRUS
Pear

PEARS ARE VALUED NOT ONLY for their sometimes edible fruits but also for their flowers, and in some cases their attractive habits – exemplified by the silvery weeping pear (*see below*). The trees are usually deciduous, and some have good autumn color. The flowers, which appear in spring, are white or pink. Fruit shapes vary from the typical pear shape to round; many varieties have been developed over the centuries for their fine-flavored fruits. Ornamental varieties include *Pyrus calleryana* (Z5b), which is thorny and develops red foliage and round, brown fruits in autumn, and the snow pear (*P. nivalis* Z7), with its silvery gray leaves – both have conical habits and flower in spring. The more compact ornamental pears are ideal for a small garden as specimens in a lawn.

Cultivation Grow pears in fertile, well-drained soil in full sun. **Prune out** any shoots that spoil the shape of the tree in late winter or early spring. **Fruiting pears** in particular may suffer from canker: areas of sunken, split bark, can kill branches as it spreads: cut back stems to healthy wood. Aphids and caterpillars may also attack the foliage.

QUERCUS
Oak

OAKS ARE LARGE, STATELY TREES, known for their longevity, with attractive foliage and fissured bark. They form a large group of deciduous and evergreen trees with a wide range of leaf shapes and colors and growth habits. Acorns ½–1¼in (1–3cm) long are borne in autumn. Many deciduous oaks are excellent for autumn color, with foliage in a variety of brilliant shades. The classic common or English oak (*Quercus robur* Z5) with the typical oak leaf is a huge, spreading tree suited only to parks or woods, but if you have a large garden, there are smaller – although still large – oaks that are well worth growing as specimen trees. Plant the sapling in its permanent position – it may not survive later transplanting.

Cultivation Oaks need deep, fertile, well-drained soil in partial shade. Evergreens prefer full sun; marginally hardy species need shelter from cold, drying winds. **Prune out** shoots that spoil the shape of the tree on planting; mature oaks need little pruning except the removal of dead wood (*see p.382*). **Sow** acorns in a seedbed or cold frame as soon as they fall (*see p.393*).

Quercus ilex (Holly oak, Holm oak)
Z7b ↕80f (t25m) ↔ 70ft (20m), evergreen, smooth gray bark, leaves silvery gray when young, thrives in coastal areas

Pyrus salicifolia 'Pendula'
Z5 ↕15ft (5m) ↔ 12ft (4m), ideal for smaller gardens, willowy, silvery felted leaves, green fruits 1¼in (3cm) long

Quercus coccinea (Scarlet oak)
Z4 ↕70ft (20m) ↔ 50ft (15m), rounded canopy, gray-brown bark, dark green leaves turn red in autumn, needs alkaline soi

Quercus laurifolia (Laurel oak)
Z7b ↕↔ 70ft (20m), rounded habit with gray-black bark, leaves bronze when young, lasts well into winter, needs alkaline soil

RHODODENDRON

Rhododendron, Azalea

DRAMATIC, SOMETIMES STRONGLY SCENTED flowers are borne on these shrubs from late winter to late autumn. The flowers vary in size and shape, but they are mainly bell-shaped, often with attractive, contrasting markings on the petals, and are carried singly or in large clusters known as trusses. This is a large and highly variable group containing thousands of hybrids and species, deciduous and evergreen, with flowers of every color. Their natural habitats include both dense forest and high alpine slopes, and they range in habit from huge trees up to 80ft (25m) tall to dwarf shrubs no more than 6in (15cm) high. All require acidic soil. The leaves vary hugely in size, from ⅛in (4mm) to 30in (75cm) long. In some species, the undersides of the leaves and young stems are covered in a dense, woolly covering of hairs or scales (called indumentum). The young growth of some can be attractive, with colors of red to bronze-brown or metallic blue-green, and many deciduous rhododendrons have strong autumn leaf colors. Rhododendrons have a variety of uses in the garden dwarf alpine species are at home in a rock garden, and larger woodland types are excellent for brightening shady spots. More compact varieties grow well in patio containers, if you do not have acidic soil. Except where noted, rhododendrons listed in this feature run a wide range of Canadian hardiness zones from 5–8. Always check with your local garden center for planting information.

Cultivation Grow in moist but well-drained, acidic soil, ideally pH 4.5–5.5. Site in dappled shade if possible, but most dwarf a pine species will tolerate full sun. Shallow planting is essential; the top of the root ball should be level with the surface of the soil. **Mulch** annually with leaf mold or acidic compost. **Deadhead** when the flowers have faded, using your forefinger and thumb to twist them to one side. Be careful not to damage the developing new buds just below, which contain the flowers for the following year. **Propagate** by layering (see p.395). If leaves are affected by powdery mildew or rusts, cut out all affected growth. Provide good drainage to avoid root rot.

Tree rhododendrons

Tree rhododendrons are very large plants, most often seen in public parks and too large to be suitable for many yards. Hardy evergreens, they are spectacular when in flower because they tend to produce the largest flower clusters of all the types of rhododendron. Some tree rhododendrons also have attractive peeling bark.

Deciduous azaleas

Azaleas have generally small to medium-sized leaves and small flowers. Most are deciduous and often color wonderfully in autumn. In spring and early summer, they are an almost solid mass of flowers in colors ranging from salmon pink to red and various shades of yellow, typically with a delicious scent. Some can grow quite tall, but they are easily controlled with occasional, but not hard, pruning.

Shrub rhododendrons

The most common and well-known type of rhododendron, these are rounded and range in size from less than 3ft (1m) to 12ft (4m). The flower clusters vary from small to large trusses in a wide range of bold colors. The added bonus with the small shrub rhododendrons is that most of them are evergreen, and their attractive leaves will therefore continue to act as a background to other plants throughout the year.

① *Rhododendron arboreum* ‡40ft (12m) ↔ 12ft (4m), tree ② *argyrophyllum* ‡20ft (6m) ↔ 8ft (2.5m), evergreen shrub ③ *arizelum* ‡↔ 25ft (8m), tree ④ *augustinii* ‡↔ 7ft (2.2m), tree ⑤ *austrinum* ‡↔ 10ft (3m), deciduous azalea ⑥ 'Azuma-kagami' ‡↔ 4ft (1.2m), evergreen azalea ⑦ 'Beauty of Littleworth' ‡↔ 12ft (4m), evergreen shrub ⑧ 'Beethoven' ‡↔ 4½ft (1.3m), evergreen azalea ⑨ 'Blue Diamond' ‡↔ 5ft (1.5m), evergreen shrub ⑩ 'Blue Peter' ‡↔ 10ft (3m), evergreen

shrub ⑪ **'Cilpinense'** ↕↔ 3½ft (1.1m), evergreen shrub ⑫ *cinnabarinum* ↕ 20ft (6m) ↔ 6ft (2m), evergreen shrub ⑬ **'Corneille'** ↕↔ 5–8ft (1.5–2.5m), deciduous azalea ⑭ **'Crest'** ↕↔ 11ft (3.5m), evergreen shrub ⑮ **'Cunningham's White'** ↕↔ 20ft (6m) evergreen shrub ⑯ **'Cynthia'** ↕↔ 20ft (6m), evergreen shrub ⑰ *davidsonianum* ↕ 12ft (4m) ↔ 10ft (3m), evergreen shrub ⑱ *falconeri* ↕ 40ft (12m) ↔ 15ft (5m), tree ⑲ *fortunei* subsp. *discolor* ↕ 20ft (6m) ↔ 10ft (3m), tree ⑳ **'Fragrantissimum'** T min. 41°F (5°C) ↕↔ 6ft (2m), evergreen shrub ㉑ *fulvum* ↕ 15ft (5m) ↔ 10ft (3m), tree ㉒ **'George Reynolds'** ↕↔ 6ft (2m), deciduous azalea ㉓ **'Glory of Littleworth'** ↕↔ 3–4ft (1–1.5m), deciduous azalea ㉔ **'Glowing Embers'** ↕↔ 6ft (2m), deciduous azalea

㉕ *Rhododendron* 'Golden Torch' ↕↔ 5ft (1.5m), evergreen shrub ㉖ 'Hatsugiri' ↕↔ 24in (60cm), dwarf evergreen azalea ㉗ 'Hinode-giri' ↕↔ 24in (60cm), dwarf evergreen azalea ㉘ 'Hinomayo' ↕↔ 24in (60cm), dwarf evergreen azalea ㉙ 'Homebush' ↕↔ 5ft (1.5m), deciduous azalea ㉚ 'Hydon Dawn' ↕↔ 5ft (1.5m), evergreen shrub ㉛ 'Irohayama' ↕↔ 24in (60cm), dwarf evergreen azalea ㉜ 'John Cairns' ↕↔ 5ft (1.5m), evergreen azalea ㉝ 'Kirin' ↕↔ 5ft (1.5m), evergreen azalea ㉞ 'Kure-no-yuki' ↕↔ 3ft (1m), evergreen azalea ㉟ 'Lavender Girl' ↕↔ 8ft (2.5m), evergreen shrub ㊱ 'Linda' ↕↔ 3ft (1m), evergreen shrub ㊲ × *mucronatum* ↕↔ 4–5ft (1.2–1.5m), semievergreen shrub ㊳ Nobleanum Group ↕↔ 15ft (5m), tree ㊴ *occidentale* ↕↔ 10ft (3m), deciduous shrub ㊵ 'Pink Pearl' ↕↔ 12ft (4m), evergreen shrub ㊶ 'Polar Bear' ↕ 15ft (5m) ↔ 12ft (4m), tree ㊷ 'President Roosevelt' ↕↔ 2m (6ft), evergreen shrub

㉙

㉚

㉛

㉜

㊲

㊳

㊴

㊵

㊹

㊺

㊻

㊼

(52)

(53)

(54)

(55)

㊸ **'Ptarmigan'** ↕↔ 36in (90cm), dwarf evergreen shrub ㊹ **'Purple Splendour'** ↕↔ 10ft (3m), evergreen shrub ㊺ ***rex* subsp. *fictolacteum*** ↕↔ 40ft (12m), tree ㊻ **'Saint Valentine'** T min. 41°F (5°C) ↕ 5ft (1.5m) ↔ 6ft (2m), evergreen shrub ㊼ **'Strawberry Ice'** ↕↔ 6ft (2m), deciduous azalea ㊽ **'Susan'** ↕↔ 10ft (3m), evergreen shrub ㊾ **'Temple Belle'** ↕↔ 6ft (2m), evergreen shrub ㊿ ***thomsonii*** ↕↔ 20ft (6m), tree (51) ***veitchianum* Cubittii Group** T min. 41°F (5°C) ↕ 5ft (1.5m) ↔ 3ft (1m), evergreen shrub (52) **'Vuyk's Rosyred'** ↕ 30in (75cm) ↔ 4ft (1.2m), evergreen azalea (53) **'Vuyk's Scarlet'** ↕ 30in (75cm) ↔ 4ft (1.2m), evergreen azalea (54) ***yakushimanum*** ↕↔ 6ft (2m), evergreen shrub (55) ***yunnanense*** ↕ 20ft (6m) ↔ 12ft (4m) tree

RHAMNUS

CULTIVATED FOR THEIR FOLIAGE, which in deciduous species usually colors well in autumn, rhamnus are mostly thorny shrubs, native to a range of habitats, from woodland, heath, and scrub to fen, bogs, and rocky places. They bear small, cup-shaped flowers, often fragrant and attractive to bees (particularly those of *Rhamnus frangula*), followed by decorative red fruits that usually ripen to purple or black. These make a very striking contrast with the leaves of white-variegated *R. alaternus* 'Argenteovariegata' (Z7b), a popular evergreen, but one that needs some shelter in cold areas. Grow rhamnus in a shrub border, or a wild or woodland garden. They also make good informal hedges.

Cultivation Grow in reasonably fertile, reliably moist soil, in full sun or partial shade. **Prune out** any crossing or misplaced shoots that spoil the shape in late winter or early spring. Trim hedges in early spring. **Sow** seed in containers in a cold frame as soon as it is ripe *(see pp.391–392)*. **Take** softwood cuttings in early summer *(see p.394)*.

RHAPHIOLEPIS

THESE ARE EVERGREEN SHRUBS with glossy, dark green foliage and fragrant flowers that look similar to apple blossoms. The white or pink flowers appear among the leaves in small clusters in spring or summer, making an eye-catching display. They are good companions to small flowering trees such as crab-apples (*Malus, see p.88*) and hawthorns (*Crataegus, p.46*). Rhaphiolepis generally grow into dense, compact shapes, around 6ft (2m) tall and wide, although there are one or two much smaller varieties. Grow in a sheltered border or next to a warm, sunny wall. Where not hardy, grow in a cool greenhouse or in containers.

Cultivation Grow outdoors in moist but well-drained soil in full sun, with shelter from cold, drying winds. If growing them in pots, use a soil-based medium and water moderately in summer, giving monthly feeds of a balanced fertilizer. **Trim** lightly after flowering, removing stems that spoil the shape of the shrub. **Take** semiripe cuttings in late summer *(see p.394)*, or layer shoots in autumn *(see p.395)*.

RHUS

Sumac

THE SHRUBS AND TREES in this group are grown for their bold, dissected leaves, which turn to vivid hues of ruby, gold, and amber as the temperature falls in autumn. The tiny flowers are borne in candlelike clusters in spring or summer; more impressive are the spikes of usually crimson fruits that then develop, although these appear only when male and female plants are grown together. Sumacs look best at the back of a shrub border or in a woodland garden, teamed with other good autumn foliage plants. Some, such as *Rhus typhina* with its craggy form, also make architectural specimens. Sumacs can be invasive; cut out suckers whenever they appear.

Cultivation Grow in reasonably fertile, moist, but well-drained soil, in full sun for best autumn color. **Prune out** shoots that are crossing or spoil the shape of the shrub in late winter or early spring. In early spring cut back stems to within 2–3 buds from the base or the main shoots. **Sow** seed in a seedbed in autumn *(see pp.391–393)*. **Take** semiripe cuttings in summer, or root cuttings in winter *(see p.394)*. Prone to coral spot, which appears as orange spots on branches. Cut affected growth out and burn it.

Rhamnus frangula (Alder buckthorn)
Z3b ↕↔ 15ft (5m), bushy, spreading habit, deciduous, tiny greenish white flowers, leaves turn red in autumn

Rhaphiolepis umbellata
T min. 41°F (5°C) ↕↔ 5ft (1.5m), slow-growing, bushy, rounded habit, flowers in early summer, berries only after long, hot summers

Rhus typhina (Staghorn sumac, Velvet sumac)
Z3 ↕ 15ft (5m) ↔ 20ft (6m), deciduous, arching, suckering shrub or tree, dense velvety coating on stems, brilliant autumn color

RIBES
Flowering currant

CLOSELY RELATED TO EDIBLE CURRANT BUSHES, most ornamental ribes have a blackcurrant- or even catlike scent, both in flower and when the leaves are crushed. These are old-fashioned, mainly deciduous shrubs, grown for their cheerful late winter or spring flowers; pink-flowered *Ribes sanguineum* is a traditional partner for yellow forsythias (*see p.58*). It is also often seen as a flowering hedge. There are ribes that flower in cerise, pale pink, white, or greenish yellow. Some species do bear fruits, although these are usually inedible. Most make large shrubs, which can be wall-trained, and there are compact varieties, including one or two with golden foliage.

Cultivation Grow in reasonably fertile, well-drained soil, in full sun. *R. laurifolium* tolerates partial shade. **Prune** after flowering, cutting back flowered shoots to strong buds or shoots lower down the stem. Prune out one or two old main branches on mature plants every three or four years. If wall-trained, after flowering or in late winter, cut back flowered shoots to within 2–4 buds of the permanent framework. Trim hedges after flowering. **Take** hardwood cuttings of deciduous ribes in winter and semiripe cuttings of evergreens in summer (*see p.394*).

***Ribes sanguineum* 'Pulborough Scarlet'**
Z6b ‡ 10ft (3m) ↔ 8ft (2.5m), upright, vigorous habit, flowers with white centers in spring, blue-black fruits

***Ribes odoratum* (Buffalo currant)**
Z2 ‡ ↔ 6ft (2m), upright, deciduous shrub, flowers in mid- to late spring, black fruits, leaves turn red and purple in autumn

Ribes laurifolium
Z7 ‡ 3ft (1m) ↔ 5ft (1.5m), spreading, evergreen, leathery leaves, flowers in late winter and early spring, tolerates semishade

ROBINIA
Black locust

ROBINIAS ARE TREES AND SHRUBS found in woodland and thickets in North America. They are usually thorny and have bright, graceful, long leaves, and, in late spring and early summer, sprays of white or pink, pealike flowers. These are followed by large, dark brown seedpods. Grow the trees as specimens in a lawn, and the shrubby species in a large shrub border, especially among darker-leaved trees or shrubs. *Robinia pseudoacacia* 'Frisia', which may be coppiced (*see p.42*) and grown as a foliage shrub, and *Acer palmatum* 'Rubrum', with dark red-purple leaves (*see pp.18–19*), make striking companions.

Cultivation Robinias like full sun in reasonably fertile soil, ideally moist but well-drained, but will tolerate dry, poor soils. Shelter from strong winds; the branches are rather brittle and break easily. **Prune out** any misplaced or crossing branches that spoil the shape of young trees in late summer or early autumn (*see p.382*). Remove any suckers (shoots growing up from the ground around the tree). **Sow** seed in a container in a cold frame in autumn (*see pp.391–392*). **Take** root cuttings (*see p.394*) in autumn.

***Robinia pseudoacacia* 'Frisia' (Black locust)**
Z4 ‡ 50ft (15m) ↔ 25ft (8m), fast-growing, suckering tree, fragrant flowers, foliage turns orange-yellow (*see inset*) in autumn

ROSA
Rose

see also
pp.150–151

SUPERB, OFTEN HIGHLY SCENTED FLOWERS in summer and autumn make roses enduring garden favorites. They are mostly deciduous shrubs, and with hundreds of colorful varieties to choose from, there is one suitable for almost any situation. Shrub roses look best mixed with other plants in borders; the miniature varieties can be grown in rock gardens and in large pots. The flowers, borne in clusters at the tips of upright, sometimes arching or trailing, thorny stems, are excellent for cutting. They vary enormously in form and size, from small single or double blooms to immense, rounded doubles. Colors range from purest white through yellows and pinks to deep blackish crimson. The red autumn fruits (hips) of some roses also make a striking display.

Cultivation Grow in an open, sunny position, in humus-rich, moist but well-drained soil **Plant** bare-root roses when dormant, from late autumn to early spring, container-grown plants at any time. **Feed** with a balanced fertilizer in spring and mulch with organic matter. **Prune** in late winter or early spring; deadhead to encourage more flowers. **Take** hardwood cuttings (see p.394) in autumn. Blackspot, powdery mildew, or rust may affect roses. Choose disease-resistant cultivars if possible.

Modern bush roses

‡ to 3ft (1m)
↔ to 3ft (1m)

These upright shrubs are useful in borders and beds, being compact and repeat-flowering with single or double flowers. They bear large flowers singly or in small clusters (hybrid tea) or small flowers in large clusters (floribunda). Prune hard, cutting the main stems of hybrid tea roses to 8–10in (20–25cm) and those of floribunda roses to 10–18in (25–45cm) above the ground, and reducing sideshoots to two or three buds.

Dwarf patio roses

‡ 24in (60cm)
↔ 24in (60cm)

Compact shrubs with a bushy habit, these roses are ideal for growing at the front of borders, in containers or in a rock garden. They produce abundant clusters of single to double, sometimes scented flowers in a wide range of colors throughout summer. Grow them in fertile soil in full sun. Only light pruning is needed: cut down the main stems and sideshoots by no more than one-third to half their length.

Groundcover roses

‡ to 24in (60cm)
↔ to 3ft (1m)

Spreading in habit, these roses have numerous stems bearing clusters of small flowers, usually double or semidouble and lightly scented. They are ideal for groundcover and also for edging paths or growing in large pots. Prune to keep plants to the desired size, cutting to an outward-facing bud. If sideshoots are overcrowded, prune to two to four buds. Every three or four years cut out the oldest wood to encourage new growth; if neglected, they can be cut back hard.

Standard roses

‡ to 6ft (2m)
↔ 5ft (1.5m)

Ideal for pots, formal schemes, or to add height in borders, these are modern bush roses top-grafted onto clear stems of rootstocks; ramblers (see pp.150–151) can be used to make weeping or trailing standards. There are two types of standards; half-standards have a stem of 2½ft (75cm) and full-standards a stem of 3½ft (1.1m). Both need permanent staking. Prune the head according to the rose type used.

Modern shrub roses

‡ 4–6ft (1.2–2m)
↔ to 6ft (2m)

A diverse group of roses, varying in size, habit, and flower type. Most are upright with flowers similar to modern bush roses, and make impressive specimen plants. Some have only one flush of blooms while others repeat-flower through the summer. Heavy pruning can spoil their character: remove dead or diseased wood and shorten main stems by up to one-third, sideshoots by half. Cut one in three old stems to the base each year.

Old garden roses

‡ 4–6ft (1.2–2m)
↔ to 6ft (2m)

A varied group, upright or arching, most flowering once (these are pruned after flowering) but some repeat-flowering, most with semi-double or double flowers, often fragrant. Position arching types so they do not crowd plants, and give only a light annual pruning, removing some older wood to encourage new shoots from the base of the shrub. Upright types require only occasional removal of thin, weak, or dead shoots.

① *Rosa* 'Amber Queen' ('Harroony') Z6 ‡↔ 24in (60cm), floribunda ② 'Angela Rippon' ('Ocaru') ‡ 18in (45cm) ↔ 12in (30cm), miniature modern bush ③ 'Anna Ford' ('Harpiccolo') ‡↔ 18in (45cm), patio ④ 'Ballerina' ‡ 5ft (1.5m) ↔ 4ft (1.2m), modern shrub ⑤ 'Belle de Crécy' Z5 ‡ 4ft (1.2m) ↔ 3ft (1m), old rose ⑥ 'Boule de Neige' Z6 ‡ 5ft (1.5m) ↔ 4ft (1.2m), old rose ⑦ 'Bourbon Queen' ‡ 8ft (2.5m) ↔ 5ft (1.5m), old rose ⑧ 'Buff Beauty' ‡↔ 4ft (1.2m), modern shrub ⑨ 'Cécile Brünner' Z6 ‡ 30in (75cm) ↔ 24in (60cm), old rose

floribunda ⑳ **'Fantin-Latour'** Z3 ‡5ft (1.5m) ↔ 4ft (1.2m), old rose ㉑ **'Felicia'** Z6b ‡5ft (1.5m) ↔ 7ft (2.2m), modern shrub ㉒ **'Fragrant Cloud'** ('Tanellis') Z6 ‡30in (75cm) ↔ 24in (60cm), hybrid tea ㉓ **'Fru Dagmar Hastrup'** Z2b ‡3ft (1m) ↔ 4ft (1.2m), old rose

⑩ **'Charles de Mills'** Z4 ‡↔4ft (1.2m), old rose ⑪ **'Chinatown'** Z6 ‡4ft (1.2m) ↔ 3ft (1m), modern shrub ⑫ **'Conservation'** ('Cocdimple') ‡↔18in (45cm), patio ⑬ **'Cornelia'** Z6 ‡↔5ft (1.5m), modern shrub ⑭ **'Crimson Glory'** Z6 ‡↔24in (60cm), hybrid tea ⑮ **'Doris Tysterman'** ‡4ft (1.2m) ↔ 30in (75cm), hybrid tea ⑯ **'Elizabeth Harkness'** ‡32in (80cm) ↔ 24in (60cm), hybrid tea ⑰ **'English Garden'** ('Ausbuff') ‡3ft (1m) ↔ 30in (75cm), modern shrub ⑱ **'English Miss'** ‡30in (75cm) ↔ 24in (60cm), floribunda ⑲ **'Escapade'** ('Harpade') ‡30in (75cm) ↔ 24in (60cm),

㉔ *Rosa* 'Frühlingsmorgen' Z5b ‡6ft (2m) ↔5ft (1.5m), modern shrub ㉕ *gallica* 'Versicolor' Z4 ‡32in (80cm) ↔3ft (1m), old rose ㉖ 'Geranium' Z6a ‡8ft (2.5m) ↔5ft (1.5m), old rose ㉗ 'Glenfiddich' Z6 ‡32in (80cm) ↔24in (60cm), floribunda ㉘ 'Graham Thomas' Z5 ‡↔4–5ft (1.2–1.5m), modern shrub ㉙ 'Great Maiden's Blush' Z4 ‡6ft (2m) ↔4½ft (1.35m), old rose ㉚ 'Hannah Gordon' ('Korweiso') Z6 ‡32in (80cm) ↔24in (60cm), floribunda ㉛ 'Iceberg' Z5 ‡32in (80cm) ↔26in (65cm), floribunda

㉜ 'Ispahan' Z5 ‡5ft (1.5m) ↔4ft (1.2m), old rose ㉝ 'Julia's Rose' Z6 ‡30in (75cm) ↔18in (45cm), hybrid tea ㉞ 'Just Joey' ‡↔30in (75cm), hybrid tea ㉟ 'Laura Ashley' ('Chewharla') ‡24in (60cm) ↔4ft (1.2m), groundcover ㊱ 'Madame Isaac Pereire' Z6 ‡7ft (2.2m) ↔6ft (2m), old rose ㊲ 'Maiden's Blush' Z3 ‡4ft (1.2m) ↔36in (90cm), old rose ㊳ 'Margaret Merril' ('Harkuly') Z6 ‡32in (80cm) ↔24in (60cm), floribunda ㊴ 'Mountbatten' ('Harmantelle') ‡4ft (1.2m) ← 30in (75cm), floribunda ㊵ 'National Trust' ‡↔24in (60cm) hybrid tea ㊶ 'Nevada' Z2b ‡↔7ft (2.2m),

modern shrub ㊷ 'Peace' ('Madame A. Meilland') Z6 ↕ 4ft (1.2m) ↔ 3ft (1m), hybrid tea ㊸ 'Perle d'Or' ↕ 4ft (1.2m) ↔ 3ft (1m), old rose ㊹ 'Pink Favorite' ↕↔ 30in (75cm), hybrid tea ㊺ 'Polar Star' ('Tanlarpost') ↕ 3ft (1m) ↔ 28in (70cm), hybrid tea ㊻ 'Pretty Polly' ('Meitonje') ↕↔ 18in (45cm), patio ㊼ 'Robin Redbreast' ('Interrob') ↕↔ 18–24in (45–60cm), groundcover ㊽ 'Rosemary Harkness' ('Harrowbond') ↕↔ 32in (80cm), hybrid tea ㊾ *rugosa* Z2b ↕↔ 3–8ft (1–2.5m), species ㊿ 'Silver Jubilee' Z6 ↕ 3½ft (1.1m) ↔ 24in (60cm), hybrid tea

(51) 'Souvenir de la Malmaison' Z6 ↕↔ 5ft (1.5m), old rose (52) 'The Fairy' Z6 ↕↔ 24–36in (60–90cm), floribunda (53) 'The Queen Elizabeth' ↕ 7ft (2.2m) ↔ 3ft (1m), modern bush (54) 'Trumpeter' ('Mactru') ↕↔ 24in (60cm), floribunda

ROSMARINUS
Rosemary

AROMATIC AND EVERGREEN, these rather angular shrubs add height and structure to a herb garden. They also grow well in pots. Native to Mediterranean regions, they suffer or die in cold wet winters. Where not hardy, bring container grown plants inside over winter. The upright types benefit from the shelter of a sunny wall, while the less hardy, prostrate forms much prefer spreading over a gravel mulch or even a stony bank or retaining wall, rather than sitting on chilly, moist soil. The leaves of rosemary are dark green, while the stems often have a grayish bloom. From midspring to early summer, and now and again in late summer, they bear clusters of blue, mauve, or white, tubular flowers toward the shoot tips. Those shown here are hardy to Zone 7.

Cultivation Grow in well-drained to dry, relatively poor soil, in full sun. **Trim** lightly but regularly to keep plants bushy and to encourage the soft, succulent young shoots that are best for cooking. **Sow** seed (*see pp.391–392*) in a container in a cold frame in spring. **Take** semi-ripe cuttings (*see p.394*) in summer.

RUBUS

↨ 10ft (3m)

THESE ARCHING SHRUBS, related to blackberries or brambles, bear simple, roselike flowers in early summer, in white, red, purple, or pink. In some, such as the thornless 'Benenden' and the spectacularly bright *Rubus spectabilis* 'Olympic Double', the flowering period is the main season of interest; these suit a wild or woodland garden. *R. biflorus* (Z6b), *R. cockburnianus* (Z6), and *R. thibetanus* (Z7b) are also grown for winter interest, with a white bloom on their prickly stems that makes them stand out. They look good with willows (*Salix, see right*) and dogwoods (*Cornus, see pp.42–43*) grown for colorful winter stems, and are best pruned hard annually.

Cultivation Grow in well-drained, reasonably fertile soil. Position in full sun for the brightest winter stems. **Prune** rubus grown for their flowers lightly, cutting back flowered shoots to strong buds or shoots lower down. Prune those grown for winter stems hard, in early spring, cutting stems to within three buds of the base, then feed and mulch. **Take** hardwood cuttings in early winter (*see p.394*).

SALIX
Willow

THIS IS A LARGE AND VARIED group of deciduous trees and shrubs. Spring catkins are one of the striking features, but they also have attractive habits, and in some cases decorative stems. Willows seen growing in the wild are often massive trees, but there are many small and medium-sized ones – the weeping *Salix caprea* 'Kilmarnock' is a favorite centerpiece for a small lawn or border. Some of the larger species, generally too vigorous for most gardens, can be grown as shrubs, cut back annually to make them compact and encourage brightly colored stems. *S. alba* 'Britzensis', for example, makes a fine winter display with mahonias (*see p.87*), Christmas box (*Sarcococca, see p.116*), and dogwoods (*Cornus, see pp.42–43*).

Cultivation Grow in any deep, moist but well-drained soil, except limy soils, in full sun. **Pruning** is rarely necessary except for those grown for winter stems; in early spring, cut these stems back to within three or four buds of the base or to a permanent stubby framework (*see right, and p.383*). **Take** greenwood cuttings in early summer, or hardwood cuttings in winter (*see p.394*). Willow cuttings root easily.

① *officinalis* ↨↔ 5ft (1.5m) ② *officinalis* 'McConnell's Blue' ↨↔ 5ft (1.5m) ③ *officinalis* Prostratus Group ↕ 6in (15cm) ↔ 5ft (1.5m) ④ *officinalis* 'Roseus' ↨↔ 5ft (1.5m)

Rubus cockburnianus (Ghost bramble)
Z6 ↨↔ 8ft (2.5m), thicket-forming, small, purple flowers in summer, black fruits, attractive but unpalatable

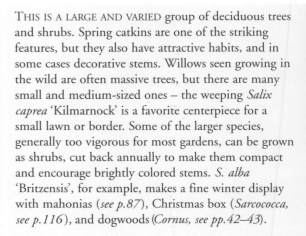

Salix helvetica (Swiss willow)
Z5 ↕ 2ft (60cm) ↔ 16in (40cm), an upright, bushy shrub, leaves gray-green above and silvery white beneath, catkins in early spring

SAMBUCUS
Elder

THESE DECIDUOUS SHRUBS AND TREES are grown for their flowers and ornamental foliage. From spring to early summer, they produce dense, flat clusters of white or creamy yellow flowers followed by black or glossy red fruits. The leaves may be blackish purple, dark green, or golden yellow, and are made up of small leaflets, deeply fringed in some cultivars. Elders are suitable for shrub and mixed borders or as specimens. Planted together, dark and yellow-leaved types contrast well. *Photinia × fraseri* 'Red Robin' (*see p.94*) with its red young foliage is also a good companion.

Cultivation Grow in reasonably fertile soil that is moist but well-drained. Position in full sun or partial shade: leaves color most strongly in full sun, but retain color better in dappled shade. **Prune** only to remove crossing or misplaced shoots, in winter or early spring; or, for the best leaf color, cut back stems to within two or three buds of the base or to a permanent framework in early spring. Prune hard to restrict size if necessary. **Sow** seed (*see pp.391–392*) in a container in a cold frame in autumn. **Take** hardwood cuttings in winter, or softwood cuttings in early summer (*see p.394*). Blackfly (*see Aphids, pp.398–399*) may infest young growth, but can be treated.

***Salix gracilistyla* 'Melanostachys'**
Z4b ↕10ft (3m) ↔ 12ft (4m), upright shrub, gray-green leaves turn glossy green, black catkins in early to midspring

COPPICING WILLOWS
Several species of willow can be cut back to the base in spring; this will produce the most brightly colored winter stems.

***Salix caprea* 'Kilmarnock'** (Kilmarnock willow)
Z5 ↕5–6ft (1.5–2m) ↔ 6ft (2m), weeping stems grafted on upright rootstock, catkins in mid- and late spring, dark green leaves

***Salix alba* 'Britzensis'**
Z2 ↕80ft (25m) ↔ 30ft (10m), large tree, annual coppicing will keep it in bounds, dull-green leaves, catkins in spring

***Sambucus racemosa* 'Plumosa Aurea'** (Red-berried elder)
Z3 ↕↔ 10ft (3m), bushy shrub, leaves are bronze when new (*see inset*) and can scorch in full sun, flowers in midspring

SANTOLINA
Lavender cotton

‡6–30in (15–75cm)
↔8–36in (20cm–1m)

COMPACT, ROUNDED, evergreen – or rather, "evergray" – shrubs, these can be used as low hedges or to edge borders, and are ideal for rock gardens, being naturally found in dry sites. They are grown principally for their fine, aromatic foliage. The long-stemmed flower heads are buttonlike, yellow or creamy yellow, surrounded by broad rings of similarly colored bracts (modified leaves) that make them more conspicuous. The plants spread to cover the ground and effectively suppress weeds. For a heady mix of scents, grow with other aromatic herbs, such as lavender (*Lavandula, see p.80*) and rosemary (*Rosmarinus, see p.114*).

Cultivation Grow in poor to reasonably fertile soil that is well-drained and in full sun. **Cut back** flowered shoots to within 1in (2.5cm) of old growth in spring. **Sow** seed (*see pp.391–392*) in containers in a cold frame in autumn or spring. **Take** semiripe cuttings (*see p.394*) in late summer and root in a propagator with bottom heat.

PRUNING SANTOLINAS
Never cut santolinas back beyond the point where you can see fresh growth shooting from old wood.

Santolina pinnata 'Sulphurea'
T min. 41°F (5°C) ‡30in (75cm) ↔ 3ft (1m), feathery, finely divided, gray-green leaves, flowers in midsummer

SARCOCOCCA
Christmas box, Sweet box

A SMALL GROUP OF TOUGH EVERGREEN shrubs, sarcococcas are invaluable in the garden in winter. Their dense forms, clothed in glossy, dark green leaves, add visual interest, bearing clusters of white flowers in early spring followed by round, shiny berries. Their greatest attraction, however, is their fragrance: the flowers are not showy, but this is more than made up for by the scent, sweet and powerful over a surprising distance. A few cut stems will scent a whole room. Grow them as a groundcover in a shade garden, or as an informal hedge.

Cultivation Grow in reasonably fertile, moist but well-drained soil, enriched with well-rotted organic matter. Position in deep or partial shade: they tolerate full sun if the soil is reliably moist. **Trim** or prune back any stems that spoil the shape of the shrub after flowering, but not too much; trimming shoots too closely may result in fewer flowers. **Sow** seed (*see pp.391–392*) in containers outdoors in autumn or spring. **Take** semiripe cuttings (*see p.394*) in late summer and provide gentle bottom heat.

Sarcococca confusa
Z7b ‡6ft (2m) ↔ 3ft (1m), dense and rounded, slow-growing shrub that is very useful for fairly dry, shady areas

SENECIO CINERARIA
Dusty Miller

see also p.325

‡↔to 24in (60cm)

THESE MOUNDING evergreen shrubs are grown chiefly for their soft, feltlike leaves, in a range of delicate shapes and shades of silvery green and gray. Yellow flower heads are produced in the second year after sowing, but the plants are often discarded after one season. The flowers are not particularly attractive, and the foliage is at its pristine best only when plants are young. They can be grown in shrub borders, but are mainly used as container plants or in bedding, where their foliage acts as a contrast to flowering plants. A classic combination is cinerarias with red salvias (*see pp.318–319*); for a more subdued effect, pair it with purple heliotropes (*see p.70*).

Cultivation Grow in reasonably fertile soil in full sun. **Trim** plants if necessary to improve the shape. **Sow** seed (*see pp.391–393*) in spring at 66–75°F (19–24°C). **Take** semiripe cuttings (*see p.394*) in mid- or late summer. Prone to rust; in bedding, affected plants are best removed to prevent it from spreading.

① *cineraria* 'Silver Dust' ‡↔ 12in (30cm), particularly bright foliage ② *cineraria* 'White Diamond' ‡12–16in (30–40cm) ↔ 12in (30cm), usually grown as perennial Both Z7b

SKIMMIA

↔ to 20ft (6m)

SKIMMIAS ARE HANDSOME evergreens, all with similar appearance but varying widely in size, with many compact varieties for the smaller garden. Clusters of starry flowers, sometimes scented, open in spring but are prominent in bud through the winter in several forms. The flowers are followed by fleshy, round, black, red, or white berries; some skimmias have male and female plants, so both are needed for fruit. The pointed leaves are dark, glossy, and aromatic. Skimmias are reliable players for winter-interest, adding structure and color next to deciduous shrubs like hamamelis (*see p.68*), and height to groupings of heathers (*Calluna, see p.31*).

Cultivation Grow in reasonably fertile, moist but well-drained soil, with well-rotted compost added. Position in light or dappled shade; *S. confusa* 'Kew Green' will tolerate full sun. **Prune** only if necessary. **Sow** seed (*see pp.391–392*) in containers in a cold frame in autumn. **Take** semiripe cuttings (*see p.394*) in late summer.

Skimmia japonica 'Rubella'
Z7 *↕↔* to 20ft (6m), male bears no fruit but has red buds in autumn and winter, flowers in mid- and late spring

SOPHORA

GROWN FOR THEIR FINE FOLIAGE and their clusters of bright flowers, these trees and shrubs need long, hot summers to flower well but are worth growing for the leaves alone. These are composed of small leaflets arranged along a central leaf stalk and have a very elegant appearance. There are both deciduous and evergreen sophoras. The pealike flowers are carried in clusters at the end of the branches, in colors that include purple-blue to white and golden yellow. Sophoras look good in a shrub border, or near a sheltered wall in cooler regions to encourage flowering. In cold areas, grow the less hardy types in pots and take under frost-free cover for the winter.

Cultivation Grow in reasonably fertile, well-drained soil, in full sun. Use a soil-based potting mix in containers, water freely in summer and feed at monthly intervals with a balanced fertilizer. **Prune** out any misplaced or crossing shoots that spoil the shape of young trees in late winter or early spring, to create a healthy framework of branches. **Sow** seed (*see pp.391–392*) in a container in a cold frame as soon as they are ripe.

Skimmia japonica
Z7 *↕↔* to 20ft (6m), variable in shape, fragrant white flowers in mid- and late spring, male and female forms

Skimmia × confusa 'Kew Green'
Z7 *↕* 1½–10ft (0.5–3m) *↔* 5ft (1.5m), a male, fruitless cultivar with aromatic leaves and fragrant white flowers in spring

Sophora davidii
Z7 *↕* 8ft (2.5m) *↔* 10ft (3m), bushy or spreading, deciduous shrub or tree, flowers late summer/early autumn when mature

SORBUS

Mountain ash, Rowan, Whitebeam

UPRIGHT, COLUMNAR, OR SPREADING trees and shrubs, sorbus have an attractive branch structure and flowers in spring or summer. Their foliage is ornamental, with leaves in a range of shapes, often coloring well in autumn, and the bark is textured when mature. The main highlight is the autumn show of berries, which are attractive to birds. These are mostly in shades of red, orange, and yellow, but some have white berries, rarely tinted pink. The thicket-forming shrub *S. reducta* (Z5) has crimson berries that become white as the leaves turn red and purple in autumn. Tolerant of air pollution, they are ideal as specimen trees in small gardens or in a border with hawthorns (*Crataegus, see p.46*) or amelanchiers (*see p.22*) for a richly colored autumn display. The Canadian hardiness zone for those shown ranges from 3–7.

Cultivation Grow in any reasonably fertile, moist but well-drained soil, in full sun or dappled shade. **Prune** out crossing or misplaced shoots in late winter or early spring, but only if necessary. **Sow** seed (*see pp.391–392*) in a container in a cold frame in autumn.

SPARTIUM JUNCEUM

Broom, Spanish broom

↔ to 10ft (3m)

THIS PLANT IS CLOSELY related to cytisus (*see p.47*) and genistas (*see p.65*), both also commonly called broom. Spanish broom is suitable for a shrub border or training against a warm, sunny wall in a coastal garden. It is an upright shrub, with slender, dark green shoots and few leaves. From early summer until early autumn, it produces masses of fragrant, pealike flowers, followed by flattened, dark brown seedpods. The intense yellow of the flowers would make a lively contrast to the similarly shaped, rich blue flowers of *Sophora davidii* (*see p.117*). Spanish broom is highly invasive in British Columbia.

Cultivation This plant likes reasonably fertile, well-drained soil; thrives in coastal areas and on alkaline soils. Needs full sun. **Trim** or prune shoots that spoil the shape of the shrub, lightly in mid- or late spring. Older specimens may be renovated by cutting back fairly hard in spring. **Sow** seed (*see pp.391–392*) in containers in a cold frame in spring or autumn. It is a plant that will often self-seed.

SPIRAEA

THERE IS A SPIRAEA FOR ALMOST any position in the garden. This varied group of semievergreen and deciduous shrubs contains many elegant and easily cultivated plants, in various sizes. They are grown mainly for their dense clusters of small, saucer-shaped or bowl-shaped flowers, carried at the branch tips in spring and summer. These range from white, pink, and yellow, to purple. Some spiraeas have colored leaves, like *Spiraea japonica* 'Goldflame', which has bronze-red young leaves that turn to bright yellow, then to mid-green; its flowers are dark pink.

Cultivation Grow in fertile, moist but well-drained soil in full sun. **Prune** most spiraeas, which flower on older wood, after flowering, cutting back the flowered shoots to strong buds or shoots lower down the shrub. Encourage new growth from the base of mature plants by cutting out about one in every three or four old stems each year. Prune *S. japonica* and its cultivars, which flower on the current year's growth, cutting them back to a permanent low framework of shoots in early spring. **Take** greenwood cuttings in summer (*see p.394*).

A LOW HEDGE
'Snowmound' is, as its name suggests, dense in habit and makes a good compact hedge. Prune immediately after flowering.

① *aria* 'Lutescens' ‡ 30ft (10m), brown-speckled red berries
② *aucuparia* ‡ 50ft (15m) ③ 'Joseph Rock' ‡ 30ft (10m)
④ *sargentiana* Z5–7 H7–5 ‡↔ 30ft (10m)

Spartium junceum
Z8, in sheltered positions may become tall and leggy; in an exposed coastal garden, winds keep growth dense

Spiraea nipponica 'Snowmound'
Z3 ‡↔ 4–8ft (1.2–2.5m), fast-growing, deciduous, smothered with white flowers in early summer

Spiraea japonica 'Anthony Waterer'
Z2b ‡ to 5ft (1.5m) ↔ 5ft (1.5m), deciduous, leaves bronze when young, often edged pink or white, flowers mid- and late summer

A SMALL GROUP OF SPREADING, deciduous and semi-evergreen shrubs, these are grown for their late winter and early spring flowers, which are small, bell-shaped, and pale yellow. The yellow buds are produced in clusters along the bare stems in autumn, opening in spring before the leaves appear. Only *Stachyurus chinensis* and *S. praecox* are reliably and widely grown; *S. chinensis* (Z7b) is the smaller of the two, while *S. praecox* has a popular variegated cultivar, 'Magpie'. Both have pointed, dark green leaves on arching, slender, glossy shoots, which are red-brown in *S. praecox* and purplish in *S. chinensis*. Grow them in a shrub or mixed border, or against a wall.

Cultivation Grow in light, moist, but well-drained, acidic soil in full sun or partial shade. Position in a spot sheltered from cold, drying winds. **Prune out** any crossing or misplaced shoots after flowering. Mature plants may be rejuvenated, when necessary, by cutting them to the base after flowering. **Sow** seed (*see pp.391–392*) in a cold frame in autumn. **Take** semiripe cuttings (*see p.394*) consisting of a sideshoot with a sliver of older stem (a "heel") attached in summer.

FORMAL SHAPES
Vigorous spiraeas such as this may seem too large for a small garden, but can be confined by regular clipping into tight, formal shapes.

Spiraea japonica 'Golden Princess' ('Lisp')
2b ‡ 6ft (2m) ↔ 5ft (1.5m), deciduous, foliage bronze-red when young, then bright yellow and red in autumn, purple-pink flowers

Spiraea × vanhouttei
Z3 ‡ 6ft (2m) ↔ 5ft (1.5m), a graceful, arching, deciduous shrub, profuse flowers almost obscure the leaves in early summer

Stachyurus praecox
Z7b ‡ 3–12ft (1–4m) ↔ to 10ft (3m), deciduous shrub, one of the first to flower in late winter and early spring

STEWARTIA

‡20–80ft (6–25m)
↔10–25ft (3–8m)

A SUCCESSION OF FLOWERS in the summer, fine autumn color, and beautifully textured bark on older specimens all make these large, evergreen or deciduous trees and shrubs worth growing. The roselike, white flowers have creamy yellow stamens in the center and are produced singly or in pairs. Stewartias are related to camellias (*see pp.32–33*) and prefer broadly similar conditions, making excellent specimen trees in a woodland setting or shady border. Try them with eucryphias (*see p.55*), which bear similar open, white flowers at different times of the year depending on the species.

Cultivation Grow in moist but well-drained, reasonably fertile, neutral to acidic soil. Position in full sun or partial shade, with shelter from strong, cold winds. Buy container-grown plants and choose the right spot first time; they resent root disturbance. **Sow** seed (*see pp.391–392*) in a cold frame in autumn. **Take** greenwood cuttings in early summer or semiripe cuttings from mid- to late summer (*see p.394*), or layer low-growing shoots in autumn (*see p.395*).

Stewartia pseudocamellia
Z5b ‡70ft (20m) ↔ 25ft (8m), peeling bark (see inset), leaves turn yellow and then orange and red, flowers in midsummer

STYRAX
Snowbell

BELL-SHAPED, PURE WHITE or pink-tinged flowers give these graceful plants their common name. A large group of deciduous or evergreen shrubs and small trees, most are compact enough to be included in almost any garden. The dainty, fragrant flowers are produced in summer on short branches formed in the previous year. The leaves are variable in shape, and some color well in autumn. Shrubby snowbells are ideal for a border with mock oranges (*Philadelphus, see p.93*), weigelas (*see p.128*), and potentillas (*see p.99*); plant trees where the flowers can be seen from below.

Cultivation Grow in moist but well-drained soil that has been enriched with well-rotted organic matter, and is preferably neutral to acidic. Position in full sun or partial shade, with protection from cold, drying winds. **Prune out** any misplaced or crossing shoots that spoil the shape of shrubs or young trees in late winter or early spring. **Sow** seed (*see pp.391–392*) as soon as ripe: this needs some care, maintaining 59°F (15°C) for three months and then keeping the seedlings frost-free until they are established. **Take** greenwood cuttings (*see p.394*) in summer.

Styrax obassia (Fragrant snowbell)
Z6 ‡40ft (12m) ↔ 22ft (7m), broadly columnar tree, downy leaves turn yellow and red in autumn, flowers early and midsummer

SYMPHORICARPOS
Snowberry

THESE DECIDUOUS SHRUBS are grown for their autumn and winter show of berries, which are usually white or rose-tinted, but are dark blue or purple in some species. In summer, they bear clusters of small, bell-shaped flowers, which are rich in nectar and attract bees and other beneficial insects to the garden. The berries last well into winter. Contact with berries may irritate the skin. Often forming thickets, these are very hardy plants and tolerant of a wide range of conditions including poor soil and pollution. They are best grown in a wild garden along a border with other shrubs, such as hawthorn (*Crataegus, see p.46*), to form a screen or mixed informal hedge.

Cultivation Grow in any reasonably fertile, well-drained soil, and position in full sun or partial shade. **Prune out** misplaced or crossing shoots that spoil the shape of the shrub in late winter or early spring (*see p.382*); reduce size by cutting back flowered stems to strong shoots lower down, after flowering. **Divide** large, clumping plants in autumn (*see p.395*). **Take** greenwood cuttings in summer, or hardwood cuttings in autumn (*see p.394*).

Symphoricarpos × *doorenbosii* 'White Hedge'
Z5 ‡5ft (1.5m) ↔ indefinite, an upright, thicket-forming shrub, flowers in mid- and late summer, densely clustered fruits

SYRINGA
Lilac

FAMOUS FOR THEIR BEAUTIFUL and exquisitely scented flowers in early summer, these deciduous shrubs, traditionally mauve-flowered, are also available in white, cream, pale yellow, pink, magenta, and wine red. Most lilacs in gardens are the familiar cultivars of *Syringa vulgaris*. With a relatively short but always eagerly anticipated season in bloom, their flowers are borne in distinctive conical clusters. These can grow quite large and suit the back of a border or a wild garden area well, or they can be pruned to a more shapely form. However there are others, such as *S. meyeri* 'Palibin', that fit into any small garden and can even be trained as standards.

Cultivation Grow in fertile soil enriched with well-rotted organic matter, preferably neutral to alkaline. Site in full sun. **Deadhead** young lilacs to prevent the plant's energy going into setting seed. **Prune out** any crossing or misshapen branches in late winter or early spring (*see p.382*). *S. vulgaris* and its cultivars can be renovated by pruning hard. **Sow** seed (*see pp.391–392*) in a cold frame as soon as ripe or in spring. **Layer** low-growing shoots (*see p.395*) in early summer.

RENOVATING LILACS
When cut back hard, old *S. vulgaris* cultivars make vigorous new growth that will need thinning. They should flower again by the third year.

Syringa meyeri 'Palibin'
Z2b ‡ 5–6ft (t1.5–2m) ↔ 4ft (1.2m), slow-growing, rounded shrub, profuse flower clusters in late spring and early summer

Syringa vulgaris var. *alba*
Z2 ‡↔ 22ft (7m), white-flowered form of this highly fragrant, spreading shrub or small tree, which usually has lilac-blue flowers

Syringa × *josiflexa* 'Bellicent'
Z4b ‡ 12ft (4m) ↔ 15ft (5m), upright shrub, flower clusters large, up to 8in (20cm) long, in late spring and early summer

Syringa vulgaris 'Primrose'
Z2 ‡↔ 22ft (7m), spreading shrub or small tree, clusters of pale, creamy yellow flowers in late spring to early summer

Syringa pubescens 'Superba'
Z3 ‡ to 20ft (6m) ↔ 20ft (6m), erect, bushy shrub, small clusters of flowers in early summer, intermittently until autumn

TAMARIX
Tamarisk

INVALUABLE IN COASTAL GARDENS, these are graceful deciduous shrubs or small trees with red-brown, arching stems. Their flowers are pink and carried in dense, plumelike sprays. Naturally found in coastal regions, tamarisks happily withstand salt-laden winds and sea spray. They have tiny, tough, feathery leaves from which little water evaporates; this makes them ideal for a windbreak or screen where winds are not cold. In a sheltered site, they grow leggy if not checked by regular pruning. Most widely seen are *Tamarix tetrandra* (Z6), flowering in mid- to late spring, and *T. ramosissima*, which flowers from late summer.

Cultivation Grow in full sun, in well-drained soil in coastal areas or in moist soil with shelter from cold, drying winds in inland gardens. **Prune** young plants almost to ground level after planting and trim regularly to stop plants becoming top-heavy (*see p.383*). Cut flowered stems of spring-flowering types back to strong new shoots; prune autumn-flowering types slightly harder, in early spring; all tolerate renovation pruning, almost to the base. **Sow** seed (*see pp.391–392*) as soon as it is ripe in containers in a cold frame. **Take** hardwood cuttings in winter or semiripe cuttings in summer (*see p.394*).

TAXUS
Yew

VERSATILE AND ADAPTABLE CONIFERS, yews are grown for their handsome evergreen foliage and sculptural forms. They have reddish brown, often peeling bark and narrow, very dark green leaves (there are also golden forms). Female plants bear red berries in autumn. Yews can be grown as freestanding trees or clipped into topiary shapes, and make possibly the best formal hedges; prostrate ones make good ground-cover. Yews grow faster than many people think and will make a dense hedge in under ten years. Unlike most conifers, they can be pruned hard into old wood, so are easy to renovate if overgrown or damaged. All parts (except the red fruits' flesh) are highly toxic.

Cultivation Grow in any except wet soil, and in any site, from full sun to full shade. **Trim** hedges and clipped shapes in summer and early autumn. Renovate in autumn to early winter. **Sow** seed (*see pp.391–393*) as soon as ripe in a cold frame or seedbed; they may take two years or more to germinate. **Take** semiripe cuttings (*see p.394*) in late summer, choosing upright shoots (except for prostrate forms), otherwise they may not form a central upright stem.

Taxus baccata 'Fastigiata' (Irish yew)
Z6 ‡ 30ft (10m) ↔ 20ft (6m), female, particularly narrow when young, a striking, smokelike column (see inset) when mature

Tamarix ramosissima 'Pink Cascade'
Z3 ‡↔ 15ft (5m), flowers in dense clusters in late summer and early autumn, on the new year's shoots

Taxus baccata 'Fastigiata Aureomarginata'
Z6 ‡ 10–15ft (3–5m) ↔ 3–8ft (1–2.5m), broadly conical tree, female, gold-variegated cultivar

Taxus baccata 'Dovastonii Aurea'
Z6 ‡ 10–15ft (3–5m) ↔ 6ft (2m), female tree with a spreading, tiered form on distinctively drooping shoots

TEUCRIUM
Germander

GROWN FOR THEIR AROMATIC FOLIAGE and attractive summer flowers, these small evergreen and deciduous shrubs are part of a large group that also includes nonwoody plants. The leaves are often gray-green with silvery undersides, and the flowers are tubular or bell-shaped, in shades of pink, yellow, or blue, and are borne in clusters in summer. A sheltered border or a sunny wall will be necessary in colder areas, but wall germanders (*Teucrium chamaedrys*) make good hedging and edging plants in milder regions. Grow with other summer-flowering shrubs that enjoy the same conditions, such as lavenders (*Lavandula, see p.80*), artemisias (*see p.25*), and rosemary (*Rosmarinus, see p.114*) for an aromatic mix.

Cultivation Grow in well-drained soil that is slightly alkaline; the smaller species require very sharply drained soil. Position in full sun. **Trim back** growth to maintain a good shape in spring or late summer, after flowering. **Take** softwood cuttings in early summer, or semiripe cuttings in late summer, rooting both in a heated propagator (*see p.394*). Overwinter young plants in frost-free conditions.

THUJA
Arborvitae

THESE CONIFERS, BOTH LARGE AND SMALL, make handsome specimen trees, and also hedges because they stand up well to clipping. They have flattened sprays of scaly, usually aromatic foliage. The white cedar, *Thuja occidentalis* (Z3) is a rounded tree that can reach 70ft (20m), with billowing branches, peeling, orange-brown bark, and apple-scented leaves. It has many different forms, and widely varying colors and sizes. 'Caespitosa', for example, is cushionlike and slow-growing, reaching only 12in (30cm) high, suitable for a rock garden. *T. plicata* (Z7) is a popular hedge, but otherwise suitable only for large gardens. It also has a range of smaller forms, like blue-green 'Hillieri', growing to just 6ft (2m).

Cultivation Grow in deep, moist but well-drained soil. Position in full sun, with shelter from cold, drying winds. **Trim** hedging in spring and late summer. **Sow** seed (*see pp.391–392*) in late winter in containers in a cold frame or take semiripe cuttings (*see p.394*) in late summer. Prone to aphids (*see pp.398–399*), bagworms, and scale insects.

THYMUS
Thyme

‡ to 1ft (30cm)
↔ to 2ft (60cm)

LOW-GROWING EVERGREEN shrubs with small, aromatic leaves and pretty flowers, thymes attract bees and other beneficial insects into the garden. They produce clusters of tiny pink, purple, or white flowers during summer. They do not like wet feet, so protect from winter moisture. Thymes can be grown with border plants, other decorative herbs such as lavenders (*Lavandula, see p.80*), and chives. They are ideal for the front or edges of a bed, and mat-forming types can be planted in crevices between paving, where stepping on them will release the scent from the foliage. In containers, perhaps with other herbs, they will trail over the edge attractively. The Canadian hardiness zone ranges from 4–7b.

Cultivation Grow in neutral to alkaline soil that is well-drained. Position in full sun. **Trim back** after flowering to keep the plants compact. **Sow** seed (*see pp.391–392*) in a container in a cold frame in spring or divide plants (*see p.395*) in spring. **Take** softwood cuttings (*see p.394*) in mid- to late summer.

Teucrium polium
Z8 ‡↔ 12in (30cm), mound-forming and deciduous, this species flowers abundantly in summer

① *occidentalis* 'Rheingold' ‡ 3–6ft (1–2m) ↔ to 3–4ft (1–1.2m), yellow leaves are tinted pink when young ② *plicata* (Western red cedar) ‡ 70–120ft (20–35m) ↔ 20–30ft (6–9m)

① *doerfleri* 'Bressingham' ‡ 4in (10cm) ② 'Doone Valley' ‡ 5in (13cm) ③ 'Peter Davis' ‡ 6in (15cm) ④ *pulegioides* 'Bertram Anderson' ‡ to 12in (30cm)

TILIA
Linden

LARGE, STATELY, DECIDUOUS trees, lindens are grown for their habit, foliage, and scented flowers. All have broadly oval to rounded, bright or dark green leaves that turn yellow in autumn. From midsummer on, they produce hanging clusters of creamy white or pale yellow flowers. These attract pollinating insects, bees in particular, into the garden. They are followed by dry fruits that are nutlike in appearance but are not edible. As the trees age, the silver-gray bark becomes fissured. Lindens can be used as specimen trees, but you need a spacious garden to accommodate one.

Cultivation Grow in moist, but well-drained soil; limes prefer alkaline or neutral soil, but will tolerate acid soils. Avoid wet sites or very dry conditions, and sites exposed to strong, cold winds. Position in full sun or partial shade. **Prune** in late winter or early spring, cutting out any crossing or misplaced shoots that spoil the shape of young trees. **Keep** seed in cold conditions for 3–5 months before sowing in containers in a cold frame in spring (*see pp.391–392*). **Aphids** attack but cannot harm lindens, but the sticky honeydew they excrete can be a nuisance as it rains from the tree in summer: do not plant lindens where they will overhang paths or parked cars.

Tilia henryana
Z7 ‡↔ to 80ft (25m), a spreading tree, leaves red-tinged when young, flowering in late summer to early autumn

Tilia oliveri
Z7 ‡50ft (15m) ↔ 30ft (10m), flowering in midsummer, this species is less troubled by aphids than many lindens

Tilia platyphyllos (Large-leaved linden)
Z5 ‡100ft (30m) ↔ 70ft (20m), a broad column of a tree, with leaves up to 6in (15cm) long, flowers in midsummer

TRACHYCARPUS
Fan palm

THESE EVERGREEN PALMS have dark green leaves made up of many pointed segments joined in a fan shape. They usually form a strong single main stem, as in the Chusan palm *Trachycarpus fortunei*, which is the most widely seen in gardens. Small yellow flowers are borne in summer in large, hanging clusters, which emerge from close to the bases of the leaves. Male and female flowers are borne on separate plants in early summer: if they are grown together, female plants produce round, blue-black fruits. Superb feature plants, Chusan palms can be grown in large containers in cold areas and brought into frost-free conditions for the winter. Grow among bamboos and ornamental grasses (*see pp.340–355*) or with ferns (*see pp.356–365*) in a sheltered courtyard.

Cultivation Grow in well-drained, fertile soil. Position in full sun or partial shade with shelter from cold, drying winds. **Pruning** is unnecessary, but trim off dead leaves (do not cut close to the trunk). **Sow** seed (*see pp.391–393*) in spring or autumn at 75°F (24°C).

Trachycarpus fortunei (Chusan palm, windmill palm)
Z7b ‡to 70ft (20m) ↔ 8ft (2.5m), seldom reaches this height in temperate gardens, generally remaining a small tree

TSUGA
Hemlock

A GRACEFUL FORM, USUALLY BROADLY conical and made up of tiers of sweeping branches, is the main attraction of these evergreen conifers. They come in almost every size you can imagine from 12in (30cm) to 100ft (30m) tall, with needlelike leaves that vary in color from bright green to blue-gray to silvery gray (often flashing pure white underneath), so there should be one to suit almost every yard or garden. In addition, *Tsuga heterophylla* (Z6), the Western hemlock, makes a fine hedge. All hemlocks grow well in shade. Male and female flowers appear in separate clusters on the same tree, and the small, hanging cones ripen in the same year as they are produced.

Cultivation Grow in moist but well-drained, preferably neutral to slightly acid soil, enriched with well-rotted organic matter on planting. Position in sun or partial shade with shelter from cold, drying winds. **Pruning** is unnecessary, as for most conifers, unless damaged growth needs to be removed. Trim hedges from early to late summer. **Sow** seed (*see pp.391–392*) in containers in a cold frame in spring or take semiripe cuttings (*see p.394*) in late summer or early autumn.

Tsuga canadensis
Z4 ‡ to 80ft (25m) ↔ to 30ft (10m), the best choice if your soil tends to be alkaline, this tree has many smaller cultivars

ULEX
Furze, Gorse

EVERGREEN AND PRICKLY, gorse is ideal for a tough barrier hedge. *Ulex europaeus* is an upright, rounded to bushy shrub with spine-tipped green shoots, and even the leaves are reduced to rigid spines, making it almost impossible to penetrate. The pealike, bright yellow blooms have a coconut-like scent, bringing a surprisingly exotic element to the spring garden. The equally spiny dwarf gorse, *U. gallii* (T min. 35°F/2°C), is more spreading in shape, reaching only 6ft (2m), and flowers from late summer. Both will suit a hot border or a sunny, sloping site, where little else will grow apart from other vigorous, drought-tolerant shrubs. Gorse is highly invasive in British Columbia.

Cultivation Grow in poor, sandy, acid to neutral, well-drained soil; plants may become very leggy on rich, fertile soils. Position in full sun. **Cut back** flowered shoots to within 1in (2.5cm) of old growth after flowering or in midspring every two or three years. **Take** semiripe cuttings in summer (*see p.394*).

Ulex europaeus 'Flore Pleno'
Z7 ‡ to 8ft (2.5m) ↔ 6ft (2m), has double flowers and does not produce seed

ULMUS
Elm

IN SPITE OF POPULAR BELIEF, there are several elms that can be grown in countries that have suffered the ravages of Dutch elm disease. These deciduous trees have appealing foliage, which turns golden yellow in autumn, and an attractive habit. They also produce clusters of tiny, red-tinted, bell-shaped flowers, usually in spring but sometimes in autumn, followed by winged green fruits. Larger elms such as *Ulmus pumila* are suitable as specimen trees in larger gardens; they also make classic "punctuation marks" for stretches of shrub borders. *U. × hollandica* 'Jacqueline Hillier' (Z5) is a shrubby elm reaching only 8ft (2.5m), and is also suitable for use as hedging.

Cultivation Grow in any well-drained soil in full sun or partial shade. **Prune out** any crossing or misplaced branches that spoil the shape of the tree in late winter or early spring. **Sow** seed (*see pp.391–392*) in containers outdoors in spring or autumn, or take softwood cuttings (*see p.394*) in summer. While Dutch elm disease is a fatal and incurable problem, the elms suggested here are partially resistant, as are Asian elms such as the Chinese elm *U. parvifolia* and its cultivars.

Ulmus pumila
Z3b ‡ 70–100ft (20–30m) ↔ 40ft (12m), bears tiny, red flowers in early spring and has lance-shaped leaves

FLOWERS, FRUITS, AND FOLIAGE are all valued in this large and widely varying group of evergreen, semievergreen, and deciduous shrubs. The flowers are pink, or pink-flushed white or cream, and in some plants intensely fragrant. They are borne in winter, spring, or summer, often in rounded clusters at the ends of the branches. The red or black berries that follow may also be ornamental; if space allows, grow several plants of the same species together to allow good pollination and a more generous show of berries. On a species such as *Viburnum opulus* (Z2b), the berries help attract wildlife into the garden. The foliage also provides interest. On some viburnums, the leaves are rough-textured, on others smooth and glossy, while many have striking, prominent veins. Most deciduous types color brilliantly in autumn and are usually grown in shrub borders or mixed borders or in woodland settings; *V. macrocephalum* (Z7b) is best grown against a wall, and *V. dentatum* (Z3) can withstand very cold weather. Viburnums run a wide range of Canadian hardiness zones from 2–8.

Cultivation Grow in any soil that is moist but well-drained. Position in full sun or partial shade, and where not hardy, shelter evergreen species from cold, drying winds. **Prune** deciduous species after flowering, lightly trimming shoots that spoil the shape of the shrub. Most deciduous types and *V. tinus* will tolerate hard pruning. Remove misplaced branches or crossing shoots from evergreens in late winter or early spring. **Sow** seed in containers in a cold frame in autumn (*see pp.391–392*), or propagate deciduous species by greenwood cuttings when the stem is a little firmer and darker (*see p.394*). Sooty molds may form on the foliage of *V. tinus* if colonized by whiteflies: control with insecticide if necessary. Remove the affected leaves of plants suffering from leaf spot.

Using viburnums in the garden

In the border *Viburnums are ideal shrubs for hedging or for a mixed border, since many, such as* V. opulus, *have an attractive, naturally rounded habit that requires little or no pruning;* 'Compactum' *is especially neat. Others are more architectural, for instance the tiered* V. plicatum *'Mariesii'.* V. davidii *is a useful evergreen for shade.*

Pinch out tips to keep head compact

As a standard *The evergreen* V. tinus *is suitable for training as a standard; underplanting will add interest beyond the viburnum's own flowering period. Training takes three or four years. Train the main stem to the desired height and pinch out the tip to encourage lots of new sideshoots to form the head. Keep pinching out sideshoots to keep it dense and rounded.*

Any shoots appearing on stem must be rubbed out

① *Viburnum acerifolium* ‡ 3–6ft (1–2m) ↔ 4ft (1.2m), deciduous ② × *bodnantense* 'Charles Lamont' ‡ 10ft (3m) ↔ 6ft (2m), deciduous ③ × *bodnantense* 'Dawn' ‡ 10ft (3m) ↔ 6ft (2m), deciduous ④ × *burkwoodii* ‡↔ 8ft (2.5m), evergreen ⑤ × *burkwoodii* 'Anne Russell' ‡ 6ft (2m) ↔ 5ft (1.5m), evergreen ⑥ × *carlcephalum* ‡↔ 10ft (3m), deciduous ⑦ *carlesii* 'Aurora' ‡↔ 6ft (2m), deciduous ⑧ 'Chesapeake' ‡ 6ft (2m) ↔ 10ft (3m), semievergreen ⑨ *davidii* ↔ 3–5ft

(1–1.5m), evergreen ⑩ *dentatum* ‡↔ 10ft (3m), deciduous ⑪ *farreri* ‡ 10ft (3m) ↔ 8ft (2.5m), deciduous ⑫ × *globosum* 'Jermyns Globe' ‡ 8ft (2.5m) ↔ 10ft (3m), evergreen ⑬ × *juddii* ‡ 4ft (1.2m) ↔ 5ft (1.5m), deciduous ⑭ *macrocephalum* ‡↔ 15ft (5m), evergreen ⑮ *opulus* 'Compactum' ‡↔ 5ft (1.5m), deciduous ⑯ *opulus* 'Xanthocarpum' ‡ 15ft (5m) ↔ 12ft (4m), deciduous ⑰ *plicatum* 'Mariesii' ‡ 10ft (3m) ↔ 12ft (4m), deciduous ⑱ *plicatum* 'Pink

Beauty' ‡ 10ft (3m) ↔ 12ft (4m), deciduous ⑲ 'Pragense' ‡↔ 10ft (3m), evergreen ⑳ *rhytidophyllum* ‡ 15ft (5m) ↔ 12ft (4m), semievergreen ㉑ *sargentii* ‡↔ 10ft (3m), deciduous ㉒ *sieboldii* ‡ 12ft (4m) ↔ 20ft (6m), deciduous ㉓ *tinus* 'Eve Price' ‡↔ 10ft (3m), evergreen ㉔ *tinus* 'Variegatum' ‡↔ 10ft (3m), evergreen

FOR A SHOWY DISPLAY OF FLOWERS in spring or summer, few shrubs are more reliable than weigelas. The flowers, bell- or funnel-shaped, come in shades of ice-cream pink to ruby red and occasionally pure white or yellow. Weigelas are deciduous and most grow to around 5ft (1.5m), making them suitable for even small backyards. They do well in almost any reasonable garden soil and can withstand neglect. If space allows, plant them with other shrubs that flower around the same time, such as potentillas (*see p.99*) or mock oranges (*Philadelphus, see p.93*). Make sure they have room to show off their arching stems.

Cultivation Grow in any fertile, well-drained soil in full sun or partial shade. Variegated types produce the best colored foliage in full sun, golden leaved forms in partial shade. **Cut back** flowered stems after flowering to strong buds or shoots lower down the shrub. Once plants are mature and growth is crowded, cut out an entire old branch or two to encourage new growth from the base. **Take** greenwood cuttings in early summer or semiripe cuttings in midsummer, or try hardwood cuttings from autumn until winter (*see p.394*).

Weigela 'Eva Rathke'
Z5 ↕↔ 5ft (1.5m), compact, upright then cascading shrub, flowers open from ruby buds to pink in late spring and early summer

Weigela florida 'Foliis Purpureis' Z5 ↕ 3ft (1m) ↔ 5ft (1.5m), low, spreading habit, tolerant of pollution, likes a warm, sunny site, flowers in late spring and early summer

Weigela 'Looymansii Aurea'
Z5 ↕↔ 5ft (1.5m), slow-growing, spreading, habit, leaf color best in partial shade, flowers in late spring and early summer

Weigela florida 'Variegata'
Z5 ↕↔ 6–8ft (2–2.5m), large, dense and bushy, tolerant of urban pollution, flowers profusely in late spring and early summer

YUCCA

PERHAPS BEST KNOWN AS A HOUSEPLANT, the yucca makes a spectacular architectural plant for the garden. Yuccas include around 40 evergreen shrubs and trees, all of which come from hot, dry deserts and plains. They usually have a sturdy, upright stem, and with maturity, some spread and become branched. Their swordlike leaves are produced in shades of mid- to dark green or blue-green. A few have cream or yellow edges. Towering spikes of bell-shaped, usually white flowers rise above the leaves in summer and autumn. Use yuccas as dramatic focal points in a border, or in containers on the patio. They grow and flower particularly well in mild coastal areas. Where not hardy, grow in a cool greenhouse.

Cultivation Grow in any well-drained soil in full sun. If growing them in pots, use a soil-based potting mix; water freely during summer and feed with a balanced fertilizer at monthly intervals. **Sow** seed in spring at 55–64°F (13–18°C) (see pp.391–392). **Take** root cuttings in winter (see p.394), or remove rooted suckers (plantlets around the main crown) in spring and replant.

Yucca gloriosa (Spanish dagger)
Z7b ↕ ↔ 6ft (2m), long, blue-green leaves mature to dark green, mature plants flower in late summer

ZAUSCHNERIA
California fuchsia

THIS EXOTIC-LOOKING SHRUB offers spectacular color late in the season when most other plants are past their peak. Evergreen in its native California, it may die back in temperate regions, but should recover. It bears show-stopping, narrow trumpets on the tips of shoots, which appear over a long period in late summer and autumn. California fuchsias thrive in hot, sunny sites with sharp drainage. Rock gardens or dry stone walls are perfect. They can also be planted in a mixed or herbaceous border alongside other late-flowering shrubs and perennials, such as hardy fuchsias (see pp.60–63), rudbeckias (see p.317), asters (see pp.192–193), and sedums (see p.324).

Cultivation Grow in reasonably fertile, well-drained soil in full sun, with shelter from cold, drying winds. **Protect** in winter in cold areas by spreading a layer of organic matter around the crown of the plant to shield from freezing weather. **Sow** seed in a container in a cold frame in spring (see pp.391–392). **Take** cuttings of strong young shoots from the base in spring, treat as softwood cuttings (see p.394), and root in a propagator.

Zauschneria californica
T min. 35°F (2°C) ↕ to 12in (30cm) ↔ 20in (50cm), evergreen or semievergreen, clump-forming

ZELKOVA

THESE STATELY TREES COMBINE a distinctive, upright, then spreading habit with dark green leaves that turn to fiery shades of yellow, orange, and red in autumn. There are about six species in the group; all are deciduous and are often confused with their close relatives, the elms (*Ulmus, see p.125*). They have tiny, green flowers in spring followed by small, green fruits. Zelkovas make handsome specimens for large gardens or open spaces, or to flank wide avenues. Good companions include lindens (*Tilia, see p.124*) and birches (*Betula, see p.28*). For smaller gardens, choose dwarf cultivars of *Z. serrata*, such as 'Goblin', which makes a 3ft (1m) tall, bushy shrub.

Cultivation Grow in deep, fertile soil that is moist but well-drained, in full sun or partial shade. Where not hardy, protect from cold, drying winds. **Prune** young trees in late winter or early spring, removing any branches that are crossing or misplaced and that spoil the shape of the tree (see p.382). **Sow** seed in containers outdoors in autumn (see pp.391–392). **Take** softwood cuttings in summer (see p.394).

Zelkova serrata
Z5b ↕ to 100ft (30m) ↔ 60ft (18m), spreading habit, smooth gray bark peels to show orange patches beneath, rich autumn color

Climbing Plants

using climbers in the garden

When planning what to plant in a border or other area of the garden, do not forget to include some climbers. They add height to a border if grown up a freestanding support or through a tree or shrub. In a small garden where there is little space to grow trees or large shrubs, climbers may be the only way to introduce some height or provide some privacy. Against a wall or fence, they extend the area of foliage and flowers on display and provide a feature or a backdrop that changes with the seasons.

Ways of using climbing plants

Climbers are perfect for covering and adding interest to bare or unsightly features in the garden, such as walls, fences, tree stumps, or outbuildings. Their bright flowers and varied foliage can provide tremendous visual impact, helping to draw the eye upward, and making full use of all the space in the garden while making it appear larger.

Clematis (*see pp.136–139*) and roses (*see pp.150–151*) offer a huge range of flower colors and sizes. Combine two or more climbers for a longer season of interest. For example, evergreen *Clematis cirrhosa* will provide cover all year round but flowers in early spring, so it works well with the pink summer blooms of *Rosa* 'New Dawn'. For scent, grow a honeysuckle (*Lonicera, see p.146*), or for vibrant autumn foliage, try one of the Virginia creepers (*Parthenocissus, see p.148*). If you want an evergreen covering, go for ivies (*Hedera, see p.142*), which are available in a myriad of leaf shapes and colors.

A pergola covered with climbing plants in flower becomes an enticing spot in any garden, and an arbor surrounded by scented plants will be a relaxing haven. Make sure you choose a plant that will suit the size

A frame of wisteria Climbers can be used to emphasise a view, or to lead the eye to a focal point in the garden, such as a statue or an urn. This metal screen is clothed with *Wisteria sinensis*, which produces masses of flowers in early summer that hang down, releasing their scent. The pendent flowers frame the statue on the bench beyond.

of the structure. Climbing roses are a classic choice – rambling roses are usually too large – but grapevines (*Vitis, see p.154*) look good on a large pergola.

If you do not have the space for a pergola or arbor, train a climber up a pillar, obelisk, or a tripod in a border or in a large container to change the pace of the planting and create a focal point. Check the mature size of the climber so that it does not outgrow the support; small or medium-sized climbers, like sweet peas (*Lathyrus odoratus, see p.145*) work well.

Climbers look natural scrambling through large trees or shrubs, perhaps adding color to a conifer. This is a good way of using a climber with a straggly habit, such as any of the *Clematis viticella* cultivars.

If you need a screen for privacy, training a climber up a fence or trellis is a decorative and speedy solution.

For all climbers, use a plant with a well-balanced shape by pruning and training it (*see p.384*). Some woody climbers, especially, bear more blooms if new stems are trained along horizontal supports each year, because this encourages flowering sideshoots.

What is a climbing plant?

The term "climber" refers to plants that in nature grow through host plants by various means to reach the light. Most climbers are perennials: some are woody and are part of the permanent structure of the garden; others are herbaceous, dying down in winter. Some are annuals and must be grown from seed each year. There are also a few evergreen climbers. Climbing plants can be self-clinging twining, scrambling, or trailing.

Self-clinging climbers have aerial roots, or adhesive pads on their shoots, that attach themselves to the surface against which they are growing. Some cling by tendril tips. These climbers do not need training into supports.

Twining climbers twine stems or coil tendrils around the support. Some, such as clematis and tropaeolums (*see p.154*), attach themselves by curling leaf stalks. Scrambling and trailing plants are

usually very vigorous with long stems that need tying into supports to help them climb. Alternatively, they can be left to ramble over walls or banks.

After planting, all climbing plants need encouragement to start climbing. Insert a stake beside the plant, angling it toward the support, and tie the shoots to the stake. Remove the stake once the plant has become established on the support (*see p.390*).

Aerial roots grow out from the stems (here of an ivy) and cling to walls, fences, and trees. If you are growing self-clinging climbers up old walls, make sure that the mortar is sound.

Tendrils Plants such as these passion flowers (*Passiflora*) and sweet peas use tendrils to enable them to climb. These quickly coil around anything they come into contact with.

Twining leaf stalks Twining leaf stalks (here on a clematis) spiral around the support, in a similar way to tendrils. Climbers with a twining habit prefer a permanent structure to grow through.

Planting sites and exposures

Dressing a tree Climbers with aerial roots or a twining habit, like this clematis, are ideal for clothing the trunks of large, mature trees. They provide extra flower power and, as they mature, may twine attractively around the branches.

When planning where to plant a climber, you will need to assess the soil and exposure. The soil at the base of a wall or fence can often be dry because it shelters the ground from most of the rain, an area known as a rain shadow. The same is true at the base of a tree or large shrub. In these situations, incorporate plenty of well-rotted compost into the soil (*see p.377*) to retain moisture before planting. Position the climber 12–18in (30–45cm) from the wall or at the edge of a tree canopy, where the soil should be less dry.

Many hardy climbers will perform well without any protection at all,

withstanding very cold conditions. A brick or stone wall, however, will give some protection from cold weather. This helps tender plants, which thrive in a south-facing exposure. Avoid placing early-flowering plants where they will catch the morning sun: if there is frost when they are in flower, the rapid thawing may damage both buds and flowers.

If the site is cast into shade for much of the day, your choice will be more limited, especially if it is also cold and north-facing, but many ivies and climbing hydrangea (*see p.143*) thrive in such conditions.

Containers

Many climbers, especially herbaceous and smaller, woody types, are happy growing in containers. You could use a container to grow a climber on a patio and train it into a trellis in the same way as for climbers growing in open ground. You could use a freestanding support such as a tripod of stakes or an obelisk in the container so that it can be moved around the garden. Containers are ideal for less hardy plants, such as jasmines. They can be taken into a heated greenhouse or conservatory for the winter.

Be prepared to fertilize and water (*see pp.386–387*) climbers in containers regularly. You may have to water them at least once or twice daily in dry weather.

Sphere made from two wire circles

Stems wound around wire

Quick topiary Make an interesting feature by training a small climber, such as a passion flower or ivy, onto a wire frame inserted into a container – there are ready-made shapes available or you could fashion your own.

ACTINIDIA

THE ATTRACTIONS OF these large, climbing plants are their deciduous foliage and, in warm climates, their flowers and fruits. They will twine through mesh, or taut wires, on a sunny wall. The large, simple leaves of variegated actinidias look like they have been splashed with white, and sometimes pink, paint. The effect is that of huge petals and is as pretty but much longer-lasting than a floral display. White, often scented flowers appear in early summer. These are followed by edible fruits provided that you have a self-fertile cultivar or have planted a male and a female close to each other. The crop needs plenty of sun to set and ripen. *Actinidia deliciosa* (Z7), the kiwi fruit or Chinese gooseberry, is the only species grown commercially.

Cultivation Choose a spot with fertile, well-drained soil in a sunny, sheltered position; full sun will encourage fruiting. **Prune** in late winter to keep within the available space (*see p.384*). **Sow** seed (*see pp.391–392*) in containers in a cold frame in spring or autumn, or take semiripe cuttings (*see p.394*) in late summer.

Actinidia kolomikta
Z3 ‡ 15ft (5m) or more, leaves emerge purple and become striped with broad bands of pink and white as they mature

AKEBIA
Chocolate vine

THE COCOA-COLORED FLOWERS of this small group of twining, woody climbers give them their common name. They hang from the branches in long clusters through early spring and, if the summer is long and hot, are followed by impressive, sausage-shaped fruits that ripen from green to purple. In milder areas, the dark green leaves of the semievergreen *Akebia quinata* do not fall in winter and become tinged purple in the cool weather. Spring interest is provided by the new leaves of the deciduous *A. trifoliata* (Z6), which are a striking bronze. Chocolate vines are splendid plants for a pergola or archway, where the spicy fragrance of the flowers can be enjoyed. They can grow quite large, so provide a sturdy support.

Cultivation Chocolate vines are not very demanding and can be grown in any moist but well-drained soil, in sun or partial shade. **Pruning** is minimal – simply trim back after flowering to keep it under control (*see p.384*). **Sow** seed (*see pp.391–392*) in containers in a cold frame, or on the windowsill, as soon as it is ripe, or take semiripe cuttings (*see p.394*) in summer.

Akebia quinata
Z5b ‡ 30ft (10m), the undersides of the leaves are blue-green and are evergreen in milder climates

AMPELOPSIS

‡ 15–40ft (5–12m)

USING TWISTING TENDRILS, these handsome, deciduous climbers can cling to walls or fences or can be trained over pergolas or old trees. They are grown for their large leaves, which give a fiery display of color in autumn. Variegated cultivars, such as *Ampelopsis glandulosa* 'Elegans' (Z3) are less vigorous than the species, so suit smaller spaces, and the white and pink mottling is a welcome splash of color on an uninteresting wall. In warm areas, following the tiny, late-summer flowers, you may get masses of ornamental pink, blue, black, or orange berries.

Cultivation Grow in any moist but well-drained soil in sun or partial shade. Fruits are more abundant in sun or if the roots are restricted in a container. **Trim** vigorous plants in spring (*see p.384*), making sure that tendrils are kept clear of roof tiles and gutters. **Sow** seed (*see p.391–392*) in a cold frame in autumn, or take softwood cuttings (*see p.394*) in summer.

Ampelopsis glandulosa var. *brevipedunculata*
Z3 ‡ 15ft (5m), the pink or purple berries change color to a clear sky blue as they ripen

BERBERIDOPSIS CORALLINA
Coral plant

THIS IS A TWINING, WOODY perennial. It has long, heart-shaped leaves with tiny spines around the edges, but it is mainly grown for its fuchsialike flowers that hang from the shoots like baubles through summer to early autumn. It is excellent scrambling through a tree, which will provide it with the ideal conditions of some shelter and partial shade. The snowy mespilus (*Amelanchier, see p.22*) or mountain ash (*Sorbus, see p.118*) make good supports since the red flowers of the coral plant bridge the gap between the spring flowers and autumn color of the tree. Alternatively, train it against a shaded, sheltered wall.

Cultivation   Plant in neutral or acidic soil and dig in plenty of well-rotted organic matter. Choose a shady area with shelter from cold winds and protect roots in winter with a thick mulch (*see p.388*). **Tie in** young shoots to their support (*see p.380*). **Trim** in late winter or early spring if it becomes too big (*see p.334*). **Sow** seed (*see pp.391–392*) in a cold frame in spring; root semiripe cuttings (*see p.394*) in late summer; or layer shoots (*see p.395*) in autumn.

CAMPSIS
Trumpet creeper, Trumpet vine

‡30fy (10m)

THE ONLY TWO CAMPSIS, *Campsis radicans* (Z5b) and *C. grandiflora* (Z7b), have been crossed to produce the popular hybrid *C. × tagliabuana*. From late summer until autumn, they produce exotic flowers, usually in shades of yellow, orange, or red, in small clusters among dark green leaves. These woody-stemmed climbers cling with aerial roots, although they will need some extra support. They are impressive growing up a wall, fence, or pergola, or through a large tree.

Cultivation   Grow in moist but well-drained soil. Where marginally hardy, they are best grown against a warm, sunny wall. **Fan out** the young stems to provide good coverage of the support and cut away misplaced shoots; it may take 2–3 years to establish a main framework of branches. You will need to tie in young shoots until the aerial roots take firm hold (*see p.380*). Once the framework is in place, prune sideshoots back to two or three buds every year, after flowering. Keep clear of roofs and gutters. **Sow** seed (*see pp.391–392*) in containers in autumn or root semiripe cuttings in summer (*see p.394*).

CELASTRUS
Bittersweet Staff vine

BITTERSWEET COMES INTO ITS OWN in autumn. When many other plants are starting to die down, it is beaded with yellow berries that split open when they are ripe to reveal pink or red seeds within, rather like tiny pomegranates. They follow discreet clusters of green flowers, but the males and females are on separate vines so you need more than one plant for fruit unless you choose a self-fertile cultivar. The most commonly cultivated are the woody, deciduous climbers: American bittersweet (*Celastrus scandens*) and Oriental bittersweet (*C. orbiculatus* Z4) and its cultivars. Oriental bittersweet can be highly invasive, and its growth is discouraged in many areas. Train *C. scandens* against a wall, fence, or pergola.

Cultivation   Bittersweet prefers full sun, but will tolerate partial shade, in any well-drained soil. It needs a strong support, so if you want to grow it through a tree choose one at least 30ft (10m) tall. **Prune** in late winter or early spring to keep it within its space (*see p.384*). **Sow** seed (*see p.391–392*) as soon as it is ripe or in spring, or take semiripe cuttings in summer (*see p.394*).

Berberidopsis corallina
Z8 ‡15ft (5m), widely available climber

Campsis × tagliabuana 'Madame Galen'
Z5b ‡30ft (10m), by far the most widely available and popular of this group of climbers

Celastrus scandens (American bittersweet)
Z3 ‡30ft (10m), bears yellow-orange fruits with red seeds

Old man's beard, Traveler's joy, Virgin's bower

see also p.214

OFTEN KNOWN AS THE QUEEN OF CLIMBERS, the climbing clematis have been favorites of gardeners for many years because of their beautiful flowers. There are hundreds to choose from with varied habits, from clump-forming herbaceous plants to evergreen scramblers up to 30ft (15m) or more that will clothe large trees. Many more are less vigorous and perfectly suited to growing on fences or through shrubs. The flowers vary widely in size, shape, and hue – from large, flat flowers to small nodding bells in soft and bold shades of white, gold, orange, and blue to pinks and scarlets, often with a contrasting boss of anthers. The foliage also varies but is delicately shaped. Some, such as *Clematis tangutica* (Z7), have attractive, silky seedheads. Clematis run the range of Canadian hardiness zones from 1–7.

Cultivation Clematis are divided into groups for pruning (*see below*), but other cultivation needs are similar for all types. **Grow** clematis in well cultivated soil with plenty of organic matter, in sun or partial shade. Climbers should be planted deeply, with the top of the rootball 3in (8cm) below the soil surface to help overcome clematis wilt, a disease that causes the plant to die back suddenly to soil level. If this happens, the stems may shoot again from buds below the surface. **Tie in** a newly planted clematis to a cane and angle it toward the permanent support to encourage the plant to cling. **Sow** seed of species when they are ripe in autumn (*see pp.391–393*) and place in a cold frame. **Take** softwood cuttings in spring or semiripe cuttings in summer (*see p.395*).

Pruning group 1

This group produces flowers in spring from the previous year's growth. The flowers are usually bell-shaped or single and ¾–2in (2–5cm) long or saucer-shaped and 1½–2in (4–5cm) across. Prune after flowering to remove dead or damaged shoots; shorten others to the allotted space. This encourages new growth in summer that will bear flowers in the following spring. Once established, vigorous montana types need regular pruning only to stop them outgrowing their space. Cut back overgrown plants hard, then leave for at least three years.

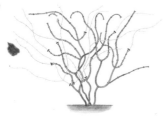

Pruning group 2

These large-flowered hybrids flower in late spring and early summer on sideshoots produced in the previous year. They are deciduous. The flowers are held upright and may be single, semidouble, or fully double, 4–8in (10–20cm) across, and are mostly saucer-shaped. In late winter or early spring, prune out any weak or damaged shoots back to their point of growth, or cut out entire shoots if they are damaged. It may be easier on a large plant to cut the sideshoots back by going over the plant with a pair of garden shears, but make sure that all the dead wood has been removed.

Pruning group 3

All the clematis in this group bear flowers on the current year's wood. The large-flowered hybrids are deciduous with single, saucer-shaped flowers, 3–6in (8–15cm) across, in summer and early autumn. Species and small-flowered hybrids flower from summer to late autumn. Their blooms may be single or double, star- or bell-shaped, or tubular and ½–4in (1–10cm) across. Prune this group in late winter or early spring by cutting all the stems back to about 12in (30cm) above the ground, just above a pair of healthy buds. Make sure that any dead growth is completely cut out.

① *Clematis* 'Abundance' ‡10ft (3m) ↔ 3ft (1m), group 3 ② 'Alba Luxurians' ‡5ft (1.5m) ↔ 3ft (1m), group 3 ③ *alpina* ‡6–10ft (2–3m) ↔ 5ft (1.5m), group 1, fluffy seedheads ④ *alpina* 'Frances Rivis' ‡6–10ft (2–3m) ↔ 5ft (1.5m), group 1, fluffy seedheads ⑤ *armandii* ‡10–15ft (3–5m) ↔ 6–10ft (2–3m), group 1, evergreen ⑥ 'Ascotiensis' ‡10–12ft (3–4m) ↔ 3ft (1m), group 3 ⑦ 'Beauty of Worcester' ‡8ft (2.5m) ↔ 3ft (1m), group 2 ⑧ 'Bees' Jubilee' ‡8ft (2.5m) ↔ 3ft

(1m), group 2, partial shade ⑨ 'Bill MacKenzie' ‡22ft (7m) ↔ 6–10ft (2–3m), group 3, fluffy seedheads ⑩ *cirrhosa* ‡8ft (2.5m) ↔ 5ft (1 5m), group 1, evergreen, silky seedheads ⑪ 'Comtesse de Bouchaud' ‡6–10ft (2–3m) ↔ 3ft (1m), group 3 ⑫ 'Doctor Ruppel' ‡8ft (2.5m) ↔ 3ft (1m), group 2 ⑬ 'Duchess of Albany' ‡8ft (2.5m) ↔ 3ft (1m), group 3 ⑭ 'Elsa Späth' ‡6–10ft (2–3m) ↔ 3ft (1m), group 2 ⑮ 'Etoile Rose' ‡8ft (2.5m) ↔ 3ft (1m), group 3 ⑯ 'Etoile Violette' ‡10–15ft (3–5m)

↔ 5ft (1.5m), group 3 ⑰ *flammula* ‡20ft (6m) ↔ 3ft (1m), group 3, prefers sheltered sun ⑱ *florida* var. *sieboldiana* ‡8ft (2.5m) ↔ good for containers, group 2 ⑲ 'Gravetye Beauty' ‡8ft (2.5m) ↔ 3ft (1m), group 3 ⑳ 'Hagley Hybrid' ‡6ft (2m) ↔ 3ft (1m), group 3, fades in sun ㉑ 'Henryi' ‡10ft (3m) ↔ 3ft (1m) group 2 ㉒ 'H.F. Young' ‡8ft (2.5m) ↔ 3ft (1m), group 2 ㉓ 'Huldine' ‡15ft (5m) ↔ 6ft (2m), group 3

24 *Clematis* 'Hybrida Sieboldii' ‡10ft (3m), group 2, prefers full sun 25 'Jackmanii' ‡10ft (3m), group 3 26 'John Warren' ‡10ft (3m), group 2 27 'Kathleen Dunford' ‡8ft (2.5m), group 2 28 'Lasurstern' ‡8ft (2.5m), group 2 29 'Lincoln Star' ‡8ft (2.5m), group 2, flowers fade in full sun 30 *macropetala* ‡10ft (3m), group 1, decorative seedheads 31 *macropetala* 'Markham's Pink' ‡10ft (3m), group 1, decorative seedheads 32 'Madame

Edouard André' ‡8ft (2.5m), group 2 33 'Madame Julia Correvon' ‡10ft (3m), group 3 34 'Minuet' ‡10ft (3m), group 3 35 *montana* ‡15–46ft (5–14m), group 1 36 *montana* f. *grandiflora* ‡10m (30ft), group 1 37 *montana* var. *rubens* ‡10m (30ft), group 1 38 *montana* 'Tetrarose' ‡15ft (5m), group 1 39 'Mrs. George Jackman' ‡8ft (2.5m), group 2 40 'Nelly Moser' ‡10ft (3m), group 2, fades in full sun 41 'Niobe' ‡6–10ft (2–3m), group 2, fades in full sun

㊷ 'Paul Farges' ‡28ft (9m), group 3 ㊸ 'Perle d'Azur' ‡10ft (3m), group 3 ㊹ 'Proteus' ‡10ft (3m), group 2 ㊺ 'Pruinina' ‡6–10ft (2–3m), group 1, decorative seedheads ㊻ *rehderiana* ‡22ft (7m), group 3 ㊼ 'Richard Pennell' ‡10ft (3m), group 2 ㊽ 'Rouge Cardinal' ‡10ft (3m), group 3, prefers full sun ㊾ *tangutica* ‡20ft (6m), group 3, decorative seedheads ㊿ 'The President' ‡10ft (3m), group 2 ○51 *tibetana* ‡6–10ft (2–3m), group 3, bright yellow, bell-shaped flowers, prefers sun

○52 'Venosa Violacea' ‡10ft (3m), group 3 ○53 'Ville de Lyon' ‡10ft (3m), group 3, best grown through an evergreen shrub, because lower foliage may become scorched ○54 *viticella* 'Purpurea Plena Elegans' ‡10ft (3m), group 3 ○55 'Vyvyan Pennell' ‡10ft (3m), group 2

CLIMBING PLANTS

CLIANTHUS
Glory pea

GROWN FOR THEIR SUMMER FLOWERS, these trailing plants are easily encouraged to climb if they are tied in regularly to their supports. The desert pea (*Clianthus formosus*) is a perennial in warm climates, but it is tender and so best grown as an annual in temperate gardens. It is a good plant for hanging baskets. Lobster claw (*C. puniceus* Z8) is hardy enough to survive a light frost, especially if given the added protection of a warm, south-facing wall and will bring a tropical look to the garden. There are some stunning cultivars available with crimson, rose pink, or pure white flowers.

Cultivation Grow in a container of gritty, soil-based potting mix and move under cover in winter, or outdoors in well-drained, fertile soil. Glory peas need full sun, shelter from cold winds, and a deep, dry, winter mulch (*see p.388*). Even with these precautions, *C. puniceus* may be damaged by winter cold but will often resprout from the base. **Little pruning** is needed trim shoots by no more than one-third, after flowering, only if it becomes necessary. **Sow** seed (*see pp.391–392*) at 64°F (18°C) in spring.

COBAEA

ONLY THE CUP AND SAUCER VINE (*Cobaea scandens*) is commonly cultivated. Although a perennial climber, it is best used as an annual where winters are cold. It has rich green leaves and creamy white, fragrant blooms that become purple as they age. Cultivars that remain white are also available. Grow this lovely plant over an arbor or an archway, where the perfume of the flowers can easily be enjoyed, or train it on a sunny wall or through a small tree. Where not hardy, grow in a cool greenhouse or plant in containers and hanging baskets and let the shoots trail over the rim.

Cultivation Grow in well-drained soil, in a sheltered spot with full sun. **Sow** seed (*see pp.391–392*) at 64°F (18°C) in spring, and plant out when the threat of frost has passed, or root softwood cuttings (*see p.394*) in summer.

DICENTRA

see also p.229

‡3ft (1m)

THESE CLIMBING PERENNIALS have unusual flowers that appear on the scrambling, slender stems throughout summer. In common with the nonclimbing, spreading or clump-forming dicentras, the flowers look as if they have been gently inflated. There are two commonly available climbing species: *Dicentra macrocapnos*, which has ferny foliage and yellow flowers into late autumn, and *D. scandens*, which has deeply lobed, mid-green leaves. They are excellent plants for walls or fences at the back of a border, or for training through a shrub or a hedge.

Cultivation Dicentras prefer moist, slightly alkaline, humus-rich soil and partial shade. They are perfect for a woodland garden or other shady spot, but will tolerate more sun in reliably damp soil. **Sow** seed (*see pp.391–392*) in containers in a cold frame as soon as it is ripe, or wait until spring. **Slugs** (*see p.398*) may leave large holes in the leaves, so it is worth protecting young plants against them.

Clianthus formosus (Desert pea)
T min. 45–50°F (7–10°C) ‡8in (20cm) ↔ 3ft (1m)

Cobaea scandens (Cathedral bells, Cup and saucer vine)
T min. 41°F (5°C) ‡30–70ft (10–20m), less if grown as an annual

Dicentra scandens (Climbing Bleeding Heart)
Z6b ‡3ft (1m), flowers may also be white or tipped with pink

ECCREMOCARPUS SCABER
Chilean glory flower

THIS FAST-GROWING, EVERGREEN climber has several cultivars. From late spring until autumn, spectacular clusters of exotic, brightly colored flowers appear. They are eye-catching clambering up a fence or wall, through a large shrub, or over an arch. The effect is especially striking when combined with other climbing plants such as morning glories (*Ipomoea, see p.142*). The light green, or gray-tinted foliage is composed of neat leaflets. Where not hardy, Chilean glory flowers are best used as annuals or as container plants, but in warm climates they can be grown as short-lived perennials.

Cultivation Grow in fertile, well-drained soil in a sunny position, or in a container of soil-based potting mix to be moved under cover in winter. **Tie in** to its support regularly (*see p.380*) until the tendrils get a firm grip. **Trim** plants grown as a perennials in early spring to fit the available space (*see p.384*). **Sow** seed (*see pp.391–392*) at 55–61°F (13–16°C) in late winter or early spring or root softwood cuttings (*see p.394*) in spring or summer in a propagator.

***Eccremocarpus scaber* Anglia Hybrids**
T min. 45°F (7°C) ↕ 10–15ft (3–5m), these cultivars are a mixed selection with red, pink, orange, or yellow flowers

FALLOPIA

THESE ENTHUSIASTIC VINES CAN GROW very fast, so if you have a vast expanse of bare wall, or an unsightly structure that needs cover quickly, they are a good choice. Before you buy, however, make sure that you have room to grow this rampant climber; in too small an area it will need constant pruning just to keep it under control. If you do have the space, these deciduous, woody plants have attractive leaves and, from late summer until autumn, bear large clusters of tiny, white flowers followed by pinkish white fruits. All fallopias are vigorous but *Fallopia japonica*, also known as Japanese knotweed, is a pernicious weed. Its underground roots can spread very quickly to take over your own, and your neighbor's, garden.

Cultivation Grow in almost any soil, in full sun or partial shade, with a strong, long-lasting support. **Trim** in early spring if it gets too big (*see p.384*). **Sow** seed (*see pp.391–392*) in containers in a cold frame in spring, or as soon as it is ripe. **Root** semiripe cuttings in summer or hardwood cuttings in autumn (*see p.394*).

Fallopia baldschuanica (Mile-a-minute plant, Russian vine)
Z5b ↕ 40ft (12m), similar to the equally popular *F. aubertii*

GELSEMIUM SEMPERVIRENS
Carolina jasmine, Carolina yellow jessamine

↕ 10–20ft (3–6m)

OF THESE TWINING PERENNIALS, *Gelsemium sempervirens* is the only common ornamental. It has handsome, glossy leaves and from spring to late summer clear yellow, perfumed flowers. Where not hardy, it needs the protection of a warm wall, or it can be grown in a container or in a temperate greenhouse. In warmer areas, it is lovely climbing over a pergola or arch, beneath which you can linger to enjoy the sweet fragrance of the flowers. All parts of the plant are toxic and have been used historically as a poison.

Cultivation Grow in well-drained soil, in full sun or semishade, with shelter from cold, drying winds. **Plant** in containers in cooler areas so it is easy to move under cover in winter. Use a soil-based potting mix and repot or top-dress annually. **Thin out** the flowered stems when they have faded. **Sow** seed (*see p.391–392*) at 55–64°F (13–18°C) in spring, or take semiripe cuttings (*see p.394*) in summer.

Gelsemium sempervirens
Z7b ↕ 10–20ft (3–6m); flower clusters 2–3in (5–8cm) across

HEDERA

Ivy

see also p.69

IVY LEAVES COME IN MANY SHAPES and shades of green, some with bright gold or silver variegation that will cheer up a dull corner. Young ivies creep flat against surfaces using aerial roots, but at maturity they become treelike, with large, bushy growths high in the air that provide a refuge for wildlife. In summer, mature ivies bear tiny flowers, followed by attractive, globe-shaped heads of black, orange, or yellow berries. These woody, evergreen climbers vary in size, hardiness, and shade tolerance, so there is bound to be one suited to your garden. Generally, *Hedera helix* and its cultivars grow well in Z5b. Grow them up a wall or tree, or let them scramble as groundcover. Contrary to popular belief, ivies do not damage walls unless there are already cracks in the mortar.

Cultivation Ivies tolerate most soils, especially alkaline, and most positions, but all grow best in fertile soil enriched with well-rotted compost. Green-leaved types thrive in shade; variegated cultivars prefer more light and some shelter from cold winds. **Prune** to fit the available space at any time of year (*see p.384*); keep clear of roofs and gutters. **Root** semiripe cuttings in summer (*see p.394*).

Hedera helix 'Anne Marie'
‡4ft (1.2m), a small cultivar best used on a sheltered wall or as a houseplant, leaves are 1½–2½in (4–6cm) across

Hedera hibernica (Atlantic ivy)
‡30ft (10m), this vigorous climber can provide fast groundcover or clothe a wall, leaves are 2–3in (5–8cm) across

Hedera helix 'Buttercup'
‡6ft (2m), compact ivy, butter yellow in sun – a good contrast for coppery bark (*see inset*), leaves 2½in (6cm) or more across

Hedera helix 'Pedata' (Bird's foot ivy)
‡12ft (4m), excellent wallcover ivy, leaves are 1½–2½in (4–6cm) across

Hedera colchica 'Dentata Variegata'
Z7 ‡15ft (5m), use as groundcover or train up a wall, leaves are 6in
(15cm) across

HUMULUS
Hops

HOPS ARE TWINING, PERENNIAL climbers, with soft, hairy shoots that die down in winter. They are admired for their large, ornamental leaves, which are often patterned with white or yellow. In summer, male and female flowers are borne on separate plants; males in clusters and females in unusual spikes that resemble papery, green pinecones. The female hop flowers are used in brewing beer, and also in fresh or dried flower arrangements. Hops are vigorous but not rampant, perfect for any area if provided with a trellis, wires, or mesh to wind around, or for growing through a large shrub or small tree.

Cultivation Grow in moist, well-drained soil in sun or partial shade. **Root** softwood cuttings in spring (*see p.394*). **Cut back** dead stems in winter, or in spring in cold areas. **If your hops look floppy,** and after watering and feeding it fails to perk up, remove a little of the outer bark at the base of one of the stems. If you see brown stripes in the tissue beneath remove the entire plant, and the soil around its roots, because it is likely to have verticillium wilt: this action will prevent the disease from spreading. If the stem seems healthy, cut it off cleanly below the wound and stay on the lookout for a possible cause.

HYDRANGEA
Climbing hydrangea

see also
pp.72–73

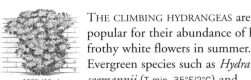

‡50ft (15m)

THE CLIMBING HYDRANGEAS are popular for their abundance of huge, frothy white flowers in summer. Evergreen species such as *Hydrangea seemannii* (T min. 35°F/2°C) and *H. serratifolia* (T min. 35°F/2°C) are great year-round plants in warm regions, with large, leathery leaves. The deciduous *H. anomala* subsp. *petiolaris* (Z5) is commonly grown in cooler areas and has the bonus of leaves that turn golden yellow in autumn. These sturdy plants will cling, using aerial roots, to large areas of wall, fence, or even old tree stumps. Once established, they grow quickly to provide invaluable cover, particularly on a shady, north- or east-facing wall where little else can thrive.

Cultivation Grow in any moist, well-drained soil in sun or shade. **Prune** to fit space after flowering (*see p.384*). **Root** softwood cuttings in early summer or hardwood cuttings in autumn (*see p.394*) or layer in spring (*see p.395*). **Mildew** (*see p.398*) and gray mold (botrytis) can be troublesome: cut back affected parts to healthy-looking wood and dispose of the trimmings, but not onto the compost pile.

Hedera helix 'Little Diamond'
‡12in (30cm), a tiny, slow-growing ivy, perfect for a rock garden,
leaves are 1½–2½in (4–6cm) across

Humulus lupulus 'Aureus' (Golden hops)
Z4 ‡20ft (6m), the golden leaves are brightest in full sun,
fragrant flowers

LAYERING SHOOTS Peg a shoot to the ground, aerial roots down, and lightly cover 6in (15cm) of the stem with soil. When rooted, cut from the parent and plant in its new position.

Hydrangea anomala subsp. *petiolaris*
‡50ft (15m), the flower heads may reach an impressive 10in
(25cm) across

IPOMOEA

Morning glory

THERE ARE ANNUAL AND PERENNIAL trailing and twining morning glories, but most are grown as annuals. Where temperatures dip below 45ºF (7ºC), grow perennial or shrubby species in a warm or temperate greenhouse. They are mostly fast-growing, twining climbers or trailing plants, with abundant trumpet- or tube-shaped flowers in reds, purples, whites, and pinks. The mid- to deep-green leaves vary in shape. Train it through a trellis in a sunny site, or up an obelisk with other climbers such as sweet peas (*Lathyrus, see facing page*) for a fine floral show. They can also be used to liven up shrubs that do not flower in summer.

Cultivation Grow in well-drained soil in full sun with shelter from cold, drying winds. **Tie** stems into their supports in the early stages of growth (*see p.380*). **Trim** perennials in spring only if they are getting too big (*see p.384*). **Sow** seed (*see pp.391–392*) singly in pots at 64ºF (18ºC) in spring. Chip each seed coat or soak in water for 24 hours before sowing to ensure germination.

① *lobata* ‡6–15ft (2–5m), perennial, grown as an annual
② *purpurea* ‡10ft (3m), annual ③ *tricolor* 'Heavenly Blue'
‡12ft (4m), annual ④ *tricolor* 'Milky Way' ‡12ft (4m), annual

JASMINUM

Jasmine, Jessamine

see also p.76

‡6–40ft (2–12m)

MANY OF THE TWINING, climbing jasmines are tender but are worth growing because of their honeyed, fragrant, usually yellow or white flowers. They are lovely in any location, but in cool climates grow jasmines in a sheltered position; grow half-hardy species as houseplants, and tender species in a warm or temperate greenhouse. The common jasmine (*Jasminum officinale* Z7), *J. beesianum* (T min. 45ºF/7ºC) and *J.* × *stephanense* (T min. 35ºF/2ºC) all bear heavily perfumed flowers in summer. Common jasmine is vigorous and may smother a small arch or a trellis.

Cultivation Grow jasmines in fertile, well-drained soil in full sun, or in containers using a soil-based potting mix. **Prune** *J. mesnyi* after flowering: cut back flowered shoots to two or three buds from the old wood. **Thin out** the old and flowered shoots from *J. officinale*; thin other jasmines after flowering (*see p.384*). **Root** cuttings in summer (*see p.394*).

Jasminum mesnyi (Primrose jasmine)
T min. 35ºF (2ºC) ‡10ft (3m) ↔ 3–6ft (1–2m), habit is naturally that of an open shrub, but it is usually trained as a climber

LAPAGERIA ROSEA

Chilean bellflower

‡15ft (5m)

THE CHILEAN BELLFLOWER is a woody, twining climber, with leathery, dark green leaves. It is prized for its exotic, fleshy, raspberry red flowers, borne in summer and late autumn. There are also luscious white and pink cultivars available. It is native to dense forest and in cultivation prefers a similarly still, shady environment. A sheltered site, close to the house for extra warmth but away from full sun, is perfect. In cold areas, the Chilean bellflower is best grown in a container and moved under cover in winter.

Cultivation Grow in well-drained, slightly acidic soil improved with plenty of well-rotted organic matter. In containers, use an acidic soil mix with added sharp sand. **Mulch** thickly over the rooting area through the winter (*see p.388*), especially in cool climates. **Trim** over-long stems to fit the available space (*see p.384*) if needed, but leave unpruned if at all possible. **Sow** seed (*see pp.391–392*) at 55–64ºF (13–18ºC) in spring, or root semiripe cuttings (*see p.394*) in summer.

Lapageria rosea
T min. 45ºF (7ºC) ‡15ft (5m), spreads by suckers, pink to red flowers born from summer to late autumn

LATHYRUS ODORATUS
Sweet pea

see also
p.269

‡6–8ft (2–2.5m)

Sweet peas are the most familiar climbers in this group, prized for their showy, usually fragrant flowers in opulent shades of red, pink, mauve, blue, and white. If they are deadheaded regularly and have the nutrients from rich soil or regular fertilizing, they will bloom from summer until late autumn. The climbers of this group are very versatile: they cling with tendrils that corkscrew tightly around almost any support. Train them on trellises, netting, wires, obelisks, through shrubs, or over an arch. *Lathyrus odoratus* is an annual, but there are other perennial peas, also with sweet-smelling flowers, such as *Lathyrus latifolius* (Z5).

Cultivation Grow in fertile soil in full sun or dappled shade. Dig lots of well-rotted organic matter into the ground. Fertilize plants every two weeks (*see p.386*). **Sow** seed (*see pp.391–393*) in a deep, preferably bottomless pots or sweet peas tubes in a cold frame, or in situ under cloches, in early spring. For earlier flowers, sow in a cold frame in autumn. **Deadhead** regularly (*see p.390*) or flowering will cease. **Slugs**, snails, and aphids (*see p.398*) are common.

Lathyrus odoratus 'Bridget'
‡6ft (2m) or more, sweetly scented

Lathyrus odoratus 'Nimbus'
‡2m (6ft) or more, delicately scented

SOWING SEED in tube pots avoids root disturbance; sow singly and cover with ½in (1cm) of soil mix almost to the rim; plant out the whole pot.

Lathyrus odoratus 'Mars'
‡6ft (2m) or more, sweetly scented. All *Lathyrus odoratus* are annuals.

Lathyrus odoratus 'Anniversary'
‡6ft (2m) or more, gently scented

Lathyrus odoratus 'Midnight'
‡6ft (2m) or more, lightly scented

Honeysuckle

see also
p.84

CLIMBING PLANTS

A CLASSIC COTTAGE-GARDEN FAVORITE, honeysuckles are valued for their delicate flowers, which are often fragrant enough to perfume the entire garden. The twining climbers are especially popular. They are very adaptable and can be trained on walls, through large shrubs or trees, or used as spreading groundcover. They are particularly lovely around a seating area where the scent can be enjoyed while you relax. There are many available that produce flowers in many shades. Snowy white and double-cream are traditional, but there are exotic, rich scarlet, coral, and gold honeysuckles available. The red or black berries can cause a slight stomach upset if they are eaten. There are also shrubby species.

Cultivation Grow in any moist but well-drained soil, in full sun or preferably partial shade, ideally with the roots in shade. **Prune** to fit the available space in early spring or after flowering. The easiest way to tidy up larger specimens is to cut them with a hedgetrimmer (*see p.384*). **Sow** seed (*see pp.391–392*) in a cold frame as soon as it is ripe. **Aphids** (*see p.398*) are fond of climbing honeysuckles.

Lonicera japonica 'Halliana'
Z6 ‡ 30ft (10m), vigorous evergreen or semievergreen, flowers from late spring to late summer, red berries in autumn

Lonicera × americana
Z6 ‡ 22ft (7m), deciduous, very fragrant flowers in summer and early autumn, red berries in autumn

Lonicera × brownii 'Dropmore Scarlet'
Z2b ‡ 12ft (4m), compact, deciduous or semievergreen, slightly fragrant flowers for a long period in summer, red berries in autumn, best grown in partial shade

TRAINING HONEYSUCKLE
Encourage the soft new shoots to climb by winding them around their support, here wires stretched up a wooden pergola post.

Lonicera × tellmanniana
Z4b ‡ 15ft (5m), deciduous, flowers from late spring to midsummer, leaves are blue-white beneath

Lonicera periclymenum 'Serotina'
Z4b ‡22ft (7m), deciduous, very fragrant flowers in mid- and late summer, red berries

LOPHOSPERMUM

THIS SMALL GROUP OF PERENNIAL CLIMBERS includes evergreen and deciduous plants. Their trumpet-shaped flowers are produced for a long period through the summer and autumn. The rose pink, or occasionally white or purple, blooms are shown off beautifully by the velvety, fresh green leaves. They cling to their support using twining leafstalks, and in warm areas are wonderful for training through shrubs and trees, or up an obelisk or trellis. They will also scramble without support as groundcover. In temperate climates, the tender species are best grown as annuals, or planted in containers and then moved under cover during the winter.

Cultivation Plant in full sun. The soil should be moist but well drained: dig some sharp sand into the planting area to improve drainage on heavy soils (*see p.377*). In a container, it is a good idea to use standard soil-based potting mix with added sharp sand. **Propagate** with seed (*see pp.391–393*) sown at 66–75°F (19–24°C) in spring, or root semiripe cuttings (*see p.394*) in summer.

‡3–6ft (1–2m)

DELICATE AND SLENDER-STEMMED, this twining climber is a herbaceous perennial with lush, bright green leaves that provide a splendid backdrop for the main attraction: the flowers. They are borne in abundance throughout the summer and autumn and are usually violet, but sometimes purple or white. Plant it so it can wind its way through a trellis, taut wires, or netting attached to any vertical surface. It is grown as an annual in cool climates, but the shorter season means it does not grow to full size; combine it with other climbers to cover a large area and prolong the display.

Cultivation Grow in moist but well-drained soil in light shade, or in sun with some shade at midday. Protect from cold, drying winds. **Deadhead** regularly (*see p.390*), and if growing it as a perennial, remove the dead top growth at the end of the season. **Sow** seed (*see pp.391–393*) at 55–64°F (13–18°C) in spring. Take softwood cuttings (*see p.394*) in spring and root in a propagator.

Lophospermum erubescens (Creeping gloxinia)
T min. 37–41°F (3–5°C) ‡4–10ft (1.2–3m), evergreen

Maurandella antirrhiniflora
T min. 41°F (5°C) ‡3–6ft (1–2m), violet flowers

Lonicera periclymenum 'Graham Thomas'
Z4b ‡22ft (7m), deciduous, very fragrant flowers in mid- and late summer, red berries

PARTHENOCISSUS
Virginia creeper

VIRGINIA CREEPERS CAN CLING strongly to almost any surface using tiny suckers at the end of their tendrils. These deciduous, woody climbers are grown for their attractive leaves that give an amazing, firelike show of color in autumn. The dense foliage has the added bonus of providing a home for a variety of beneficial wildlife. Tiny, summer flowers may be followed by mildly toxic black berries. These are vigorous vines that can be trained to cover walls, fences, and any unsightly garden structures, or can be used to scramble through a large tree. Virginia creepers are easily controlled, but be careful where they climb because the suckers can leave unsightly marks on walls and fences.

Cultivation Grow in fertile, well-drained soil in sun or shade; grow *P. henryana* in partial shade. **Support** young plants until they firmly attach themselves (*see p.380*). **Trim** in winter and summer to keep within bounds (*see p.384*) and clear of gutters and roofs. **Sow** seed (*see pp.391–392*) in pots in a cold frame in autumn, or take softwood cuttings in summer or hardwood cuttings in winter (*see p.394*).

PASSIFLORA
Passionflower, Granadilla

DESPITE THEIR TROPICAL APPEARANCE, some of these mostly evergreen climbers, notably the blue passionflower (*Passiflora caerulea*), can be grown outdoors in cool climates. They climb using tendrils, so need the support of stretched wires, netting, trellises, or a large shrub. They are good all-around plants, with pleasing foliage, and unusual and exotic flowers through summer and autumn that are followed by edible, but not always tasty, fruits. Where not hardy, grow in containers or in a cool to warm greenhouse.

Cultivation Grow in soil that is moist but well-drained, in full sun or partial shade, or in tubs of soil-based potting mix. Give shelter from cold winds and apply a winter mulch (*see p.388*) if grown outside in cold areas. **Root** semiripe cuttings (*see p.394*) in summer or layer (*see p.395*) in spring or autumn.

Passiflora caerulea (Blue passionflower)
Z7 ‡ to 30ft (10m), flowers from summer to autumn, orange-yellow fruits

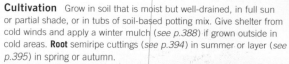

① *henryana* Z6b ‡30ft (10m) ② *tricuspidata* (Boston ivy) Z5b ‡70ft (20m) ③ *tricuspidata* 'Lowii' Z5b ‡70ft (20m) ④ *tricuspidata* 'Veitchii' Z5b ‡70ft (20m)

Passiflora 'Star of Bristol'
T min. 41°F (5°C) ‡ to 12ft (4m), flowers from summer to autumn, bright orange fruits

Passiflora caerulea 'Constance Elliot'
Z7 ‡ to 30ft (10m), fragrant flowers from summer to autumn, orange-yellow fruits

...siflora × exoniensis
...n. 41°F (5°C) ‡ to 20ft (6m), downy, rich green leaves, flowers in
...ner followed by yellow, banana-shaped fruits

PILEOSTEGIA VIBURNOIDES

THIS WOODY CLIMBER is valued for its sprays of starry, creamy white flowers that are borne from late summer to autumn, and its leathery, evergreen leaves that are up to 6in (15cm) long. This vigorous plant can cling to almost any surface with aerial roots and will make short work of covering a large tree trunk, fence, or wall. It can also be grown over a sturdy pergola or arch. Use its rich green foliage as a background for showy spring- and summer-flowering annuals such as morning glories (*Ipomoea, see p.144*) and sweet peas (*Lathyrus, see p.145*). It is also a good plant to combine with deciduous climbers such as clematis (*see pp.136–139*), as well as being invaluable for shady north- and east-facing walls.

Cultivation Grow in any soil in sun or shade. **Trim** in early spring to keep it under control (*see p.384*). **Root** semiripe cuttings (*see p.394*) in summer or layer shoots (*see p.395*) in spring.

PLUMBAGO
Leadwort

PLUMBAGO IS GROWN for its large clusters of simple, flat flowers. There are annuals, perennials, and shrubs in the group, but the evergreen climbers are most commonly cultivated. Their bright, matte green leaves provide the perfect foil for the sky blue, pure white, or deep rose pink flowers. In mild climates, grow plumbago over a pergola or arch, or against a wall. Where temperatures fall below 45°F (7°C), it is best grown in a container placed in a sheltered, sunny spot, and moved under cover during the cold winter months.

Cultivation Grow in fertile, well-drained soil in full sun, or in containers of soil-based potting mix, and top-dress or repot in spring. **Tie** shoots of young plants (*see p.380*) into the support as they grow to create a permanent framework of well-spaced stems. **Prune** in early spring once fully established; cut back sideshoots to within two or three buds of the main branches. **Sow** seed (*see pp.391–392*) at 55–64°F (13–18°C) in spring or take semiripe cuttings (*see p.394*) in midsummer. **Whiteflies** may attack if the plant is grown under glass or moved under cover through winter.

Pileostegia viburnoides
Z7 ‡ 20ft (6m), flower clusters are up to 6in (15cm) across

Plumbago auriculata (Cape leadwort)
T min. 41°F (5°C) ‡ 10–20ft (3–6m) ↔ 3–10ft (1–3m), flower clusters from summer to late autumn are up to 6in (15cm) across

...ssiflora 'Amethyst'
...nin. 41°F (5°C) ‡ to 12ft (4m), flowers from late summer to autumn
...nge fruits

see also
pp.110–113

THE GLORIOUS DISPLAYS PRODUCED by climbing and rambling roses are some of the delights of the summer garden, but the thorny, arching stems will need some form of support and, in most cases, regular tying in. Climbers tend to have stiff stems, with the flowers, often scented, carried singly or in clusters. Some have one main show of blooms on wood produced the previous year, while others flower in succession on the current season's growth. Ramblers are generally more rampant and have more flexible stems. The sometimes scented flowers are usually borne in clusters in one main flush on the previous year's growth. Both types can be trained against walls and fences or over pergolas and other ornamental structures (see below).

Cultivation Roses tolerate a wide range of conditions, but prefer fertile soil in a sunny site. Plant bare-root roses while dormant, from late autumn to early spring. Container-grown roses can be planted at any time. **Water** well after planting and keep watered until established. **Prune** sideshoots of climbers back to two or three buds in autumn or spring once the basic framework is established; cut one or two old stems to the base every three or four years to encourage new growth. Ramblers produce shoots from the base, so cut out one in three main stems after flowering each year. **Take** hardwood cuttings (see p.394) in autumn. Plants may be affected by mildew, blackspot, or rust. If possible choose a disease-resistant variety and improve air circulation around the plant.

Covering an arch with a rose

Climbing or rambling roses look particularly good when trained over an arch an arrangement that also makes it easy to enjoy the scent of the flowers. The arch must be strong enough to bear the weight of the numerous shoots and flowers in summer. Check, too, that it is securely anchored into the ground. Tie in the stems as they grow, spreading them evenly over the frame. This is much easier done while the shoots are still young and flexible, especially on climbers. Deadhead faded blooms regularly to encourage more flowers on those varieties that produce a succession.

Training a rambler into a tree

Ramblers with pliant, far-reaching stems will scramble into trees to provide a spectacular display. Check first that the tree can support the mass of growth, especially if choosing a vigorous rose. Plant the rose at least 3–4ft (1–1.2m) away from the trunk, and add plenty of organic matter to the planting hole to aid moisture retention. Site the rose on the windward side so that shoots are blown toward the tree, and train it into the tree up a length of rope leading from a stake at the rose's roots to a low branch. Protect the bark with a piece of rubber hose. No further training should be needed.

Growing a climber up a pillar or tripod

Roses trained up structures such as pillars, tripods, or obelisks add useful height to a bed or border. Choose one of the less vigorous climbers to reduce the need for pruning. Keeping stems close to the horizontal encourages the development of flowering sideshoots so, where possible, train stems in a spiral fashion around the pillar or tripod. Tie in stems regularly as they grow, while they are still young and flexible. Once they start to stiffen up, they are liable to break easily. Prune out any unwanted or overlong stems as necessary.

① *Rosa* 'Albertine' Z6 ‡15ft (5m) ↔ 12ft (4m), rambler ② 'Aloha' ‡10ft (3m) ↔ 8ft (2.5m), climber ③ 'American Pillar' ‡15ft (5m) ↔ 12ft (4m), rambler ④ *banksiae* 'Lutea' Z6 ‡↔ 20ft (6m), rambler ⑤ 'Breath of Life' ('Harquanne') Z6 ‡8ft (2.5m) ↔ 7ft (2.2m), climber ⑥ 'Chaplin's Pink Climber' ‡15ft (5m) ↔ 8ft (2.5m), climber ⑦ 'Climbing Iceberg' ‡↔ 10ft (3m), climber ⑧ 'Compassion' ‡10ft (3m) ↔ 8ft (2.5m), climber ⑨ 'Danse du Feu' ‡↔ 8ft (2.5m), climber

② ③ ④ ⑤ ⑧ ⑨ ⑩ ⑪ ⑭ ⑮ ⑯ ⑰ ⑳ ㉑ ㉒ ㉓

⑩ **'Dortmund'** Z5 ↕10ft (3m) ↔ 6ft (2m), climber ⑪ **'Dublin Bay'** ('Macdub') Z6 ↕↔7ft (2.2m), climber ⑫ **'Félicité Perpétue'** Z6 ↕15ft (5m) ↔ 12ft (4m), rambler ⑬ *filipes* **'Kiftsgate'** ↕30ft (10m) ↔ 20ft (6m), rambler ⑭ **'Gloire de Dijon'** ↕15ft (5m) ↔ 12ft (4m), climber ⑮ **'Golden Showers'** Z6 ↕ 10ft (3m) ↔ 6ft (2m), climber ⑯ **Handel'** ('Macha') ↕10ft (3m) ↔ 7ft (2.2m), climber ⑰ **'Madame Grégoire Staechelin'** ↕20ft (6m) ↔ 12ft (4m), climber ⑱ **'New Dawn'** ↕10ft (3m) ↔ 8ft (2.5m), climber ⑲ **'Paul's Lemon Pillar'** ↕12ft (4m) ↔ 10ft (3m), climber ⑳ **'Pink Perpétué'** ↕10ft (3m) ↔ 8ft (2.5m), climber ㉑ **'Rosy Mantle'** ↕8ft (2.5m) ↔ 6ft (2m), climber ㉒ **'Sander's White Rambler'** ↕↔ 12ft (4m), rambler ㉓ **'Zéphirine Drouhin'** ↕10ft (3m) ↔ 6ft (2m), thornless climber

SCHISANDRA

SCHIZOPHRAGMA

‡20ft (6m)

see also
p.114

RUBUS IS A LARGE GROUP of climbers and shrubs, which includes blackberries and raspberries. The ornamental climbers are mainly slender, prickly, or bristly evergreens. The dark green foliage is felted white on the undersides. The clusters of flat, usually pink summer flowers are similar to those of wild roses and are followed by glossy fruits. Some species are very vigorous and are best reserved for wild and woodland gardens. Other species are well behaved and splendid grown with other climbers such as jasmine (*Jasminum, see p.144*).

Cultivation Grow in well-drained soil in sun or partial shade. The young stems need tying into their support regularly to keep them neat (*see p.380*). **Trim** large species only if necessary keep them in check, after flowering (*see p.384*). **Root** semiripe cuttings of evergreens in summer or hardwood cuttings of deciduous species in early winter (*see p.394*). **Gray mold** can result in fuzzy, fungal growth on any part of the plant; remove affected areas promptly to prevent spreading.

‡10–30ft (3–10m)

IF YOU HAVE A LARGE AREA to cover, schisandras are good all-arounders with attractive flowers, foliage, and fruits. These twining, woody, usually deciduous climbers have glossy, mid-green leaves and pretty, white, or red flowers. They are borne in spring and summer, and are followed by bright bunches of pink or red berries if a male and female plant are grown together. Train them through trees, or over a trellis attached to walls or fences. They can be grown with plants such as golden hops (*Humulus lupulus* 'Aureus', *see p.143*) for a spectacular color contrast.

Cultivation Grow in fertile, moist, well-drained soil in sun or partial shade. **Tie in** the shoots of young plants until they begin to twine (*see p.380*), encouraging them to form a regularly spaced framework. Once this is accomplished, maintain it by cutting back sideshoots to within three or four buds of the main stems in early spring. **Sow** seed (*see pp.391–392*) in pots in a cold frame when ripe, or root semiripe cuttings (*see p.394*) in summer.

THESE WOODY, DECIDUOUS climbers are in the same family as hydrangeas (*see p.143*). The resemblance can be clearly seen in their huge, flat clusters of creamy white, subtly fragrant flowers. They are borne in abundance in midsummer, against a background of dark green leaves. The foliage of some cultivars is mottled silver or edged with pink. These variegated plants provide unusual groundcover when grown without support in the dappled shade under deciduous trees and shrubs. Train schizophragmas up walls or large tree trunks, to which they cling strongly using aerial roots. These large climbers are heavy when mature, so choose a suitably sturdy support that will not collapse under the weight.

Cultivation Grow in moist, well-drained, humus-rich soil in sun or partial shade. **Tie in** the shoots of young plants to their support until the aerial roots take hold (*see p.380*). **Trim** them in spring if they outgrow their space (*see p.384*). **Root** semiripe cuttings (*see p.394*) in late summer.

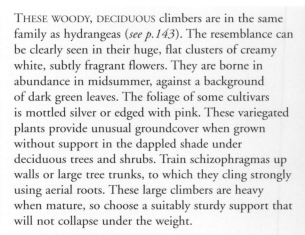

Rubus henryi var. *bambusarum*
Z6 ‡10ft (6m), evergreen, white hairy shoots have sharp spines, bears black fruits in autumn

Schisandra rubriflora
Z7b ‡30ft (10m), vigorous, young shoots are red, flowers in late spring and summer, fleshy fruits in autumn (*see inset*)

Schizophragma integrifolium
Z5b ‡40ft (12m)

SOLANUM

THIS HUGE GROUP OF PLANTS contains varieties that are annuals, perennials, shrubs, and trees, but the climbing solanums are especially popular. They are grown for their bell- or trumpet-shaped flowers in regal blues and purples, or pure white, from spring through autumn. In some years, shiny, round berries may follow. Although solanums count potatoes and eggplant among their number, most of the ornamental species are toxic if eaten: be careful because the decorative fruits can be very appealing to children. Solanums need a warm, sunny wall to thrive in temperate climates. Where not hardy, grow in a cool or temperate greenhouse.

Cultivation Grow in well-drained soil in full sun. **Mulch** (see p.388) over winter, particularly young plants. In cold areas, use containers of soil-based potting mix and move under cover in winter. **Tie in** shoots regularly (see p.380). **Prune** back sideshoots to within two or three buds of main branches in late winter. **Sow** seed (see pp.391–392) at 64–68°F (18–20°C) in spring or root semiripe cuttings (see p.394) in summer in a propagator.

THUNBERGIA

VALUED FOR THEIR ABUNDANCE of exotic, brightly colored flowers, the tropical, perennial climbers are grown as annuals or in pots and taken under cover in winter. The blooms come in shades of gold, orange, or blue and are borne against a background of soft green leaves. Their slender, twining stems can wind around a freestanding arch or obelisk, or through a shrub. Otherwise attach a trellis, wires, or netting to a fence or wall to provide a support that they can scramble up. Create a fabulous, jewel-like display through summer by growing thunbergias with other annual climbers, such as sweet peas (*Lathyrus, see p.145*), on a single support.

Cultivation Grow in a reasonably sheltered site in moist, well-drained soil and full sun. In containers, use a soil-based potting mix. **Train** the young plants toward their support (see p.380). **Trim** thunbergias only if they are taking up too much room (see p.384). **Sow** seed (see pp.391–392) at 61–64°F (16–18°C) or take semiripe cuttings (see p.394) in summer.

Thunbergia mysorensis
T min. 55–59°F (13–15°C) ‡20ft (6m), flowers in spring

① *crispum* 'Glasnevin' T min. 45°F (5°C) ‡20ft (6m)
② *rantonnetii* 'Royal Robe' T min. 45°F (7°C) ‡3–6ft (1–2m)
– both flower from summer to autumn

Thunbergia alata (Black-eyed Susan vine)
T min. 45–50°F (7–10°C) ‡5–6ft (1.5–2m) as an annual, flowers from summer to autumn, often raised from seed

Thunbergia grandiflora (Blue trumpet vine, Sky vine)
T min. 55–59°F (13–15°C) ‡15–30ft (5–10m), flowers are occasionally white

TROPAEOLUM

see also
p.333

‡20–28ft (6–9m)

THESE WOODY, EVERGREEN climbers are widely available. They are grown for their glossy, dark green leaves and immaculate white, perfumed flowers in mid- and late summer, which, on *Trachelospermum asiaticum*, age to yellow. Where marginally hardy, train them against a warm wall: trellises or horizontal wires, attached 2in (5cm) away from the wall, provide perfect support for twining stems. Where not hardy, grow in a container and move under cover in winter. The mature plants can be used to support spring- and summer-flowering annuals, such as tropaeolums (*see right*), to create a stunning mass of color.

Cultivation Choose a spot with fertile, well-drained soil, in sun or partial shade, with shelter from cold, drying winds. **Mulch** (*see p.388*) over winter, particularly young plants. For containers use a soil-based potting mix. **Trim** back long shoots in spring if you find the plant is outgrowing its support (*see p.384*). **Root** semiripe cuttings in summer (*see p.394*).

CLIMBING TROPAEOLUMS use long, twining leafstalks to scale fences, trellises, or pergolas. They can also scramble through shrubs, or without support grow as groundcover. In summer, they are decorated with masses of flamboyant flowers, often in glowing shades of red and yellow. Some cultivars have the bonus of variegated foliage. Many species are tender, but even the perennials can be grown successfully as annuals in cold climates. The climbing nasturtiums (*Tropaeolum majus* and some cultivars) flower best on poor soil and are a useful stopgap in neglected plots. The leaves and flowers of annual species are edible and can be used as a peppery addition to salads.

Cultivation Grow these plants in moist but well-drained soil in full sun. **Tie in** young stems to their support (*see p.380*) to encourage them in the right direction. **Sow** seed of perennials in containers in a cold frame when ripe. Annual seed needs temperatures of 55–61°F (13–16°C) in early spring, or can be sown in situ in midspring (*see pp.391–393*). **Blackflies** can smother shoots; pick or wash them off.

Tropaeolum speciosum (Flame nasturtium)
Z8 ‡10ft (3m), perennial, prefers acidic soil, flowers are followed by blue berries in red, papery jackets; mulch in winter

Trachelospermum jasminoides (Confederate jasmine, Star jasmine) T min. 35°F (2°C) ‡28ft (9m), aging flowers remain pure white, bronze winter foliage

Tropaeolum peregrinum (Canary creeper)
T min. 41°F (5°C) ‡8–12ft (2.5–4m), annual, the flowers are said to resemble flying canaries

Tropaeolum tuberosum 'Ken Aslet'
T min. 35°F (2°C) ‡6–12ft (2–4m), perennial, lift tubers and store in a frost-free place until spring (as for dahlias, *see pp.222–223*)

VITIS
Grape

‡22ft (7m) to 50ft (15m)

THE ORNAMENTAL GRAPES in this group, unlike those grown for fruits or to make wine, are valued for their large leaves, which turn brilliant shades of bright red or plum purple in autumn. Some bear edible grapes; others bear small, unpalatable blue-black fruits. Strong tendrils fasten these vigorous, woody, deciduous climbers to the nearest support. Train against a wall or fence, or through a large shrub or tree. Grapes make an attractive covering for an arbor or pergola, especially over an eating area, because the leafy growth provides cool shade.

Cultivation Grow vines in well-drained, neutral, or slightly alkaline (limy) soil, in full sun or semishade. **Prune** in winter and again in summer if growth needs to be restrained (*see p.384*). If your vine is more formally trained against a wall, prune sideshoots to two or three buds from the main framework in winter. **Sow** seed (*see pp.391–392*) in a cold frame in autumn or spring or take hardwood cuttings (*see p.394*) in winter. **Mildew** (*see p.398*) can be troublesome.

WISTERIA
Wisteria

THESE ELEGANT CLIMBERS are cultivated for their showy, pealike flowers. Before you buy, check the stem for a healthy graft union: seedling plants (those growing on their own roots) take years to bloom and then often bear few, or no, flowers. The fragrant flowers are borne in long clusters in spring or early summer and are followed by green, beanlike pods. These woody, deciduous, twining climbers can be trained over a sturdy arch or pergola or against a wall. Wisterias can grow very large if they are on too rich a soil. Prune plants twice a year to keep them within bounds and maximize flowering. A low-maintenance option is to scramble wisteria through a large tree where it will need no pruning.

Cultivation Grow in moist but well-drained soil, in sun or semi-shade. **Tie in** shoots (*see p.380*) to form a permanent framework. Keep the main stems horizontal. **Trim** sideshoots in late summer to 4–6 leaves, or about 6in (15cm), from the main branches. Shorten again in winter, to 2–3 buds. **Leaf spot** (*see p.399*) can be a problem.

Wisteria floribunda ‘Alba’
Z6 ‡28ft (9m) or more, flower clusters up to 24in (60cm) long open from base to top, followed by velvety, green pods

Vitis coignetiae (Crimson Glory Vine)
Z5 ‡50ft (15m), widely available, dark green leaves are up to 12in (30cm) long; bears unpalatable blue-black fruits

Wisteria floribunda ‘Multijuga’
Z6 ‡28ft (9m) or more, flower clusters up to 12in (30cm) long open from base to tip, followed by velvety, green pods

Wisteria brachybotrys ‘Shiro-kapitan’
Z7 ‡28ft (9m) or more, foliage is softly hairy, flower clusters to 6in (15cm) long, occasionally produces double flowers

Flowering Plants

using flowering plants

Flowering plants are the mainstay of the garden, providing the "understory" of planting in borders and a varied complement to more permanent trees and shrubs. This chapter covers the huge range of nonwoody, or herbaceous, plants, apart from grasses (*see pp.340–355*) and ferns (*see pp.356–365*). Herbaceous perennials, annuals, biennials, and bulbs – including alpines, some succulents, garden orchids, and herbs – provide a great deal of color in the garden, particularly in spring and summer.

A plant for every place

There is a huge variety of flowering plants, and you can find some to furnish any part of the garden. Before selecting plants, think about your soil and conditions in different parts of the garden – whether the soil is dry or moist, alkaline or acid, and how much sun or shade each area receives. It is easier to grow plants that are suited to the particular bed, border, or container in your garden than to try to alter the conditions to suit the plants.

Most flowering plants will tolerate a fairly wide range of soil conditions, but some have specific requirements that, if not met, will result in poor growth. For instance, rhododendrons require an acidic soil (one that is alkaline-free), otherwise the leaves will turn yellow, and the plant will eventually die. Heaths and heathers also require acidic soil, and although the winter heath (*Erica carnea*) and its cultivars will tolerate slightly alkaline conditions, the best results are still obtained by growing them in acidic soil.

The amount of sun and shade in different parts of your garden will determine which plants you can grow where. Shade may be cast by existing buildings, or by trees and shrubs that are already established. Most perennials and annuals need full sun to flower well, whereas foliage plants such as hostas and lungworts (*Pulmonaria*) and many bulbs tolerate shady conditions.

How wet or dry your soil is will also influence the plants that can be grown. You can fill shady areas with moist soil by a pond or stream with moisture-loving plants like primroses, whereas plants such as lavender need dry soil in an open, sunny position.

Summer is the peak for most flowering plants, but a few provide welcome color in autumn and winter. With careful choices you can have something in flower for almost twelve months of the year.

Plants in a shady site Many people regard shady sites as problem areas, but there is a wide choice of flowering plants available that can be grown in shady sites to create a charmingly natural planting effect. Here, the bold foliage of *Hosta sieboldiana* contrasts well with the narrower leaves and white flowers of *Primula pulverulenta* 'Bartley' growing under trees by a pool. These plants both thrive in the moist soil beside water.

Designing a planting plan

The best way to plan a planting design is to decide on the plants you would like to grow and then choose cultivars in colors you wish to predominate. Color is always important (*see right*), but consider also the texture and the shapes of leaves and stems. You can evoke different moods with the types of plants that you choose. For example, lots of bright colors and small leaves could create a cottage-garden effect, whereas large-leaved plants and pale shades look more contemporary.

Find out the mature height and spread of each plant before planting it.

To determine the distance you should leave between any two plants, add the spreads of both plants, and divide by two. Generally taller plants are best at the back of the border and shorter ones at the front, but placing some taller ones near the middle or front gives an undulating effect and can prevent the planting design from looking too flat. They will also partly obscure other plants, creating an element of mystery.

Don't forget to mix in some early-spring bulbs and autumn-flowering plants such as asters and rudbeckias to prolong the flowering display.

Architectural plants Architectural plants with strong outlines are ideal as specimen plants or massed for bold effects. Here a modern, formal water cascade mirrors the clean shapes of the leaves and flowers of *Zantedeschia aethiopica*.

Planting in groups For the greatest impact, particularly in borders, plant in groups of three, five, or seven. This creates bold drifts of color that are much more effective than the piecemeal effect of combining single plants of each variety.

Form and texture Selecting the right planting combinations can create wonderful contrasts in color, form, and texture. Here the upright, swordlike foliage and orange flowers of montbretia (*Crocosmia*) stand above and contrast well with the rounded, softer foliage and lime yellow flowers of *Alchemilla mollis*. Planting combinations like this can often happen by happy accident.

Painting with plants

The subject of color in the garden is a very personal one, but you should not be dogmatic about it. Experiment with different color combinations between adjacent plants and in a border as a whole, and don't be afraid to move plants if the colors do not work together. You could create very harmonious effects by using tones of the same or similar colors, or make exciting contrasts with different hues, but aim for an overall balance.

Reds, yellows, and oranges are vibrant, hot colors that liven up the border; for a cool, reflective mood choose shades of white, blue, and purple. The apparent size of a border or garden can be affected by color. Hot hues draw the eye so distances appear shorter. Cool shades seem to recede into the distance, making a border look longer.

Light, the season, and time of day alter the effect of color. Often white and pastel shades look lost among bright colors and appear washed out in intense sunlight, but become almost luminous in evening twilight.

Subtle hues The complementary shades of *Eryngium bourgatii* and stachys in tones of blue and lilac bring a cooling and restful atmosphere to the border. The spiky foliage of the eryngium contrasts well with the softer foliage of the stachys.

Clashing contrast For a lively planting, grow large swaths of hot-colored plants. Here red salvias shout out above a contrasting clump of *Heliotropium* 'Blue Wonder'.

Flowers with fragrance

Scent gives many flowering plants an added dimension. Flower scents vary from deliciously fresh sweet peas (*Lathyrus odorata*) to the musky aroma of phlox. Some plants have scented leaves; try artemisias, mint, and some geraniums. The perfume of many flowers is stronger in the cool of the evening and can be more intense in a corner or an enclosed area; place a seat there to catch the full fragrance or plant below a window so that the balmy air can float indoors.

Added attraction The scent of many plants attracts butterflies (here on marjoram flowers), bees, and other insects to the flowers and to your garden. Many of them help to pollinate the plants. Other scented plants that attract insects include red valerian (*Centranthus ruber*), heliotropes, *Iris graminea*, evening primrose (*Oenothera biennis*), stocks (*Matthiola*), and tobacco plant (*Nicotiana*).

perennials

What is an herbaceous perennial?

An herbaceous perennial, commonly called a perennial, is a nonwoody plant that grows and flowers over several years. Some perennials are evergreen, but in most, the top-growth dies down in winter while the roots remain alive. In spring, new growth starts up again from the base, or crown. The majority of perennials are long-lived plants that will thrive for years, but some, such as flax (*Linum*), are short-lived, lasting only three or four years. These short-lived plants tend to seed themselves quite freely around the garden, so there is often no need to buy replacements for plants that are growing older.

Perennials demonstrate an immense variety of sizes, shapes, colors, scents, textures, and habits and are among the most versatile of garden plants. They range from tall plants, like *Cephalaria gigantea*, which reach up to 6ft (2m) in one season to small plants, for example some hardy geraniums, which are no more than 6in (15cm) tall and make good groundcover plants.

Perennials encompass not only traditional border plants but also alpines and rock-garden plants, water-garden plants, and succulents.

Large perennial Some perennials, like these lupines, make a tremendous amount of growth in a season, forming large architectural plants and bringing a touch of height and drama to the garden. Large-flowered cultivars can be top-heavy, so will need staking to prevent them from flopping over or their brittle stems being broken in the wind.

Dainty alpine This rock jasmine (*Androsace carnea*), which grows to no more than a few centimeters tall, is shown off at its best in a graveled raised bed or the scree of a rock garden.

Choosing perennials for the garden

Because they are so versatile, you should be able to find a perennial for any purpose or site you need, with an appropriate height and spread for the amount of space you have available.

You can create pleasing planting designs by using plants with different growth habits. A spreading perennial contrasts well with one of strong, upright growth, while mound-forming plants lend a softer feel to the border. Dense clumps of bright color combine well with airy flower sprays of plants such as gypsophila. There are carpeting perennials that can be used as groundcover or under roses.

Most perennials are valued for their flowers: these vary as much as the habits and provide much of the seasonal color in the garden, from the elegant blooms of lilies and blowsy poppies to the daintiness of pinks (*Dianthus*). Choose flowers that fit in with your preferred planting style. In general, flowers of species are more delicate in appearance, whereas cultivars are larger and more showy.

Some perennials are chosen mainly for their foliage. Foliage usually lasts longer than the flowers, so consider the potential of leaf shape, size, and texture in your garden design, since it will extend the period of interest. This is especially important in a small garden.

Try planting cultivars with variegated leaves, and look for contrasts of glossy or matte and hairy or waxy textures. Use small-leaved plants with those that have large or strongly shaped leaves, or you can choose strappy iris leaves with the star-shaped leaves of astrantias. Bear in mind that some perennials have foliage in hues other than green, such as heucheras.

Handsome foliage Here variegated *Hosta fortunei*, *H. fortunei* var. *obscura*, and *H.* 'Carol' form a bold combination of foliage, the variegated forms highlighted by the plain greens. Hostas have attractive flowers held above the foliage in summer.

Trailing habit Use trailing perennials, such as this *Aurinia saxatilis* 'Dudley Nevill', to add an air of informality, and to soften the hard edges of raised beds, low walls, or steps.

In beds and borders

The way herbaceous perennials are used in beds and borders has changed over time as well as with fashions in gardening. Traditionally, they were grown on their own in long, formal borders, each backed by a hedge or fence. This worked well if you had a large yard with plenty of room to grow perennials, trees, and shrubs in separate borders. Now, with yards getting smaller, there is not often the space to grow plants separately in this way. We tend to create mixed borders, incorporating the perennials with trees, shrubs, and perhaps some climbers and annuals.

Formal herbaceous borders usually have straight edges, and the planting is graded, with lower plants at the front and taller ones at the back. In mixed borders, a more informal approach to planting works well. In this situation, perennials are often used to fill the gaps between the shrubs while they are still young, and the gradation of plant height is less strictly followed.

Island beds are a modern way of growing perennials. These are plots surrounded by lawn, paving, or gravel, so they can be viewed from all sides. They are usually planted with the taller plants in the middle, tapering to shorter ones at the edges of the bed. Plants tend to grow better in island beds because they are in a more open situation. Include a couple of striking specimen plants, such as cannas or yuccas, to give the bed a focal point.

Herbaceous border
This traditional herbaceous border contains euphorbias, daylilies (*Hemerocallis*), phloxes, and lilies, and is designed to be at its glorious flowering peak in midsummer. All these plants are easily grown and are planted in bold groups of three to five plants. Some taller plants are grown at the front of the border to add a little variation in pace.

Cottage planting
This style of planting is relaxed and informal, and features annuals and perennials that are allowed to seed themselves freely. This bed includes traditional cottage-garden plants such as aquilegias, euphorbias, fennel (*Foeniculum*), irises, and scabious. There is little need to worry about the relative heights and spreads of plants since spontaneity is all part of the charm.

Seasonal interest

While we rely on perennials to fill the garden with color throughout summer, they can also provide a lot of interest even when not in flower in spring, autumn, and even in winter.

Fresh foliage emerging from barren soil and unfurling after a long winter is a welcome sight and a promise of things to come. At the other end of summer, many perennials have interesting seedheads and some have berries. Don't be in a hurry to cut down the old growth in autumn – birds will appreciate the seeds, and the old stems can look very attractive, especially when covered with frost. Beneficial insects may also make a home among the old stems in winter.

Summer beauty Anise hyssop (*Agastache foeniculum*) is upright and anise-scented with purple flowers from midsummer.

Mellow autumn In autumn, the seedheads, held on tall stems, turn a parchment brown and give some structure to the border.

Winter frost In early winter, shimmering hoarfrost encrusts the seedheads, altering their appearance once again.

Naturalistic plantings

Some perennials, especially those that are species rather than cultivars, look very good in naturalistic settings, appearing to grow as they would in the wild. You might create a woodland mood under some trees, or a meadow in grass, or a naturalistic planting in a border. Such plantings require a lot of planning to achieve the desired effect. Make beds in informal, irregular shapes to blend in with the surroundings.

Plant drifts that intermingle or create substantial clumps of some plants to imitate how plants grow naturally. Because the planting style is fairly loose, you can add new plants anytime but avoid creating a fussy effect with a lot of different, single plants.

Woodland display Here the huge leaves of *Gunnera manicata* form a dramatic backdrop for the dark, purple-black foliage and deep scarlet flowers of *Lobelia* 'Queen Victoria'.

annuals and biennials

What are annuals and biennials?

Annuals are plants that germinate, flower, set seed, and die all within one year. Hardy annuals can withstand frost. Those that are damaged or killed by frost and low temperatures are half-hardy annuals. If raised under glass, they can be planted out in the spring when all danger of frost has passed.

Biennials need two growing seasons to complete their life cycle. The first year they produce leafy growth, then flower in the following year. Tender perennials, which need protection in winter, are often treated as annuals in cooler climates to avoid overwintering them under glass.

As annuals and biennials grow and flower in one season, they are perfect for providing color very quickly and inexpensively. They also offer a wide range of flower forms and growth habits. As fillers among young shrubs or creating a colorful display in an empty border, they are unrivaled. Hardy annuals are the easiest of all because they can be scattered and sown outdoors where they are to flower.

Annual poppies (*Papaver*) fill the garden with color all summer long and are available in delightful shades of scarlet, orange, pink, and white. Sow seeds in shallow drills or just scatter them in a patch and cover them lightly. Thin the seedlings when they are 1in (2.5cm) tall. If you leave the seedheads on, they will seed themselves over the garden.

Biennial foxgloves (*Digitalis*) require two seasons to reach flowering size. The long spikes of flowers come in a wide variety of colors and are ideal for giving a cottage-garden look to a border.

Planning annual beds and borders

Formal bedding A formal bedding design is a great addition to a garden in the right setting. Either raise your own plants or buy young plants from the garden center. This bold, flowing scheme is made up of *Celosia* 'New Look' among *Petunia* 'Pink Wave'. To keep the display at its peak and to encourage more new blooms, remove the fading flowers regularly so that the plants do not set seed.

A bed or border devoted to annuals and biennials, whether informal or formal, is usually a mass of flower, and since it lasts for only one season, you can experiment with confidence. For an informal bed, you could choose a limited palette of colors, such as reds and oranges, or pinks, purples, and blues, and sow in broad drifts that intermingle. Alternatively, mix up the seed before you sow it to obtain a completely random riot of color.

Formal bedding plans tend to consist of half-hardy annuals and biennials planted in symmetrical or stylized patterns. These are most often seen in public parks, but on a smaller scale they can look very striking in your own garden. Think about what design you want to achieve before getting the seed or the plants. Select one or two colors and a simple pattern, such as a crescent, an undulating curve, or a checkerboard, and either plot it out on some graph paper or trace it out on the soil with some sand. Formal bedding designs do need more maintenance to keep them neat and tidy and looking good, but the rewards are worthwhile.

Whatever sort of annual bed or border you would like, plan it carefully before sowing so that the flowering periods of the different plants overlap and provide interest over a long season. Half-hardy annuals past their peak can be replaced with homegrown or bought plants to create different effects.

Although foliage is not the most prominent feature of annuals, don't forget to mix leaf shapes and textures.

Using annuals and biennials around the garden

Annuals are excellent in mixed borders among perennials, trees, and shrubs. Because they have few or no special soil needs and such a brief life span, they will not interfere with the growth of surrounding plants.

Take advantage of trailing annuals such as nasturtiums, and biennials such as the spring-flowering wallflowers (*Erysimum*), to provide speedy ground-cover and add variety to the established borders. You could also try leaving space in a mixed or herbaceous border

and plant a different selection of annual and biennials each year.

If you have just moved into a new house with a sparsely planted garden, growing a selection of annuals is an inexpensive way of filling the garden with color, while you plan the more permanent features and planting. New trees, shrubs, and perennials will take several seasons to fill out and fill the borders, so use annuals and biennials in between them to provide temporary color and to keep the weeds down.

Informal planting
With informal planting designs you are aiming to create a mixture of plants growing happily together in an apparently naturalistic fashion. Take care in positioning your informal area – it might look odd alongside a formal water feature, for example. The mixture of old-fashioned annuals and biennials here includes sunflowers, foxgloves, and poppies.

Annual edging These pot marigolds (*Calendula officinalis*) are low enough to be used as an edging around a vegetable plot. The bright flowers attract beneficial insects to the garden and these help with pollination and controling pests.

Annuals for cutting

Almost all annual flowers can be cut and arranged indoors. If you have a vegetable garden or an out-of-the-way plot, sow an area with annuals so that you can cut them without spoiling the display in the main garden. Keep them in water in a cool place, and they will last for days, or even weeks. Some, such as statice (*Limonium*) and helichrysum, can be cut and hung up in an airy spot for use in dried arrangements.

Cutting flowers *Zinnia elegans* 'Whirligig' is a flamboyant flower borne on a tall stem, so is ideal for cutting. Cut the flowers just as they are opening so that they last longer once put in water. Trim off any leaves below the water line.

Annuals and biennials in containers

With their short growing season, annuals and biennials, and tender perennials, are ideal for temporary containers, either on their own or mixed with other plants. The planted containers can form a focal point, be moved around so that the plants are seen to their best advantage, and are perfect for filling gaps in a border.

Any container is suitable, from a pot or a tub to a windowbox or a hanging basket, providing that it has drainage holes in the base. Assess how sunny the site is going to be in order to decide which plants to grow. Then select a container that looks good in the site, and that complements the plants you

want to grow. Containers in hot, sunny places or exposed windy sites will dry out quickly. They need to be watered every day in hot weather, so take this into account when choosing a location. If necessary, use cultivars with compact growth so that they are not blown about in windy conditions.

Hanging baskets and windowboxes are perfect for trailing plants. Good choices are geraniums (upright and trailing), fuchsias, and impatiens. Others to try include petunias, marigolds (*Tagetes*), lobelia, and alyssum. Heliotropes mixed with showier plants, especially near the house, will give off a delightful scent.

Potful of charm This pot is overflowing with *Viola tricolor*. This delightful annual will flower for many weeks over summer; deadheading will prolong flowering.

Hanging basket A riot of different shades of pink, and both bold and delicate flowers, this hanging basket includes diascias, lobelia, geraniums, phloxes, and verbenas.

bulbs

What are bulbous plants?

A bulbous plant is a perennial that has a food storage organ – a swollen part of the stem or root – that enables the plant to remain dormant until conditions are favorable for growth. The term *bulbous plants* is commonly used to describe true bulbs, corms, tubers, and rhizomes – all different types of food-storage organs.

A true bulb consists of tightly packed modified leaves on a reduced stem; you can see the "leaves" when you slice open an onion. Corms are enlarged underground stems; tubers are formed from swollen roots or underground stems.

Other bulbous plants store food in creeping, underground stems, called rhizomes; these may be thick and stubby, as in bearded irises, or long and thin, as with lily-of-the-valley (*Convallaria*).

Simple bulb (daffodil)

Stem (here of tulip) grows from bud in center of bulb

Scaly bulb (lily)

True bulb There are two types of true bulb: a simple bulb has tightly packed leaves and a papery skin, or tunic; a scaly bulb has loosely packed leaves, or scales, and dries out more quickly.

Stem tuber (cyclamen)

Tuber Shoots emerge from buds at the top of the tuber; stem tubers have more buds than root tubers. Root tubers are replaced by fresh ones each year, but stem tubers get bigger each season.

Corms and cormlets (gladiolus)

Corm (colchicum)

Corm One or two buds arise on the corm surface. Usually, a new corm forms at the base of the stem each year. Small cormlets may also develop around the old corm and can be removed to grow on.

Where to grow bulbs

Summer highlights
Many summer-flowering bulbs, including lilies and montbretias (*Crocosmia*), are tall plants with striking flowers that are ideal for use in mixed borders with herbaceous perennials. This border in high summer has a touch of drama provided by the bold, showy flower heads of alliums. They contrast well with the more delicate blooms of columbines (*Aquilegia*) and catmint (*Nepeta*).

Bulbous plants are generally not too fussy about soil conditions, as long as they have well-drained soil, and many are very hardy. You can grow bulbs in any aspect except deep shade. Many bulbs prefer hot, sunny sites, but those from woodland habitats thrive in light, dappled shade; the hardy cyclamens tolerate even dry shade. Some bulbs are delicate enough for the rock garden.

Bulbs look good if planted in large groups. For maximum impact, plant up a formal bed with spring bulbs in different colors. Once they die down, lift and store them in a cool, dark place to make way for summer bedding.

For a more informal display, use the bulbs among other perennials, so that the dying foliage will be hidden by the perennials. Don't think of bulbs as

plants only for spring; choose bulbs with different flowering periods and you can have a beautiful display from the earliest snowdrops (*Galanthus*) to richly colored cyclamens in autumn.

Formal bedding Plant spring bulbs, like these tulips, in large blocks to bring a splash of color to the garden. They also look good with wallflowers (*Erysimum*) and forget-me-nots (*Myosotis*).

Naturalizing bulbs in the garden

If left undisturbed in the ground in a site that suits them, many bulbs will naturally increase to form large clumps, and then drifts, of color. Making use of this natural method of reproduction is a simple way to bring seasonal color to new areas of the garden. Once they are planted, the bulbs will come up year after year with very little attention.

Sea of daffodils Here, bright yellow daffodils flower beneath an ornamental cherry tree (*Prunus* x *yedoensis*) in full bloom to create a pretty spring garden. The showy blooms of bulb cultivars look spectacular under specimen trees in the garden, while the more delicate flowers of species bulbs are a more appropriate choice in native woodland, small copses, or under fruit or nut trees.

The easiest way to naturalize bulbs is to grow them in grass. After flowering, the grass needs to be left uncut for about six weeks to allow the foliage to die down. In this way, the bulbs draw energy from the foliage and build up food reserves and flower buds for the following year. Think first about how often you wish to mow an area of lawn.

Early-flowering bulbs, like snowdrops, are suitable for a lawn that will be cut from spring. Later-flowering bulbs such as some daffodils may suit an area that can be left unmown for longer, perhaps around the edge of a lawn or on a grassy bank. Some bulbs, such as the snake's head fritillary (*Fritillaria meleagris*), thrive when planted in a wildflower meadow that is not cut until late summer or early autumn.

Choose vigorous bulbs since they will have to put up with competition from the grass roots. The best way to achieve a natural effect is to scatter the bulbs and plant them where they fall. As long as the bulbs are at least 4in (20cm) apart, they should flower well.

Spring- and autumn-flowering bulbs also thrive under deciduous trees where they can flower either before or after the leaf canopy is at its most dense. Plant them under individual specimen trees in the garden, or in loose drifts in a woodland setting.

In woodland Some bulbs look most at home in a natural woodland setting; this effect could be achieved in a small area with just a few trees and shrubs. Carpet the ground with low-growing bulbs, punctuated with larger ones, like this giant lily (*Cardiocrinum*), which likes moist shade.

Using bulbs in containers

Most bulbs grow well in windowboxes and other containers because they enjoy the free drainage. Aim to choose a container that suits the size of the bulbs. A lily, for example, will need a deep pot to balance its height when fully grown, while small bulbs such as crocuses look appealing grown in wide, shallow bowls or pans.

Planting one species of bulb to each container provides dense clumps of flower; you can place containers of different bulbs together as they come into flower. If you wish to plant a mixture of bulbs in one container, plant them in layers with larger bulbs at the bottom and smaller ones at the

too for a succession of bloom. Spring bulbs are likely to be among the earliest flowers in the garden, so place them where you can see them easily, perhaps by the front door, outside a window, or to form a focal point. Have pots of fragrant bulbs such as hyacinths close to the house where the scent can be easily enjoyed.

Once the flowers are over, move the pots to a less prominent area, or remove the bulbs and temporarily plant them in a corner of a bed, while the foliage dies down. This frees up the pots to use for other plants. When the foliage is dead, lift the bulbs to store them or plant them in a border.

Classic beauty Some bulbs have elegant blooms and foliage that work well in a traditional or formal style. This terracotta urn, backed by a hornbeam (*Carpinus*) hedge, is simply planted with tulips.

Forcing bulbs

The best way to bring color and fragrance into the home in the dark days of winter is to force bulbs in pots (*see also p.288*). Growing them in relatively warm conditions indoors makes them flower earlier than usual. Hippeastrums, with their giant, exotic blooms, scented hyacinths, and daffodils are all suitable for forcing.

Plant the bulbs in autumn in a soilless bulb or cuttings medium. Keep them watered until just moist in a cool, dark place for a few weeks until a good root system has formed. Check the bulbs regularly and bring them into the light when they have made about 1in (2.5cm) of growth.

ACAENA

Bidi-bidi, New Zealand burr

THESE LOW, CREEPING herbaceous perennials form dense mats of evergreen foliage by virtue of their rooting stems. This makes for good groundcover in a rock garden or at the front of a flower border, but these plants can be invasive. In summer, the plant is covered with round flower heads, which later develop into the characteristic, spiny, red burrs for which these plants are known. New Zealand burrs are valued for their colorful leaves: *Acaena caesiiglauca* (Z7) has glaucous blue foliage, and *A. microphylla* 'Kupferteppich' (Z7) has bronze leaves and bright red burrs. Other mat-forming plants that combine well with them include *Sedum rupestre* and *S. obtusatum* (*see p.324*).

Cultivation Grow in reasonably fertile soil in full sun or part shade. If necessary, curb a spreading plant by pulling out unwanted rooted stems. **Sow** seed (*see pp.391–392*) in containers in a cold frame in autumn. **Make** new plants by digging up rooted stems and transplanting them to a new position, in autumn or early spring.

Acaena '**Blue Haze**'
Z7 ‡ 4–6in (10–15cm) ↔ 3ft (1m), steely gray-blue foliage lasts throughout the year and sets off the dark red burrs in summer

ACANTHUS

Bear's breeches

WITH THEIR TALL SPIKES of unusual flowers above the striking spiny, dark green foliage, acanthus make valuable architectural plants for the herbaceous or mixed border. The individual tubular flowers, each up to 2in (5cm) long, come in combinations of white, green, yellow, pink, or purple, and are borne on spikes up to 4ft (1.2m) tall. These are produced from late spring to midsummer, and can be cut and dried for indoor display. Leave a few spikes on the plant over winter, however, since they look good when covered in frost. Acanthus are vigorous herbaceous perennials and associate well with other perennials such as hardy geraniums (*see pp.250–251*) and phloxes (*see p.306*).

Cultivation Grow in any reasonably fertile soil in sun or partial shade, although they do best in deep, fertile, well-drained soil. **Remove** dead foliage and old flower spikes in late winter or early spring. **Sow** seed in pots in a cold frame (*see pp.391–392*) in spring, or divide clumps in spring or autumn (*see p.395*). **Take** root cuttings in winter (*see p.394*). **Powdery mildew** may mar leaves, but only in very dry conditions.

① *hirsutus* Z8 ‡ 6–14in (15–35cm) ② *hungaricus* Z7b ‡ 2–4ft (60–120cm) ③ *mollis* Z6b H112–7 ‡ 5ft (1.5m) ④ *spinosus* Z5 ‡ 5ft (1.5m)

ACHILLEA

Yarrow

THE FERNY, GRAY-GREEN FOLIAGE and flat-topped flower heads of yarrows are mainstays of the cottage-style garden or herbaceous border. Low-growing types are ideal for rock gardens. Herbaceous perennials, yarrows quickly form spreading, drought-resistant clumps suited to most soil types, including alkaline and gravelly soils. Their summer flower heads, in a wide range of colors, attract bees, butterflies, and other beneficial insects, making them a good choice for wildflower borders. The flower heads can be dried for indoor decoration. Grow with other herbaceous perennials such as lythrums (*see p.283*), phloxes (*see p.306*), and sidalceas (*see p.325*). Contact with the foliage may aggravate some skin allergies.

Cultivation Grow in moist, but well-drained soil in an open site in full sun, although most yarrows tolerate a wide range of soils and conditions. **Remove** faded flowers to encourage more to follow. **Sow** seed outdoors (*see pp.391–393*) in situ, or divide clumps every 2–3 years in spring (*see p.395*) to increase stock and maintain vigor. In dry, overcrowded conditions, powdery mildew may spoil foliage.

Achillea '**Moonshine**'
Z3b ‡↔ 24in (60cm), once the bright yellow flowers open in summer, 'Moonshine' puts on a fine display well into autumn

Achillea × *lewisii* 'King Edward'
Z5 ‡3–5in (8–13cm) ↔ 9in (23cm) or more, shows pale yellow
flower heads from early summer, ideal for a rock garden

Achillea filiper dulina 'Gold Plate'
Z3 ‡4ft (1.2m) ← 18in (45cm), this classic variety, with golden
yellow flower heacs in summer, is also one of the tallest

Achillea 'Forncett Candy'
Z4 ‡34in (85cm) ↔ 18in (45cm), the pale pink flower heads fade
to almost white as they age

Achillea 'Fanal'
Z4 ‡30in (75cm) ↔ 24in (60cm), bold crimson flower heads are
ideal cutting material; a contrast to gray or silvery plants

Achillea nobilis subsp. *neilreichii*
Z4 ‡12–18in (30–15cm) ↔ 18in (45cm) or more if allowed to
spread, ivory flowe heads above aromatic gray foliage

ACONITUM

Aconite, Monkshood

MONKSHOODS ARE NAMED for their hooded flowers, which come in shades of lilac, blue, and pale yellow. These are arranged on tall spires held well above the clumps of divided green foliage. The flowers, which appear from early summer to autumn depending on variety, attract bees and butterflies into the garden. Monkshoods are spreading herbaceous perennials, at their best in reasonably moist beds and borders where they associate well with other perennials such as achilleas (*see p.167*), hemerocallis (*see p.258*), phloxes (*see p.306*), and delphiniums (*see p.224*). The flowers are good for cutting, but be careful handling this plant as all parts are toxic if eaten, and contact with the foliage may aggravate some skin allergies.

Cultivation Monkshoods prefer cool, moist, fertile soil in partial shade, but most soils are tolerated, as is full sun. **Stake** taller monkshoods to prevent them from falling over. **Cut down** the previous year's growth in late winter or early spring. **Sow** seed (*see pp.391–392*) in pots in a cold frame in spring. Divide clumps every three years in autumn or late winter to maintain vigor (*see p.395*).

Aconitum × cammarum 'Bicolor'
Z3b ‡ to 4ft (1.2m) ↔ 12in (30cm), an unusual monkshood, flowers in mid- and late summer

Aconitum carmichaelii 'Arendsii'
Z3b ‡ to 4ft (1.2m) ↔ 12in (30cm), flowers in early and midautumn

Aconitum 'Ivorine'
Z4 ‡ 36in (90cm) ↔ 18in (45cm), a choice variety for a cool, moist site, flowers in early summer

Aconitum 'Bressingham Spire'
Z3b ‡ 36–39in (90–100cm) ↔ 12in (30cm), a long-flowering monkshood, from midsummer to autumn

ACTAEA
Baneberry, Bugbane

THIS GROUP OF PLANTS, which now includes those formerly known as cimicifugas, comprises a range of clump-forming perennials for woodland gardens, shady borders, or streamsides. All have attractive foliage and flowers, and in some cases fruits. Plumes or spires of small, white or pink-tinged flowers appear above the foliage from midspring to late summer and autumn. Varieties such as *Actaea alba* (Z4), *A. rubra*, and *A. spicata* also develop clusters of shiny white, red, or black berries, which are highly poisonous. The divided leaves are usually green, but some of the bugbanes (*Cimicifuga*), for instance *Actaea simplex* 'Brunette', are prized for their bronze or purple foliage. Bugbanes combine well with other perennials such as sidalceas (*see p.325*), goldenrods (*Solidago, see p.327*), and rudbeckias (*see p.317*).

Cultivation Grow in moist, fertile soil, enriched with well-rotted organic matter, in partial shade. Keep well watered in dry spells. **Sow** seed in containers in a cold frame in autumn (*see pp.391–393*); divide plants in spring (*see p.395*).

Actaea rubra
Z4 ↕18in (45cm) ↔ 12in (30cm), the white flowers, followed by red berries, enliven areas of light shade in woodland

ADONIS
Pheasant's eye

THE SOLITARY FLOWERS of these relatively obscure, clump-forming perennials and annuals have a delicate anemone-like appeal. Some, such as *Adonis amurensis* (Z5), appear from late winter to spring, before the fine, ferny foliage has had time to develop. *Adonis brevistyla* and *A. vernalis* (Z5) also bloom in spring and, like many flowers at this time of year, come in shades of white and yellow. These three are all perennial. Good early-flowering companions include cyclamens (*see p.221*), doronicums (*see p.231*), and snowdrops (*see p.247*). *A. aestivalis* is a charming annual that opens its red flowers in midsummer. Adonis vary in their cultivation requirements, suiting either cool, shady, woodland conditions or sunny, open sites. Check soil conditions before you buy.

Cultivation Grow *A. amurensis* and *A. brevistyla* in cool, humus-rich, acidic soil in shade; *A. aestivalis* needs well-drained, alkaline soil in sun. **Sow** seed *(see pp.391–393)* in a cold frame as soon as ripe; germination is slow. Perennial adonis do not respond well to being divided. Susceptible to slug damage.

Actaea (Cimicifuga) simplex
Z4 ↕3–4ft (1–1.2m) ↔ 24in (60cm), feathery spires of flowers appear in late summer and autumn

Actaea (Cimicifuga) simplex 'Brunette'
Z4 ↕3–4ft (1–1.2m) ↔ 24in (60cm), has flower plumes like those of *A. simplex* (*see left*) but tinged with pink

Adonis brevistyla
Z5 ↕8–16in (20–40cm) ↔ 8in (20cm), a faint flush of blue on the outside of the petals adds to the charm of this adonis

AEGOPODIUM PODAGRARIA
Bishop's weed, Goutweed

OF THE FIVE OR SO SPECIES of bishop's weed, most are invasive weeds that spread by underground stems, but the variegated cultivars of *Aegopodium podagraria* are worthy of the garden. *A. podagraria* 'Variegatum' makes a decorative groundcover, spreading over those moist, shady areas of the garden where little else will grow. The leaves are up to 4in (10cm) across. In early summer, it produces clusters of white flowers, but its main value lies in its foliage. Confining this perennial to poor soil, where other plants will not thrive, prevents it from becoming troublesome. Alternatively, grow it in an island bed on its own. Other plants that enjoy similar conditions include bergenias (*see p.198*) and hardy geraniums (*see pp.250–251*).

Cultivation Bishop's weed can be grown in any soil, even very poor ground, in full or partial shade. **Removing** fading flowers before they set seed and slicing off unwanted growth with a spade help to confine its spread. **Divide** rhizomes in autumn or spring (*see p.395*).

Aegopodium podagraria 'Variegatum'
Z4 ‡12–24in (30–60cm) ↔ indefinite

AETHIONEMA
Stone cress

CLUSTERS OF DAINTY FLOWERS, in cheerful shades of red, pink, creamy white, and pure white, are the main reason for growing these annuals and evergreen or semievergreen, woody-based perennials. The flowers are produced on short stems from spring to early summer. The leaves are small, usually stalkless, and rather fleshy. They tend to be short-lived plants, and it is best to increase them from cuttings every two or three years to make sure they perform well. As tiny plants, they are obvious candidates for the front of an herbaceous border or as part of a rock garden. Try growing them with dicentras (*see p.229*), *Euphorbia polychroma* (*see p.242*), and doronicums (*see p.231*).

Cultivation These plants grow best in fertile, well-drained, alkaline soil in full sun, but they also tolerate poor, acidic soils. **Sow** seed (*see pp.391–393*) in containers in a cold frame in spring; sow seed of annuals in autumn directly where they are to grow. **Take** softwood cuttings (*see p.394*) in late spring or early summer.

① *armenum* Z5 ‡6–8in (15–20cm), perennial, flowers in late spring ② *grandiflorum* Z5 ‡8–12in (20–30cm), perennial, flowers in late spring and early summer

AGAPANTHUS
African blue lily

VIGOROUS AND CLUMP-FORMING, these large perennials bear round or pendent heads of bell-shaped flowers in deep shades of blue and violet blue, or in white, from midsummer to early autumn. They generally have handsome, long, strappy leaves. The majority of hybrids are deciduous, while some species are evergreen. The blooms make excellent cut-flower displays, although if they are left on the plant attractive seedheads will follow. These late-flowering perennials also look particularly good in containers.

Cultivation Agapanthus prefer fertile, moist but well-drained soil, in full sun. Mulch them in late autumn, in cold areas, with a layer of well-rotted organic matter. **Container-grown** plants are best in soil-based potting mix. Water them freely during summer; sparingly in winter. During summer, apply a balanced liquid fertilizer until flowering commences. *A. campanulatus* 'Albovittatus' does better under cover if winters are very cold. **Sow** seed (*see pp.391–393*) when they are ripe or in spring. Keep the seedlings in a frost-free cold frame for their first winter. Most seedlings do not come true to type. **Divide** large clumps (*see below and p.395*) in spring.

DIVIDING A ROOTSTOCK
Use a clean, sharp knife to trim off damaged root tissue and old stems. Dust the cuts with fungicide to avoid rot.

Agapanthus campanulatus (Lily of the Nile)
Z7b ‡24–48in (60–120cm) ↔ 18in (45cm), deciduous, gray-green leaves, flowers (often white) in mid- and late summer

THESE PERENNIALS ARE GROWN for their long-lasting, loose spikes of small, tubular flowers, which are up to 12in (30cm) long and borne from midsummer until autumn. These are erect, bushy plants, with lance-shaped to oval, aromatic leaves. *Agastache barberi* 'Tutti-Frutti' (Z6) has strongly aromatic foliage and pinkish red flowers and can be grown as an annual where winters are harsh, as can the rosy-flowered *A. mexicana.* (Z7) Suitable for herbaceous and mixed borders, agastaches associate well with perennials such as yarrows (*see p.166*) and phloxes (*see p.306*).

Cultivation Grow these plants in fertile, well-drained soil in full sun. In warm areas, the less hardy species will survive winter conditions outside if they are planted in a sheltered site. In cold areas, overwinter young plants in frost-free conditions. **Sow** seed (*see pp.391–393*) in early spring. Take semiripe cuttings (*see p.394*) in late summer. **Powdery mildew** may be a problem on the leaves in dry summers; keep the soil thoroughly watered, but avoid splashing the foliage.

Agapanthus **'Bressingham White'**
Z7b ‡36in (90cm) ↔ 24in (60cm), flowers in mid- and late summer

Agapanthus **'Blue Giant'**
Z7b ‡4ft (1.2m) ↔ 24in (60cm), flowers in mid- to late summer

Agapanthus campanulatus **'Albovittatus'**
Z7b ‡24–48in (60–120cm) ↔ 18in (45cm), broad leaves with bold white stripes, flowers in mid- and late summer

Agastache foeniculum (Anise hyssop)
Z6 ‡3–5ft (90–150cm) ↔ 12in (30cm), flowers from midsummer to early autumn

AGROSTEMMA
Corn cockle

‡2–3ft (60–90cm)
↔ 1ft (30cm)

AT ONE TIME, THE CORN COCKLE was a weed in cornfields, but today this delightful annual is used to bring summer color to the garden. The purple to plum pink or white flowers are borne on slender, downy stems, and are set off by the thin, gray-green leaves. The corn cockle's delicate, lax appearance works best in a cottage-style garden, wildflower meadow, or annual border – or try it in containers. Growing it with other types of hardy annuals allows you to create a bright tapestry of color. The flowers are suitable for cutting and attract bees.

Cultivation Grow in poor, well-drained soil in full sun. Too fertile a soil results in leaf growth at the expense of flowers. **Sow** seed in the soil where it is to grow (*see pp.391–393*) in early spring or autumn, and thin seedlings to 9–12in (23–30cm) apart. The rather lax growth often needs staking with twiggy sticks (*see p.390*). **Remove** fading flowers to prolong flowering, or leave on to allow plants to self-seed.

AJUGA
Bugleweed

BUGLES MAKE EXCELLENT GROUNDCOVER in shade or partial shade, particularly in moist ground. They have a dense, spreading habit and can carpet large areas quickly, yet are easy to pull up if they start to grow into other plants. A few are annuals but, for the most part, those grown in gardens are evergreen or semi-evergreen perennials. The leaves of some bugles have a metallic sheen, but for added color, choose those that are tinted bronze or purple-red, or splashed with cream and pink. From late spring until early summer, the mats of foliage are studded with short spikes of usually blue or mauve flowers. Undemanding and easy to grow, bugleweeds are a good choice for the edge of a shady border or for growing under shrubs.

Cultivation Grow in any moist but well-drained soil in partial shade or part-day sun. *Ajuga reptans* and its cultivars tolerate poor soils and full shade. **Separate** rooted stems to make new plants, or take softwood cuttings in early summer (*see p.394*). In overcrowded, dry conditions, powdery mildew and southern blight may spoil leaves. After flowering, remove flower stems and excess growth to avoid problems.

Ajuga reptans 'Multicolor'
Z3 ‡ 6in (15cm) ↔ 24–36in (60–90cm), evergreen, tolerates full shade but needs some sun to bring out colors in its leaves

Agrostemma githago 'Milas'
‡ 24–36in (60–90cm) ↔ 12in (30m), annual, flowers grow to 2in (5cm) across

Ajuga reptans 'Catlin's Giant'
Z3 ‡ 6in (15cm) ↔ 24–36in (60–90cm), the dark blue flower heads grow to 8in (20cm) tall on this large-leaved evergreen

Ajuga reptans 'Atropurpurea'
Z3 ‡ 6in (15cm) ↔ 24–36in (60–90cm), these lustrous evergreen leaves go well with shade-loving primroses

ALCEA
Hollyhock

AN OLD-FASHIONED, COTTAGE GARDEN FAVORITE, hollyhocks are short-lived perennials or biennials. The tall, showy spires of flowers, up to 8ft (2.5m) tall, come in a variety of shades including shell pink, apricot, lemon, cerise, white, and purplish black. The flowers, especially if single, are attractive to butterflies and bees. At their most impressive when grown at the back of a border or along a wall or fence, hollyhocks associate well with cottage-garden favorites with soft colors and billowing outlines, such as rambling roses (*see pp.150–151*) and lilacs (*Syringa, p.121*). Mingle the brightest types with delphiniums (*see p.224*).

Cultivation Grow in reasonably fertile, well-drained soil in full sun. In exposed places, stems may require staking. **Treat** as annuals or biennials (sow one year to flower the next year) to limit the spread of hollyhock rust, the most common disease, which causes orange-brown spots on the leaves. Rust-resistant varieties are available. **Sow** seed (*see pp.391–393*) of annuals at 55°F (13°C) in late winter or where it is to grow in spring. For biennials, sow in midsummer where plants are to flower and thin out or transplant small seedlings, as necessary, in autumn.

ALCHEMILLA
Lady's mantle

‡2–24in (5–60cm)
↔ 8–30in (20–75cm)

THE MOST WIDELY GROWN plant in this group of perennials, all with grayish green leaves and frothy, luminous yellow flowers, is *Alchemilla mollis*. Drought-tolerant and clump-forming, it makes excellent groundcover. The flowers appear for long periods from early summer and are good for cutting, and for drying. Most other alchemillas, such as *A. erythropoda* (Z4), are smaller. Lady's mantle self-seeds prolifically unless fading flowers are removed before they set seed. Grow it in beds and borders or along paths to soften hard lines. It associates well with shrub roses (*see pp.110–111*) and penstemons (*see p.304*), and contrasts beautifully with blue flowers.

Cultivation Grow in any reasonably fertile soil in sun or partial shade. **Deadhead** *A. mollis* and cut back foliage after flowering for fresh leaves. **Sow** seed (*see pp.391–393*) in pots in a cold frame in spring, or divide plants (*see p.395*) in early spring or autumn.

CRYSTAL DROPS The downy leaves retain beads of sparkling dew and raindrops.

① *rosea* Chater's Double Group Z3 ‡ 8ft (2.5m) ↔ to 24in (60cm), vigorous, flowers in bright or pale shades ② *rosea* 'Nigra' Z3 ‡ to 6ft (2m) ↔ to 24in (60cm)

Alchemilla alpina (Alpine lady's mantle) Z4 ‡ 3–5in (8–13cm) ↔ to 20in (50cm), leaves with silvery undersides, flowers in summer, good for a rock garden

Alchemilla mollis Z4b ‡ 24in (60cm) ↔ 30in (75cm), velvety gray-green leaves and yellow-green flowers from early summer to early autumn

ALLIUM
Ornamental onion

THESE DISTINCTIVE, BULBOUS perennials bear dramatic, round, or pendent clusters of bell- or star-shaped flowers in spring and summer. Some of these are up to 12in (30cm) across; some dry well for use in winter flower arrangements. Alliums range in size from small, rock-garden species to 6ft (2m) giants, but most plants are 1–3ft (30–90cm) tall. Show off their bold flower heads in borders, among other flowering perennials, or punching through a drift of grasses. Chives (*Allium shoenoprasum*) and *A. cernuum* are good edging plants. Alliums include the edible onions, and so the strappy or cylindrical foliage has a pungent onion aroma when crushed; it often withers before the flower heads open.

Cultivation Grow in fertile, well-drained soil in full sun. **Plant** bulbs to two or three times their own depth in autumn. **Remove** offsets of bulbs in autumn and divide clumps (*see p.395*) in spring. **Downy mildew**, an off-white fungus, may cause leaves to wither and rot into the bulbs in damp conditions; space plants farther apart. Dig up and destroy bulbs attacked by onion fly and thrips.

Allium cristophii (Star of Persia)
Z5 ‡12–24in (30–60cm) ↔ 6–7in (15–19cm), flower heads to 8in (20cm) in early summer, gray-green basal leaves

DEADHEADING ALLIUMS
Seedheads may be left on for winter interest, or cut close to the ground for drying. Cutting faded flower heads before they produce seed helps to conserve energy in the bulb for next year.

Allium karataviense (Turkistan allium)
Z4 ‡4–10in (10–25cm) ↔ 4in (10cm), broad, flat leaves, purple or gray-green with red edges, flowers in summer

Allium moly (Golden garlic)
Z3 ‡6–10in (15–25cm) ↔ 2in (5cm), gray-green flat leaves, medium flowers in summer, naturalizes rapidly into drifts

Allium 'Globemaster'
Z5 ‡32in (80cm) ↔ 8in (20cm), gray-green basal leaves, dramatic flower heads to 6–8in (15–20cm) in summer

Allium cernuum (Nodding onion, Wild onion)
Z3 ‡ 12–24in (30–60cm) ↔ 2in (5cm) vigorous, narrow dark green leaves, stiff stems, mid- to deep pink flowers in summer

Allium caeruleum (Blue allium)
Z2 ‡ 24in (60cm) ↔ 1in (2.5cm), mid-green leaves clasp the stem, small flower heads appear in early summer

ALSTROEMERIA
Peruvian lily

WIDELY GROWN FOR CUT FLOWERS, these vigorous, tuberous perennials are stalwarts of many a mixed and herbaceous border. The flowers appear in summer, usually in small clusters at the ends of the stems; they are available in such a wide range of shades that there is bound to be one to suit virtually any color scheme. The long, strappy leaves are mid- to gray-green. Try growing alstroemerias combined with shrub roses (see pp.110–113), sunflowers (Helianthus, see p.256), and border phloxes (see pp.306–307). The Canadian hardiness zone ranges from 6–8.

Cultivation Alstroemerias like moist but well-drained soil, in sun or partial shade. **Plant** the long tubers 8in (20cm) deep in late summer or early autumn, and handle them carefully, because they break easily. The plants resent being disturbed, so leave them to form large clumps. **Protect** them with a dry mulch in winter (see p.388). **Sow** seed (see pp.391–392) in a container in a cold frame when it is ripe; transplant seedlings to small pots; and plant out from the pots to avoid root disturbance. **Divide** large, established clumps (see p.395) in autumn or early spring, if needed. Slugs can attack (see p.398); remove and destroy plants infected by viruses (see p.399).

Allium flavum (Small yellow onion)
Z4 ‡ 4–14in (10–35cm) ↔ 2in (5cm), leaves clasp stems, small heads of tiny flowers droop as they open in summer

Allium unifolium
Z4 ‡ 12in (30cm) ↔ 2in (5cm), short, gray-green basal leaves that die before small flower heads appear in spring

① **aurea** ‡ 3ft (1m) ↔ 18in (45cm) ② **ligtu** hybrids ‡ 20in (50cm) ↔ 30in (75cm) ③ **pelegrina** ‡ ↔ to 24in (60cm) ④ **psittacina** ‡ 3ft (1m) ↔ 18in (45cm)

ALTHAEA

‡5ft (1.5m)
↔18in (45cm)

THESE WOODY-BASED PERENNIALS and annuals are similar to hollyhocks (*see Alcea, p.173*), but, unlike hollyhocks, they have smaller flowers, which are on stalks. The blooms appear from midsummer until early autumn in shades of lilac, deep pink, or rose pink sometimes with darker eyes. Althaeas have dark green leaves with lobed or toothed edges and pale undersides. The stems are strong and wiry and rarely need supporting. These are pretty plants for a mixed or herbaceous border as well as a wildflower garden. Grow them with other summer-flowering perennials, like daylilies (*see Hemerocallis, p.258*) and loosestrife (*see Lysimachia, p.283*).

Cultivation These plants tolerate a range of conditions, but do best in fertile, moist but well-drained soil. **Sow** seed of perennials in rows outdoors (*see pp.391–393*) in midsummer and transplant seedlings in early autumn; for annuals, sow seed in pots in late winter, or directly in the ground in midspring. **Rust**, orange-brown spots, may afflict the leaves; pick them off and destroy them. *A. rosea* is less susceptible.

Althaea cannabina (Mallow)
Z4 ‡6ft (2m) ↔ 24in (60cm), perennial

ALYSSUM

LOW MASSES OF BRIGHTLY COLORFUL FLOWERS make this large group of tufted or mat-forming, evergreen perennials, and sometimes erect annuals, prized in the garden. The flowers open in early summer, in shades of pale and golden yellow, pale to deep rose pink, or white, and are occasionally honey-scented. The small leaves form rosettes and are colored gray to silvery gray, sometimes with white hairs. Alyssums are spreading, although never invasive, so can be put to many uses. Try them at the front of a border, in a rock garden, or even in soil-filled crevices in a wall. They look very effective when planted with other carpeting plants, for example *Arabis × arendsii* 'Rosabella', which has rose pink flowers.

Cultivation Grow the plants in well-drained, reasonably fertile soil with added grit, in full sun. A light trim after flowering maintains a compact shape. **Sow** seed (*see pp.391-393*) in a container in autumn or spring. **Root** greenwood cuttings – new shoots that are beginning to firm up – as for soft stem-tip cuttings, in early summer (*see p.394*).

Alyssum wulfenianum
Z5 ‡4–6in (10–15cm) ↔ to 20in (50cm), erect or prostrate evergreen

AMARANTHUS

‡1–5ft (30cm–1.5m)
↔12–30in (30–75cm)

THESE ERECT OR PROSTRATE, bushy annuals or short-lived perennials have red, purple, or green stems and large, shapely leaves – some, especially in cultivars of the annual *Amaranthus tricolor*, in bright hues of purple, maroon, bronze, gold, and red. From summer until early autumn, they produce hanging clusters up to 24in (60cm) long of crimson-purple, red, maroon, gold, rose pink, or cream flowers that look like woolly tassels. In autumn, colored seedheads follow. They are commonly grown as annuals in summer bedding. Try them next to plants with large leaves or flowers of strongly contrasting colors. Some can be grown in containers and hanging baskets.

Cultivation Grow them in moist, reasonably fertile, well-drained soil, in full sun. **Keep** well watered in dry spells during summer to prolong flowering. **Sow** seed (*see pp.391–393*) in midspring in containers or, in milder areas, directly in the garden where plants are to grow. Thin the seedlings to 24in (60cm) apart.

COLLECTING SEED
When the flowers begin to change color, gently run your fingers down the tassels to dislodge the seed.

Amaranthus caudatus (Love-lies-bleeding, Tassel flower)
‡3–5ft (1–1.5m) ↔ 18–30in (45–75cm), annual, leaves up to 6in (15cm), tolerates poor soil

× AMARYGIA PARKERI

‡3ft (90cm)
↔ 12in (30cm)

THE PARENTS OF THIS HYBRID are *Amaryllis belladonna* (*see right*) and *Brunsvigia*. Opening on bare, sturdy stems before the leaves appear, its large, pink or white flowers make an eye-catching addition to the summer garden. The leaves, which are up to an impressive 18in (45cm) long and grow from the base of the plant, are semierect and strappy. In colder areas, the plant benefits from the shelter at the foot of a warm wall, or in an herbaceous or mixed border. Grow it with other bulbous perennials, such as crinums (*see p.218*), and perennials such as achilleas (*see p.166*).

Cultivation Plant bulbs from early to late summer with the necks just above soil level, in full sun in sandy soil that has been enriched with well-rotted organic matter. **Water** freely during summer and apply a well-balanced fertilizer monthly. **Remove** offsets to replant (*see p.395*) from congested plants just before they come into growth in summer. The leaves are prone to scorch. If flowers fail, aphids and bulb flies may have eaten the bulb; dig up and discard affected plants.

AMARYLLIS BELLADONNA

STATELY, SCENTED, AND SHOWY, the clusters of flowers of this bulbous perennial open on sturdy stems in the autumn. It has strappy, fleshy leaves, up to 16in (40cm) long which are produced after the flowers open. Where not reliably hardy, grow it at the base of a sunny, sheltered wall. Where winter temperatures regularly fall below 23°F (−5°C), this plant is best grown in a cool greenhouse or in a conservatory. It looks attractive partnered with other autumn-flowering plants, such as coneflowers (*see Rudbeckia, p.317*), and autumn-flowering bulbs, for example autumn crocuses (*see Colchicum, p.215*).

Cultivation Plant the bulbs just below soil level when they are dormant, in late summer or in spring. **Outdoors**, grow them in reasonably fertile, well-drained soil in full sun and protect the foliage from frost. **Indoors**, they need a soil-based potting mix with additional sharp sand, and full light. In the growing season, water well and apply a balanced fertilize monthly. **Remove** offsets (*see p.395*) in spring and grow them indoors for 1–2 seasons before planting them out. Amaryllis are prone to slug damage (*see p.398*), leaf scorch, and aphids.

Amaranthus caudatus 'Viridis'
‡3–5ft (1–1.5m) ↔ 18–30in (45–75cm), annual, green flowers fade to cream as they age

× *Amarygia parkeri* 'Alba'
T min. 41°F (5°C)

Amaryllis belladonna
Z8 ‡24in (60cm) ↔ 4in (10cm), each flower is up to 4in (10cm) across

ANACYCLUS

‡↔ 12in (30cm)

APPEALING, DAISY FLOWERS and feathery foliage are the attractions of these creeping, low-growing annuals and herbaceous perennials. The flowers, which are usually white with yellow centers, are borne on short stems in summer, held just above a low mound of foliage; the leaves are finely cut and attractive in their own right. Anacyclus dislike cold, wet conditions, and are most suited to growing in a rock garden, raised bed, or alpine trough; a top-dressing of sharp sand over the soil will help keep their stems dry and also enhances their sun-loving, Mediterranean look.

Cultivation Grow in gritty, sharply drained soil in full sun, with shelter from excesive winter moisture. If growing in containers, use a mix of equal parts soil-based potting mix, leaf mold, and sharp sand or grit. **Sow** seed in an open frame in autumn (*see pp.391–393*). **Take** softwood cuttings in spring or early summer (*see p.394*).

ANAGALLIS
Pimpernel

‡ to 8in (20cm)
↔ to 16in (40cm)

THE DEEP BLUE OR DEEP PINK flowers of these annuals and evergreen perennials are produced in late spring and summer, and are borne in such profusion that they almost completely hide the leaves. The flowers are open and saucer-shaped. Pimpernels are low-growing or mat-forming, with branching stems and mid-green leaves. The largest grow to only around 10in (25cm) tall and look good in a rock garden or at the front of a border. Tiny varieties like *Anagallis tenella* 'Studland' are ideal plants for shallow pots and bowls.

Cultivation Grow pimpernels in fertile, moist, but well-drained soil or gritty potting mix, in full sun. Pimpernels are short-lived so it is best to propagate them every three or four years. **Divide** in spring (*see p.395*). **Sow** seed in a container in a cold frame in spring (*see pp.391–392*). **Take** stem-tip cuttings of named varieties in spring or early summer (*see p.394*). Overwinter young plants in a cool greenhouse and plant out only when any danger of frost has passed.

Anagallis monellii (Blue pimpernel)
Z7b ‡ 4–8in (10–20cm) ↔ to 16in (40cm), perennial, red- and pink-flowered forms are available

Anacyclus pyrethrum var. *depressus*
Z4 ‡ 2in (5cm) or more ↔ 4in (10cm), perennial, leaves gray-green, flowers on short, slender stems, petals red on reverse

Anagallis tenella 'Studland'
Z6 ‡ 2–4in (5–10cm) ↔ to 16in (40cm), perennial, bright green leaves tend to be obscured by the scented flowers

ANAPHALIS
Pearly everlasting

THESE MEDIUM-HEIGHT, SPREADING or upright perennials have woolly, gray foliage, and clusters of papery, "everlasting" white flowers produced from midsummer until autumn. They are very popular for cutting and drying. The smaller varieties suit a rock garden; grow the more upright varieties in a herbaceous or mixed border. They are ideal plants for a white-themed scheme, since the flowers and silvery foliage provide several months of color. Pearly everlasting is also especially useful in locations that are too moist for growing other gray- or silver-leaved foliage plants that prefer better-drained soils. To dry the flowers, cut them soon after they are open and hang upside down in bunches in a light, airy place.

Cultivation Grow in reasonably fertile soil that is fairly well-drained, but does not dry out during hot spells in summer. They prefer full sun but will tolerate partial shade. **Divide** plants in early spring (see p.395). **Sow** seed in a container in a cold frame in spring (see pp.391–392). **Take** stem-tip cuttings in early summer (see p.394).

ANCHUSA
Alkanet

ALKANET FLOWERS HAVE A DEPTH OF BLUE that is not often seen in other plants. The small, but numerous flowers are produced in spring and early summer on branching stems, which are upright in taller cultivars or prostrate in the dwarf, mound-forming types, in shades of indigo, clear gentian blue, or ultramarine, some with a white center. Bees love them. The leaves are long and thin, coarse, and often bristly. Alkanets may be annual, biennial, or perennial. The taller ones give a vivid accent to a herbaceous or mixed border. Dwarfer types, such as *Anchusa cespitosa*, bring jewel-like brilliance to a rock garden or alpine trough.

Cultivation Grow in any moist but well-drained soil that is moderately fertile, in full sun. Most alkanets resent excessive winter moisture. Dwarf types in particular must have free-draining, gritty potting mix or soil. **Stake** taller anchusas if necessary as they grow (see p.390). **Deadhead** after the first flush of flowers to encourage more later on. **Cut back** top-growth after flowering to encourage new growth that will overwinter. **Sow** seed in a container in a cold frame in spring (pp.391–392). **Take** basal cuttings in spring, or root cuttings in winter (see p.394). May suffer from mildew (see pp.398–399).

Anchusa capensis 'Blue Angel'
↕8in (20cm) ↔ 6in (15cm), biennial often grown as an annual, leaves bristly, flowers in summer

margaritacea Z4 ↕↔ 24in (60cm), flowers midsummer to early
umn ② *triplinervis* Z3 ↕32–36in (80–90cm) ↔ 18–24in
–60cm), flowers in mid- and late summer

Anchusa azurea 'Loddon Royalist' (Italian bugloss)
Z3b ↕36in (90cm) ↔ 24in (60cm), perennial, forms densely flowering clumps, rarely needs staking, flowers in early summer

Anchusa cespitosa
Z5b ↕2–4in 5–10cm) ↔ 6–8in (15–20cm), perennial, ground-hugging, flowers in spring

ANDROSACE
Rock jasmine

‡10in (25cm)
↔ 12in (30cm)

THESE PRETTY PERENNIALS make dense cushions or mats of evergreen foliage that is smothered in small pink or white flowers. The flowers are tubular and appear singly or in clusters from late spring to late summer. The cushion-forming species from high mountainous regions are ideal for an alpine house (an unheated, well-ventilated greenhouse) where they are easily protected from winter moisture. The rest, however, are suitable for rock gardens, dry-stone walls, and alpine troughs, and look good with other cushion-forming plants such as saxifrages (*see pp.320–321*). The Canadian hardiness zone ranges from 4–6.

Cultivation Grow in vertical crevices in walls in moist, well-drained soil in full sun. In containers, use a soil-based potting mix with extra grit, and add a collar of grit at the neck of the plant.. **Top-dress** the soil surface with grit (*see p.386*) to protect plants from moisture, which causes fungal disease. **Sow** seed in a cold frame when ripe or in autumn (*see pp.391–393*). Take single rosettes as cuttings in early to midsummer; water from below to avoid wetting the rosettes.

① *carnea* subsp. *lagger-i* ‡2in (5cm) ② *lanuginosa* ‡ to 4in (10cm) ③ *pyrenaica* ‡1½–2in (4–5cm) ④ *villosa* var. *jacquemontii* ‡ to 1½in (4cm)

ANEMONE
Windflower

THIS LARGE AND VERSATILE GROUP of perennials has delightful flowers from spring to autumn, and displays a wide range of habits, sizes, and tolerance for different situations. The flowers vary from pink, blue, and violet to red and yellow. They are usually saucer- to cup-shaped with a central boss of stamens and are either solitary or in clusters. Leaves are mid- to dark green with toothed edges. Anemones are divided into three main groups: spring-flowering types, growing in woodland and pastures, some with tubers or rhizomes; tuberous Mediterranean species, flowering in spring or early summer; and larger, tall herbaceous perennials, flowering in late summer and autumn.

Cultivation Grow in moist, well-drained soil in sun or partial shade. Plant in autumn or spring and mulch with well-rotted organic matter (*see p.388*) for winter protection. **Sow** seed (*see pp.391–393*) in containers in a cold frame when ripe; germination may be slow and erratic. **Divide** (*see p.395*) autumn-flowering anemones in autumn or spring. Separate tubers of tuberous species in summer when they are dormant. Foliage may be disfigured by powdery mildew (*see p.398*).

Anemone pavonina
Z8 ‡10in (25cm) ↔ 10in (15cm), red, pink, or purple flowers in spring; needs sun and good drainage

Anemone × *hybrida* 'Max Vogel' (Japanese anemone)
Z4 ‡4–5ft (1.2–1.5m) ↔ indefinite, prefers moist, humus-rich soil, in sun or light shade, flowers from late summer to midautumn

Anemone nemorosa (Windflower, Wood anemone)
Z4 ‡3–6in (8–15cm) ↔ 12in (30cm) or more, this creeping, spring-flowering anemone grows under hedges or deciduous trees

ANETHUM GRAVEOLENS

Dill

THE AROMATIC GREEN AND BLUE-GREEN FOLIAGE of dill is its distinctive feature, complemented in midsummer by its flattened clusters of greenish yellow or yellow flowers. Dill is annual or biennial and has hollow, ridged stems and anise-scented leaves that are finely divided into threadlike leaflets. The seeds and leaves have many culinary and medicinal uses. Dill looks at its best grown with other herbs in a vegetable or herb garden, but the fine, ferny foliage also acts as a wonderful contrast to perennials with bolder leaves such as hostas *(see pp.260–261)*. The dwarf *Anethum graveolens* 'Fern Leaved' grows to only 18in (45cm) and is suitable for pots on a windowsill.

Cultivation Grow in fertile, well-drained soil in full sun with shelter from strong, cold winds. **Water** freely during dry spells in summer to prevent running to seed. **Sow** seed *(see pp.391–393)* from spring to midsummer for a succession of fresh foliage. Young plants do not transplant well; thin seedlings to 4in (10cm) apart. If you have limited space, sow a pinch of seed in a large pot and grow on the patio.

STAKING TALL PLANTS
Tall anemones are easily blown over. Stake them early in the season, pushing the supports well into the ground and raising them as the plant grows and fills out

Anemone vitifolia (Grapeleaf anemone)
Z4b ↕ 3ft (1m) ↔ indefinite, the white flowers, excellent in light shade, appear in late summer and early autumn

Anemone hupehensis 'Bressingham Glow'
Z3 ↕ 24–36in (60–90cm) ↔ 16in (40cm), mid- to late-summer-flowering anemone spreads well once established

Anemone blanda 'Radar'
Z5 ↕ ↔ 6in (15cm), grows from knobby tubers and prefers sun or partial shade and well-drained soil; flowers in spring

Anemone blanda 'White Splendour'
Z5 ↕ ↔ 6in (15cm), like 'Radar' *(see left)* in every respect, except that it has white flowers

Anethum graveolens
↕ 24in (60cm) or more ↔ 12in (30cm), annual

FLOWERING PLANTS

ANGELICA

‡3–8ft (1–2.5m)
↔ 3–4ft (1–1.2m)

ARCHITECTURAL ANGELICAS bring height and drama to a garden. Clump-forming perennials and biennials, their majestic stems are topped with umbrella-shaped flower clusters, followed by attractive seedheads. The flowers are lime yellow on *Angelica archangelica* and open in early summer; those of *A. gigas* (Z4) appear in late summer and, like the stems, are a striking red-purple. Grow them in borders, or as specimens in a woodland setting. They also thrive in damp soil along streams or pond edges.

Cultivation Grow in deep, moist, fertile soil in full sun or partial shade. *Angelica archangelica* dies after flowering, but if the fading flowers are cut off before the seedheads form it may survive and flower for a second year. It may also self-seed freely. **Sow** seed (*see pp.391–393*) in a container in a cold frame as soon as it is ripe; do not cover with potting mix or grit – it needs light to germinate. **Transplant** the seedlings while small since larger plants resent root disturbance. They will take around two years to flower from seed. Slugs and snails may be troublesome (*see p.398*).

Angelica archangelica
Z4 ‡6ft (2m) ↔ 4ft (1.2m), the leaf stalks of this aromatic herb can be candied for use in sweets and cake decoration

ANOMATHECA

‡6–12in (15–30cm)
↔ 2in (5cm)

CLOSELY RELATED TO FREESIAS, this small group of perennials bears delicate flowers in shades of red, green, and pure white. These appear in late spring and early summer and are followed by brown seedheads containing scarlet seeds. Like freesias, anomathecas grow from corms. Where not hardy, they are best grown in a container in a cool or cold greenhouse or conservatory. Plant them at the front of a sheltered border; they make splendid companions for late-flowering tulips.

Cultivation Plant corms in spring 2in (5cm) deep in free-draining, sandy, reasonably fertile soil, in full sun. If growing in containers, use a soil-based potting mix. **Water** well and apply a balanced fertilizer at monthly intervals during the growing season. Keep the corms completely dry while dormant. **Divide** clumps in spring, as necessary (*see p.395*). **Sow** seed (*see pp.391–393*) at 55–61°F (13–16°C) in spring, but allow up to two years for the seedlings to flower.

Anomatheca laxa
Z8 ‡6–12in (15–30cm) ↔ 2in (5m), each corm produces up to six flowers in early summer

ANTHEMIS

AROMATIC FOLIAGE AND DAISY FLOWERS are the chief attributes of these clump-forming and mat-forming perennials. The golden-eyed, yellow, or white flowers are produced in succession from late spring until late summer and are often excellent for cutting. Anthemis enjoy sunny, well-drained conditions, the smaller types such as *A. punctata* (Z7) making valuable plants for the rock garden. In borders, their finely cut foliage, sometimes silver-gray, can look effective next to other filigree-leaved plants such as artemisias (*see p.25 and p.189*) and argyranthemums (*see p.24*). Alternatively, contrast anthemis with bold, sword-leaved plants such as irises (*see pp.264–267*) and yuccas (*see p.129*).

Cultivation Grow in reasonably fertile, well-drained soil in full sun. *Anthemis sancti-johannis* and *A. tinctoria* are short-lived plants. **Cut back** hard, to the new shoots at the base, after flowering to encourage new growth and increase longevity. **Sow** seed (*see pp.391–392*) in pots in a cold frame in spring. **Divide** in spring (*see p.395*) to make new plants or take basal cuttings in spring or late summer (*see p.394*).

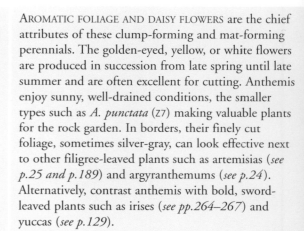

Anthemis tinctoria 'E.C. Buxton' (Golden chamomile)
Z3 ‡8–28in (45–70cm1) ↔ 24–36in (60–90m), flowers are produced in abundance all summer, if deadheaded regularly

ANTHERICUM

WITH GRACEFUL, NARROW LEAVES to 16in (40cm) long, these rhizomatous perennials are ideal for naturalizing in grass. In late spring and early summer, the clumps of mid- or gray-green leaves produce delicate, lilylike, white flowers in small clusters on slender stems. The flowers are at their largest, up to 1¼in (3cm) across, in *Anthericum liliago* var. *major* (Z7) In autumn, these are followed by decorative brown seedheads. Anthericums are excellent naturalized with other wildflowers, or in a herbaceous or mixed border. They look good alongside early summer-flowering oriental poppies (*Papaver, see p.299*). The flowers are also excellent for cutting.

Cultivation Grow in any fertile, well-drained soil in full sun. **Sow** seed (*see pp.391–393*) in a container in a cold frame in autumn or spring. Seedlings may take up to three years to flower. Alternatively, increase stock by dividing (*see p.395*) in spring as growth begins, although the new plants may not flower until the following year.

ANTHRISCUS

THE DAINTY FLOWER HEADS AND LACY FOLIAGE of *Anthriscus sylvestris*, better known as cow parsley or Queen Anne's lace, introduce an airy, natural charm into the garden from midspring until early summer. This is the most commonly grown ornamental of the various annual, biennial, and perennial types of anthriscus, although the annual *A. cerefolium*, chervil, is an anise-flavored herb. Cow parsley's tiny, white or creamy white flowers are followed by flat seedheads. The delightful, dark-leaved *A. sylvestris* 'Ravenswing' has flower heads with a tinge of pink. Usually biennial, but sometimes a short-lived perennial, it is particularly at home in meadow-style plantings. In the herbaceous border, team it with spiky flowered stachys (*see p.328*), veronicas (*p.337*), or salvias (*p.318*).

Cultivation Grow in any moist but well-drained soil, in full sun or partial shade. It self-seeds prolifically. **Sow** seed (*see pp.391–392*) in a container in a cold frame in spring or autumn. If grown well away from other cow parsleys, 'Ravenswing' produces dark-leaved seedlings.

Anthemis sancti-johannis
Z4 ↕ 24–36in (60–90cm) ↔ 24in (60m), a short-lived but free-flowering plant, best supported in exposed sites

Anthericum liliago (St Bernard's lily)
Z7 ↕ 24–36in (60–90cm) ↔ 12in (30m), this is a versatile plant for naturalistic and sophisticated garden designs

Anthriscus sylvestris 'Ravenswing'
Z4 ↕ 3ft (1m) ↔ 12in (30cm), like all cow parsleys, this self-seeds, but select only those with dark, purple-brown foliage

FLOWERING PLANTS

Snapdragons

APPEALINGLY SHAPED FLOWERS, usually in a riot of bright colors, make snapdragons a cheerful garden plant. They belong to a group of annuals and perennials that flower from early summer until autumn. The most popular are those grown as annuals in bedding or as cut flowers. Although technically short-lived perennials, the best flowers are usually obtained in their first year, so new plants should be bought, or raised from seed, each spring. The dark green leaves will be almost entirely hidden by the flowers when plants are grown closely together, in blocks or with other summer-bedding plants. There are trailing types especially bred for hanging baskets too. If you have a rock garden, try growing some of the lesser-known, more delicate, shrubby snapdragons.

Cultivation Grow in fertile, well-drained soil in full sun. Shrubby species require very well-drained soil and shelter from strong, cold winds. **Remove** fading flowers to prolong the flowering display. **Sow** seed of *A. majus* cultivars at 61–64°F (16–18°C) in early spring, and of shrubby species in a container in autumn or spring (*see pp.391–393*).

Antirrhinum pulverulentum
Z8 ‡6–8in (15–20cm) ↔ 8–12in (20–30cm), very small and creeping, needs shelter and dislikes cold, wet conditions

Antirrhinum hispanicum
Z7b ‡8in (20cm) ↔ 18in (45cm), dwarf, compact, good for small rock gardens or an alpine trough, dislikes winter moisture

Antirrhinum majus **Madame Butterfly Series**
Z6b ‡24–30in (60–75cm) ↔ 18in (45cm), perennial grown as annual, good as cut flowers, long-lasting with tall stems

Antirrhinum braun-blanquetii
Z7 ‡↔ 18in (45cm), a bedding type, very densely packed flowers, ideal for containers

AQUILEGIA
Columbine

THE NODDING, BONNETLIKE FLOWERS of columbines are invaluable in informal planting designs, from a sunny cottage garden to a lightly shaded woodland area. From late spring, and in some cases until late summer, mostly bell-shaped flowers with spurred petals are borne singly or in small clusters on long stalks. Columbines are upright, vigorous perennials, and the larger species, including *Aquilegia vulgaris,* are at home in dappled shade or massed in a border with upright flowering plants such as lupines (*see p.280*), delphiniums (*see p.224*), and other perennials. The alpine columbine is best grown in a rock garden in sharply drained soil.

Cultivation Grow the larger types in fertile, moist but well-drained soil in full sun or partial shade. Grow alpine species in well-drained soil in full sun and mulch (*see p.388*) with sand. **Sow** seed in a container in a cold frame as soon as it is ripe (*see pp.391–392*). Seed of alpine species may take two years to germinate. Columbines do self-seed freely if seed is allowed to ripen on the plants, so do not be hasty in cutting back stems in autumn.

Aquilegia McKana Group
Z3 ‡30in (75cm) ↔ 24in (60cm), flowers from late spring to midsummer, vigorous but short-lived

Aquilegia fragrans
Z4 ‡6–16in (15–40cm) ↔ 6–8in (15–20cm), fragrant flowers tinged blue in early summer, needs rich soil, tolerates light shade

Aquilegia vulgaris 'Nivea'
Z3 ‡36in (90cm) ↔ 18in (45cm), gray-green foliage, flowers in late spring and early summer

Aquilegia vulgaris 'Nora Barlow'
Z3 ‡36in (90cm) ↔ 18in (45cm), vigorous, with uncharacteristic spurless, double pompon flowers

Aquilegia alpina (Alpine aquilegia)
Z4 ‡18in (45cm) sometimes more ↔ to 12in (18in), flowers in late spring, prefers rich soil in sun or partial shade

ARABIS
Rock cress

THESE SMALL, MAT-FORMING, evergreen or semi-evergreen perennials can bring color to poor or dry sites where many other plants would not survive. Loose clusters of cross-shaped flowers are borne on slender stems during late spring and early summer. The leaves are often hairy, and on some cultivars are variegated white or yellow. Rock cress is very easy to grow, and *Arabis alpina* subsp. *caucasica* (Z3) is a good groundcover option for dry soils. It is often used as a spreading plant in a rock garden, at the edge of a border, or in crevices in a wall.

Cultivation Grow rock cress in any well-drained soil in full sun. It will tolerate poor, infertile soils, even in very hot or dry conditions. **Protect** *A. blepharophylla* 'Fruhlingszauber' from winter moisture (*see p.372*). **Site** vigorous species, such as *A. alpina* subsp. *caucasica*, with care as they may swamp small neighbors. **Trim** with shears, after flowering, to keep plants dense and neat. **Sow** seed (*see pp.391–392*) in a container in autumn and give seedlings the protection of a cold frame. Alternatively, take softwood cuttings (*see p.394*) in summer.

Arabis procurrens 'Variegata'
Z5 ‡ 2–3in (5–8cm) ↔ 12–16in (30–40cm), evergreen or semi-evergreen, remove stems with nonvariegated leaves

ARCTOTIS
African daisy

SILVERY LEAVES AND A SOUTH AFRICAN origin mark out these annuals and perennials as heat-loving plants. Long, sturdy stems support the daisies from midsummer until autumn. They are brightly colored orange, white, or creamy yellow; the petals are often marked near the base with a contrasting shade. The flowers have a tendency to close on cloudy days or in midafternoon, although modern varieties have been bred to stay open longer. African daisies are often used as an annual in summer bedding displays, and are wonderful in gravel gardens or containers.

Cultivation Grow in sharply drained, but preferably moist soil in full sun. **Sow** seed (*see pp.391–393*) at 61–64°F (16–18°C) in early spring or autumn. After gemination, prick seedlings out into individual 4in (10cm) pots to minimize root disturbance before planting out. **Root** stem cuttings (*see p.394*) at any time – this is the best method for propagating plants with especially fine flowers, because seed may not come true.

Arabis alpina subsp. *caucasica* 'Variegata'
Z3 ‡ 6in (15cm) ↔ 20in (50cm) or more, when the fragrant flowers have finished, cream-margined evergreen leaves appear

Arabis blepharophylla 'Frühlingszauber'
Z5 ‡ 4in (10cm) ↔ 8in (20cm), mat- or cushion-forming evergreen, short lived if subjected to winter moisture

Arctotis fastuosa (Monarch of the veldt)
T min. 41°F (5°C) ‡ 12–24in (30–60cm) ↔ 12in (30cm), grow as a bedding plant in cool climates, with flowers 4in (10cm) across

Arctotis fastuosa 'Zulu Prince'
T min. 41°F (5°C) ↕ 12–24in (30–60cm) ↔ 12in (30cm), silver
foliage combines with brightly marked white flowers

ARENARIA
Sandwort

MOST OF THE SANDWORTS are low-growing or spreading perennials; some of them are evergreen, although there are a few annual species. All have narrow, grayish green leaves, borne on wiry stems that can form loose mats or dense cushions. From late spring until early summer, they bear a profusion of small, cup-shaped, usually white flowers. Sandworts, which come from mountainous regions, thrive in a rock garden or the crevices of dry-stone walls. They are excellent, too, for planting between paving to soften the hard edges and will transform a bare patio if grown in this way with other mat-forming plants such as aubrietas (*see p.195*) and arabis (*see p.186*).

Cultivation Grow in moist, but well-drained, sandy or poor soil, in full sun. *Arenaria balearica* grows well in partial shade; *A. tetraquetra* needs very well-drained soil. **Divide** plants (*see p.395*) in early spring. **Sow** seed (*see pp.391–392*) in a cold frame in autumn, or take new shoots from the base and treat as softwood cuttings (*see p.394*) in early summer.

① *balearica* (Corsican sandwort) Z5b ↕ ½in (1cm) ↔ 12in
(30cm) or more ② *montana* Z4 ↕ 1–2in (2–5cm) ↔ 12in
(30cm), flowers in late spring to early summer

ARGEMONE
Prickly poppy

↕ 3–5ft (1–1.5m)
↔ to 16in (40cm)

AS YOU MIGHT EXPECT from its common name, an argemone resembles a cross between a thistle and a poppy. This group of annuals and short-lived perennials form clumps of gray-green, often very spiky leaves. The main attraction, though, is their paper-thin, white, yellow, or mauve flowers that are borne from summer to autumn, and are followed by very spiny seedpods. Complement their coloring by planting them with other silver-leaved plants such as artemisias (*see p.25*) or mulleins (*Verbascum, see p.336*) in a hot, sunny border or gravel garden. Perennial argemones are often grown as annuals. All species self-seed freely.

Cultivation Argemones like very poor, gritty or stony soil in full sun. **Deadhead** regularly (*see p.390*) to prolong the flowering period. **Sow** seed (*see pp.391–392*) at 64°F (18°C) in early spring, and prick out seedlings into 5in (10cm) pots. **Plant out** as soon as possible after the last frost because established plants resent disturbance.

Argemone mexicana (Devil's fig, Mexican poppy)
↕ 3ft (1m) ↔ 12–16in (30–40cm), annual, scented flowers, up to
3in (8cm) across, appear in late summer and early autumn

ARMERIA

Sea pink, Thrift

THRIFTS ARE A DELIGHTFUL group of clump-forming perennials, familiar to some as seaside plants. They are loved for their small and fluffy, rounded flower heads in late spring to summer, borne at the tips of slender stems above grassy foliage. Flower colors range from white to pale and dark pink. These are ideal plants for growing in a rock garden or at the front of a mixed border. They also make a decorative edging plant alongside a path and thrive between cracks in paving. Try growing them in a trough with other small rock-garden plants like haberleas (*see p.254*) and rhodiolas (*see p.316*).

Cultivation Grow in well-drained, poor to reasonably fertile soil in an open spot in full sun. **Sow** seed in a pot or tray (*see pp.391–393*) in a cold frame in spring or autumn. **Divide** plants in early spring (*see p.395*).

① *maritima* 'Splendens' (Sea thrift) Z4 ‡ to 8in (20cm) ↔ to 12in (30cm) ② *pseudarmeria* Z5 ‡ to 20in (50cm) ↔ 12in (30cm)

ARNEBIA PULCHRA

Prophet flower

THE FUZZY-HAIRY FOLIAGE of this arnebia has a certain similarity to that of the lungworts (*Pulmonaria, see p.314*), but it is the small clusters of trumpet-shaped, summer flowers for which this plant is grown. These are golden yellow, with purple-black spots at the base of the petals, which fade as the petals age. *Arnebia pulchra* is a short-lived, clump-forming perennial and is easy to grow. It suits a wide range of sites, from rock gardens to the front of a mixed border. Try combining it with other herbaceous perennials such as evening primroses (*Oenothera, see p.294*), arenarias (*see p.187*), and armerias (*see left*).

Cultivation Grow *A. pulchra* in partial shade in moist but well-drained soil. It will tolerate full sun so long as the soil is reliably moist. **Sow** seed in a container in a cold frame as soon as it is ripe (*see pp.391–392*). **Take** root cuttings in winter or divide plants in spring (*see pp.394–395*) to increase stock.

Arnebia pulchra
Z7 ‡↔ to 12in (30cm)

ARTEMISIA

Mugwort, Sagebrush, Wormwood

see also p.25

GARDENERS ARE ATTRACTED by artemisias' silvery and aromatic, ferny foliage, which is shown to advantage when set beside plants with bold or plain leaves. Most artemisias have a bushy habit, but there are some creeping or spreading forms, such as *Artemisia stelleriana* 'Boughton Silver', which make good groundcover plants. The majority are perennial, and a few are classed as shrubs (*see p.25*). If the small and insignificant flowers spoil the overall appearance, snip these off as they appear in summer. Artemisias make splendid partners for many plants, including silver-leaved shrubs such as lavenders (*see p.80*), and plants with purple, pink, or red flowers. They also look good at the base of roses (*see pp.110–113 and 150–151*).

Cultivation Grow in well-drained, fertile soil in full sun. Improve heavy soils before planting by digging in plenty of coarse grit. **Cut back** in spring to maintain a compact habit. **Divide** plants in spring or autumn (*see p.395*). **Sow** seed in containers in a cold frame in spring (*see pp.391–392*). **Take** greenwood or heel cuttings in summer, slightly later than softwood cuttings when the stem is a little firmer (*see p.394*).

Artemisia schmidtiana 'Nana' (Silvermound) Z4 ‡3in (8cm) ↔ 12in (30cm), low, compact plant with silky, silvery foliage that is ideal for rock gardens and troughs

ARTHROPODIUM

THE GRASSY, BLUE- OR GRAY-GREEN leaves and small, starry flowers in midsummer are the main points of interest of this little-known group of evergreen and deciduous perennials. Relatives of the lily, arthropodiums grow from short rhizomes, producing leaves that are up to 10in (25cm) long. The pendulous, white, pale violet, or blue flowers are borne in loose clusters and have a wiry delicacy. *Arthropodium candidum* and *A. milleflorum* are the hardiest and two most commonly grown plants in this group, suiting sunny rock gardens or sheltered herbaceous and mixed borders, where they mix well with foliage plants such as tradescantias (*see p.331*).

Cultivation Grow in fertile, well-drained, gritty soil in full sun. Where marginally hardy, grow at the base of a warm, sheltered wall, or in a cold or cool greenhouse. **Sow** seed in containers in a cold frame in autumn or early spring (*see pp.391–392*). **Divide** plants in early spring (*see p.395*). Young plants should be overwintered in frost-free conditions. New growth is vulnerable to slugs (*see p.398*).

Artemisia pontica (Roman Wormwood)
Z5b ‡ 16–32in (40–80cm) ↔ 36in (90cm), forms dense, all-year groundcover, but it is highly invasive

Artemisia 'Powis Castle'
Z5b ‡ 24in (60cm) ↔ 36in (90cm), silvery artemisia forms a fine, billowing clump of foliage but may not survive severe winters

Artemisia stelleriana 'Boughton Silver' (Dusty Miller)
Z4b ‡ to 6in (15cm) ↔ 12–36in (30–45cm), good for groundcover in well-drained sites, and an attractive plant for large pots

Arthropodium milleflorum
T min. 41°F (5°C) ‡ to 20in (50cm) ↔ to 8in (20cm), the bluish or grayish green foliage is spangled with flowers in midsummer

FLOWERING PLANTS

ARUM

Lords and ladies

‡6–20in (15–50cm)
↔ 6in (15cm)

WITH THEIR ARROW-SHAPED LEAVES emerging in late autumn and winter, these tuberous perennials make good foliage plants at a time of year when fresh growth is particularly welcomed. Reaching 14in (35cm) long, the leaves can be glossy green and have pale green or cream marbling. Between late spring and summer, leaflike flowers are produced in pale green, white, or yellow. Enclosed within is a prominent spike that bears persistent, bright orange-red berries later in the year. The best and largest leaves are produced in light shade, but a sunny, open site is needed for the plant to flower well. All parts of the plant are toxic.

Cultivation Grow in a sheltered site in well-drained soil enriched with organic matter. **Plant** tubers up to 6in (15cm) deep in autumn or spring. **Divide** after flowering to make new plants (*see p.395*).

Arum italicum 'Marmoratum'
Z5b ‡12in (30cm) ↔ 6in (15cm), marbled leaves through to late spring, flowers in early summer, berries last to autumn

ARUNCUS

Goatsbeard

‡ to 6ft (2m)
↔ to 4ft (1.2m)

FEATHERY PLUMES OF FLOWERS are borne above mounds of handsome, heavily veined leaves from early to midsummer. Goatsbeards belong to a small genus, related to filipendulas (*see p.244*) and spiraeas (*see p.119*), containing just a few species, all perennial. The tiny cream or white flowers that form the plumes may be either male or female, with the females subsequently producing small green seedpods that will scatter seed freely if they are not deadheaded. Both seedheads and flower heads are popular for indoor arrangements. In the garden, this clump-forming plant thrives in moist soil and suits being grown at the edge of a pond or in damp woodland. *Aruncus aethusifolius* (Z4) is a small, very compact form.

Cultivation Grow in moist, fertile soil, in partial shade. **Plant out** in autumn or early spring. **Sow** seed in containers (*see pp.391–393*) placed in a cold frame. **Lift and divide** in spring or autumn every two or three years to make new plants and maintain vigor (*see p.395*).

Aruncus dioicus
Z3b ‡6ft (2m) ↔ 4ft (1.2m), will tolerate drier conditions than other types, but much prefers a fairly damp site

ASARINA PROCUMBENS

Creeping snapdragon, Wild Ginger snapdragon

‡2in (5cm) ↔ to 24in (60cm)

THE DELICATE, PALE YELLOW flowers of this trailing, evergreen perennial closely resemble those of the snapdragon (*see Antirrhinum, p.184*), giving rise to its common name. Appearing from early summer until early autumn, the flowers have deep yellow throats with light purple veining and reach 1½in (3.5cm) long. They are borne above gray-green leaves that are soft, hairy, and slightly sticky. Asarina's trailing habit makes it a favorite for growing as a groundcover over the edge of a shady wall, a raised bed, or the stony slopes of a rock garden. The plant tends to be short lived but seeds itself freely about the garden.

Cultivation Grow in well-drained soil enriched with well-rotted organic matter. **Plant** in partial shade for best results. **Sow** seed in early spring (*see pp.391–392*) at a temperature of 61°F (16°C).

Asarina procumbens
Z5 ‡2in (5cm) ↔ to 24in (60cm)

ASCLEPIAS
Milkweed, Silkweed

COLORFUL CLUSTERS OF FLOWERS are produced by this large group of perennials (and a few shrubs) in such abundance that they attract great numbers of butterflies and bees. The flowers range in color from purple-pink, deep pink, and orange-red to yellow and appear from midsummer until autumn. They are followed by fruits that split when ripe to reveal rows of seeds with long, silky hairs, hence the common name of silkweed. The leaves and tips of the stems contain a milky sap, which can irritate skin. Milkweeds like a variety of sites from sunny borders to pondsides; many are suited to wildflower plantings.

Cultivation Most grow well in fertile, well-drained soil in full sun, although *A. incarnata* prefers fairly moist conditions. Some are slow to begin growth in spring. **Sow** seed in spring in containers in a cold frame (*see pp.391–392*). **Divide** in spring to make new plants (*see p.395*) and, if necessary, keep clumps under control. Some, especially *A. hallii* and *A. syriacus*, spread quickly by underground suckers and can be invasive.

ASPHODELINE
Jacob's rod

‡3–5ft (1–1.5m)
↔12in (30cm)

STRIKING SPIRES OF YELLOW OR WHITE starry flowers emerge in spring and summer, rising above the clumps of blue-green, grassy leaves. These herbaceous biennial and perennial plants, natives of the Mediterranean, grow from swollen, fleshy roots (rhizomes), which allow them to withstand dry conditions. They thrive in dry, sunny sites such as banks and well-drained beds and borders. Good companions include many annuals, such as the corn marigold (*Chrysanthemum segetum*), eryngiums (*see p.238*), and other Mediterranean plants like rosemary (*p.114*) and phlomis (*p.306*).

Cultivation Grow in reasonably fertile, well-drained soil in full sun. **Mulch** for winter protection in very cold areas by spreading a thick layer of straw, bark chips, or other organic matter over clumps in late autumn. **Sow** seed in a container (*see pp.391–393*) in a cold frame in spring. **Divide** plants (*see p.395*) in late summer or early autumn, taking care not to damage the roots.

ASPHODELUS
Asphodel

GROWN FOR THEIR SLENDER SPIKES of delicate flowers in shades of white or pink, asphodels, like their close cousins asphodelines (*see left*), are excellent plants for a dry, sunny border. Those grown in gardens are mostly perennial, but there are also some annuals. The flowers open in late spring and early summer and often have attractive, contrasting markings on the petals. The tall flower stems rise up from dense tufts of grassy foliage. Natives of warm, well-drained, sometimes quite barren places, asphodels need a sheltered site and free-draining soil in cool climates where winters tend to be wet. A beautifully bold plant for naturalistic plantings.

Cultivation Grow in well-drained soil in full sun. **Sow** seed in a container (*see pp.391–393*) in a cold frame in spring. *Asphodelus fistulosis* is generally grown as an annual and needs to be raised from seed each year. **Divide** plants (*see p.395*) in late summer or early autumn, taking care not to damage the roots.

Asclepias incarnata (Swamp milkweed)
Z4 ‡4ft (1.2m) ↔ 24in (60cm), likes a moist site and grows well near streams and pools

Asphodeline lutea (Yellow asphodel, King's spear)
Z6 ‡5ft (1.5m) ↔ 12in (30cm), fragrant flowers in late spring, the spires of seedpods are also attractive

Asphodelus albus
Z7b ‡36in (90cm) ↔ 12in (30cm), clumping perennial, flowers in mid- or late spring

ASTERS BRING CHEER TO THE LATE-SUMMER and autumn garden with masses of daisylike flowers, which give *Aster novi-belgii* types the name of Michaelmas daisy. Varying in hue from sky blue to white, scarlet, pink, and lavender, all with bright golden centers, flowers are carried at the tips of the stems, either singly or in clusters. Asters are mostly perennial but also include a few annuals, biennials, and shrubby types; they range from tiny alpines no more than 6in (15cm) tall to upright, clumps of 4ft (1.2m) or more. There are asters for most positions in a garden, since they grow naturally in both moist woodland and mountainous areas. Try smaller asters at the front of borders or in rock gardens; taller ones look best in a mixed border. Flowering times vary slightly. Some such as *A.* × *frikartii* and *A. thomsonii* put on a particularly long display. All asters mentioned here are hardy to Zones 3–5.

Cultivation Asters grow in a variety of sites from open sun to partial shade. Plant them according to which of the three cultivation groups they fall into. **Group 1** needs moist, fertile, well-cultivated soil in sun or partial shade. **Group 2** needs open, well-drained, moderately fertile soil, and a position in full sun. **Group 3** needs moist, moderately fertile soil in partial shade. **Support** taller asters to prevent them from flopping over (*see below*); this is best done in early spring. **Cut down** old stems in autumn, making it easier to give plants a winter mulch, or if preferred leave and cut down in winter or early spring. **Divide** clumps (*see p.395*) every three to four years, both to give more plants and to maintain vigorous growth, especially for *A. novae-angliae* and *A. novi-belgii* cultivars. **Sow** seed (*see pp.391–393*) in spring or autumn in a cold frame. Gray mold (botrytis) and powdery mildew can affect plants, particularly in cultivars of *A. novi-belgii*; remove infected parts. *Aster amellus* and *A.* × *frikartii* types are generally trouble free.

How to stake asters

Stakes and twine This is the most inexpensive method of staking. Space the stakes evenly around the plants and among clumps and weave the twine around them, keeping it taut, to provide support. This may look unsightly at first but both stakes and twine will soon be completely hidden by the foliage and flowers. Put a cap on all stakes to prevent accidental damage to your eyes. L-shaped linking stakes are a commercial alternative, adaptable to any size of clump and easy to store.

Twiggy sticks These branching sticks are the most versatile method of staking. The garden may look a little like a forest immediately after they are put in; but they are soon hidden once the plants grow and cover them. The tops of the sticks can be bent over, providing additional support for the plants to grow through. The sticks should last for several seasons. Use any thin, twiggy stick for support or try stems from tall shrubs like buddleja (see p.29) that are pruned in early spring, just when staking is needed.

Grow-through supports These consist of a mesh or grid of rigid plastic across a hoop supported by four legs. The support is simply pushed into place over the plant, which grows through the mesh. Grow-through supports can gradually be raised as plants become taller. It is essential to get this type of support in place over the aster early in the season, when the plant has made about 12in (30cm) of growth. Grow-through supports are easily removed when the old stems are cut back in autumn.

① *Aster alpinus* ‡10in (25cm) ↔ 18in (45cm), Gp 2 ② *amellus* 'King George' ‡↔ 18in (45cm), Gp 2 ③ *cordifolius* 'Silver Spray' ‡4ft (1.2m) ↔ 18in (45cm), Gp 3 ④ × *frikartii* 'Mönch' ‡28in (70cm) ↔ 14–16in (35–40cm), Gp 2 ⑤ × *frikartii* 'Wunder von Stäfa' ‡28in (70cm) ↔ 14–16in (35–40cm), Gp 2 ⑥ *lateriflorus* 'Horizontalis' ‡2ft (60cm) ↔ 1ft (30cm), Gp 3 ⑦ *novae-angliae* 'Harrington's Pink' ‡4ft (1.2m) ↔ 2ft (60cm), Gp 1 ⑧ *novi-belgii* 'Carnival' ‡2ft (60cm) ↔ 3ft

(90cm), Gp 1 ⑨ *novi-belgii* 'Chequers' ‡2ft (60cm) ↔ 3ft (90cm), Gp 1 ⑩ *novi-belgii* 'Jenny' ‡1ft (30cm) ↔ 18in (45cm), Gp 1 ⑪ *novi-belgii* 'Kristina' ‡1ft (30cm) ↔ 18in (45cm), Gp 1 ⑫ *novi-belgii* 'Lady in Blue' ‡1ft (30cm) ↔ 20in (50cm), Gp 1 ⑬ *novi-belgii* 'Little Pink Lady' ‡15in (40cm) ↔ 20in (50cm), Gp 1 ⑭ *novi-belgii* 'Marie Ballard' ‡3ft (90cm) ↔ 2ft (60cm), Gp 1 ⑮ *novi-belgii* 'Patricia Ballard' ‡3ft (90cm) ↔ 2ft (60cm), Gp 1 ⑯ *novi-belgii* 'Schöne von Dietlikon' ‡to

3ft (1m) ↔ 18in (45cm), Gp 1 ⑰ *novi-belgii* 'Snowsprite' ‡10–12in (25–30cm) ↔ 18in (45cm), Gp 3 ⑱ *pilosus* var. *demotus* ‡4ft (1.2m) ↔ 18in (45cm), Gp 3 ⑲ *pilosus* 'Monte Cassino' ‡3ft (1m) ↔ 1ft (30cm), Gp 1 or 3 ⑳ *pyrenaeus* 'Lutetia' ‡ 2ft (60cm) ↔ to 3ft (1m), Gp 2 ㉑ *sedifolius* ‡4ft (1.2m) ↔ , Gp 2 ㉒ *thomsonii* 'Nanus' ‡18in (45cm) ↔ 10in (25cm), Gp 3 ㉓ *turbinellus* ‡4ft (1.2m) ↔ 2ft (60cm), Gp 2

WITH THEIR PLUMES OF TINY, STARRY flowers, astilbes bring both elegance and texture to the garden. The flower heads, in shades of white, cream, pink, and red, are produced in summer and, if left on the plant to fade, turn a rich russet brown, extending the period of interest from autumn into winter. The cut flowers also last well in water in arrangements. Handsome, mid- to dark green, divided leaves add to the attractions of these clump-forming perennials. They particularly suit damp sites close to ponds and streams, or in bog gardens, and combine well with daylilies (*see Hemerocallis, p.258*), ferns (*see pp.356–365*), and grasses (*see pp.340–355*).

Cultivation Grow in moist soil enriched with plenty of well-rotted organic matter in sun or partial shade. Astilbes will not thrive in soils that dry out in summer. **Divide** plants in late winter or early spring every three or four years to maintain vigor (*see p.395*). The flowers and young leaves can, occasionally, be damaged by late frost. Foliage may also be marred by a grayish white coating of powdery mildew, mainly if plants are in too dry a site.

Astilbe 'Straussenfeder'
Z3b ↕ 36in (90cm) ↔ 24in (60cm), flowers in late summer and early autumn, young foliage has a bronze tint

Astilbe × arendsii 'Fanal'
Z3b ↕ 24in (60cm) ↔ 18in (45cm), the crimson flower plumes appear in early summer

Astilbe chinensis 'Purpurlanze' (Spiraea)
Z3b ↕ 4ft (1.2m) ↔ 36in (90cm), vigorous, flowers in late summer and early autumn, tolerates drier conditions than most

Astilbe × arendsii 'Irrlicht'
Z3b ↕↔ 18in (50cm), flowers in late spring and early summer, somewhat smaller than many astilbes

ASTRANTIA
Hattie's pincushion, Masterwort

THE DELICATE AND DISTINCTIVE FLOWER HEADS that grace these clump-forming perennials are, in fact, composed of an outer circle of papery bracts (modified leaves) and a central cluster of small, 5-petaled true flowers. In early and midsummer, strong stems hold the blooms of white, pink, or red well above the foliage. *Astrantia* 'Sunningdale Variegated' (Z5) has leaves with creamy yellow margins, at their most striking early in the season. The flowers look attractive in dried flower arrangements. Astrantias make good companions for many other herbaceous perennials, including asters (*see pp.192–193*), astilbes (*see left*), and rudbeckias (*see p.317*).

Cultivation Grow in moist, fertile soil, enriched with well-rotted organic matter, in sun or partial shade. 'Sunningdale Variegated' needs full sun for the best foliage color. **Remove** faded flowers if you do not want plants to self-seed. **Divide** plants in spring (*see p.395*) to maintain vigor and make new plants. **Sow** seed in a container in a cold frame as soon as it is ripe (*see pp.391–392*). **Powdery mildew** may spoil the leaves in dry or overcrowded sites (*see p.399*).

Astrantia major 'Rubra'
Z5 ‡ 24in (60cm) ↔ 18in (45cm), will tolerate slightly drier conditions

AUBRIETA
Aubretia

‡ 2in (5cm)
↔ 24in (60cm)

MATS OR LOW HUMMOCKS of pink, magenta, mauve, and purple flowers, make aubretia a mainstay of the spring rock garden and border edge. It is a useful plant, too, for growing in crevices in walls. When in bloom, the small, cross-shaped flowers, which may be single or double, obscure the evergreen foliage, although in silver- or gold-variegated aubretias such as 'Argenteovariegata' and 'Aureovariegata' this also makes a good show after the flowers have faded. This spreading perennial is most popularly combined with rock-garden plants of a similar habit, such as soapworts (*Saponaria, see p.319*) or saxifrages (*see pp.320–321*).

Cultivation Grow in reasonably fertile, well-drained soil, preferably neutral to alkaline in full sun. **Cut back** hard after flowering to maintain a compact habit and prevent the center from becoming straggly and bare. **Sow** seed (*see pp.391–393*) in a cold frame in spring or autumn; named cultivars rarely come true to type. **Take** softwood cuttings in early summer (*see p.394*).

Astrantia 'Hadspen Blood'
Z5 ‡ 24in (60cm) ↔ 18in (45cm), one of the darkest of all astrantias and useful for adding depth of color to planting designs

Astrantia major 'Alba'
Z5 ‡ 24in (60cm) ↔ 18in (45cm), the delicate white flowers will enliven a shady corner

Aubrieta × cultorum 'Joy'
Z4 ‡ 2in (5cm) ↔ 24in (60cm), mat-forming variety with double flowers in spring

BAPTISIA

False indigo, Wild indigo

FALSE INDIGO IS A VIGOROUS, clump-forming perennial that sends up tall spires of royal blue, purple, or white pealike flowers in early summer, followed by large, puffy seedpods that last into the autumn months. Grown in an informal border, it can be used to add height to a wildflower garden, but also thrives when grown among other clump-forming plants of medium height, benefiting from their support. Grow it toward the center of a traditional border with other robust perennials such as lupines (*see p.280*), eryngiums (*see p.238*) and Oriental poppies (*see Papaver, p.299*), or mix with tall grasses such as calamagrostis (*p.344*), *Stipa gigantea* (*see p.355*), and miscanthus (*see p.350*).

Cultivation Grow in full sun in a well-drained, sandy soil. Take care to choose the right site, because the plants resent root disturbance once established. Plants grown in open or windy sites usually benefit from staking. **Sow** seed (*see pp.391–392*) in pots in a cold frame as soon as it is ripe. **Divide** (*see p.395*) in early spring, keeping the sections of rootball as intact and large as possible.

BEGONIA

MOST BEGONIAS USED IN THE GARDEN produce spectacular flowers – either in individual size or their sheer number – in whites, yellows, apricots, and pinks, through to bright orange, cerise, and rich reds. There are also types grown chiefly for their heavily patterned foliage. The most familiar are the small, fibrous-rooted *Begonia semperflorens* (T min. 50°F/10°C) plants, widely used for bedding and containers. Larger types make useful plants for summer accents in borders and in patio containers; use trailing begonias for hanging baskets. Where not hardy, grow in a temperate or warm greenhouse.

Cultivation Grow in fertile, well-drained soil in full sun or partial shade. In pots, use a multipurpose soil mix; keep well watered, and apply a balanced fertilizer monthly. **Deadhead** to prolong the flowering period. **Cut back** semperflorens kinds in autumn; lift and pot them up if necessary; and bring them under glass; place in good light and water moderately until spring. **Lift tubers** before first frost and store over winter; in spring, pot them up, and start into growth by watering. **Sow** seed (*see pp.391–392*) in late winter or early spring at 70°F (21°C). **Take** stem-tip cuttings (*see p.394*) in spring or summer.

Begonia 'Illumination Orange'
T min. 50°F (10°C) ↕ 24in (60cm) ↔ 12in (30cm), tuberous, trailing habit, huge, vivid flowers in summer

Baptisia australis (False indigo)
Z3b ↕ 5ft (1.5m) ↔ 24in (60cm), erect to spreading, flowers in early summer followed by pods, both are good for cutting

Begonia sutherlandii (Hardy orange begonia)
T min. 50°F (10°C) ↕ 18in (45cm), tuberous-rooted, trailing, small but many-flowered, tubers must be lifted and stored each winter

Begonia 'Can-can'
T min. 50°F (10°C) ↕ 36in (90cm) ↔ 18in (45cm), tuberous, upright habit, flowers to 7in (18cm) across in summer

Begonia 'Apricot Delight'
T min. 50°F (10°C) ‡24in (60cm) ↔ 18in (45cm), tuberous,
upright with pendent flowers from early summer to midautumn

BELLIS
Daisy, Double daisy

ALTHOUGH BELLIS ARE IN FACT PERENNIALS, they are
very often grown as biennials; with wallflowers (*see
Erysimum, p.239*) and forget-me-nots (*Myosotis,
p.287*), they form a classic triumvirate of spring
bedding. Their small, perky flower heads, to 3in
(8cm) across, in white tinged with maroon, pink,
or red, are borne from late winter until late summer.
These highly bred varieties of the lawn-type daisy
make great cottage-garden plants and are also good for
containers. Those with tight, pompon flower heads
can also have a formal, old-fashioned charm; use them
to fill beds in a potager, herb, or knot garden, before
summer salads, herbs, or bedding plants go in.

Cultivation Grow in well-drained soil, in full sun or partial shade.
Deadhead to prolong the flowering display of bedding plants, or to
prevent plants grown as perennials from self-seeding. **Sow** seed
(*see pp.391–393*) in containers in early spring, or outdoors in early
summer where the plants are to grow – or, if raising bedding for the
next year, in a nursery bed. **Divide** plants grown as perennials just after
flowering (*see p.395*).

Bellis perennis Tasso Series (English daisy)
Z5b ‡↔ 2–8in (5–20cm), flowers to 2½in (6cm) across, grow in
early summer or buy in late summer to flower next spring

Begonia 'Crystal Brook'
T min. 50°F (10°C) ‡6in (15cm) ↔ 3ft (1m), fibrous-rooted
perennial, small and spreading, overwinter under cover in pots

Begonia 'Président Carnot' (Angelwing begonia)
T min. 50°F (10°C) ‡5–6ft (1.5–2m) ↔ 2ft (60cm), pink flowers in
summer, good leaf color, cut back in spring, overwinter in pots

BERGENIA

Elephant's ears, Pigsqueak

AS THEIR COMMON NAME so aptly describes, bergenias have large, glossy or leathery, tough leaves, and the plant spreads to make an excellent groundcover. Bergenias are evergreen perennials that produce clusters of creamy pink to purple-pink flowers on sturdy stems in spring and early summer. The rounded leaves are usually mid- to dark green but many, such as 'Ballawley', turn bronze-red in winter. Bergenias can be grown at the front of a border or in a woodland garden, but they may need cutting back if they spread too far. They are particularly useful for covering dry and shady areas in the shadows of walls or shrubs and trees. The Canadian hardiness zone ranges from 3b–6.

Cultivation Grow in well-drained soil enriched with well-rotted organic matter, in full sun or partial shade. Poorer soils enhance the winter leaf color. **Slice down** with a spade to remove growth exceeding the allotted space. **Divide** old, leggy-looking clumps every three to five years after flowering or in autumn (see p.395), replanting healthy sections of rhizome with roots and one or more leaves. Pick off any foliage that develops dark leaf spots (see p.399).

① 'Ballawley' ‡24in (60cm), winter foliage shown
② 'Silberlicht' ‡12–18in (30–45cm) ③ *stracheyi* ‡6–12in
(15–30cm) ④ 'Sunningdale' ‡12–18in (30–45cm)

BIDENS FERULIFOLIA

THIS POPULAR, SPREADING PERENNIAL has fresh, finely divided leaves and a succession of flowers from midsummer to autumn. Although it is a perennial, it is usually treated as an annual because it grows quickly and is short-lived. It has star-shaped, bright yellow flowers, but flowers can be orange or orange-red forms. Its sprawling habit makes it a good choice for growing in hanging baskets or wall pots where the stems will tumble over the edge of the container. Bidens look cheerful with other summer bedding plants that enjoy similarly warm, well-drained conditions, such as felicias (see p.244) and marigolds (see Tagetes, p.329). They do well in a gravel garden with rock roses (see Cistus, p.40).

Cultivation Grow in reasonably fertile, moist but well-drained soil, in full sun. If growing them in hanging baskets or other containers, water regularly during summer and apply a balanced fertilizer weekly. **Sow** seed at 55–64°F (13–18°C) in spring (see pp.391–393). **Take** stem-tip cuttings after flowering in autumn (see p.394). **Cut back** plants in autumn and overwinter in a frost-free greenhouse, keeping the plants on the dry side until spring.

Bidens ferulifolia (Tickseed)
Z8 ‡ to 12in (30m) ↔ to 30in (90cm), slender, spreading stems

BLETILLA

‡12–24in (30–60cm)
↔ 24in (60cm)

THESE ORCHIDS ARE NATIVE to temperate regions of China and Japan. They have delicate, bell-shaped, magenta flowers that are arranged in upright clusters, with up to 12 flowers on each cluster. The narrow, mid-green leaves that spring up from the bulbous, fleshy rootstock die back in winter. Bletillas look charming in a sheltered woodland setting with other small, spring-flowering plants, such as *Anemone blanda* (see p.180). They can also be grown in a raised bed, bringing their exquisite flowers close to eye level. Mulch in winter, lift and store dry and cool, or grow in an alpine house or cold greenhouse

Cultivation Grow in in partial shade, in moist but well-drained soil enriched with well-rotted organic matter, or in soil-based potting mix with added leaf mold. **Mulch** in autumn with a layer of organic matter at least 2in (5cm) thick to protect from cold. Alternatively, lift and overwinter in a frost-free place. **Divide** in early spring (see p.395).

Bletilla striata
Z5b ‡↔ 12–24in (30–60cm), fleshy underground storage organs known as pseudobulbs, flowers from spring to early summer

BOLTONIA

‡to 6ft (2m)
↔24in (60cm)

THERE ARE AROUND EIGHT SPECIES of these perennials, all of which thrive in moist, sunny sites. They have masses of daisy flowers in shades of white, lilac, or pinkish purple with canary yellow centers. The flowers are set off by blue-green or mid-green, sometimes finely toothed foliage. Their loose, relaxed appearance is ideal for a wild garden, or they can add a light, airy feel to a border. The flowers are also good for cutting. Boltonias are tolerant of most garden soils and will put up with partly shaded conditions. Plant alongside other tall perennial daisies, such as Michaelmas daisies (*see Aster, pp.192–193*) and rudbeckias (*p.317*). Stonecrops (*see Sedum, p.324*) are also good companions.

Cultivation Grow in any reasonably fertile, moist, well-drained soil, in full sun or partial shade. **Divide** plants in spring every two or three years to maintain their vigor (*see p.395*). **Sow** seed in containers in a cold frame in autumn (*see pp.391–392*). Can be susceptible to powdery mildew (*see pp.398–399*) in dry conditions.

Boltonia asteroides
Z4 ‡6ft (2m) ↔ 3ft (1m), glaucous, blue-green leaves become greener with age, flowers in late summer to midautumn

BORAGO
Borage

BORAGE GROWS WILD IN ROCKY PLACES in western and southern Europe. They are robust plants with hairy stems and leaves, and flower for long periods over summer, producing nodding heads of intensely blue, or occasionally white, starry flowers. *Borago pygmaea* (Z6) is a shade-loving perennial, suitable for a rock or gravel garden, growing to about 24in (60cm) tall and wide. The annual, common borage, *B. officinalis*, needs sun and tolerates dry places. It has cucumber-flavored leaves that are often added to fruit cups, alcoholic drinks, and salads, and the flowers make a pretty garnish. It looks attractive growing with mint, sage, and feverfew, but may be too rough for a small, neat herb garden; if so, it looks fine in a border. All species self-seed freely.

Cultivation Grow in any reasonably well-drained soil, in full sun or partial shade. **Sow** seed of *B. officinalis* where you want it to grow in spring (*see pp.391–393*). **Take** cuttings of young sideshoots of *B. pygmaea* in summer (*see p.394*) and overwinter the young plants in a cold frame.

Borago officinalis (Borage)
‡24in (60cm) ↔ 18in (45cm), freely branching annual, will flower until the first frosts, attractive to bees

BOYKINIA

ORIGINATING IN MOIST WOODLAND and mountain regions, boykinias are clump-forming perennials with dark green foliage that is occasionally tinted bronze when young. The mounds of round to kidney-shaped leaves that develop around the base of the plants make good groundcover. In spring or summer, lax clusters of crimson or white, bell-shaped flowers rise above the leaves on long stalks. Boykinias thrive in cool, moist soil in partial shade. In the garden, they are best suited to a shady border or rock garden, or woodland edge. Pair them with violas (*see p.338*), or grow in clumps among other low, informal perennials that are not too vigorous and enjoy similar conditions, such as heucheras (*see p.259*) and dicentras (*p.229*). Small species also grow well in troughs and sinks.

Cultivation Grow in fertile, acidic soil, or acidic soil mixt with added grit, in partial shade. **Divide** in spring (*see p.395*). **Sow** seed in containers in a cold frame as soon as it is ripe (*see pp.391–392*).

Boykinia jamesii
Z6 ‡↔ 6in (15cm), flowering in mid- and late spring, the frilled flowers have green centers

BRACHYCOME IBERIDIFOLIA
Swan River daisy

THESE DROUGHT-TOLERANT PLANTS are grown for their cheerful, scented daisylike flowers. Borne in summer, they may be white, pinkish purple, or blue, with bright golden yellow or, in the Splendour Series, jazzy black centers and white, lilac-pink, or purple flower heads. The soft foliage is green or downy gray, often finely divided and feathery. Grow these drought-tolerant bushy or spreading annuals in summer bedding, or let them spill over the edges of containers such as windowboxes and large pots.

Cultivation Grow in fertile, well-drained soil and position in a sheltered spot in full sun. Use a soil-based potting mix if growing them in containers, water freely during summer and apply a balanced fertilize weekly. **Pinch out** the tips of young plants to encourage a bushy habit and plenty of flowers. **Sow** seed (*see pp.391–393*) at 64°F (18°C) in spring, and plant out in early summer when any threat of frost has passed.

Brachycome iberidifolia
‡to 18in (45cm) ↔ 14in (35cm), annual, the flowers are usually purplish blue, but may be white or violet pink

BRODIAEA

THESE PLANTS ARE PERENNIALS, growing from corms (*see p.164*), which in early summer produce funnel-shaped flowers in shades of violet, lilac, deep purple, or pink. The flowers are carried in large, open clusters, with each flower on its own short stalk, at the top of tall stems, and are excellent for cutting. Strappy, blue-green or mid-green leaves grow from the base of the plant, often dying back before the flowers emerge. They look similar to agapanthus (*see p.171*), but smaller. Grow brodiaeas at the front of a border, or in a rock garden or raised bed, in mild areas, or in shallow pots and bowls where they need to be stored under cover over winter.

Cultivation Grow in light, well-drained soil in full sun or partial shade. **Plant** corms 3in (8cm) deep in autumn. **Water** freely when plants are in full growth, but keep warm and dry after they die down in summer. **Protect** with a winter mulch of well-rotted organic matter (*see p.388*) in frost-prone areas, or bring container-grown plants under cover. **Sow** seed (*see pp.391–392*) at 55–61°F (13–16°C) as soon as ripe. Remove offsets (*see p.365*) when the corms are dormant.

Brodiaea californica
Z8 ‡20in (50cm) ↔ 3in (8cm), the flowers may be violet, lilac, pink, or white in this species

BROWALLIA
Amethyst flower, Bush violet

GROWN FOR THEIR MASS of deep blue and pure white flowers, these are woody-based perennials that flower profusely in their first year and are more often grown as annuals. Each flower is a tube opening to a flat face, up to 3in (8cm) across in some selections. They are produced during summer either singly or in small clusters where the leaves join the stems. The leaves are narrow and pointed, and feel slightly sticky. Outdoors, these plants combine well with other summer bedding plants such as heliotropes (*see p.70*), pelargoniums (*see pp.300–303*) or marigolds (*Tagetes, see p.329*). They make fine container plants, and are also popular as winter container plants indoors.

Cultivation Grow in fertile, well-drained soil, in full sun or partial shade. Use a soil-based potting mix if growing them in containers; water freely during summer; apply a balanced fertilizer at weekly intervals. **Sow** seed (*see pp.391–393*) at 64°F (18°C) in early spring for summer flowering or in late summer for winter-flowering container plants. Aphids and whiteflies may be a problem under cover (*see pp.398–399*).

Browallia speciosa 'White Troll'
T min. 59–61°F (13–16°C) ‡to 10in (25cm) ↔ 10in (25cm), this is half the height of *B. speciosa*

BRUNNERA MACROPHYLLA

Siberian bugloss

‡18in (45cm)
↔24in (60cm)

THIS CLUMP-FORMING perennial and its cultivars have both delicate flowers and attractive foliage. In mid- and late spring, they produce clusters of small, usually bright blue flowers similar to those of forget-me-nots (*Myosotis, see p.287*). The softly hairy leaves on the stems are broadly lance shaped, those at the base larger and more heart shaped. Excellent for woodland areas beneath deciduous trees and shrubs, brunneras also make good groundcover in borders – especially those with patterned foliage that remain attractive once flowering is over. Grow them with other spring-flowering perennials such as leopard's bane (*see Doronicum, p.231*).

Cultivation Grow in reasonably fertile soil that is moist but well drained, preferably in a cool site in part shade. Dig in well-rotted organic matter when planting. **Divide** established plants (*see p.395*) in spring. **Sow** seeds (*see pp.391–392*) in a container in a cold frame in early spring. Take root cuttings in winter (*see p.394*).

Brunnera macrophylla ('Langtrees')
Z3b, spotted form is easy to grow, tolerating moderate variation in soil moisture and some morning sun

Brunnera macrophylla 'Dawson's White'
Z3b ‡18in (45cm) ↔ 24in (60cm), wide creamy edges of the leaves help to brighten the light shade that this plant needs, slightly less easy to grow than other forms and needs richer soil

THESE ARE FINE, FAST-GROWING GROUNDCOVER plants. They are fairly vigorous, and the tips of the spreading shoots root easily when they come into contact with the soil, extending the plant ever farther. In spring or early summer, erect stems bear clusters of flat-faced flowers. These are purple when they first open, later maturing to clear blue. There are about 15 species, including annuals, perennials, and subshrubs. The leaves are mid- to dark green, variably shaped, and generally rough or hairy. These plants are at home in a woodland or wild garden, or in a border with other spreading, spring-flowering plants such as aubrietas (*see p.195*) or with bulbs.

Cultivation Grow in a fertile, well-drained soil that is neutral to alkaline. Position in full sun, but preferably with some shade around midday. **Sow** seed (*see pp.391–392*) in containers in a cold frame in autumn or spring. **Divide** perennials (*see p.395*) in early spring . **Take** stem-tip cuttings (*see p.394*) of subshrubs in summer.

Buglossoides purpurocaerulea
Z7 ‡24in (60cm) ↔ variable, perennial species, with underground rhizomes, flowers in late spring and early summer

BULBOCODIUM VERNUM
Spring meadow saffron

THIS PLANT RESEMBLES the autumn crocus (*Colchicum, see p.215*) but with flowers that appear in spring or even in late winter in mild areas. These are pinkish purple and turn from funnel- to star-shaped as the petals open. The leaves follow soon after, but do not reach their full height, 6in (15cm), until after the flowers are finished. Although the spring meadow saffron is fully hardy, it has the reputation of being rather fussy, resenting excessive winter moisture, but it should thrive in sunny rock gardens, raised beds, and well-drained borders. It also grows well in pots. Pair it with other spring-flowering bulbs such as crocuses (*see p.220*) and small daffodils (*Narcissus, see pp.288–289*).

Cultivation Plant corms 3in (8cm) deep in autumn, in full sun or partial shade, in soil enriched with well-rotted organic matter. **Sow** seed in a pot in a cold frame in autumn or spring (*see pp.391–392*). Offsets from corms can be removed in summer (*see p.395*).

Bulbocodium vernum (Spring meadow saffron)
Z5 ‡ 1½–3in (4–8cm) ↔ 2in (5cm)

BUPHTHALMUM SALICIFOLIUM
Oxeye daisy

WITH FLOWERS LIKE CHRYSANTHEMUMS, *Buphthalmum salicifolium* is an easy-to-grow perennial suitable for most garden soils, including alkaline soils. It produces masses of bright yellow daisies from early summer and into autumn, when they almost completely hide the dark green, willowy leaves. The flowers last well when cut, making them useful for indoor arrangements. The plant forms spreading clumps. Well suited to a wildflower planting, this is also a good plant for the front of an informal herbaceous border with other perennials like achilleas (*see p.167*), phloxes (*see p.306*), and monardas (*see p.286*), or try growing it among hostas (*see pp.260–261*) to brighten dappled shade.

Cultivation Grow in poor soil in full sun or partial shade; tall plants may need to be supported. **Divide** mature plants in early spring (*see p.395*). **Sow** seed in a container in a cold frame in spring (*see pp.391–392*).

Buphthalmum salicifolium
Z3b ‡ 24in (60cm) ↔ 18in (45cm)

CALANDRINIA

THESE FLESHY-LEAVED PERENNIALS form mats of evergreen foliage topped with long-lasting displays of vivid, purple-red, pale pink, or purple flowers in summer. *Calandrinia umbellata* tends to be short lived and is often treated as an annual or as a biennial – where the seeds are sown one year to flower the following year, just like wallflowers (*Erysimum, see p.239*). Each flower lasts for just two days, but there are always plenty to continue the display into late summer. Rock purslanes are drought-tolerant plants for the rock garden, associating well with small pinks (*Dianthus, see pp.226–227*) and other plants with gray or silvery foliage.

Cultivation Grow in slightly acidic soil that is sharply drained and in full sun. **Sow** seed at 61–64°F (16–18°C) in early spring (*see pp.391–393*), or in autumn, planting out the following spring. **Take** stem-tip cuttings in spring (*see p.394*). If growing the plant as a perennial, take cuttings regularly, as it can be short lived. Young plants may need protection from slugs and snails (*see p.398*).

Calandrinia umbellata (Rock purslane)
Z7b ‡ ↔ 6–8in (15–20cm), blue or gray-green leaves, flowers to ¾in (2cm) across in summer

CALCEOLARIA
Pouch flower, Slipper flower, Slipperwort

THE CURIOUS FLOWERS of calceolarias always arouse interest, with their vivid colors and strange balloon or pouch shapes. They are a group of annuals and perennials that generally flower throughout spring and summer, depending on when the seeds are sown. On flowering, they form massed or loose clusters of red, orange to yellow, even rich brown blooms, which are often spotted. The bedding forms like 'Bright Bikinis' are short lived and can be prone to frost damage, but they make striking spring and summer container plants. The hardier perennial and alpine species are ideal for a rock garden or trough.

Cultivation Grow in light, reasonably fertile soil in sun or partial shade. They require cool, moist conditions to flower freely. Grow alpine species like *C. arachnoidea* in moist, gritty soil and protect from winter moisture. **Sow** seed of hardy and alpine species, which must be exposed to cold, in containers outdoors in a cold frame in autumn (*see pp.391–393*). Top-dress alpine seeds with grit rather than potting mix. Sow seed of 'Bright Bikinis' and other bedding types at 64°F (18°C) in late summer or spring. Do not cover the tiny seeds with mix; cover the pots with plastic wrap (*see below right*).

Calceolaria tenella
Z7b ‡2in (5cm) ↔ to 12in (30cm), perennial, forms creeping mats of pale, evergreen foliage, flowers in summer

Calceolaria arachnoidea
T min. 35°F (2°C) ‡8–10in (20–25cm) ↔ to 6in (15cm), evergreen alpine perennial, white-hairy leaves, flowers from summer to autumn

KEEPING SEED MOIST
Surface-sow seed of non-alpine species, then cover with plastic wrap. Remove as soon as seed germinates.

Calceolaria 'Bright Bikini'
Z7b ‡8–18in (20–45cm) ↔ 6–12in (15–30cm), bedding biennial with compact growth and dense flower clusters in summer, perfect for a patio pot or windowbox

Calceolaria 'Walter Shrimpton'
Z7b ‡4in (10cm) ↔ 9in (23cm), evergreen perennial, glossy, dark green, leafy rosettes, flowers in summer

CALENDULA OFFICINALIS

English marigold, Pot marigold

THIS ANNUAL CALENDULA is the one most widely grown in gardens: they are exceptionally easy, fast-growing plants that bear a succession of vibrant orange, yellow, soft cream, or apricot, daisylike flowers from summer to autumn. The wide range of cultivars includes many with double or "pompon" flowers, varying from compact, dwarf plants to taller forms. All make good cut flowers. Pot marigolds continue flowering throughout autumn into mild winters, and although annual, they can survive into the following year. They make excellent, robust plants for hardy annual borders, and are equally useful in bedding or in containers. Plants self-seed prolifically so they can be enjoyed year after year.

Cultivation Sow seed outdoors in spring or autumn where plants are to grow (*see pp.391–393*), in sun or partial shade. Thin out seedlings to 6in (15cm) apart. Autumn-sown seedlings will benefit from cloche protection to keep off the worst of the winter weather. **Deadhead** flowers regularly to prolong flowering (*see p.390*).

Calendula officinalis
‡ 12–18in (30–75cm) ↔ 12–30in (30–45cm), annual, softly hairy, aromatic leaves, flowers 4in (10cm) across

CALLA PALUSTRIS

Bog arum, Water arum, Water dragon

‡ 8–10in (20–25cm)
↔ 6–20in (15–50cm)

THIS EASY-TO-GROW PERENNIAL is an excellent marginal aquatic plant and looks particularly attractive growing along slow-moving stream edges. It spreads through shallow water – no more than 10in (25cm) deep – by means of creeping underground stems (rhizomes) below the soil. In midsummer, large white "hoods" appear that surround the conelike flower clusters, which in autumn develop into spikes of scarlet berries. The leaves remain on the plant during mild winters. Contact with the foliage may cause skin allergies, so wear gloves when handling the plant.

Cultivation Grow bog arums in very moist soil at the edge of a stream or pond. **Plant** in aquatic planting baskets using humus-rich, acidic soil or directly into mud in shallow water, which should be still or slow moving. Position the plants in full sun to encourage more flowers. **Divide** (*see p.395*) in spring, severing the underground stems carefully. **Sow** seed (*see pp.391–392*) in late summer in containers submerged in shallow water.

Calendula officinalis 'Fiesta Gitana'
‡ 12in (30cm) ↔ 12–18in (30–45cm), dwarf annual, double flowers in a variety of warm shades, sometimes bicolored

Calla palustris
Z4 ‡ 10in (25cm) ↔ 24in (60cm)

CALOCHORTUS

Fairy lantern, Mariposa

‡ to 28in (70cm)

SHYLY NODDING, BUT EYE-CATCHING, cup-shaped flowers, produced in spring and summer, are the key attraction of these bulbous perennials. The flower colors range from shades of white to pale pink or yellow, all bearing distinctive, contrasting markings on the insides of the petals. The leaves are long and strappy and mid- to gray-green in color. Calochortus look good in herbaceous or mixed borders with other bulbs such as late-flowering tulips (*see pp.334–335*).

Cultivation Plant bulbs 4–6in (10–15cm) deep in autumn, in full sun, in free-draining soil. In areas of heavy rainfall or on heavy soils, it is better to grow them in pots and place them in a cold frame to keep dry because the bulbs may rot in winter moisture. In pots, use a soil-based potting mix with added grit for good drainage. **Water** bulbs in pots freely when growing, but keep dry when the bulbs are dormant in winter. **Sow** seed in a cold frame as soon as it is ripe (*see pp.391–392*). Some species produce bulbils in the joints between stems and leaves, as lilies do (*see p.274*), and these can be grown on in late spring or early summer.

① *amabilis* Z7 ‡ 8–20in (20–50cm), flowers spring to early summer ② *umpquaensis* ‡ 8–12in (20–30cm), grown only as a specimen plant in a cold greenhouse

CALTHA PALUSTRIS

Kingcup, Marsh marigold

THIS MOISTURE-LOVING PERENNIAL and its cultivars display striking yellow or white flowers in spring and early summer, which are followed by architectural, heart-shaped leaves up to 6in (15cm) in diameter. The plants spread by means of underground stems (rhizomes), and prefer a moist soil at the edge of water, although they will thrive in nonaquatic garden sites provided that the soil remains reliably moist. *Caltha palustris* will tolerate being grown in water up to 9in (23cm) deep, but prefers more shallow water or a boggy soil. Grow them with other moisture-loving plants such as mimulus (*see p.286*), or with bright pink waterside primulas (*see pp.312–313*).

Cultivation Marsh marigolds prefer an open site with constantly moist soil in full sun. When planting in water, use an aquatic planting basket and top with gravel. **Divide** plants (*see p.395*) in late summer or early spring. Marsh marigolds are prone to powdery mildew (*see pp.398–399*) when conditions are hot and dry, especially when they are growing in soil rather than water.

① *palustris* Z3 ‡ 4–16in (10–40cm) ↔ 18in (45cm)
② *palustris* 'Flore Pleno' Z3 ‡↔ 10in (25cm)

CAMASSIA

Quamash

THESE BULBOUS PERENNIALS are grown for their tall spikes of large flowers, in sky blue or creamy white. These are borne in late spring and early summer amid clumps of strappy, prominently veined, gray-green leaves. There are many types to choose from, but all are very similar. Grow them near the front or in the middle of a border, in a wildflower or meadow planting, or in containers. The frilly flower spikes would contrast well with the drumstick flowers of alliums such as 'Globemaster' (*see p.174*), perhaps underplanted with soft yellow cowslips (*Primula veris, see pp.312–313*). The flowers are ideal for cutting, lasting well in indoor arrangements.

Cultivation Plant bulbs 4in (10cm) deep in autumn, in moist but well-drained soil enriched with well-rotted organic matter, in full sun or partial shade. In heavy clay soils, fork in grit before planting to improve drainage. **Protect** with a winter mulch in cold areas (*see p.388*). **Sow** seed (*see pp.391–392*) in a container in a cold frame as soon as it is ripe, or remove bulb offsets (*see p.395*) in summer when the bulbs are dormant.

Camassia leichtlinii (Large camas)
Z4 ‡ 2–4½ft (60–130cm), flowers in late spring

Bellflower

CAMPANULAS ARE OLD FAVORITES in cottage gardens for their pretty tubular, bell- or star-shaped flowers. They are borne in clusters, or occasionally singly, in a range of shades from white to lavender, sky blue, and soft lilac-pink. Campanulas form a large group of perennial, biennial, or annual plants and vary greatly in habit from spreading mats no more than 2in (5cm) tall, and clump-forming or trailing plants, to upright giants 5ft (1.5m) tall. Smaller species are best for rock gardens or raised beds. Tall campanulas can punctuate mixed borders or be naturalized in wildflower beds.

Cultivation To make cultivation easy, campanulas are divided into groups. **Group 1** need fertile, well-drained, slightly alkaline soil, in sun or partial shade. Taller species require staking. Cut back after flowering to encourage more flowers later. **Group 2** are rock-garden species that need well-drained soil in sun or partial shade. **Groups 3 and 4** are alpine or tender plants that are not often grown in temperate gardens. **Rust**, a fungal disease that causes orange or brown patches to develop on leaves or stems, may afflict some campanulas. Remove affected foliage and thin out congested growth of affected plants.

Campanula alliariifolia (Ivory bells)
Z4 ‡12–24in (30–60cm) ↔ 18in (45cm), clump-forming perennial, flowers from midsummer to early autumn, group 1

SOWING SEED To make sure that you sow the fine seed evenly, mix it first with some horticultural silver sand. Don't use builder's sand; it may contain chemicals that inhibit seed germination.

Campanula lactiflora 'Loddon Anna'
Z3 ‡4–5ft (1.2–1.5m) ↔ 24in (60cm), upright perennial, flowers from early summer to early autumn, group 1

Campanula glomerata 'Superba' (Clustered bellflower)
Z3 ‡24in (60cm) ↔ indefinite, perennial, spreading clumps of upright stems, flowers throughout summer, group 1

Campanula persicifolia 'Telham Beauty' (Peach bellflower)
Z3b ‡↔ 36in (90cm), rosette-forming perennial with upright stems, flowers in early and midsummer, group 1

Campanula 'G.F. Wilson'
Z4 ‡ to 4in (10cm) ↔ to 8in (20cm), mound-forming perennial,
flowers in mid- and late summer, group 2

CANNA

‡ to 7ft (2.2m)
↔ 20in (50cm)

THESE STRIKING PERENNIALS bring a touch of the exotic to any garden and height to otherwise low borders. They have dramatic foliage, with large leaves in shades of purple-brown to mid-green, sometimes with attractive veining, as well as showy, gladioli-like flowers. The flowers appear in pairs from midsummer to early autumn, in bright shades of scarlet to golden yellow. Cannas have underground stems (rhizomes), which suffer frost damage except in the warmest parts of British Columbia; lift and store the plants over winter or grow them as annuals.

Cultivation Grow cannas in sheltered borders in fertile soil and full sun. Plant outside after all threat of frost is past, in early summer. **Water** well during summer and apply a phosphate-rich fertilizer monthly to encourage flowers. Deadhead regularly to prolong flowering. **Lift** the plants in autumn, cut them down, and store the rhizomes in barely moist peat or leaf mold in frost-free conditions. **Sow** seed (*see pp.391–393*) in spring or autumn at 70°F (21°C). **Divide** the rhizomes (*see p.395*) in early spring, making sure that each piece has a healthy bud before replanting it.

Canna 'Durban'
T min. 35°F (2°C) ‡ 4ft (1.2m) ↔ 20in (50cm), bears burnt orange
flowers in late summer

Campanula carpatica 'Weisse Clips' (syn. 'White Clips')
Z4 ‡ 8in (20cm) ↔ 12–24in (30–60cm), clump-forming perennial,
flowers throughout summer, group 2

Canna 'Assaut'
T min. 35°F (2°C) ‡ 6ft (2m) ↔ 20in (50cm), purple-brown leaves,
flowers from midsummer to autumn

Canna 'Rosemond Coles'
T min. 35°F (2°C) ‡ 5ft (1.5m) ↔ 20in (50cm), flowers from
midsummer to early autumn

CARDAMINE
Bittercress

CARDIOCRINUM
Giant lily

CATANANCHE
Blue cupidone, Cupid's dart

A LARGE GROUP, the bittercresses include both dainty garden plants, mostly perennial, and invasive weeds, mostly annual. Ornamental types are grown for the four-petaled flowers that they bear in late spring and early summer. The flowers are in shades of pale purple, lilac, white, and occasionally pink. The leaves are variable, sometimes made up of smaller leaflets, and may be lance shaped and toothed in some species, rounded or kidney shaped in others. The small, compact types are ideal for growing in a rock garden or at the front of a border with other plants that flower in late spring, such as camassias (*see p.205*). Other, larger species suit woodland gardens.

THESE STATELY PLANTS grow to around 12ft (4m) in ideal conditions, so be careful where you plant them. Grow a small group as a specimen planting in woodland or in a shady border. They are bulbous perennials, related to lilies (*Lilium, see pp.274–277*). Trumpet-shaped, scented white flowers, occasionally tinged with maroon-purple or green at the base, are borne in clusters in summer. The stems are strong and stout, and the leaves glossy green and heart shaped. The bulbs die after flowering, but leave many offsets (*see p.164*) that will flower in four or five years: the spectacular show is well worth the wait.

GROWN FOR THEIR BRIGHT summer flowers, this is a small group of annuals and perennials. Their flowerheads, up to 2in (5cm) across, are similar to those of cornflowers (*Centaurea, see facing page*) and are good for cutting and drying. Produced from midsummer until autumn, they may be lilac-blue, yellow, or white with purple centers. Grasslike, hairy leaves grow from the base. Grow *Catananche caerulea* as an annual with other summer bedding plants like asters (*see pp.192–193*), annual rudbeckias (*see p.317*), and impatiens (*p.263*); *C. caespitosa* is a plant of high, dry meadows, and is best grown in pots and over-wintered under cover to protect it from winter wet.

Cultivation Grow in moist soil that has been enriched with plenty of well-rotted organic matter. Position in full sun or partial shade. **Divide** plants (*see p.395*) in spring or after flowering. **Sow** seed in containers in a cold frame in autumn or spring (*see pp.391–392*).

Cultivation Plant bulbs just below the soil surface in autumn, in a moist but well-drained, deep, fertile soil. Site in a sheltered spot in partial shade; they will not do well in hot, dry places. **Apply** a balanced fertilizer two or three times during the growing season to encourage the development of offsets. Top-dress annually with well-rotted organic matter. **Divide** and grow on the bulb offsets (*see p.395*) or sow seed in a deep tray (*see pp.391–392*) in a cool shady place as soon as ripe; seed-raised plants may take seven years to flower.

Cultivation Grow in any well-drained soil: *C. caespitosa* can be short-lived, particularly if grown in heavy soil. Position in full sun. **Sow** seed (*see pp.391–393*) in a container in a cold frame in early spring or in drills outside in midspring. **Divide** plants grown as perennials in spring (*see p.395*). **Take** root cuttings in winter (*see p.394*) of plants grown as perennials. If powdery mildew is a problem (*see pp.398–399*), avoid wetting the leaves.

Cardamine pratensis 'Flore Pleno' (Lady's smock)
Z5 ‡8in (20cm) ↔ 12in (30cm), flowers in late spring and has glossy dark green leaves; produces many plantlets at the base

Cardiocrinum giganteum
Z7 ‡5–12ft (1.5–4m) ↔ 18in (45cm), often has 20 strongly scented flowers in each cluster, on tall stems (*see inset*)

Catananche caerulea 'Bicolor'
Z4 ‡20–36in (50–90cm) ↔ 12in (30cm), this perennial is treated as an annual or biennial because it flowers best when young

CELMISIA
New Zealand daisy

IDEAL FOR A ROCK GARDEN, New Zealand daisies are a large group of perennials grown for their attractive evergreen foliage and cheerful daisies. They flower freely in spring and summer, but also have long, thin, leathery leaves, which are silvery green and make them worthwhile for the rest of the year. The flowerheads are around 2in (5cm) across and are borne on dense, whitish, woolly stems in early summer. They are white, sometimes tinged pink or purple, with yellow centers. Grow them among small shrubs such as lavenders (*Lavandula*, see p.80) and lavender cotton (*Santolina*, see p.116).

Cultivation Grow in moist but well-drained, slightly acidic soil, in sun or partial shade. Grow smaller species in an alpine house in a mix of acidic soil, leaf mold, and sharp sand and shelter under glass in winter. **Divide** plants (see p.395) in spring or take individual rosettes of leaves with roots and treat as cuttings in spring (see p.395). **Sow** seed (see pp.391–392) in a container in a cold frame as soon as it is ripe: New Zealand daisies hybridize freely in the garden, but produce few viable seeds.

CENTAUREA
Hardheads, Knapweed

STRIKING, THISTLELIKE FLOWER HEADS, which last for many weeks over summer, are the main attraction of this group of plants, which includes annuals, biennials, and perennials. Characteristically rounded, the flower heads may be purple, pink, blue, or yellow, and are often deeply and sometimes darkly fringed; they attract bees and butterflies. The leaves, which are not particularly attractive, are sometimes toothed and occasionally gray-green beneath. Try centaureas in a wildflower garden, or among other bright herbaceous perennials such as achilleas (see pp.166–167), daylilies (*Hemerocallis*, see p.258), phloxes (see p.306), or loosestrifes (*Lythrum*, see p.283).

Cultivation Most will tolerate some drought and can be grown in well-drained soil in full sun. Taller varieties may need support in the border. **Grow** selections of *C. macrocephala* and *C. montana* in moist but well-drained soil; they tolerate some shade. **Divide** perennials (see p.395) in spring or autumn. **Sow** seed in containers in a cold frame (see pp.391–392) in spring. Powdery mildew may be a problem (see pp.398–399) in dry summers; avoid wetting the leaves.

SUPPORTING PLANTS
Once plants are growing, place a ring of short stakes around each and tie string securely around them. The foliage will soon hide them completely.

Centaurea hypoleuca 'John Coutts'
Z5 ‡ 24in (60cm) ↔ 18in (45cm), clump-forming perennial, flowers are long-lasting and fragrant in summer

Celmisia spectabilis
Z8 ‡↔ to 12in (30cm), tufted, clump-forming New Zealand daisy that flowers in early summer

Centaurea dealbata 'Steenbergii' (Persian cornflower)
Z4 ‡↔ 24in (60cm), easy-to-grow, clump-forming perennial, needs support, flowers in midsummer, excellent for cutting

Centaurea cyanus (Cornflower)
‡ 8–32in (20–80cm) ↔ 6in (15cm) upright annual, flowers from late spring to midsummer, white and pink forms exist

POPULAR FOR THEIR BRIGHT, SHOWY FLOWERS, these upright, bushy annuals and herbaceous perennials are the stars of late summer and autumn. They are grown primarily for border displays, for cutting, and for exhibition (specialty mail-order suppliers offer hundreds of cultivars suitable for showing). Chrysanthemums come in a wide range of glowing colors from ivory to pink, crimson, and gold, with blooms that vary vastly in shape, size, and form. Petals may, for instance, be reflexed, incurved, or spoon-shaped. There are ten chrysanthemum flower head categories all together. Some, especially the huge exhibition varieties, can be demanding since rain may damage the flowers and many are not hardy. Those classed as Rubellum Group chrysanthemums, such as 'Clara Curtis', are among the easiest to grow and are ideal for beds and borders, as are the many hardy pompon and spray types, which include the 'Pennine' cultivars. Annual *Chrysanthemum segetum* (corn marigold) and *C. carinatum* put on a long, colorful display and mix well with other annuals. Check at the nursery for hardiness.

Cultivation Check the plant label or supplier's catalog for growing requirements and hardiness when buying. **Plant** from late spring in a sheltered site in full sun, in fertile, moist, but well-drained soil. **Support** tall varieties with canes and tie in regularly. Pinch out (*see below*) to improve plant shape and flowering. **Water** freely during dry spells and apply a balanced fertilizer every 7–10 days from midsummer until the buds begin to show some color. **Lift** nonhardy types after the first frost and store in a frost-free place for winter. Hardy chrysanthemums can remain in the ground.

Pinch pruning chrysanthemums

Pinch pruning a plant – taking out the growing tip or tips – encourages it to produce plenty of sideshoots from the buds in the leaf axils (where leaf stalk joins stem) lower down the stem. This results not only in a bushier, more attractive shape, but also in extra flowers on plants such as chrysanthemums and fuchsias. The more frequently a plant is pinch pruned, the greater the number of sideshoots and flowers it will produce. This is a technique much used by show exhibitors, but it can also be worthwhile in the garden, especially in containers, where you may want to maintain a more compact style of growth. For the greatest success, plants need to be growing strongly, so if necessary apply a balanced fertilizer regularly.

Next generation of shoots have all their tips taken out

Stems branch after pinch pinching

Shoot tip only is removed

1 When the plant is 6–8in (15–20cm) high, pinch out the tip of the shoot just above a leaf joint, using your finger and thumb. Remove only the small tip to encourage the maximum number of flower-bearing sideshoots (known as breaks).

2 Side buds grow and develop into shoots. When these shoots have developed four leaves, repeat the pinching (called the second stop). Pinch pruning stimulates shoots from the tip and lower down the stem, creating a much bushier plant.

3 Keep pinching out the tips of the shoots until the plant is furnished with plenty of bushy growth. Stop pinching in early autumn to let flowering shoots develop. Here, several plants have been pinch pruned into a spectacular, colorful display.

① *Chrysanthemum* 'Alison Kirk' ‡4ft (1.2m) ↔ 16in (40cm) ② 'Autumn Days' ‡4ft (1.2m) ↔ 30in (75cm) ③ 'Brietner's Supreme' ‡4ft (1.2m) ↔ 30in (75cm) ④ 'Bronze Fairie' ‡↔ 30in (60cm) ⑤ 'Bronze Hedgerow' ‡5ft (1.5m) ↔ 30–39in (75–100cm) ⑥ 'Bronze Yvonne Arnaud' ‡4ft (1.2m) ↔ 24–30in (60–75cm) ⑦ 'Buff Margaret' ‡4ft (1.2m) ↔ 24–30in (60–75cm) ⑧ *carinatum* 'Court Jesters' ‡2ft (60cm) ↔ 1ft (30cm), annual ⑨ 'Clara Curtis' ‡30in (75cm)

↔ 2ft (60cm), Rubellum Group ⑩ 'George Griffiths' ‡5ft (1.5m) ↔ 3ft (1m), good for showing
⑪ 'Madeleine' ‡4ft (1.2m) ↔ 30in (75cm) ⑫ 'Maria' ‡18in (45cm) ↔ 12–24in (30–60cm) ⑬ 'Marion'
‡4ft (1.2m) ↔ 30in (75cm) ⑭ 'Marlene Jones' ‡3ft (1m) ↔ 2ft (60cm) ⑮ 'Pavilion' ‡4½ft (1.3m)
↔ 24–30in (60–75cm), good for showing ⑯ 'Pennine Alfie' ‡4ft (1.2m) ↔ 30in (75cm) ⑰ 'Pennine
Flute' ‡4ft (1.2m) ↔ 30in (75cm) ⑱ 'Pennine Oriel' ‡4ft (1.2m) ↔ 24–30in (60–75cm) ⑲ 'Purple

Pennine Wine' ‡4ft (1.2m) ↔ 30in (75cm) ⑳ 'Roy Coopland' ‡4½ft (1.4m) ↔ 2ft (60cm)
㉑ 'Salmon Fairie' ‡12–24in (30–60cm) ↔ 24in (60cm) ㉒ 'Satin Pink Gin' ‡4ft (1.2m)
↔ 30–39in (75–100cm), good for showing ㉓ 'Wendy' ‡4ft (1.2m) ↔ 24–30in (60–75cm)
㉔ 'Yvonne Arnaud' ‡4ft (1.2m) ↔ 24–30in (60–75cm)

CIRSIUM

Plumed thistle, Creeping thistle

THE OPULENT, JEWEL-LIKE SHADES sported by the flowers of the cirsium deserve a place in every garden. The hues range from deep crimson-purple to rich reds, yellows, and sometimes white. The flowers, up to 1¼in (3cm) across, are carried singly or in small clusters over dark green, prickly leaves in summer and autumn. Cirsiums belong to a large group of perennials and biennials; some form clumps, others spread by means of underground stems (rhizomes) and can be invasive. Cirsiums look dramatic grown among fine grasses (*see pp.340–355*) or with other summer-flowering perennials such as coreopsis (*see p.217*), phloxes (*see p.306*), and cranesbills (*Geranium, see pp.259–251*). They also blend in well in naturalistic borders or wildflower gardens.

Cultivation Cirsiums need moist but well-drained soil, in full sun. **Deadhead** to avoid self-seeding if growing cirsiums in a formal garden. **Sow** seed (*see pp.391–393*) in a cold frame in spring or divide plants (*see p.395*) in autumn or spring.

Cirsium rivulare 'Atropurpureum'
Z5 ‡ 4ft (1.2m) ↔ 24in (60cm), clump-forming perennial, flowers in early and midsummer

CLARKIA

Godetia

THESE HARDY ANNUALS are widely grown for their satiny, paper-thin flowers borne in abundance over many weeks in summer. There are many species and an ever-increasing number of cultivars, offering both single or double flowers. These come in soft pastel hues and brighter shades of red, purple, and salmon pink. Easy-to-grow, the bushy plants have a maximum height of 20in (50cm) and spread of 12in (30cm), and have green to gray-green leaves. Clarkias make ideal cut flowers. They look good in annual borders with other annuals like corn cockles (*Agrostemma, see p.172*), California poppies (*Eschscholtzia, see p.241*), and pot marigolds (*Calendula, see p.204*).

Cultivation Well-drained, slightly acidic and moderately fertile soil, in sun or partial shade, suits clarkias. They dislike hot, humid spots. Avoid fertilizing all but poor soils before sowing to avoid leaf growth at the expense of flowers. **Sow** seed (*see pp.391–393*) in autumn or spring in shallow drills where they are to grow; clarkias do not like being transplanted. **Thin** seedlings to 6in (15cm) apart. Protect autumn-sown seedlings with a cloche over winter.

Clarkia 'Sundowner'
‡ 30in (75cm) ↔ 18in (45cm), annual, good for cutting, grow in full sun

CLEMATIS

Old man's beard, Virgin's bower

see also pp.136–139

THERE ARE A FEW CLEMATIS that are herbaceous perennials, forming open, sometimes woody-based plants smothered in delicate, often scented flowers. These appear in summer to late autumn. All the herbaceous clematis have very attractive, dark, mid- or gray-green leaves that vary in shape. Their soft stems require some support to stop them from flopping over with the weight of the flowers. Plant these clematis in large containers or towards the centers of herbaceous or mixed borders among other summer-flowering perennials such as achilleas (*see p.167*) and hardy geraniums (*see pp.250–251*).

Cultivation These clematis require full sun in fertile soil that has been enriched with well-rotted organic matter. **Prune** (*see pp.382–383*) the previous year's growth back to two or three buds, about 6–8in (15–20cm) from the base of the plant, before new growth starts in early spring. **Support** the stems with thin, twiggy sticks. **Mulch** with a layer of garden compost or well-rotted manure in late winter. **Divide** in spring (*see p.395*) or take semiripe cuttings (*see p.394*) in summer.

Clematis integrifolia
Z5 ‡ ↔ 24in (60cm), flowers in summer, followed by silvery brown, silky seedheads

Clematis heracleifolia 'Wyevale'
Z5 ‡30in (75cm) ↔ 3ft (1m), open bush, scented, light to midblue flowers that are 1¼ in (4cm) long in summer

CLEOME
Spider flower

THE CURIOUSLY SPIKY FLOWERS and sharply spined stems of the flowers reveal how this plant gained its common name. Of the many species, only the bushy annuals are widely grown. These produce upright stems to 5ft (1.5m) tall, with hairy leaves. They bear dense clusters of white, pink, red, or violet-purple, scented flowers from early summer to early autumn. Cleomes make good gap-fillers in beds and borders where they are useful for extending color into late summer and autumn. Alternatively, grow in large containers or with other annuals such as clarkias (*see facing page*) and rudbeckias (*see p.317*). The long stems of cleomes make them ideal for cutting.

Cultivation Grow cleomes in full sun, in light, fertile, free-draining – preferably sandy – soil. **Water** freely in dry weather. In containers, use a soil-based potting mix; water the plants regularly; and feed them with a balanced fertilizer at weekly intervals. **Deadhead** fading flowers regularly to prolong flowering. **Sow** seed at 64°F (18°C) in spring (*see pp.391–393*); harden off and plant out seedlings after the last frost.

COLCHICUM
Autumn crocus, Naked lady

AUTUMN CROCUSES ARE A LATE-SEASON TREASURE, their flowers emerging seemingly from nowhere in autumn before the leaves appear. A few appear in spring. The flowers are fragrant and come in delicate shades of lilac pink or white. The strappy leaves of these bulbous perennials last from winter to spring. Sizes vary from large cultivars such as 'The Giant' with a height of 8in (20cm) and spread of 4in (10cm) to the tiny *Colchicum kesselringii*, which, with a height and spread of 1in (2.5cm), is best grown as an alpine. Large-leaved colchicums such as 'Autumn Queen' sprawl untidily after the wind or rain and should be grown in the shelter of deciduous shrubs. Naturalize others such as *C. speciosum* and *C. autumnale* in grass. The Canadian hardiness zone for colchicums ranges from 4–6. All parts are highly toxic.

Cultivation Plant the corms 4in (10cm) deep, in deep, fertile, well-drained, moisture-retentive soil, in summer or early autumn. Choose an open, sunny site. Small alpine species need gritty, sharply draining soil. **Apply** a low-nitrogen fertilizer before growth starts. **Divide** large clumps (*see p.395*) in summer.

Clematis recta (Ground clematis)
Z4 ‡3–6ft (1–2m) ↔ 30in (75cm), clump-forming, heavily scented flowers from midsummer to autumn, decorative seedheads

Cleome hassleriana 'Colour Fountain'
T min. 39°F (4°C) ‡4ft (1.2m) ↔ 18in (45cm), annual, with scented flowers in violet pink, rose red, or white to 4in (10cm) in

① *autumnale* 'Album' ‡4–6in (10–15cm)
② *byzantinum* ‡5in (13cm) ③ *speciosum* 'Album' ‡7in (18cm) ④ 'Waterlily' ‡5in (13cm)

FLOWERING PLANTS

CONSOLIDA
Larkspur

‡ to 4ft (1.2m)
↔ to 14in (35cm)

CLOSELY RELATED TO DELPHINIUMS, these slender-stemmed annuals produce daintier versions of the tall flower spikes over a period of many weeks during summer. The flowers may be in shades of blue, lilac blue, pink, or white. They are good for cutting, especially those of longer-stemmed types, and may also be dried. The foliage is feathery and downy, usually rounded, and mid- to dark green in color. They are excellent plants for growing with other hardy annuals, such as marigolds (*Calendula, see p.204*), clarkias (*see p.214*), and coneflowers (*Rudbeckia, see p.317*). Larkspurs make charming additions to a cottage garden or annual border.

Cultivation Larkspurs grow best in full sun and with their roots in light, fertile, well-drained soil. **Support** may be necessary with stakes or twiggy sticks. Pay attention to watering in dry weather, because the soil must not dry out. **Remove** fading flowers to prolong flowering. **Sow** seed (*see pp.391–393*) directly in the garden in spring or autumn, with protection where marginally hardy.

CONVALLARIA MAJALIS
Lily-of-the-valley

FAMED FOR THEIR STRONG FRAGRANCE, the dainty white flowers of this small, creeping perennial are borne on arching stems in late spring to early summer. Lily-of-the-valley has mid- to dark green leaves and makes an excellent groundcover in a woodland garden or moist, shady border. It spreads by means of underground stems (rhizomes) and rapidly forms new colonies in favorable conditions. To show off these plants at their best, grow them under deciduous shrubs so that their bell-shaped flowers stand out against a background of newly opening spring leaves. Forms with pink flowers or variegated leaves are available.

Cultivation A shady position in moist, fertile soil that has been enriched with well-rotted organic matter is best for lily-of-the-valley. **Lift** some of the rhizomes and pot them up in autumn for a display of fragrant flowers indoors. Replant them outdoors after flowering in the spring. **Sow** seed (*see pp.391–393*) in containers in a cold frame as soon as it is ripe.

CONVOLVULUS
Bindweed, Morning glory

DO NOT CONFUSE THESE annuals and perennials with the pernicious, choking weed that shares their common name. These plants produce flowers in several shades, from white, blue, and creamy white, often with a contrasting colored center, and are suitable for mixed borders, rock gardens, and sunny banks. The more compact forms grow to only around 12in (30cm) tall. *Convolvulus sabatius* is good in containers, including hanging baskets. The perennials are short lived and are often treated as annuals. Grow convolvulus with annuals such as marigolds (*Calendula, see p.204*) and larkspurs (*see far left*).

Cultivation These trouble-free plants require poor to moderately fertile, well-drained soil and a sunny, sheltered site. **Deadhead** flowers to prolong the flowering period into autumn. **Container-grown** plants require soil-based potting mix and frequent watering in dry weather. Apply a balanced fertilizer weekly. **Sow** seed (*see pp.391–393*) of annuals directly in the garden in midspring, or in autumn with protection where marginally hardy.

Consolida 'Frosted Skies'
‡ 12–18in (30–45cm) ↔ 6–9in (15–23cm), annual, semidouble flowers in summer, prefers heavy soil, needs staking

Convallaria majalis
Z2 ‡ 9in (23cm) ↔ 12in (30cm), fragrant, waxy flowers are held in graceful sprays, good for cutting

Convolvulus tricolor 'Royal Ensign' (Dwarf morning glory)
T min. 41°F (5°C) ‡ 12in (30cm) ↔ 9–12in (23–30cm), bushy, short-lived perennial or annual, flowers throughout summer

Convolvulus sabatius (Ground morning glory)
‡ 6in (15cm) ↔ 20in (50cm), trailing, slender-stemmed perennial,
ale to deep lavender flowers from summer to early autumn

COREOPSIS

Tickseed

‡ to 30in (75cm)
↔ to 24in (60cm)

BOTH THE PERENNIALS AND ANNUALS are grown for their bright, daisylike, summer-long flowers. Masses of single or double flowers, all in shades of gold, are produced on stems rising above fine foliage. The flowers not only attract bees into the garden, they also make successful cut flowers. Many of the perennials are short lived, however, and are grown as annuals – usually flowering freely in their first year from seed sown in spring. Grow them in a sunny border with perennials such as achilleas (*see p.167*) and phloxes (*see p.307*). Species shown here are hardy to Canadian Zones 4–5.

Cultivation Fertile, well-drained soil and a position in full sun or partial shade are required for this plant. **Remove** fading flowers to prolong flowering. **Stake** taller-growing plants to support the flower stems. **Sow** seed (*see pp.391–393*) in a seedbed outdoors in spring or indoors at 55–61°F (13–16°C) in late winter or early spring; sow in small batches from early spring to early summer for a longer succession of flowers. **Divide** (*see p.395*) perennials in early spring.

① *auriculata* 'Schnittgold' ‡ 32in (80cm) ↔ 24in (60cm), flowers in early to midsummer ② 'Sunray' ‡ 18–36in (45–90cm) ↔ 18in (45cm), flowers late spring to late summer

CORYDALIS

LOW-GROWING AND CLUMP-FORMING, the numerous perennials, annuals, and biennials are favored for their distinctive flowers. These occur in shades of blue, white, and red, and are borne in clusters above the foliage in the spring, summer, or autumn. The ferny leaves are usually mid- to light green and in a few species, such as *Corydalis lutea* and *C. ochroleuca*, are evergreen. The perennials have tuberous ('George Baker') or rhizomatous roots. Some species will self-seed freely. They are best grown in a border or rock garden, but often survive in soil-filled cracks in walls and paving. Some corydalis require a dry, dormant summer period and protection from winter moisture, and are best grown in shallow pots in an unheated greenhouse or cold frame. The Canadian hardiness zone ranges from 4–6.

Cultivation All need free-draining, moderately fertile soil enriched with well-rotted organic matter. Some corydalis prefer sun, others like partial shade. **Sow** seed (*see pp.391–393*) in pots in an open frame as soon as it is ripe; germination can be erratic. **Divide** spring-flowering species in autumn, summer-flowering ones in spring (*see p.395*).

① *flexuosa* ‡ 12in (30cm) ↔ 8in (20cm) ② *lutea* ‡ 16in (40cm) ↔ 12in (30cm) ③ *ochroleuca* ‡↔ 12in (30cm) ④ *solida* 'George Baker' ‡ 10in (25cm) ↔ 8in (20cm)

COSMOS ARE INVALUABLE plants for informal gardens. They include easy-to-grow tuberous perennials and annuals favored for their attractive crimson red, pink, or white, bowl- or saucer-shaped flowers, produced on long, graceful stems in summer. The perennial chocolate cosmos (*Cosmos atrosanguineus*), with reddish brown stems and spoon-shaped, dark green leaves, has velvety, chocolate-scented flowers from midsummer until autumn. It needs winter protection once the foliage dies back. Grow them with other border plants such as phloxes (*see p.306*) and gray-leaved plants like santolinas (*see p.116*) to contrast with the dark flowers. Sow the annual *C. bipinnatus* in a drift, or plant to fill mid- and late-summer gaps in a border.

Cultivation Grow in reasonably fertile soil that is moist but well drained, in full sun. Deadhead to prolong flowering. **Lift** and store tubers in autumn and keep in frost-free conditions. **Sow** annuals where they are to grow in spring or autumn in milder gardens, or in pots (*see pp.391–393*). Thin seedlings to 6in (15cm).

TALL, BUT WITH AN AIRY PRESENCE, these woody-based annuals or perennials are grown for their handsome, wavy-edged leaves and sprays of tiny, often white, sometimes fragrant flowers, which attract bees. The flowers appear from late spring to midsummer, carried on strong stems above undulating, dark green or blue-gray foliage. The large leaves are decorative when young, but tend to die down in mid- to late summer. While crambes are magnificent in a mixed border, taller species, such as *Crambe cordifolia*, need lots of space. They are a good choice for coastal sites because the tough foliage withstands sea spray and salt-laden winds. Grow them with old garden roses (*see pp.110–113*) and philadelphus (*see p.93*).

Cultivation Grow crambes in deep, fertile, well-drained soil in full sun, although they also tolerate poor soil and partial shade. Shelter from strong winds. **Sow** seed (*see pp.391–393*) in a pot in a cold frame in spring or autumn. **Divide** plants (*see p.395*) in early spring. **Clubroot**, a persistent, soil-borne disease that can affect crambes, wallflowers, and other members of the cabbage family, causes deformed roots and stunted plants. Dig out and burn affected plants.

‡20in–5ft (50cm–1.5m)
↔6–12in (15–30cm)

REMINISCENT OF LILIES, crinums belong to a large group of stately, deciduous and evergreen bulbous perennials. They are grown for their showy, white and pink flowers that are often scented; these are borne on long, leafless stalks from spring to autumn, depending on the species. The long, strappy leaves are a glossy, light to mid-green. Crinums are best grown outside in a warm, sheltered border with other perennials like *Anemone hupehensis* and forms of *A. × hybrida* (*see pp.180–181*), border phloxes (*see p.306*) and daylilies (*Hemerocallis, see p.258*).

Cultivation Plant in spring with the neck of each bulb just above soil level, in deep, fertile soil that is moist but very well-drained, and enriched with well-rotted organic matter. Choose a position in full sun, preferably by a wall. **Water** generously when crinums are in growth and keep moist after flowering. **Divide** large clumps of the huge bulbs in spring (*see below and p.395*) to increase your stock.

EMERGING SHOOTS
The soft, new foliage of crambes shooting from the woody crowns give interest to a border in spring.

DIVIDING CRINUMS
Lift a clump of bulbs in spring and shake off the excess soil. Pull or cut it apart and replant well-developed, healthy offsets.

① *atrosanguineus* Z7b ‡30in (75cm) ↔ 18in (45cm)
② *bipinnatus* 'Sea Shells' ‡to 3ft (90cm) ↔ 18in (45cm), annual, with ferny foliage, good for cutting

Crambe cordifolia
Z5 ‡to 8ft (2.5m) ↔ 5ft (1.5m), perennial, bristly leaves to 14in (35cm) across, flowers from late spring to midsummer

Crinum × powellii 'Album'
Z8 ‡5ft (1.5m) ↔ 12in (30cm), deciduous, up to ten fragrant flowers per stem from late summer to autumn

CROCOSMIA
Montbretia

PERFECT FOR HOT-COLORED BORDERS, these eye-catching perennials produce arching sprays of flowers in vivid shades of scarlet, orange, and yellow, as well as bicolors in red and orange. From mid- to late summer, long-lasting flowers are held on wiry stems that may be branched or unbranched – they are good for cutting. Crocosmias are robust, forming clumps of flat, swordlike, often ribbed leaves that stand erect but fan out slightly, making a strong accent in a bed or border. Established clumps spread to around 2ft (60cm). Plant crocosmia corms in a shrub border or with other late-summer perennials, such as Michaelmas daisies (*Aster, see pp.192–193*), rudbeckias (*see p.317*), and sedums (*see p.324*).

Cultivation Plant corms in spring, 3–4in (8–10cm) deep, in soil enriched with well-rotted organic matter, in sun or partial shade. In frost-prone gardens, plant the corms close to a sheltered wall **Divide** congested clumps in spring or autumn every three or four years to maintain the vigor of the plants (*see right and p.395*).

DIVIDING A CLUMP
Dig up a clump of corms; prise apart with your hands or a spade. Separate the healthy corms, trim off the top-growth, and replant.

Crocosmia masoniorum
Z8 ‡ 4ft (1.2m), pleated leaves and upward-facing flowers on unbranched spikes in midsummer

Crocosmia × crocosmiiflora 'Star of the East'
Z6 ‡ 28in (70cm), flowers from late summer to early autumn on branched stems

Crocosmia 'Lucifer'
Z5 ‡ 3–4ft (1–1.2m), flowers 2in (5cm) long in midsummer on sparsely branched spikes

Crocosmia × crocosmiiflora 'Gerbe d'Or'
Z6 ‡ 24–30in (60–75cm), also called 'Golden Fleece', flowers on arching stems from mid- to late summer

NOT JUST A WELCOME SIGN OF SPRING, some crocuses also extend the season well into autumn. This is a large group of dwarf perennials that grow from corms, producing flowers at the same time as, or just before, the narrow, grassy foliage. The flowers come in vivid or pastel shades from yellow to lilac, purple, and white and are sometimes striped or shaded. The leaves are mid-green with a central, silver-green stripe. Crocuses are easy to grow and look best planted in drifts at the front of a border or naturalized in short grass for carpets of color. Grow them with spring-flowering bulbs like dwarf narcissi (*see pp.288–289*) or autumn-flowering hardy cyclamens (*see p.221*).

Cultivation Most prefer gritty, not too rich, well-drained soil in full sun or partial shade. **Plant** in situ; spring-flowering types 3–4in (8–10cm) deep in autumn, autumn-flowering ones in late summer. Autumn crocuses can be planted densely in containers and brought indoors to flower. **Divide** cormlets (*see p.395*) while the plants are dormant and replant them, or leave to self-seed freely. **Rodents** may feed on the corms; deter them by covering groups of corms at planting with a layer of chicken wire before replacing the soil.

Crocus chrysanthus 'Snow Bunting'
Z3 ‡3in (8cm) ↔ 2in (5cm), scented flowers in early spring, up to four per plant

Crocus speciosus
Z4 ‡4–6in (10–15cm) ↔ 2in (5cm), autumn-flowering crocus, which increases rapidly; flowers produced before the leaves

Crocus chrysanthus 'Gipsy Girl'
Z3 ‡3in (8cm) ↔ 2in (5cm), flowers in early spring

Crocus sieberi 'Hubert Edelsten'
Z3 ‡2–3in (5–8cm) ↔ 1in (2.5cm), flowers in late winter to early spring

Crocus sieberi 'Albus'
Z3 ‡2–3in (5–8cm) ↔ 1in (2.5cm), flowers ¾–1¼in (3–4.5cm) long with deep yellow throats, in early spring

CYCLAMEN

CYCLAMEN BRING WINTER CHEER to gardens and windowboxes. The elegant flowers of these tuberous perennials are held aloft on leafless flower stalks. They are produced, depending on the species, from autumn until late winter and vary in hue from white to pink to carmine red. The leaves are heart-shaped to rounded, attractively marked with silver zones or patterns; they last through winter into spring. Grow these hardy cyclamens under trees, or at the front of a shrub border with early bulbs such as snowdrops (*Galanthus, see p.247*) and spring-flowering crocuses (*see facing page*); they also do well in a rock garden, raised bed, or container. Do not confuse them with winter-flowering cyclamens sold as houseplants.

Cultivation Plant the corms 1–2in (2.5–5cm) deep in well-drained, humus-rich, fertile soil. They prefer dryish conditions in summer. **Mulch** (*see p.388*) with leaf mold every year after the leaves die down. **Rodents** can be deterred by placing a layer of chicken wire over the tubers at planting time before replacing the soil.

Cyclamen cilicium
Z6 ‡2in (5cm) ↔ 3in (8cm), pink or white flowers in autumn, stained carmine-red at the mouth, strongly patterned leaves

CYNARA

‡5–6ft (1.5–2m)
↔ 4ft (1.2m)

THESE IMPOSING, ARCHITECTURAL plants have great presence in a border. The clump-forming perennials produce tall, thistlelike flower heads in shades of blue and violet from summer until autumn. The unopened buds of the globe artichoke (*Cynara scolymus* Z7b) are edible, and the flowers can be dried and used in indoor arrangements. The boldly cut, silver or grayish green leaves arch elegantly in the manner of a fountain, making this an impressive foliage plant for the back of a mixed or herbaceous border with other perennials such as veronicas (*see p.337*), salvias (*see p.318*), or daylilies (*Hemerocallis, see p.258*). Cynaras also attract bees and other pollinating insects into the garden.

Cultivation Grow in any reasonably fertile soil that is well drained and in full sun. Where temperatures fall below 5°F (-15°C), protect with a mulch of organic matter (*see p.388*). **Sow** seed (*see pp.391–393*) in a container in a cold frame or divide plants (*see pp.395*) in spring. New shoots are vulnerable to slugs and snails.

PLANTING CYCLAMEN
To ensure flowers in the first year, plant tubers in root growth, with the tops just visible at soil level. Fill in with soil and firm gently.

Cyclamen hederifolium
Z7 ‡4–5in (10–13cm) ↔ 6in (15cm), sometimes scented flowers in mid- and late autumn, before the patterned leaves

Cyclamen coum
Z5 ‡ 2–3in (5–8cm) ↔ 4in (10cm), compact white, pink, or carmine-red flowers in winter or early spring, variegated leaves

Cynara cardunculus (Cardoon)
Z7b ‡5ft (1.5m) ↔ 4ft (1.2m), spiny leaves, woolly gray stems, flowers early to late summer, leaf stalks and midribs edible

DAHLIAS ARE DESERVEDLY POPULAR GARDEN PLANTS, putting on a bravura performance from midsummer until the first frosts of autumn, in shades from white to vivid yellow, orange, scarlet, pink, and purple. In addition to bringing welcome color as summer plants fade, the blooms are good for cutting, and a few cultivars have rich, chocolate-colored foliage. Dahlias, which grow from tubers, are perennials. In permanent plantings, reserve spaces for them because tubers cannot be set out until late spring or early summer, except in mild, frost-free areas. The smaller bedding types are often treated as annuals and grown from seed each year; they are superb for edging borders or growing in containers. Dahlia flowers come in a striking range of shapes, sizes, and forms, which, as well as brightening gardens and cut-flower arrangements, have great appeal for show exhibitors. There are several categories including singles and fully doubles, with collarettes and waterlilies somewhere in between. Cactus types have spiky, quill-shaped petals, while pompons and balls have a pleasing geometry. The giant decoratives may have flowers the size of a dessert plate. All dahlias shown here are tender and should be lifted for the winter, except in the mildest parts of Zone 8.

Cultivation   Grow in full sun in deep, fertile soil enriched with plenty of well-rotted manure or compost. Bedding dahlias tolerate less rich conditions. In milder areas, tubers can be left in the ground, covered with a dry mulch over winter. **Plant out** young plants in leaf when the threat of frost has passed in early summer – dormant tubers a little earlier – and lift in midautumn (*see below*). **Support** with sturdy stakes inserted at planting and tie in new growth regularly. Bedding dahlias do not need staking. **Water** well in dry periods, and apply nitrogen-rich fertilizer regularly during the growing season; from midsummer switch to a high-potassium fertilizer to encourage flowering. **Cut** flowers regularly for a succession of blooms; for large flowers restrict the plants to two or three shoots. **Propagate** by starting tubers into growth in spring in a greenhouse or cold frame. Divide the tuber into sections, each with a growing shoot, and pot up each as a new plant. Slugs (*see p.398*) and earwigs (*see p.397*) may eat the leaves and flowers.

Storing dahlias over winter

❶ *In midautumn, ideally after the foliage has been blackened by the first frost, cut the old stems back, taking care to leave about 6in (15cm) of stem attached to each tuber. Loosen the soil and lift the tubers out gently. Clean off any excess soil from the tubers and attach a label to each around one of the stems.*

❷ *Store the tubers upside-down for about three weeks in a frost-free place, to allow moisture to drain from the stems, which are hollow. When the stems have dried out, put the tubers in a cool, frost-free place and cover with a layer of bark chips. Keep them dry until spring, but inspect them occasionally for disease.*

❸ *In spring, about six weeks before the last frosts, plant out dormant tubers. Before planting tall types, insert a sturdy 3ft (1m) stake in the planting hole. Add soil around the tuber so that the crown, where the stem and tubers are joined, is 1–2in (2.5–5cm) below soil level. Shoots will show in about six weeks.*

① *Dahlia* **'Bishop of Llandaff'** ‡3½ft (1.1m) ↔ 18in (45cm), chocolate-colored foliage ② **'Candy Cane'** ‡3–4ft (1–1.2m) ↔ 2ft (60cm), miniature waterlily ③ **'Clair de Lune'** ‡3½ft (1.1m) ↔ 2ft (60cm), collerette ④ **'Conway'** ‡3½ft (1.1m) ↔ 2ft (60cm), small semicactus ⑤ **'Corton Olympic'** ‡4ft (1.2m) ↔ 2ft (60cm), giant decorative ⑥ **'Davenport Sunlight'** ‡4ft (1.2m) ↔ 2ft (60cm), medium semicactus ⑦ **'David Howard'** ‡↔ 3ft (90cm), miniature decorative ⑧ **'Fascination'**

‡2ft (60cm) ↔ 18in (45cm), annual bedding ⑨ 'Hamari Accord' ‡4ft (1.2m) ↔ 2ft (60cm), large semicactus ⑩ 'Hamari Gold' ‡4ft (1.2m) ↔ 2ft (60cm), giant decorative ⑪ 'Hillcrest Royal' ‡3½ft (1.1m) ↔ 2ft (60cm), medium cactus ⑫ 'Nina Chester' ‡3½ft (1.1m) ↔ 2ft (60cm), small decorative ⑬ 'Noreen' ‡3ft (1m) ↔ 18in (45cm), pompon ⑭ 'Pontiac' ‡4ft (1.2m) ↔ 2ft (60cm), semicactus ⑮ 'Preston Park' ‡↔ 18in (45cm), annual bedding ⑯ 'Rhonda' ‡3½ft (1.1m) ↔ 2ft (60cm), pompon ⑰ 'Rokesly Mini' ‡3ft (1m) ↔ 18in (45cm), semi cactus ⑱ 'Small World' ‡3½ft (1.1m) ↔ 2ft (60cm), pompon ⑲ 'So Dainty' ‡3½ft (1.1m) ↔ 2ft (60cm), miniature semicactus ⑳ 'White Alva's' ‡4ft (1.2m) ↔ 2ft (60cm), giant decorative ㉑ 'Wootton Cupid' ‡3½ft (1.1m) ↔ 2ft (60cm), miniature ball ㉒ 'Wootton Impact' 4ft (1.2m) ↔ 2ft (60cm), semicactus ㉓ 'Zorro' ‡4ft (1.2m) ↔ 2ft (60cm), giant decorative

DELPHINIUM

HANDSOME AND UNUSUAL, this spreading perennial loves moisture. In late spring, pink or white flowers are borne in clusters at the tips of sturdy, hairy stems that can grow to 6ft (2m) in height. It is only when the flowers begin to fade that the rounded, long-stemmed leaves, which are up to 24in (60cm) across, begin to unfurl. This impressive foliage turns scarlet in autumn before dying down over winter. *Darmera peltata* is a large plant that needs plenty of space, and although it will grow in a shady border, darmeras prefer sites in bog gardens or by water. Try it with other moisture-loving plants like astilbes (*see p.194*) or primulas (*see pp.312–313*), or plant a group of them together to emphasise their striking forms.

Cultivation This plant prefers moist or boggy soil in sun or shade, but it will tolerate drier soil in shade. **Sow** seed (*see pp.391–392*) in containers in a cold frame in spring or autumn, or divide plants (*see p.395*) in spring.

WITH THEIR TOWERING SPIKES of flowers, delphiniums are perfect for adding height and form to a border. The blooms are borne in early and midsummer, in a wide range of colors from creamy whites through lilac pinks, sky blues, and deepest, darkest indigo. The mid-green leaves form clumps around the bases of the flower stems. The garden delphiniums are usually herbaceous perennials. Their flower spikes make the stems top heavy and prone to snapping in winds, so they need support and a sheltered position. This can often be provided by placing them at the back of a border by a wall or fence. Small species and dwarf varieties are suited to more exposed areas. Belladonna types are easier to grow.

Cultivation Delphiniums like fertile, moist but well-drained soil in full sun. Provide support with sturdy bamboo stakes (*see below, facing page*). **Deadhead** regularly (*see p.390*) and you may be rewarded with another flush of flowers later in the summer, but do not expect them to be as spectacular as the first. **Sow** seed (*see pp.391–393*) at 55°F (13°C) in early spring. **Slugs** and snails (*see p.398*), and powdery mildew (caused by damp leaves and dry soil) can be troublesome.

Delphinium 'Bruce'
Z4 ‡6ft (2m) ↔ 24–36in (60–90cm), clump-forming perennial

Darmera peltata (Umbrella plant)
Z6 ‡6ft (2m) ↔ 3ft (1m) or more

AUTUMN FOLIAGE

Delphinium 'Fanfare'
Z4 ‡7ft (2.2m) ↔ 24–36in (60–90cm), clump-forming perennial

Delphinium 'Sungleam'
Z4 ‡5ft (1.5m) ↔ 24–36in (60–90cm), clump-forming perennial

Delphinium nudicaule (Larkspur)
Z5 ↕24–36in (60–90cm) ↔ 8in (20cm), short perennial grown as
an annual, flowers in midsummer only

Delphinium 'Em ly Hawkins'
Z4 ↕5½ft (1.7m) ↔ 24–36in (60–90cm), clump-forming perennial

SUPPORTING A STEM
Insert a stake as tall as the
full height of the plant and
begin tying in the stem when
it is about 12in (30cm) tall,
with a figure-eight loop.

Delphinium 'Blue Fountain'
Z4 ↕2–3ft (60–90cm) ↔ 24–36in (60–90cm), clump-forming
perennial, good for small or windy gardens

Delphinium 'Blue Nile'
Z4 ↕5½ft (1.7m) ↔ 24–36in (60–90cm), clump-forming perennial

Delphinium 'Mighty Atom'
Z4 ↕5ft (1.5m) ↔ 3ft (1m), clump-forming perennial, flowers and
stems may be deformed if too many flowers are pollinated

DIANTHUS
Carnation, Pink

‡3–36in (8–90cm)
↔8–16in (20–40cm)

THE MAIN GARDEN PLANTS IN THIS GROUP of evergreen perennials and annuals are pinks and border carnations. In summer, both bear a profusion of bright flowers above narrow, silvery leaves. The flowers, which last well when cut, are single or double in many shades of pink, white, carmine, salmon, and mauve, often with darker, contrasting markings on the petals. Some are fragrant, particularly the rich, spicy "clove-scented" cultivars. Pinks are smaller than carnations and have fewer petals, but other than this their flowers and growth habits are similar. Smaller pinks, including the alpine types like *Dianthus* 'Little Jock', are excellent in rock gardens and troughs. The perpetual carnations, grown in greenhouses for cut flowers, are the tallest in the group. Sweet William (*D. barbatus* Z4) is a short-lived perennial usually grown as a biennial from seed sown in summer; plants flower in the following year. All dianthus shown here run the range of Canadian hardiness zones from 3–5b.

Cultivation All dianthus require a well-drained, neutral to alkaline soil enriched with well-rotted manure or compost. Position plants in full sun. Alpine cultivars, especially, benefit from sharp drainage in alpine troughs and raised beds. **Plant out** young plants in spring and early summer and apply a balanced fertilizer in spring. **Support** tall cultivars in spring using thin stakes and string. **Deadhead** to encourage plants to produce more flowers and maintain a compact growth habit (*see p.390*). Annuals and biennials are discarded after flowering.

Increasing pinks

Taking pipings is an easy way to propagate all kinds of Dianthus, *but especially pinks. Choose nonflowering shoots. Hold a shoot near the base and sharply pull out the tip. The shoot should break easily at a leaf joint, giving a cutting or piping about 3–4in (8–10cm) long with three or four pairs of leaves. Remove the lowest pair of leaves and insert the pipings in pots containing equal parts rooting medium and sharp sand. Place in a shady spot, keep moist, and when they have rooted, after three or four weeks, pot up the young plants separately.*

Layering border carnations

❶ *Loosen the soil around the plant and mix in equal parts sharp sand and peat-free potting mix. Select nonflowering sideshoots and remove all but the top four or five leaves on each shoot. Below a bud, cut into the stem along its length to form a tongue (see inset). Wounding the stem in this way encourages roots to form. Dust the cut surface with hormone rooting powder.*

❷ *Push the tongue of each shoot into the prepared soil and pin down with a piece of bent wire. Tie the leafy part of the shoot to a stake so it is held upright and the cut is held open. Water lightly, cover the shoot with soil, and put a stone over it to retain moisture. Check if roots have formed after five or six weeks. Separate and lift the layers from the parent plant and plant out.*

① *Dianthus alpinus* 'Joan's Blood' ‡3in (8cm) ↔ 4in (10cm), alpine pink ② 'Becky Robinson' ‡18in (45cm) ↔ 16in (40cm), scented pink ③ 'Bovey Belle' ‡18in (45cm) ↔ 16in (40cm), scented pink ④ 'Brympton Red' ‡18in (45cm) ↔ 1ft (30cm), pink ⑤ 'Christine Hough' ‡5ft (1.5m) ↔ 1ft (30cm), carnation ⑥ 'Christopher' ‡15in (38cm) ↔ 1ft (30cm), pink ⑦ 'Dad's Favourite' ‡18in (45cm) ↔ 1ft (30cm), pink ⑧ 'Dainty Dame' ‡4in (10cm) ↔ 8in (20cm), alpine

pink ⑨ *deltoides* 'Leuchtfunk' ‡8in (20cm), ↔ 1ft (30cm), pink ⑩ 'Doris' ‡18in (45cm) ↔ 16in (40cm), scented pink ⑪ 'Forest Treasure' ‡2ft (60cm) ↔ 16in (40cm), carnation ⑫ 'Golden Cross' ‡2ft (60cm) ↔ 16in (40cm), carnation ⑬ 'Gran's Favourite' ‡18in (45cm) ↔ 16in (40cm), scented pink ⑭ 'Haytor White' ‡18in (45cm) ↔ 16in (40cm), scented pink ⑮ 'Houndspool Ruby' ‡18in (45cm) ↔ 16in (40cm) pink ⑯ 'La Bourboule' ‡8in (20cm), ↔ 1ft (30cm), scented alpine pink

⑰ 'Little Jock' ‡8in (20cm), ↔ 1ft (30cm), scented alpine pink ⑱ 'London Brocade' ‡18in (45cm), scented pink ⑲ 'Mrs Sinkins' ‡18in (45cm) ↔ 1ft (30cm), scented pink ⑳ 'Musgrave's Pink' ‡18in (45cm) ↔ 1ft (30cm), pink ㉑ Pierrot ('Kobusa') ‡to 5ft (1.5m) ↔ 1ft (30cm), perpetual carnation ㉒ 'Valda Wyatt' ‡18in (45cm) ↔ 16in (40cm), scented pink ㉓ 'Warden Hybrid' ‡4in (10cm) ↔ 8in (20cm), alpine pink

FLOWERING PLANTS

DIASCIA

FOR THEIR LENGTH OF FLOWERING ALONE, these annuals and semievergreen perennials are worthy of any garden. Loose, densely packed flower heads bloom from early summer to mid-autumn above heart-shaped, mid-green leaves. The main flush of flowers is in early summer, but if you trim back plants after this, they produce another flush later in summer. The color range includes shades of apricot, deep pink, rose pink, purplish pink, or salmon pink. Try growing diascias at the front of a herbaceous border, under roses, or in a rock garden. Most are creeping or mat-forming, but some diascias have a trailing habit which makes them excellent in containers. Diascias are not reliably hardy, so take cuttings to make sure that you have them for the next year.

Cultivation Diascias prefer moist but well-drained, fertile soil, in full sun. Water in dry periods. **Sow** seed (see pp.391–393) at 61°F (16°C) as soon as it is ripe, or in spring. Take semiripe cuttings in late summer (see p.394). Overwinter young plants in frost-free conditions.

① *barberae* 'Blackthorn Apricot' Z7 ② *barberae* 'Fisher's Flora' Z7 ③ *fetcaniensis* Z8 ↕10in (25cm) ↔ 20in (50cm)
④ *rigescens* Z6b ↕12in (30cm) ↔ 20in (50cm)

DICENTRA

see also p.140

↕to 4ft (1.2m)
↔ 18in (45cm)

THIS GARDEN FAVORITE is grown both for its finely cut foliage and its heart-shaped flowers. Most are perennials and form compact clumps with ferny, often grayish leaves and arching stems from which the flowers are suspended. Flowers are produced from spring to early summer in a range of shades from red, purple, and deep pink to white or yellow. Dicentras are also at home in a mixed border, cottage-garden planting, or in woodland garden. They may die down early in dry summers. Their delicate flowers and foliage contrasts nicely with the broad young foliage of hostas (see pp.260–261).

Cultivation Most decentras thrive in partial shade and moist, fertile, slightly alkaline soil enriched with well-rotted compost. *D. chrysanthus* needs a dry, sunny site; *D. spectabilis* tolerates sun if in moist soil. **Sow** seed (see pages 391–393) in a container in a cold frame as soon as it is ripe, or in spring. **Divide** the fleshy-rooted plants (see p.395) carefully in spring or after the leaves die down.

Dicentra formosa (Wild bleeding heart)
Z4 ↕18in (45cm) ↔ 24–36in (60–90cm), spreading perennial, leaves glaucous below, late spring and early summer flowers fade to white

PINK-FLOWERED FORM

Dicentra spectabilis (Bleeding heart, Lyre flower)
Z3 ↕to 4ft (1.2m) ↔ 18in (45cm), clumping perennial, light green leaves, flowers in late spring and early summer

Dicentra cucullaria (Dutchman's breeches)
Z4 ↕to 8in (20cm) ↔ 10in (25cm), tuberous perennial, compact clumps, white or pink flowers in early spring, needs gritty soil

Dicentra spectabilis 'Alba'
3 ‡ to 4ft (1.2m) ↔ 18in (45cm), robust, clump-forming perennial, light green leaves, flowers from late spring until midsummer

DICTAMNUS ALBUS
Burning bush, Dittany, Gas plant

‡16–36in
(40–90cm)
↔ 24in (60cm)

THIS TALL, WOODY-BASED perennial is grown for its dense spikes of fragrant flowers, produced above lemon-scented foliage in summer. The leathery leaves are composed of light green leaflets. Volatile, aromatic oils produced by the flowers and ripening seedpods can be ignited in hot weather, giving rise to the common name of burning bush. This clumping plant mixes well in a herbaceous or mixed border with other tall perennials such as achilleas (*see p.167*), phloxes (*see p.306*), daylilies (*Hemerocallis, see p.258*) and loosestrifes (*Lythrum, see p.283*). Contact with the foliage may cause skin irritation aggravated by sunlight (photodermatitis).

Cultivation Grow this plant in any well-drained, reasonably fertile soil, in full sun or partial shade. **Sow** seed (*see pp.391–393*) in containers in a cold frame as soon as it is ripe. **Divide** plants (*see p.395*) in autumn or spring; bear in mind that the woody rootstocks may take some time to get established again.

① *albus* Z3, white or pinkish white flowers
② *albus* var. *purpureus* purplish pink flowers

DIERAMA
Angel's fishing rod, Wandflower

ONE OF THE MOST DELICATE-LOOKING and mobile plants in the garden, dieramas carry their flowers on long, gently arching stems, so slender that they move in every breeze. The funnel- or bell-shaped flowers in shades of coral pink to red, bright pink, or purple-pink, are borne in succession and hang from the stems on individual flower spikes. The fine, grassy, green to gray-green leaves of these evergreen perennials grow from tufts at the base and can be up to 30in (90cm) long. Grow dieramas with other summer-flowering perennials such as acanthus (*see p.166*), penstemons (*see p.304*), phloxes (*see p.306*), and salvias (*see p.313*).

Cultivation Plant the corms 2–3in (5–8cm) deep in spring; site them in well-drained soil enriched with compost, in a sheltered site in full sun. Do not let plants dry out in summer. Cover them with a protective dry mulch over winter. Young plants take some time to settle, but once established grow freely. **Sow** seed (*see pp.391–393*) in a seedbed or in containers in a cold frame as soon as it is ripe. **Divide** clumps (*see p.395*) in spring.

Dierama pulcherrimum
Z7b ‡3–5ft (1–1.5m) ↔ 24in (60cm), flowers pale to deep magenta-pink, occasionally white or purple-red, in summer

Foxglove

CLASSIC GARDEN PLANTS, foxgloves form a large group of biennials and short-lived perennials. Their imposing flower spikes come in a variety of shades, from the classic purple of *Digitalis purpurea* to pink, white, and yellow, and appear from spring through to midsummer in the second year. They are striking plants, with one or more leafy rosettes at the base, and flower stems often reaching 5ft (1.5m) or more. Use them to give height to a mixed or a herbaceous border with other early-flowering perennials such as dicentras (*see p.229*) and doronicums (*see facing page*) or in a woodland planting. They self-seed prolifically, adding a natural charm to the garden. All foxgloves are toxic.

Cultivation Grow in almost any soil and situation, except extremely wet or dry conditions. Most prefer soil enriched with well-rotted compost in partial shade. **Deadhead** after flowering if you do not want the seedlings springing up everywhere. **Collect** the seed and sow in containers in a cold frame in late spring (*see pp.391–393*). The leaves might be disfigured (*see p.399*) by leaf spot and powdery mildew: avoid splashing the foliage when watering and pick off affected leaves.

Digitalis grandiflora
Z3 ‡ to 3ft (90cm) ↔ 18in (45cm), clumping biennial or perennial, le up to 10in (25cm), flowers in early and midsummer

SELF-SOWN SEEDLINGS
Check for seedlings at the foot of each plant in early autumn. Lift them with a trowel so each retains a ball of soil around its roots and replant them 12in (30cm) apart.

Digitalis davisiana
Z8 ‡ to 28in (70cm) ↔ 18in (45cm), perennial with underground stems (rhizomes), flowers in early summer

Digitalis × mertonensis
Z3 ‡ to 3ft (90cm) ↔ 12in (30cm), clump-forming perennial, flowers in late spring/early summer, comes true from seed

Digitalis purpurea Excelsior Group
Z4 ‡ 3–6ft (90cm–2m) ↔ to 24in (60cm), biennial or perennial, at their best when grown annually from seed, good for cut flowers

DODECATHEON
American cowslip, Shooting stars

‡ to 16in (40cm)
↔ 10in (25cm)

THESE PERENNIALS MAKE an impressive display in spring and summer. They thrive alongside ponds and at the edge of bog gardens, as well as in rock gardens and mixed and herbaceous borders. Their cyclamen-like flowers, in shades of purple pink, reddish purple, magenta pink, lavender, or white, are borne in clusters on long, arching stems. They have basal rosettes of lance or spoon-shaped leaves. After flowering in summer, the plants become dormant. Grow with other spring and early summer-flowering perennials like doronicums (*see right*), lupines (*see p.280*), and poppies (*Papaver, see p.299*).

Cultivation Grow these in well-drained, moist but not waterlogged, soil enriched with well-rotted compost in sun or partial shade. Keep them well watered during the growing season. **Sow** seed (*see pp.391–393*) as soon as it is ripe in a container and place in an open cold frame, although it will need exposure to cold before germination can take place. **Divide** plants in spring (*see p.395*). **Protect** the young leaves from slugs and snails (*see p.260*).

DORONICUM
Leopard's bane

LEOPARD'S BANE ARE GROWN FOR their delightful single or double yellow flowers. They are held, on their own or in small clusters, on slender stems high above the leaves. These perennials flower for several weeks over spring. Some species are bulbous and have tubers or rhizomes (*see p.164*). Leopard's bane look quite at home in a woodland garden; alternatively, plant them in a herbaceous border with daffodils (*Narcissus, see pp.288–289*), pulmonarias (*see p.314*) and primulas (*see pp.312–313*). They are also good for cutting.

Cultivation Grow in moist soil enriched with well-rotted compost, in part or dappled shade. *D. orientale* and its cultivars are vulnerable to root rot, especially on heavy clay soils that are wet in winter: dig in plenty of coarse grit to improve drainage on heavy soils. Raising the soil level by 2–3in (5–8cm) can also help. **Water** well in the growing season and deadhead to prolong flowering. **Sow** seed in containers in a cold frame in spring (*see pp.391–393*). **Divide** plants in early autumn (*see p.395*). Powdery mildew may affect the leaves if the soil is dry but the air is damp; avoid splashing leaves when watering.

DRABA
Whitlow grass

THESE DELICATE ALPINES ARE usually found in mountainous areas. The garden plants in this group are mat- or cushion-forming perennials that produce a mass of yellow or white flowers in spring or early summer. The tiny, green to gray-green leaves form tight, evergreen or semievergreen rosettes. They are best grown in a rock garden or raised bed, although some need protection from winter moisture in temperate climates. In the autumn, place a sheet of glass or clear plastic over each plant, supported by short stakes, then put a stone on top to hold it in place. Alternatively, grow the plant in a shallow pot, or pan, and move it over winter into a well-ventilated cold frame or unheated greenhouse.

Cultivation Grow drabas in gritty, sharply drained soil in full sun, with a gravel mulch. If growing them in pots, use soil-based potting mix with added grit. Avoid wetting the foliage. **Sow** seed in an open frame in autumn; they need a cold winter to germinate (*see pp.391–393*). **Take** rosettes of larger species as cuttings in late spring (*see p.394*).

① ...*entatum* Z8 ‡ ↔ to 8in (20cm), 2–5 white flowers per stem in late ... ② *pulchellum* 'Red Wings' Z5 ‡ 14in (35cm) ↔ 8in (20cm), ...owers per stem in late spring and early summer

Doronicum 'Miss Mason'
Z4 ‡ 5–24in (13–60cm) ↔ 24in (60cm), clumps spread by underground stems (rhizomes), flowers in mid- and late spring

Draba mollissima
Z4 ‡ 3in (8cm) ↔ 8in (20cm), hummock-forming evergreen, gray-green, hairy leaves, flowers in late spring

DRACOCEPHALUM
Dragon's head

THE ANNUALS AND PERENNIALS in this group are grown for their sagelike, tubular flowers in shades of white and blue. The flowers are produced from early to midsummer in spikes up to 12in (30cm) or more long. Their leaves are often aromatic. Originating in rocky, grassy regions and dry woodland areas, they make a bright and colorful addition to free-draining, mixed or herbaceous borders, and rock gardens. They associate well with such plants as poppies (*Papaver, see p.299*) or hardy geraniums (*see pp.250–251*). Annuals combine well with grasses and are useful gap-fillers in borders. Some will naturalize in partial shade.

Cultivation Well-drained, moderately fertile soil and full sun are the requirements for these plants, although some shade from the midday sun is also needed. *Dracocephalum forrestii* requires sharply drained soil and protection from excessive winter moisture. *D. ruyschiana* tolerates dry soil. **Sow** seed (*see pp.391–393*) of annuals in midspring directly in the soil. Thin seedlings to around 6in (15cm) apart. **Divide** mature clumps (*see p.395*) or sow seed of perennials in autumn or spring in containers in a cold frame. **Take** new shoots from the base and treat as softwood cuttings (*see p.394*) in mid- or late spring.

DRYAS
Mountain avens

MATS OF PLEASING, EVERGREEN FOLIAGE distinguish these prostrate, low-growing, woody-based perennials. The oaklike, leathery leaves have a whitish down on their undersides. The plants are also valued for their large white or yellowish flowers produced from spring to early summer. Upright or nodding, they have a central boss of golden stamens and are borne singly at the tips of slender stems. Pinkish, feathery seedheads follow. An open, sunny site at the front of a border suits these easy-to-grow, carpeting plants. They will also happily scramble over rocks in a rock garden or even colonize dry-stone walls. There are small types suitable for growing in troughs with other dwarf alpines, such as drabas (*see p.231*).

Cultivation Grow these plants in well-drained soil enriched with well-rotted compost. They will grow in full sun or partial shade. **Add** plenty of grit to maintain good drainage. **Sow** seed (*see pp.391–393*) in a container in a cold frame as soon as they are ripe, or take softwood cuttings (*see p.394*) in early summer. **Lift**, detach, and transplant rooted stems in spring.

ECHINACEA
Coneflower

WITH THEIR LARGE DAISIES in shades of purple, rose pink, or white, these tall perennials from dry prairies, open woodland, and gravelly hillsides make an eye-catching display in a late-summer border. The large central cone standing proud of its petals gives rise to the plant's common name and may be brownish yellow to ocher. Each daisy is up to 6in (15cm) across and is held on stout, upright stems. The flowers persist for about two months and they also make a long-lasting cut flowers. The leaves reach up to 8in (20cm) in length. Grow these undemanding plants in a border with other late-flowering perennials, such as sedums (*see p.324*) and rudbeckias (*see p.317*). The seedheads continue looking attractive into winter.

Cultivation Coneflowers need deep, fertile, well-drained soil enriched with well-rotted compost and full sun, although they tolerate some shade. **Cut back** the stems as the flowers fade for more blooms. **Sow** seed (*see pp.391–393*) in spring. **Divide** in spring or autumn (*see p.395*). **Take** root cuttings (*see p.394*) in late autumn.

Dracocephalum argunense
Z4 ↕ 18in (45cm) ↔ 12in (30cm), clump-forming perennial, hairy leaves 2–3in (5–8cm) long, flowers in midsummer

Dryas octopetala (Mountain avens)
Z3 ↕ 4in (10cm) ↔ 36in (1m), mat-forming, flowers in late spring or early summer, suitable for the rock garden

Echinacea purpurea 'Green Edge'
Z3b ↕ 5ft (1.5m) ↔ 18in (45cm), flower heads 5in (13cm) across from midsummer to early autumn

FROSTED SEEDHEADS

...inacea purpurea
‡ 5ft (1.5m) ↔ 18in (45cm), stems sometimes red-tinted, flowers are (13cm) across and borne from midsummer to early autumn

Echinacea purpurea 'White Lustre'
Z3b ‡ 32in (80cm) ↔ 18in (45cm), flowers from midsummer to early autumn

Echinacea purpurea 'Magnus'
Z3b ‡ 5ft (1.5m) ↔ 18in (45cm), extra-large flowers are 7in (18cm) across and borne from midsummer to early autumn

Echinacea purpurea 'Kim's Knee High'
Z3b ‡ 18–24in (45–60cm) ↔ 12–24in (30–60cm), ur usually compact, dwarf habit, flowers from midsummer to early autumn, drought-tolerant, can be grown in containers

Echinacea purpurea 'Robert Bloom'
Z3b ‡ 4ft (1.2m) ↔ 20in (50cm), flowers from midsummer to early autumn

ECHINOPS
Globe thistle

GROWN FOR THEIR THISTLELIKE FLOWERS that appear from midsummer until autumn, these perennials, biennials, and annuals are very undemanding plants. The flowers can be up to 1½in (4cm) across, often have bristly bracts (modified leaves), and are usually blue or white and carried on stout stems. Globe thistles usually form clumps and often have dissected foliage that is spiny and grayish white. The flowers are also good for cutting and drying. Plant them in a wild garden, or grow them with other perennials such as echinaceas (*see p.232*), monardas (*see p.286*), and phloxes (*see p.306*).

Cultivation Globe thistles are best grown in poor, well-drained soil in full sun, but they will tolerate almost any situation. **Remove** fading flowers to prevent self-seeding. **Sow** seed in a seedbed in midspring (*see pp.391–393*). **Divide** established plants from autumn to spring or take root cuttings in winter (*see pp.394–395*).

ECHIUM

THIS IS A LARGE GROUP OF ANNUALS, biennials, and evergreen perennials, with charming flowers that appear from early to late summer in shades of deep blue, pink, purple, or white. They are carried either on large, impressive spikes, or in dense clusters close to the stems. The bristly, hairy leaves are usually borne in basal rosettes and on the stems. Grow echiums in borders with echinaceas (*see p.232*), chrysanthemums (*see pp.212–213*), and phloxes (*see p.306*). Wear gloves when handling echiums because contact with the bristly foliage may irritate your skin.

Cultivation Grow these plants in reasonably fertile, well-drained soil, in full sun. **Protect** the perennials in winter in colder areas by covering them with mulch. As a precaution, it is also wise to take cuttings of perennials in summer (*see p.394*). **Sow** seed at 55–61°F (13–16°C) in summer and overwinter the seedlings in a frost-free greenhouse or cold frame; annuals can be sown in spring where they are to grow (*see pp.391–393*).

EPILOBIUM
Willow herb

THE COTTAGE GARDEN FAVORITES from this large group of annuals, biennials, and perennials produce clusters of white or pink flowers from the bases of the leaves over several weeks from summer through autumn. They can be invasive if allowed to self-seed, like their wildflower cousin the rosebay willow herb, but are easy to control by regular deadheading. There are great variations in height and spread: some grow to around 5ft (1.5m), spreading to 3ft (90cm), and are best in a mixed or herbaceous border. The smaller ones, suitable for a rock garden, have a height and spread of around 12in (30cm).

Cultivation Grow in soil enriched with well-rotted compost in sun or partial shade. The smaller, alpine species benefit from some shade around midday. **Remove** fading flowers to encourage more blooms and prevent self-seeding. **Sow** seed in containers in a cold frame as soon as they are ripe or in spring (*see pp.391–393*). **Divide** established plants in autumn or spring or take softwood cuttings in spring (*see pp.394–395*). Willow herb is prone to damage from slugs and snails (*see p.398*) and to powdery mildew on the leaves.

![Echinops ritro 'Veitch's Blue']

***Echinops ritro* 'Veitch's Blue'**
Z3 ‡to 3ft (90cm) ↔ 18in (45cm), compact perennial, leaves have white, downy undersides, flowers in late summer

***Echium vulgare* 'Blue Bedder'**
Z3 ‡18in (45cm) ↔ 12in (30cm), evergreen biennial with upright, bushy habit, light blue flowers age to bluish pink

① *angustifolium* var. *album* Z4 ‡5ft (1.5m) ↔ 3ft (90cm), strong, spreading perennial ② *glabellum* Z5b ‡↔ 8in (20cm), semievergreen, mat-forming, cream or pink flowers, likes cool, damp shade

EPIMEDIUM
Barrenwort

THE FOLIAGE IS PRIZED AS MUCH AS THE FLOWERS with these perennials. The mid- to light-green leaves are lost in autumn in some species or after new leaves have formed in others. They often develop attractive tones in autumn and occasionally bronze tips on the new leaves in spring. From spring until early summer, loose clusters of saucer- to cup-shaped flowers, often with spurs, are produced in a range of colors including gold, beige, white, pink, crimson, and purple. They make excellent groundcover plants, especially under trees where little else will grow.

Cultivation Grow epimediums in fertile soil, enriched with well-rotted compost, in partial shade. Provide shelter from strong, cold winds. **Sow** seed in a container in a cold frame as soon as it is ripe (*see pp.391–393*). **Divide** established plants in autumn or just after flowering (*see p.395*). Good hygiene in the garden is important (*see pp.396–399*) because epimediums can be at risk from vine weevils eating the leaves and mosaic virus, which causes stunted, mottled growth. Destroy any plants afflicted by virus.

SPRING PRUNING Use shears to clip old leaves to the ground in late winter or early spring, before the new flower spikes appear, to encourage new growth, except for *E. perralderianum*.

Epimedium × *youngianum* 'Niveum'
Z4 ‡8–12in (20–30cm) ↔ 12in (30cm), deciduous, redish leaf stalks, colored foliage when young, flowers mid- to late spring

Epimedium acuminatum
‡12in (30cm) ↔ 18in (45cm), clumping evergreen, leaf undersides with powdery bloom, flowers in midspring to early summer

Epimedium pinnatum subsp. *colchicum*
Z5 ‡12–16in (30–40cm) ↔ 10in (25cm), slow-spreading, evergreen, white or red hairy leaves, late spring flowers

Epimedium 'Versicolor'
Z5 ‡↔ 12in (30cm), evergreen, young leaves copper-red and brown (*inset*) turning mid-green, flowers in mid- and late spring

FLOWERING PLANTS

EPIPACTIS
Helleborine

These orchids come mainly from temperate regions of the northern hemisphere, where they favor marshes, meadows, woodland and even dunes. They require damp, shady conditions or a woodland setting. They have fleshy underground stems, or rhizomes, which produce twisted stalks bearing loose or dense clusters of flowers from spring to early summer. Some of the blooms are greenish white while others are brown-tinted and streaked with violet, white, or pink. Epipactis usually have ribbed, mid-green leaves that are to 8in (20cm) in length.

Cultivation Epipactis require soil enriched with well-rotted compost; it must be moist but well drained, and in partial or deep shade. Given favorable conditions, they will spread freely by sending out creeping rhizomes. **Divide** clumps (see p.395) in early spring, making sure that each piece of rhizome has at least one healthy growing point before replanting. **Slugs** and snails (see p.398) may be attracted to the fleshy flowers and shoots.

ERANTHIS HYEMALIS
Winter aconite

WINTER ACONITES PROVIDE A SPLASH OF GOLD to signal the end of winter. Their buttercup-like flowers bloom from late winter to early spring; each appears to sit on an elegant ruff of finely dissected leaves. The leaves at the bases are broader and deeply lobed. These clump-forming perennials grow from knobby tubers just below soil level in damp, shady places. They look best under deciduous shrubs or trees where, once established, they rapidly spread to form a carpet of color, especially on alkaline soils. Winter aconites also naturalize well in grass and combine well with other winter- and early-spring bulbs, such as snowdrops (*Galanthus, see p.247*). Contact with the sap may aggravate skin allergies.

Cultivation Fertile soil that does not dry out in summer and a position in full sun or light, dappled shade are required here. **Plant** the tubers 2in (5cm) deep in autumn. Dried-out tubers will not thrive. *E.pinnatifida* needs acidic soil in a raised bed. **Sow** seed (see pp.391–393) in containers in a cold frame in late spring. Lift and divide large clumps (see p.395) in spring after flowering.

EREMURUS
Desert candle, Foxtail lily

MAJESTIC FLOWER SPIKES densely covered in pink, white, or golden, starry flowers soar skyward in spring and early summer. Usually, these clump-forming perennials produce only one flowering stem from each crown. Their long, fleshy, strappy leaves deteriorate quickly, however, so foxtail lilies are best placed toward the middle or back of a border among shrubs or herbaceous perennials, where the dying foliage will be hidden from view. The flowers are long-lasting when cut. Since grasslands and semideserts are the natural home of foxtail lilies, their large, starfish-shaped, fleshy rootstocks are prone to rot in damp conditions.

‡3–10ft (1–3m) ↔ to 4ft (1.2m)

Cultivation Plant in well-drained, fertile soil, in full sun with shelter from winds. To improve drainage on heavy clay soils, dig in plenty of coarse grit around the planting area; fork extra into the bottom of the planting hole. **Support** in exposed sites. **Sow** seed (see pp.391–393) in containers in a cold frame in autumn or late winter. **Divide** plants after flowering (see p.395); handle the brittle rootstocks gently.

Epipactis gigantea (Giant helleborine)
Z5 ‡ 12–16in (30–40cm) ↔ to 5ft (1.5m), loose terminal spikes of up to 15 flowers from late spring to early summer

Eranthis hyemalis (Winter aconite)
Z4 ‡ 2–3in (5–8cm) ↔ 2in (5cm), rapid colonizer especially in alkaline soils, flowers ¾–1¼in (2–3cm) across

① *himalaicus* ‡ 4–6ft (1.2–2m) ↔ 24in (60cm), green leaves, flowers late spring to early summer ② *robustus* ‡ 10ft (3m) ↔ 4ft (1.2m), blue-green leaves, flowers in early and midsummer. Both Z5

ERIGERON
Fleabane

LONG-LASTING, SINGLE OR DOUBLE DAISIES are
borne over many weeks in summer by the annuals,
biennials, and perennials in this group. The flowers
are available in a wide range of shades, from white,
pink, purple, or blue to yellow or orange. All have
a bright yellow eye and are borne singly or in small
clusters. The leaves are found mostly at the bases of
the plants, are sometimes spoon-shaped, and mid- or
light green. Erigerons range from low-growing alpines
to medium-sized clumps, so need a position at the
front of a border. They also stand up well to salt-laden
winds, making them invaluable in coastal gardens.
The flowers last well if they are cut when fully open.

Cultivation Erigerons prefer fertile, well-drained soil that does not
dry out in summer in sun, preferably with some shade around midday.
Alpine species need sharply drained soil and protection from winter
moisture. **Stake** taller species. **Remove** fading flowers regularly for more
flowers; cut down old growth in autumn. **Divide** plants every 2–3 years
in late spring (see p.395). **Take** root cuttings (see p.394) in spring or
detach new shoots near the base and treat as softwood cuttings.

Erigeron karvinskianus (Mexican daisy)
Z5b ‡ 6–12in (15–30 m) ↔ 3ft3ft (1m) or more, suitable
for cracks in walls or paving, white flowers fade to pink

Erigeron 'Dunkelste Aller'('Darkest of all')
Z4 ‡ 24in (60cm) ↔ 18in (45cm), clump-forming border perennial,
flowers in early and midsummer

Erigeron 'Quakeress'
Z4 ‡ 24in (60cm) ↔ 18in (45cm), clump-forming border perennial,
clusters of single flowers in early and midsummer

Erigeron aureus 'Canary Erd'
Z5 ‡ to 4in (10cm) ↔ to 6in (15cm), hairy-leaved perennial, flowers
in summer, needs protection from winter moisture

FLOWERING PLANTS

ERINUS
Fairy foxglove

DAINTY, OPEN FLOWERS in shades of pink, purple, or white are borne in clusters by these trouble-free plants. There are only two species, which are semi-evergreen, short-lived perennials. The leaves are lance- to wedge-shaped, softly textured, and produced in rosettes. Fairy foxgloves are ideal for alpine or rock gardens, or for growing in crevices in old walls or between gaps in paving. If you let them, they will self-seed themselves around the garden.

Cultivation Grow these plants in light, reasonably fertile soil that is well drained, in full sun or partial shade. **Sow** seed in the ground where they are to grow or in containers in a cold frame in autumn (*see pp.391–393*). **Take rosettes** as cuttings in spring (*see p.394*).

Erinus alpinus (Alpine liverwort)
Z5 ‡3in (8cm) ↔ 4in (10cm), sticky leaves, pink, purple, or white flowers from late spring to summer

ERODIUM
Heron's bill, Stork's bill

THE FOLIAGE AND LONG FLOWERING PERIOD of the annual and perennial erodiums make them valuable plants for the garden. The flowers resemble those of cranesbills (*Geranium, see pp.250–251*) and are produced singly from the joints of leaves and stems or in clusters at the ends of the stems. Flower hues range from pink to purple, and occasionally yellow or white. The curious, pointed seedpods give the plant its common name. Grow the smaller species in a rock garden and the taller ones in a mixed or herbaceous border with other summer-flowering perennials such as achilleas (*see p.166*), geraniums, phloxes (*see p.306*), or among shrub roses (*see pp.110–113*).

Cultivation Grow the plants in well-drained soil that is neutral to alkaline, in full sun. **Protect** the smaller species from excessive winter moisture. In an alpine house, grow in a mix of loam, leaf mold, and grit. **Sow** seed as soon as it is ripe in containers in a cold frame (*see pp.391–393*). **Divide** plants in spring or take stem cuttings in late spring or early summer (*see pp.394–395*).

① ***glandulosum*** Z5b ‡4–8in (10–20cm) ↔ 8in (20cm), perennial, flowers in summer ② ***manescaui*** Z4 ‡8–18in (20–45cm) ↔ 8in (20cm), perennial, flowers summer to autumn

ERYNGIUM
Eryngo, Sea holly

SEA HOLLIES ARE STRIKING, ARCHITECTURAL plants that add interest to any border; some can be naturalized in a wildflower meadow. Most form basal rosettes of leaves that are often spiny, with attractive silvery white veins. From midsummer to autumn, they bear thistlelike flowers on branched stems. These consist of round to cone-shaped heads of tiny flowers, that are surrounded by conspicuous ruffs, also usually silvery white. Grow smaller sea hollies in a rock garden and taller ones in a herbaceous border, where their skeletal forms can be enjoyed through winter. The flowers can be dried, but cut them before they are fully open for best effect. Eryngiums are a large group of annuals, biennials, and deciduous and evergreen perennials.

Cultivation All sea hollies prefer well-drained soil in full sun, but some like poor to moderately fertile soil and protection from winter moisture, whereas others need moist, rich soil. **Sow** seed as soon as they are ripe in containers in a cold frame (*see pp.391–393*). **Divide** plants in spring – they can be slow to re-establish; take root cuttings of perennials in winter (*see pp.394–395*). Despite their spines, sea hollies are prey to slugs and snails.

Eryngium* × *oliverianum
Z5 ‡3ft (90cm) ↔ 18in (45cm), clumping perennial, dark green spiny leaf rosettes, blue stems, flowers midsummer to early autumn

Eryngium alpinum (Alpine sea holly)
Z4 ‡28in (70cm) ↔ 18in (45cm), rosette-forming perennial, mid-green, spiny leaves, flowers steel blue or white in midsummer to early autumn, keep soil moist but protect from winter moisture

THE MOST COMMONLY GROWN wallflowers are those used as spring bedding plants. They are usually grown as biennials from seed sown in summer or plants bought bare-rooted in autumn. The fragrant flowers are produced in pastel and brilliant hues of scarlet, orange, and gold, with some purples. Wallflowers spread only 8–24in (20–60cm), so are ideal for containers, a rock garden, or the front of a mixed border. Use with spring-flowering plants such as forget-me-nots (*Myosotis, see p.287*), primulas (*see pp.312–313*), and tulips (*see pp.334–335*).

Cultivation Grow in poor to reasonably fertile, well-drained, slightly alkaline soil, or soil-based potting mix with added grit, in full sun. **Trim** perennials lightly after flowering to keep them compact. **Soak** bare-root plants in a bucket of water for an hour before planting. **Sow** seed of perennials in containers in a cold frame in spring; and of biennials in early summer. Transplant to flowering positions in autumn (*see pp.392–393*). **Take** softwood cuttings from woody-based perennials in summer (*see p.394*). Wallflowers are susceptible to white rust, downy mildew, and clubroot, so plant them in a different spot each year and maintain good garden hygiene (*see pp.396–399*).

Eryngium × tripartitum
Z4 ‡2–3ft (60–90cm) ↔ 20in (50cm), clumping perennial, dark green toothed leaves, flowers midsummer to early autumn

Eryngium variifolium
Z5 ‡12–16in (30–40cm) ↔ 10in (25cm), clumping evergreen, flowers mid- to late summer, protect from winter moisture

① 'Bowles' Mauve' Z4 ‡30in (75cm) ② 'Bredon' Z6 ‡12in (30cm) ③ 'John Codrington' Z6 ‡10in (25cm) ④ *linifolium* 'Variegatum' Z6 ‡18in (45cm)

ERYTHRONIUM
Dog-tooth violet, Trout lily

THE ELEGANT, DROOPING FLOWERS of these perennials are produced from spring until early summer, singly or in clusters on slender, upright stems. They have distinctive, swept-back petals, in shades of purple, violet, pink, yellow, or white, and conspicuously long stamens. The broad leaves grow from the base and may be glossy or glaucous; some have a strong bronze marbling, as in *Erythronium dens-canis*, or are veined with white. The common name derives from the long-pointed, toothlike bulbs from which these clump-forming perennials grow. Natives of meadows and woodlands, they thrive in a rock garden or beneath deciduous trees, and also if naturalized with other bulbs such as dwarf narcissi (*see pp.288–289*) and crocuses (*see pp.220–221*).

Cultivation These plants like deep, fertile soil that does not dry out, in partial or light, dappled shade. Plant the bulbs at least 4in (10cm) deep in autumn; keep them slightly damp if stored before planting. **Divide** established clumps (*see right and p.395*) after flowering.

Erythronium 'Pagoda'
Z4 ‡6–14in (15–35cm) ↔ 4in (10cm), vigorous, leaves glossy green and bronze, clusters of up to 10 flowers in spring

DIVIDING CLUMPS
After the leaves wither, lift the bulbs carefully with a fork; separate the offsets, and replant them.

Erythronium californicum 'White Beauty'
Z4 ‡6–14in (15–35cm) ↔ 4in (10cm), vigorous, soon forms a large clump, bears clusters of up to 3 flowers in spring

Erythronium revolutum (Western trout lily)
Z6 ‡8–12in (20–30cm) ↔ 4in (10cm), clusters of up to four flowers in midspring, sometimes slow to establish, but self-seeds freely once it is settled, leaves heavily marbled bronze

Erythronium dens-canis (Dog-tooth violet)
Z4 ‡4–6in (10–15cm) ↔ 4in (10cm), pink, white, or lilac flowers with blue or purple-blue anthers singly in spring, naturalizes well in grass

ESCHSCHOLZIA
California poppy

IN FIERY SHADES OF ORANGE, gold, and scarlet, and sometimes cream, white, pink, or purple, the tissue-thin, satiny flowers of California poppies are carried singly on slender stems. They may be simple and cup-shaped, double, or even ruffled. Although they open fully only in sun, the flowers are still colorful when closed and are good for cutting. The ferny foliage is light to blue-green. The most commonly grown are the summer-flowering hardy annuals – often in a border with other annuals such as clarkias (*see p.214*) and annual phloxes (*see p.306*) or in a gravel garden. *Eschscholzia californica* cultivars also do well in containers and hanging baskets. Their fragile appearance belies their robust nature; they self-seed freely, even into cracks in paving or concrete.

Cultivation These poppies thrive in a poor, well-drained soil, in full sun. **Sow** seed (*see pp.391–393*) of annuals where they are to grow in spring or early autumn. Repeat sowings at two or three week intervals to provide a succession of flowers. Thin to around 6in (15cm) apart

WIRE SUPPORT
California poppies tend to sprawl. A chicken wire cage over young plants provides support and will soon be entirely hidden by the foliage.

Eschscholzia caespitosa
↕↔ to 6in (15cm), diminutive tufted annual, threadlike leaves, scented flowers in summer, useful edging plant

Eschscholzia californica (California poppy)
↕ to 12in (30cm) ↔ to 6in (15cm), annual, variable habit, often sprawling, flowers orange, red, white, and gold in summer

EUCOMIS
Pineapple flower, Pineapple lily

↕ 6–30in (15–75cm)
↔ 6–8in (15–20cm)

THESE STRIKING PLANTS are grown for their unusual clusters of flowers in late summer and early autumn. The starry flowers are usually pale greenish white or white, but what sets them apart is the tuft of green bracts leaves, similar to that on a pineapple, that tops each tight cluster. The flowers are followed by long-lasting seedpods. In mild or sheltered places, grow these bulbous perennials at the base of a warm wall or in a sunny border, where the upright stems and strappy leaves contrast well with bold foliage plants such as hostas (*see pp.260–261*). Elsewhere, grow them in containers so they can be overwintered under cover.

Cultivation Plant the bulbs 6in (15cm) deep in fertile, well-drained soil in full sun. **Mulch** in winter (*see p.388*) with a layer of organic matter. **In pots**, use a soil-based potting mix with added coarse grit for drainage, and water freely during active growth. **Sow** seed (*see pp.391–393*) at 61°F (16°C) in autumn or spring or remove bulb offsets (*see p.395*) in spring.

Eucomis bicolor
Z7 ↕ 12–24in (30–60cm) ↔ 8in (20cm), maroon-spotted, light green stems and leaves

EUPATORIUM

Joe Pye plant

ADORED BY BEES AND BUTTERFLIES, the clusters of tiny flowers on upright, leafy stems are the attraction of the hardy eupatoriums. The flowers come in shades of white, pink, violet, or purple and are mostly borne from summer until early autumn. There are many, varied annuals and perennial eupatoriums that are worthy of the garden, with leaves that differ in shape and shade. The large, hardy, herbaceous perennials such as *Eupatorium cannabinum* (z4) look lush in large borders, with grasses (*see pp.340–355*) or in a wild or woodland garden. *E. purpureum* is even taller and has similarly strong stems that need no support.

Cultivation Eupatoriums thrive in any soil, providing it remains moist, in full sun or partial shade. **Deadhead** fading flowers. **Divide** hardy species (*see p.395*) and take softwood cuttings of tender species (*see p.394*) in spring. Sow seed in spring (*see pp.391–393*).

EUPHORBIA

Milkweed, Spurge

see also p.57

THE FLAMBOYANT, ACID YELLOW BRACTS characteristic of many garden spurges contrast dramatically with other plants, and are sure to always catch the eye. The bracts, which are really modified leaves, surround tiny flowers, borne in clusters at the stem tips. As well as acid yellow, plants with bracts in warm shades of red, orange, purple, or brown are available. The leaves are usually green to blue-green. This huge and incredibly varied group includes annuals, biennials, evergreen and semievergreen perennials, and succulents; you can find a euphorbia to suit almost any garden situation. Spurges can be short-lived, particularly in wet soils; luckily, many such as *Euphorbia polychroma* self-seed freely about. All parts of euphorbias are toxic.

Cultivation Most herbaceous euphorbias like either well-drained, light soils in full sun or moist, humus-rich soils in light, dappled shade. **Sow** seed (*see pp.391–393*) in containers in a cold frame. **Divide** plants in early spring (*see p.395*). Tender and succulent species should be overwintered in a cool greenhouse or conservatory.

Euphorbia schillingii
Z7b ↕ 3ft (1m) ↔ 12in (30cm), clump-forming perennial for moisture and light shade, flowers from midsummer to midautumn

Eupatorium purpureum (Joe Pye plant)
Z3 ↕ 7ft (2.2m) ↔ 3ft (1m), clump-forming perennial, flowers from midsummer to early autumn, prefers alkaline soil

Euphorbia polychroma (Cushion spurge)
Z4 ↕ 16in (40cm) ↔ 24in (60cm), perennial, likes sun, flowers midspring to midsummer, good groundcover, can be invasive

BEWARE OF THE SAP
All euphorbias exude a milky sap that irritates the skin, so wear gloves when handling the plants.

Euphorbia griffithii 'Fireglow'
Z4 ↕ 30in (75cm) ↔ 3ft (1m), perennial, light shade, autumn leaves red and gold, flowers early summer, can be invasive

EXACUM AFFINE
Persian violet

FRAGRANT, SUMMER FLOWERS in shades of lavender blue or, less frequently, rose pink or white are borne by this annual, or short-lived perennial. The blooms are set off against glossy leaves in a small, bushy, evergreen plant that achieves a maximum height and spread of 12in (30cm). Persian violets, often grown as house or conservatory plants, are best grown outdoors in containers for a summer display and overwintered in a greenhouse. In milder areas, they can also be grown as summer bedding or to fill in mixed beds and borders. Try them with plants such as asters (*see pp.192–193*), begonias (*see pp.196–197*), and petunias (*see p.306*).

Cultivation Position Persian violets in full sun, in moderately fertile, well-drained soil. For plants in containers, mix sharp sand with a soil-based potting mix to improve the drainage. **Water** well and feed with a balanced fertilizer at weekly intervals in summer. **Sow** seed (*see pp.391–393*) at 64°F (18°C) in early spring.

Euphorbia dulcis 'Chameleon'
Z7 ‡↔ 12in (30cm), spreading perennial, tolerates dry shade, dark green or bronze leaves in autumn, flowers in summer

Euphorbia palustris (Marsh spurge)
Z6 ‡↔ 36in (90cm), vigorous perennial, prefers moist soil, leaves yellow and orange in autumn, flowers in late spring

Euphorbia myrsinites (Myrtle spurge)
Z4 ‡ 4in (10cm) ↔ 12in (30cm), evergreen succulent, trailing stems, flowers in spring, needs good drainage and sun

Exacum affine (Persian violet)
T min. 45–50°F (7–10°C) ‡↔ 9–12in (23–30cm)

FELICIA
Blue daisy

MASSES OF DAISIES OF PURE BLUE, or occasionally white, mauve, or lilac, smother felicias throughout summer, making the annuals a popular choice for bedding and containers, including hanging baskets. Low-growing perennials are suitable for rock gardens or at the base of a warm, sunny wall. The plentiful, tiny leaves are gray- or mid-green in summer; those of *Felicia amoena* 'Variegata' (T min. 37–41°F/3–5°C) have bright creamy white edges.

Cultivation Grow felicias in poor to moderately fertile, well-drained soil, in full sun. They do not thrive in damp conditions. For plants in containers, use a soil-based potting mix; then water them well in summer; and feed at weekly intervals with a balanced fertilizer. **Pinch back** young shoots regularly to encourage a bushy habit. **Sow** seed (*see p.391–393*) at 50–64°F (10–18°C) in spring. Take softwood cuttings (*see p.394*) in late summer and overwinter the young plants in frost-free conditions under cover.

FILIPENDULA

FROM A DISTANCE, THE FLOWERS of filipendulas look like a cloud of foam floating above a sea of bright green leaves. At closer quarters, their unusual, musky fragrance can be detected. These perennials bear large heads of fluffy white, cream, pink, or red flowers on branching stems in late spring and summer. They thrive in damp soil, so are most at home in soil that stays moist through summer. Try them with other moisture-loving perennials such as eupatoriums (*see p.242*) or hostas (*see pp.250–251*). *Filipendula vulgaris* (Z4) tolerates drier conditions, and prefers alkaline soils in full sun; it has dark green, ferny leaves, which look good with lupines (*see p.280*) and poppies (*Papaver, see p.299*).

Cultivation Grow filipendulas in moderately fertile, moist but well-drained soil, in sun or partial shade. Planting gold-leaved cultivars in shade results in a stronger color. **Sow** seed (*see pp.391–393*) in autumn in pots and place them in a cold frame, or sow in spring at 50–55°F (10–13°C). **Divide** plants (*see p.395*) in autumn or spring. Take root cuttings (*see p.394*) from late winter until early spring.

Filipendula rubra 'Venusta'
Z3 ‡ 6–8ft (2–2.5m) ↔ 4ft (1.2m), spreading to large clumps, flowers in early and midsummer, becoming paler as they age

Felicia amelloides 'Santa Anita'
T min. 37–41°F (3–5°C) ‡↔ 12–24in (30–60cm), subshrub, often grown as annual, 2in (5cm) flowers from summer to autumn

Filipendula palmata
Z3 ‡ 4ft (1.2m) ↔ 24in (60cm), clump-forming, variable leaves to 12in (30cm) long with densely woolly, white undersides, pale to deep pink flowers 8in (20cm) across borne in midsummer

FOENICULUM VULGARE
Fennel

THE LARGE, BILLOWING CLUMPS of green or purple filigree foliage make fennel a star in bed and borders, where the finely cut leaves contrast well with broad-leaved plants or large flowers. Try purple fennel with the huge, dusky pink blooms of the oriental poppy, 'Patty's Plum'. Fennel is perhaps best known as an aromatic herb with a strong anise flavor, and all parts have the strong aroma of anise. This perennial reaches a height of 6ft (2m) and spread of 18in (45cm) from large, deep, edible roots. During mid- and late summer, flat clusters of tiny, yellow flowers appear, followed by large, aromatic seeds. Herb fennel and ornamental fennels both work well in borders or in a herb garden.

Cultivation Fennels prefer fertile, moist but well-drained soil, in full sun. **Deadhead** flower heads before the seeds form to prevent prolific self-seeding. **Sow** seed (*see pp.391–393*) in spring at 55–64°F (13–18°C) or outdoors where the plants are to grow.

FENNEL SEEDHEADS Seed can be collected from fennel, although the plant is promiscuous and may interbreed with any closely related species, such as dill, grown nearby, so the seedlings may yield herbs with an indeterminate flavor.

Foeniculum vulgare 'Purpureum'
Z6 ‡ 6ft (2m) ↔ 18in (45cm), bronze-purple foliage when young, turning glaucous green with age

FRAGARIA
Strawberry

IN THE RUSH FOR THE DELICIOUS, early-summer fruits, the ornamental cultivars of the perennial strawberry plants should not be overlooked. These bear clusters of up to ten pink or white flowers from late spring until midautumn. *Fragaria vesca* 'Variegata' (Z5) has attractively variegated, cream and gray-green leaves. Strawberries increase by means of stems that creep along the ground, producing young plantlets at their tips. They spread rapidly, but they are not invasive, which makes them very useful as a weed-suppressing groundcover. Strawberries are vigorous plants: some cultivars can be used for groundcovers or to edge beds and borders, in cracks and crevices of paving, containers, or hanging baskets.

Cultivation Fertile, moist but well-drained soil, in full sun or partial shade is required. Strawberries prefer neutral to alkaline soils, but will tolerate acidic soil. **Sow** seed (*see pp.391–393*) in spring at 55–64°F (13–18°C). **Remove** and transplant rooted runners in late summer.

Fragaria 'Pink Panda'
Z5 ‡ 4–6in (10–15cm) ↔ indefinite, flowers to 1in (2.5cm) across, borne from late spring to midautumn, rarely bears fruit

FRANCOA
Bridal wreath

WIDELY GROWN AS A FLOWER FOR CUTTING, bridal wreath has graceful, dainty flower spikes of pink or white that give an airy feeling to a border. The main flowering period of these few evergreen perennials is summer, but often the plants produce a second flush of flowers in autumn. They are 24–36in (60–90cm) tall, and have attractive rosettes of softly hairy leaves with wavy edges that spread to about 18in (45cm). Bridal wreath happily seed themselves about without becoming invasive. Place them in mixed borders with plants such as persicarias (*see p.305*), phloxes (*see p.306*), and daylilies (*Hemerocallis, see p.258*), or use them in containers or as edging plants.

Cultivation Undemanding, these plants like moist but well-drained soil that has been enriched with well-rotted compost, in full sun or partial shade. **Water** freely in summer and apply a balanced feed every four weeks. **Divide** plants (*see p.395*) in spring. **Sow** seed (*see pp.391–393*) at 59–75°F (15–24°C) in spring.

Francoa sonchifolia
Z7b ‡ 24–36in (60–90cm) ↔ 18in (45cm)

FRITILLARIA
Fritillary

ELEGANT, NODDING BELLS are the common feature of this diverse group of perennial bulbs. The flowers come in muted shades such as soft green, tawny reds, and purples, often with strikingly patterned petals, and are borne in spring and early summer, singly or in clusters. Fritillaries vary from diminutive, delicate types only 3in (8cm) tall to more robust species with sturdy stems up to 5ft (1.5m). Crown imperials thrive in mixed borders. The more demure snake's head fritillary (*F. meleagris*) can be naturalized in moist meadows or in the dappled shade under trees and shrubs. Alpine species can be tricky to grow and need sharp drainage and usually alpine-house conditions.

Cultivation Plant the bulbs at four times their depth. Fritillarias differ in their needs, but most garden plants need fertile, well-drained, moisture-retentive soil in full sun, or moist, humus-rich soil in light shade. **Divide** large clumps (*see p.395*) in late summer. Smaller species such as *F. acmopetala* produce numerous but tiny bulblets (called "rice"); treat them like seeds and grow on in a seed tray (*see pp.391–393*).

Fritillaria imperialis (Crown imperial)
Z5 ↕ 5ft (1.5m) ↔ 10–12in (25–30cm), orange, red, or yellow flowers in early summer, needs fertile soil in full sun

GAILLARDIA
Blanket flower

THESE PLANTS HAVE CHEERFUL, LARGE DAISIES that appear all throughout summer and well into autumn. The flowers, which are up to 5½in (14cm) across, are yellow, crimson, or orange with contrasting bosses in purple, brown, red, or yellow. These are held on long stems up to 36in (90cm) tall above bushy plants with soft, hairy, long leaves. Cultivars of the short-lived perennial *Gaillardia × grandiflora* are most commonly grown of the group, which also includes annuals and biennials. They brighten up containers or mixed or annual borders; try them with pinks (*Dianthus, see p.226–227*), pot marigolds (*Calendula, see p.204*), and rudbeckias (*see p.317*). Gaillardias are also good for cutting.

Cultivation Gaillardias prefer fertile, well-drained soil in full sun; they will also tolerate poor soils. **Deadhead** regularly to encourage more flowers. **Cut back** perennials to around 6in (15cm) in late summer to encourage fresh growth at the base. **Sow** seed (*see pp.391–393*) at 55–64°F (13–18°C) in early spring. Seed of annuals can also be sown in situ in late spring or early summer. **Divide** perennials (*see p.395*) in spring or take root cuttings (*see p.394*) in winter.

Fritillaria meleagris (Snake's head fritillary)
Z4 ↕ 12in (30cm) ↔ 2–3in (5–8cm), purple or white flowers in spring, needs moist, enriched soil in sun or light shade

Fritillaria acmopetala
Z5 ↕ 16in (40cm) ↔ 2–3in (5–8cm), robust, flowers in late spring, needs fertile, well-drained soil in full sun

Gaillardia 'Dazzler'
Z3 ↕ 24–34in (60–85cm) ↔ 18in (45cm), short-lived perennial, mid-t... gray-green leaves, flowers from early summer to early autumn

GALANTHUS
Snowdrop

SNOWDROPS NEED LITTLE INTRODUCTION: this hugely popular flower is a welcome sight in late winter and early spring, appearing when little else is in flower. There are hundreds of different kinds with subtly different petal shapes and green markings; snowdrop fanciers, called galanthophiles, will travel miles to see new forms. Each snowdrop bulb usually produces a single, white, pendent flower on an arching flower stalk. Some have scented flowers. Most snowdrops are vigorous and easily grown, often forming large clumps, and spread by self-seeding. They look particularly good if naturalized in grass. *Galanthus reginae-olgae* (Z7b) flowers in autumn. All parts of the plant are mildly toxic; contact with the bulbs may irritate the skin.

Cultivation Soil enriched with well-rotted compost that does not dry out in summer, in sun or partial shade, suits snowdrops. **Divide** clumps of bulbs every 3–4 years to stop the plants becoming congested and losing vigor; this is done in spring after flowering while the bulbs are "in the green" (*see below*). Snowdrops cross-pollinate freely so may not come true to type from seed.

Galanthus 'Atkinsii'
Z4 ‡8in (20cm) ↔ 3in (8cm), flowers 1¼in (3cm) long appear in late winter

GALAX URCEOLATA
Wandflower

THIS EVERGREEN PERENNIAL IS GROWN for its elegant wands of small white flowers produced in late spring and summer, followed by rich, red-bronze foliage in autumn. The flower spikes are up to 10in (25cm) tall and the leaves up to 3in (8cm) across. It spreads by creeping roots and makes a useful groundcover under shrubs in a shady bed or border or in a woodland garden. It is also happy in a large rock garden. Try it with other shade-loving, early summer-flowering perennials, such as geraniums (*see pp.250–251*), lupines (*see p.280*), and poppies (*Papaver, see p.299*).

Cultivation This plants thrives in moist, acidic soil in partial shade; make sure that the roots will not dry out. **Mulch** annually in spring with pine needles or leaf mold. **Sow** seed (*see pp.391–393*) in containers of acidic (ericaceous) potting mix in an open frame outdoors in autumn. **Separate** rooted runners in early spring: carefully dig up the rooted stem; trim back the stub; and transplant the divided pieces where required.

DIVIDING SNOWDROPS
Snowdrops should be divided "in the green" while they still have leaves and shortly after the flowers have faded. Carefully dig up the clumps with a fork, pull apart the bulbs, and replant individually or in small groups where required.

Galanthus 'S. Arnott'
Z4 ‡8in (20cm) ↔ 3in (8cm), strongly honey-scented flowers, 1–1½in (2.5–3.5cm) long, in late winter and early spring

Galanthus nivalis 'Flore Pleno'
Z3 ‡4in (10cm), robust, double-flowered, spreads rapidly from offsets, honey-scented, irregular flowers in winter

Galax urceolata
Z6 ‡12in (30cm) ↔ 3ft (1m)

GALEGA

Goat's rue, French lilac

‡1–5ft (30cm–1.5m)
↔ 2–3ft (60–90cm)

THE TALL, FLOPPY stems of these bushy, spreading perennials are very graceful, but tend to fall over other plants unless staked. The many clusters of pealike flowers come in shades or bicolors of white, blue, and mauve. Viewed from a distance, the mass of small flowers creates a vivid wash of color over the bright green foliage. Flowering usually in summer, but also in spring or autumn, galegas are best in borders with summer-flowering plants like lychnis (*see p.282*), lythrums (*see p.283*), monardas (*see p.287*), and sunflowers (*see p.256*). They also naturalize well and are good for cutting. *Galega officinalis* (Z6) is most often seen in gardens.

Cultivation Galegas thrive in any moist soil in full sun or partial shade. **Deadhead** to prevent self-seeding; cut back to ground level after flowering. **Sow** seed, soaked overnight, of species (*see pp.391–393*) in containers in a cold frame in spring. **Divide** cultivars (*see p.395*) between late autumn and spring.

Galega 'His Majesty'
Z6 ‡ to 5ft (1.5m) ↔ 3ft (1m), flowers from early summer to early autumn; 'Lady Wilson' has similar flowers, 'Alba' is a white form

GALTONIA

‡ to 4ft (1.2m)
↔ 4in (10cm)

LIKE A LATE-SUMMER HYACINTH, *Galtonia candicans* has tall, elegant spikes of pure white, slightly fragrant flowers. The only commonly grown species, it is particularly useful in the garden, and deserves wider recognition, because few bulbs of this beauty flower at this time of year. The gray-green, strappy leaves are quite fleshy. This trouble-free, bulbous perennial mixes well with grasses and other perennials like dicentras (*see p.229*), lythrums (*see p.283*), monardas (*see p.287*), poppies (*Papaver, see p.299*), rudbeckias (*see p.317*), and sedums (*see p.324*). *G. viridiflora* (Z7b) has pale green, trumpet-shaped, nodding flowers.

Cultivation Fertile, well-drained soil that is reliably moist in summer, in full sun, suits galtonias. **Lift** the bulbs in late autumn in areas with severe winters, and overwinter in pots in a frost-free greenhouse or conservatory. Alternatively, leave the bulbs in the soil and cover with a deep winter mulch (*see p.388*). **Sow** seed in a container (*see pp.391–393*) in a cold frame as soon as it is ripe. **Divide** large clumps (*see p.395*) and replant in early spring.

Galtonia candicans
Z6 ‡ 3–4ft (1–1.2m) ↔ 4in (10cm), tubular flowers open from the base of the flower spike in late midsummer

GAURA LINDHEIMERI

THE SUMMER AND AUTUMN FLOWERS of this gracious perennial would soften any border with their light, airy growth. Each bloom nestles inside the leaves and is short-lived but soon replaced by another, keeping up a continuous display for several weeks. This trouble-free plant forms a bushy clump. *Gaura lindheimeri* has several pretty cultivars – 'Corrie's Gold' has gold-edged leaves and 'Siskiyou Pink' has pinkish flowers. 'Whirling Butterflies' is named after the shape of its reddish flowers; it forms a smaller clump, and is very free-flowering. Gauras contrast well with late-flowering perennials that have large, fleshy blooms, like chrysanthemums (*see pp.212–213*), rudbeckias (*see p.317*), and sedums (*see p.324*).

Cultivation Any fertile, moist but well-drained soil, in full sun will do; drought and partial shade are tolerated. **Sow** seed (*see pp.391–393*) in containers in a cold frame from spring until early summer. **Divide** clumps (*see p.395*) in spring to increase stock. Take softwood cuttings in spring or heel cuttings in summer (*see p.394*).

Gaura lindheimeri
Z6 ‡ to 5ft (1.5m) ↔ 36in (90cm), pinkish buds open at dawn to white flowers fading to pink, late spring to early autumn

GAZANIA

THE BRIGHT AND CHEERY, sunflower-like blooms of
these small annuals or evergreen perennials are most
often seen in summer bedding displays, windowboxes,
and patio containers in climates with frosty winters.
Hybrids are usually grown and are treated as annuals
with other bedding plants like marigolds (*see p.204
and p.329*) and geraniums (*see pp.300–303*). The
summer flowers come in a wide range of bold colors,
often with darker centers and markings on the petals.
They need a sunny site because they close up on dull
days. The dark green, hairy foliage is a good contrast
to the flowers. Gazanias grow well in coastal areas.

Cultivation Grow gazanias in light, sandy, well-drained soil, in full
sun. **Remove** dead blooms to prolong flowering. **Sow** seed at 64–68°F
(18–20°C) in late winter or early spring (*see pp.391–393*). **Take** new
shoots from the base and treat as softwood cuttings (*see p.394*) in late
summer or early autumn. Overwinter the new plants in frost-free
conditions; these may suffer from gray mold (botrytis) if poorly
ventilated, and aphids may be a problem – remove any plants that
are severely infested.

Gazania 'Talent Yellow'
Z8 ‡↔ to 10in (25cm), vigorous evergreen perennial, gray felty
leaves, flowers in summer

Gazania Mini Star Series
Z8 ‡ to 8in (20cm) ↔ to 10in (25cm), compact, tuft-forming, evergreen perennial, white silky hairs
beneath leaves, summer flowers may be bright yellow, orange, copper, bronze, white, pink, and beige

GENTIANA
Gentian

IT IS THE INTENSE BLUE, trumpet- or bell-shaped
flowers that draw gardeners to gentians, but there are
also white-, yellow- and occasionally red-flowered
forms. Flowering times vary, from late spring (*G.
acaulis*), summer (*G. saxosa*), late summer (*G.
septemfida*), to autumn (*G. sino-ornata*). Gentians are
a large and varied group, but perennials are usually
grown; they may be deciduous, evergreen, or
semievergreen, and range from low mats and trailing
types to clumping or upright forms. Many are alpines,
needing rock-garden conditions; a few suit herbaceous
borders, such as the relatively tall, shade-loving
G. asclepiadea (z7) with late-summer flowers.
Autumn-flowering gentians have rosettes of leaves.
Hardiness zone ranges from 3–5, except where noted.

Cultivation Most need light but rich, well-drained but moist soil, in
full sun only where summers are cool. Provide partial shade in warmer
areas. Autumn-flowering gentians need neutral to acidic soil. **Sow** seed
(*see pp.391–393*) of species as soon as it is ripe in a cold frame.
Divide rooted offshoots (*see p.395*) carefully in spring.

① *acaulis* ‡3in (8cm) ↔ 12in (30cm) ② *saxosa* ‡3in (8cm)
↔ 4in (10cm) ③ *septemfida* ‡6–8in (15–20cm) ↔ 12in (30cm)
④ *sino-ornata* Z6 ‡ to 3in (8cm) ↔ 6–12in (15–30cm)

GERANIUM
Cranesbill

EASY-TO-GROW, VERSATILE, AND LONG-FLOWERING, few plants are as useful in the garden as hardy geraniums. The genus contains about 300 annuals, biennials, and herbaceous perennials, some of them semievergreen or evergreen. The flowers are delicate and abundant, with colors ranging from white, shades of pink and purple, to blue, often with contrasting veins. Leaves are usually rounded or palmlike (palmate) and are frequently aromatic. Some types have colorful autumn foliage. They are often confused with the genus *Pelargonium* (*see pp.300–301*), which is commonly called geranium. Cranesbills are found in many habitats, except in very wet areas, and can be grown almost anywhere in the garden, and in pots. There are compact varieties to 6in (15cm) tall, suitable for a rock garden, and plants of 4ft (1.4m) or more for mixed and herbaceous borders. Mat-forming species like *Geranium macrorrhizum* are useful as groundcover, including on slopes, where the dense root system helps to prevent soil erosion. All hardy geraniums shown here run a range of Canadian hardiness zones from 4–6b, except where noted.

Cultivation Grow the larger species and hybrids in fertile soil in full sun or partial shade. Small species need a well-drained site in full sun. Avoid soils that are excessively wet in winter. **Water** plants well during dry spells and apply a liquid fertilizer monthly. **Trim off** the faded blooms and foliage after the first flush of flowers in early or midsummer to encourage fresh leaves and another show of flowers. **Sow** seed (*see pp.391–393*) of hardy species outdoors in containers as soon as it is ripe or in spring. Seed of half-hardy species is sown at 55–64°F (13–18°C) in spring. **Divide** overgrown clumps in spring (*see p.395*). **Take** basal cuttings (the base of the stem and a small piece of the crown) in spring. Treat them in the same way as soft-tip cuttings (*see p.394*).

Using geraniums in the garden

Woodland planting *Loose, spreading shapes and plentiful flowers, even in dappled shade, make cranesbills an appropriate choice for the woodland garden. Here, the airy foliage and dainty pink flowers of* G. endressii *make an effective contrast to the solid forms of the tree trunks. This species, together with* G. himalayense *and* G. macrorrhizum *and their cultivars, and* G. nodosum, *all make good cover in any shady site.*

Groundcover Geranium × magnificum *is used here as ground-cover under climbing roses. Roses and geraniums are a classic garden combination. A geranium's vigorous, spreading habit camouflages bare soil and hides dull rose stems – and its small, saucer-shaped flowers are good foils to the showier rose blooms. Their characteristic blue, mauve, and pink hues harmonize with many rose colors. Here, a profusion of rich violet blooms makes an eye-catching contrast to the bright scarlet roses.*

① *Geranium* '**Ann Folkard**' ‡24in (60cm) ↔ 3ft (1m) ② *asphodeloides* ‡12–18in (30–45cm), ↔ 12in (30cm), evergreen ③ × *cantabrigiense* ‡12in (30cm) ↔ 24in (60cm), evergreen, aromatic ④ × *cantabrigiense* '**Biokovo**' ‡12in (30cm) ↔ 30–36in (75–90cm), evergreen ⑤ *cinereum* '**Ballerina**' ‡6in (15cm) ↔ 12in (30cm), evergreen, needs good drainage ⑥ *cinereum* var. *subcaulescens* ‡6in (15cm) ↔ 12in (30cm), evergreen, needs good drainage ⑦ *clarkei* '**Kashmir White**' ‡18in (45cm)

↔ indefinite ⑧ *dalmaticum* ‡6in (15cm) ↔ 20in (50cm), evergreen ⑨ *endressii* ‡18in (45cm) ↔ 24in (60cm), evergreen ⑩ *erianthum* ‡18–24in (45–60cm) ↔ 12in (30cm), good autumn leaf color ⑪ *himalayense* ‡12–18in (30–45cm) ↔ 24in (60cm) ⑫ *himalayense* 'Gravetye' ‡12in (30cm) ↔ 24in (60cm) ⑬ *ibericum* ‡20in (50cm) ↔ 24in (60cm) ⑭ *macrorrhizum* ‡20in (50cm) ↔ 24in (60cm), aromatic ⑮ *macrorrhizum* 'Ingwersen's Variety' ‡20in (50cm) ↔ 24in (60cm), semievergreen

⑯ *maculatum* ‡24–30in (60–75cm) ↔ 18in (45cm) ⑰ *maderense* ‡↔ 4–5ft (1.2–1.5m), T min. 41°F (5°C) evergreen ⑱ × *magnificum* ‡↔ 24in (60cm) ⑲ *nodosum* ‡12–20in (30–50cm), ↔ 20in (50cm) ⑳ *orientalitibeticum* ‡12in (30cm) ↔ 3ft (1m) ㉑ × *oxonianum* ‡32in (80cm) ↔ 24in (60cm), evergreen ㉒ × *oxonianum* 'Southcombe Star' ‡32in (80cm) ↔ 24in (60cm), evergreen ㉓ × *oxonianum* 'Winscombe' ‡↔ 18in (45cm), evergreen

GEUM
Avens

LOOKING RATHER LIKE BUTTERCUPS or small roses, the bold flowers of geums come in attractive shades of red, orange, and yellow. They appear from late spring into summer and are held above clumps of deep green, divided, wrinkled leaves. The smaller geums are suitable for growing in a rock garden, while the larger ones are almost tailor-made for the front of a sunny border. Combine them with other herbaceous perennials such as the closely related potentillas (*see p.311*), which have a similar style of flower, and cranesbills (hardy geraniums *see pp.250–251*).

Cultivation Grow most geums in fertile, well-drained soil in full sun. *Geum rivale* and its cultivars need more moisture and plenty of organic matter, but avoid soil that becomes waterlogged in winter. **Sow** seed in containers in a cold frame in spring or autumn (*see pp.391–393*). 'Lady Stratheden' and 'Mrs J. Bradshaw' generally come true from seed, but the majority of the larger geums cross-pollinate freely and produce unpredictable offspring. **Divide** other named varieties (*see p.395*) to be sure that new plants are true to type.

Geum montanum
Z3 ‡ 6in (15cm) ↔ to 12in (30cm), smaller geum ideally suited to a rock garden; it flowers in spring and early summer

***Geum* 'Lady Stratheden'**
Z5 ‡ 16–24in (40–60cm) ↔ 24in (60cm), good for a sunny border, where its large flowers will be produced all summer

***Geum* 'Red Wings'**
Z5 ‡ to 24in (60cm) ↔ to 16in (40cm), the semidouble, bright red or scarlet flowers appear very freely throughout summer

GLADIOLUS

WITH THEIR TALL, STRONGLY UPRIGHT spikes of summer flowers, gladioli can look especially striking in cut-flower displays as well as in the garden. The funnel-shaped flowers open from the bottom of the stem upward and come in shades of white, red, pink, yellow, orange, and some bicolors, sometimes with dainty splotches on the lower petals. Gladioli grow from corms, with long, swordlike leaves arranged in fans. Many need a warm, sheltered wall or border to thrive. They are sometimes grown in rows in the vegetable garden specifically for cutting. Most gladioli are hardy wherever the soil does not freeze deeply in winter. Where not hardy, dig up in autumn and replant in spring.

Cultivation Grow in fertile, well-drained soil in full sun. **Plant** corms 4–6in (10–15cm) deep in spring. In heavy soil, fork coarse grit into the planting area. Large-flowered kinds need staking. Where not hardy, **lift** corms in autumn, dry them for a few weeks, then remove all leafy remains. **Separate** the corms, discarding the old, dried-up, dark brown ones, and store over winter in a cool, frost-free place. Check occasionally and remove any that show signs of mold.

***Gladiolus* 'Elvira'**
‡ 32in (80cm) ↔ 3–4in (8–10cm), each corm produces two or three slender flower spikes in early summer, ideal for cutting

Gladiolus tristis
↕ 1½–5ft (45–150cm) ↔ 2in (5cm), pale yellow or creamy white flowers in spring, strong evening scent

Gladiolus communis subsp. *byzantinus*
Z4b ↕ to 3ft (1m) ↔ 3in (8cm), vigorous, spreading, flowers in early summer, mulch over winter in cold areas

SUPPORTING GLADIOLI
Tall varieties must be tied to stakes from midsummer. Use soft twine every 8in (20cm), taking care not to damage or restrict emerging flowers.

Gladiolus 'Anna Leorah'
↕ 5½ft (1.6m) ↔ 6in (15cm), each towering flower spike is densely packed with pink-edged blooms from early to late summer

GLECHOMA
Ground ivy

THE CREEPING NATURE of these perennials makes them useful groundcover plants, especially in partially shaded areas. The small, toothed leaves appear on long, slender stems, which readily root into the soil. Some forms can be invasive and need to be checked from time to time. The small, violet blue flowers are borne from spring through summer. Good companions include bugles (*Ajuga*, see p.172), corydalis (*see p.217*), lamiums (*see p.269*), violets (*see p.338*), and snowdrops (*Galanthus, see p.247*). The white-marbled leaves of *Glechoma hederacea* 'Variegata', the most commonly grown type, make a good foil for summer bedding plants such as pelargoniums (*see pp.300–303*) and fuchsias (*see pp.60–63*) in container displays, and mixes well with silver-leaved helichrysums.

Cultivation Grow in reasonably fertile, well-drained soil in full sun or partial shade. **Divide** plants in spring or autumn (*see p.395*), or take softwood cuttings in late spring (*see p.394*).

Glechoma hederacea 'Variegata'
Z4 ↕ to 6in (15cm) ↔ to 6ft (2m) or more, the trailing foliage makes an all-year display in hanging baskets and windowboxes

GUNNERA

THE FOLIAGE OF GUNNERAS is one of gardening's sensations. Although there are diminutive mat-forming gunneras like *Gunnera magellanica* (Z8), which is no more than 6in (15cm) tall, it is the giant rhubarb, *G. manicata* (Z6), for which this group of perennials is famed. This plant reaches a majestic 8ft (2.5m) or more within a season. The undersides of the rhubarb-like leaves and their thick stalks are coarsely spined. The flower spikes are also attractive in some species. Large-leaved specimens make excellent architectural plants for stream- or pondsides, but in large gardens only. They combine well with other moisture-loving plants, such as astilbes (*see p.194*). The small gunneras are best in a rock garden.

Cultivation Grow in deep, permanently moist soil in sun or partial shade in a sheltered position. In cold areas, protect their crowns in winter with a covering of the old leaves. **Increase** large species by taking cuttings of leafy, basal buds, with a section of root attached, in spring. **Divide** small species in spring (*see p.395*). **Sow** seed (*see pp.391–393*) in containers in a cold frame as soon as it is ripe.

Gunnera tinctoria
T min. 41°F (5°C) ‡5ft (1.5m) ↔ 6ft (2m), the enormous leaves and rusty flower heads are smaller than those of the hardier G. manicata

GYPSOPHILA

THE DIFFUSE, STARRY SPRAYS of small, white or pink summer flowers of gypsophilas will be familiar to anyone who buys cut flowers. They make an airy filler for indoor arrangements and in the garden. Small types are ideal for rock gardens or for tumbling over retaining walls; the annual and larger perennial gypsophilas such as *G. paniculata* (Baby's breath) suit borders. The clouds of flowers look good with many herbaceous perennials, for example coreopsis (*see p.217*), cranesbills or hardy geraniums (*see p.250*), and geums (*see p.252*). Popular cultivars include 'Bristol Fairy' and 'Perfecta', with double white flowers, and 'Flamingo', with lilac pink double flowers. All are good for cutting.

Cultivation Grow in deep, light, preferably alkaline soil that is sharply drained and in full sun. **Sow** seed of annuals where they are to flower in spring (*see p.393*), and thin out seedlings to around 6in (15cm) apart. Seed of perennials should be sown at 55–64°F (13–18°C) in spring (*see pp.391–392*). **Take** root cuttings of perennials in winter (*see p.394*) as an alternative way of making new plants.

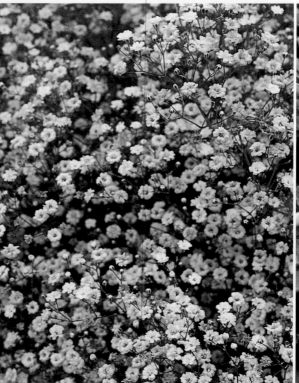

Gypsophila 'Rosenschleier'
Z3 ‡16–20in (40–50cm) ↔ 3ft (1m), also known as 'Rosy Veil' for its billowing clusters of pale pink, semidouble flowers

HABERLEA

SUITED TO A SHADY ROCK GARDEN, these stemless, evergreen perennials can gradually colonize an area with their rosettes of dark green leaves, which are brightened in spring and early summer by loose clusters of nodding, trumpet-shaped flowers. These appear in shades of lavender blue or pale violet blue. Haberleas, which grow only to about 6in (15cm), are ideal for growing in the pockets of a drystone wall, in rock crevices, or in an alpine house (a well-ventilated, cold greenhouse). They combine well with a wide range of other rock plants.

Cultivation Grow in moist, but well-drained, preferably alkaline soil in full or partial shade. In an alpine house, grow them in free-draining, soil-based potting mix. Once planted, they resent root disturbance. **Protect** from excessive winter wet; haberleas prefer to be planted on their sides to prevent water from accumulating in the crowns of the plants. **Sow** seed at 55–64°F (13–18°C) in spring (*see pp.391–392*). **Divide** clumps of rosettes in early summer (*see p.395*). Slugs and snails may attack the foliage (*see p.398*) of plants outside.

Haberlea rhodopensis 'Virginalis'
Z5 ‡6in (15cm) ↔ to 10in (25cm), leaves are softly hairy

HACQUETIA EPIPACTIS

THE BRIGHT, EARLY FLOWERS of this species are composed of a central boss of tiny, yellow true flowers surrounded by bright green bracts (modified leaves). They are borne in dense clusters from late winter to midspring. The plant has glossy, green leaves that only fully develop once the flowers are finished. This is a small clump-forming perennial for a damp, shady site. An ideal position would be a damp rock garden in shade or a woodland border with plants such as snowdrops (*Galanthus, see p.247*), dwarf daffodils (*Narcissus, see pp.288–289*), anemones (*see p.181*), winter aconites (*Caltha, see p.205*), and corydalis (*see p.217*). Other natural companions include hellebores (*see p.257*) and epimediums (*see p.235*).

Cultivation This plant will thrive in any reliably moist but not waterlogged, neutral to acidic soil, that has been enriched with well-rotted compost. **Sow** seed in a container in a cold frame as soon as it is ripe or in autumn (*see pp.391–392*). **Divide** plants in spring (*see p.395*) to increase stock and to maintain vigor, or take root cuttings in winter (*see p.394*).

HELENIUM
Sneezeweed

A TOP CHOICE FOR THE AUTUMN BORDER, heleniums make a superb late-flowering contribution to the garden. Their daisy flowers, in wonderfully hot colors, appear over a long period from summer to autumn. These relatively tall, clump-forming perennials slowly spread over the years to create bold expanses of color in shades of yellow, bronze, orange, and red. The flowers are good for cutting and also attract bees and other beneficial insects into the garden. Grow in a herbaceous border with such late-flowering perennials such as sedums (*see p.324*), rudbeckias (*see p.317*), and asters (*see pp.192–193*). Contact with foliage may aggravate skin allergies.

Cultivation Grow in any fertile, moist but well-drained soil in full sun. **Provide** support for tall varieties. **Divide** clumps every few years in autumn or spring (*see p.395*) to increase stock or maintain vigor. **Sow** seed (*see pp.391–392*) of species in containers in a cold frame in spring. **Propagate** cultivars by taking new shoots from the base of the plant in spring and treating them as softwood cuttings (*see p.394*).

Helenium 'Moerheim Beauty'
Z3b ↕36in (90cm) → 24in (60cm), flowers from early to late summer

Hacquetia epipactis
Z6 ↕2in (5cm) ↔ to 6in (15cm), a fascinating color combination that will help light up damp areas in shade

Helenium 'Crimson Beauty'
Z3b ↕36in (90cm) ↔ 24in (60cm), the shaggy, red flowers take on a brownish tinge with age

Helenium autumnale (Sneezeweed)
Z3b ↕to 5ft (1.5m) ↔ 18in (45cm), flowers from late summer to mid-autumn; use twiggy sticks to support stems

HELIANTHUS
Sunflower

‡ to 15ft (5m)
↔ to 4ft (1.2m)

A FAVORITE FOR CHILDREN'S gardens, these annuals and perennials are grown for their dramatic height and often huge, bright, daisylike flower heads. These appear in summer and autumn in shades of yellow, red, bronze, and mahogany, and are borne singly or in loose clusters. The flowers of some annuals may measure up to 12in (30cm) across. Despite their coarse foliage, they make showy plants for the border; some of the dwarfer annuals also do well in containers. Sunflowers are good for cutting; they attract pollinating insects into the garden, and the seedheads may provide food for birds. Tall types make a good, fast-growing summer screen.

Cultivation Grow in reasonably fertile soil that is well drained, neutral to alkaline and in full sun. Tall types, especially those with large, heavy heads, will need support. **Sow seed** (see pp.391–393) of perennials in containers in a cold frame in spring. Sow annuals at 61°F (16°C) in spring. **Divide** (see p.394) and replant perennials every two to four years in spring or autumn to maintain vigor.

① **'Lemon Queen'** annual, ‡ 5½ft (1.7m) ② **'Monarch'** Z5 ‡ to 6ft (2m) ③ **'Soleil d'Or'** Z5 ‡ to 6ft (2m) ④ **'Velvet Queen'** annual, ‡ 5ft (1.5m)

HELIOPSIS
Ox eye, False sunflower

ORIGINATING IN THE DRY PRAIRIES of North America, these clump-forming perennials are valuable for their long flowering period and for being relatively trouble-free. Their cheerful, golden yellow, daisies, up to 3in (8cm) in diameter, are produced from midsummer through to early autumn. Ox eyes have stiff, branching stems to 3ft (1m) tall, clothed with mid- or dark green foliage. The flowers may be single or double. These are useful plants in a mixed or a herbaceous border; grow them with other colorful perennials such as achilleas (see p.167), rudbeckias (see p.317), hardy geraniums (see pp.250–251), and campanulas (see p.206).

Cultivation Grow in reasonably fertile, well-drained soil enriched with well-rotted compost, in full sun. The taller types may need supporting with twiggy sticks or stakes. **Divide** plants (see p.394) every two to three years to maintain vigor. **Sow seed** (see pp.391–392) in a container in a cold frame in spring. **Take** cuttings of new shoots at the base of the plant in spring and treat as softwood cuttings (see p.394). Young shoots are prone to slug damage (see p.398).

Heliopsis helianthoides **'Sommersonne'**
Z4 ‡ 36in (90cm) ↔ 24in (60cm), deep gold flowers sometimes flushed orange-yellow, good for cut flowers

HELLEBORUS
Hellebore

HELLEBORES ARE STARS OF THE WINTER garden. All species in this group of mainly evergreen perennials are grown for their handsome, glossy foliage that sets off the exquisite flowers in subtle shades of purple, pink, green, white, and cream, many with contrasting spots. The flowers are extremely long-lasting; some face outward, others look gracefully to the ground, and a few are scented. Hellebores are most effective when grown in groups in a mixed or shrub border or in a natural woodland setting. Grow them with winter-flowering shrubs like witch hazels (*Hamamelis*, see p.68), Christmas box (*Sarcococca*, see p.116), and viburnums (see pp.126–127).

Cultivation Hellebores tolerate a fairly wide range of soil types and conditions. Most prefer neutral to alkaline soil in sun or shade. Avoid dry or waterlogged soils. **Dig in** plenty of well-rotted compost before planting, and mulch with a layer of organic matter in autumn. **Sow seed** (see p.391–392) in containers in a cold frame as soon as it is ripe; named forms will not come true. Hellebores self-seed freely. **Divide** (see p.394) in early spring or late summer.

SEEDLINGS
Lift and transplant self-sown seedlings found at the base of a plant in spring, when each has at least one true leaf.

Helleborus foetidus (Stinking hellebore)
Z6 ‡ to 32in (80cm) ↔ 18in (45cm), deeply cut foliage, unpleasant smell, flowers from midwinter to midspring

Helleborus × *hybridus* (Lenten rose)
Z6 ↕↔ to 18in (45cm), flowers, in white, purple, yellow, green, or pink, from midwinter to midspring, remove old, tattered leaves before the flowerbuds open

Helleborus argutifolius (Corsican hellebore)
Z6 ↕ to 4ft (1.2m) ↔ 3ft (90cm), overwintering leaves, shallow pale green flowers in late winter and early spring

Helleborus × *hybridus* Slaty blue
Z6 ↕↔ 18in (45cm), usually grown from seed, flowers from midwinter to midspring

Helleborus niger 'Potter's Wheel' (Christmas rose)
Z4 ↕ to 12in (30cm) ↔ 18in (45cm), overwintering leaves, particularly large flowers from early winter to early spring

Helleborus × *hybridus* Ashwood Garden hybrids
Z6 ↕↔ 18in (45cm), variously spotted and speckled, some double flowers in midwinter to midspring

HEMEROCALLIS
Daylily

‡ 10in–4ft (25cm–1.2m)
↔ 12in–4ft (30cm–1.2m)

THE EXOTIC BLOOMS of daylilies last for only one day – hence the name – but more buds open to take their place. Thousands of cultivars are available, with blooms in dazzling hues from white, gold, and apricot to orange, red, and blue; they vary in shape from spidery or flat to very full doubles. Deciduous, evergreen, or semievergreen, these easy-to-grow, clump-forming perennials flower from spring to late summer, adding height and long-lasting color to a border. Many flower repeatedly through the season (remontant). They are especially successful in drifts in a wild garden. Dwarf daylilies are good in containers.

Cultivation Daylilies like fertile, moist but well-drained soil; most need full sun for best color but also grow in partial shade. **Divide** plants (see p.395) every 2–3 years to maintain vigor; divide or plant evergreens only in spring. Maggots of hemerocallis gall midges may infest and kill early buds; destroy abnormally swollen buds at once.

HEPATICA

THIS SMALL GROUP OF EARLY-FLOWERING perennials is related to anemones (see p.180). Their solitary, bowl- or star-shaped flowers are unusual in that they open from late winter until early spring, before the leaves have fully developed. The flowers come in shades of white, pale pink to crimson, pale blue to mauve, and purple, and are often mottled or marbled. The leaves are often purple underneath and sometimes marbled in silver or white. They form basal rosettes to 5in (13cm) across and last all summer after the flowers fade. Hepaticas do well in moist soil in partial shade, such as in a woodland planting, a shady corner of a rock garden, or combined with small spring bulbs.

Cultivation Hepaticas grow well in partial shade, in heavy, neutral to alkaline soils, but will also thrive in well-drained soils that have been enriched with well-rotted compost. **Top-dress** with a layer of leafmold or garden compost around the plants in spring or autumn. Hepaticas do not transplant well since they resent root disturbance. **Sow** seed (see pp.391–393) in a cold frame as soon as it is ripe. Divide plants in spring (see p.395); divisions are slow to reestablish.

① 'Gentle Shepherd' ‡ 26in (65cm) ② 'Golden Chimes' both Z3b ‡ 36in (90cm) ③ 'Lemon Bells' ‡ 4ft (1.2m) ④ 'Marion Vaughn' both Z3b ‡ 34in (85cm)

Hepatica nobilis
Z5b ‡ 4in (10cm) ↔ 6in (15cm), slow-growing, domed, semievergreen, white, pink, blue, or purple flowers in early spring

Hepatica nobilis var. *japonica*
Z5b ‡ to 3in (8cm) ↔ 6in (15cm), slow-growing, semievergreen, flowers white, pink, or blue in early spring, suits alpine troughs

HESPERIS MATRONALIS
Dame's violet, Sweet rocket

‡ to 36in (90cm)
↔ 18in (45cm)

THE SWEET-SCENTED FLOWERS of hesperis are borne on tall, swaying stems above rosettes of hairy, dark green leaves. Only the biennial or the short-lived perennial, *Hesperis matronalis*, and its cultivars are usually grown. The blooms are usually lilac or purple, appear in late spring to early summer, and have an intensely spicy fragrance in the evening. Some cultivars have double flowers, and they are all good for cutting. Hesperis is usually grown as a biennial and freely self-seeds. It works well in a cottage garden, herbaceous border, or wild garden, with other early flowerers, such as poppies (*Papaver, see p.299*). Hesperis can be invasive.

Cultivation Grow this plant in fertile, moist but well-drained soil that is neutral to alkaline, in sun or partial shade. **Sow** seed (*see pp.391–393*) in spring or early summer, in spare ground, or where the plants are to grow, and plant out in autumn.

HEUCHERA
Coral flower

RICHLY COLORED FOLIAGE is the chief feature of heucheras. Evergreen and semievergreen, the lobed, rounded, or scalloped leaves are often tinted bronze or purple, are mottled or marbled, and have bold veins. They form neat mounds, above which rise airy spikes of dainty flowers in shades of pink to almost pure white from early to midsummer. They are good for cutting and drying, and attract bees into the garden. Commonly used as groundcover in borders and as edging for pathways, heucheras also look good in borders, and woodland and rock gardens. Contrast the foliage with that of plants like *Stachys byzantina* (*see p.328*) or *Choisya ternata* 'Sundance' (*see p.40*).

Cultivation Heucheras prefer a neutral, fertile soil that is moist but well drained, in sun or partial shade. They tolerate deep shade if the soil is moist. **Sow** seed of species in containers (*see pp.391–393*) in a cold frame in spring. **Divide** all types each autumn (*see below and p.395*) to stop the woody rootstock from pushing up from the soil. Black vine weevil larvae may eat the roots, causing the plant to wilt; destroy affected plants immediately.

Heuchera cylindrica 'Greenfinch'
Z4 ‡ to 36in (90cm) ↔ 24in (60cm), mound-forming, often hairy leaves, flowers from midspring to midsummer

Hesperis matronalis var. *albiflora*
Z4, flowers 1¼–1½in (3–4cm) across, attractive to insects, seedlings are white if no other hesperis are grown nearby

DIVIDE CLUMPS of heucheras each year to prevent them from becoming too woody and sparse at the center.

Heuchera micrantha 'Palace Purple'
Z4 ‡↔ 18–24in (45–60cm), mound- or clump-forming, leaves to 6in (15cm), flowering in early summer, pink seedheads

Heuchera 'Red Spangles'
Z3 ‡ 20in (50cm) ↔ 10in (25cm), clumping, kidney-shaped, dark green leaves marbled pale green, flowers all summer

HOSTA
Plantain lily

HOSTAS ARE AMONG THE MOST IMPRESSIVE OF FOLIAGE PLANTS, their ribbed, sometimes huge, leaves appearing in shades of green, yellow, blue-green, and blue-gray. In many cultivars, they are edged or banded with white or cream. In summer, spires of trumpet-shaped flowers are held well above the foliage. These herbaceous perennials grow naturally along rocky streamsides, and in woodland and alpine meadows. Most form clumps, but a few spread by underground stems. All make excellent groundcover plants because the dense, overlapping leaves block out light from the soil surface, preventing weed seeds from germinating. They are ideal, too, for shady sites, but if planted under trees will need plenty of well-rotted compost added to the soil to retain moisture. Hostas also look effective in pots, where they are easier to protect against slug damage. Their lush, rounded foliage looks especially pleasing by ponds, or when contrasted with tall, spiky plants, such as grasses. The neat, small-leaved cultivars are good for growing in rock gardens. Most hostas are hardy to Zone 4, but some may survive in Zone 3b.

Cultivation Grow hostas in fertile, moist but well-drained soil, sheltering them from cold, drying winds. Never let the soil dry out and water plants thoroughly during dry spells. Most hostas prefer a site in full or partial shade, although yellow-leaved and variegated cultivars have better leaf color in sun. Strong sunshine, however, may cause scorch leaves. **Mulch** (*see p.388*) between plants in spring to help conserve soil moisture. **Propagate** by division in spring (*see p.395*). Hostas are prone to damage from slugs and snails, and protective measures generally need to be taken (*see below*). The roots of container-grown plants may be eaten by black vine weevil larvae (*see p.398*).

Preventing slug and snail damage

The leaves of hostas are stunning, but they also often prove irresistible to slugs and snails, which leave irregular holes and silvery slime trails. It is not uncommon to find some leaves completely shredded after slugs have been feasting at night. There are several ways to control them without resorting to the use of slug pellets, which may harm beneficial wildlife such as birds and raccoons (*see p.397*). Slug traps can be purchased, or you can construct a "slug pub" (*see below*) by sinking a container in the ground and filling it with beer to attract slugs and snails. Coarse grit, gravel, crushed eggshells, or cocoa shells spread around the plants before the leaves emerge in spring may act as a deterrent: they dislike crossing rough surfaces. Renew when necessary. Collect slugs and snails at nightfall with the aid of a flashlight, especially in damp weather.

Band of copper Containers can offer hostas a degree of protection. As a further barrier, stick adhesive copper tape, available at garden centers, around the pot rim. The copper produces a natural electric charge to which mollusks are sensitive and will not cross.

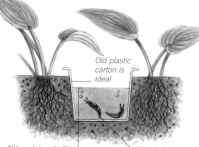

Old plastic carton is ideal

Fill container half to three-quarters full

Dead slugs can be composted

Slug pub A slug pub is an organic way to catch slugs and snails. Attracted by the smell of the beer, they fall into the container and drown. Sink the container in the ground with the rim about 1in (2.5cm) above soil level to prevent beneficial beetles from falling in.

① *Hosta* 'Aureomarginata' ‡20in (50cm) ↔ 3ft (1m), tolerates sun or partial shade ② 'Blue Blush' ‡8in (20cm) ↔ 14–16in (35–40cm), lavender blue flowers ③ 'Emerald Tiara' ‡14in (35cm) ↔ 26in (65cm), violet flowers ④ *fortunei* var. *albopicta* ‡22in (55cm) ↔ 3ft (1m) ⑤ *fortunei* var. *aureomarginata* ‡22in (55cm) ↔ 3ft (1m), tolerates sun or partial shade ⑥ 'Francee' ‡22in (55cm) ↔ 3ft (1m) ⑦ 'Frances Williams' ‡24in (60cm) ↔ 3ft (1m), grayish white flowers ⑧ 'Golden

Prayers' ‡14in (35cm) ↔ 24in (60cm) ⑨ 'Halcyon' ‡4–16in (35–40cm1) ↔ 28in (70cm), lavender-gray flowers ⑩ 'Honeybells' ‡30in (75cm) ↔ 4ft (1.2m), fragrant, white or lavender-blue-striped flowers ⑪ *lancifolia* ‡18in (45cm) ↔ 30in (75cm), purple flowers, red-dotted stems ⑫ 'Love Pat' ‡18in (45cm) ↔ 3ft (1m), off-white flowers ⑬ 'Regal Splendor' ‡30in (75cm) ↔ 3ft (1m) ⑭ 'Royal Standard' ‡24in (60cm) ↔ 4ft (1.2m), fragrant ⑮ 'September Sun' ‡26in (65cm) ↔ 3ft (1m)

⑯ 'Shade Fanfare' ‡18in (45cm) ↔ 24in (60cm) ⑰ *sieboldiana* var. *elegans* ‡3ft (1m) ↔ 4ft (1.2m) ⑱ 'Sum and Substance' ‡30in (75cm) ↔ 4ft (1.2m), pale lilac flowers ⑲ *undulata* ‡3ft (1m) ↔ 18in (45cm), mauve flowers ⑳ *undulata* var. *univittata* ‡18in (45cm) ↔ 28in (70cm) ㉑ *ventricosa* ‡20in (50cm) ↔ 3ft (1m) ㉒ *venusta* ‡2in (5cm) ↔ 10in (25cm) ㉓ 'Wide Brim' ‡18in (45cm) ↔ 3ft (1m)

HYACINTHOIDES
Bluebell

BLUEBELLS ARE FAMILIAR TO US as a shimmering blue carpet of flowers in woods in late spring. They can become invasive, but are easy to control by digging up unwanted bulbs. The small flowers, usually violet blue but occasionally white or pink, are held on sturdy stems above strappy, mid-green foliage. Plant the English bluebell (*Hyacinthoides non-scripta* Z6) in dappled shade *en masse* beneath deciduous trees; the flower color will seem all the more intense. Assure yourself when buying that the bulbs have not been collected from the wild. The larger, more robust Spanish bluebell (*H. hispanica*) tolerates sun and drier conditions. Bluebells may be naturalized in grass or in a wild garden, but in a border *H. hispanica* is may become a nuisance.

Cultivation Plant bu bs 3in (8cm) deep in autumn, in reasonably fertile soil that is well-drained, in partial shade. Remove flowers as they fade to prevent sel²-seeding, except where planted in woodland. **Sow** seed (*see pp.391-393*) in a container in a cold frame as soon as it is ripe or divide clumps in summer (*see p.395*).

① *hispanica* (Spanish bluebell) Z4 ‡16in (40cm) ②
hispanica 'Excelsior' Z4 ‡20–22in (50–55cm)

HYACINTHUS
Hyacinth

POSSIBLY THE MOST SWEETLY SCENTED of all spring-flowering bulbs, hyacinths are grown for their densely packed flower heads in white, pink, red, yellow, and shades of purple. Each sturdy flower stem rises up above the deep green, strappy leaves. All cultivated forms derive from *H. orientalis*, growing 8–12in (20–30cm) tall. Use them in formalized spring bedding displays, with polyanthus (*Primula, see pp.312–313*), winter-flowering pansies (*Viola, see p.338*) and tulips (*see pp.334–335*). Hyacinths can be forced to flower earlier in pots than outdoors.

Cultivation **Plant** bulbs 4in (10cm) deep and 3in (8cm) apart in autumn. Grow in well-drained, reasonably fertile soil in sun or partial shade. Protect container-grown bulbs from excessive winter moisture. **For forcing,** plant specially prepared bulbs in containers in autumn; use bulb fiber in bowls with no drainage holes. Keep in a cool, dark place for 6 weeks and bring into light and warmth when shoots are 1in (2.5cm) tall. After flowering, plant forced bulbs outside in a secluded spot; they go on to produce smaller, less showy flower clusters.

① *orientalis* 'Blue Jacket' flowers in early spring
② *orientalis* 'City of Haarlem' flowers in late spring
All Z4b

IBERIS
Candytuft

CLUSTERS OF SMALL, OFTEN SCENTED FLOWERS almost conceal candytuft's low mounds of spoon-shaped, dark green leaves. This group of spreading perennials and bushy annuals flowers in shades of white, purple, red, or pink from late spring until early summer. Evergreen *Iberis sempervirens* (Z3), 12in (30cm) tall, produces round heads of densely packed, white flowers, while compact *I. umbellata* has flower heads in pinks and purples. Perennial forms are fine for rock gardens and walls, where their growth can spread and tumble, hiding hard edges. Grow the annuals as bedding, at the front of borders or in containers; good companions include other hardy annuals such as clarkias (*see p.214*) and nigellas (*p.291*).

Cultivation **Grow** in poor to reasonably fertile soil that is moist but well-drained, in sun. After flowering, trim perennials back to neaten. **Sow** seed of annuals where they are to grow (*see p.393*), in spring or autumn. Sow seed of perennials in containers in a cold frame in autumn (*see pp.391-392*). **Take** softwood cuttings in late spring, or semi-ripe cuttings in summer (*see p.394*).

Iberis umbellata Fairy Series
‡6–12in (15–30cm) ↔ to 9in (23cm), annual, with a mixture of pink, lilac-purple, and white, scented flowers

IMPATIENS

Impatiens, Balsam, Busy Lizzie

FREE-FLOWERING EVEN IN SHADE, impatiens are among the most useful plants for long-lived summer color. They produce a profusion of flowers, in reds, purples, pinks, and white, and many bicolors, from early summer until well into autumn. Most grown in gardens are either annuals, or tender perennials grown as annuals – used as summer bedding plants and discarded at the end of the season. All have brittle, almost succulent stems with fleshy leaves. The New Guinea hybrids and *Impatiens walleriana* (T min. 50°F/10°C) varieties are invaluable both in borders and containers in shady spots; try some of the more unusual types in a windowbox or in pots on a patio to bring their flowers nearer the eye.

Cultivation Grow in soil enriched with well-rotted organic matter in partial shade, with shelter from cold winds. In pots, use soil-based potting mix and keep well watered; apply a balanced fertilizer every week. **Sow** seed (*see pp.391–393*) at 61–64°F (16–18°C) in early spring **Take** softwood cuttings (*see p.394*) in spring and summer to overwinter. Moulds (*see pp.398–399*) may affect flower buds in damp conditions; pick them off promptly and healthy ones should follow.

INULA

THESE ROBUST, HERBACEOUS PERENNIALS produce a mass of yellow, daisies with prominent, yellow centers and narrow, dainty petals. The flowers are borne either singly or in flat-topped clusters throughout summer. The leaves are large at the base, becoming progressively smaller up the stem. Heights vary from *Inula ensifolia* 'Compacta' (Z4), only 6in (15cm) tall and suitable for a rock garden, to towering species such as *I. magnifica* (Z5), growing to 6ft (2m) tall, which with their rather coarse foliage suits the back of a border or a wild garden. Those of medium height can be grown in an informal border, with other cheerful, summer-flowering perennials. Some species can become invasive, but are quite easy to control by digging out unwanted clumps.

Cultivation Grow all but rock-garden species in deep, fertile soil that is well drained, in full sun or partial shade. **Divide** perennials (*see p.395*) in spring or autumn. **Sow** seed (*see pp.391–393*) in containers in a cold frame in spring or autumn. The taller species may need support. **Powdery mildew** can be a problem in dry conditions.

IPHEION

THE STARRY FLOWERS OF THESE PLANTS sit like jewels among their grassy leaves in spring. This is a small group of bulbous perennials whose blue, violet, or white flowers are often strongly honey-scented. Most other parts of the plant, especially the leaves, smell of onions when crushed. The most commonly grown species, *Ipheion uniflorum*, is small but sturdy and quickly clump-forming. These are beautiful plants for a rock garden; use them in a border to underplant herbaceous perennials such as hostas (*see pp.260–261*) and peonies (*see p.298*). They need winter protection in colder areas if grown in pots and bowls, they can be brought under cover in winter.

Cultivation Grow in reasonably fertile, well-drained soil enriched with well-rotted compost, or in soil-based potting mix, in full sun. Plant the bulbs 3in (8cm) deep, 2in (5cm) apart in autumn. **Provide** a protective mulch (a thick layer of organic matter) where temperatures regularly fall below 14°F (-10°C). **Divide** (*see p.395*) in summer, when the plants are dormant. **Sow** seed (*see pp.391–393*) in containers in a cold frame as soon as it is ripe, or in spring.

① *balsamina* Tom Thumb Series T min. 41°F (5°C) ‡to 12in (30cm), double-flowered annual ② *niamniamensis* 'Congo Cockatoo' T min. 59°F (15°C) ‡36in (90cm), erect habit

Inula hookeri
Z4 ‡24–30in (60–75cm) ↔ 24in (60cm), softly hairy stems and leaves, flowers from late summer to midautumn

Ipheion uniflorum 'Wisley Blue'
Z5 ‡6–8in (15–20cm), leaves produced in late autumn, scented solitary flowers in spring

IRISES PRODUCE THEIR DISTINCTIVE, HANDSOME FLOWERS mainly from midwinter to midsummer on plants that vary greatly in height. Diminutive types such as *Iris danfordiae* and *I. histrioides* unfold their petals even when snow is on the ground. These are bulbous irises (Z5), one of the many types included in this wide-ranging genus. Other irises grow from rhizomes, fleshy stems that creep on or below the soil surface. Those with this kind of rootstock include the widely grown bearded irises (range from Z3–7), with stiff, swordlike leaves shooting from fat surface rhizomes. They are at their peak in early summer. Beardless irises (range from Z3–7) lack the decorative tuft on the lower petals of the bearded types, but their flowers are often beautifully marked. They include early summer-flowering Siberian irises (which grow from below-soil rhizomes), and moisture-loving water, or flag, irises. Those classed as crested irises (generally Z4) also spread by rhizomes and produce showy but relatively flat flowers. There are many more garden-worthy irises besides. All are perennial, and on a few the strappy leaves are evergreen. Taller irises have a stately presence in mixed or herbaceous borders. Smaller varieties tend to be best suited to a rock garden, raised bed, or container. Always check with your garden center for zonal information.

Cultivation Different types of iris require different growing conditions, so check the label carefully when you buy. **Plant** bearded irises in well-drained soil in sun (*see below*). Moisture-loving species need the soil to be damp at all times and suit bog gardens or pond margins. Most types grow well in slightly neutral to slightly acid soil, but a few have special requirements: *I. laevigata* and Pacific Coast irises, for instance, need acid soil, and winter-flowering *I. unguicularis* needs alkaline soil as well as a sheltered site. **Remove** faded flowers and spent flower stems if unsightly, for example on bearded irises, but leave them if you want the decorative seedheads, as with *I. foetidissima*. **Divide** rhizomes from midsummer until early autumn (*see below*). **Sow** seed in containers in spring or autumn (*see pp.391–393*). Bearded irises are susceptible to rot if the soil is not sufficiently well drained.

How to divide iris rhizomes

❶ *Lift the iris (here Iris pseudoacorus) and wash the soil from the roots. Split the clump apart with your hands or an old knife. Make sure there is one good rhizome with roots and leaves for each new clump.*

❷ *Use a sharp knife to trim the rhizome carefully. Discard any pieces that do not have any new shoots. Trim the roots by up to one-third, then cut down the leaves to 6in (15cm) to prevent wind rock. The leaves can act like sails.*

How to plant irises

Water irises *should be replanted in a basket if destined for a pond, or in damp ground. In baskets, use aquatic medium and a top-dressing of gravel to prevent the medium from washing away.*

Bearded irises *need to be planted with the roots in the soil but the rhizomes set on the surface, 5in (13cm) apart. Firm in and water to settle the soil around the roots. Water regularly until established.*

① *Iris* 'Alcazar' ‡24–36in (60–90cm), bearded ② 'Annabel Jane' ‡4ft (1.2m), bearded, late spring ③ *aucheri* 'Austrian Sky' ‡16–18in (40–45cm), bulbous, late winter or spring ④ 'Blue Denim' ‡16–18in (40–45cm), bulbous, late winter or spring ⑤ 'Braithwaite' ‡24–36in (60–90cm), bearded, early summer ⑥ *bulleyana* ‡14–18in (35–45cm), Siberian, early summer ⑦ 'Cantab' ‡4–6in (10–15cm), dwarf bulbous, late winter ⑧ *chrysographes* ‡16–20in (40–50cm), Siberian, early

summer ⑨ *confusa* ‡3ft (1m), crested, midspring ⑩ *danfordiae* ‡3–6in (8–15cm), dwarf bulbous, late winter ⑪ *decora* ‡12in (30cm), beardless, best raised from seed, early summer ⑫ *delavayi* ‡5ft (1.5m), Siberian, summer ⑬ *douglasicna* ‡6–28in (15–70cm), beardless, late spring ⑭ 'Early Light' ‡3ft (1m), bearded, midspring ⑮ *ensata* ‡36in (90cm), bulbous water iris, midsummer ⑯ 'Eyebright' ‡12in (30cm), bearded, early spring ⑰ *foetidissima* ‡12–36in (30–90cm), beardless, seedheads in autumn, purple flowers tinged yellow in early summer ⑱ *forrestii* ‡14–16in (35–40cm), Siberian, early summer ⑲ 'George' ‡5in (13cm), bulbous, early spring ⑳ *graminea* ‡8–16in (20–40cm), beardless, scented, late spring ㉑ 'Harmony' ‡4–6in (10–15cm), bulbous, late winter ㉒ *histrioides* Major' ‡4–6in (10–15cm), dwarf bulbous, early spring ㉓ *innominata* ‡6–10in (15–25cm), beardless, early summer

㉔ 'Jane Phillips' ‡ 24–36in (60–90cm), bearded, early summer ㉕ 'Joyce' ‡ 5in (13cm), dwarf bulbous, early spring ㉖ 'Katherine Hodgkin' ‡ 5in (13cm), dwarf bulbous, late winter ㉗ *kerneriana* ‡ 12–20in (30–50cm), beardless, early summer ㉘ *lacustris* ‡ 2in (5cm), crested, late spring ㉙ *laevigata* ‡ 32in (80cm), beardless water iris, early summer ㉚ *laevigata* 'Variegata' ‡ 32in (80cm), beardless water iris, early summer ㉛ 'Langport Flame' ‡ 12–18in (30–45cm), bearded, midspring ㉜ *magnifica* ‡ 12–24in (30–60cm), bulbous, mid-spring ㉝ *missouriensis* ‡ 8–20in (20–50cm), beardless, early summer ㉞ 'Natascha' ‡ 5in (13cm), bulbous, early spring ㉟ *orientalis* ‡ 36in (90cm), beardless, late spring ㊱ *pallida* 'Variegata' ‡ 4ft (1.2m), bearded, late spring ㊲ 'Red Revival' ‡ 24–36in (60–90cm), bearded, scented, late spring, later flushes ㊳ *prismatica* ‡ 16–32in (40–80cm), beardless, early summer ㊴ *pseudacorus* ‡ 3–5ft (90cm–1.5m),

beardless water iris, midsummer ④⓪ **'Queechee'** ‡24–36in (60–90cm), bearded, early summer
④① *ruthenica* ‡8in (20cm), beardless, scented, late spring ④② **'Sable'** ‡24–36in (60–90cm), bearded,
early summer ④③ *setosa* ‡6–36in (15–90cm), beardless, late spring ④④ *sibirica* **'Anniversary'** ‡30in
(75cm), Siberian, midspring ④⑤ *sibirica* **'Butter and Sugar'** ‡28in (70cm), Siberian, mid-spring
④⑥ *sibirica* **'Ruffled Velvet'** ‡22in (55cm), Siberian, early summer ④⑦ *sibirica* **'Shirley Pope'**

‡34in (85cm), Siberian, early summer ④⑧ *sibirica* **'Wisley White'** ‡3ft (1m), Siberian,
early summer ④⑨ *tectorum* ‡10–16in (25–40cm), crested, early summer ⑤⓪ *tenax* ‡8–14in
(20–35cm), beardless, midspring ⑤① *unguicularis* ‡12in (30cm), beardless, fragrant, late winter
⑤② *unguicularis* **'Mary Barnard'** ‡12in (30cm), beardless, midwinter ⑤③ *variegata* ‡8–20in
(20–45cm), bearded, midsummer

KNAUTIA

‡ 5ft (1.5m)
↔ 18in (45cm)

THESE CHARMING PLANTS are particularly suited to growing in a cottage garden or a wildflower area, where their exuberant habit lends an air of informality to the planting. Garden knautias are perennials, but there are annual species. They have basal rosettes of simple, broad leaves that last through the winter and tall, slender stems. From summer to autumn, these bear numerous, long-lasting, bluish lilac to purple flowers, similar to those of scabious (*see p.322*), that wave gracefully in the breeze and attract bees. If the plants flower profusely for 2–3 years, they may become exhausted and have to be replaced.

Cultivation Grow in any moderately fertile, well-drained soil, preferably alkaline, and in full sun. Knautias can be prone to rot in wet soils during winter. **Dig in** plenty of coarse grit to improve drainage permanently on heavy clay soils. Raising the level of the soil by 2–3in (5–8cm) can also help to improve drainage. **Sow** seed (*see pp.391–393*) in containers or take cuttings (*see p.394*) from the base of the plant in spring.

Knautia macedonica
Z5 ‡ 24–32in (60–30cm) ↔ 18in (45cm), flowers ½–1¼in (1.5–3cm) across in mid- and late summer

KNIPHOFIA
Red-hot poker, Torch flower

THE SPIKY FLOWER HEADS IN BRAZEN HUES and erect habit of these striking perennials reveal how they became known as red-hot pokers. Most form large clumps with arching, strappy, light green or blue-green leaves. During summer, strong stems soar up to 6ft (2m) and bear flower spikes composed of many small, tubular flowers. They may be in shades of scarlet, orange, gold, white, or greenish white – some flower spikes are bicolored red. There are also dwarf kniphofias that are no more than 20in (50cm) tall. Use these plants in borders to provide a vertical contrast to plants with broad foliage such as hostas (*see pp.260–261*).

Cultivation Grow in fertile, well-drained, preferably sandy soil with plenty of well-rotted compost added to it before planting. Kniphofias prefer a sandy soil in full sun or partial shade. **Protect** young plants in the first winter by putting a layer of straw or leaves over deciduous plants, or tying together the stems of evergreens. **Sow** seed (*see pp.391–393*) in containers in a cold frame in spring. **Divide** (*see p.395*) established clumps in late spring.

Kniphofia ‘Green Jade’
Z6 ‡ to 5ft (1.5m) ↔ 24–30in (60–75cm), evergreen, flowers fade to cream then white in late summer and early autumn

Kniphofia ‘Bees’ Sunset’
Z6 ‡ 3ft (90m) ↔ 2ft (60m), deciduous, flowers early to late summer

iphofia 'Ice Queen'
‡o 5ft (1.5m) ↔ 30in (75cm), deciduous, green buds open to pale
ose, then to ivory, in late summer to early autumn

iphofia 'Royal Standard'
‡36–39in (90–100cm) ↔ 2ft (60cm), deciduous, scarlet buds,
vers in mid- and late summer

LAMIUM
Deadnettle

THIS GROUP OF ANNUALS AND PERENNIALS are grown
mainly for their very decorative foliage; they make
good plants among shrubs and larger, vigorous
perennials. The leaves are roughly textured and, in
some plants, are mottled or tinted. Lamiums have the
distinctive square stems of plants belonging to the
nettle family but fortunately no stings. From late
spring until summer, the two-lipped flowers are
borne either singly or in tiers in dense clusters or
spikes. Easily grown, the larger species can be invasive
in very rich soils, less so in poorer soils. Lamiums look
particularly good at the front of a border or in a
woodland setting with light, dappled shade. Lamiums
are hardy to Zones 3–5.

Cultivation Grow vigorous species in moist but well-drained soil
in shade. Dig out the spreading underground stems (rhizomes) if
needed, to keep them away from less robust plants. Less vigorous
lamiums prefer sharply drained soil in full sun or partial shade.
Trim straggly plants with shears in early spring or in summer after
flowering. **Sow** seed (see pp.391–393) in autumn or spring in pots in
a cold frame; take stem-tip cuttings (see p.394) in early summer.

① *galeobdolon* 'Hermann's Pride' ‡2ft (60cm) ↔ indefinite
② *maculatum* ‡8in (20cm) ↔ 3ft (1m) ③ *maculatum* 'Album'
④ *maculatum* 'Beacon Silver' both ‡6in (15cm) ↔ 2ft (60cm)

LATHYRUS VERNUS
Spring vetchling

see also
p.145

‡↔ 18in (45cm)

THIS DENSE, CLUMP-FORMING
herbaceous perennial is related to
the climbing sweet pea (*Lathyrus
odorata*). However, despite the plant's
pealike appearance it does not climb.
In spring, it bears one-sided clusters of 3–6 flowers,
poised above dark to mid-green pointed leaflets. The
plant dies back in summer after flowering. Since the
spring vetchling grows only 8–18in (20–45cm) tall
and spreads to only 18in (45cm), it is suitable for
rock gardens and woodland settings. It can also be
grown in herbaceous and mixed borders, but the
plants should be placed near the back of the border
so that they are hidden when their foliage dies back.
There is also a fine pink- and white-flowered form,
Lathyrus vernus 'Alboroseus'.

Cultivation Spring vetchlings prefer well-drained soil in full sun or
partial shade. They will tolerate poor soil but resent being disturbed or
transplanted. **Sow** seed (see pp.391–393) in pots in spring or directly
into the soil where they are to grow.

Lathyrus vernus
Z4–9, ‡8–18in (20–45cm) ↔ 18in (45cm), flowers are ¾in (2cm)
across

Mallow

see also
p.81

‡most to 4ft (1.2m)
↔ 24in (60cm)

THE ANNUAL MALLOWS have very similar flowers to the shrubby types, and like them grow vigorously and flower very profusely in a single season, but once seed is set, they die. They produce masses of showy, open, funnel-shaped flowers in shades from white to pale pink to reddish or purple pink. The leaves are mid- to dark green with heart-shaped bases. The flowers are also good for cutting. Mallows grow wild in dry, rocky places and in the garden they thrive in sunny herbaceous borders or summer bedding displays. For a traditional cottage-garden look, grow them with other annuals such as calendulas (*see p.204*), clarkias (*see p.214*) and nasturtiums (*Tropaeolum, see p.333*).

Cultivation Grow in ideally light to moderately fertile soil, in full sun. The plants can grow quite tall, and so may need supporting with twiggy sticks in exposed gardens. **Sow** seed in containers under glass in midspring, or slightly later outside where plants are to grow (*see pp.391–393*).

Lavatera trimestris 'Silver Cup'
‡30in (75cm) ↔ 18in (45cm), annual, one of the brightest colored mallows, with large flowers in summer

Lavatera trimestris 'Mont Blanc'
‡20in (50cm) ↔ 18in (45cm), compact annual that does not need staking, very dark green foliage, flowers in summer

Lavatera cachemiriana
Z8 ‡8ft (2.5m) ↔ 4ft (1.2m), short-lived, woody perennial grown as an annual, flowers in summer, good as temporary hedge

Lavatera trimestris 'Pink Beauty'
‡to 24in (60cm) ↔ to 18in (45cm), annual, soft, hairy leaves, flowers measure 3–4in (8–10cm) across, excellent for cutting, easily raised from seed to flower from early summer until early autumn

LEUCANTHEMUM

ROBUST AND CLUMP-FORMING, these perennials and annuals bloom for long periods in summer through to early autumn and the dense flower heads are carried singly at the ends of long stems, well above the foliage. The flowers are excellent for cutting. The dark green leaves are long and toothed. *Leucanthemum vulgare* (Z4) is the common marguerite or ox-eye daisy, a classic plant for meadows and wild gardens, while *L. × superbum* cultivars (Z5) are what used to be called *Chrysanthemum maximum* – also white-flowered but usually with fancy petal details. Grow them in a wild or informal area, or in mixed or herbaceous borders to lighten planting schemes in which richer colors predominate.

Cultivation Grow in reasonably fertile soil that is well-drained, in full sun or partial shade. Taller plants may need support with twiggy sticks. **Divide** perennials in early spring or late summer (*see p.395*). **Sow** seed of annuals where plants are to grow, in spring. Sow seed of perennials in containers in a cold frame in spring or autumn (*see pp.391–393*).

Leucanthemum × superbum 'Phyllis Smith'
Z5 ‡36in (90cm) ↔ 24in (60cm), sturdy perennial with single flowers 4–5in (10–13cm) across, excellent for cutting

LEUCOJUM
Snowflake

SIMILAR TO SNOWDROPS, although some are larger, these bulbous perennials flower at various times of year, giving more scope for pairing them with other plants. The flowers have attractive greenish spots on the tips of the petals. The slender, strappy leaves grow direct from the bulbs. The larger species are good in a border or near water, while the smaller species are ideal for a rock garden or alpine trough. *Leucojum vernum* (Z5) and *L. aestivum* (Z4), both spring-flowering, associate well with other bulbs, such as crocuses (*see p.220*) and narcissus (*see pp.288–289*). *L. autumnale* (Z5b) and *L. roseum* (Z7) both small and flowering in autumn, look good planted with dainty schizostylis (*see p.323*).

Cultivation Plant bulbs 3–4in (8–10cm) deep in autumn, in moist but well-drained soil in full sun. Add plenty of organic matter for *L. aestivum* and *L. vernum*, which need soil that retains moisture reliably. **Sow** seed in a container in a cold frame in autumn (*see pp.391–392*), or remove well-rooted offsets (*see p.395*) once the leaves have died down.

Leucanthemum × superbum 'Wirral Supreme'
Z5 ‡36in (90cm) ↔ 30in (75cm), strong-stemmed perennial with glossy leaves and dense, double flower heads

Leucanthemum × superbum 'Cobham Gold'
Z5 ‡24in (60cm) ↔ 30in (75cm), robust perennial, double flower heads on short stems, dark green leaves

Leucojum aestivum 'Gravetye Giant'
Z4 ‡36in (90cm) ↔ 3in (8cm), the largest of the snowflakes, flowers are faintly chocolate-scented, likes moisture

FLOWERING PLANTS

LEWISIA

THESE POPULAR, HARDY ALPINES are grown for the pretty, often bright colors of their flowers. There are both deciduous and evergreen kinds, forming either rosettes or tufts of fleshy leaves. The deciduous species are more commonly native to high meadows or to grassland and will die down after flowering; the evergreens are found in shady crevices among rocks. Lewisias have many-petaled flowers in shades of pink, peach, magenta, purple, yellow or white – they are often striped. They bloom for many weeks in spring and summer. Grow them in a rock garden or in crevices in a dry-stone wall, with other rock plants and perhaps aubrietas (see p.195).

Cultivation Grow in reasonably fertile, sharply drained, neutral to acidic soil, in full sun or partial shade. Protect all lewisias from winter wet. In containers, grow in equal parts loam, leafmold, and sharp sand. **Sow** seed in containers in a cold frame in autumn (see pp.391–392). Seed of L. cotyledon hybrids produces plants that may look different to their parents. Evergreens may produce plantlets around the main rosette of leaves, which can be removed and potted up in early summer. Prone to attack from slugs and snails (see p.398).

Lewisia brachycalyx
Z6 ↕↔ to 3in (8cm), deciduous perennial, flowers with pale pink on short leafless stems in late spring and early summer

LIATRIS
Blazing star, Gayfeather

THE TALL FLOWER SPIKES OF LIATRIS are unusual in that they open from the top of the spike downward, instead of from the bottom up, giving them a distinctive bottle-brush shape that is emphasized by the threadlike appearance of the tightly packed flowers. These are produced on stiff stems in shades of purple, reddish purple, blue purple, or white, and are highly attractive to bees. Liatris grow wild on prairies and in open woodland. In the garden, they provide late-summer color in a border. The flowers are good for cutting, too. Try growing them with perennials with open-faced flowers, such as erigerons (see p.237), coreopsis (see p.217), and geums (see p.252), to accentuate their striking form.

Cultivation Grow in light, reasonably fertile, moist but well-drained soil in full sun. L. spicata needs soil that is reliably moist. In heavy soils, plant on a layer of coarse gravel to improve drainage, or plants may rot in wet winters. **Divide** in spring (see p.395). **Sow** seed in a container in a cold frame in autumn (see pp.391–392). Prone to attack by slugs and snails (see p.398), and mice.

Lewisia cotyledon **hybrids**
Z3b ↕ 6–12in (15–30cm) ↔ 8–16in (20–40cm), evergreen perennial, yellow, orange, or pink flowers in late spring to summer

Lewisia 'George Henley'
Z3b ↕ 4in (10cm) ↔ 4in (10cm), evergreen perennial, small rosettes, flower stems with many flowers from late spring to summer

Liatris spicata 'Kobold'
Z4 ↕ to 5ft (1.5m) ↔ 18in (45cm), broad, long-lasting flower spikes in late summer and early autumn

LIBERTIA

VALUED FOR THEIR STRIKING FORMS, libertias have stiff, narrow, evergreen leaves that are a feature all year round. At the base, the leaves are leathery and long; those on the stem are smaller and more sparse. In late spring and summer, libertias produce slender spires of saucer-shaped, white, yellow-white or blue flowers. These are followed by shiny, light brown seedheads, which are useful in flower arranging. The leaves and seeds of *Libertia ixioides* are tinted orange in late autumn and winter. These clump-forming, tender perennials should be grown toward the front of a mixed or herbaceous border; they make perfect partners for the garden tradescantias (*see p.331*), and also look good with bronze-tinted grasses.

Cultivation Grow in reasonably fertile soil enriched with well-rotted compost, in full sun. Where marginally hardy, protect with a thick mulch in winter. **Divide** in spring (*see p.395*). **Sow** seed in containers outdoors as soon as it is ripe (*see pp.391–393*).

LIGULARIA

THESE ARCHITECTURAL PLANTS are large, robust, clump-forming perennials grown for their pyramid-shaped spikes of flowers, produced in shades of yellow and orange from midsummer until early autumn. Each individual flower is daisylike, often with a contrasting center. The large, usually rounded or kidney-shaped, mid-green leaves are equally bold. Ligularias look imposing grown in a mixed or herbaceous border, with other moisture-loving perennials such as astilbes (*see p.194*), daylilies (*Hemerocallis, p.258*) and border phloxes (*p.306*). Tall species, such as *Ligularia przewalskii,* (Z4) need to be at the back of planting schemes. They also look very striking by a stream or pond, where they will enjoy the damp conditions.

Cultivation Grow in reasonably fertile, deep, and reliably moist soil, in full sun or partial shade. Provide shelter from strong winds; taller plants may need staking. **Divide** in spring or after flowering (*see p.395*). **Sow** seed of species outdoors in autumn or spring (*see pp.391–393*).

Ligularia 'Gregynog Gold'
Z5b ‡ to 6ft (2m) ↔ 3ft (1m), rounded to heart-shaped leaves, flowers with brown centers in late summer and early autumn

Libertia grandiflora
T min. 35°F (2°C) ‡ to 36in (90cm) ↔ 24in (60cm), forms dense clumps, flowers early spring to early summer

Ligularia 'The Rocket'
Z4 ‡ 6ft (2m) ↔ 3ft (1m), sturdy black stems, large, boldly toothed leaves with purple veins, tall "candles" of flowers with orange-yellow centers, flowers in early and late summer

LILIUM

Lily

LILIES HAVE LONG GRACED GARDENS, both in the West and in the East, where many originate. Their appeal lies in their extravagant, often fragrant, summer blooms, which can measure up to 3in (8cm) across and more than 4in (10cm) long. There are about 100 species; all are perennial bulbs. Some of the earliest in cultivation are among the most demanding, for instance the Madonna lily, *Lilium candidum*, which can be disease prone. Others have definite preferences for acidic or alkaline soil. Modern hybrids, however, tend to be vigorous, disease resistant, and less fussy about soil. Lilies are available in most colors except blue, and the flowers come in four distinct shapes: trumpet, funnel, bowl, and turkscap. One of the easiest ways to grow them is in a container on the patio where their perfume is readily appreciated. Most do well in sunny borders; some, such as *L. martagon*, prefer a shady woodland garden. A few dwarf species are at home in rock gardens. Asiatic and Martagon lilies are generally hardy to Zone 3; other lilies may be more tender or more tolerant of warmer winters.

Cultivation Grow in any well-drained soil enriched with well-rotted compost or in containers in a soil-based potting mix. On heavy clay soils, improve drainage by digging in plenty of coarse grit in the planting hole. Most lilies prefer full sun, but some tolerate partial shade. **Plant** bulbs in autumn or spring at a depth of 2–3 times their height; the distance between should be three times the diameter of the bulb. **Water** regularly during dry spells in summer and apply a high-potassium fertilizer in the growing season. **Stake** tall varieties in exposed sites. **Deadhead** fading flowers before seed sets to maintain the plant's vigor. **Sow** seed (*see pp.391–392*) as soon as it is ripe in pots in a cold frame. **Detach** stem bulbils and bulblets from those cultivars that produce them (*see below*). Plants, including the flowers, may be eaten by slugs and snails (*see p.398*), and lily beetles. Pick off and destroy the distinctive, bright orange beetles.

Propagating from bulblets

Lilies such as L. auratum, L. longiflorum, *and* L. speciosum *naturally produce bulblets (small rooted bulbs that will grow into flowering plants in 3–4 years). These form below ground at the base of the main stem. Lift the parent plant in autumn, remove the bulblets and replant the mature bulb. Prepare pots of moist soil-based potting mix. Insert the bulblets to twice their own depth, and cover the mix with a layer of grit. Label and keep in a frost-free place before planting out the young lilies in the following autumn.*

Propagating from bulbils

Bulbils are tiny bulbs that form where the leaf stalks join stems of lilies such as L. bulbiferum, L. chalcedonicum, L. lancifolium, *as well as* L. × testaceum, *and their hybrids. They ripen in summer, and will produce flowering plants in 3–4 years. Take them only from healthy plants because bulbils can transfer disease. Fill a pot with moist, soil-based mix and press the bulbils into the surface. Cover with a ½in (1cm) layer of coarse sand and label. Grow on in a frost-free place until planting out the following autumn.*

① *Lilium* African Queen Group ‡5–6ft (1.5–2m), scented ② 'Angela North' ‡28–48in (70–120cm) ③ 'Ariadne' ‡2½–4½ft (80cm–1.4cm), scented ④ *auratum* var. *platyphyllum* ‡5ft (1.5m), scented ⑤ Bellingham Group ‡6–7ft (2–2.2m), increases rapidly, acidic soil, partial shade ⑥ 'Black Beauty' ‡4½–6ft (1.4–2m), scented ⑦ 'Bright Star' ‡3–5ft (1–1.5m), scented, alkaline soil ⑧ *bulbiferum* var. *croceum* ‡16–60in (40–150cm) ⑨ *canadense* ‡3–5½ft (1–1.6m) ⑩ *candidum*

‡3–6ft (1–2m), scented, neutral to alkaline soil ⑪ 'Casa Blanca' ‡3–4ft (1–1.2m), scented
⑫ *chalcedonicum* ‡2–5ft (60cm–1.5m), unpleasantly scented but thrives in any soil, sun or shade,
⑬ Citronella Group ‡3–5ft (1–1.5m) ⑭ 'Connecticut King' ‡3ft (1m) ⑮ × *dalhansonii* ‡3–5ft
(1–1.5m), unpleasantly scented ⑯ *davidii* var. *willmottiae* ‡6ft (2m) ⑰ *duchartrei* ‡24–39in
(60–100cm), scented ⑱ 'Enchantment' ‡24–39in (60–100cm), easy to grow, good for cutting ⑲ 'Fire

King' ‡3–4ft (1–1.2m), good in containers ⑳ *formosanum* var. *pricei* ‡4–12in (10–30cm),
scented, ㉑ Golden Splendor Group ‡4–6ft 1.2–2m), scented ㉒ 'Grand Paradiso' ‡36in
(90cm) ㉓ *grayi* ‡3–5½ft (1–1.7m), scented, needs moist, acidic soil

㉔ *hansonii* ‡ 3–5ft (1–1.5m), scented, partial shade, early summer ㉕ *henryi* ‡ 3–10ft (1–3m), neutral to alkaline soil partial shade, late summer ㉖ 'Journey's End' ‡ 3–6ft (1–2m), late summer ㉗ 'Lady Bowes Lyon' ‡ 3–4ft (1–1.2m) ㉘ *lancifolium* ‡ 2–5ft (60cm–1.5m), acidic soil but tolerates some lime, late summer and early autumn ㉙ *longiflorum* ‡ 16–39in (40–100cm), lime-tolerant, partial shade ㉚ *mackliniae* ‡ 12–24in (30–60cm) ㉛ 'Magic Pink'

‡ 1.2m (4ft) ㉜ *martagon* ‡ 3–6ft (90cm–2m), rank scent, well-drained soil, sun or partial shade ㉝ *martagon* var. *album* ‡ 3–6ft (90cm–2m), rank scent, well-drained soil, sun or partial shade ㉞ *medeoloides* ‡ 16–30in (45–75cm), acid soil, partial shade ㉟ *monadelphum* ‡ 3–5ft (1–1.5m), scented, early summer ㊱ 'Mont Blanc' ‡ 24–28in (60–70cm) ㊲ *nanum* ‡ 2½–12in (6–30cm), scented, acidic soil, partial shade ㊳ *nepalense* ‡ 24–39in (60–100cm), acidic soil, partial shade, early to midsummer

39 *pardalinum* ‡5–8ft (1.5–2.5m) **40** 'Peggy North' ‡4–5ft (1.2–1.5m) **41** Pink Perfection Group ‡5–6ft (1.5–2m), scented **42** *pomponium* ‡3ft (1m), rank scent, alkaline soil **43** *pyrenaicum* ‡12–39in (30–100cm), rank scent, neutral to alkaline soil **44** 'Red Night' ‡28–39in (70–100cm) **45** *regale* ‡2–6ft (60cm–2m), scented, full sun, midsummer **46** 'Rosemary North' ‡36–39in (90–100cm) **47** *rubellum* ‡12–32in (30–80cm), acid soil, partial shade, early summer **48** *speciosum* var. *rubrum* ‡3–5½ft (1–1.7m), scented, acidic soil, partial shade, late summer and early autumn **49** 'Star Gazer' ‡3–5ft (1–1.5m) **50** 'Sterling Star' ‡3–4ft (1–1.2m) **51** 'Sun Ray' ‡3ft (1m) **52** *superbum* ‡5–10ft (1.5–3m), acidic soil, late summer and early autumn **53** *tsingtauense* ‡28–39in (70–100cm), acidic soil

LIMNANTHES DOUGLASII
Poached egg plant

THIS IS A FAST-GROWING ANNUAL with sweetly scented flowers similar to those of buttercups from summer to autumn. It has yellow, glossy flowers with white tips on the petals. Although annual, it does self-seed prolifically – once you sow it, you will never be without it. The flowers are rich in nectar and so are attractive to bees and hoverflies. Hoverflies are good allies to have in the garden as they consume many aphids over the summer. The poached egg plant makes neat, bright splashes of color at the front of a border – perhaps with other vividly colored annuals, such as calendulas (*see p.204*) and nasturtiums (*Tropaeolum, see p.333*) – at a path edge, or scattered among paving. It makes an attractive rockery plant, although you will almost certainly find yourself weeding out surplus self-set seedlings.

Cultivation Grow in fertile, moist but well-drained soil, in full sun. **Sow** seed (*see pp.391–393*) where plants are to grow in spring or autumn. Protect autumn sowings with cloches in colder areas.

LINARIA
Toadflax

THIS IS A LARGE GROUP of annuals, biennials, and herbaceous perennials. Their stems, which can be erect, trailing, or branched, are clothed with clusters of flowers that look like tiny snapdragons. They bloom abundantly from spring to autumn, in hues of white, pink, red, purple, orange, and yellow. The smaller species suit a rock garden, scree bed (a sharply drained area with a deep layer of stone chips and a thin layer of soil), or wall crevice. Taller annuals and perennials, such as *Linaria vulgaris*, (Z4) are a popular choice for the foreground of borders, forming soft masses of color that act as foils to plants with bolder flowers; they also grow well in gravel beds. The Canadian hardiness zone ranges from 4–8.

Cultivation Grow in reasonably fertile, well-drained soil, in full sun. **Divide** perennials in early spring (*see p.395*). **Sow** seed of annuals where they are to flower in early spring (*see p.393*). Thin the seedlings to around 6in (15cm). Sow seed of perennials in containers in a cold frame in early spring (*see pp.391–392*). **Take** softwood cuttings of perennials in spring (*see p.394*).

LINUM
Flax

see also
p.82

THESE ANNUALS, BIENNIALS, AND PERENNIALS produce clouds of brilliantly colored, saucer-shaped flowers on graceful, wiry stems. The flowers appear for many weeks from early to late summer, and are mainly in pale primary colors – yellow, blue, or red – or white. The flowers of *Linum perenne* (Z5) last for only one day, but are replaced by more flowers the next day. The perennials tend to be short-lived, but are easy to raise from seed. The smaller flaxes are at home in a rock garden, while the larger ones make a stunning display *en masse* in borders; grow them in drifts among other herbaceous plants with soft outlines, such as hardy geraniums (*see pp.250–251*) and monardas (*see p.287*).

Cultivation Grow in light, reasonably fertile soil enriched with well-rotted organic matter in full sun. Smaller alpine species need sharply drained soil and protection from winter moisture. **Sow** seed in spring or autumn. Annuals can be sown where they are to grow; sow perennials in containers in a cold frame (*see pp.391–393*). **Take** stem-tip cuttings of perennials in early summer (*see p.394*).

Limnanthes douglasii
↕↔ 6in (15cm) or more, annual, sprawling habit, ferny, yellow-green leaves

① *alpina* ↕↔ 6in (15cm) ② *dalmatica* ↕ 3ft (1m) ↔ 24in (20cm) ③ *purpurea* 'Canon Went' ↕ to 36in (90cm) ↔ 12in (30cm) ④ *vulgaris* ↕ to 36in (90cm) ↔ 12in (30cm)

Linum perenne (Perennial flax)
↕ 4–24in (10–60cm) ↔ 12in (30m), relative of the flax used for linseed oil and linen, short-lived perennial but seeds freely

Linum flavum 'Compactum' (Golden flax)
Z5 ↕ ↔ 6in (15cm), upright perennial, dark green leaves, dense flowers that open in summer sun

LOBELIA

ANNUAL BEDDING LOBELIA IS EXTREMELY POPULAR, producing masses of flowers in the familiar blues, but also pink, purple, and white. Use it in summer beds, as edging, or trailing from hanging baskets and windowboxes. Planted around the edges of containers, they are perfect partners for fuchsias (*pp.60–63*) and other summer bedding. There are also perennial lobelias, which are effective beside water, or in a mixed or herbaceous border. They usually bear flowers in erect spikes, in jewel-like shades of azure, violet, carmine red, and scarlet. The aquatic *Lobelia cardinalis* (z4) does well in bog gardens or wildlife ponds.

Cultivation Grow in deep, fertile, reliably moist soil, in sun or partial shade. *L. cardinalis* can be grown in baskets (*see p.381*) in water 3–4in (8–10cm) deep. Bedding lobelia flowers for longer in shade. In containers, apply a weekly feeding with a balanced fertilizer. **Protect** perennials in cold areas with a thick winter mulch (*see p.388*). **Divide** perennials in spring; aquatics in summer (*see p.395*). **Sow** seed of perennials as soon as ripe; annuals in late winter, at 55–64°F (13–18°C) (*see pp.391–393*). Prone to slug damage (*see p.398*).

Lobelia 'Bees' Flame'
Z5 ↕ 30in (75cm) ↔ 12in (30cm), clump-forming perennial, dark leaves, tall flower spikes in mid- and late summer

LOBULARIA
Sweet alyssum, Sweet Alison

FROM SUMMER UNTIL EARLY AUTUMN, sweet alyssum forms cushions of densely packed, 4-petaled flowers in shades of white, pink, rose pink, mauve, and deep purple. In some cultivars, the flowers are honey scented. There are both annuals and perennials in the group and their long-flowering season and colorful blooms make them a popular choice in the garden. They originate from maritime areas and thus thrive in similar conditions – light soil and full sun – in gardens. Sweet alyssum is a useful edging plant for borders and in raised beds; white-flowered forms are often grown with blue trailing lobelia for a jaunty, nautical display. Gravels beds and cracks and crevices in paving also suit it well, and it will often self-seed into sunny niches.

Cultivation Grow in light, reasonably fertile soil that is well drained and in full sun. Trim the plants after the first flush of blooms has faded to encourage more flowers later on. **Sow** seed where plants are to grow (*see pp.391–393*) in late spring.

Lobularia 'Royal Carpet'
↕ 4in (10cm) ↔ 12in (30cm), annual, grow in pots or raised beds to appreciate the sweet scent of the flowers

FLOWERING PLANTS

LUNARIA
Honesty, Satin flower

FLOWERS, SEEDPODS, AND LEAVES are all decorative in this small group of plants. They bear purple or white flowers in late spring and early summer, followed by flat, translucent seed capsules, the sides of which reveal a satiny inner membrane. The seedpods last quite well into autumn, although for use in dried flower arrangements they are usually cut in late summer and dried indoors to avoid any damage from autumn weather. The leaves vary in shape and have toothed edges. Annual, biennial, or perennial, honesty self-seeds easily and naturalizes well in a wild garden. It can also be grown in a shrub border or with herbaceous perennials like aquilegias (*see p.185*), lupines (*see p.280*) and poppies (*Papaver, see p.299*).

Cultivation Grow in fertile, moist but well-drained soil, in full sun or partial shade. **Divide** *L. rediviva* (*see p.395*) in spring. **Sow** seed (*see pp.391–393*) in a seedbed: *L. rediviva* in spring, and *L. annua* in early summer. If plants are stunted, pull one up to see if the roots are knobbly and deformed; if so, burn all affected plants; they may have clubroot (*see Crambe, p.218*), a persistent soil-borne disease.

COLLECTING SEED
When the capsules become thin and papery, the seeds will be ripe. Peel the papery sides away and pick the seeds from the central membrane.

Lunaria annua 'Alba Variegata'
Z4 ‡ to 36in (90cm) ↔ to 12in (30cm), the white flowers will be followed by silvery seedpods inside and out

LUPINUS
Lupine

THE ENDURINGLY POPULAR FLOWER SPIKES of lupines provide some of the brightest colors in the early-summer garden. There are plenty to choose from, in almost any color and even bicolors; they last well when cut. The attractive foliage is mid-green with lance-shaped leaflets; a rain shower will leave it starred with small, silvery droplets. Most lupines grown in gardens are stately perennials, to be paired with other classic herbaceous plants such as delphiniums (*see pp.224–225*) and Oriental poppies (*Papaver orientale, p.299*). However, there are smaller-flowered, less formal, low-growing annuals.

Cultivation Grow in reasonably fertile, well-drained soil in full sun or partial shade. **Deadhead** (*see p.390*) for a second flush of flowers. **Sow** seed, after soaking for 24 hours, in spring or autumn, outside or in containers in a cold frame (*see pp.391–393*). **Take** cuttings of new shoots of named varieties in midspring (*see p.394*). Snapdragons are likely to be attacked by slugs and snails (*see p.398*). It is worth taking precautions against these pests.

Lunaria rediviva (Perennial honesty)
Z6 ‡ 24–36in (60–90cm) ↔ 12in (30cm), fragrant flowers; seedpods of this species are more fawn-colored than silvery

Lunaria annua 'Variegata'
Z4 ‡ to 36in (90cm) ↔ to 12in (30cm), as well as white-edged leaves, this has more deeply colored flowers than *L. annua*

Lupinus 'The Chatelaine'
Z3 ‡ 36in (90cm) ↔ 30in (75cm), this crisp combination is popular and among the brightest of the bicolored forms

Lupinus 'Beryl, Viscountess Cowdray'
Z5 ‡36in (90cm) ↔ 30in (75cm), this is something of a rarity but worth seeking out for its rich red flowers

Lupinus 'Noble Maiden'
Z3 ‡36in (90cm) ↔ 30in (75cm), the densely packed flower spikes make a strong impact in the border

Lupinus 'Chandelier'
Z3 ‡36in (90cm) ↔ 30in (75cm), restrained creamy yellow spikes like church candles allow the form and foliage to shine

Lupinus Russell hybrids
Z3 ‡36in (90cm) ↔ 30in (75cm), among the earliest and most reliable hybrids, these have a wide color range

Lupinus regale 'The Page'
Z4 ‡36in (90cm) ↔ 30in (75cm), more open flower spikes let some lupines to look at home in an informal garden design

LYCHNIS
Campion, Catchfly

CAMPIONS HAVE BRIGHT SUMMER FLOWERS in shades of vivid scarlet, purple, and pink as well as in white. The flowers are usually tubular or star-shaped and borne singly or in small clusters. The erect flower stems make them ideal for cutting. Butterflies find the flowers attractive, so they are a good choice for a wild garden. The leaves may be hairy. Campions are biennial or perennial. Smaller species are pretty in rock gardens, and the taller ones are best in informal borders with other perennials including aquilegias (*see p.185*), lupines (*see pp.280–281*), and Oriental poppies (*Papaver orientale, see p.299*). Some campions, such as *Lychnis chalcedonica*, have brittle stems and need the support of twiggy branches.

Cultivation Campions thrive in reasonably fertile soil that is well drained, in full sun or partial shade. Gray-leaved species produce the best leaf color in well-drained soil in full sun. **Remove** fading flowers regularly. **Sow** seed in containers (*see pp.391–392*) in a cold frame when it is ripe or in spring. **Divide** plants (*see p.395*) or take cuttings (*see p.394*) from new shoots at the base in spring.

Lychnis chalcedonica (Jerusalem cross, Maltese cross)
Z4 ‡3–4ft (90cm–1.2m) ↔ 12in (30cm), perennial, flowers in early and midsummer, self-seeds freely

Lychnis coronaria (Rose campion)
Z3b ‡32in (80cm) ↔ 18in (45cm), biennial or short-lived perennial, flowers in late summer, self-seeds freely

LYSICHITON
Skunk cabbage

THESE STRIKINGLY SHAPED, COLORFUL perennials flower in early spring. Dense spikes of tiny, greenish flowers are surrounded by elegantly sculptural, hooded bracts (modified leaves). These are followed by clusters of large, glossy, mid- to dark green leaves springing directly from the ground. The yellow skunk cabbage, *Lysichiton americanus*, is larger than the white-flowered *L. camtschatcensis* (Z7), which has 16in (40cm) hoods and leaves up to 39in (100cm) long; it has a height and spread of 30in (75cm). Both plants have a musky, almost unpleasant, smell. Their native habitat is beside water, so grow them by a pond or stream along with *Caltha palustris* (*see p.205*) and other moisture-loving marginal plants.

Cultivation Fertile soil enriched with plenty of well-rotted organic matter, at the edge of a stream or pond, in full sun or partial shade will suit these aquatic marginals. Allow sufficient space for the leaves to develop without swamping other plants. **Remove** offsets (*see p.395*) at the bases of the main stems in spring or summer.

Lysichiton americanus (Yellow skunk cabbage)
Z7 ‡3ft (1m) ↔ 4ft (1.2m), the hooded flowers are up to 16in (40cm) long, leaves up to 48in (120cm) long

LYSIMACHIA
Loosestrife

LOOSESTRIFES ARE A LARGE AND VARIED GROUP that includes many herbaceous perennials and some evergreens. Flowers appear from mid- to late summer, and may be star-, saucer- or cup-shaped; they are usually white or yellow, but sometimes are pink or purple. Larger loosestrifes are suitable for planting in damp herbaceous and mixed borders along with other moisture-loving perennials such as astilbes (*see p.194*), daylilies (*Hemerocallis, see p.258*), and border phloxes (*see pp.306–307*). They are happy in a bog garden or by pond margins and also look at home when naturalized in a woodland garden. Creeping Jenny (*Lysmachia nummularia*) makes a good groundcover plant. Yellow-flowered *L. punctata* can spread and become a problem, but is less invasive on dryish soil.

Cultivation Grow these plants in soil that is well drained but enriched with well-rotted organic matter, in full sun or partial shade, and in a site that does not dry out in summer. **Support** tall species with twiggy pea sticks. **Sow** seed in containers outdoors (*see pp.391–393*) in spring or divide plants in spring or autumn (*see p.395*).

Lysimachia nummularia (Creeping Jenny)
Z4 ↕ to 2in (5cm) ↔ indefinite, mat-forming evergreen, rooting stems spread rapidly, cup-shaped, bright yellow flowers

LYTHRUM
Loosestrife

EVEN LONGER-FLOWERING THAN THEIR NAMESAKES (*see left*), these upright annuals and perennials are valued for their slender spikes of pretty flowers in shades of purplish pink, or occasionally white. Individual flowers are up to ¾in (2cm) wide, with 4–8 petals, and are borne along the ends of tapering, square stems in summer to autumn. The leaves are up to 4in (10cm) long and sometimes add to autumnal displays by turning yellow. Some of these loosestrifes flourish at the margins of streams and ponds; a few species are noxious weeds and should not be planted where they could escape into natural wetlands. For a colorful, natural display, combine non-invasive loosestrifes with astilbes (*see p.194*), bergamots (*Monarda, see p.286*), montbretias (*Crocosmia, see p.219*), and phloxes (*see p.306*).

Cultivation These loosestrifes thrive in any fertile, moist soil in full sun. **Remove** fading flowers to prevent self-seeding. **Sow** seed at 55–64°F (13–18°C) in spring (*see pp.391–393*) or divide plants in spring (*see p.395*). Take cuttings from new shoots at the base of the plant (*see p.394*) in spring or early summer.

Lysimachia clethroides (Gooseneck loosestrife)
Z4 ↕ 36in (90cm) ↔ 24in (60cm), spreading, hairy leaves, flower heads appear mid- to late summer

Lysimachia ciliata 'Firecracker'
Z4 ↕ 4ft (1.2m) ↔ 24in (60cm), flowers in midsummer

Lythrum virgatum 'The Rocket'
Z4 ↕ 32in (80cm) ↔ 18in (45cm), clump-forming perennial, leaves 4in (10cm) long, flowers from early to late summer

FLOWERING PLANTS

MACLEAYA
Plume poppy

THESE MAJESTIC HERBACEOUS perennials are grown for their handsome foliage and graceful plumes of tiny, petalless flowers. The feathery flower plumes, in buff-white, cream, or soft apricot to coral pink, are carried on erect blue- or gray-green stems from early to midsummer and appear to almost float above the foliage. The fine leaves, in gray-green to olive green, are deeply lobed and may be up to 10in (25cm) across. Plume poppies can grow quite tall, up to 8ft (2.5m), so are best planted at the back of a border, where they have great presence; they can be invasive, however. Grow them in a spacious border with other summer-flowering perennials; they can also be used to create superbly subtle effects with tall grasses.

Cultivation Grow in any soil that is moist but well drained, in full sun or partial shade. Provide shelter from cold, drying winds. **Divide** plants in spring or autumn. **Sow** seed (*see pp.391–393*) in containers in a cold frame in spring **Take** root cuttings in winter (*see p.394*) or separate the rhizomes (*see p.395*).

Macleaya microcarpa 'Kelway's Coral Plume'
Z4 ‡ 7ft (2.5m) ↔ 3ft (1m), gray-green leaves are 5- to 7-lobed, buff to coral pink flowers in early and midsummer

MALVA
Mallow

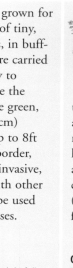

‡ 8in–4ft (20cm–1.2m)
↔ 9–24in (23–60cm)

MALLOWS ARE EASY AND REWARDING plants to grow and flourish on the poorest of soils. This colorful group of annuals, biennials, and woody-based perennials produce leafy spikes of pink, purple, blue, or white flowers throughout summer on upright plants. The flowers are bowl- or saucer-shaped and last for many weeks, making mallows useful plants for mixed, annual, and herbaceous borders alike. Use them as gap-fillers among other summer-flowering plants such as campanulas (*see p.206*), phloxes (*see p.306*), and lilies (*see pp.274–277*), or for a more informal look, with flowering grasses such as *Lagarus ovatus* (*see p.349*).

Cultivation Grow in any moist but well-drained soil in full sun. Provide some support especially if growing in very fertile soil. Perennial cultivars and species are often short-lived, but they self-seed freely. **Sow** seed of annuals where the plants are to grow, or in containers, in spring or early summer (*see pp.391–393*). **Take** cuttings of new young shoots from perennials in spring (*see p.394*).

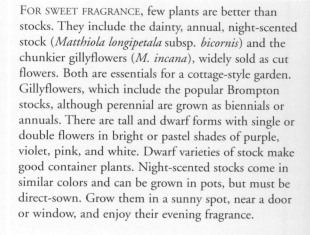

① *moschata* Z4 ‡ 36in (90cm) ↔ 24in (60cm), erect perennial
② *sylvestris* 'Primley Blue' Z4 ‡ to 8in (20cm) ↔ 12–24in (30–60cm), prostrate perennial

MATTHIOLA
Stock, Gillyflower

FOR SWEET FRAGRANCE, few plants are better than stocks. They include the dainty, annual, night-scented stock (*Matthiola longipetala* subsp. *bicornis*) and the chunkier gillyflowers (*M. incana*), widely sold as cut flowers. Both are essentials for a cottage-style garden. Gillyflowers, which include the popular Brompton stocks, although perennial are grown as biennials or annuals. There are tall and dwarf forms with single or double flowers in bright or pastel shades of purple, violet, pink, and white. Dwarf varieties of stock make good container plants. Night-scented stocks come in similar colors and can be grown in pots, but must be direct-sown. Grow them in a sunny spot, near a door or window, and enjoy their evening fragrance.

Cultivation Grow in any moist but well-drained soil in full sun; *incana* types tolerate partial shade. Tall forms may need some support. **Sow** seed (*see pp.391–393*) of *incana* types for summer flowering in early spring at 50–64°F (10–18°C) and for spring-flowering outdoors in summer; overwinter in a cold frame to plant out the following spring. Sow night-scented stocks in situ and thin to 4–6in (10–15cm) apart.

Matthiola incana Cinderella Series
Z7b ‡ 8–10in (20–25cm) ↔ to 10in (25cm), double flowers held in dense spikes 6in (15cm) tall, in late spring to summer

MECONOPSIS

‡ to 8ft (2.5m)
↔ to 3ft (1m)

THIS COSMOPOLITAN GROUP of plants includes both the cheerful yellow Welsh poppy (*Meconopsis cambrica*) and the sapphire-blue Himalayan poppy (*M. betonicifolia*). Meconopsis grow best where there are cool, damp summers; long hot summers are not ideal. If you have a suitable site – a cool, moist woodland garden, or a sheltered border that mimics these conditions, with soil rich in humus or leaf mold – you can grow any meconopsis, in eye-catching shades of turquoise and faded denim, pomegranate pink, and clear yellows. Their silky flowers, with yellow or cream stamens, appear from early to midsummer. The plants may be short-lived, but all are worth it; some self-seed.

Cultivation Grow in moist but well-drained, slightly acidic soil, in partial shade, with shelter from cold winds. **Divide** established plants after flowering (*see p.395*). **Sow** seed (*see pp.391–393*) in containers in a cold frame as soon as ripe, overwintering seedlings in the frame, or in spring. Sow thinly, on the surface of the medium.

① *betonicifolia* Z4 ‡ 4ft (1.2m) ② *cambrica* Z4 ‡ 18in (45cm), grows but very dry soils ③ *napaulensis* Z8 ‡ 8ft (2.5m), evergreen *sheldonii* Z7 ‡ 4–5ft (1.2–1.4m)

MELISSA OFFICINALIS
Lemon balm

‡ to 4ft (1.2m)
↔ to 18in (45cm)

THE LEAVES OF THIS POPULAR HERB give off a clear, fresh lemon aroma when they are crushed or brushed in passing. Apart from their scent, these bushy, upright perennials (Z3) are grown mainly for their attractive nettlelike foliage, which is hairy and light to bright green, or splashed with golden yellow in variegated forms. The young shoots are popular ingredients in potpourri and herb teas. In summer, the plants also produce spikes of small, tubular, two-lipped, whitish flowers, which attract bees. Grow balms in a herbaceous or mixed border or with other herbs in a herb garden. While they enjoy full sun, these plants are also useful for dry shade.

Cultivation Grow in any poor soil in full sun, with protection from winter moisture. **Cut back** hard after flowering to encourage a fresh flush of foliage and to prevent self-seeding. Variegated forms are better trimmed back before flowering to encourage bright foliage (*see below*). **Divide** plants (*see p.395*) as growth starts in spring, or in autumn. **Sow** seed in containers in a cold frame in the spring (*see pp.391–393*) or transplant self-sown seedlings.

TRIMMING LEMON BALM Harvesting shoot tips for potpourris will also encourage a new flush of leaves and help prevent self-seeding.

Melissa officinalis 'Aurea' (Golden lemon balm)
Z3, hairy stems, off-white flowers in summer

MELITTIS MELISSOPHYLLUM
Bastard balm

‡ 8–28in (20–70cm)
↔ 20in (50cm)

THIS HERBACEOUS PERENNIAL is grown for its tubular flowers produced in late spring and early summer. They occur in shades of pink and purple, or white with creamy white, marked with pink or purple, and they stud the stems, appearing in the leaf joints. The oval leaves are hairy and wrinkled; they have an aromatic or honeyed scent. Grow bastard balm in a cool border with other plants that are happy in light shade, such as bergenias (*see p.198*) and aquilegias (*see p.185*), or in a woodland garden. Its flowers will attract bees and other pollinating insects into the garden.

Cultivation Grow in reasonably fertile, moist but well-drained soil, in partial shade. **Divide** plants (*see p.395*) in spring as new growth begins. **Sow** seed in a container in a cold frame as soon as it is ripe, or in spring (*see pp.391–393*).

Melittis melissophyllum
Z7 ‡ 8–28in (20–70cm) ↔ 20in (50cm), may become invasive

MIMULUS
Monkey flower

THE NUMEROUS HYBRID MIMULUS are grown as annuals for their bright flowers that bring color to containers or borders from early summer through autumn. These resemble snapdragons and are trumpet-shaped or tubular, in a variety of colors, and usually heavily freckled with a contrasting hue. The pale- to dark green leaves often have silvery hairs. Mimulus often have a creeping habit, but may be upright and bushy; some are perennial. Most prefer moist or even boggy soil; *Mimulus luteus* and *M. ringens* (Z4) thrive in shallow water at pond edges.

Cultivation These plants need very moist soil in sun or semishade, although *M. cardinalis* will tolerate drier soil; the bedding hybrids and *M. aurantiacus* require well-drained ground and sun. Mimulus is short-lived, so it is worth propagating regularly. **Sow** seed (*see pp.391–393*) of hardy species in containers in a cold frame in autumn or spring; sow tender bedding at 43–54°F (6–12°C) in spring. **Root** softwood cuttings in early summer (*see p.394*). **Divide** perennials (*see p.395*) in spring. **Slugs** (*see p.398*) can cause damage.

① *aurantiacus* Z7b ‡↔ 3ft (1m) ② *cardinalis* Z6b ‡ 3ft (1m) ↔ 2ft (60cm) ③ *lewisii* Z6 ‡ 2ft (60cm) ↔ 18in (45cm) ④ *luteus* Z7 ‡ 1ft (30cm) ↔ 2ft (60cm)

MOLUCCELLA LAEVIS
Bells of Ireland, Shell flower

‡ 36in (90cm) ↔ 9in (23cm)

THE EXTRAORDINARY, LEAFY FLOWERS and pale green foliage are the attractions of this commonly cultivated annual – a favorite with flower arrangers. In late summer, it produces spikes up to 12in (30cm) tall that, near the tips, bear tiny, white or pink flowers cupped in large, green collars (called calyces). The calyces become white-veined and papery as the seeds develop and can be used in dried flower arrangements. The flowers are also fragrant. Moluccellas can be used to provide an eye-catching addition to a border of more common bedding plants such as French marigolds (*Tagetes, see p.329*) or heliotropes (*see p.70*).

Cultivation Moluccellas will grow in any moist, but well-drained soil in full sun. **Sow** seed (*see pp.391–393*) at 55–64°F (13–18°C) in early or midspring, or in situ in late spring.

Moluccella laevis
‡ 3ft (1m) ↔ 9in (23cm), annual, fragrant white to pale purplish flowers, stalks can be dried, prefers well-drained soil

MONARDA
Bee balm, Bergamot

‡ 3ft (90cm) ↔ 18in (45cm)

WITH SPIDERY FLOWER HEADS and lush foliage, monardas enhance any garden. Most widely grown are the clump-forming, herbaceous perennials, but there are a few annuals. From midsummer to early autumn, they produce clusters of tubular flowers, in shades of crimson, pink, white, or violet, at the tips of the stems. The leaves are mid- to dark green, with prominent, dark veins, and are often flushed purple. The whole plant is highly aromatic; both the leaves and flowers are used in the fragrance industry. Use these splendid plants in any border where they will attract bees and other pollinating insects to the garden.

Cultivation Any moist but well-drained soil that does not dry out in summer is suitable – in full sun or dappled shade. **Sow** seed (*see pp.391–393*) in a container in a cold frame, in spring or autumn. **Divide** plants (*see p.395*) in spring before new growth begins. **Slugs** may attack in spring. Powdery mildew may become a problem in dry weather (*see p.398*); mildew-resistant cultivars are available.

① 'Cambridge Scarlet' Z3b ‡ 36in (90cm) ↔ 18in (45cm), clump-forming perennial ② 'Croftway Pink' Z3b ‡ 36in (90cm) ↔ 18in (45cm), clump-forming perennial

MUSCARI
Grape hyacinth

THESE BULBOUS PLANTS, although rarely more than 8in (20cm) in height, are very versatile. In spring, and occasionally in autumn, they bear tight clusters of tiny flowers that are usually blue, but sometimes yellow, white, purple, or even black. Some species are very fragrant. The flower heads are held above clumps of fleshy, blue-, gray- or mid-green leaves. Plant grape hyacinths in large groups in a border, or in carpets beneath deciduous shrubs and trees. They are often grown naturalized in grass with other colorful, spring-flowering bulbs such as daffodils (*Narcissus, see pp.288–289*) and tulips (*see pp.334–335*). Some species are invasive in favorable conditions; be sure that they do not encroach on other plants.

Cultivation Plant the bulbs 4in (10cm) deep in autumn, in any well-drained soil, in sun or dappled shade. **Lift and divide** (*see p.395*) clumps every five or six years, in summer, to maintain vigor and improve flowering. **Sow** seed in containers in a cold frame in autumn (*see pp.391–393*). **Viruses** may be a problem; destroy any plants that are stunted, distorted, or marked with yellow streaks or patches.

Muscari macrocarpum
Z6 ‡ 4–6in (10–15cm) ↔ 3in (8cm), spreading clumps, spring flowers are strongly fragrant, prefers hot, dry summers

Muscari armenicanum 'Blue Spike'
Z3 ‡ 8in (20cm) ↔ 2in (5cm), may form large clumps and become invasive, mid-green leaves in autumn, flowers in spring

MYOSOTIS
Forget-me-not

A LARGE GROUP OF ANNUALS, biennials, and short-lived perennials grown for their delightful flowers and hairy leaves. Most forget-me-nots have blooms in shades of blue, with white or golden eyes, but pink, yellow, or white varieties are available. The biennial *Myosotis sylvatica* (Z4) and its cultivars, widely used in bedding designs and containers, are also easy to grow in borders. The water forget-me-not (*M. scorpioides* Z5) is happiest in mud or shallow water, and some of the small, mat-forming perennials, like the alpine forget-me-not (*M. alpestris* Z4), prefer very sharply drained conditions. Nearly all self-seed freely, so can be left to create large drifts of color in wildflower gardens.

Cultivation Forget-me-nots thrive in any moist but well-drained, not too fertile, soil, in sun or semishade. **Sow** seed (*see pp.391–393*) of all myosotis in situ in spring; seed of annuals and biennials can be sown in a cold frame in summer for earlier flowers in the following year. Seed of *M. scorpioides* should be sown in pondside mud. **Divide** plants (*see p.395*) when they are dormant. **Mildew** can create white patches on the foliage (*see p.393*) in damp conditions.

Myosotis 'Indigo'
Z3 ‡ 12in (30cm) ↔ 6in (15cm), biennial, one of the darkest blue cultivars, flowers from midspring to midsummer

Daffodil

DAFFODILS AND NARCISSI ARE THE HARBINGERS OF SPRING. The flowers, in cheerful yellows, creams, and white, occasionally tinged with pink or a hint of green, are a welcome sight after a long winter. The range of species and cultivars runs into thousands, varying enormously in height and flower shape, with flowers that may be borne singly or several per stem. All are bulbous perennials. The tall, showy varieties look splendid growing among shrubs, in borders, or as spring bedding along with clumps of polyanthus primroses. The smaller types are preferred for more naturalistic plantings and are often at their most effective in drifts in grass or in a woodland setting, where they will gradually spread if left undisturbed. Dwarf types are suitable for rock gardens. Some, including many of the jonquil, tazetta, and poeticus narcissi, are fragrant. Grow these where you can catch their delicious scent, such as in a trough by the door, or in a windowbox. Daffodils also make excellent cut flowers. Some may also be "forced," (*see below*), grown indoors, to flower early, usually for Christmas. Daffodils can be grown in most areas of Canada, down to Zone 4, or Zone 3b with good snow cover.

Cultivation Daffodils and narcissi tolerate a wide range of soil types, but most grow best in fertile, well-drained soil that is moist during the growing season. Position them in full sun or partial shade. **Plant** the bulbs to twice their own depth in autumn, slightly deeper in light, sandy soils and when naturalizing them in grass. **Water** late-flowering daffodils during dry spring weather to encourage good blooms. **Deadhead** faded flower heads before the seedheads form, but leave the foliage to die down naturally. This helps the bulb build up food reserves for the following year, needed for the formation of flower buds. **Feed** foliage until it dies down with a high-potassium fertilizer to encourage subsequent flowering. If daffodils are being grown in grass, delay mowing until the foliage has died down. **Lift and divide** bulbs (*see p.395*) if flowering deteriorates, usually where bulbs become congested after four or five years. The tiny young bulbs can be grown on into new plants, which need three to four years to begin flowering. Poor flowering, or "blindness," may also be due to bulbs not having been planted deeply enough, and replanting may be necessary. Stunted, mottled, or streaked foliage is a sign of virus attack, and infected plants are best dug up and destroyed.

Forcing daffodil bulbs

❶ Mix some washed gravel with a little charcoal. Fill the container three-quarters full of gravel. Make a gentle dip in the surface with your finger and place a bulb (here Grand Soleil d'Or) in it, "nose" upward. Plant the remaining bulbs, making sure they do not touch.

❷ When you have finished planting, add water until it is just below the bottom of the bulbs. Unless you have prepared bulbs, which can be left in the light, cover the container with a black plastic bag, tie it with string, and stand in a cool, dark place.

❸ Check the bulbs after about four weeks to see if they need more water. After 8–10 weeks, the bulbs should have grown about 1in (1–2cm) and can be brought into the light. As the plants grow taller, support any weak leaves or stems by tying them to stakes.

① *Narcissus* '**Actaea**' ‡18in (45cm), late spring, scented ② '**Baby Moon**' ‡10–12in (25–30cm), late spring ③ *bulbocodium* ‡4–6in (10–15cm), midspring, can be naturalized in grass, suitable for growing in a rock garden ④ '**Cassata**' ‡16in (40cm), midspring ⑤ '**Cheerfulness**' ‡16in (40cm), midspring, scented ⑥ '**Dove Wings**' ‡12in (30cm), early spring ⑦ '**February Gold**' ‡12in (30cm), early spring, can be naturalized in grass, suitable for forcing ⑧ '**Fortune**' ‡18in (45cm), midspring

9 'Golden Ducat' ‡14in (35cm), mid-spring 10 'Grand Soleil d'Or' ‡18in (45cm), midspring, scented, suitable for forcing 11 'Hawera' ‡7in (18cm), late spring 12 'Ice Follies' ‡16in (40cm), mid-spring, prolific 13 'Jack Snipe' ‡8in (20cm), early and midspring, increases rapidly 14 'Jenny' ‡12in (30cm), early and midspring, can be naturalized in grass, suitable for forcing 15 'Liberty Bells' ‡12in (30cm), midspring 16 'Little Beauty' ‡6in (15cm), dwarf, early spring 17 'Mount Hood' ‡18in (45cm), early spring 18 'Pencrebar' ‡7in (18cm), midspring, scented 19 *romieuxii* ‡3–4in (8–10cm), early spring 20 'Salome' ‡18in (45cm), midspring, produces consistently good-quality flowers 21 'Sweetness' ‡16in (40cm), midspring, vigorous, scented, long-lasting as a cut flower 22 'Thalia' ‡14in (35cm), midspring, scented 23 *triandrus* ‡4–10in (10–25cm), midspring

FLOWERING PLANTS

NEMESIA

ANNUAL NEMESIAS ARE POPULARLY used as riotous summer bedding or container plants. They are easy to grow and produce abundant, brightly colored flowers in an assortment of blues, reds, pinks, yellows, oranges, and whites. Many are bicolored. The showy, almost trumpet-shaped, two-lipped flowers are borne singly or in short terminal racemes. They are good for cutting. *Nemesia caerulea* (T min. 41°F/5°C), a woody-based perennial, is suitable for a raised bed or herbaceous border, and is often used as a container plant.

Cultivation Grow in any moist but well-drained soil in full sun. Nemesias may suffer from root rot in wet soils. **Pinch out** the growing tips of annuals to promote a bushy habit and plenty of flowers. Be sure that plants in pots are watered regularly. **Sow** seed at 59°F (15°C) from early to late spring, or in autumn (*see pp.391–393*). **Take** softwood cuttings from perennials in late summer (*see p.394*) and overwinter young plants in frost-free conditions.

① *denticulata* ‡10in (25cm), annual ② *strumosa* **Carnival Series** ‡7–9in (17–23cm), dwarf annual with large blooms

NEMOPHILA

THE SLENDER, FLESHY STEMS OF NEMOPHILAS carry large, open flowers with distinctively marked petals. The flowers are saucer-shaped and usually blue or white, with veins, tints, patches, or centers in contrasting shades of blue, purple, white, or yellow. The showy blooms are set off by feathery, mid- or gray-green leaves. Nemophilas are low-growing annuals that bloom for several weeks in early to midsummer, with more flowers being produced in cool, moist conditions. They are useful for edging a path or filling gaps in the front of a border. Neat and compact, they also suit any type of container, or a rock garden that has moisture-retentive soil.

Cultivation Grow in any moist but well-drained soil, or in soil-based potting mix, in full sun or partial shade. **Water** well during dry spells, or plants may stop flowering. **Sow** seed where it is to grow outdoors in spring or autumn (*see pp.391–393*), in shallow drills about 6in (15cm) apart. Thin the seedlings along the rows to about the same distance. Will also self-seed freely.

Nemophila maculata (Five-spot baby)
‡↔ 6–12in (15–30cm), annual, named for the markings at the tips of its five petals, sometimes veined in mauve also

NEPETA
Catmint

THE CATMINT BEST KNOWN for its strongly aromatic leaves is catnip (*Nepeta cataria* Z4), which cats find hypnotic, but there are other varieties widely grown in gardens that are less appealing to cats. They are perennials with soft, silvery gray foliage and small, erect flower spikes in white and shades of blue, purple, and sometimes yellow. Most have a loose, spreading habit and act as good groundcover plants since the dense growth suppresses weeds. They can be used to line a broad, sunny path where their scent can be enjoyed while walking; some tiny species also suit a rock garden. Taller catmints are best sited in a mixed or herbaceous border.

Cultivation Grow in any well-drained soil in full sun or partial shade. The more loosely growing, taller nepetas may benefit from staking (*see p.390*). **Trim** the plants after flowering to maintain a compact habit and encourage more flowers. **Divide** plants in spring or autumn (*see p.395*). **Sow** seed in a container in a cold frame in autumn (*see pp.391–392*).

① *govaniana* Z6 ‡3ft (1m) ↔ 24in (60cm) ② *sibirica* Z3 ‡3ft (1 ↔ 18in (45cm) ③ **'Six Hills Giant'** Z4 ‡3ft (1m) ↔ 24in (60cm) *subsessilis* Z5 ‡ to 3ft (1m) ↔ 12in (30cm)

NERINE

THESE BULBOUS PERENNIALS have the most unlikely flowers for autumn – delicate, trumpet-shaped clusters in bright pink, or occasionally crimson or orange-red. They cannot help but lend an invigorating, airy feel to the garden at a time when most other plants are fading. Nerines enjoy well-drained, dry conditions, and usually flourish under a south- or west-facing wall or in a sheltered rock garden. In most, only once the flowers open or even die down do the strappy, mid-green leaves start to emerge, making the bare-stemmed flowers stand out even more dramatically; they are stunning seen in isolated groups against dark soil, pale stone, or painted masonry. Alternatively, plant them with other late-flowering bulbs, such as schizostylis and *Scilla scilloides* (*see p.323*).

Cultivation Plant in well-drained soil in full sun in early spring. Try to site them carefully, because they are best left undisturbed to form a large clump. Where marginally hardy, provide a deep, dry mulch (a layer of straw or compost spread over the growing area) for protection. May need protection against slugs (*see p.393*).

NICOTIANA

Tobacco plant

THE PERFUMED, TRUMPET-SHAPED FLOWERS are the main reason for growing this group of annuals, biennials, and perennials. The flowers, in shades of lime green, red, pink, apple green, and white, last for many weeks throughout summer and autumn. They usually open fully only in the evening, when they release their heady scent, but some newer cultivars will open during the day if sited in partial shade. Most tobacco plants have sticky, mid-green leaves. Although some are herbaceous perennials, most are usually grown as annuals and are raised from seed every year. Plant in groups for the best effect and site them on a patio or near the house so that their rich evening fragrance can waft across and into windows and doorways. Contact with the foliage can irritate the skin.

Cultivation Grow in any moist but well-drained soil in full sun or partial shade. **Stake** tall plants in exposed positions. **Sow** seed at 64°F (18°C) in spring on the surface of the compost (*see pp.391–392*); they need light to germinate.

NIGELLA

Love-in-a-mist, Devil-in-a-bush

NIGELLA HAS BEEN GROWN IN GARDENS for centuries and today is available in several colors – white, mauve, rose pink, deep pink, and yellow – as well as the original blue. Some seed mixtures, such as the popular Persian Jewels, produce flowers in several harmonizing shades. These bushy annuals flourish on rocky slopes and wastelands, and will grow almost anywhere. Their dainty summer flowers sit within a hazy ruff of feathery foliage (the "mist" of the common name), and are followed by inflated seedpods, equally good for cutting. Sky-blue 'Miss Jekyll' with yellow and orange eschscholzias (*see p.241*) makes a fine and fast-growing, summery contrast. Both of these easy plants fill your garden with color; they self-seed freely.

Cultivation Grow in any well-drained soil in full sun. **Sow** seed where it is to grow (*see pp.391–393*) in shallow drills about 6in (15cm) apart and thin seedlings to about the same distance. Seed can be sown in spring or autumn, but autumn-sown seedlings benefit from protection over winter.

Nerine bowdenii
Z8 ‡18in (45cm) ↔ 3in (8cm), robust plant, broad leaves to 12in (30cm) long, faintly scented flowers

① 'Lime Green' ‡ 24in (60cm) ↔ 10in (25cm), upright annual ② *sylvestris* T min. 45°F (7°C) ‡ to 5ft (1.5m) ↔ to 24in (60cm), perennial in mild areas, strongly perfumed

Nigella damascena 'Miss Jekyll'
‡ to 20in (50cm) ↔ 9in (23cm), annual, self-seeded offspring may flower in different shades, good for cutting

FLOWERING PLANTS

NYMPHAEA
Waterlily

WITH THEIR JEWEL-LIKE, OFTEN FRAGRANT, BLOOMS, waterlilies bring an exotic touch to garden ponds and pools. These herbaceous, submerged, aquatic plants grow from tubers or rhizomes (underground stems) that run at or just below the soil surface. There are hardy and nonhardy waterlilies, all of which flower in summer. Hardy varieties have mostly white, yellow, or crimson flowers that float on the surface and open during the day. Nonhardy tropical waterlilies bloom either in the day or at night and the flowers, which include shades of blue, are held above the water. Waterlilies look stunning in large ponds, and there are dwarf varieties to suit small ponds, even those in containers such as half-barrels. Their handsome leaves cover the water and provide shade for fish and also have the effect of reducing algal growth in the water by cutting out sunlight. Hardy waterlilies survive even when water is frozen: the old foliage dies and new leaves grow in spring. Tender tropical waterlilies are treated as annuals in cool climates or overwintered in damp sand at a minimm of 50°F (10°C) after being a r-dried for a few days. Regular attention is needed to keep waterlilies flowering freely. In general, hardy waterlilies can be grown to Zone 3.

Cultivation Grow in still water in full sun at the correct depth for the variety; waterlilies will not thrive in moving water. **Plant** hardy types in early summer in aquatic soil – or ordinary garden topsoil is usually suitable – in planting baskets lined in burlap. Insert the rhizomes just under the soil surface and top-dress with gravel to help keep soil in place. **Submerge** the basket so that it sits with 6–10in (15–25cm) of water above it. It can be placed on a stack of bricks if the pond is too deep. Once the plant is established, gradually lower the basket, allowing the leaves to grow to the surface between each move, until it sits at the right depth. Most waterlilies grow at a depth of 12–18in (30–45cm), but a few prefer shallower or deeper planting (see below). In a natural pond lined with mud, you can plant directly into the mud. **Remove** fading flowers, if possible, to encourage further flowering. **Cut off** dead or dying foliage to prevent rotting and giving off poisonous gases that can harm fish. **Divide** established plants after three or four years (see below).

How to divide and replant waterlilies

Waterlilies grow vigorously and will eventually become overcrowded and exhausted. A sure sign of this is when their leaves begin to stand out of the water instead of resting on the surface, and plants start to produce fewer flowers than normal.

If this is the case, they need dividing. This is best done in spring when plants are starting into growth, preferably in late spring, when the warmer water and longer daylight hours ensure that the plants will re-establish quickly.

❶ Lift a mature clump during spring, when the new leaves are beginning to show. Dip the plant in fresh water to remove any soil or algae from the roots.

❷ Using a sharp knife, cut the rhizome into several sections, with each having 2–3 buds. Trim off any coarse or damaged roots, and pot each section.

❸ Plant in a basket with the crown just below soil level. Top with a layer of gravel. Place the basket in shallow water until the plant is established.

① *Nymphaea alba* ↔ 5½ft (1.7m), water depth 1–3ft (30–90cm) ② 'American Star' ↔ 4–5ft (1.2–1.5m), water depth 1½–4ft (45cm–1.2m) ③ 'Attraction' ↔ 4–5ft (1.2–1.5m), water depth 1½–4ft (45cm–1.2m) ④ 'Aurora' ↔ 3–5ft (90cm–1.5m) ⑤ 'Escarboucle' ↔ 4–5ft (1.2–1.5m), flowers 6–7in (15–18cm) across, water depth 1–2ft (30–60cm) ⑥ 'Fabiola' ↔ 5ft (1.5cm), water depth 6–12in (15–30cm) ⑦ 'Fire Crest' ↔ 4ft (1.2m) ⑧ 'Froebelii' ↔ 36in (90cm), water depth 6–12in (15–30cm)

⑨ 'Gonnère' ↔ 3–4ft (90cm–1.2m), water depth 8–18in (20–45cm) ⑩ 'James Brydon' ↔ 3–4ft (90cm–1.2m) ⑪ 'Laydekeri Fulgens' ↔ 4–5ft (1.2–1.5m) ⑫ 'Marliacea Albida' ↔ 3–4ft (90cm–1.2m) ⑬ 'Marliacea Carnea' ↔ 4–5ft (1.2–1.5m) ⑭ 'Marliacea Chromatella' ↔ 4–5ft (1.2–1.5m) ⑮ 'Norma Gedye' ↔ 4–5ft (1.2–1.5m), water depth 1–3ft (30–90cm) ⑯ 'Odorata Sulphurea Grandiflora' ↔ 3–4ft (90cm–1.2m) ⑰ 'Pink Sensation' ↔ 4ft (1.2m) ⑱ 'Pygmaea Helvola' ↔ 10–16in (25–40cm), flowers 2–3in (5–8cm) across, water depth 3–6in (8–15cm) ⑲ 'René Gérard' ↔ 5ft (1.5m) ⑳ 'Rose Arey' ↔ 4–5ft (1.2–1.5m) ㉑ tetragona ↔ 10–16in (25–40cm), water depth 3–6in (8–15cm) ㉒ 'Vésuve' ↔ 4ft (1.2m), flowers 7in (18cm) across ㉓ 'Virginalis' ↔ 3–4ft (90cm–1.2m) All are hardy waterlilies

FLOWERING PLANTS

OENOTHERA

Evening primrose, Sundrops

THE DELICATE, PAPERY FLOWERS of evening primrose grace the garden from late spring until summer's end. Although short-lived, they are borne in such profusion that new flowers constantly unfurl to replace their predecessors. This varied group includes annuals, biennials, and perennials that produce yellow, white, or pink flowers. Some have the additional attraction of decorative, red or coral flower buds that form subtle color contrasts with the open flowers. Heights range from low-growing species suitable for rock gardens or raised beds, such as *Oenothera macrocarpa*, to border plants such as the tall, graceful wands of *O. biennis* (Z4), which attains a height of 3–5ft (1–1.5m) and spreads to 24in (60cm). Grow these in mixed or herbaceous borders, or in pots.

Cultivation Grow in well-drained soil in full sun – rock plants in a site not prone to excessive winter wet. **Divide** perennials (*see p.395*) in early spring, or take softwood cuttings (*see p.394*) from late spring to midsummer. **Sow** seed in pots in a cold frame (*see pp.391–392*), of perennials in early spring and of biennials in early summer.

Oenothera macrocarpa
Z5 ‡6in (15cm) ↔ 20in (50cm), vigorous perennial with hairy, branching, red-tinted stems, flowers in late spring

OMPHALODES

Navelwort

SPRAYS OF BLUE OR WHITE FLOWERS, similar to those of forget-me-nots (*Myosotis, see p.287*) are produced in spring and summer. The flowers are held on long, wiry, upright stems, which look like tiny lights, particularly when they shine out in shade. This small group of annuals, biennials, and perennials, some evergreen or semievergreen, have a spreading habit that makes a good groundcover. Some are suitable for shady borders where the plant choice is limited; companions could include hostas (*see pp.260–261*), carexes (*p.345*), or *Arum italicum* 'Pictum' (*p.190*). The annual *O. linifolia* and *O. luciliae* (Z7b) prefer sun: grow them in a raised gravel bed or rock garden to enjoy the dainty flowers close up.

Cultivation Grow *O. cappodocica* and *O. verna* in moist, fertile soil in partial shade. *O. linifolia* and *O. luciliae* require sun and well-drained soil or gritty potting mix, which must be alkaline for the latter. **Sow** seed (*see pp.391–393*) in spring; annuals where they are to grow, and perennials in pots in a cold frame. **Divide** perennials (*see p.395*) in early spring. Prone to damage by slugs and snails (*see p.398*).

Oenothera fruticosa 'Fyrverkeri'
Z4 ‡12–36in (30–90cm) ↔ 12in (30cm), perennial or biennial, purple-brown flushed leaves, flowers from late spring to late summer

Oenothera speciosa 'Rosea'
Z6 ‡↔ 12in (30cm), spreading perennial, flowers from early summer to autumn, can be invasive, dislikes winter moisture

Omphalodes cappadocica 'Cherry Ingram'
Z7 ‡10in (25cm) ↔ 16in (40cm), evergreen perennial, flowers that are larger than those of the species, in early spring

OPHIOPOGON
Lilyturf

THE GRASSY LEAVES OF THESE PLANTS range in color
from an unusual shade of near-black to light green
with cream, yellow, or white margins. In summer,
they produce small clusters of bell-shaped, lilac, pink,
or white flowers, followed by glossy, round, blue or
black seedpods. Their unusual hues associate well
with many other plants, including small grasses (*see
pp.340–355*) such as *Lagarus ovatus*, brizas and
carexes. Blue fescue (*Festuca*) makes a striking
contrast to the dark 'Nigrescens'. Alternatively, use
as a groundcover plant. Although all are evergreen
perennials, they can be raised from seed as summer
bedding each year – the dark-leaved forms, planted
en masse, form a stark contrast to brighter bedding,
such as flame-colored begonias (*see p.196*).

Cultivation Grow in moist, but well-drained soil that is slightly
acidic, in full sun or partial shade. **Divide** plants in spring (*see p.395*)
as the new growth appears. **Sow** seed in containers in a cold frame
(*see pp.391–392*) as soon as it is ripe. Slugs (*see p.393*) can damage
young leaves.

ORIGANUM
Marjoram, Oregano

see also
p.91

BEST KNOWN AS CULINARY HERBS, marjorams have
eye-catching flowers, aromatic foliage, and varied
habits that make them useful and ornamental garden
plants. These perennials have tiny flowers that are
usually pink, surrounded by bracts (modified leaves)
which determine the dominant color, in shades of
purple, pink, or green. The justly popular *Origanum
laevigatum* 'Herrenhausen' has branched stems to
18in (45cm) tall, clothed with leaves that are flushed
purple when young, and dense clusters of flowers
with red-purple bracts. *O. marjorana* (Z7b), *O. onites*
(Z7), and *O. vulgare*, which has a gold-leaved form, are
the well-known culinary herbs. Grow marjorams in a
mixed or herbaceous border or herb garden, and
smaller species in a rock garden, as edging, or in
paving crevices.

Cultivation Grow in full sun in well-drained and, preferably,
alkaline soil. **Cut back** flowered stems in spring. **Divide** (*see p.395*)
or take cuttings (*see p.394*) in spring. **Sow** seed (*see pp.391–393*)
in pots in autumn or at 50–55°F (10–13°C) in spring.

Ophiopogon planiscapus 'Nigrescens'
Z6 ‡ 8in (20cm) ↔ 12in (15cm), purplish white flowers borne in
summer, followed by round, dark blue-black fruits

Ophiopogon jaburan 'Vittatus'
Z7b ‡ 24in (60cm) ↔ 12in (30cm), white, sometimes lilac-tinted
flowers in late summer and oblong, violet-blue fruits

① *laevigatum* Z5 ‡ 20–24in (50–60cm) ↔ 18in (45cm) woody-
based perennial ② *vulgare* Z3 ‡↔ 12–36in (30–90cm), woody-
based perennial

FLOWERING PLANTS

ORNITHOGALUM

Star-of-Bethlehem

GLISTENING, SILVERY WHITE FLOWERS that shine through the dusk of evening are the key charm of these bulbous perennials. The flowers are cup-, star-, or funnel-shaped, occasionally scented, and borne on sturdy stems in spring and summer. Each thick, long leaf curls attractively to a point, and some have a silver stripe down the center. Plants vary in height from *Ornithogalum lanceolatum* (Z6), which is only 2–4in (5–10cm) tall, to *O. pyramidale* (Z7), which can reach up to 48in (120cm). Smaller species are suitable for a rock garden. Both *O. nutans* and *O. umbellatum* (Z4) can be invasive; they are best naturalized in short grass or at the base of shrubs. Tender species can be grown in containers and moved under cover in winter.

Cultivation Plant hardy bulbs in autumn, 4in (10cm) deep in reasonably fertile, well-drained soil in full sun; some tolerate partial shade. Tender bulbs are best planted in spring, for summer flowers; keep frost-free over winter. On heavy clay soils, plant bulbs on a layer of coarse grit to improve drainage. **Lift** and separate offsets (*see p.395*) when the bulbs are dormant in summer.

OSTEOSPERMUM

BEGUILING DAISIES WITH A SATIN SHEEN and soft evergreen foliage make these plants worthy of any border. Several new cultivars are brought out each year in an ever-increasing range of colors. The petals are sometimes spoon-shaped and either white washed with a delicate shade of violet, pink, lilac, or blue, or saturated with a single hue, from cream or magenta to purple. The central boss of each flower has a contrasting tint. Osteospermums can bloom from late spring until autumn. They include annuals and subshrubs, but perennials are most commonly grown in borders. Where not hardy, grow as annuals. Osteospermums can get straggly after a few years but are easily increased from cuttings to replace old plants.

Cultivation Grow in light, moderately fertile, well-drained soil, in a warm, sheltered site in full sun. **Remove** fading flowers regularly. **Take** softwood cuttings in late spring and semiripe cuttings in late summer (*see p.394*). **Sow** seed at 64°F (18°C) in spring (*see pp.391–393*).

Osteospermum 'Nairobi Purple'
T min. 45°F (7°C) ‡6in (15cm) ↔ 36in (90cm), spreading subshrub, flowers flushed white beneath

① *narbonense* Z7b ‡12–36in (30–90cm), long leaves are gray-green, flowers in late spring and early summer ② *nutans* Z5 ‡8–24in (20–60cm), flowers borne in spring

Osteospermum 'Buttermilk'
T min. 45°F (7°C) ‡↔ 24in (60cm), upright subshrub, toothed mid-green leaves have pale yellow edges, flowers are bronze-yellow

Osteospermum jucundum
T min. 45°F (7°C) ‡4–20in (10–50cm) ↔ 20–36in (50–90cm), clumping perennial, flowers have bronze undersides

OXALIS
Shamrock, Sorrel

LOW CLUMPS OF PRETTY, CLOVERLIKE LEAVES provide a fine setting for these plants' small flowers. These appear in spring and summer, and may be funnel-, cup-, or bowl-shaped and tinted in shades of pink, yellow, and reddish purple. In cloudy weather, the flowers close up. Some oxalis are spreading weeds, and some of the ornamental types can also be invasive and are best planted in isolation. Bulbous perennials, these plants may spring from tubers, rhizomes, or true bulbs. Many oxalis thrive in the free-draining soil of a rock garden or in a container. Others, such as *Oxalis acetosella* (Z4) and *O. oregana* (Z7b) are happy in woodland or shady sites where they have plenty of space to spread.

Cultivation Woodland species need moist, humus-rich, fertile soil in sun or partial shade; hardy species need moderately fertile, humus-rich, well-drained soils in full sun. For plants in containers, use a soil-based potting mix with extra grit for good drainage. **Sow** seed at 55–64°F (13–18°C) in late winter or early spring (*see pp.391–393*). **Divide** plants (*see p.395*) in spring.

PACHYSANDRA

GOOD GROUNDCOVER PLANTS, these low, bushy perennials quickly spread to create an evergreen, or semievergreen, carpet of dark or gray-green foliage. These leaves are sometimes toothed and cluster at the tips of upright, fleshy stems. *Pachysandra terminalis* 'Variegata' has pleasing white leaf margins. In spring to early summer, pachysandras produce small spikes of greenish white female, and white male, flowers. These are easy plants to grow and look very much at home in shady areas or at the feet of flowering shrubs, for example rhododendrons (*see pp.104–107*) and camellias (*see pp.32–33*). Pachysandras spread particularly freely where the soil is moist and the conditions are humid.

Cultivation Any soil is suitable – except very dry soil – in full sun or partial shade. Soil enriched with plenty of organic matter is best. **Divide** established plants (*see p.395*) in spring or take softwood cuttings (*see p.394*) in early summer.

Osteospermum 'Whirlygig'
T min. 45°F (7°C) ‡↔ 24in (60cm), spreading subshrub, petals are slate or powder blue on reverse, flowers have slate blue central boss

Oxalis adenophylla
Z5 ‡ 4in (10cm) ↔ to 6in (15cm), true bulb, prefers sun and free-draining soil such as a raised bed or rock garden

Pachysandra terminalis
Z4 ‡ 8in (20cm) ↔ indefinite, evergreen, leaves to 4in (10cm) long, male flowers in early summer

PAEONIA
Peony

see also
p.92

↕↔ 14–40in
(34–110cm)

WITH THEIR SPECTACULAR BLOOMS and bold, lush foliage, the many herbaceous perennial peonies remain a classic choice for any border. The flowers open from large buds, usually in early summer, and vary from single cups, some with golden stamens, to showy doubles. They range in size from 2in (5cm) to an impressive 8in (20cm) or more. The large leaves of these clump-forming plants are usually blue-, gray-, or dark green, and deeply divided. Think carefully before you plant peonies – they are long-lived plants, and suffer if moved once they are established.

Cultivation Grow in fertile, moist but well-drained soil, and dig in well-rotted compost before you plant. Choose a position in full sun or partial shade. **Support** stems of peonies with very large flowers. **Take** root cuttings (*see p.394*) in winter or divide the tuberous roots in autumn or early spring (*see p 395*). **Peony wilt** may cause stems to blacken and flop: if a brown patch or gray, fuzzy fungal growth develops around the bases, cut affected stems back to healthy growth, beneath the soil if necessary.

RING STAKES
provide support for the huge flowers: simply let young stems grow up through the gaps.

Paeonia lactiflora 'Sarah Bernhardt'
Z4 ↕↔ 36–39in (90–100cm), vigorous, with mid-green leaves and erect stems, fragrant flowers are over 8in (20cm) across

Paeonia lactiflora 'Festiva Maxima'
Z4 ↕↔ 36–39in (90–100cm), abundant mid-green leaves, fragrant flowers on strong, erect stems are over 8in (20cm) across

Paeonia cambessedesii (Majorcan peony)
Z8 ↕↔ 18–22in (45–55cm), leaves are purple-red beneath with purple veins, flowers up to 4in (10cm) in mid- and late spring

Paeonia mlokosewitschii (Caucasian peony)
Z5 ↕↔ 26–36in (65–90m), erect stems, leaves hairy beneath, flowers up to 5in (13cm) in late spring and early summer

PAPAVER
Poppy

THESE COTTAGE-GARDEN FAVORITES are beloved by gardeners for their bright, papery, summer blooms. As well as the classic blood red, poppies come in glowing oranges, and more subtle pinks, yellows, and white; many are smudged black at the bases of their petals. Each flower is short lived, but is followed by many more, and later by striking, pepper-pot seedheads. The light to mid-green, often hairy or bristly, ferny leaves are very distinctive, even as seedlings. The flowers of annuals and biennials are generally more delicate than the bold, brash blooms of the perennial oriental poppies (all z3). Large poppies look good in any border; annuals thrive in a rock or gravel garden and self-seed freely.

Cultivation Grow in fertile, well-drained soil in full sun. **Sow** seed (*see pp.391–393*) in spring: annuals and biennials in situ; perennials in a cold frame. **Avoid** high-nitrogen fertilizers because they may cause flowers to fall early. **Cut back** oriental poppies after flowering for a second flush later in summer. **Divide** perennials (*see p.395*) in spring, or raise them from root cuttings (*see p.394*) in autumn and winter. **Mildew** (*see p.398*) may be troublesome in damp summers.

POPPY SEEDHEADS scatter their tiny seeds like pepper pots; they last well into winter and are excellent for drying.

Papaver orientale 'Cedric Morris'
‡18–36in (45–90cm) ↔ 24–36in (60–90cm), clumping perennial, hairy, gray leaves, 6in (16cm) flowers late spring to midsummer

Papaver rhoeas 'Mother of Pearl'
‡36in (90cm) ↔ 12in (30cm), annual, downy leaves, summer flowers in dove gray, pink, and lilac-blue

Papaver orientale 'Black and White'
‡18–36in (45–90cm) ↔ 24–36in (60–90cm), clumping perennial, bristly leaves, flowers late spring to midsummer

Papaver orientale 'Beauty of Livermere'
‡18–36in (45–90cm) ↔ 24–36in (60–90cm), clumping perennial, flowers to 8in (20cm) across in late spring to midsummer

Papaver rhoeas Shirley Series
‡36in (90cm) ↔ 12in (30cm), annual, downy leaves, single to double flowers in yellow, pink, orange, and red in summer

PELARGONIUM

Geranium, Flowering geranium

THESE POPULAR PLANTS ARE commonly called geraniums, but are quite different from the hardy geraniums or cranesbills (*see pp.250–251*). Geraniums have deservedly been garden favorites for many years. There is a huge range to choose from, with not only beautiful flowers but attractive, multicolored, and often fragrant leaves as well. Geraniums are generally used as bedding plants, or in hanging baskets and other containers, producing dense clusters of bright flowers from summer until autumn. Flower forms vary from the double, heavily frilled 'Apple Blossom Rosebud' to the delicate 'Bird Dancer', and colors range from orange to pink, red, or purple, in soft and restrained or bold and vivid shades. Most geraniums form upright, bushy plants with rounded or divided leaves, but there are also trailing forms (details of main types are given below). Geraniums are generally hardy to 36°F (2°C); some, particularly the scented-leaved types, may overwinter at the base of a warm wall in Zone 8.

Cultivation Grow in fertile, well-drained soil, or in a soil-based or soilless potting mix. Position most plants in full sun; zonal geraniums will tolerate some shade. **Deadhead** regularly. **Apply** a high-potassium fertilizer through the summer to encourage plenty of flowers. **Lift** the plants in autumn, and keep them almost dry in a frost-free place over winter. Cut back the top-growth by about one-third and repot the plants in late winter as growth begins. **Cuttings** can be taken in spring, summer, and autumn (*see p.394*), but these will need to be kept in a frost-free place over winter; alternatively young plants and plug plants (*see p.393*) are widely available in garden centers in early summer. **Sow** seed (*see pp.391–392*) with bottom heat in spring. Geraniums are generally trouble-free, but in pots they are susceptible to attack by black vine weevils (*see p.398*). If plants suffer from gray mold (botrytis), cut out all affected parts and discard.

Ivy-leaved geraniums

These trailing perennials make a spectacular show in containers such as windowboxes and hanging baskets, or even as small climbers, if tied into suitable supports. They have clusters of single or double flowers in shades of red, pink, mauve, and purple or white. As their name suggests, they resemble ivy in both their habit and in the shape of their stiff, fleshy, evergreen leaves 1–5in (2.5–13cm) long, which are lobed and occasionally pointed.

Scented-leaved geraniums

Plant these in containers where you can touch them easily so that the leaves release their scent, or along a path where you will brush against them. Each cultivar has its own delicious perfume, from sweet to spicy or citrus. These geraniums are grown mainly for their leaves, which are usually mid-green, occasionally variegated, ½–5in (1.5–13cm) long, and varying in shape. The flowers, in shades of mauve, pink, purple, and white, are usually not very large.

Regal geraniums

Bushy, evergreen, and usually grown under glass, these bear dense clusters of single or double flowers to 1½in (4cm) across, in red, pink, purple, orange, white, or reddish black, often with more than one shade. The rounded leaves are up to 3½in (9cm) long. Some plants become quite large and should be cut back in spring. Those described as unique types have larger leaves, sometimes divided and often scented; angel types have smaller leaves and flowers.

Zonal geraniums

The most popular of all the types, zonal geraniums are long-established favorites for patio containers, bedding, or house plants. They are bushy, evergreen perennials with short-jointed stems. The round leaves are marked with zones of dark bronze-green or maroon; those of fancy-leaved cultivars may be tricolored, with white or green, bronze, silver, and gold. The flowers are single to fully double, in white and many shades of orange, purple, pink, and scarlet.

① *Pelargonium* '**Alberta**' ‡20in (50cm) ↔ 10in (25cm), zonal ② '**Amethyst**' ‡12in (30cm) ↔ 10in (25cm), ivy-leaved ③ '**Ann Hoystead**' ‡18in (45cm) ↔ 10in (25cm), regal ④ '**Apple Blossom Rosebud**' ‡16in (40cm) ↔ 10in (25cm), zonal ⑤ '**Bird Dancer**' ‡8in (20cm) ↔ 6in (15cm), zonal ⑥ '**Caligula**' ‡5in (13cm) ↔ 4in (10cm), zonal ⑦ '**Clorinda**' ‡20in (50cm) ↔ 10in (25cm), cedar-scented leaves ⑧ '**Coddenham**' ‡5in (13cm) ↔ 4in (10cm), zonal ⑨ *crispum* '**Variegatum**' ‡8in

(20cm) ↔ 6in (15cm), lemon-scented leaves ⑩ **'Crystal Palace Gem'** ‡18in (45cm) ↔ 12in (30cm), zonal ⑪ **'Dale Queen'** ‡16in (40cm) ↔ 8in (20cm), zonal ⑫ **'Dolly Varden'** ‡12in (30cm) ↔ 6in (15cm), zonal ⑬ **'Fair Ellen'** ‡16in (40cm) ↔ 8in (20cm), spicy scented leaves ⑭ **'Flower of Spring'** ‡24in (60cm) ↔ 10in (25cm), zonal ⑮ **Fragrans Group** ‡10in (25cm) ↔ 8in (20cm), pine-scented leaves ⑯ **'Francis Parrett'** ‡5in (13cm) ↔ 4in (10cm), zonal ⑰ **'Freckles'** ‡↔ to 12in (30cm), zonal ⑱ **'Friesdorf'** ‡8in (20cm) ↔ 5in (13cm), zonal ⑲ **'Golden Wedding'** ‡↔ 24in (60cm), zonal ⑳ **'Graveolens'** ‡24in (60cm) ↔ 16in (40cm), lemon-rose-scented leaves ㉑ **'Happy Thought'** ‡18in (45cm) ↔ 10in (25cm), zonal ㉒ **'Irene'** ‡18in (45cm) ↔ 12in (30cm), zonal ㉓ **'Ivalo'** ‡12in (30cm) ↔ 10in (25cm), zonal ㉔ **'Lachskönigin'** ‡12in (30cm) ↔ 8in (20cm), ivy-leaved

㉕ *Pelargonium* 'Lady Plymouth' ‡16in (40cm) ↔ 8in (20cm), eucalyptus-scented leaves
㉖ 'Lavender Grand Slam' ‡16in (40cm) ↔ 8in (20cm), regal ㉗ 'L'Elégante' ‡10in (25cm) ↔ 8in (20cm), ivy-leaved ㉘ 'Lemon Fancy' ‡16in (40cm) ↔ 8in (20cm), citrus-scented leaves
㉙ 'Leslie Judd' ‡16in (40cm) ↔ 8in (20cm), regal ㉚ 'Mabel Grey' ‡14in (35cm) ↔ 6in (15cm), lemon-scented leaves ㉛ 'Madame Fournier' ‡5in (13cm) ↔ 4in (10cm), zonal

㉜ 'Mr. Everaarts' ‡8in (20cm) ↔ 5in (13cm), zonal ㉝ 'Mr. Henry Cox' ‡12in (30cm) ↔ 5in (13cm), zonal ㉞ 'Mrs. Pollock' ‡12in (30cm) ↔ 6in (15cm), zonal ㉟ 'Mrs. Quilter' ‡16in (40cm) ↔ 6in (15cm), zonal ㊱ Multibloom Series ‡↔ 12in (30cm), zonal ㊲ 'Old Spice' ‡12in (30cm) ↔ 6in (15cm), spicy-scented leaves ㊳ 'Orsett' ‡28in (70cm) ↔ 20in (50cm), spicy mint-scented leaves ㊴ 'Paton's Unique' ‡18in70 (45cm) ↔ 8in (20cm), unique ㊵ 'Paul Humphries' ‡12in (30cm)

↔ 8in (20cm), zonal ④ 'Pixie Rose' ‡12in (30cm) ↔ 8in (20cm), zonal ④ 'Polka' ‡20in (50cm) ↔ 10in (25cm), unique ④ 'Purple Emperor' ‡16in (40cm) ↔ 8in (20cm), regal ④ 'Robe' ‡18in (45cm) ↔ 8in (20cm), zonal ④ 'Rollisson's Unique' ‡18in (45cm) ↔ 8in (20cm), unique ④ 'Rouletta' ‡24in (60cm) ↔ 8in (20cm), ivy-leaved ④ 'Royal Oak' ‡16in (40cm) ↔ 12in (30cm), spicy-scented leaves ④ 'Schöne Helena' ‡16in (40cm) ↔ 10in (25cm), zonal ④ 'Sefton' ‡16in

(40cm) ↔ 8in (20cm), regal ⑤ 'Strawberry Sundae' ‡24in (60cm) ↔ 12in (30cm), regal ⑤ 'The Boar' ‡24in (60cm) ↔ 10in (25cm), trailing ⑤ 'Timothy Clifford' ‡5in (13cm) ↔ 4in (10cm), zonal ⑤ 'Tip Top Duet' ‡16in (40cm) ↔ 8in (20cm), angel ⑤ *tomentosum* ‡36in (90cm) ↔ 30in (75cm), peppermint-scented leaves ⑤ Tornado Series ‡10in (25cm) ↔ 8in (20cm), ivy-leaved

FLOWERING PLANTS

THESE FLAMBOYANT PLANTS bring color to the garden from midsummer, often lasting until the first frosts. Upright spires produce a continuous succession of tubular flowers, similar to foxgloves, in rich hues of purple, scarlet, pink, yellow, and white; many are bicolored. This is a large group of mostly evergreen, bushy but neat perennials. They range from dwarf kinds around 6in (15cm) tall, that are suitable for rock gardens, to taller border plants of 24in (60cm) or more; these may need staking (*see below and p.390*). The leaves may be narrow and up to 3in (8cm) long or oval, from 5in (13cm) long.

Cultivation Border penstemons like fertile, well-drained soil in full sun or partial shade; dwarf and shrubby species need gritty, sharply drained, poor to moderate soil. **Protect** plants with a dry mulch in winter in frost-prone areas. **Deadhead** unless seed is needed. **Sow** seed (*see pp.391–393*) in late winter or spring at 55–64°F (13–18°C). **Take** softwood cuttings in early summer or semiripe cuttings in midsummer (*see p.394*). **Divide** plants (*see p.395*) in spring.

Penstemon 'Chester Scarlet'
Z6 ↕24in (60cm) ↔ 18in (45cm), large leaves and flowers 2–3in (5–8cm) long from midsummer to midautumn

SUPPORTING CLUMPS
Put stake and twine or metal supports in place before penstemons grow too tall so that they can develop a natural habit.

Penstemon 'Apple Blossom'
Z5 ↕↔ 18–24in (45–60cm), narrow leaves, white-throated flowers from midsummer to early or midautumn

Penstemon 'Evelyn'
Z7 ↕18–24in (45–60cm) ↔ 12in (30cm), bushy, narrow leaves, flowers 1–1¼in (2.5–3cm), midsummer to midautumn

Penstemon 'Stapleford Gem'
Z7 ↕to 24in (60cm) ↔ 18in (45cm), large leaves, flowers 2–3in (5–8cm) long from midsummer to early autumn

Penstemon 'Pennington Gem'
Z7 ‡ to 30in (75cm) ↔ 18in (45cm), narrow leaves, flowers 2–3in
(5–8cm) long from midsummer to early or midautumn

PERSICARIA
Fleeceflower

SHORT, BOTTLEBRUSH BLOOMS – made of tiny pink, white, or red, funnel- or bell-shaped flowers that cluster tightly on wiry stems appear from summer to autumn. Persicarias also have pleasing foliage: with broad, long-stalked leaves at the base and smaller leaves clothing the fleshy stems. Many of these clump-forming perennials and annuals spread by means of creeping stems and can become invasive, but they are easily kept under control if necessary. Ranging in height from 2in (5cm) to 4ft (1.2m), most are medium sized and make an undemanding, weed-suppressing groundcover. Grow persicarias with phygelius (*see p.95*), and perennials like hardy geraniums (*see pp.250–251*) and monardas (*see p.287*). Contact with all parts may irritate skin.

Cultivation Any moist soil in full sun or partial shade suits this plant; the best flower color is obtained in full sun. *Persicaria bistorta* tolerates dry soil. **Sow** seed (*see pp.391–393*) in a container in a cold frame in spring. **Divide** perennials in spring or autumn (*see p.395*).

PETRORHAGIA

CLOSELY RELATED TO GYPSOPHILA (*see p.254*) and dianthus (*see pp.226–227*), these perennials and annuals are grown for their clusters of white, or occasionally pink or yellow, flowers that are borne all through summer. The delicate flowers are held on the tips of wiry stems above grassy leaves. Petrorhagias are best grown in a sunny position at the front of a mixed or herbaceous border, on a sunny bank, or against a wall. You could also grow them in a rock garden with other low alpines, such as dianthus and saxifrages (*see pp.320–321*). Try planting petrorhagias in an alpine trough where the stems and flowers can be allowed to spill out and soften the trough's hard edges.

Cultivation Petrorhagias thrive in any poor to reasonably fertile, well-drained soil in full sun. **Sow** seed (*see pp.391–393*) in a container in a cold frame in autumn. **Take** stem-tip cuttings (*see p.394*) in early summer. Slugs and snails (*see p.398*) can be a problem.

Petrorhagia saxifraga (Tunic flower)
Z5 ‡ 4in (10cm) ↔ 8in (20cm), mat-forming perennial, long-lasting white or pink flowers – ½in (1cm) across – in summer

Persicaria bistorta 'Superba' (Bistort)
Z4 ‡ to 36in (90cm) ↔ 18in (45cm), semievergreen, mat-forming perennial, autumn leaves brown, flowers over long period

Penstemon 'White Bedder'
Z7 ‡ 24in (60cm) ↔ 18in (45cm), large leaves, flowers become tinged pink as they age, from midsummer to midautumn

FLOWERING PLANTS

PETUNIA

STAPLE BEDDING AND CONTAINER PLANTS, petunias are prized for their showy, velvety flowers borne from late spring to late autumn. They may be single or double, and often brightly veined or striped with a contrasting color; the choice of forms increases every year. There are two groups: Grandiflora types have large flowers up to 4in (10cm) across and include the Surfinias and others that are less weather-resistant. The bushier, and often more resilient, Multifloras bear masses of smaller blooms, to 2in (5cm) across. Trailing petunias are perfect for hanging baskets. Use Multifloras to carpet large beds or borders. Petunia leaves and stems are sticky and hairy. Many petunias are perennial, but most are grown as annuals. They may survive winters in the mildest parts of Zone 8.

Cultivation Petunias enjoy light, well-drained soil or potting mix in full sun. Feed plants in containers with a tomato fertilizer every 10–14 days. **Deadhead** regularly (see p.390) to keep them in bloom. **Sow** seed (see pp.391–393) at 55–64°F (13–18°C) in autumn or mid-spring, or root softwood cuttings (see p.394) in summer. Overwinter seedlings under cover; plant out when all danger of frost has passed.

① **Surfinia Purple** ‡9–16in (23–40cm) ↔ 12–36in (30–90cm)
② **Surfinia White** ‡9–16in (23–40cm) ↔ 12–36in (30–90cm), both, although Grandifloras, tolerate wet weather without damage

PHLOMIS

see also
p.94

THE HERBACEOUS PERENNIAL phlomis are good year-round plants. Although the silvery or gray-green, sage-like leaves die down in winter, the attractive seedheads remain to provide interest through the barest months. In spring, white-woolly young shoots emerge, to form an erect or spreading clump of foliage. Clusters of hooded flowers, somewhat like the dead nettle (*Lamium, see p.269*), are borne on tall stems in summer, and are usually white, dusty pink, or soft yellow. Phlomis is a very good choice of plant for hot, dry areas – for example, beside a patio or in a gravel garden – because their hairy leaves help them to retain moisture. They are also lovely planted in groups to form softly colored mounds in a warm, sunny border. There are also shrubby types of phlomis.

Cultivation Grow in any fertile, well-drained soil in full sun, although *Phlomis russeliana* and *P. samia* will tolerate some shade. **Sow** seed (see pp.391–393) at 55–64°F (13–18°C) in spring. **Divide** (see p.395) large clumps, ideally in spring, but also in autumn.

Phlomis russeliana
Z5 ‡36in (90cm) ↔ 30in (75cm), upright, hairy leaves up to 8in (20cm) long, flowers from late spring to early autumn

PHLOX

PHLOXES ARE TREASURED for their flat, blue, milky-to bright pink, or red flowers, which are borne in fat clusters at the tips of tall stems. They are a diverse group that include spreading to erect, evergreen and herbaceous perennials, and some annuals. Spring-flowering, dwarf varieties, such as *Phlox subulata*, are perfect in a rock garden; early summer-flowering plants, such as 'Chattahoochee', prefer a woodland area, where their pale flowers seem to glow in the shade. Tall, midsummer-flowering phloxes, such as perennial *P. maculata* or *P. paniculata*, make a colorful addition to a sunny border. Annual bedding phloxes (forms of *P. drummondii*) flower from late spring to autumn.

Cultivation Perennial border phloxes prefer well-drained soil in sun or partial shade; annuals and rock garden types need well-drained soil in full sun. Woodland phloxes such as *P. divaricata* require moist soil and shade. **Deadhead** (see p.390) *P. maculata* and *P. paniculata* regularly. **Sow** seed (see pp.391–393) of annuals at 55–64°F (13–18°C) in spring; that of perennials in containers in a cold frame when ripe, or in spring. **Divide** (see p.395) tall plants in spring or in autumn, or take root cuttings (see p.394) in autumn or winter.

Phlox divaricata 'Chattahoochee'
Z4 ‡6in (15cm) ↔ 12in (30cm), short-lived, semievergreen perennial, prostrate, purplish leaves, flowers summer and early autumn

Phlox 'Kelly's Eye'
Z5b ‡4in (10cm) ↔ 12in (30cm), evergreen, mounding perennial, long narrow leaves, flowers in late spring to early summer

Phlox maculata 'Omega'
Z3b ‡36in (90cm) ↔ 18in (45cm), herbaceous perennial, fragrant flowers in early and midsummer

Phlox paniculata 'Graf Zeppelin'
Z3 ‡4ft (1.2m) ↔ 24–39in (60–100cm), herbaceous perennial, ideal for a border, scented flowers summer to midautumn

THINNING SHOOTS
Pinch out one-third of the shoots at the base to reduce congestion and the chance of powdery mildew, and ensure strong, healthy growth.

Phlox paniculata 'Harlequin'
‡4ft (1.2m) ↔ 24–39in (60–100cm), herbaceous perennial, ideal for border, fragrant flowers from summer to midautumn

Phlox paniculata 'Windsor'
Z3 ‡4ft (1.2m) ↔ 24–39in (60–100cm), herbaceous perennial, ideal for a border, flowers from summer to midautumn

Phlox subulata 'Liliacina'
Z3 ‡2–6in (5–15cm) ↔ 20in (50cm), dense, mat-forming, evergreen perennial, flowers in late spring and early summer

PHUOPSIS STYLOSA

PHYSALIS
Ground cherry

PHYSOSTEGIA
Obedient plant

THIS IS A MAT-FORMING PERENNIAL with slender, branching stems bearing clusters of up to eight narrow, pointed leaves that have a musky fragrance. Over many months in summer, it produces a profusion of round heads of tiny, pink flowers at the tips of the stems. These are delicately scented. Phuopsis spreads by rooting stems and makes a good ground-cover plant at the front of a border or on a sunny bank. You could also try it in a rock garden with other alpines such as phloxes (*see p.306*) and saponarias (*see p.319*).

‡24–30in (60–75cm)
↔ 36in (90cm)

WITH THEIR STRIKING SEEDHEADS, this group of upright, bushy annuals and perennials bring welcome color to the garden in autumn. Clusters of tiny, white or cream flowers appear in the summer, but it is the seedheads that give these plants their impact. Vivid orange or scarlet, papery lanterns, or calyces, enclose bright red, gold, or purple berries. These lanterns retain their color well when dried for decorative use or they may be left on the plant through winter to decay into skeletons, revealing the berries inside. The leaves often have silvery hairs. Physalis can be invasive in rich soils.

VALUABLE IN THE LATE-SUMMER BORDER, the upright, herbaceous perennials in this group form dense clumps. Their flower spikes rise up in midsummer, crowded with almost stalkless blooms in shades of pink, lilac-pink, magenta-pink, or white. The flowers usually face in one of two directions; if they are moved on the stalks, the flowers remain in their new position, earning them the name of obedient plant. Like deadnettles (*Lamium, see p.269*), to which they are related, physostegias have square stems. The variably shaped leaves often have toothed edges. Physostegias spread by underground stems (rhizomes) and can be invasive in rich soils, but are well behaved in poor soils. Combine them with perennials such as phlomis (*see p.306*) and persicarias (*see p.305*). They are also good for cutting.

Cultivation This plant needs reasonably fertile, moist but well-drained soil, in full sun or partial shade. **Cut back** the top-growth after flowering to maintain a compact habit. **Sow** seed (*see pp.391–393*) in a container in an open cold frame in autumn. **Divide** established plants (*see p.395*) or take stem-tip cuttings (*see p.394*) from spring until early summer.

Cultivation Any well-drained soil in full sun or partial shade will suit these plants. **Cut** stems for drying as the calyces begin to color. **Sow** seed (*see pp.391–393*) of perennials in containers in a cold frame in spring; sow seed of annuals where they are to grow in midspring. **Divide** perennials (*see p.395*) in spring.

Cultivation Moderately fertile soil that is reliably moist, in full sun or partial shade, suits these plants. **Sow** seed (*see pp.391–393*) in a container in a cold frame in autumn. **Divide** plants (*see p.395*) in winter or early spring before growth starts.

Phuopsis stylosa
Z6 ‡6in (15cm) ↔ 20in (50cm) or more, individual flowers are ½–¾in (1.5–2cm) long

Physalis alkekengi (Chinese lantern, Japanese lantern)
Z4 ‡24–30in (60–75cm) ↔ 36in (90cm) or more, vigorous perennial, spreads by underground stems, lanterns 2in (5cm) across

Physostegia virginiana 'Vivid'
Z3b ‡12–24in (30–60cm) ↔ 12in (30cm), toothed leaves to 5in (13cm) long, flowers from midsummer to early autumn

PLATYCODON GRANDIFLORUS
Balloon flower

LARGE BUDS LIKE MINIATURE BALLOONS give this plant its common name. The several cultivated forms of this perennial are grown for the pretty flowers borne in late summer, in blue, lilac-purple, pale pink, or white. The balloon flower varies in habit but most form neat, compact clumps with toothed, blue-green leaves. These are lovely plants for a large rock garden or a border, and are also good for cutting. Try them with other herbaceous perennials, such as achilleas (*see p.167*), physostegias (*see left*), and lythrums (*see p.283*). Once they are well-established, the plants should not be moved because they do not recover well if their roots are disturbed.

Cultivation The balloon flower prefers deep, fertile, well-drained but reliably moist soil, in full sun or partial shade. **Support** the stems if necessary in exposed positions (*see p.390*). **Sow** seed (*see pp.391–393*) in pots in a cold frame in spring. **Divide** plants (*see p.395*) in summer. You can also try removing shoots that have rooted at the base in early summer and using them as cuttings (*see p.394*).

POLEMONIUM
Jacob's ladder

NAMED FOR THEIR DISTINCTIVE LEAVES, these mostly clump-forming annuals and perennials are favorites in cottage gardens. The leaves are composed of many paired leaflets, which resemble the rungs of a ladder, and are produced in rosettes, from which spring erect stems. The cup-, bell-, or saucer-shaped flowers are borne in spring and summer and are either solitary or held in small clusters at the stem tips. Usually blue or white, they can be purple, pink, or yellow. Taller species look good in a mixed or herbaceous border, with other spring- or summer-flowering perennials such as aquilegias (*see p.185*) or tradescantias (*see p.331*), while small ones look best in a rock garden. *Polemonium caeruleum* can be naturalized in grass in a wildflower garden.

Cultivation Taller species thrive in any well-drained but moist soil in full sun or partial shade. Small species prefer very gritty, sharply drained soil in full sun. **Deadhead** regularly to prolong flowering. **Sow** seed (*see pp.391–393*) in a container in a cold frame in autumn or spring. **Divide** plants (*see p.395*) in spring.

Polemonium 'Lambrook Mauve'
Z3b ‡↔ 18in (45cm), rounded mounds of neat leaves, free-flowering in late spring and early summer

Platycodon grandiflorus
Z3b ‡ to 24in (60cm) ↔ 12in (30cm), compact clump, flowers to 2in (5cm) across

Polemonium caeruleum (Greek valerian, Jacob's ladder)
Z3b ‡ 12–36in (30–90cm) ↔ 12in (30cm), leaves 16in (40cm) long, flowers, rarely white, in early summer

Polemonium pauciflorum
Z6 ‡↔ to 20in (50cm) short-lived, leaves to 6in (15cm) long, red-tinted flowers single or in clusters early to late summer

POLYGALA

Milkwort, Seneca, Snakeroot

BY FAR THE MOST WIDELY GROWN in gardens are the tiny rock polygalas, with their rich flower colors. *Polygala calcarea* (Z7b) and its varieties flower in particularly distinctive marine blues; use them to create pools of color over pale stone chips or, for a more unusual effect, dark slate or colored glass pebbles. Commonly known as milkwort, this species was once used in herbal tonics for nursing mothers. *P. chamaebuxus* flowers in a mix of yellows; it also has white and bicolored forms. Both these polygalas are evergreen, with small, leathery leaves, and flower in late spring and early summer. Grow them in a rock garden, or in an alpine trough or sink garden.

Cultivation Grow in moist but well-drained soil in full sun or dappled shade. In containers, use a soilless multipurpose medium, and top-dress with a layer of grit. **Sow** seed in containers in a cold frame in autumn (*see pp.391–392*). **Take** softwood cuttings in early summer or semi-ripe cuttings in mid- to late summer (*see p.394*).

Polygala chamaebuxus var. grandiflora
Z7 ‡2–6in (5–15cm) ↔ 12in (30cm), spreading evergreen, purple "wings" are plain yellow in the species

POLYGONATUM

Solomon's seal

ARCHING, LEAFY STEMS dripping with pendent flowers are the defining characteristic of most Solomon's seals – vigorous, clump-forming perennials with creeping, fleshy roots that thrive in shade. With their drooping habit, even the tallest ones have a shy look that is perfect for a woodland garden. The bell-shaped, subtly fragrant flowers that hang from the stems in spring and early summer are creamy white or sometimes pink, with green markings, and are followed by red or black berries. Plant Solomon's seal among shrubs or beneath trees, or use them in pots on a shady patio to create a lush, textural display together with hostas (*see pp.260–261*) and ferns (*see pp.356–365*).

Cultivation Grow in moist soil or soil-based potting mix enriched with well-rotted compost, in deep or partial shade. **Divide** large species (*see p.395*) as growth begins in spring, but take care not to damage brittle young shoots. **Sow** seed in containers in a cold frame in autumn (*see pp.391–393*).

Polygonatum hirtum
Z4b ‡4ft (1.2m) ↔ 24in (60cm), erect zigzag stems, flowers from late spring to midsummer, blue-black berries

DEEP PLANTING
Deep, humus-rich soil suits these plants best; plant them with the top of the rootball a little below the surface.

Polygonatum hookeri
Z5 ‡4in (10cm) ↔ 12in (30cm), small, creeping perennial, flowers in late spring and early summer, needs rich soil

Polygonatum × hybridum 'Striatum'
Z4 ‡36in (90cm) ↔ 10in (25cm), brightens dark areas, flowers in late spring, the berries that follow are black

POTENTILLA

Cinquefoil

see also
p.99

CINQUEFOIL IS A REFERENCE to the five-petaled flowers. The heavily veined foliage of these herbaceous perennials is very reminiscent of the foliage of strawberry plants. These plants are valued both for their brightly colored flowers and mid- to dark green foliage. Their saucer-shaped, single or double blooms are borne throughout summer and into early autumn. The smaller types suit a rock garden, while the taller, clump-forming potentillas are popular choices for beds, borders, and cottage gardens. When planted with other late-flowering favorites such as asters (*see pp.392–393*) and chrysanthemums (*see pp.212–213*), they continue to warm up the fading garden into autumn with fiery shades of blood red, burnt orange, and golden-yellow.

Cultivation Grow in full sun and well-drained soil; flowering is better on poorer soils. **Divide** (*see p.395*) in autumn or spring. **Sow** seed in containers in a cold frame in autumn or spring (*see pp.391–392*).

Potentilla 'Monsieur Rouillard'
Z3b ‡18in (45cm) ↔ 24in (60cm), bears semidouble, satin-petaled flowers from early to late summer

Polygonatum stewartianum
Z6b ‡8–36in (20–90cm) ↔ 10in (25cm), flowers from late spring to midsummer, followed by red berries with white spots

Potentilla 'Gibson's Scarlet'
Z3b ‡18in (45cm) ↔ 24in (60cm), extremely popular, flowers to 1¼in (3cm) across from early to late summer

Potentilla megalantha
Z4 ‡6–12in (15–30cm) ↔ 6in (15cm), widely available, hairy leaves, flowers from mid- to late summer

FLOWERING PLANTS

PRIMULA
Primrose

THERE IS A PRIMULA FOR ALMOST EVERY LOCATION in the garden. This diverse group of herbaceous perennials grows naturally in a wide range of habitats from boggy marshes to woodland and alpine areas, and most primulas are long-flowering and easy to grow. Many bloom in early spring and early summer, although a few flower in late winter onward. Their delicate clusters of flowers come in an appealing range of colors from deep purple and maroon through to pink, scarlet, and several shades of yellow, cream, and white. Occasionally the flowers, stems, and foliage are covered with a white or yellow meal, or "farina." Garden primulas are divided into three groups: candelabra, auricula, and polyanthus (*see below*), although these groups do not include all species. Polyanthus types are easiest to grow. Compact varieties make a bright display in containers, while more robust ones are suitable for the herbaceous border or cottage garden, or can be naturalized in lawns. Many primulas enjoy the dappled shade of the woodland edge and work well planted with other woodland plants, such as lilies (*see pp.274–275*) and trilliums (*see p.332*). Water-loving candelabras thrive in bog gardens or on the banks of streams and ponds. Primulas shown here are hardy to Zones 3–5, except where noted.

Cultivation Grow primulas in full sun or partial shade, for the most part in moisture-retentive soil. **Dig in** plenty of well-rotted organic matter (such as leaf mold, manure, or garden compost) before planting. Mix coarse grit into the soil or compost before planting alpine species, since these require sharp drainage. **Water** plants well in dry weather. **Deadhead** the flowers as they fade to prevent unwanted self-seeding, or allow seedheads to develop to collect your own seed. **Sow** seed as soon as it is ripe (*see pp.391–392*). Scatter those of hardy species on the soil's surface in pots or trays and place in a cold frame. **Divide** hybrids and cultivars, which will not come true from seed, between autumn and spring (*see p.395*). Black vine weevil grubs (*see p.398*) may eat roots, especially in pots.

Candelabra primulas

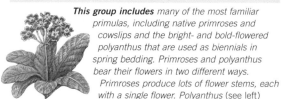

These grow best in moist soil in a shady glade or at the edge of a pond. Robust perennials, they produce their rings of flowers, in many different colors, all the way up their sturdy stems. Candelabra primulas are deciduous and die back in autumn. Once established, plants will freely scatter their seed, which germinates quite easily and eventually make a large and colorful colony. Unwanted seedlings are easy to control by weeding, or can be transplanted in spring to other parts of the garden.

Auricula primulas

The beautiful markings and colorings of many auriculas are a result of several hundred years of selection by enthusiasts. Developed originally for showing, these evergreen primulas, with rather leathery leaves, have been highly bred. Show types need the protection of an alpine house, as do many alpine auriculas, although these will also thrive in rock gardens. Those classed as border auriculas are the ones to choose for general garden cultivation. They particularly suit rock garden plantings and can look good in troughs.

Polyanthus group

This group includes many of the most familiar primulas, including native primroses and cowslips and the bright- and bold-flowered polyanthus that are used as biennials in spring bedding. Primroses and polyanthus bear their flowers in two different ways. Primroses produce lots of flower stems, each with a single flower. Polyanthus (see left) have one central, sturdy stem topped by a cluster of flowers. When grown together in the garden, the two types will freely hybridize and may produce unique seedlings.

① *Primula* 'Adrian' ‡1ft (30cm) ↔ 10in (25cm), alpine auricula ② *allionii* ‡4in (10cm) ↔ 8in (20cm), evergreen, flowers late winter ③ *auricula* var. *albocincta* ‡8in (20cm) ↔ 10in (25cm), evergreen ④ *auricula* 'Blairside Yellow' ‡20in (50cm) ↔ 1ft (30cm), border auricula ⑤ *auricula* 'Orb' ‡6in (15cm) ↔ 10in (25cm), show auricula ⑥ *beesiana* ‡↔ 2ft (60cm), candelabra ⑦ 'Buckland Wine' ‡4in (10cm) ↔ 10in (25cm), polyanthus ⑧ *bulleyana* Z5–8 H8–5 ‡↔ 2ft

(60cm), candelabra ⑨ **Crescendo Series**, ↕↔6in (15cm), annual ⑩ *denticulata* var. *alba* ↔ 18in (45cm), drumstick ⑪ *elatior* ↕1ft (30cm) ↔ 10in (25cm), evergreen, suits woodland ⑫ *flaccida* ↕20in (50cm) ↔ 1ft (30cm) ⑬ *florindae* Z3–8 H8–1 ↕4ft (1.2m) ↔ 3ft (1m), fragrant cowslip, for bogs and streams ⑭ *frondosa* ↕6in (15cm) ↔ 10in (25cm) ⑮ **Gold-laced Group** ↕10in (25cm) ↔ 1ft (30cm), polyanthus ⑯ **'Guinevere'** ↕5in (13cm) ↔ 10in (25cm), polyanthus ⑰ **'Inverewe'** ↕↔2ft

(60cm), semievergreen, candelabra ⑱ *marginata* **'Linda Pope'** ↕6in (15cm) ↔ 1ft (30cm), evergreen ⑲ *prolifera* ↕↔ 2ft (60cm), candelabra, moist shade ⑳ *rosea* Z3–8 H8–1 ↕↔ 8in (20cm) ㉑ *veris* ↕↔ 10in (25cm), evergreen, fragrant cowslip ㉒ *vialii* ↕2ft (60cm) ↔ 1ft (30cm), moist shade ㉓ *vulgaris* subsp. *sibthorpii* ↕8in (20cm) → 14in (35cm), suits woodland ㉔ **'Wanda'** ↕6in (15cm) ↔ 16in (40cm), evergreen, long-flowering

PULMONARIA
Lungwort

‡6–18in (15–45cm)
↔18–36in (45–90cm)

OFTEN HANDSOMELY SPOTTED in silver or white, the deciduous or evergreen leaves were said in medieval times to resemble lung tissue and were used in remedies for chest complaints. Today, pulmonarias are invaluable as groundcover that spreads slowly by underground stems (rhizomes). Pulmonaria flowers are a welcome sight in the late-winter garden, and the display continues until late spring or early summer. The delicate blooms may be blue, pink, red, or white and are held above the foliage in small clusters; they attract bees into the garden. Show off the flowers beneath deciduous trees and shrubs or with bulbs for a jeweled carpet in spring. The Canadian hardiness zone ranges from 4–6.

Cultivation Grow in moist, but not wet, humus-rich soil in full or dappled shade; *Pulmonaria officinalis* tolerates sun. **Cut back** after flowering to promote new foliage. **Divide** (*see p.395*) every three to five years to keep plants healthy. **Sow** seed (*see pp.391–393*) outdoors when ripe. **Powdery mildew** may spoil leaves in dry weather.

PULSATILLA

AMONG THE MOST BEAUTIFUL of perennial alpine plants, pulsatillas have fine, ferny foliage, large, silky flowers, and round, fluffy seedheads. The leaves, buds, and petals are often covered with soft, silvery down. In spring and early summer, blooms appear in white or shades of yellow, pink, and purple – usually with a large, central boss of golden stamens. As the seedheads develop, the flower stems grow even taller. Pulsatillas form clumps in a rock garden or at the front of a border, if you have well-drained soil. Grow them with other spring-flowering plants such as aubrietas (*see p.195*) or scillas (*see p.323*). In areas with heavy soil, it is best to grow pulsatillas in containers so they can enjoy free-draining soil and be moved easily to a position sheltered from the worst of the winter snow and rain.

Cultivation Pulsatillas prefer fertile, very well-drained, sandy soil in full sun. They resent being disturbed; plant them out while they are young and site them carefully so they do not have to be moved. **Sow** seed (*see pp.391–393*) as soon as it is ripe in a cold frame. **Take** root cuttings (*see p.394*) in winter.

Pulsatilla halleri
Z3 ‡8in (20cm) ↔ 6in (15cm), violet-purple to lavender-blue flowers that are 3½in (9cm) across in late spring

① 'Lewis Palmer' ‡↔ 16in (40cm) ② *rubra* 'Redstart' ‡16in (40cm) ↔ 36in (90cm) ③ *saccharata* ‡12in (30cm) ↔ 24in (60cm) ④ 'Sissinghurst White' ‡↔ 16in (40cm)

Pulsatilla vernalis
Z4 ‡↔ 4in (10cm), semievergreen, flowers to 2½in (6cm) across, requires sharp drainage and protection from winter moisture

Pulsatilla vulgaris (Pasque flower)
Z3 ‡4–8in (10–20cm) ↔ 8in (20cm), young leaves hairy, pale to deep purple flowers 2½–4½in (4–9cm) across, rarely white, in spring

PUSCHKINIA SCILLOIDES

THIS LITTLE BULB'S FLOWER looks very much like a snowdrop, with each delicate white, or very pale blue, petal marked with a thin, dark blue stripe. The blooms are borne in thick spikes on arching stems in spring. Each bulb has two leaves. *Puschkinia* var. *libanotica* (Z4) has smaller, pure white flowers. Puschkinias spread freely in a rock garden or can be used for a pretty display beneath deciduous trees and shrubs before the leaf cover becomes too dense. They are easily naturalized in short grass with other bulbs for a colorful carpet in spring. In common with other rock-garden or alpine plants, puschkinias can be successfully grown in containers; they enjoy the well-drained conditions, especially while they are dormant.

Cultivation This plant likes any well-drained soil in full sun or dappled shade. **Sow** seed (*see pp.391–393*) in a container in a cold frame in spring or autumn; seedlings may take 2–3 years to reach flowering size. **Divide** clumps of bulbs (*see p.395*) as leaves die down in summer.

RANUNCULUS
Buttercup, Crowfoot

THERE ARE HUNDREDS OF TYPES of buttercup – some are annuals and biennials – but herbaceous perennials are by far the most common; some are evergreen. They are variable in habit, with widely ranging needs, so there should be one suited to any spot in the garden. Buttercups all bear cupped flowers, with bold central stamens, in spring, summer, or occasionally in autumn. They are mainly golden yellow, but white, pink, orange, or scarlet varieties are available.

Cultivation Buttercups have a wide range of cultivation requirements. **Most species** are fine in fertile, moist but well-drained soil, in sun or semishade. **Woodland** buttercups, which often have bronze-tinted leaves, need rich, moist soil in shade. **Alpine** plants are small, with relatively large flowers, and require full sun and sandy, sharply drained soil, as do many of the tuberous buttercups. **Aquatic** or bog plants are often tall and have lots of lush, bright green leaves. They need wet soil at the edge of a stream or pond. **Sow** seed (*see pp.392–393*) of most buttercups in a container in a cold frame as soon as it is ripe. Alpine seed is best sown while it is unripe; its germination can be erratic and may take several years. **Divide** (*see p.395*) all but alpines, in spring or autumn.

Ranunculus ficaria var. *albus* (Lesser celandine)
Z5 ‡2in (5cm) ↔ 8in (20cm), woodland type, early-spring flowers fade from pale yellow to white, may spread rapidly

Puschkinia scilloides
Z4 ‡8in (20cm) ↔ 2in (5cm), larger clumps will quickly form

Ranunculus aconitifolius 'Flore Pleno' (Fair maids of France, White bachelor's buttons) Z5 ‡24in (60cm) ↔ 18in (45cm), flowers late spring and early summer

Ranunculus ficaria 'Brazen Hussy' (Lesser celandine)
Z5 ‡2in (5cm) ↔ 12in (30cm), woodland type, flowers are bronzed underneath and borne in early spring, may spread rapidly

RHEUM
Rhubarb

‡4–8ft (1.2–2.5m)
↔ 2–6ft (60cm–2m)

THESE IMPRESSIVE, clump-forming perennials have bold, handsome foliage and feathery flower plumes. The huge, rounded leaves, which are up to 36in (90cm) across, often emerge crimson-purple from bright red buds in spring. They mature to a glossy, dark green but often retain a scarlet flush, especially on the undersides. In summer, large plumes of tiny pink, pale green, or cream flowers are held above the foliage on thick, hollow stems. Rheums revel in moist conditions: use them to create a lush display by a stream or pond, in damp borders or in woodland gardens. Although this group includes edible rhubarb, the leaves of both edible and ornamental varieties are toxic if eaten.

Cultivation Rheums need deep, damp soil that has been enriched with organic matter, in sun or shade. **Mulch** (*see p.388*) in spring to retain moisture. **Sow** seed (*see pp.391–393*) in pots in a cold frame in autumn. **Divide** the large, woody rhizomes (*see p.395*) in early spring.

Rheum palmatum 'Atrosanguineum'
Z4 ‡ 8ft (2.5m) ↔ 6ft (2m), plumes of flowers up to 6ft (2m) tall in early summer

RHODIOLA

AS LONG AS THEY ARE GROWN in full sun, these perennials will thrive and are useful for bringing subtle color and texture into a rock or gravel garden, or to the front of a bed or border. They form clumps of straight stems clothed in fleshy, gray-green leaves that complement plants with white flowers or silver foliage, such as artemisias (*see p.25 and p.189*). Each stem is topped by a fluffy flower head of many tiny, starry, yellow, green, orange, or crimson flowers. As well as flowers in late spring or summer, both the buds and seedheads provide ornamental displays.

Cultivation Grow rhodiolas in any reasonably fertile soil in full sun. **Sow** seed (*see pp.391–393*) in containers in a cold frame in spring or autumn. **Divide** the rhizomes (*see p.395*) in spring or early summer.

Rhodiola rosea (Roseroot)
Z3 ‡ 1½–12in (5–30cm) ↔ 8in (20cm), variable habit, leaves to 1½in (4cm) with reddish green tips, flowers in summer

RODGERSIA

‡3–6ft (90cm–2m)
↔ 30in–6ft (75cm–2m)

A SUPERB CHOICE FOR MOIST SOIL, these vigorous, clump-forming perennials are valued for their fabulous foliage and tall flower spikes. The giant leaves are up to 36in (90cm) across, and are dark green and glossy. They are often boldly veined or wrinkled, especially when young, and occasionally tinged purple or bronze. Some varieties also display rich, reddish brown autumn tints. The flower stems are often dark purple and bear fluffy clusters of tiny, sometimes scented, blooms in summer, in shades of pink or white. Grow rodgersias by the edge of a pond or stream, or in a moist border.

Cultivation Reliably moist soil, enriched with well-rotted compost, in full sun or partial shade, with shelter from cold, drying winds is required. Drier soil is tolerated in shadier areas. **Mulch** (*see p.388*) with a thick layer of organic matter in spring to help retain soil moisture. **Sow** seed (*see pp.391–393*) in containers in a cold frame in spring. **Divide** (*see p.395*) plants in early spring.

Rodgersia pinnata 'Superba'
Z5 ‡4ft (1.2m) ↔ 30in (75cm), new purple foliage matures to dark gre
stalks reddish green, flowers in mid- and late summer

ROSCOEA

DESPITE THEIR EXOTIC, ORCHIDLIKE flowers, these tuberous perennials thrive in cool climates. They are invaluable in moist, shady borders where they are used to add a long season of bright color to areas that are usually the preserve of shade-loving foliage plants, such as ferns (*see pp.356–365*), hostas (*see pp.260–261*), and Solomon's seal (*Polygonatum, see p.310*). Most roscoeas bear flowers all summer and into autumn, in shades of white, gold, or purple, occasionally with contrasting marks on their petals. They often start to bloom before the arching leaves, which reach up to 16in (40cm) long, are fully grown.

Cultivation Roscoeas prefer a cool, sheltered, shaded site, in moist but well-drained, moderately fertile soil. Dig in plenty of well-rotted organic matter. **Plant** tubers 6in (15cm) deep in winter or early spring. In very cold areas, plant tubers even deeper: the extra insulation of the soil helps them survive temperatures down to -4°F (-20°C). **Mulch** thickly (*see p.388*) in winter where marginally hardy. **Sow** seed as soon as it is ripe (*see pp.391–393*) in containers. **Divide** established plants (*see p.395*) in spring.

RUDBECKIA
Coneflower

THIS LARGE GROUP OF ANNUALS, biennials, and perennials are grown for their large, brightly colored daisies in late summer and autumn. They bloom in many shades from burnt orange to vivid yellow and last for many weeks – seeming to glow in the golden autumn light. The prominent, conical centers may be black, brown, or green and give the plant its common name. Rudbeckias form leafy clumps with the flowers at the tips of sturdy, upright stems. The perennial *Rudbeckia hirta* (Black-eyed Susan Z3) and its cultivars are often used as annual bedding. Very easy to grow, rudbeckias provide a wonderful late burst of color; try them with sedums (*see p.324*) and Michaelmas daisies (*Aster, see pp.192–193*). They are also good for cutting.

Cultivation Reliably moist, heavy but well-drained, moderately fertile soil, in full sun or partial shade, is needed. **Sow** seed (*see pp.391–393*) of perennials in containers in a cold frame in early spring. Sow seed of annuals at 61–64°F (16–18°C) in spring and plant out young plants when all threat of frost has passed. **Divide** established plants (*p.395*) in spring or autumn

Rudbeckia laciniata
Z3 ‡ 5–10ft (1.5m–3m) ↔ 3ft (1m), loosely clumping perennial, flowers 3–6in (8–15cm), midsummer to early autumn

Roscoea cautleyoides
Z7 ‡ 22in (55cm) ↔ 6in (15cm), leaves 6in (15cm) tall at flowering, midsummer flowers are yellow, white, or purple

Rudbeckia 'Herbstsonne'
Z3 ‡ 6ft (2m) ↔ 36in (90cm), rhizomatous perennial, flowers 4–5in (10–13cm) across in midsummer to early autumn

Rudbeckia maxima
Z4 ‡ 5ft (1.5m) ↔ 18–24in (45–60cm), perennial, large, waxy, gray-green leaves, flowers from midsummer to autumn

SALPIGLOSSIS

SELECTED FOR THEIR CHEERFUL, funnel-shaped flowers, this small group of annuals brings bold color to summer beds and containers. The flowers, with heavily veined and strikingly marked petals, come in a variety of bright shades, from rich red to yellow, bronze, violet-blue, and purple. They are produced in the leaf joints of the slender, branching stems and last from summer through autumn. Grow with other bright summer bedding, such as geraniums (*see pp.300–301*) or salvias (*see right*), or use them to fill gaps in herbaceous and mixed borders. Salpiglossis are excellent plants for containers.

‡to 24in (60cm)
↔ to 12in (30cm)

Cultivation Grow in reasonably fertile, moist, but well-drained soil in full sun. In containers, use a soil-based potting mix; water freely during summer and apply a balanced fertilizer every two weeks. **Remove** fading flowers to prevent seed forming and prolong the flowering period. Provide thin twiggy sticks for support in open sites. **Sow** seed at 64–75°F (18–24°C) in spring or autumn (*see pp.391–392*). In very mild areas, sow seed outdoors where plants are to grow (*see p.393*).

SALVIA
Sage

THE CULINARY SAGE (*Salvia officinalis* Z6), grown for its pungent leaves, is attractive enough for borders. They usually thrive in sunny borders or a wildflower meadow, with elegant flower spires in clear blues and reds. Brightly colored salvias grown as annuals and biennials are good in borders, bedding, and containers; the bushier plants in subtler colors, such as the clary sages, are attractive in an informal or a herb garden. Hairy, woolly, or even white-mealy leaved salvias are more demanding, best grown in rock gardens or raised beds. Many species attract bees, and some have medicinal uses.

Cultivation Grow in reasonably fertile, well-drained soil, in sun or partial shade. Small species with hairy leaves need sharply drained soil in full sun and protection from winter moisture. **Divide** perennials (*see p.395*) in spring. **Take** cuttings from new shoots in spring or early summer (*see p.394*). **Sow** seed of annuals at 61–64°F (16–18°C) in spring. Sow annuals and biennials in situ in spring.

Salvia argentea (Silver sage)
Z5 ‡36in (90cm) ↔ 24in (60cm), rosette-forming biennial or perennial, woolly leaved, protect from winter moisture

***Salpiglossis* Casino Series**
‡to 24in (60cm) ↔ to 12in (30cm), annual, compact and branching, with flowers to 2in (5cm) across

***Salvia coccinea* 'Lady in Red'** (Texas sage)
‡16in (40cm) ↔ to 12in (30cm), erect, bushy annual with flowers ¾in (2cm) long from summer to autumn

***Salvia patens* 'Cambridge Blue'**
Z8 ‡18–24in (45–60cm) ↔ 18in (45cm), erect perennial with true blue flowers from midsummer to midautumn

via discolor

in. 41°F (5°C) ‡18in (45cm) ↔ 12in (30cm), erect perennial bearing
es of very dark indigo flowers in late summer and early autumn

SANGUISORBA
Burnet

FOR AN UNUSUAL SUMMER HIGHLIGHT in a moist
border or corner of a garden, this small group of tall,
clump-forming perennials is ideal. The wiry stems
clothed with attractive leaves produce bottlebrush-like
spires of small, fluffy flowers in red, pink, white, or
greenish white, with prominent stamens. The leaves
are composed of toothed leaflets that are heavily
veined and sometimes grayish. Burnets are suitable
for mixed and herbaceous borders or particularly for
naturalizing in a damp meadow or wildflower garden
as they form spreading clumps. The flowers and foliage
are good for cutting. Grow them with other perennials
and with tall ornamental grasses (*see pp.340–355*).

Cultivation Grow in any reasonably fertile soil that is moist but
well-drained, in sun or partial shade. Taller species may need some
support. In ideal conditions, plants may become invasive but can be
controlled by regular division (*see p.395*) in spring or autumn. **Sow** seed
in a container in a cold frame in spring or autumn (*see pp.391–392*).

SAPONARIA
Soapwort

The sap of soapwort was once used for laundering
clothes as well as medicinally for skin complaints.
This group of sprawling and upright perennials is now
grown for its profusion of tiny, pink to deep pink
flowers in summer and autumn, as well as its ground-
covering ability and for keeping down weeds. The
plants thrive in sunny, dry sites. The low-growing,
mat-forming species are excellent for the front of a
border, perhaps spilling over paving or in a rock
garden. Grow taller ones with old-fashioned, pastel
perennials such as pinks (*Dianthus, pp.226–227*).

Cultivation Grow border perennials in reasonably fertile soil that
is well drained and neutral to alkaline, in full sun. Compact species
such as *S. caespitosa* require sharply drained soil in a rock garden
or between paving. Cut *S. ocymoides* hard back after flowering to
maintain a compact habit. **Divide** border perennials (*see p.395*) in
autumn or spring. **Sow** seed in containers in a cold frame in spring or
autumn (*see pp.391–392*). **Take** softwood cuttings in early summer
(*see p.394*). Saponarias may be damaged by slugs and snails; lay
traps or pick them off by hand (*see p.398*).

Salvia fulgens
T min. 41°F (5°C) ‡20–39in (50–100cm) ↔ 16–36in (40–90cm),
woody-based perennial with downy leaves and flowers in summer

Sanguisorba canadensis
Z3 ‡to 6ft (2m) ↔ 3ft (1m), hairy leaves, flower spikes, to 8in
(20cm) long, from midsummer to midautumn

Saponaria ocymoides (Rock soapwort)
Z3 ‡3in (8cm) ↔ 18in (45cm), mat-forming perennial, flowers in
summer, can swamp small plants

A STAPLE OF THE ROCK GARDEN, saxifrages are mostly low-growing plants that make dense mounds or mats of foliage, carpeting the ground or cascading down walls. There are more than 400 species, including evergreen, semievergreen, or deciduous perennials, biennials, and a few annuals, many of which come from cool, mountain regions. Arising from the foliage are masses of delicate, star- or saucer-shaped flowers in shades from white to lemon, bright yellow to rose, and indigo. In some, the tiny rosettes of leaves are attractive by themselves. Apart from rock gardens, saxifrages are grown in raised beds, alpine troughs, and in alpine houses (unheated, well-ventilated greenhouses). They are also often used to soften walls and paving (*see below*). A few larger and more vigorous types, such as London pride (*Saxifraga* × *urbium*) and *S. fortunei*, make good path edgings or groundcover in borders and woodland gardens. The botanical categories applied to saxifrages are many and various but, for gardens, plants can be divided into four main groups (*see below*). Saxifrages shown here are hardy to Zones 5–7b, except where noted.

Cultivation Saxifrages fall into four broad groups for cultivation. **Group 1** need moist, well-drained soil in deep or partial shade. Suitable for borders and rock gardens. **Group 2** prefer humus-rich soil (with plenty of organic matter added), but with sharp drainage. Neutral to alkaline soil in light shade is best. Suitable for rock gardens, crevices, scree beds (sloping areas where soil is mixed, and usually covered, with gravel or stone chips), or alpine houses. **Group 3** like fertile, well-drained, neutral to alkaline soil, with their roots moist. They tolerate full sun in cool areas. Suitable for rock gardens or alpine troughs. **Group 4** require fertile but sharply drained, alkaline soil in full sun. Suitable for rock gardens, troughs and alpine houses. Some will not tolerate winter moisture. **Sow** seed (*see pp.391–392*) in autumn in containers and put in a cold frame. **Divide** herbaceous types in spring (*see p.395*). Single rosettes can be detached and rooted as cuttings (*see p.394*) in late spring and early summer.

Planting saxifrages in paving

When laying paving, leave gaps for vigorous saxifrages. They will spread over the edges of the slabs, giving the paving a soft, naturalistic look. Before planting, incorporate sandy medium into the soil in the planting gaps. This helps the roots to penetrate easily and also improves drainage. Water well until the plants are established.

Planting in wall crevices

❶ *Mix equal parts of soil, sand, and leaf mold. Scrape out space in a crevice, put a stone in the bottom, and add a 1in (2.5cm) layer of mixture. Ease in the roots of the plant. Sprinkle another 1in (2.5cm) layer of potting mix over the roots.*

❷ *To hold the plant in place, cap the potting mix with a small stone that slopes down into the rockface. Add more plants, around 4in (10cm) apart. Cover the roots of the last plant with medium and trickle in water to settle the soil around the roots.*

① *Saxifraga* 'Apple Blossom' ‡6in (15cm) ↔ indefinite, suitable for crevices and borders, group 4 ② 'Aureopunctata' ‡12in (30cm) ↔ indefinite, good for hanging baskets, group 3 or 4 ③ *burseriana* ‡2in (5cm) ↔ 6in (15cm), group 3 or 4 ④ 'Cloth of Gold' ‡4in (10cm) ↔ 12in (30cm), group 2, best in shade ⑤ *fortunei* ↔ 12in (30cm), group 1 ⑥ × *geum* ‡↔ 8in (20cm), group 1 ⑦ *granulata* ‡8–14in (20–35cm) ↔ 6in (15cm), group 1, tolerates full sun in moist soil

8 'Gregor Mendel' ‡4in (10cm) ↔12in (30cm), group 3, can be grown in crevices 9 'Hindhead Seedling' ‡2in (5cm) ↔6in (15cm), group 3 or 4 10 'Jenkinsiae' ‡2in (5cm) ↔8in (20cm), group 3 11 'Kathleen Pinsent' ‡↔8in (20cm) group 1 12 'Mount Nachi' ‡6in (15cm) ↔indefinite, group 3 or 4 13 *oppositifolia* Z2 ‡1in (2.5cm) ↔8in (20cm), group 3 14 *paniculata* Z2 ‡6in (15cm) ↔10in (25cm), group 4 15 *sancta* ‡2in (5cm) ↔8in (20cm), group 3 16 *sempervivum* ‡4in (10cm) ↔8in (20cm), cushion-forming, group 4 17 'Southside Seedling' ‡12in (30cm) ↔8in (20cm), group 3 or 4 18 *spathularis* ‡20in (50cm) ↔indefinite, group 3 or 4 19 'Stansfieldii' ‡4in (10cm) ↔8–9in (20–23cm) group 3 or 4 20 'Tricolor' ‡↔12in (30cm), group 1, good for hanging baskets 21 'Tumbling Waters' ‡4in (10cm) ↔12in (30cm), group 3 22 'Variegata' ‡12in (30cm) ↔indefinite, group 3 or 4 23 'Wisley' ‡4in (10cm) ↔6in (15cm), group 4

SCABIOSA

Pincushion flower, Scabious

AS THE COMMON NAME SUGGESTS, the centers of these plants' flowers look like pincushions. Whether you choose to grow the annuals, biennials, or perennials, each bears masses of delicate, solitary, sometimes fragrant flowers in summer to autumn. Shades range from lilac, purple, or white to deep crimson. Most of the leaves cluster at the bases of the stems. All attract bees and other beneficial insects into the garden. The tall-stemmed species, such as *Scabiosa caucasica,* which has a height and spread of 24in (60cm), are good for cutting. Scabious blend in well in informal or cottage-garden plantings, in mixed borders, or in containers.

Cultivation Scabious prefer well-drained, moderately fertile soil that is neutral to slightly alkaline, in full sun and with protection from excessive winter moisture. **Sow** seed (*see pp.391–393*) of annuals at 43–54°F (6–12°C) in early spring or where they are to flower in mid-spring. Sow seed of perennials in containers in a cold frame as soon as it is ripe, or in spring. **Deadhead** regularly to encourage more flowers. **Divide** established plants (*see p.395*) or take stem-tip cuttings (*see p.394*) of perennials in spring.

Scabiosa caucasica 'Miss Willmott'
Z4 ‡36in (90cm) ↔ 24in (60cm), clump-forming perennial, flowers from mid- to late summer

SCAEVOLA

UNUSUAL, FAN-SHAPED FLOWERS in shades of purple-blue, lilac, or blue are produced by scaevolas in large numbers between spring and autumn. The flowers are borne singly or in clusters on slender stems, above spoon-shaped, mid-green leaves. Most are short-lived, mainly evergreen perennials. The perennial *Scaevola aemula* and its cultivars are most commonly grown in gardens. It is the only species that can be grown in temperate regions outdoors in summer and is generally treated as an annual. Grow scaevolas in mixed borders, in hanging baskets, or in large containers, where they make attractive specimen plants that can be moved under cover for winter.

Cultivation Scaevolas require a well-drained, reasonably fertile soil, in full sun or partial shade. Use a soil-based potting mix for plants grown in containers; water freely in summer; and feed with a balanced fertilizer at monthly intervals. **Sow** seed (*see pp.391–393*) at 66–75°F (19–24°C) in spring, or take softwood cuttings (*see p.394*) in late spring or summer.

Scabiosa 'Butterfly Blue'
Z4 ‡↔ 16in (40cm), hairy, herbaceous perennial with branched stems, flowers to 1½in (4cm) across in mid- and late summer

Scaevola aemula (Fairy fan-flower)
T min. 41°F (5°C) ‡↔ to 20in (50cm), erect or prostrate, hairy stems, purple-blue or blue flowers to 1in (2.5cm) across in summer

SCHIZANTHUS
Butterfly flower, Poor man's orchid

EXOTIC-LOOKING, ORCHIDLIKE FLOWERS that almost smother the entire plant and last for many weeks throughout summer make this an excellent summer bedding plant. There is a wide range of flower colors to choose from, including yellows, purples, pinks, reds, and white. The flowers also last well when cut. The spreading, bushy foliage is attractively fernlike, with leaves made up of deeply lobed leaflets. This group of mostly annuals and some biennials thrives with other summer bedding plants such as marigolds (*Calendula, see p.204*), salvias (*see pp.318–319*), or fuchsias (*see pp.60–63*), in mixed borders or containers.

Cultivation Full sun and reasonably fertile soil is needed to grow schizanthus. For plants in containers, use a soil-based potting mix; water them well in summer; and apply a balanced fertilizer at weekly intervals. **Support** flowering stems with sticks if necessary. **Pinch back** the young shoots to encourage a bushy habit. **Sow** seed (*see pp.391–393*) at 61°F (16°C) in spring for summer flowers; for spring flowers in containers, sow in late summer and overwinter the seedlings in frost-free conditions.

Schizanthus × *wisetonensis* 'Hit Parade'
↕↔ 9–12in (23–30cm), annual with white, pink, gold, purple, or scarlet flowers to 3in (8cm) across from spring to autumn

SCHIZOSTYLIS COCCINEA
Kaffir lily

TALL SPIKES OF DELICATE, SHIMMERING flowers in hot shades of red, pink, or scarlet make the kaffir lily a welcome addition to any garden. They resemble the gladiolus and are borne on stems up to 24in (60cm) in height, in late summer, autumn, or early winter, when there is little else in flower. A native of southern Africa, this vigorous, clump-forming perennial and its cultivars spread by means of underground stems (rhizomes). Try placing it in mixed borders with other late-flowering plants – for example Michaelmas daisies (*Aster, see pp.192–193*) or coneflowers (*Rudbeckia, see p.317*) – in containers, in waterside plantings, or by a sunny wall. The flowers are excellent for cutting.

Cultivation Grow in moist but well-drained, fertile soil in full sun. **Support** the flower stems if necessary with sticks in exposed gardens. **Protect** the plants with a mulch of organic matter in winter when the flowers are finished. **Divide** clumps (*see p.395*) in spring to maintain their vigor. **Sow** seed (*see pp.391–392*) at 55–61°F (13–16°C) in spring

Schizostylis coccinea 'Major'
Z7b ↕ 24in (60cm) ↔ 12in (30cm), flowers 2–2½in (5–6cm) across are borne on stiff stems in late summer

SCILLA
Squill

↕ 3–48in (8–12cm)
↔ 2–4in (5–10cm)

THE DAINTY, DIMINUTIVE FLOWERS of scillas are extremely eye-catching, often with attractive, contrasting markings to the petals. They may be star- or bell-shaped, mostly in shades of blue but sometimes in purple or white, and are borne in loose or tight clusters amid strappy leaves in spring, summer, and autumn. Scillas are bulbous plants that will grow in a wide range of conditions and, if left to their own devices, will self-seed freely. Naturalize the bulbs in grass, in rock or gravel gardens, or grow them in mixed borders, beneath deciduous shrubs and trees where they will receive plenty of light before the woody plants put on leaves. Scillas are also suitable for coastal gardens.

Cultivation Plant bulbs 3–4in (8–10cm) deep in late summer or early autumn, in well-drained, humus-rich, fertile soil that is in full sun or partial shade. **Sow** seed (*see pp.391–392*) in pots and place in a cold frame. **Divide** and pot up offsets (*see p.395*) when the bulbs are dormant in summer.

① *bifolia* Z3 ↕ 3–6in (8–15cm) ② *peruviana* 'Alba' Z8 ↕ 12in (30cm) ③ *scilloides* Z4 ↕ 8in (20cm) ④ *siberica* 'Spring Beauty' Z3 ↕ 8in (20cm)

SEDUM
Stonecrop

SEDUMS BRING A RANGE OF TEXTURES and shapes to a garden; there are hundreds of annuals and perennials, many of which are succulent. There are low, creeping plants with tiny flowers that hug the ground, such as the common stonecrop (*Sedum acre* Z4), which thrives in a rock or gravel garden, or in the crevices of paving or stone walls. The tall herbaceous perennials usually form architectural clumps, with large, flat heads of pink or white flowers. These provide late-season color in summer and autumn, attract butterflies, and their tawny seedheads persist through winter. Sedums are often vigorous and very easy to grow.

Cultivation Sedums like moderately fertile, neutral to alkaline, well-drained soil in full sun, although vigorous plants tolerate light shade. **Trim** spreading species after flowering to keep them neat. Support sedums with heavy flower heads early on to stop the stems collapsing outward. **Divide** (*see p.395 and right*) large herbaceous plants every 3–4 years in spring to improve flowering. **Sow** seed in containers in a cold frame in autumn (*see pp.391–393*). **Take** softwood cuttings of perennials (*see p.394*) in early summer. **Rot** may occur in wet.

LIFT LARGE SEDUMS with care as the fleshy growth is very brittle. Pull a clump into pieces the size of a large hand; discard old, woody growth. Replant.

Sedum 'Ruby Glow'
Z3 ↕10in (25cm) ↔ 18in (45cm), low, spreading, deciduous perennial, flowers from midsummer to early autumn

Sedum spathulifolium 'Cape Blanco'
Z6 ↕4in (10cm) ↔ 24in (60cm), mat-forming, evergreen perennial, powdery bloom on leaves, summer flowers, stands light shade

Sedum (syn. *Hylotelephium*) *populifolium*
Z5 ↕8–12in (20–30cm) ↔ 18in (45cm), deciduous perennial with lax stems, fragrant flowers in late summer and early autumn

Sedum spathulifolium 'Purpureum'
Z6 ↕4in (10cm) ↔ 24in (60cm), vigorous, mat-forming, evergreen perennial, golden flowers in summer, tolerates light shade

Sedum spectabile 'Brilliant' (Ice plant)
Z4 ↕↔ 18in (45cm), clumping, deciduous perennial, flower heads 6in (15cm) across in late summer, seedheads persist, needs support

SEMPERVIVUM
Hens and chicks

THESE EVERGREEN SUCCULENTS are grown for their fleshy rosettes of leaves, which are often flushed red or purple, and sometimes thickly covered in hairs. There are numerous varieties with leaves of differing colors, sizes, and shapes. Although each plant is small, they spread across the soil by rooting stems, or runners, that produce new plantlets to form large mats of densely packed rosettes. In summer, white, yellow, red, or purple flowers cluster on sturdy, fleshy stems. After a rosette flowers, it dies, but the gap is quickly filled by a new offset. Hens and chicks need only shallow soil, so thrive in rock or gravel gardens or containers with other alpines such as saxifrages (*see pp.320–321*) or pinks (*Dianthus, see pp.226–227*).

Cultivation Hens and chicks grow in full sun, in poor sharply drained soil. In an alpine house, grow in soil-based potting mix with plenty of added sand. Shield hairy hens and chicks from winter moisture to avoid rot. **Sow** seed (*see pp.391–393*) in pots in a cold frame in spring. **Rooted offsets** can be detached in spring or early summer; they establish more quickly if kept out of direct sun.

SENECIO
see also p.116

THERE ARE HUNDREDS OF SENECIOS, including annuals and biennials, shrubs, trees, and climbers. The shrubs are often grown in the garden for their foliage; the clump-forming annuals and perennials are valued for their daisylike flowers. They bloom from early summer until late autumn in shades of white, yellow, blue, crimson, and purple; usually with a golden yellow center. Since senecios are so varied, check the plant label or with the nursery about each plant's specific needs before you buy. Generally, annuals are used as summer bedding or in containers; small perennials in rock or gravel gardens, and larger varieties in borders or areas devoted to wildflowers. Where not hardy, grow in a cool greenhouse; move container-grown senecios under cover in winter.

Cultivation Senecios may need gritty or moist, poor or moderately fertile, well-drained soil, in full sun or partial shade. **Sow** seed (*see pp.391–393*) in spring at 66–75°F (19–24°C); seed of bog plants and alpines can be sown in a cold frame. **Take** softwood cuttings (*see p.394*) of perennials in early summer.

SIDALCEA
False mallow, Prairie mallow

FROM EARLY TO MIDSUMMER, these annuals and perennials produce tall spires of long-lasting flowers, rather like those of hollyhocks. The petals are thin and silky, sometimes fringed round the edges, and in clear shades of pink, purple-pink, or white. They often produce a second flush of blooms in autumn if the fading flowers are cut back before seeds develop. Another bonus is that the dense clumps of attractive, lobed or serrated, round leaves cover the soil and suppress weeds. Use sidalceas to add height to a bed or border; they also are excellent for cutting.

Cultivation A site in full sun, with moderately fertile, neutral to acidic, moist but well-drained soil, enriched with well-rotted organic matter, is best. Sidalceas tolerate a range of soils, but do not like to be too wet, especially in winter. **Mulch** (*see p.388*) with straw or bracken in winters without snow cover. **Cut back** stems hard after the first flowering. **Sow** seed (*see pp.391–393*) in a container in a cold frame in spring or autumn. **Divide** (*see p.395*) in spring or autumn. **Remove** leaves affected by rust (orange-brown spots); thin the foliage to improve air circulation and help prevent a recurrence.

① *arachnoideum* (Cobweb houseleek) Z4 ‡3in (8cm) ↔ 12in (30cm), pink flowers ② *tectorum* (Hens and chicks) Z4 ‡6in (15cm) ↔ 20in (50cm), red-purple flowers

Senecio pulcher
T min. 35°F (2°C) ‡8–24in (145–60cm) ↔ 20in (50cm), perennial, flowers in mid- to late autumn

Sidalcea malviflora 'Oberon'
Z6 ‡4ft (1.2m) ↔ 18in (45cm), rounded or kidney-shaped leaves, flowers in early and midsummer

FLOWERING PLANTS

SILENE

Campion, Catchfly

THERE ARE HUNDREDS of these annuals, biennials, and deciduous and evergreen perennials. They are grown for their pretty flowers, which have delicately notched or split petals. In summer, erect stems bear blooms, singly or in clusters, in shades from dark pink to pure white. Most campions are easy to grow; many are prolific self-seeders. This makes them an excellent choice for a wildflower garden. If they are regularly deadheaded, smaller perennials can be used in a rock or gravel garden; place taller varieties in beds and borders. Annuals are often used as summer bedding. Some catchflies have sticky hairs on their leaves that trap insects – hence the common name.

Cultivation Grow these plants in moderately fertile, neutral to alkaline, well-drained soil, in full sun or dappled shade. Smaller alpine species need sandy, sharply drained soil. *Silene hookeri* prefers acidic soil. **Sow** seed (*see pp.391–393*) of perennials in a cold frame in autumn. Sow hardy annuals in situ in autumn or spring; tender varieties at 61–66°F (16–19°C) in spring. Harden them off and plant out when the threat of frost has passed. **Take** new shoots from the base in spring and treat as softwood cuttings (*see p.394*).

Silene schafta
Z3b ‡ 10in (25cm) ← 12in (30cm), clumping, semievergreen perennial, flowers in late summer and autumn, good for rock gardens

SILYBUM MARIANUM

Blessed thistle, Milk thistle

‡ 5ft (1.5m)
↔ 24–36in (60–90cm)

THIS TALL, PRICKLY BIENNIAL forms an impressive rosette of glossy, dark green, spiny leaves up to 20in (50cm) long in its first year, that are spectacularly veined and marbled with white. In the second year, large, slightly scented flower heads appear throughout the summer and autumn. If you wish to keep the leaf variegation at its best and prolong the life of the plant, pinch out the flowers as they form. Silybums are excellent in groups in borders, where their architectural foliage contrasts with softer, round-leaved plants. Plant it singly in a gravel garden, so its handsome form can be appreciated.

Cultivation Silybums prefer well-drained, neutral or slightly alkaline soil, in full sun. They dislike wet winters, so provide shelter if possible to avoid rot. **Sow** seed (*see pp.391–393*) in situ, in spring or early summer, then thin seedlings to 24in (60cm) apart. If grown for foliage, sow seed under cover in late winter or early spring; pot up into 3½in (9cm) pots; harden off and plant out in spring.

Silybum marianum
Z5 ‡ 5ft (1.5m) ↔ 36in (90cm), self-seeding, spiny, glossy dark green leaves are white-veined and marbled

SISYRINCHIUM

PRETTY, STAR- OR CUP-SHAPED FLOWERS are produced by these annuals and perennials in profusion over many weeks in spring or summer. They bloom in rich blues and mauves, or subtle yellows and whites, singly at the tips of stems or in tall flower spikes. The long leaves, sometimes variegated with creamy white stripes, form grassy clumps or large, irislike fans. The spiky foliage complements that of ornamental grasses (*see pp.340–355*) or provides a textural contrast to plants with feathery or broad leaves. Smaller varieties are best in a rock or gravel garden where they can be left to self-seed and will not get swamped by large, vigorous plants; the tall sisyrinchiums are able to hold their own in a border.

Cultivation Poor to moderately fertile, neutral to alkaline, well-drained soil in full sun, is required, with protection from extreme winter moisture which encourages root rot. Some small or half-hardy plants are best grown in pots and moved under cover in damp winters. **Sow** seed (*see pp.391–393*) in a container in a cold frame in spring or autumn. **Divide** clumps (*see p.395*) in spring.

PLANT SISYRINCHIUMS with their crowns slightly above soil level. This allows water to drain away quickly in wet weather and reduce the risk of rot in the crowns.

Sisyrinchium striatum 'Aunt May'
Z7 ‡ 20in (50cm) ↔ 10in (25cm), clumping perennial, flowers 1in (2.5cm) across borne in early and midsummer

SMILACINA
False Solomon's seal

THE LUSH FOLIAGE OF THESE VIGOROUS perennials is much like that of Solomon's seal (*Polygonatum, see p.310*) – hence the common name. The resemblance ends when they burst into bloom from midspring to midsummer, producing dense clusters of tiny, starry flowers at the tips of arching stems. The flowers are creamy white and have a delicate scent that hangs in the still, moist air of a woodland garden. Green berries follow that ripen to red in autumn, at the same time as the leaves of many smilacinas turn a rich yellow. In favorable conditions, these trouble-free plants can be invasive but are easily dug up if they spread too far. Use smilacinas with other shade-loving plants, for example ferns (*see pp 356–365*).

Cultivation Smilacinas thrive in moderately fertile, preferably slightly acidic soil that has been enriched with well-rotted compost. Choose a position in full or dappled shade that is sheltered from cold winds. **Sow** seed (*see pp.391–393*) in containers in a cold frame in autumn. **Divide** the rhizomes of established plants (*see p.395*) in spring.

SOLIDAGO
Goldenrod

THE WARM YELLOW FLOWERS of these vigorous, woody-based perennials glow in the golden light of late summer and autumn. They are borne in spikes or clusters, densely packed with tiny blooms, on stiff, upright stems. The leaves are usually mid-green. Species goldenrods can be invasive, and although they can be controlled by digging them out, they are best reserved for wildflower gardens. Happily, many less unruly hybrids, with larger flower heads, are available. They add late color to the garden and are excellent for cut flowers. Use them with other autumn flowers such as rudbeckias (*see p.317*) and asters (*see pp.192–193*), and among earlier-flowering plants for a prolonged seasonal display.

Cultivation Goldenrods thrive in poor to moderately fertile, preferably sandy, well-drained soil, in full sun. **Deadhead** regularly to prevent self-seeding. **Divide** (*see p.395*) plants every three or four years in autumn or spring to keep them healthy: discard the old, woody centers. **Powdery mildew** is common in dry summers.

× SOLIDASTER LUTEUS

‡36in (90cm)
↔ 32in (80cm)

THIS HYBRID IS A CROSS between a solidago and an aster: as you might expect, it combines elements of both plants. Much like goldenrod (*see left*), it bears a profusion of tiny blooms in dense clusters from midsummer through to autumn. The flowers themselves are daisy-like and similar to those of an aster (*see pp.192–193*). They open a pale, creamy yellow with a darker center, then fade as they age. The plant forms a clump with erect stems. Like both its parents, this perennial is a splendid choice for adding late-summer color to a border and makes an excellent cut flower.

Cultivation Moderately fertile, well-drained soil, in full sun or dappled shade, suits this plant. Take care not to overfertilize the soil, because this encourages foliage at the expense of flowers. **Divide** clumps in autumn or spring (*see p.395*) every three or four years to maintain vigor and discard the congested, woody centers. Take new shoots from the base in spring and treat as softwood cuttings (*see p.394*). **Powdery mildew** is common in dry summers.

AUTUMN FOLIAGE

Smilacina racemosa (False spikenard)
Z4 ‡36in (90cm) ↔ 24in (60cm), clump-forming, leaves downy underneath, green-tinged flowers in mid- and late spring

Solidago 'Goldenmosa'
Z4 ‡30in (75cm) ↔ 18in (45cm), compact bush, wrinkled foliage, 12in (30cm) long flower spikes in late summer and early autumn

× *Solidaster luteus* 'Lemore'
Z5 ↔ 32in (80cm), more spreading habit and a paler yellow than the species

STACHYS

Betony, Hedge nettle, Woundwort

CARPETS OF LARGE, FELTED OR VELVETY LEAVES are the main attraction of these plants. Held on square stems, the leaves are usually covered in fine hairs; in some species, leaves are aromatic. Stachys include many spreading perennials that make excellent groundcover plants, for example *Stachys byzantina* of which 'Silver Carpet' is a nonflowering form ideal for edging. Their silvery foliage will complement many border plants: try crocosmias (*see p.219*), penstemons (*see p.304*), and shrub roses (*see pp.110–113*). The flower spikes, in white or shades of pink, purple, or gold, appear in summer and attract bees, butterflies, and other beneficial insects into the garden. Low-growing species, like *Stachys candida*, are good for dry banks or gravel gardens.

Cultivation Grow in well-drained, reasonably fertile soil in full sun. Smaller rock garden species need very sharply drained soil **Sow** seed (*see pp.391–392*) in a container in a cold frame in autumn or spring. **Lift and divide** entire plants (*see p.395*) in spring, as growth starts, or cut off and replant rooted sections from the outside of large clumps.

Stachys byzantina (Lambs' ears, Lambs' tongues)
Z3b ↕18in (45cm) ↔ 24in (60cm), mat-forming perennial, woolly pink-purple flowers from early summer to early autumn

SYMPHYTUM

Comfrey

↕↔ 1–6ft (30cm–2m) or more

PRIZED FOR THEIR SHADE tolerance, these hairy, clump-forming perennials make useful groundcover in a shady border or woodland garden. Although essentially coarse plants, they have decorative, crinkly foliage and pretty, long-lasting flowers. These are tubular or bell-shaped, in shades of bright blue, pale blue, cream, pale yellow, purple-violet, or white, and are borne in clusters amid the foliage from late spring to late summer. The leaves may be plain green, cream- or gold-variegated. Pick a site carefully because all but the variegated species can be invasive. They thrive under trees or in borders, where little else will grow.

Cultivation Grow in moist soil in sun or shade, or in dry shade. **Remove** flowers from variegated species for the best foliage color. **Divide** plants (*see p.395*) in spring; comfrey spreads by underground stems (rhizomes) and will reshoot from a tiny bit of stem left in the soil. Comfrey leaves make a rich, if smelly, liquid fertilizer: fill a bucket one-third full with leaves and top up with water. Cover and leave for 2–3 weeks, then use diluted one part comfrey liquid with two parts water.

Stachys candida
Z6 ↕6in (15cm) ↔ 12in (30cm), spreading, flowers in summer, needs excellent drainage and protection from winter moisture

***Stachys macrantha* 'Superba'**
Z5 ↕24in (60cm) ↔ 12in (30cm), erect, hairy perennial, rosettes of dark green leaves, flowers early summer to early autumn

***Symphytum* 'Hidcote Blue'** Z6 ↕↔ 8in (145cm), hairy, erect then lax stems, red buds, flowers to ½in (1.5cm) long in mid- and late spring that fade with age, large leaves

...mphytum caucasicum
‡↔ 24in (60cm) clump-forming hairy perennial, erect then lax stems,
...settes of leaves, flowers early to late summer

TAGETES
Marigold

FOR LENGTH OF FLOWERING AND SHOW of color, marigolds have few rivals, and make excellent subjects for a formal bedding display. The many annuals and perennials are usually treated as annuals and sown in spring. Germination is swift, and they start flowering just a few weeks after sowing. The flowers, in a wide range of shades from deep orange to bright yellow, are produced from early summer until the first frosts of autumn. In some forms, flowers are single, often with contrasting darker markings on the petals; in others they resemble carnations. The ferny foliage is usually strongly aromatic. Taller African marigolds, with pompon flowers, are best grown in a border, but others, including French marigolds, are equally at home in containers or borders.

Cultivation Any reasonably well-drained soil in full sun will suit marigolds. **Deadhead** regularly to prolong the flowering period and water freely in dry weather. If growing marigolds in containers, water them well, and apply a balanced fertilizer at weekly intervals. **Sow** seed (*see pp.391–393*) at 70°F (21°C) in spring.

Tagetes 'Lemon Gem'
‡9in (23cm) ↔ to 16in (40cm), annual, flowers to 1in (2.5cm)
across from late spring to early autumn

TANACETUM
Pyrethrum

MOST SPECIES IN THIS LARGE, DIVERSE group of annuals and perennials have finely cut, pungently aromatic leaves and daisylike flowers in early and midsummer. Some flower heads have a prominent central disk, and others have small, double pompons. The ferny leaves are very decorative. *Tanacetum balsamita* (Z7) smells minty and is an ingredient of potpourri. Some species, such as *Tanacetum haradjanii* (Z7), are suitable for a rock garden, while others species, such as forms of *T. parthenium* (Z3), can be grown in a herb garden or as an edging to mixed or herbaceous borders. Pyrethrums also make interesting plants for raised beds and containers.

Cultivation Grow these plants in any well-drained soil in full sun. Dwarf and silver-leaved species prefer sharply drained soil. **Cut back** the flowers of *T. coccineum* after flowering to encourage a further flush of blooms. Feverfew self-seeds prolifically. **Sow** seed at 50–55°F (10–13°C) in early spring (*see pp.391–393*). **Divide** perennials (*see p.395*) or take new shoots from the base and treat as cuttings (*see p.394*) in spring. **Chrysanthemum** eelworm in the roots may cause leaves to turn brown and die from the base; destroy affected plants.

① *haradjanii* ‡ to 6in (15cm), mat-forming evergreen, tiny yellow daisies in late summer ② *parthenium* (Feverfew) ‡18–24in (45–60cm) bushy perennial, flowers in summer

330 THALICTRUM

Meadow rue

‡ 8ft (2.5m)
↔ 24in (60cm)

THALICTRUMS ARE A LARGE GROUP of moisture-loving perennials with delicate, gray-green foliage and airy clouds of tiny flowers from early to late summer. The numerous flowers may be colored white, pink, and purple to yellow, often with showy central stamens, which create a fluffy effect from a distance. The leaves are composed of many fine-textured leaflets. They are mostly upright plants, although some, such as *Thalictrum kiusianum* (Z4), are mat-forming. Taller species are excellent in mixed and herbaceous borders with perennials like achilleas (*see p.166*), sidalceas (*see p.325*), and goldenrod (*Solidago, see p.327*), or in a woodland planting. Small ones add grace to a shady rock garden.

Cultivation Grow in partial shade, in moist soil enriched with well-rotted organic matter. Small species like well-drained soil in cool, partial shade. **Stake** taller plants. **Sow** seed (*see pp.391–393*) in a container when ripe or in early spring. **Divide** plants (*see p.395*) as growth begins in spring. Powdery mildew can be a problem in dry soil.

***Thalictrum delavayi* 'Album'**
Z5 ‡ 4ft (1.2m) or more ↔ 24in (60cm), erect clumps, leaves up to 14in (35cm) long, flowers midsummer to early autumn

TIARELLA

Foam flower

FROTHY SPIRES OF TINY FLOWERS appear to float above the foliage of these herbaceous perennials. The white or pinkish white flowers are borne over a long period from late spring to midsummer. The foliage is also a valuable feature of these plants, being oval to heart-shaped and pale to mid-green with bristly hairs. In autumn, the leaves turn reddish copper. Since the foliage is so dense and some species have a spreading habit, foam flowers make attractive and effective groundcover plants, particularly in a shady border or a woodland garden. They combine well with other shade- or moisture-loving perennials such as coral flowers (*Heuchera, see p.259*), hostas (*see pp.260–261*), and speedwells (*Veronica, see p.337*).

Cultivation Foam flowers thrive in any moist soil that has been enriched with well-rotted compost, in deep or partial shade. **Protect** the crowns from excessive winter moisture. **Sow** seed in a container (*see pp.391–393*) in a cold frame as soon as they are ripe. **Divide** plants (*see p.395*) in spring.

Thalictrum aquilegiifolium
Z5 ‡ to 3ft (1m) ↔ 18in (45cm), erect clumps, leaves up to 12in (30cm) long, flowers in early summer

***Thalictrum delavayi* 'Hewitt's Double'**
Z5 ‡ 4ft (1.2m) or more ↔ 24in (60cm), leaves up to 14in (35cm) long, long-lasting flowers from midsummer to early autumn

***Tiarella cordifolia* (Foam flower)**
Z4 ‡ 4–12in (10–30cm) ↔ to 12in (30cm), hairy leaves bronze-red in autumn, flower spikes 4–12in (10–30cm) long in spring

TOLMIEA MENZIESII
Piggyback plant

‡12–24in (30–60cm)
↔ 3–6ft (1–2m)

THE APPEAL OF THIS FAST-GROWING, clump-forming perennial lies in its foliage. Its softly hairy, usually light green, pretty leaves produce new plantlets at the points where the leaf stalks and leaf blades meet, hence the name of piggyback plant. From late spring to early summer, it bears long clusters of up to 50 slightly scented flowers with purple-brown petals. *Tolmiea menziesii* and its cultivars spread by means of creeping stems. Use it as groundcover in a woodland setting with perennials such as coral flowers (*Heuchera, see p.259*) and foam flowers (*see facing page*).

Cultivation Plant this perennial in moist soil in partial or deep shade. Full sun can scorch the leaves. For a container-grown plant, use a soil-based potting mix; water freely during the growing season; and apply a balanced fertilizer weekly. **Sow** seed (*see pp.391–393*) in a container in a cold frame in autumn, or divide (*see p.395*) in spring. You could also try removing plantlets and rooting them in the same way as a cutting (*see below and p.394*).

TRADESCANTIA

THE HARDY TRADESCANTIAS are very useful, clump-forming perennials, and although each flower is short-lived, they are produced in profusion in summer and much of autumn. The blue, purple, rose pink, rose red, or white blooms stud the mounds of matte green, or occasionally purple-tinged, grassy foliage. Grow these easygoing plants in a mixed border, perhaps married with ornamental grasses such as hakonechloas (*see. p348*), or with other herbaceous perennials. Tradescantias are familiar as houseplants with trailing stems and evergreen, often striped or purple leaves, such as Wandering Jew (*T. fluminensis*). Tender species work well with fuchsias or impatiens, or tumbling over the edges of hanging baskets, windowboxes, or pots.

Cultivation Hardy species prefer moist, fertile soil, in full sun or partial shade. **Cut back** hard after flowering to prevent seed setting and for a further flush of flower. **Divide** hardy tradescantias in spring or autumn (*see p.395*).

TRICYRTIS
Toad lily

TOAD LILIES HAVE SPECTACULAR FLOWERS, produced in white, shades of pinkish white, or green flushed white or yellow, and frequently spotted with contrasting markings in pink or purple. They are star- or funnel-shaped and borne singly or in small clusters during summer and autumn. The leaves are often glossy, dark green to pale green and usually clasp erect or arching stems. Some foliage is spotted or has prominent veins. Toad lilies are herbaceous perennials and particularly suitable for woodland gardens and shady borders. Try combining them with other perennials that enjoy moist, shady situations such as Solomon's seal (*Polygonatum, see p.310*).

Cultivation Toad lilies prefer moist but well-drained, humus-rich soil, in partial shade. In colder areas, grow late-flowering species in a warm, sheltered shrub border, protected from wind and frost, which could damage late flowers. **Mulch** thickly with organic matter over the growing area in winter to protect the plants from severe frosts. **Sow** seed as soon as it is ripe in a cold frame and overwinter seedling plants in frost-free conditions (*see pp.391–393*). **Divide** plants (*see p.395*) in early spring while they are still dormant.

ROOTING PLANTLETS
In mid- to late summer, cut off a plantlet below the leaf; fold the leaf as shown. Pot in rooting medium so the leaf is just covered.

Tolmiea menziesii 'Taff's Gold'
Z7 ‡12–24in (30–60cm) ↔ 3–6ft (1–2m) leaves up to 5in (13cm) long, particularly prone to sun scorch

① 'J.C. Weguelin' ‡16–24in (40–60cm) ↔ 18–24in (45–60cm) ② 'Purewell Giant' ‡↔ 18in (45cm) – both flower from early summer to early autumn Both Z3b

① *formosana* Z4 ② *hirta* 'Alba' Z5 ‡to 32in (80cm)
③ *macrantha* subsp. *macranthopsis* Z8; all ‡to 32in (80cm)
④ *ohsumiensis* Z7 ‡to 20in (50cm)

FLOWERING PLANTS

Wake robin, Wood lily, Trinity flower

THESE SPRING-FLOWERING PLANTS of the woodland floor are prized for their curious three-petaled flowers held above the foliage, also grouped in threes. A small group of deciduous perennials, they are clump-forming and vigorous once established. The flowers, in white and shades of pink, dark red, and yellow, are held at the tips of slender stems in spring and summer. The rich or dark green leaves are sometimes mottled or marbled with silver or purple. Trilliums can be slow to start but once established resent being disturbed, so site them carefully. They are suitable for moist, shady borders or woodland gardens, alongside plants such as hostas (*see pp.260–261*).

Cultivation Grow in moist soil, preferably slightly acidic soil, in deep or partial shade. **Divide** plants (*see p.395*) after flowering, preferably by lifting small, rooted sections; try to keep the central clump undisturbed. **Sow** seed as soon as it is ripe in containers in a cold frame (*see pp.391–393*). Plants may take up to seven years to reach flowering size from seed. Young leaves can be damaged by slugs and snails, so lay traps or pick off by hand (*see p.398*).

Trillium cernuum
Z6 ‡ to 24in (60cm) ↔ to 10in (25cm), pendent flowers with prominent centers, flowers in spring

Trillium chloropetalum
Z6 ‡ to 16in (40cm) ↔ to 8in (20cm), with thick red-green stems and fragrant flowers in spring

Trillium luteum
Z6b ‡ to 16in (40cm) ↔ to 12in (30cm), leaves palely mottled, stalkless sweet-scented flowers in spring

Trillium grandiflorum (Great white trillium)
Z4 ‡ to 16in (40cm) ↔ to 12in (30cm), vigorous, with the largest flowers to 3in (8cm) long, in spring

Trillium rivale
Z6 ‡ to 5in (13cm) ↔ to 6in (15cm), dwarf species with leaves only 1¼in (3cm) long, flowers in spring

TROLLIUS
Globeflower

‡to 36in (90cm)
↔ 24in (60cm)

RELATED TO BUTTERCUPS, these moisture-loving perennials take their common name from their bowl-shaped flowers. Flower color ranges from pale cream to deep orange, with all shades in between. The flowers may be single, semidouble, or double, and appear from late spring to early summer, borne on tall stems; single flowers often have prominent central stamens. The rosettes of mid-green leaves are divided and often deeply cut, and may be glossy. Grow in a moist border, bog garden, or beside a pond or stream, with plants that enjoy similar conditions, like *Caltha palustris* (*see p.205*) or lysichitons (*see p.282*).

Cultivation Grow in very moist soil, in full sun or partial shade. Cut back stems after the first flush of flowers to encourage more later in the season. **Divide** plants (*see p.395*) as new growth begins or after flowering. **Sow** seed (*see pp.391–392*) in a container in a cold frame as soon as it is ripe, or in spring; it can take two years to germinate.

TROFAEOLUM
Nasturtium

see also p.154

NASTURTIUMS ARE THE MOST FAMILIAR of these vigorous, scrambling annuals and half-hardy perennials, grown for their cheerful, spurred flowers from summer until the first frosts of autumn. The trumpet-shaped flowers are borne in a variety of warm colors from red to orange and yellow, many bicolored or with contrasting markings on the petals. The round or lobed, light to mid-green leaves are held on long stalks. The bushy plants are best with other annuals or as border gap-fillers. Those with trailing stems scramble over the ground or climb; use them to clothe new structures quickly over the summer. Semitrailing types are ideal for hanging baskets. Tender perennials grown in pots may be overwintered under cover. Leaves and flowers of annuals are edible.

Cultivation Grow in moist but well-drained soil, in sun or partial shade. Water plants in pots freely in summer; apply a balanced fertilizer weekly. **Sow** seed (*see pp.391–393*) of annuals where they are to grow, in midspring; sow seed of perennials in a container in a cold frame as soon as ripe. Watch out for blackfly (*see Aphids, p.398*).

lium sessile (Toadshade)
‡to 12in (30cm) ↔ to 8in (20cm), patterned leaves and dark, less flowers in late spring

Trollius × cultorum 'Orange Princess'
Z3b ‡to 36in (90cm) ↔ 18in (45cm), glossy leaves, large at the base of the plant, flowers in late spring and early summer

① *majus* Alaska Series (Nasturtium) ‡to 12in (30cm), annual, variegated leaves ② *polyphyllum* T min. 35°F (2°C) ‡2–3in (5–8cm), trailing perennial, blue-green leaves

Tulip

↕min. 4in (10cm)
↕max.30in (75cm)

TULIPS HAVE BEEN PRIZED FOR CENTURIES for their brilliantly colored spring flowers. They were one of the first of the many bulbous perennials to be introduced into Western gardens from the eastern Mediterranean. Single or double, they come in a dazzling array of colors, often fascinatingly flushed or streaked with other shades. Petals may be frilled, fringed, pointed, waisted, or tinged with green, as in the viridiflora types such as 'Spring Green'. The species tulips, for instance *Tulipa sprengeri*, *T. tarda*, and the Greigii types, are often the smallest and among the easiest to grow. They suit borders, rock gardens, and areas of naturalistic planting. The taller, more highly bred hybrids put on an eye-catching display, but flowers can diminish over the years and are best lifted (*see below*) or treated as annuals. All are excellent in pots. Tulips need a long winter and thrive in Canadian hardiness Zones 4–8. Check with your garden center for planting times.

Cultivation Grow in well-drained, fertile soil in full sun. All tulips dislike heavy damp soil. Plant at twice the bulb's own depth in late autumn. **Deadhead** to prevent seedheads forming, thereby concentrating the plant's energy into developing the bulb and next year's flower bud within. **Apply** a balanced liquid fertilizer every two weeks after flowering until the foliage withers, to build up the bulb. **Lift** bulbs (except for small species tulips) once the foliage has died down (*see below*), and discard or separate small offsets. **Plant** large bulbs in late autumn. Grow on offsets in a spare corner until they reach flowering size (up to seven years). **Aphids** may spread an untreatable virus that causes petal streaking, which, although sometimes attractive, usually triggers a plant's decline.

Planting tulip bulbs for easy lifting

Most tall, hybrid tulip bulbs are best lifted once the foliage withers, then dried (if possible in a greenhouse or cold frame), and stored until autumn. This, to some extent, mimics their natural ripening process in the wild and helps bulbs perform well for years, especially on heavy soils. Species tulips, including the Greigii and Kaufmanniana types, need not be lifted.

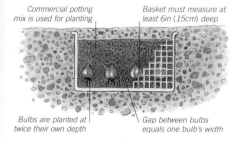

Commercial potting mix is used for planting

Basket must measure at least 6in (15cm) deep

Bulbs are planted at twice their own depth

Gap between bulbs equals one bulb's width

◁ ❶ *Planting tulips in a basket means that they can be easily lifted after flowering and stored when not in season. Use a container with plenty of drainage holes in the bottom – a lattice basket for pond plants is ideal. Lift carefully, so as not to damage roots that have grown through the basket. Bury the basket in a resting place in the garden so the top of it is just below the soil surface. Remember to label the basket and water it in well.*

▷ ❷ *Tulips planted directly in the soil can be gently lifted with a fork. Shake off any soil and leave them in a dry place, such as a garden shed, to dry off. Once dry, remove any old soil, withered leaves and flaking skin. Any bulbs showing signs of disease should be thrown away. Keep the bulbs in a cool, dark, and dry place. Check them at intervals to prevent disease from spreading. Replant in autumn for flowering the following spring.*

① *Tulipa acuminata* ↕20in (50cm), early and midspring ② 'Ancilla' ↕6in (15cm), midspring, good for rock gardens ③ 'Angélique' ↕12in (30cm), midspring, suitable for bedding or borders ④ 'Apeldoorn' ↕24in (60cm), midspring ⑤ *biflora* ↕4in (10cm), late winter to spring, fragrant ⑥ 'Carnaval de Nice' ↕16in (40cm), late spring ⑦ 'China Pink' ↕20in (50cm), late spring ⑧ *clusiana* var. *chrysantha* ↕12in (30cm), early and midspring ⑨ 'Douglas Bader' ↕18in (45cm),

late spring ⑩ *linifolia* ‡8in (20cm), early and midspring ⑪ *linifolia* **Batalinii Group** ‡14in (35cm), late winter to late spring ⑫ **'Madame Lefeber'** ‡14in (35cm)), early spring, large blooms, may need staking ⑬ **'Mount Tacoma'** ‡16in (40cm), late spring ⑭ **'Oriental Splendour'** ‡12in (30cm), early spring, leaves marked bluish purple ⑮ *praestans* **'Van Tubergen's Variety'** ‡20in (50cm), early and midspring, easy to grow ⑯ **'Prinses Irene'** ‡14 n (35cm), midspring, good for cut flowers

⑰ **'Purissima'** ‡14in (35cm), midspring ⑱ **'Queen of Night'** ‡24in (60cm), late spring ⑲ *sprengeri* ‡20in (50cm), early summer, wi self-seed in sun or partial shade ⑳ **'Spring Green'** 16in (40cm), late spring ㉑ *tarda* ‡6in (15cm), early and midspring ㉒ *turkestanica* ‡12in (30cm) early and midspring, unpleasant fragrance ㉓ **'West Point'** ‡20in (50cm), late spring ㉔ **'White Parrot'** ‡22in (55cm), late spring

Mullein

THESE STATELY PLANTS are grown for their tall flower spikes, densely set with saucer-shaped blooms from summer to autumn. The short-stemmed flowers occur usually in shades of yellow but are occasionally purple, scarlet, brownish red, or white. While the individual flowers are short lived, there are always more opening to sustain the display. Most garden mulleins are vigorous, rosette-forming plants that are useful in any border, particularly in gravel and cottage gardens. The often woolly, silvery rosettes of leaves remain attractive into winter. They are not generally long-lived, being biennials, short-lived perennials, and some annuals. Mulleins self-seed prolifically if allowed to do so, although the seedlings may not come true.

Cultivation Grow in well-drained, alkaline soil in full sun. Tall plants may require support especially in rich soil. **Sow** seed (*see pp.391–393*) of perennials in containers in a cold frame in late spring or early summer. Sow seed of biennials in early summer to flower the following year. **Divide** perennials (*see p.395*) in spring. **Take** root cuttings (*see p.394*) in winter.

Verbascum 'Cotswold Queen'
Z5 ‡4ft (1.2m) ↔ 12in (30cm), semievergreen, upright perennial with gray-green leaves, flowers from early to late summer

Verbascum 'Gainsborough'
Z5 ‡to 4ft (1.2m) ↔ to 12in (30cm), semievergreen perennial, gray-green rosettes, tall flower spikes from early to late summer

Verbascum chaixii 'Album'
Z6 ‡3ft (1m) ↔ 18in (45cm), rosette-forming perennial, flower spikes to 16in (40cm) mid- to late summer

Verbascum 'Letitia'
Z5 ‡to 10in (25cm) ↔ to 12in (30cm), dense, bushy evergreen, flower spikes to 4in (10cm) long all summer

Verbascum nigrum (Dark mullein)
Z3 ‡36in (90cm) ↔ 24in (60cm), rosette-forming, semievergreen or evergreen perennial, flowers midsummer to early autumn

VERBENA

THIS LARGE GROUP OF ANNUALS AND PERENNIALS are invaluable in a summer garden, with dense clusters of small flowers in shades of red, blue, pink, lilac, and violet borne on stiff, square stems. All are long flowering, but only a few are reliably hardy. Verbenas fall into two main groups: hardy perennials, such as *Verbena bonariensis*, will grow quite tall and bring height and an airy aspect to a border, while the shorter perennials tend to sprawl. Grown as annual bedding they will add color to containers and hanging baskets as well as the edges of borders. Grow perennials with tall plants like *Cynara cardunculus* (*see p.221*) and annuals with bedding plants such as geraniums (*see pp.300–303*).

Cultivation Moist but well-drained soil in full sun is best for verbenas. In containers, use a soil-based or soilless potting mix – water well in summer, apply a balanced fertilizer at weekly intervals. **Sow** seed (*see pp.391–393*) at 64–70°F (18–21°C) in early spring. **Divide** perennials (*see p.395*) in spring and take stem-tip cuttings (*see p.394*) in late summer. Powdery mildew can be a problem.

VERONICA
Speedwell

THE SLENDER, GRACEFUL SPIRES of veronica carry small, outward-facing flowers in intense or pastel shades of blue, pink, purple, or white. The numerous annuals and perennials in this group are mostly mat- or cushion-forming, but sometimes upright and branching. Their long or rounded leaves have toothed edges and are mid- to dark green, sometimes felted. Speedwells flower over a long period, from spring to autumn, and are excellent garden plants, especially for the front of a sunny border. They make good partners for shrubby or perennial plants such as lavenders (*see p.80*) and hardy geraniums (*see pp.250–251*). The smaller types are best grown in a rock garden.

Cultivation Alpine speedwells require sharply drained, poor to moderate soil, in full sun and protection from winter moisture for those with felted leaves. Others like any fertile soil in full sun or partial shade. **Sow** seed (*see pp.391–393*) in a container in a cold frame in autumn. **Divide** perennials (*see p.395*) in spring or autumn. Veronicas may suffer from powdery mildew in dry weather; remove affected parts.

Veronica austriaca 'Kapitän'
Z5 ‡ to 12in (30cm) ↔ to 16in (40cm), mat-forming perennial with flower spires 4–6in (10–15cm) long all summer

ariensis Z7b ‡ to 6ft (2m), perennial, flowers late summer to apply a winter mulch ② x *hybrida* 'Peaches and Cream' 5°F (2°C) ‡ to 18in (45cm), sprawling perennial grown as annual

Veronica gentianoides
Z4 ‡↔ to 18in (45cm), mat-forming perennial, dark green leaves, pale blue or, more rarely, white flowers in early summer

Veronica spicata 'Rotfuchs' (syn. 'Red Fox')
Z3 ‡↔ to 12in (30cm), mat-forming perennial, spreads by rooting stems, flowers from early to late summer

Pansy, Violet

THE RICHLY COLORED AND OPEN "FACES" of these well-loved flowers bring cheer to the garden all year round. Hundreds of forms are available, with flowers in hues of gold, orange, crimson, purple, black, blue, lilac, and white; many are bicolored and or even tricolored. Traditional violas are compact, tufted perennials, with dainty, often scented flowers, such as the classic English violet, *Viola odorata* (Z5). This is an evergreen perennial with a strong, sweet scent and is a good groundcover for a shady spot. Garden pansies include the brasher, large-flowered hybrids, mostly unscented; they are grown as bedding, and include winter-flowering forms. There are also annual violas. Violas look pretty as border edging or in hanging baskets and other containers.

Cultivation Violas like fertile, humus-rich, moist but well-drained soil, in full sun or partial shade. Violas can be short-lived, so it is best to raise new plants regularly. **Sow** seed (*see pp.391–393*) in late winter for summer flowers, or in summer for winter or spring flowers. **Take** softwood cuttings of perennials (*see p.394*) in spring or late summer.

Viola 'Nellie Britton'
Z6 ‡6in (15cm) ↔ 12in (30cm), clump-forming, evergreen perennial, abundant flowers, 1in (2.5cm) across, all summer

Viola 'Jeannie Bellew'
Z6 ‡8–9in (20–23cm) ↔ 10–12in (25–30cm), bushy, spreading perennial, flowers from midspring to midautumn

Viola 'Jackanapes'
Z5 ‡5in (13cm) ↔ 12in (30cm), clump-forming, short-lived, evergreen perennial, ¾in (2cm) flowers in late spring and summer

DEADHEAD regularly to prolong flowering. Cut out faded flowers near the base of the stalks to encourage new shoots to grow.

Viola 'Rebecca'
Z5 ‡4in (10cm) ↔ 10in (25cm), spreading perennial, heavily scented flowers – tinged blue in cold conditions – in summer

Viola tricolor (Heartsease, Johnny-jump-up)
Z4 ‡3–5in (8–13cm) ↔ 4–6in (10–15cm), annual, biennial, or short-lived evergreen perennial, flowers from spring to autumn

WALDSTEINIA
Barren strawberry

EXCELLENT AS GROUND COVER for a shady spot, waldsteinias quickly carpet the earth with small tufts of lush, green foliage, which resembles that of the strawberry plant (*Frageria, see p.245*). The foliage is in turn smothered in bright yellow flowers, either singly or in small, loose clusters, from late spring to early summer. These trouble-free, herbaceous or semi-evergreen perennials cover the ground by means of creeping stems (rhizomes) that spread underground and produce a weed-suppressing mat. They can be invasive in favorable conditions, so choose a site carefully. Waldsteinias are happy in a woodland garden, at the front of shady mixed beds, borders, or banks, or in herbaceous borders.

Cultivation Any moderately fertile soil in full or partial shade suits this undemanding plant. **Divide** mature plants (*see p.395*) in early spring. **Sow** seed (*see pp.391–393*) in containers in spring or autumn and place in a cold frame overwinter.

ZANTEDESCHIA
Calla lily

THESE IMPOSING, ARCHITECTURAL PERENNIALS have lush foliage and elegant, funnel-shaped blooms. The flowers are borne in spring and summer on stems up to 36in (90cm) tall and are usually clear yellow, although white, pink, lilac, or dark purple forms are available. The large, mid- to dark green leaves are arrow-shaped and sometimes spotted. *Zantesdeschia aethiopica* (T min. 35°F/2°C) can be grown in moist borders, where it can form large clumps, or as a marginal aquatic in water up to 12in (30cm) deep, in a 10–12in (25–30cm) aquatic basket filled with heavy loam.

Cultivation *Z. aethiopica* needs moist soil, enriched with organic matter, in full sun. In frost-prone areas, protect the crowns with a deep winter mulch. *Z. elliotiana* is best raised in pots under frost-free glass and stood outside for summer display. Use a soil-based potting mix and apply a balanced fertilizer weekly. **Divide** (*see p.395*) in spring. **Sow** seed (*see pp.391–393*) at 70–81°F (21–27°C).

...nia ternata
...cm) ↔ 24in (60cm), vigorous semievergreen, leaves to 2½in
...lowers up to ½in (1.5cm) across

Zantedeschia aethiopica 'Green Goddess'
T min. 35°F (2°C) ↕36in (90cm) ↔ 24in (60cm), clumping, evergreen in mild areas, 6–8in (15–20cm) flowers late spring to midsummer

Zantedeschia elliottiana (Golden calla)
T min. 50°F (10°C) ↕24–36in (60–90cm) ↔ 8in (20cm), erect habit, leaves to 8in (45cm) long, flowers 6in (15cm) long in summer

Bamboos and Grasses

using grasses in the garden

Most gardeners have a grass lawn or an area of turf in their gardens, but there is also a wonderful array of ornamental grasses that can be used in the borders. They are very architectural plants, with arching or upright stems, feathery or tufted flower heads, and subtly shaded seedheads. Ornamental grasses are easy to grow and bring constant movement and grace to the garden as well as soothing sounds as they rustle in the wind. Many grasses will remain attractive well into autumn and winter.

What is a grassy plant?

Ornamental grasses include several groups of grasslike plants. True grasses include lawn grasses; they may be annual or perennial and most have flower heads formed of many tiny flowers in clusters or spikes. Bamboos are very large, handsome, evergreen grasses. Many are vigorous, and once established can spread over a large area. The grasslike sedges and rushes are usually much smaller, often with colored or variegated foliage.

Many grassy plants thrive in most situations. True grasses often tolerate very dry conditions, whereas rushes and sedges prefer moister soils. Before planting, however, it is a good idea to incorporate plenty of well-rotted compost in dry soils to ensure moisture retention. Heavier clay soils need coarse grit dug in to improve drainage. Grasses require little further attention apart from cutting down old foliage, where needed, in early spring.

True grasses, like this Yorkshire fog, vary greatly in color and habit, but are grown for their flower spikes and seedheads, and sometimes for their colored stems.

Bamboos, such as this *Bambusa multiplex*, are true grasses but have attractive, segmented woody stems or canes, and up to 20 pairs of long, thin, delicate, divided leaves.

Rushes have tightly packed, upright leaves rising straight out of the soil. They prefer moist or wet soil, like this flowering rush, *Butomus umbellatus*, which grows in pond margins.

Sedges are low-growing, usually perennial and evergreen, and valued for their foliage, such as this carex, 'Silver Sceptre'. Sedge stems are triangular and feel distinctly ridged.

Planting ideas

Ornamental grasses, bamboos, and sedges can be used in a wide variety of ways. Larger grasses such as pampas grass (*Cortaderia, see p.346*) and *Stipa gigantea (see p.355)* are excellent as specimens planted on their own in a lawn or in a hot, gravel garden. If you have the space, you could have an entire border dedicated to grasses. It is possible to create many wonderful contrasts of foliage color, shape, and height, by planting drifts of grasses to form a border that shimmers and changes with every passing breeze. Vary the pace by placing tall, bold grasses next to fine-leaved ones.

Grasses and sedges also look good in mixed or herbaceous borders. They provide the perfect contrast to the broad leaves of hostas or the bright colors of flowering annuals and perennials, such as cirsiums (*see p.214*). The slender stems of grasses make them semitransparent so that you can glimpse other flowering plants through them, giving a light, airy feel to the planting. Taller grasses can be planted in clumps at intervals to act as focal points in a bed, or grown as a specimen or a screen – bamboos with colored stems are a good choice.

In a container Many grasses thrive in containers. Choose one that tones with or complements the color of the foliage – here the bronze of an old coal scuttle highlights the same tint in a carex.

In a raised bed Smaller grasses look particularly good in a raised bed. Here festucas, *Holcus mollis*, and acorus, in grays and blues, along with astilbes and stachys, echo the hue of the wood pilings.

In a mixed border
Grasses can look particularly good grown among herbaceous perennials in a mixed bed or border. The finer foliage of the grasses contrasts well with the more static shapes and bolder colors of flowering perennials and shrubs. Dwarf grasses, such as festucas, also make an elegant edging for a border.

Extending the display

One of the advantages of growing grasses in the garden is that many of them are late-flowering, and so extend the season of interest into autumn with their fluffy or feathery flower heads silhouetted against clear autumn skies. Some also provide autumn color when their architectural foliage turns brown or bronze and holds these russet tones through the winter, giving the garden some structure during the bleakest months of the year.

The flower heads also are long lasting and look just as graceful when they go to seed. They can look stunning when encrusted with frost. Most grasses are then cut down in spring; you could cover the gap until they grow back by planting spring-flowering bulbs.

Leaving grasses uncut during winter provides a much-needed food source – the seeds – for birds. Beneficial insects such as beetles also like to shelter in the bases of the plants until spring.

Winter interest
Miscanthus sinensis 'Zebrinus' is a great specimen plant that looks as good in winter as it does in summer. The dark green and yellow, banded leaves turn a subtle brown-bronze, the maroon flower heads fade to silver, and the lax stems remain unbroken despite winter winds.

Keeping bamboos within bounds

Unless you have a large garden, you should choose bamboos with care. Some have fibrous root systems that form compact clumps. Others will colonize the soil using underground stems, or rhizomes. As these spread through the soil, they push new canes up at intervals to form new clumps and can overwhelm other plants in a border. Spreading bamboos are best grown as specimen plants in an island bed so that their rhizomes are kept in check by mowing the lawn around them. You could also confine them by sinking a continuous barrier, made from concrete or flexible plastic, into the ground, but it may be easier to chop the roots back (*see right*).

Controlling spreading roots with a spade Dig a 12in (30cm) deep trench around the base of the plant to uncover the roots. Using a spade with a sharpened blade, chop through the roots on the inside wall of the trench, and remove them. Fill in the trench with sand so that it will be easier to do this again next year. Alternatively, chop through the roots of unwanted offshoots and dig them out.

ALOPECURUS
Foxtail grass

FOXTAIL GRASSES MAKE LOW, loose, spreading clumps of flat leaves, and in spring and summer bear dense, narrow, hairy spikes of flowers that resemble a fox's tail. Although spreading, they are not invasive, so are suitable for borders and for rock gardens. The tall flowering stems, rising above the basal tufts of leaves, make them interesting plants for growing in containers on the patio. The blue-green perennial *Alopecurus lanatus*, with its leaves covered in fine hairs, dislikes winter moisture and is best in alpine-style rock gardens. The fine striped foliage of the perennial *A. pratensis* 'Aureovariegatus' acts as a perfect contrast to plants with large, flat leaves, such as hostas (*see pp.260–261*). There are also annual foxtail grasses.

Cultivation Grow in gritty well-drained soil in sun or partial shade. On heavier soils, dig coarse grit into the planting area to improve the drainage. **Cut back** the old foliage in spring to get the best foliage effect from new growth. **Sow** seed (*see pp.391–392*) in containers in a cold frame as soon as it is ripe, or in spring. **Lift** and divide the plants (*see p.395*) carefully in spring or early summer.

Alopecurus pratensis 'Aureovariegatus'
Z4 ‡ to 4ft (1.2m) ↔ 16in (40cm), produces pale green to purple spikes of flowers from midspring to midsummer

BRIZA
Quaking grass

‡ to 3ft (90cm)
↔ 12in (30cm)

THE DELICATE SHIMMERING effect created by the drooping heads of these grasses in the smallest summer breeze adds movement and interest to any border or rock garden, and gives the plants their common name. The flowers, almost hoplike, are tinged red-brown or purple when young and turn straw-colored in autumn. They are popular for dried flower displays, either in their natural state or dyed. The loose tufts of narrow leaves vary in color from light green to blue-green. There are three commonly grown quaking grasses: the largest, *Briza media* (Z4b), at 60–90cm (2–3ft), is a perennial, while *B. maxima* (*see below*) and *B. minor*, the smallest at 18in (45cm), are annuals.

Cultivation All types require a well-drained soil. Grow the annual species in any such soil with a site in full sun; perennial species will tolerate a range of soils and a position in sun or partial shade. **Sow** seed of annuals where they are grown in spring (*see pp.391–393*). **Divide** perennials (*see p.395*) from midspring to midsummer.

Briza maxima (Greater quaking grass)
‡ 18–24in (45–60m) ↔ 10in (25cm), annual, flower heads from late spring to late summer

CALAMAGROSTIS
Feather reed grass

THE MOST WIDELY GROWN REED GRASSES are cultivars of *Calamagrostis × acutiflora*. These are perennial grasses, generally slow-spreading and clump-forming, with particularly soft and elegant plumes of flowers in subtle shades. Their upright, architectural forms add height to herbaceous or mixed borders, while their open habits allow you to see other plants growing behind them. They are attractive throughout the year, coming into growth early and bearing open clusters of summer flowers, which slowly compress to become narrow seedheads that are retained through the autumn. 'Karl Foerster' (Z4) has pink-bronze flowers fading to buff; 'Stricta' (Z5) has red-brown flowers; and 'Overdam' (*see below*) has purplish summer flowers that fade to grayish pink.

Cultivation Grow in moist soil, ideally enriched with plenty of well-rotted compost, but all but the poorest soils are tolerated. Position in sun or partial shade. **Leave** the season's growth uncut for winter effect, then cut down in early spring, before new growth starts. **Divide** overgrown clumps in spring (*see p.395*).

Calamagrostis × acutiflora 'Overdam'
Z4 ‡ to 4ft (1.2m) ↔ 24in (60cm), pale yellow edges and stripes on the leaves, which fade to pink-flushed white as they age

CAREX
Sedge

THESE GRASSY, TUFTED perennials are grown mainly
for their form, and the colors or markings on their
long, narrow leaves. There are many sedges in shades
of copper or russet, and others striped with gold or
silvery white. Mixed groups – for example, rich yellow
Carex elata 'Aurea' next to the red-brown *C. flagellifera*
(Z6) – create unusual color contrasts. Some also have
attractive clusters of flowers, drooping in *C. pendula*,
or spiky seedheads, like *C. greyi* (Z4). Most are
evergreen, some deciduous, and while some prefer a
damp spot, others are not fussy at all.

Cultivation Sedges can be grouped by their differing cultivation
requirements. **Group 1** will thrive in any soil in sun or partial shade.
Group 2 needs a moist, fertile, but well-drained alkaline soil and a
position in sun or partial shade. **Group 3** includes *C. flagellifera* and
C. siderosticha 'Variegata' and requires fertile, moist or wet soil in
sun or partial shade. **Cut back** deciduous species in spring. Trim
out any dead leaves on evergreen species in summer. **Divide** plants
(*see p.395*) between midspring and early summer. Aphids (*see p.398*)
occasionally attack the bases of the stems.

Carex oshimensis 'Evergold'
Z6b ‡12in (30cm) ↔ 14in (35cm), group 2, evergreen

MULCHING CAREX with gravel
or bark gives a decorative finish
and will help protect some
varieties in winter. Spread the
mulch over the root area during
mild, moist autumn weather.

Carex elata 'Aurea' (Bowles' golden sedge)
Z5 ‡to 28in (70cm) ↔ 18in (45cm), group 3, deciduous

Carex testacea
T min. 41°F (5°C) ‡to 5ft (1.5m) ↔ 24in (60cm), group 1,
evergreen

Carex pendula (Weeping sedge)
Z4 ‡to 4½ft (1.4m) ↔ to 5ft (1.5m), group 3, evergreen,
self-seeds freely

BAMBOOS AND GRASSES

CHUSQUEA

THIS LARGE GROUP OF BAMBOOS forms dense clumps of glossy, solid canes. They make distinctive evergreen specimens in a lawn or in a woodland garden, or can be grown with large ferns, such as *Woodwardia radicans* (*see p.365*), for dramatic, contrasting foliage effects. They are a good choice for a coastal garden. The hardy types, the most popular being *Chusquea culeou*, typically reach 20ft (6m). The stems are yellowish, with long, tapering, papery white leaf sheaths. These stay on the plant for the first year, giving an attractive striped appearance to the young canes. Clusters of sideshoots grow from the leaf joints, bearing many thin, mid-green leaves. When leaves fall from the lower part of older canes, the branching growth and leaf stalks remain at the tips, giving them a "whiskery" look.

Cultivation Grow in well-drained soil, enriched with plenty of well-rotted compost. Position in sun or partial shade, with shelter from cold, drying winds. **Divide** clumps (*see p.395*) in spring.

CORTADERIA
Pampas grass, Tussock grass

LARGE AND STATELY EVERGREEN GRASSES, these are grown for their arching, ornamental foliage and large, feathery plumes of flowers in shades of white and silver. They form dense clumps of stiff, narrow, leaves with sharp edges (take care when siting it in family gardens), with flowers held on strong, upright stems above the foliage. The plumes can be used fresh or dried in flower arrangements. Pampas grass has a "retro" image and still looks somewhat kitschy in a lawn or front garden, but it makes an end-piece to a border, perhaps in front of a dark green hedge that will highlight its silvery plumes, or can be used to add often needed height and drama to a modern planting design of perennials and grasses.

Cultivation Grow in fertile, well-drained soil in full sun with plenty of space to develop. **Protect** the crowns of young plants in their first winter, and plants of all ages in cold areas, with a winter mulch. **Cut back** the old and dead growth in late winter or early spring; take care because the leaf edges are sharp. **Sow** seed (*see pp.391–392*) with bottom heat in spring. **Divide** (*see p.395*) in spring.

CUTTING DOWN PAMPAS
Wearing gloves, cut back old stems with shears in early spring. Be careful not to damage emerging new growth.

Cortaderia selloana 'Sunningdale Silver'
Z7 ‡10ft (3m) or more ↔ to 8ft (2.5m), weather-resistant plumes from late summer

Chusquea culeou (Chilean bamboo)
T min. 41°F (5°C) ‡to 20ft (6m) ↔ 8ft (2.5m), canes become very chunky, up to 1¼in (3cm) across

Cortaderia selloana 'Pumila' (Dwarf pampas grass)
Z7 ‡to 5ft (1.5m) ↔ to 4ft (1.2m), flower heads open in late summer

Cortaderia selloana
Z7 ‡8–10ft (2.5–3m) ↔ 5ft (1.5m), flower spikes, often flushed pink or purple, from late summer

DESCHAMPSIA
Hair grass

CLOUDLIKE, AIRY FLOWER HEADS and graceful habits make these perennial grasses worth including in any garden. The tussocks of threadlike leaves may be evergreen or deciduous. Many of the hair grasses grown in gardens are cultivars of *Deschampsia cespitosa*, with flowers from silvery reddish brown to gold, changing color as they age in autumn. This species grows up to 6ft (2m) tall, although it has several more compact varieties; *D. flexuosa* (Z5), at 24in (60cm), also suits smaller gardens. All are effective alongside plants with open clusters of flowers, such as *Campanula lactiflora* (*see p.206*); the soft lilac-pink flowers of *C.* 'Loddon Anna', for example, make a perfect contrast to the golden flowers of *D. cespitosa* 'Goldtau'.

Cultivation Best in neutral to acidic soil. Dig in plenty of well-rotted organic matter if your soil is light and sandy, to help retain moisture. Position in sun or part shade. **Prune** old flower heads in spring before new growth begins. **Sow** seed in spring or autumn where plants are to grow (*see p.393*). **Divide** (*see p.395*) in spring or early summer.

FARGESIA

THESE CLUMP-FORMING BAMBOOS have slender, arching stems and lance-shaped leaves growing from purplish sheaths. The large, striking *Fargesia murielae* makes a fine focal point or a hardy hedging or screening plant. The stems are white-powdery when young, maturing to yellow-green and then yellow. They arch under the weight of the leaves, which are up to 6in (15cm) long, with drawn-out tips. The leaf sheaths age to pale brown. For wonderful foliage contrast, grow it next to the bold gunnera (*see p.254*), although you will need a fair amount of space to accommodate both plants. The similarly large *F. nitida* (Z5) has very slender, purplish canes and long, narrow leaves, which give it a more airy, delicate appearance.

Cultivation Grow in fertile, moisture-retentive soil. Position *F. nitida* in dappled shade with shelter; *F. murielae* will tolerate full sun and windy sites. **Divide** established clumps (*see p.395*). Take root cuttings (*see p.394*) of lengths of underground stem (rhizomes) in spring.

FESTUCA
Fescue

FESCUES ARE A LARGE, VARIED GROUP, deciduous and evergreen, mostly suited to sunny positions. They are grown mainly for the narrow, arching, smooth leaves, but also bear flower heads that fade to golden shades. The densely tufted evergreen perennial *Festuca glauca* and its many new cultivars are very popular; the larger *F. amethystina* (Z4), which turns purplish after flowering, is also attractive. Grow fescues as edging or to provide a contrast to other smallish plants with bolder leaves: most are too small to make specimen plants. Blue flowers, like those of felicias (*see p.244*), complement the steely blue of *F. glauca*, while silver foliage plants, such as *Stachys byzantina* (*see p.328*), make a wonderful contrast. A mulch of dark, chipped slate would complete a striking, urban look.

Cultivation Grow fescues in poor to moderately fertile, well-drained soil, in full sun. **Sow** seed (*see pp.391–392*) from autumn until spring in containers in a cold frame. **Divide** and replant (*see p.395*) in spring every two to three years to maintain good foliage color and keep plants vigorous.

Deschampsia cespitosa 'Goldtau' (Tussock grass)
Z4 ↕↔ to 30in (75cm), reddish silver young flower heads mature from early to late summer to golden yellow

Fargesia murielae (Umbrella bamboo)
Z5b ↕ to 12ft (4m) ↔ to 5ft (1.5m)

Festuca glauca (Blue fescue)
Z3b ↕ to 12in (30cm) ↔ 10in (25cm) evergreen, violet to blue-green flower heads in early and midsummer

GLYCERIA MAXIMA

Manna grass

THIS IS A DENSE, VIGOROUS, spreading perennial. Unusually for grasses, it grows naturally not just along the damp edges of ponds or streams but also in shallow water, to a depth of 30in (75cm). There are many forms, but the only one widely grown is *Glyceria maxima* var. *variegata*. This has narrow, strappy leaves; tinged with pink when they emerge in spring, they later become deep green striped with white. Plumelike clusters of green to purplish green flowers appear in mid- and late summer on reedlike stems. It is useful for shading and softening the edges of a large pond, or in problem sites with wet soil, but with its invasive, spreading habit it may best be grown in a container or planting basket.

Cultivation Grow *G. maxima* var. *variegata* in any moisture-retentive soil, or in water to 6in (15cm) deep, planted in an aquatic basket to restrict the spread of the roots. It also needs full sun. **Divide** plants in spring (*see p.395*).

Glyceria maxima var. *variegata*
Z6 ‡32in (80cm) ↔ indefinite, can become invasive both in ponds and in damp soil

HAKONECHLOA MACRA

Japanese forest grass

THIS BRIGHTLY COLORED GRASS brings warmth and light to low-level plantings or the front of a border, forming a dense mound of narrow, arching, pale green leaves and producing reddish brown flower spikes in summer. It is a deciduous perennial, flushed with orange and rust in autumn and slowly spreading to form mats. The leaves remain on the plant well into winter and often keep their color, forming a bright splash in winter. This is one of the most attractive ornamental grasses to grow in containers on a patio, forming a neat, bushy mop of gently arching foliage that will almost completely cover its pot. There are several cultivars with differing variegation.

Cultivation Grow in fertile soil enriched with well-rotted organic matter, or soil-based potting mix, in full sun or partial shade. **Cut off** the old foliage in autumn if its winter show is not wanted, or in spring. **Divide** plants (*see p.395*) in spring.

Hakonechloa macra 'Aureola'
Z5 ‡14in (35cm) ↔ 16in (40cm), leaves flushed red in autumn, is best grown in partial shade

HELICTOTRICHON

FORMING TUSSOCKS OF LEAVES in shades of blue-gray or mid- to light green, these grasses come from open sites, often with poor soils. They are particularly suited to the conditions offered by rock gardens or gravel plantings but are happy in borders with well-drained soil. There are many species, both deciduous and evergreen, and all perennial. In summer, upright or nodding clusters of flowers glisten in the light; these age to a straw color. *Helictotrichon sempervirens* is especially popular, forming a dense, fine clump of tightly rolled leaves. Its flattened spikes of flowers, tinged with purple, have a graceful, nodding habit. These grasses make good specimens and associate well with purple or silver foliage plants.

Cultivation Grow in well-drained, poor to moderately fertile soil, preferably alkaline, in full sun. **Cut back** dead foliage and flowers in spring. **Sow** seed (*see pp.391–392*) in spring in containers in a cold frame or on a windowsill. **Divide** (*see p.395*) in spring. Rust (*see p.399*) can be a problem, particularly in damp summers.

Helictotrichon sempervirens (Blue oat grass)
Z4b ‡to 4ft (1.4m) ↔ 24in (60cm), evergreen, gray-blue leaves fade in autumn, flower spikes in early and midsummer

HORDEUM
Barley

THIS GROUP OF ORNAMENTAL GRASSES contains about 20 annual and perennial species and includes the cereal crop, barley. The narrow leaves may be flat or rolled and range from light to mid-green or blue-green. Flowers are produced in dense, cylindrical, or flattened spikes with distinctive long bristles. The type most often grown in gardens is *Hordeum jubatum*, which has spikes up to 5in (13cm) long of silky, bristled flowers. Squirrel tail grass is often grown as an annual with hardy annuals such as cornflowers (*Centaurea, see p.209*), creating a fluffy look for a garden bordering open countryside. Many species are good to use in dried flower arrangements. They also look good in a wild garden or meadow planting, or among blue campanulas (*see pp.206–207*).

Cultivation Grow in moderately fertile, well-drained soil, in full sun. **Sow** seed where it is to grow (*see pp.391–393*) in spring or autumn. **Cut** flowerheads for drying before they are fully mature.

Hordeum jubatum (Foxtail grass)
‡ 20in (50cm) ↔ 12in (30cm), annual or perennial, red-purple-flushed flowers early to midsummer, then fade to beige

LAGURUS OVATUS
Hare's tail

‡ to 20in (50cm)
↔ 12in (30cm)

THIS ANNUAL GRASS grows naturally in open spaces in the Mediterranean region. It is valued for the appealing, softly hairy flower heads that give it its name. These are pale green, tinged with purple, and mature to a pale, creamy buff color in late summer and autumn. The flat, narrow leaves are pale green. A small and unassuming plant, hare's tail has most impact when planted in groups. It is best grown in drifts or among other hardy annuals such as calendulas (*see p.204*), cosmos (*see p.218*), and annual chrysanthemums (*see pp.212–213*). It also makes a useful gap-filler in herbaceous borders. The flower heads can be used in fresh or dried flower arrangements.

Cultivation Prefers light, sandy soil that is well-drained and moderately fertile. **Position** in full sun. **Sow** seed (*see pp.391–393*) in spring where the plants are to grow, or in containers in a cold frame in autumn. **Pick** flowerheads for drying before they are fully mature.

Lagurus ovatus
‡ to 20in (50cm) ↔ 12in (30cm), annual, pale green, purple-tinged panicles turn pale buff as they mature

LUZULA
Woodrush

VALUED FOR THEIR TOLERANCE of shade, these rushes provide good groundcover in woodland or mixed borders. Woodrushes are mostly evergreen perennials from heaths, moors, and scrubby woodland, forming tussocks of grassy leaves with white hairs on them, particularly along the edges. Clusters of tiny flowers are produced in spring or summer. The greater woodrush, *Luzula sylvatica*, will grow in dry shade and makes an excellent, weed-suppressing ground-cover. Its leaves are glossy, dark green, and in mid-spring and early summer it bears chestnut brown flowers in open clusters. Snowy woodrush, *L. nivea* (Z4), has pure white flowers, in early and midsummer.

Cultivation Grow in poor to reasonably fertile, well-drained soil. Position in partial or deep shade; woodrushes can be grown in full sun where the soil is always moist. **Sow** seed (*see pp.391–392*) in containers in spring or autumn. **Divide** plants (*see p.395*) between spring and early summer.

Luzula sylvatica 'Aurea'
Z5 ‡ to 32in (80cm) ↔ 18in (45cm), yellow-green leaves become bright, shiny yellow in winter, needs light, dappled shade

Wood millet

MISCANTHUS

MAINLY WOODLAND GRASSES, these are a small group of annuals and perennials. The leaves are sometimes quite broad, and yellow-green to light green. Open, delicate flower clusters appear from spring to midsummer. Milium adds a bright splash of color to herbaceous borders or the dappled shade at the edge of a woodland. Plants with dark green leaves, such as astilbes (*see p.194*) or some hostas (*see pp.206–261*), will highlight the leaf color. *Milium effusum* 'Aureum', is named for E. A. Bowles, a famous gardener and writer. Its smooth, flat, arching, golden leaves are at their best in early spring, fading slightly as summer goes on. Miliums associate well with other grasses such as pennisetums (*see facing page*) or woodrushes (*Luzula, see p.349*).

Cultivation Grow in fertile, moist but well-drained soil with plenty of organic matter. Position in partial shade; may be grown in sun if the soil remains moist at all times. **Sow** seed (*see pp.391–393*) outdoors in spring. **Divide** plants (*see p.395*) in early spring and early summer.

GRACEFUL SPECIMEN PLANTS in a lawn or in borders, these wonderful grasses add height without over-powering other plants. They bring movement and a rustling sound in the lightest breeze. Although they look delicate, the flowering stems stand up well to wind; this and their often fine autumn color gives them added value late in the season. Miscanthus form large clumps of arching, narrow, light green foliage. Many cultivars of eulalia grass (*Miscanthus sinensis*, Z4) are widely grown. During late summer and autumn, they produce large, distinctive tassels of silky, hairy flowers, some red-tinted, others silvery. These grasses are deciduous, but the dying foliage of many develops russet or golden tints in autumn.

Cultivation Tolerant of most conditions, but they grow best in fertile, moist but well-drained soil in full sun. May be slow to settle in. **Protect** from excessive winter moisture. **Cut** old foliage to the ground in early spring before growth starts. **Sow** seed (*see pp.391–392*) in spring in a cold frame or on the windowsill. **Divide** plants (*see p.395*) as new growth emerges in spring.

Miscanthus sinensis 'Zebrinus' (Zebra grass)
Z4 ‡ to 4ft (1.2m) ↔ 4ft (1.2m), the most spreading of several striped cultivars, lighter bands on leaves in summer

Milium effusum 'Aureum' (Bowles' golden grass)
Z5 ‡ to 24in (60cm) ↔ 12in (30cm), perennial with slender, nodding, golden flower spikes from late spring to midsummer

DIVIDING A LARGE CLUMP
Cutting up the rootball and replanting will both rejuvenate the center of the clump and help control its spread. A saw may be needed for tough roots.

Miscanthus sinensis 'Gracillimus' (Maiden grass)
Z4 ‡ 4½ft (1.3m) ↔ 4ft (1.2m), dense, fine leaves with good bronze tints in autumn, may not flower in cooler summers

Miscanthus sinensis 'Silberfeder'
Z4 ‡ to 8ft (2.5m) ↔ 4ft (1.2m), abundant flower heads that age to silv and are retained into winter, particularly dislikes wet soil

MOLINIA CAERULEA
Purple moor grass

THIS SPECIES IS THE ONLY ONE grown in gardens, but there are a number of different varieties. These are tall and slender grasses, making excellent structural plants for mixed and herbaceous borders, or for the far edges of informal ponds. They are grown for their attractive habits, forming clumps of narrow, dark green leaves, and for dense, purple flower spikes, which are held on graceful, arching, golden stems over a long period from spring to autumn. The flower heads and leaves in some cultivars turn glorious shades of golden yellow in autumn, but the flowering stems do not usually last into winter. A beautiful way to highlight the purple flowers and yellow-tinted stems is by growing tall, pale blue delphiniums (*see pp.238–239*) behind them.

Cultivation Grow in any moist but well-drained soil, preferably acid to neutral, in full sun or partial shade. **Sow** seed (*see pp.391–393*) in spring in containers in a cold frame or on the windowsill. **Divide** plants (*see p.395*) in spring and pot up until they become established and then replant in the garden.

PENNISETUM

THESE ORNAMENTAL GRASSES are grown for their feathery clusters of flowers or overarching stems, produced in summer and autumn, and popular in fresh and dried flower arrangements. Several types of these clump-forming perennials and annuals are grown. The evergreen fountain grass, *Pennisetum alopecuroides*, up to 5ft (1.5m) tall, has flat, dark green leaves, with bottlebrush-shaped, bristly flower heads in yellowish green to dark purple. The smaller, deciduous fountain grass, *P. orientale* (z7), has distinctive, pink flower heads and combines well with Mediterranean plants such as lavenders (*Lavandula, see p.80*). Feathertop, *P. villosum* (T min. 41°F/5°C), although a deciduous perennial, is often grown as an annual.

Cultivation Grow in light, reasonably fertile soil in full sun. **Cut back** dead growth in spring. **Sow** seed (*see p.391–392*) in heat in early spring. **Divide** plants (*see p.395*) in late spring or early summer.

Molinia caerulea subsp. *arundinacea*
Z4 ‡ to 5ft (1.5m) ↔ 16in (40cm), this subspecies and its cultivars are particularly noted for their autumn color

Pennisetum alopecuroides 'Hameln'
Z5 ‡↔ 20in (50cm), compact and early flowering, dark green leaves turn golden yellow in autumn

Pennisetum villosum (Feathertop)
T min. 41°F (5°C) ‡↔ 24in (60cm), flat leaves, soft flowerheads in late summer and early autumn, maturing to purple

PHALARIS ARUNDINACEA

Reed canary grass, Ribbon grass

THIS SPREADING PERENNIAL and it cultivars are widely grown. It is an erect, evergreen grass with flat leaves. From early to midsummer, it bears narrow clusters of silky, pale green flowers that age to buff. It makes highly effective groundcover, crowding out weeds, and looks at home planted by a pond or stream. This grass can be invasive, so needs plenty of space or firm control: it requires lifting and dividing regularly when grown in small gardens or in mixed borders. There are several variegated cultivars. *Platycodon grandiflorus* (*see p.309*) is a striking plant to grow alongside these grasses – its blue flowers will be highlighted by the bright white stripes on the foliage.

Cultivation Tolerates any soil in full sun or partial shade. Contain its spread if necessary by planting t in a sunken, bottomless half-barrel. **Cut back** the dead foliage in spring. Variegated types may revert to plain green foliage in midsummer; cut down all but young shoots in early summer to encourage new variegated foliage. **Divide** plants (*see p.395*) from midspring to midsummer.

***Phalaris arundinacea* var. *picta* (Gardener's garters)**
Z3b ‡ to 3ft (1m) ↔ indefinite, variable, white-striped leaves, classic pond- and stream-side plant where space is not a problem

PHYLLOSTACHYS

Black, Golden, or Zigzag bamboo

VALUED FOR THEIR GRACEFUL forms, fine stems, and rustling foliage, these medium to large, evergreen bamboos can be included in almost any garden. They spread by underground stems (rhizomes) to form slowly expanding clumps, but can become invasive in mild areas. Phyllostachys can be grown in shrub borders or in containers outdoors. They also thrive in woodland gardens and have become popular as an elegant alternative to traditional hedging plants. These bamboos are particularly noted for their grooved, beautifully colored stems: brilliant yellow in *Phyllostachys aureosulcata* 'Aureocaulis' (Z7) or purple in *P. violascens* (Z7b). They often grow in a zigzag fashion and have a branching habit, bearing fairly small leaves.

Cultivation Grow in well-drained soil enriched with well-rotted compost. Position in full sun or dappled shade. In containers, use a soil-based potting mix and apply a liquid fertilizer monthly. **Shelter** from cold, drying winds that can scorch leaf edges. **Cut out** some of the old canes each year. **Divide** clumps (*see p.395*) in spring.

***Phyllostachys aurea* (Golden or Fishpole bamboo)**
Z7 ‡ 6–30ft (2–10m) ↔ indefinite, stiffly upright young canes are bright to mid-green, maturing to brownish yellow

***Phyllostachys nigra* (Black bamboo)**
Z7 ‡ 10–15ft (3–5m) ↔ 6–10ft (2–3m), arching, slender young canes are green, turning to shiny black over two years

MOST PLEIOBLASTUS ARE DWARF only in relation to other bamboos, most being 3–5ft (1–1.5m) in height, although the pygmy bamboo, *Pleioblastus pygmaeus* (Z7b) grows to only 16in (40cm) tall. This generally reduced stature, however, makes them ideal bamboos for containers, as they will not appear top-heavy. Growing them in large pots also has the advantage of restraining their vigorously spreading habit; the pygmy bamboo is a particular offender in this respect. *P. auricomus* and *P. variegatus* are naturally more restrained, especially in cooler climates. They make dense thickets of erect, leafy canes, and while they will thrive in open woodland glades, enjoying the shelter, they should be used cautiously in borders.

Cultivation Grow in moist, well-drained soil enriched with well-rotted organic matter. Position in full sun or partial shade, sheltered from cold, drying winds that may scorch leaf edges. **Restrain** their spread by confining the roots if necessary (*see p.343*). **Take** root cuttings in spring and plant out widely spaced, keeping the soil reliably moist until plants are established.

GROWN FOR THEIR ERECT, WOODY CANES, this small group of vigorous, thicket-forming bamboos require quite a bit of space, such as in a woodland or wild garden. They do have features that strongly recommend them in spite of this, making excellent screening plants to hide structures, such as sheds or compost piles. Cooler climates help keep them clump-forming rather than invasive, but *Pseudosasa amabilis* (Z5) may look ragged if not sheltered. The leaf sheaths tend to remain on the stems, giving a striped appearance. The leaves are generally large, lance-shaped, and mid- or dark green. Rarely, lax clusters of small spikelike green flowers are produced. Unlike many bamboos, these often survive flowering, although they are weakened.

Cultivation Grow in moist but well-drained, fertile soil; *P. japonica* tolerates poor, dry, or wet soils. Position in sun or partial shade. **Divide** the clumps (*see p.395*) in spring and keep the divisions moist until they are well established. **Cut back** plants if they flower, and apply fertilizer and a deep organic mulch.

‡ to 6ft (2m)
↔ indefinite

THESE THICKET-FORMING bamboos are small to medium in height, and grown as much for their handsome foliage as for their canes. The leaves are large and turn white and dry around the edges from autumn onward, giving a variegated appearance. Sasas are useful groundcover plants or as a hedge, if you have the space. The moderately spreading *Sasa veitchii* is invaluable under trees, tolerating deep shade: its natural habitat is in moist hollows in woodland. More rampant is the broad-leaved *S. palmata* (Z6b); the purple-streaked canes of *S. palmata* var. *nebulosa* are attractive, but this is a bamboo to plant only where there is plenty of space.

Cultivation Tolerant of most sites and soils, except for dry soils in full sun. Dig in well-rotted compost before planting. Contain its spread by growing in a large tub sunk in the soil. **Divide** plants (*see p.395*) in spring, or cut off pieces of rhizomes (underground stems).

① *auricomus* Z7b ‡ to 5ft (1.5m) ↔ 5ft (1.5m), leaves edged with fine bristles ② *variegatus* Z7b ‡ 30in (75cm) ↔ 4ft (1.2m), leaves hairy, pale green canes

Pseudosasa japonica (Arrow bamboo)
Z8 ‡ 20ft (6m) ↔ indeterminate, canes are olive green when young and mature to pale beige, stands up well to winds

Sasa veitchii
Z6 ‡ 4–6ft (1.2–2m) ↔ indefinite, slender, purple canes are smooth and round with a fine bloom, bristly sheaths protect new leaves

SCHOENOPLECTUS
Club-rush

THIS GROUP OF SEDGES includes both annuals and evergreen perennials, suitable for a bog garden or as aquatic plants in still or gently moving water. They are valued mainly for their stems and for their grassy leaves. Growing in planting baskets around the edges of a pond, the narrow foliage makes an interesting textural contrast to the broader leaves of water irises (*see pp.264–267*). The brown flowers, which are borne from early to late summer in clusters, are a fairly low-key display. Among the most widely grown is the variegated club-rush *Schoenoplectus lacustris* 'Zebrinus': striking stems are reminiscent of tiny tide-marker poles rising from the water.

Cultivation Grow in fertile, wet soil or in water to a depth of up to 12in (30cm), in a position in full sun. **Restrict** growth in small ponds by cutting back the roots every year. **Cut out** any plain green stems to the ground on variegated rushes. **Propagate** by uprooting and planting out sections of underground stem (rhizome) from midspring to midsummer.

Schoenoplectus lacustris 'Zebrinus'
Z5 ‡ 3ft (1m) ↔ 24in (60cm), perennial, almost leafless stems arise at intervals from rhizomes

SEMIARUNDINARIA

‡ 22ft (7m)
↔ 6ft (2m)

THESE ARE TALL, UPRIGHT bamboos, forming thickets in warmer climates, but clumps in cooler climates. These bamboos are at home in a woodland garden, making elegant companions to slender, small-leaved trees such as birches (*Betula, see p.28*). Their strongly vertical forms also make fine informal screens if you have the space. The leaf sheaths often hang onto the canes by the bases for some time before falling. *Semiarundinaria fastuosa* (Z7) is widely grown. The lower levels of its canes are bare of leaves, making it ideal to position among lower plants in a shrub border. The glossy, mid-green canes have purple-brown stripes that are most prominent when the leaves are young.

Cultivation Grow in well-drained, reasonably fertile soil, adding plenty of well-rotted compost. Position in full sun or light shade. **Divide** clumps (*see p.395*), or uproot and plant out sections of underground stem (rhizome) in spring. Young shoots may be damaged by slugs (*see p.398*).

Semiarundinaria fastuosa (Narihira bamboo)
‡ to 22ft (7m) ↔ 6ft (2m) or more, glossy, mid-green leaves, sheaths reveal a polished, deep red interior when they open

SPARTINA
Cord grass, Marsh grass

ADAPTABLE AND HARDY, these herbaceous perennial grasses are found in swamps, marshes, and wet prairies. They are grown for their arching leaves and make excellent groundcover at the margins of ponds. In damp soil, they spread quickly by underground stems (rhizomes); they tolerate all but the driest soils, however, and the drier the soil, the easier they are to contain. Cord grasses tolerate salty conditions well, making them useful in coastal gardens. Grow prairie cord grass, *S. pectinata* (Z4), alongside late-flowering perennials that come from similar habitats, such as heleniums (*see p.255*) and rudbeckias (*see p.317*); the bright golden yellow to brown, autumn color of the grass is a perfect contrast to the yellows, oranges, and rich reds of these flowers.

Cultivation Grow in reasonably fertile, damp to well-drained soil with plenty of well-rotted organic matter added to it. They prefer full sun but tolerate light, dappled shade. **Cut down** the old foliage in early spring. **Divide** clumps (*see p.395*) in spring. Young shoots may be damaged by slugs (*see p.398*).

Spartina pectinata 'Aureomarginata'
Z4 ‡ to 6ft (2m) ↔ indefinite, retains its yellow autumn leaves and elegant silhouette during winter

STIPA

Feather grass, Needle grass, Spear grass

THIS LARGE GROUP OF PERENNIAL grasses includes evergreen and deciduous types that form lax tufts of narrow foliage, above which tall flower stems rustle and wave. The growth habit alone is appealing; the flowering display in summer and early autumn is spectacular, ranging from the ethereal, drooping flowers of *Stipa arundinacea* to the feathery, upright *S. tenuissima* (Z7) and the towering stems of *S. gigantea*. Elegant in dried flower arrangements, many age to rich golden yellow and russet, keeping their colors into winter. There is a range of shapes and sizes suitable for use in most situations. Plant *S. gigantea* in a border with the tall, open *Verbena bonariensis* (*see p.337*) to lend an airy feel to the planting scheme; both add height without obscuring other plants.

Cultivation Grow in any reasonably fertile soil that is well-drained, in full sun. Dig in some coarse grit on heavier soils to improve drainage. **Cut back** deciduous species in early winter or spring. **Sow** seed in containers in spring (*see pp.391–392*). **Divide** plants (*see p.395*) from midspring to early summer.

Stipa gigantea (Giant feather grass, Golden oats)
Z8 ‡ to 8ft (2.5m) ↔ 4ft (1.2m), evergreen or semievergreen, purple-green flowers are gold when ripe in summer

Stipa calamagrostis
Z7 ‡ 3ft (1m) ↔ 4ft (1.2m), deciduous, blue-green leaves, summer flowerheads are silvery and buff to purplish-tinted

UNCINIA

Hook sedge

GENERALLY GROWN FOR THEIR shiny, richly colored, grassy leaves, these evergreen sedges are small perennials with a loosely tufted habit, at home in damp places. Upright, triangular to cylindrical stems bear flowers in narrow spikes, with male flowers at the top and female flowers beneath them, followed by the hooked, nutlike fruits that give the plants their common name. The most widely grown hook sedges are the russet-leaved *Uncinia rubra* and the smaller *U. unciniata*, both of which resemble the New Zealand species of carex (*see p.345*) in many ways. Uncinias look very attractive surrounded by a gravel mulch, although the soil below must be moisture-retentive. Where not hardy, grow frost-tender species in a cool greenhouse.

Cultivation Grow in reasonably fertile, but well-drained soil, containing plenty of well-rotted organic matter. Position in full sun or dappled shade. **Sow** seed (*see pp.391–392*) in heat in spring. **Divide** well-grown plants (*see p.395*) between spring and midsummer.

Uncinia rubra T min. 35°F (2°C) ‡ 12in (30cm) ↔ 14in (35cm), greenish red or reddish brown foliage, russet, then dark brown to black flowers in mid- to late summer

using ferns in the garden

Ferns are frequently underrated as foliage plants. They can create an impact on both a large and small scale: their outlines are bold and architectural whether used singly or *en masse*, and their leaves, or fronds, can be crimped, curled, or lacy, and provide attractive contrasts when combined with other plants. In an area of deep or dappled shade, or by the side of a pond or stream, ferns bring atmosphere to the garden and, in some cases, year-round color.

How to use ferns in the garden

The mood that you want to create in the garden will determine where you plant ferns and how you combine them with other plants. You can create interesting effects by interspersing the fine foliage of ferns with other leafy plants, such as irises (*see pp.264–267*) or hostas (*see pp.260–261*).

In a formal setting, plant shuttlecock ferns (*Matteuccia, see p.363*) behind a low hedge of trimmed boxwood (*Buxus, see p.30*); the clean, horizontal lines of the hedge create an elegant contrast with the skyward thrust of the ferns' tall, upright fronds.

For informality, group ferns by a pool or in a bog garden, where the delicate fronds contrast strikingly with the coarser foliage of other moisture-loving plants such as rodgersias (*see p.316*) and gunneras (*see p.254*).

Ferns can make lush groundcover in a shady or semishady spot under trees and shrubs, providing an interesting understory. Choose tall, arching ferns, for example the male fern (*Dryopteris filix-mas*) or the soft shield fern (*Polystichum setiferum, see p.365*), to screen bare or leggy stems of shrubs. Once the fronds open in spring, they create dense shade to suppress weeds.

A touch of mystery The ferns planted alongside and in-between these steps help to soften the hard lines of the stone and blend well with the mossy surfaces. They thrive in the cool, shady conditions below the walls, giving a quiet and natural feel to this obscure corner. Many ferns thrive in crevices in walls and stonework, and this planting exploits that natural tendency.

Another option is to create a fernery, dedicated to ferns of different types. Choose a shady corner backed by a wall or mossy bank where few other plants grow and plant it thickly with ferns, in the ground and wall crevices.

Ferns also flatter flowering plants, particularly woodland plants that prefer similarly damp and shady conditions. Try mixing them with early-flowering lungworts (*Pulmonaria, see p.314*) in dappled shade.

Fascinating foliage

The foliage of ferns displays a striking variety of shapes and habits, from stiff and upright to gracefully arching. Some fronds are leathery and glossy, while others are more fragile, for example adiantums (*see p.360*).

Ferns also possess foliage in a range of different shades of green and with subtle hues of silver and bronze. Some have colored spring foliage, such as the sensitive fern (*Onoclea sensibilis*,

see p.363) and Wallich's wood fern (*Dryopteris wallichiana*, *see p.363*). Clumps of several types of fern combine to create stunning contrasts of form and texture.

Many ferns are very attractive in spring as their new fronds begin to unfurl; they often have a brown, furry coating, which glows in the low spring sunshine and makes them excellent companions for bulbous plants.

Divided frond This European chain fern (*Woodwardia radicans*) is an example of a highly divided, classically shaped fern frond.

Broad frond Strappy, undivided leaves characterize some ferns, such as this glossy hart's tongue fern (*Asplenium scolopendrium*).

Leafy frond Some ferns, like this Japanese holly fern (*Cyrtomium falcatum*), have fronds that are shaped more like conventional leaves.

Colored frond Color variation in ferns may be subtle as with the silvery white undersides of the fronds of this lip fern (*Cheilanthes argentea*).

What is a fern?

Ferns are perennial foliage plants – some are evergreen and others are deciduous. Unlike most other plants, which flower and then set seed, ferns reproduce by means of tiny spores. Spore cases form on the undersides of the fronds and, when ripe, the spores fall to the soil, where they eventually germinate if the soil is moist.

Propagating ferns from spores is not straightforward. An easier method to

increase most ferns is by lifting and dividing clumps in the same way as other plants (*see p.395*). Some ferns, such as *Asplenium bulbiferum* and some polystichums, form bulbils on the fronds. Detach a frond of bulbils and peg it on to a tray of rooting medium. Keep it watered, warm, and light until plantlets form and have rooted, then detach and pot up the plantlets when they are large enough to handle.

Fern spores The spore cases that may appear on the undersides of fronds vary in color and pattern. The ripening spores shown here are on *Polypodium vulgare*. When spore clusters are ripe, they darken. After the spores have been shed, the underside of the frond will feel rough to the touch.

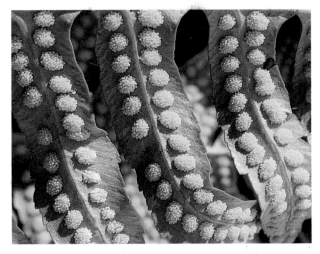

Choosing a suitable planting site

Ferns are generally easy to grow in moist, shady areas. As they are quite tough, their needs are minimal, and they need very little maintenance once they are established. Most ferns need a site in dappled, partial, or full shade – strong sunlight can scorch the thin fronds. The cold winds that blow over exposed sites can also cause scorching. Choose a sheltered position. The few exceptions to this include lip ferns (*Cheilanthes*) and some polypodiums (*see p.364*), which tolerate drier conditions and sun. Some ferns will grow in rock crevices on a shady wall.

Good garden soil that is rich in organic matter is best for most ferns. Before planting, dig in as much well-rotted compost as you can to help the soil retain plenty of moisture. Most ferns require neutral to alkaline soils although there are some, such as the hard ferns (*Blechnum, see p.361*) and cryptogrammas (*see p.362*), which prefer acidic conditions.

Humidity is also important for ferns to thrive, which is why damp corners, bog gardens, and pond-side areas with sheltered, still air, often provide ideal conditions for lush foliage growth.

Woodland native Many ferns, such as this hard fern (*Blechnum spicant*), naturally grow in established woodland where the shady conditions retain moisture in the soil. You can create a similar effect in your garden.

Select a place shaded by woodland shrubs and arrange old branches and stumps from a managed woodland to give a natural effect. Plant ferns in crannies and pockets between the stumps. Once the ferns are established, this area will give the romantic illusion of an area of ancient woodland.

ADIANTUM
Maidenhair fern

GRACEFUL, OFTEN FINELY DIVIDED FOLIAGE is the most desirable characteristic of this large group of evergreen, semievergreen, and deciduous ferns often grown as house plants. The fronds are usually mid-green, but may be paler green or even bronze-pink when young. They have black or brown-black stems, which stand out well against the foliage. These ferns can spread widely by underground stems (rhizomes). They require shady areas, such as under trees or large shrubs, and also flourish beside water. Show off the delicate foliage by contrasting it with the bold foliage of plants such as hostas (*see pp.260–61*).

Cultivation Grow hardy ferns in moist but well-drained, reasonably fertile soil in partial or deep shade. *A. capillus-veneris* likes moist, alkaline soil. **Cut** old foliage from deciduous species in late winter or early spring. **Divide** rhizomes in early spring every three or four years. Pull apart the rhizomes to obtain about three new ferns and replant, or grow them on in a pot of soil-based potting mix (*see also p.395*).

ASPLENIUM
Spleenwort

THIS HUGE AND VARIED GROUP OF FERNS includes evergreens and semievergreens. The green fronds range in shape and texture from fine and feathery to long, pointed, and glossy. The hen-and-chicken fern (*Asplenium bulbiferum* (Z8) is one of many with fronds composed of tiny leaflets. Spleenworts grow from erect, sometimes creeping, rhizomes. Plant small species in wall crevices, or in a rock garden or alpine trough. Grow larger species in woodland or among shrubs in a shady border.

Cultivation These ferns need partial shade and moist but well-drained soil, enriched with plenty of well-rotted compost. Most need an acidic soil, but *A. ceterach*, *A. scolopendrium*, and *A. trichomanes* prefer alkaline soils. **Divide** hardy species (*see p.395*) in spring every four or five years to obtain new plants with at least two leaves; replant them or pot up in soil-based potting mix. **In wet** winters, *A. scolopendrium* is prone to rust disease; if you see orange or brown patches, remove the affected fronds.

Asplenium ceterach (Rusty-back fern)
Z5 ‡6in (15cm) ↔ 8in (20cm), evergreen fronds up to 8in (20cm), rusty brown scales on undersides, prefers alkaline soil

Adiantum venustum (Evergreen maidenhair fern)
Z6 ‡6in (15cm) ↔ indefinite, evergreen fronds 6–12in (15–30cm) long, bright bronze-pink in late winter and early spring

Asplenium scolopendrium (Hart's tongue fern)
Z7 ‡18–28in (45–70cm) ↔ 24in (60cm), evergreen, fronds 16in (40cm) or more long, prefers alkaline soils

Asplenium trichomanes (Maidenhair spleenwort)
Z4 ‡6in (15cm) ↔ 8in (20cm), evergreen or semievergreen, fronds 4–8in (10–20cm) long, rusty red spores on undersides

ATHYRIUM
Lady fern

THE LACY-LEAVED FRONDS of *Athyrium filix-femina* and its cultivars, and the silvery green, deeply divided fronds of *A. niponicum* (Z5) mean that these deciduous lady ferns are decorative plants for shady areas. The midribs are reddish in color, contrasting sharply with the foliage. The ferns are found growing wild in moist woodlands or forests, and they also look best grown in a woodland setting in the garden. You can create a natural-looking habitat for them by placing old logs in a shady border and planting the lady ferns among them as if they were growing among fallen trees.

Cultivation Grow lady ferns in moist, fertile soil that is neutral to acidic and enriched with plenty of well-rotted organic matter. Choose a site that is both shaded and sheltered. Lady ferns will tolerate all but the driest sites. **Divide** hardy species in spring every four or five years. Use a spade to cut up larger clumps, obtaining several new plants with two or three leaves each. Replant the new pieces in prepared ground.

BLECHNUM
Hard fern

SOME SPECIES OF HARD FERNS have spectacular foliage, which bursts upward and outward in a fountain shape, sometimes from a small "trunk." This trunk is in fact an upright rhizome, up to 36in (90cm) tall, and covered in black scales; the fronds grow out from the top. Other species, such as *Blechnum penna-marina* have creeping rhizomes and are more suitable as groundcover plants. Hard ferns are generally evergreen, with tough fronds standing through the winter. They flourish in moist soil under trees or in shady borders. The smaller species are also suitable for a shady corner in a rock garden.

Cultivation Hard ferns like moist soil, preferably acid, enriched with well-rotted organic matter to retain moisture. **Grow** hard ferns in pots of bark-based potting mix or acidic medium mixed with plenty of sharp sand or grit. Hard ferns need partial to deep shade. **Grow** tender species in large pots and keep them in frost-free conditions over winter; in mild areas, they may survive winter outdoors if protected with straw held in place with netting. **Divide** *B. penna-marina* and *B. spicant* in spring (*see p.395*); other species can be divided but take longer to reestablish.

Blechnum spicant (Deer fern)
Z5 ‡3–6ft (90cm–2m) ↔ indefinite, trunklike rhizomes, fronds up to 3ft (1m) long with scaly stalks

Athyrium filix-femina 'Frizelliae' (Tatting fern)
‡8in (20cm) ↔ 12in (30cm), fronds 4–8in (10–20cm) long

Blechnum penna-marina
T min. 50°F (10°C) ‡4–8in (10–20cm) ↔ indefinite, fronds are 4–8in (10–20cm) long and glossy or matt, depending on the form

Blechnum gibbum (Miniature tree fern)
T min. 50°F (10°C) ‡↔ to 36in (90cm), trunklike rhizomes, fronds 36in (90cm) or more long, spectacular conservatory plant

CRYPTOGRAMMA CRISPA
Parsley fern

‡6–9in (15–23cm)
↔ 6–12i (15–30cmn)

THIS DELIGHTFUL SMALL FERN is grown for its delicate foliage. The only cryptogramma commonly grown in gardens, it has deciduous fronds that turn an attractive, bright rust-brown during autumn. The old fronds usually persist all through winter. Since it is a fairly low-growing fern, the parsley fern is suitable for growing in a shaded crevice of a rock garden or at the front of a shady border. The lacy, pale green fronds make a good contrast to darker and bolder foliage on plants such as astilbes (*see p.194*) and rodgersias (*see p.316*).

Cultivation This fern prefers partial or full shade in fertile soil that has been enriched with well-rotted organic matter to help retain moisture. The soil should be acidic or neutral; if your soil is alkaline grow the fern in a container or a raised bed that contains acidic potting mix mixed with plenty of grit or sharp sand, or a bark-based medium. **Remove** the faded fronds in spring before new ones grow. The parsley fern is deep-rooted and difficult to propagate by division.

Cryptogramma crispa
Z2 ‡9in (23cm), sterile fronds shorter

CYSTOPTERIS
Bladder fern

THE FINELY DIVIDED FRONDS of the bladder ferns make them a valuable asset in the garden. Bladder ferns are deciduous; their fronds grow in clumps or rosettes from fleshy stems (rhizomes), which may creep or grow upright above ground. The fronds tend to be pale or gray-green. These ferns will be happy in shady areas of a rock garden or in a shady border under shrubs or trees. They also blend in well in a border or woodland area that is dedicated to ferns; such a planting will highlight their differing textures, forms, and shades of green, and make a restful feature.

Cultivation Grow in fertile, moist soil, incorporating well-rotted compost to help retain moisture in partial or full shade. Provide shelter from cold, drying winds. **Divide** rhizomes in spring (*see p.395*), planting them in the ground. **Alternatively**, increase them by using the bulbils that ripen on the undersides of the fronds in late summer or early autumn (*see p.359*); one frond should produce many plants. Once they have rooted, transfer the plants to 3in (8cm) pots of soil-less potting mix; keep them in frost-free conditions over the winter; and plant them out in spring.

Cystopteris fragilis (Brittle bladder fern)
Z4 ‡↔ 8in (20cm), clump-forming with upright rhizomes, fronds are 6–18in (15–45cm) long

DICKSONIA

SPECTACULAR, TREELIKE FORMS and dramatic foliage distinguish these very large semievergreen or evergreen ferns. They have thick, furry "trunks" formed from a mass of old stems and leaf bases. Each stem can be up to 24in (60cm) in diameter and has only a few roots – most of its nutrients are derived in the wild from decaying matter that collects in the fronds. The large, leathery fronds grow to 10ft (3m) and sprout from the top of the stem. The new fronds have a furry protective coating as they unfurl in spring (*see inset, below*). Dicksonias grow to their full height only in favorable conditions; they are very slow-growing and so are quite expensive. If you invest in one, take good care of it. Show it to its best advantage as a specimen or with other ferns in a shady border.

Cultivation Dicksonias need fertile soil in partial or full shade. In spells of hot, dry weather, hose the trunk with water daily. **Protect** the trunk and leaves in winter by attaching wire netting loosely around the trunk and over the crown and stuffing the gap with straw. **Cut off** old fronds in early spring. These ferns are difficult to propagate.

Dicksonia antarctica (Soft tree fern)
T min. 45°F (7°C) ‡ to 20ft (6m), usually much less ↔ 12ft (4m), flourishes in a mild, damp climate sheltered from wind and sun

DRYOPTERIS
Buckler fern

THIS LARGE GROUP OF FERNS, popular in cultivation, produce long, elegant fronds, often in a conical shape. Many retain their leaves over winter in mild, sheltered conditions, although they die down in less favorable climates. The evergreen fronds of the golden male fern (*Dryopteris affinis* Z7) are pale green when young, contrasting with golden brown midribs. *D. erythrosora* (Z6) has copper foliage in spring, turning dark green, with green midribs. The midribs of *D. wallichiana* are covered with dark brown or black scales, and are particularly striking in spring against the new yellow-green fronds; these age to dark green. With their distinctive shapes, they add height to a mixed fern border or look good as foliage plants in a shady, herbaceous border.

Cultivation Grow these ferns in partial shade in soil with plenty of well-rotted organic matter to retain moisture. **Shelter** from cold, drying winds. **Divide** mature plants (*see p.395*) in spring or autumn every five or six years; use a spade for older clumps.

MATTEUCCIA

SHUTTLECOCK-SHAPED ROSETTES of upright, gently arching fronds are characteristic of the three or four species in this group of deciduous ferns. During mid- to late summer, smaller, dark brown fronds appear in the center of each rosette; these are fertile fronds, while the green ones around the edge are sterile. The ferns spread by creeping stems (rhizomes) from which more fronds sprout. They are striking foliage plants for a damp, shady border in woodland or by water, and work well with other shade-loving plants such as rhododendrons (*see pp.104–107*).

Cultivation Grow these ferns in moist but well-drained soil, incorporating well-rotted organic matter to help retain moisture. Matteuccias prefer neutral to acidic soil in partial shade. If your soil is alkaline, grow them in containers or raised beds containing acidic potting medium mixed with plenty of grit or sharp sand, or a bark-based medium. **Divide** established clumps (*see p.395*) in early spring to obtain four or five new plants, each with at least two or three vigorous fronds.

ONOCLEA SENSIBILIS
Sensitive fern

‡ to 3ft (1m)
↔ indefinite

UPRIGHT AND ARCHING FRONDS up to 3ft (1m) long are produced by this single, deciduous fern. Its name derives from the fact that all its top-growth dies down at the first frost. In spring, its new, sterile fronds are sometimes pinkish bronze; these turn pale green. They are very deeply divided, giving them a feathery appearance. In late summer, a number of fertile fronds with a contrasting, stiffly upright habit grow to 2ft (60cm). The sensitive fern thrives by the edge of water or in shady borders in damp soil. Try it with other shade- and damp-loving plants such as candelabra primulas (*see pp.312–313*).

Cultivation Plant this fern in a sheltered site away from cold, drying winds. The sensitive fern prefers moist, fertile, acidic soil in light, dappled shade; the fronds will be scorched if they are exposed to strong sun. **Divide** established clumps (*see p.395*) in spring; be sure that each new clump has at least two or three fronds.

Dryopteris wallichiana (Wallich's wood fern)
T min. 45°F (7°C) ‡36in (90cm), sometimes to 6ft (2m) ↔30in (75cm), upright rhizome, deciduous fronds 36in (90cm) or more long

Matteuccia struthiopteris (Ostrich fern, Shuttlecock fern)
Z3 ‡5½ft (1.7m) ↔ to 3ft (1m), sterile green fronds 4ft (1.2m) long

Onoclea sensibilis
Z3b ‡24in (60cm) ↔ indefinite, sterile fronds

POLYPODIUM

OSMUNDAS ARE IMPOSING, DECIDUOUS FERNS, with upright, blue-green or bright green fronds, which fade to yellow or brown in autumn. In the center of these sterile fronds are erect, fertile fronds that contrast pleasingly with the surrounding green foliage. In the royal fern (*Osmunda regalis*), they are brown or rust-colored; the cinnamon fern (*O. cinnamomea* Z4) is named after the rich color of its fertile fronds. Use these large, architectural ferns as specimen plants in a mixed border or by a pond or stream. The royal fern also makes an excellent container plant provided that it is watered regularly, especially in warm weather. The plant's roots are fibrous, absorbing lots of water and, as osmunda fiber, they are used as potting mix for orchids.

Cultivation Osmundas like moist, fertile, preferably acidic soil in light, dappled shade. The royal fern does require a wet soil, but will do well in sun as long as the soil is moist. **Divide** established clumps (*see p.395*) in autumn or early spring using a spade.

THESE ADAPTABLE FERNS make excellent groundcover with their spreading habit and beautiful, sculptural fronds. Many produce relatively long, arching fronds randomly from the creeping stems, or rhizomes. The fronds reach 24in (60cm) in the case of the southern polypody (*Polypodium cambricum* Z7). Some have spores on the undersides of the fronds in contrasting colors. Unlike most ferns, polypodiums are also drought-tolerant and are happy in full sun. The mostly evergreen ferns in this group look particularly good growing in mixed borders or on a bank where ground cover is required. Their spreading habit helps to suppress weeds.

Cultivation Grow polypodiums in well-drained, moderately fertile soil, with plenty of well-rotted organic matter added. On heavy clay soils, dig in coarse grit or sand to improve drainage. *P. cambricum* prefers a neutral to alkaline soil. **Site** in full sun or partial shade and provide shelter from cold, drying winds. **Divide** in spring or early summer (*see p.395*) when the plants are four or five years old.

Osmunda regalis (Flowering fern, Royal fern)
Z4 ‡6ft (2m) ↔ 12ft (4m), sterile fronds are 3ft (1m) or more long

Polypodium vulgare (Common polypody)
Z7 ‡12in (30cm) ↔ indefinite, thin to leathery fronds are 16in (40cm) long

Polypodium glycyrrhiza (Licorice fern)
Z5 ‡12in (30cm) ↔ indefinite, mid- to dark green fronds up to 14in (35cm) long, rhizomes have a sweet licorice taste

POLYSTICHUM
Christmas fern, Shield fern, Holly fern

THE FINE FOLIAGE OF THESE FERNS is usually arranged in shapely "shuttlecocks," forming exuberant bursts of often dark green fronds. The fronds tend to be highly intricate, especially in the soft shield fern (*Polystichum setiferum*) and its cultivars, and the leaflets may end in a sharp bristle, hence a common name of holly fern. This large group of mostly evergreen ferns includes plants that are 16in–4ft (40cm–1.2m) tall. These all combine well with other ferns or with other woodland plants such as hydrangeas (*see pp.72–73*) in a well-drained woodland planting. The smaller shield ferns are best displayed in a shady rock garden.

Cultivation Holly ferns prefer fertile soil enriched with well-rotted organic matter, in deep or partial shade. **Protect** the crowns from excessive winter moisture with a mulch of organic matter. In early spring, remove any dead fronds. **Divide** the rhizomes in spring. In late summer or early autumn, detach fronds with bulbils for propagation (*see p.359*). Once they have rooted, transfer to 3in (8cm) pots of soilless potting mix with added grit; keep frost-free; and plant out in spring.

THELYPTERIS PALUSTRIS
Marsh fern

↕24in (60cm)
↔ to 3ft (1mt)

THIS IS A DECIDUOUS FERN of swamps and bogs. If there is good light in summer, fertile fronds, which are longer than the sterile ones, are produced. Spores are borne in abundance on the undersides of the leaflets, creating a brown haze over the ferns in late summer. Try growing this fern with other moisture-loving plants such as hostas (*see pp.260–261*), primulas (*see pp.312–313*), and marsh marigolds (*Caltha, see p.205*) at the edge of a pond. The marsh fern can be invasive, spreading by long, creeping underground stems (rhizomes), so allow it plenty of space, but it is also easy to keep under control by digging out unwanted pieces.

Cultivation Grow the fern in any reliably moist, moderately fertile soil. **Dig in** well-rotted organic matter to increase moisture retention, in sun or partial shade. **Divide** in spring or summer (*see p.395*), replant, and keep well watered, especially in summer.

WOODWARDIA
Chain fern

LARGE, SPREADING, AND ARCHING plants, the chain ferns are so-called because the spores are arranged on the undersides of the fronds in a chainlike formation. This small group of ferns includes evergreen and deciduous species. The intricate fronds are particularly attractive as they unfurl in spring. On their upper surfaces, small bulbils may be produced over the summer near the tips. The chain fern is ideal for covering a shady bank that has moist soil. It looks particularly natural near water, and it combines well with bold foliage plants, such as gunneras (*see p.254*), that also like moist soil.

Cultivation Chain ferns like neutral, reasonably fertile, damp soil in partial shade. In cold areas, shelter the ferns from cold, drying winds. **Protect** chain ferns over winter, where marginally hardy, with a mulch of straw held in place with netting. **Divide** the plants in spring using a spade (*see p.395*) or sharp knife; replant the pieces in a similar site. Alternatively, propagate from bulbils in late summer or early autumn (*see p.359*). Once they have rooted, pot the new ferns into 3in (8cm) pots of soilless potting mix; keep them frost-free over winter; and plant them out in spring.

Polystichum setiferum 'Pulcherrimum Bevis'
Z7 ↕ 24–32in (60–80cm), very rarely fertile

Thelypteris palustris
Z4 ↕24in (60cm) ↔ 3ft (1m), fertile fronds longer

Woodwardia radicans (European chain fern)
Z8 ↕6ft (2m) ↔ 10ft (3m) evergreen, each leaflet to 12in (30cm) long

CARING FOR PLANTS

If you choose plants for your garden wisely, you can reduce the amount of work you have to do to maintain them, but they will perform at their peak only if you give them a certain amount of attention, particularly in the growing season. In this chapter, you are guided through the basic principles of caring for garden plants, from assessing where to plant them and what to look for when you buy them to all aspects of caring for them once they are in the ground. There are also guidelines on easy ways to increase stocks of your favorite plants.

planning your garden

Whether adapting an existing garden or designing one from scratch, there are many things to consider before rushing out and buying lots of plants. Taking time at the planning stage will help you to avoid making costly mistakes and practically guarantee that you end up with your ideal garden.

First, make a rough sketch of your garden, preferably to scale on squared paper. Then list the things you want to include, how you want it to look, how you intend to use it (*see box, right*). With this information in mind, take another look at your sketch and see what changes need to be made.

Moving into a new house and then creating a garden completely from scratch can seem daunting. It does however have the great advantage of giving you complete freedom to develop your own design. Unlike an established garden that may be full of plants, a bare plot of freshly laid sod gives few clues as to what plants can be grown successfully. It is essential to take into account the garden's location, effect of the local climate (*see p.371*), and soil type (*see pp.376–377*) before buying any plants.

If you are redesigning an existing garden, don't be too hasty in your initial assessment of the site: you may inadvertently remove some useful plants and features. Make changes gradually, over a full year if possible, adapting existing features to your plan.

Flowers and foliage come in an infinite palette of shades, providing the opportunity to experiment with color designs, and moods in the borders. Do your homework before buying trees, shrubs, climbers, and perennials since these can be expensive and will form the permanent structure of the garden. By comparison, many annuals and biennials – including bedding plants – last for one growing season and are much less expensive, so you can make changes from year to year, if you wish.

When organizing the layout of your borders, try to show each plant to its best advantage. It is important not to place new plants too close together: allow room for them to reach their full size, even if it leaves a few gaps at first.

Good planning insures a long season of color.

Assessing your priorities in the garden

- How will you use your garden?
- Do you enjoy gardening or just want a place in which to relax?
- Do you want to maximize your planting space or increase the amount of hard landscaping for a low-maintenance option?
- Is an outdoor entertaining or dining area needed?
- Informal or formal? Which garden style do you prefer?
- What should the mood of the garden be – restful or vibrant?
- If children use the garden, do they need their own play area?
- Are new paths or steps needed?
- Are you happy to grow fruit and vegetables among other plants, or do you want a kitchen garden?
- Is there space for a utility area for a shed and compost bins? (Hide them behind hedges or trellises.)
- Do you want a pond or some sort of water feature ?

◁ **Night lights** Carefully positioned lighting allows you to continue using and enjoying the garden during the evening. Here, gentle spotlights create a pool of light that picks out the colors and textures of the plants and rocks in this naturalistic pond.

Fruit and vegetables can be combined with ornamental plants to create some stunning planting effects. Also, by growing the plants together in borders, they will be less susceptible to attack from pests and diseases.

Quiet corners After a busy day, enjoy the peace and quiet of a secluded corner filled with scented plants. An old railroad tie resting on a stone boulder and a brick pillar makes a simple but comfortable bench.

Choosing a style of planting

The plants are the most important element in a garden. No matter how many ornamental features you may include, the space will still look bare until the plants are in place, bringing movement and life into the garden.

There are many styles of planting to choose from and thousands of plants with which to plan a design. If you are looking for inspiration, one of the best ways to discover what style or theme would suit your yard is to visit gardens that are open to the public. Wandering around your neighborhood and looking at other people's gardens will give you a good idea of different layouts and of which plants would be most happy growing in the local soil and climate.

Extending the interest over several seasons is the key to getting the most out of a small garden. Ideally, each plant you choose should remain attractive over many months, for example displaying spring blooms or autumn leaf color as well as flowers.

△ **Formality and order** Large areas of hard landscaping are often a feature of formal gardens, but although it allows for easy maintenance it can look clinical. A balance can be struck with planting. Here, bricks have been set into a sweep of stone slabs to warm up the color and to add texture, while the hard edges of the paving are softened by the large drifts of restrained planting that spill over onto the stone.

▷ **Informal charm** The free-flowing charms of the cottage garden call for an unforced naturalness and spontaneity, created by intermingling plants so that they appear to jostle for space. The plants take center stage and are allowed to self-seed where they will. Given a free rein, they will grow together to create borders of great charm.

Ponds and water features

Informal pond Unlike formal ponds, which are regular in shape, an informal pond is designed to look as natural as possible. To help it blend into the rest of the garden, the edges may be lined with rocks, cobblestones, or slate. Plants that grow in the shallow water around the edge ("marginals") conceal the outline of the pond completely, creating a lush appearance.

A water feature always adds an extra dimension to a garden, whether it is a formal or natural pond, or a half-barrel of water. It is also a magnet for wildlife – birds will bathe in the shallows, while frogs and toads, which help to control slugs and snails, will become regular visitors.

Consider the style of pond you prefer and how it relates to the overall plan of your garden. Ponds are not easy to move once installed. To help visualize it in detail, mark the outline on the ground using rope or a length of hose. Avoid siting the pond under a tree because falling leaves will foul the water.

If you want to keep fish, ask your aquatic supplier to recommend numbers for your size pond.

A bubble fountain is a safe option if you have young children. A pump circulates water from a shallow tank to splash over a tray of cobblestones so you can enjoy the sound of water without any danger.

Using containers

Bring color right up to the windows of your house by planting containers with an ever-changing selection of plants, from spring bulbs and summer bedding to shrubs and small trees. Choose planters, pots, and windowboxes in materials that enhance, not compete with, the planting. Roots will quickly become restricted within the confines of a container, so replenish the nutrients in the medium and water regularly.

Bulbs in containers Most bulbs can be grown successfully in containers. These pink tulips, top-dressed with moss, should be planted out in the garden after flowering.

Using color in the garden

Garden flowers come in an infinitely varied and dazzling array of colors and shades. However, foliage, bark, stems, berries, and seedheads can be colorful, too, and foliage and bark often have a longer season of interest than flowers. How you combine color is a matter of personal preference, but there are a few ways to be sure of successful planting designs. Many designers use a color wheel for inspiration. This is simply a circle divided into six wedges, colored in this order: yellow, green, blue, purple, red, and orange. Colors adjacent to each other on the wheel create harmonious effects, while colors opposing each other on the wheel make for lively contrasts. Yellows through reds are warm and stimulating; while greens to purples are restful and cool.

Restricting the color palette can produce a more pleasing effect than using very many colors, which often looks too fussy. Strong colors attract the eye and can be used for specimen plants. Color can be used to set a mood – reds, golds, and oranges, typical of a hot, intense design, are exciting and dominant; while blues, soft pinks, and whites are soothing and subtle.

Hot reds and yellows *Kniphofia caulescens*

Cool blues *Delphinium* Blue Fountains Group

Foliage and form

Contrasting leaves With so many colors, shapes, and textures available, it is possible to make dramatic planting designs with foliage alone. Here, luxuriant hostas and feathery ferns combine to great effect with colorful shrubs.

Growing beautiful flowers is one of gardening's obvious pleasures, but you can have great fun designing with plants grown specifically for their attractive growth habits and strikingly shaped or colored foliage. Unlike a brief burst of flower color, a foliage plant will offer a long season of interest. Plants with different types of foliage can be used to build up three-dimensional layers of texture, giving even a narrow border a feeling of depth and movement.

Create a collage of leaf shapes and sizes by planting spiky specimens, such as grasses and yuccas, next to round-leaved cultivars, such as hostas (*see pp.260–261*) and bergenias (*see p.198*). Look for subtle contrasts in leaf texture, such as glossy or hairy leaves, as well as striking variegation and complementary colors, from silver and cream to purple and gold.

Seasonal interest

The huge choice of herbaceous and bedding plants available makes planning a beautiful summer garden relatively easy. Colorful borders need not be a transient pleasure – there are many plants that provide interest over a longer period, such as the peony (*see below*). As well as creating a permanent framework, trees and shrubs are often blessed with attractive spring blossoms, followed in autumn by good leaf color or berries and hips. There may also be attractive stems or bark to enjoy in winter. Keep the color coming with spring bulbs, beginning in late winter with snowdrops (*Galanthus, see p.247*).

Spring The emerging shoots of *Paeonia mlokosewitschii* glow in the spring sun.

Late spring Over the next couple of months, the elegant leaves turn blue-green.

Early summer Lemon flowers appear, each one measuring up to 5in (13cm) across.

Autumn Seed pods split open to reveal brilliant-red fruits and black seeds.

climate and location

Not only does the weather dictate when certain jobs can be tackled in the garden, but the local climate will determine the types of plants that will thrive in your plot. Although many plants are adaptable, choosing ones that are most suited to your particular locality and exposure in the garden is fundamental to success. Providing suitable conditions for all the plants and matching as closely as possible their natural habitats is both challenging and satisfying.

The weather – temperature, frost, snow, rain, humidity, sun, and wind – affects how plants grow and will dictate the length of the growing season. Only when the weather turns milder can we plant out tender bedding or start sowing seed outdoors. Colder areas tend to have later springs, sometimes weeks later than warmer areas farther south, as well as shorter growing seasons. Inland regions are often drier than areas by the coast. Although plants have to contend with salt spray and strong winds, coastal areas are also generally much milder.

You don't have to travel far, however, to discover significant variations in climate. There is a huge difference between the growing conditions on a sheltered valley floor compared to the exposed slopes of the surrounding hills. In the same way, while most of your garden may be warm and sunny, it may contain a range of different microclimates, where the growing conditions are modified by factors such as the shelter of warm wall or the heavy shade cast by an evergreen tree. Such areas in the garden will need to be treated and planted differently.

Since the local climate will dictate which kinds of plants you can grow successfully, it is worth taking some time to find out what weather patterns you can expect over the course of the year. Consider joining a gardening club – gardeners are always willing to share their experiences with like-minded people, and they will be a valuable source of information.

Assessing your garden

Before making any changes it is worth assessing your garden to give yourself an idea of the plants you can grow.

◆ How high above sea level are you? The higher you are, the colder it is because of exposure to strong winds.

◆ Does the garden face north or south? This will have a bearing on how much sun the garden gets.

◆ How shady is the garden? Is there heavy shade cast by established trees and shrubs or by the house?

◆ Is the garden on a slope? Cold air will gather at the bottom of a slope to cause a frost pocket (*see p.372*).

◆ Does it get very cold in the winter or very hot in summer? Temperature extremes can stress plants, and you may have to take extra care of them.

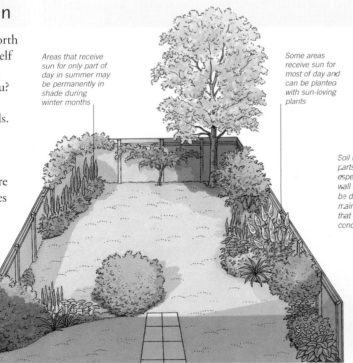

Areas that receive sun for only part of day in summer may be permanently in shade during winter months

Some areas receive sun for most of day and can be planted with sun-loving plants

North-facing garden The shade cast by the house keeps the air cool and the soil moist.

Shade cast by deciduous tree is more dense in summer and spring than during autumn, when it loses leaves

Soil in some parts of garden, especially next to wall or fence, will be dry and suited mainly to plants that tolerate such conditions

South-facing garden is warm and sunny, but the soil may dry out in summer.

The dangers of frost and cold

One of the greatest hazards that a gardener has to contend with is frost, especially in spring and autumn. An unexpected spring frost can destroy flower buds, ruining the display for the year. Tender, new shoots are also susceptible. Still, clear nights often signal that a frost is on the way, and quick action can protect vulnerable plants. Bring them under cover, or loosely wrap them in some horticultural fleece, newspapers, or similar insulating material.

The incidence of late spring frosts in your area will determine the time at which it is safe to plant out tender plants, such as summer bedding. The onset of autumnal frosts determines the end of their growing season.

Where there are low points in the garden, frost pockets (*see below*) may form. If there is a hollow or depression in the garden, avoid growing fruit there and choose plants that are hardy (*see right*) and will not suffer in low temperatures.

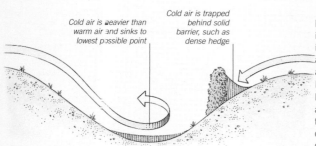

Cold air is heavier than warm air and sinks to lowest possible point

Cold air is trapped behind solid barrier, such as dense hedge

Frost pocket Cold air is denser than warm air; it always flows downhill and becomes trapped in any slight dip or hollow. Frost also collects at the bases of fences, walls, and closely planted, thick hedges, or large objects such as a statue or solid seat.

Hardiness of plants

The hardiness of a plant refers to its ability to withstand year-round climatic conditions in a specific area. The Canadian hardiness zones are given for all plants in this book, except for tender plants (which are given a minimum temperature) and annuals.

Hardiness zones are based on a wide range of climatic variables, including not only minimum winter temperature, but also length of the frost-free period, snow cover, and maximum wind speed.

All hardiness zone ranges given in this book are intended as approximate guides and should not be considered definitive.

Hardiness may be modified through cultural practices (*see below*).

Snowy shrub Although it looks pretty, heavy snow can weigh down branches, causing them to break. After a snowfall, either brush it off the plant or let additional snow cover it. If more snow is forecast, tie vulnerable branches into the main stem – this works well with conifers.

Helping plants to survive the winter

Small or immature plants need protection to help them survive a severe winter. Protect top-growth by covering plants with horticultural fleece, burlap, bubble plastic, or layers of newspaper.

Wrapping plants, such as tree ferns, in dry bracken or straw will trap any warm air escaping from the soil and provide valuable insulation on a cold night. When temperatures are above freezing, unwrap the plants to give them a chance to breath and prevent the build-up of molds and pests. A thick mulch of garden compost spread over the crowns of plants, such as herbaceous perennials that

have died down over winter, will give protection from several degrees of frost. A mound of dried leaves, held in place over the plant with chicken wire, works well too.

Glass or plastic cloches, or cold frames are excellent for keeping excessive winter rain, snow, or frost off plants. On exposed sites, protect plants with windbreaks or mesh netting supported on stakes.

Frost-tender plants (*see above, right*) should be taken into a greenhouse or conservatory with a controlled growing environment that regulates temperature, humidity, and ventilation.

Bell cloches As well as making an attractive feature in the border, these bell cloches offer effective winter protection for less hardy plants. Glass cloches are beautiful, but very expensive and vulnerable to breakage – plastic ones, like these, do the job just as well.

Winter coat Wrapping containers with burlap (*see above*) or with bubble plastic protects the roots from freezing. This is a useful technique where the container is too large to take indoors. A double or triple layer of wrapping offers good protection from severe cold and frost.

Wind and its effect on your garden

Strong winds can have positive benefits, helping to disperse pollen and seeds. However, they can be a destructive force causing damage to plants, especially young ones that have yet to become established. They can also discourage beneficial insects that help to control pests. Although they have a cooling effect on plants, strong winds increase the rate at which water vapor is lost from plants' leaves (called desiccation), causing browning and leaf drop.

When woody plants are exposed to strong winds, their top-growth becomes unbalanced, making the plants appear one-sided. The tips of shoots and leaves are also at risk of being damaged, or scorched. The higher the wind speed, the more

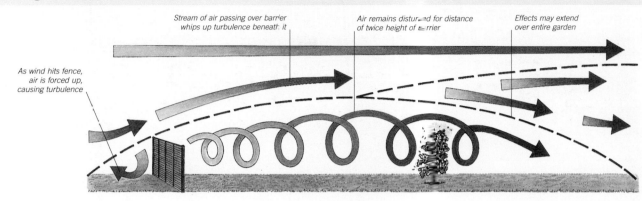

Stream of air passing over barrier whips up turbulence beneath it

Air remains disturbed for distance of twice height of barrier

Effects may extend over entire garden

As wind hits fence, air is forced up, causing turbulence

damage is done, with stems being broken and, in severe cases, entire plants being uprooted.

Protect vulnerable plants with a windbreak. Choose a material that will allow about 50 percent of the wind to pass through, because a solid structure will create problems of its own (*see above*). Hedging plants are ideal, or choose open-weave fencing or special windbreak netting. For best protection, a windbreak should be 12ft (4m) tall, but a lower one would work well for smaller plants.

Action of wind The movement of air over leaf surfaces increases the rate of rapid water loss from the leaves. These effects are most severe in winter, since water lost from leaves cannot be replaced when the soil is frozen. Strong winds will rock any tall, unstaked plants until their roots become loosened in the soil, and greenhouses and other garden structures may be damaged. On light, sandy soil, there is a risk of the topsoil being blown away.

The effects of shade

Shady areas of the garden often have dryish soil, and plants have to cope with low light levels. The ground under trees poses a real challenge to gardeners, because some types of tree and hedges, such as conifers and other evergreens, cast deep shadow and take lots of water and nutrients from the soil. The soil at the base of walls and fences can also be shady and dry. However, if the soil is enriched by digging in plenty of well-rotted manure or garden compost (*see p.377*), and any overhanging plants are judiciously pruned, a number of beautiful plants that can be grown, for example *Cyclamen hederifolium* (*see p.221*). You may also have areas of cool, moist,

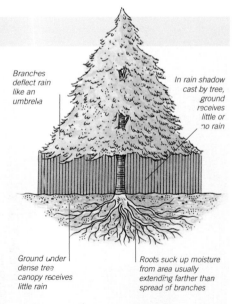

Branches deflect rain like an umbrella

In rain shadow cast by tree, ground receives little or no rain

Ground under dense tree canopy receives little rain

Roots suck up moisture from area usually extending farther than spread of branches

dappled shade – often under deciduous trees. In such conditions, there are plenty of woodland plants that will thrive.

Providing shelter

If you are planting on an exposed site, most young plants, especially evergreen shrubs and perennials, will require protection from strong winds and fierce sun until their root systems become established. If the garden does not enjoy the natural shelter of trees and hedging plants (*see above*), there are several temporary measures you can take.

Open-weave fencing provides a suitable solution, as does planting fast-growing climbers to cover trellis panels. For an instant and economical fix, make a small windbreak using mesh and stakes (*see right*). For best results, erect the shelter on the windward side of the plant or, if sun is the problem, on the sunny side.

Temporary shelter Staple a length of fine mesh (available from garden centers) or burlap sacking to two long stakes. Push the stakes firmly into the ground around the plant. If the site is very windy, you may need to insert extra stakes to stabilize the structure. Remove the shade or windbreak as soon as the plant becomes established.

buying plants

The old saying, "You get what you pay for," is never truer than when buying plants. Young plants do not have the resources to survive too many shocks, and so it is essential they get a good start in life. Buying quality plants from a reputable nursery is always money well spent. You may be tempted by trays of on-sale bedding, but they may have been on the shelf for ages, starved of food and water, so they will never grow as vigorously as good-quality stock.

When selecting a plant, look for one that is well-balanced, with plenty of healthy growth and, where appropriate, lots of flower buds If the plant shows any signs of pests or disease, choose another one. Yellowing leaves may signify a lack of nutrients, a sign that the plant has not been looked after very well. Wilting leaves are caused by a lack of water; if the potting mix dries out too often the plant becomes stressed and vulnerable to pests and diseases. Gently knock the plant out of its pot and take a look at the root system. Do not buy it if the roots are tangled and crammed tight – it has become pot-bound (*see facing page*) and probably will not grow properly.

Bare-root plants

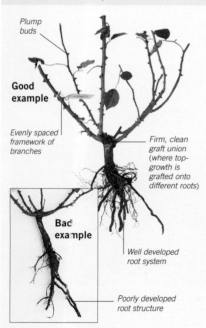

Plump buds

Good example

Evenly spaced framework of branches

Firm, clean graft union (where top-growth is grafted onto different roots)

Bad example

Well developed root system

Poorly developed root structure

Bareroot plants, like this rose, should have a good root system to support the plant. To encourage fibrous, feeding roots to form, trim the longest of the thick roots back hard.

Woody plants, including deciduous trees, shrubs, and roses, are often sold as bare-root plants. Grown in the ground rather than in pots, they are less expensive to produce in bulk, and the nurseries can pass on their savings to their customers. The plants also tend to be bigger and stronger than similarly priced container plants. Bare-root plants are available in nurseries, but they are generally sold by mail order.

The plants are dug up in their dormant season, cleaned of soil, wrapped for mailing and sent out in time for planting, preferably in autumn or early spring; they are unlikely to survive transplanting if bought and planted when in leaf. Unwrap them as soon as they arrive and plant without delay to prevent the roots drying out.

Container-grown plants

Most plants are now available in containers, from summer bedding in plastic strips to large shrubs and trees in pots. The big advantage to buying plants grown in this way is that the root system remains undisturbed during planting so that there is no check on growth. These advantages, however, come at a premium price.

Most hardy container-grown plants can be planted out at any time of year. The exception is tender summer bedding, which often goes on sale in early spring. If you cannot resist buying, grow the plants on under cover, and move them outdoors after the last frost, usually in late spring or early summer.

When choosing a container-grown plant beware of neglect – signs include algal growth on the compost, pests and disease, a stunted appearance, dry compost, and yellowing leaves. If you can, gently knock the plant out of its container and inspect the root system. If it looks pot-bound (*see facing page*), don't buy it.

Leaves look fresh with no signs of wilting

Sickly pot plant

Unbalanced growth

This impatiens has yellowing leaves

Healthy, blemish-free, lush foliage (here, pansies) with no long roots growing out of drainage holes

Healthy root system guarantees that this holly gets off to good start

Healthy shrub Look for strong, bushy growth.

Healthy bedding has lots of flower buds.

Pot-bound plants

Pot-bound roots may be visible on surface of potting mix

Pot-bound root ball The tangled mass of roots indicates that this plant has been in its pot for too long. Such severe constriction may inhibit the plant's ability to take up water and nutrients.

Before buying a plant, do not be shy about gently knocking it out of its pot to check the root system. If lots of roots are growing through the drainage holes, or you find a solid mass of roots growing around the outside of the root ball, then the plant is pot-bound. In this state, the plant's growth will have been severely stunted, and it may never fully recover and thrive.

If you find you have purchased a pot-bound plant, tease out the roots carefully and cut off some of the thicker sections. This will encourage new roots to venture out into the surrounding soil. Before planting it, soak the root ball in a bucket of water for a couple of hours and water the planting hole.

Aquatic and water-garden plants

Always be careful to introduce only healthy plants into a pond, otherwise the delicate ecosystem may be disturbed by pests or diseases carried in on the plants. Choose those with clean, green leaves and a good crown (the point where the leaves and roots meet) with several buds. If leaves are slimy or yellow, or if the water the plants are growing in is murky, then select another plant.

The best time to buy water-garden, or aquatic, plants is in late spring and early summer so that they have a chance to become established before winter sets in. Most aquatic plants tolerate being out of the water for only a short time. Take them home in a plastic bag and put them into the pond as soon as possible.

Leaves of this water hawthorn are lush, green, and float well

Stems are sturdy

New shoots

Basket is top-dressed with gravel to prevent loss of medium

Aquatic plants help keep the pond healthy.

Balled-and-burlapped plants

Wrapping stops roots from drying out

Evergreens, like this conifer, are often sold balled-and-burlapped

Balled-and-burlapped plants are grown in open ground rather than in pots. They are lifted with a ball of roots and soil wrapped in net or burlap. Many shrubs and trees are sold in this way in spring and autumn by nurseries, often by mail order. Check that the root ball feels firm and evenly moist, with the wrapping intact. Soak the burlapped root ball in water for an hour, then unwrap and plant immediately.

Bulbous plants

Spring-flowering bulbs, corms, and tubers are sold in autumn, whereas summer-flowering cultivars will be available in spring. Always buy bulbs as soon as they go on sale, when they will be in prime condition (firm, plump, and blemish- and rot-free). The longer you delay, the more dried out they will become, and the plants will not perform as well. Inspect the bulbs and reject any that show signs of disease, such as soft patches.

Healthy, firm bulb (Narcissus) is firm and plump, with clean, unbroken skin, or tunic

Unhealthy bulb lacks tunic and shows dark spots indicative of disease

Mail-order plants

If buying plants by mail order, always deal with a reputable supplier, placing your order early to get the ones you want. The plants will be sent out in special packs, such as molded, snap-shut containers, designed to keep them moist. As soon as the plants arrive, open the package and check the plants, making sure that they are healthy and the ones you ordered. Pot up the plants in potting mix and grow on for planting.

Plants are kept moist in sealed plastic bag

Healthy plants with no sign of pests and diseases, ready to grow on

soils and compost

Soils are made from minute particles of rock and organic matter that has been weathered and broken down over time. Fertile soil is essential for healthy plant growth and success in the garden. The soil supports the plant, supplying it with water, air, and nutrients. Not every type of soil is suitable for the widest range of plants, but almost any soil can be improved over the years, especially if good garden compost is worked into it on a regular basis.

Treat the soil well and you should be able to grow a wide range of plants successfully.

It is important to know what type of soil you have in your garden so that you can grow plants that thrive in it. It is relatively easy to determine your soil type (*see right*) and its pH (*see facing page*). The soil within the garden, however, can vary so you may have to choose different plants to suit each site.

To make sure that your plants get off to a good start, it is a worthwhile investment to condition the soil (*see facing page*) before planting with plenty of well-rotted organic matter, such as homemade garden compost (*see p.378*) or commercial soil conditioners.

Types of garden soil

The soil type you have largely dictates the plants you can grow. Soils in different sites, or even in different parts of a garden, vary in terms of their fertility, ease of cultivation, and how easy it is for plant roots to penetrate. There are several basic kinds of garden soil.

Loam has an ideal balance of clay and sand particles. It is the perfect growing medium – rich in nutrients and with a friable, crumbly texture that allows good drainage and water-retention. Calcareous (chalky) soil is very free-draining and quick to lose moisture. It is reasonably fertile and alkaline.

Clay soil is often very fertile but slow-draining. Heavy clay soil can be difficult to work. If you open up its structure by digging in grit and organic matter, clay soil can support vigorous plant growth. Peat soil is acidic and in winter can become waterlogged. It is high in organic matter and, if well-drained, provides good growing conditions. Add lime to grow more types of plants on it.

Sandy soil feels gritty and light, is easy to work, and warms up quickly in spring. Very free-draining, it dries out fast; nutrients can be washed out easily by rain and by watering, so it needs regular additions of organic matter and fertilizer.

Silty soil is neither gritty nor sticky but silky to the touch. It holds less water than clay soils; it is prone to compaction when wet. Improve it by adding plenty of well-rotted organic matter. Silty soil is also reasonably fertile.

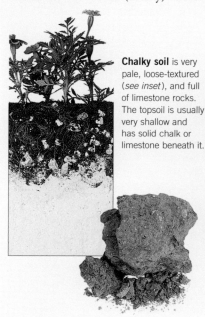

Chalky soil is very pale, loose-textured (*see inset*), and full of limestone rocks. The topsoil is usually very shallow and has solid chalk or limestone beneath it.

Clay soil is heavy, cold, and sticky when wet. In dry conditions, it sets like concrete and then cracks. Clay has a very fine texture (*inset*) and rolls into a soft ball that is shiny if smoothed.

Peat soil is spongy and holds a lot of water. Its very dark color shows it is rich in decomposed organic matter, parts of which are still visible (*see inset*).

What is soil pH?

Before buying any plants, check the pH of your soil to be sure that they will thrive in it. The pH reflects the level of acid in the soil. Soils lying over limestone or chalk are rich in lime and known as alkaline, but soils over sands become acid. Soil pH is measured on a scale of 1–14. Neutral soil, in which most plants thrive, has a pH of 7; soils of more than pH7 are alkaline, and those of less than pH7 are acidic. Soil testing kits, which indicate pH by reacting with soil and changing color (*see right*), are available from garden centers.

Soil pH affects the solubility of vital nutrients in the soil and their availability to plants. Acidic and alkaline soils vary in the amounts of nutrients they contain. Plants like or tolerate different levels of lime, so some, such as azaleas and many ericas, thrive only on acidic (called lime-free) soils and others, such as clematis and pinks, are happy in alkaline soils. The optimum soil pH for plant growth is within pH5.5–7.5.

pH scale and soil testing kits

Strongly alkaline soil: unsuitable for some ornamental plants, especially acid-lovers such as camellias and rhododendrons

8

7 — Neutral pH

Slightly acidic soil: best for many ornamental plants

6

5

4

Strongly acidic soil: unsuitable for most plants

Conditioning the soil

There are many soil-conditioning materials available from garden centers. The best are bulky organic materials, like manures, composted bark, or garden compost, which improve the soil structure so that it drains freely but retains moisture in dry weather. Manures and compost also replace some of the nutrients taken up by plants or washed out of the soil. Organic matter must be well-rotted; if not, it will deplete the soil of nutrients as it rots.

The more organic matter you add to the soil, the more organisms such as bacteria and worms will populate the soil, help to work it, and improve its structure.

Well-rotted horse manure is one of the best soil conditioners but can be hard to obtain. Making garden compost is easy and costs nothing (*see p.378*). Spent mushroom compost contains rotted manure and peat. It also has some lime, so do not use it where acid-loving plants are grown. Seaweed is an excellent conditioner because it makes the soil more friable and is rich in trace elements. Composted straw and leaf mold use otherwise wasted resources, but they take two years to rot. Pelleted chicken manure adds vital nutrients but has no conditioning value since the pellets have little bulk.

Incorporating manure or other well-rotted organic matter into the soil is most effectively done by digging it in during autumn. Scatter a thick layer all over the bed and fork it in (*see right*). Alternatively, leave it as a surface mulch. This will help to protect the roots of vulnerable plants over winter, and in the course of the year, the material will be incorporated into the soil by worms and other beneficial soil organisms.

The importance of good soil drainage

The amount of water available to plants through their roots depends on the type of soil (*see facing page*) and how free-draining it is. In well-structured soils, like loam, sufficient water and air is held in the spaces, or pores, between the soil particles to supply most plants adequately. A soil with poor structure may dry out very quickly or become waterlogged.

For example, finely textured clay soils hold most moisture, but it is

bound up in such a way that it is unavailable to plants. The large pores of sandy soils make water easily available to plant roots, but it drains away quickly. Peat soils can become waterlogged, and compacted silt and clay soils often are poorly drained.

Digging in well-rotted organic matter (*see above, right*) will improve the structure of both clay and sandy soils. Drainage can also be improved by adding gravel (*see right*).

Improving soil drainage with gravel
You can greatly improve the drainage of heavy clay and silty soils by incorporating coarse grit or gravel into the soil. Digging in the gravel will open up the structure and facilitate the flow of water through the soil. Spread a good 2–3in (5–8cm) layer over the area and dig it in with a fork. Any smaller amount will be ineffective. The gravel should make an instant and permanent improvement to the soil aeration and drainage, making it easier for plant roots to penetrate and extract the moisture and nutrients that they need.

Making garden compost

Rotted compost is dark, friable, and odorless.

Even in the smallest garden, it is worth making your own compost – it enables you to recycle waste and return it to the garden in a form unsurpassed for improving soil structure and fertility. It also saves you the expense of buying commercial soil conditioners.

To make good garden compost, you first need a suitable container.

You can easily make a compost bin at home from builder's pallets or old wood. The bin should be 3–5ft (1–1.5m) square, with solid sides to retain heat and moisture. It should also have a cover; a piece of old carpet will do.

The best compost is made from mixing fast-rotting material, such as grass clippings and vegetable trimmings, with drier material, such as straw and shredded newspaper, which is slower to decompose. Avoid adding meat or dairy products, which attract vermin. Try to add materials in well-mixed layers.

Compost takes about a year to rot down, but the process can be speeded up if the heap is turned at least once to mix the contents thoroughly. The easiest way to do this, if space allows, is to have two bins, so you can turn the contents of one bin into the other. Properly maintained compost generates heat, so be careful when handling an active compost heap.

Garden compost ingredients

Almost any materials of organic origin can be recycled into compost. You can add any plant waste, except noxious perennial weeds, from the garden into the heap. Seedheads must be removed because seeds will survive and cause problems in the future; any diseased material should not be composted.

Shred woody prunings, thick, fibrous stems, newspapers, and cardboard. Vegetable kitchen waste can also be used, but meat, fish, and dairy products will attract vermin. You can also add manure and autumn leaves. Do not use thick layers of grass clippings; they inhibit air movement.

Grass clippings need to be mixed with coarser material like straw or paper.

Woody prunings are slow to rot and must first be shredded into small pieces.

Annual weeds with the seedheads removed are usable, as well as dandelion leaves.

Kitchen waste of vegetable material only – to avoid attracting vermin.

Natural fibers, such as 100 percent wool or cotton, rot quickly if cut into small pieces.

Woolen carpet must be cut into pieces and mixed with green stuff to break it down.

Feathers rot better if they are taken out of the pillow and mixed with other waste.

Newspapers, torn into strips, are good for mixing with soft grass clippings.

How to make leaf mold

Autumn leaves rot slowly and if you have large quantities, you can compost them separately in an open bin made from a wooden frame and wire netting (*see right*) or in sealed plastic sacks with a few holes punched in them. The resulting leaf mold takes about two years to form. It is very crumbly and makes an excellent mulch (*see p.388*) and soil conditioner.

Leaf mold bin is open to the elements.

Using a worm bin

Worms feed on organic matter and eject the waste in the form of worm casts. This process can create a fine, crumbly, nutrient-rich compost that can be used in potting mixes and as a top-dressing or plant feed.

You can buy a kit complete with worms, or make your own wormery from a dustbin. Drill drainage holes in the base and stand the bin on some bricks. Put a 6in (15cm) layer of garden soil in the bottom and add a large potful of worms; redworms or African night crawlers are best. Top with a small layer of garden or kitchen waste, allowing the worms to digest each layer before adding more. Worms don't like citrus fruits or onions, but do like lime, such as crushed egg shells. When the bin is full, sieve out the worms and start again.

planting basics

Give your plants a good start in life, and there is every chance that they will grow strong and healthy. The first and most important step is to create a welcoming environment for their roots, encouraging them to spread out into the surrounding soil where they will take up water and nutrients.

Good planting practice results in healthy plants.

All plants appreciate being planted in a suitable and well-prepared site. Generally, the better the soil, the quicker they will become established. It is best to choose plants that are suited to the conditions you can offer. For example, if the soil in your garden is very light and dries out quickly, you can do much to improve its condition by enriching it with well-rotted organic matter, such as farmyard manure or garden compost (*see p.377*). If you then opt for plants that require rich, moist soil, they will struggle and flower indifferently. You will have far better results with plants that need free-drainage and tolerate dry conditions.

First, clear the plot of any weeds that could compete with your plants for water and nutrients.

Make sure that each plant has room to grow to its full size. Check the mature height and spread on the care label and mark it out around each planting hole. Fill the gaps with bedding plants until they mature. If a plant outgrows its space, transplant it in autumn or spring: dig it up, saving as much of the root mass as possible, and replant it in a previously prepared site.

Plants always look more natural in a border when grouped in odd numbers because the brain automatically sorts even numbers into pairs.

Many trees and shrubs are planted in the same way as those grown in containers (*see right*), but bare-root and balled-and-burlapped plants (*see pp.374–375*) require slightly different treatment.

Plant bare-root plants as soon as possible after purchase, in spring or autumn. Even with careful handling, they may suffer some root damage. To encourage new growth, cut damaged roots back hard; to compensate for the loss of roots, trim top-growth back hard.

Plant balled-and-burlapped plants in autumn or spring. Soak the root ball, remove the netting, and tease out the roots. Plant these and bare-roots with the old soil mark level with the surface.

Planting container-grown trees and shrubs

Container-grown plants can be planted (*see below*) at any time, so long as the soil is not waterlogged or frozen, but the best results are from autumn or spring planting. If you plant in summer you must keep the roots watered while the plant establishes itself. Before planting, prune out any dead or diseased growth and awkwardly placed shoots. Scrape away the top layer of medium from the pot to remove any weed seeds, then stand it in its pot in a bucket of water for two hours to soak the root ball thoroughly.

Dig a good-sized planting hole. Fill the hole with water and allow it to seep away. Next, fork a thick layer of well-rotted farmyard manure or garden compost into the bottom of the hole to give the plant a good start. Shrubs also appreciate some slow-release fertilizer. If the soil gets very wet in winter, improve the drainage by forking in coarse grit. Gently knock off the pot and place the plant in the prepared hole.

Planting at the correct depth is crucial to avoid a check in growth. With a few exceptions – such as some clematis (*see pp.136–139*) which like to be planted deep – you should keep the plant at the same depth as it was in its container.

It also helps to enrich the removed soil by mixing it with well-rotted organic matter. If the plant needs support, insert stakes, taking care not to damage the root ball, and tie in the main stem.

How to plant a container-grown tree or shrub
❶ Soak the plant's root ball in a bucket of water for 1–2 hours before planting. Dig a hole that is at least twice as wide and one-and-a-half times deeper than the root ball. Fork in plenty of well-rotted organic matter and, if it is needed for improved drainage, some coarse grit.

❷ Set the plant at the same depth as its original pot. Use a stake to check that the root ball is level with the soil surface.

❸ Fill in the hole with soil. Use your heel to firm the soil around the plant to remove air pockets.

❹ Water the plant well to settle the soil, even if it is raining. Apply a 2in (5cm) layer of well-rotted compost or bark as a mulch over the root area to help retain moisture and suppress weeds.

Planting nonwoody plants

The principles of planting are much the same for perennials, annuals, and other bedding plants as for shrubs (*see p.379*). However, these plants are more prone to drying out, so should be planted without delay. Some plants are sold in pots (*see below*), but bedding plants are usually sold in modular trays, with one seedling per module to keep the roots intact during planting. As soon as you buy bedding plants, give them a good soaking and plant them or, if there is still a risk of frost, pot them up separately to grow on under cover until it is safe to plant them out.

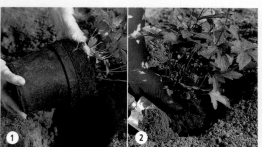

Planting a perennial
❶ *Dig a planting hole and loosen the soil around the edges. Mix some well-rotted organic matter or general fertilizer into the removed soil. Gently knock out the plant while holding the crown in one hand.*
❷ *Tease out the roots and hold the root ball level with the surface. Fill in the hole, and firm with your fingers. Water well and mulch; keep watered until plant is established.*

Planting climbers

The soil at the base of a wall or fence can be extremely dry because it is in a rain shadow, where rain rarely reaches the soil. When planting a climber, you should first improve the soil's moisture-retention by digging in plenty of well-rotted organic matter (such as garden compost). Follow the technique for planting a container-grown shrub (*see p.379*), but make sure that the planting hole is at least 12–18in (30–45cm) away from the wall. Don't forget to angle the top of the root ball toward the wall, while keeping the crown of the plant level with the soil surface.

Before planting, fix up a support. The easiest system is horizontal wires threaded through galvanized vine eyes in the wall, or trellis panels (*see p.390*) attached to slats.

Training a climber Once the climber has been planted, separate out the shoots and tie them into the supports, using garden twine. Stakes pushed into the ground and angled to the wall will encourage the shoots to grow toward it.

Planting bulbs

There are a couple of important points to remember when planting bulbs. First, most should be planted at a depth equivalent to three to five times their size (deeper in light than in heavy soils). For example, if a bulb stands 2in (5cm) tall, then there should be at least 4in (10cm) of soil on top of it, and the planting hole should therefore be at least 6in (15cm) deep. Some bulbs, such as nerines and some lilies, prefer to have their tops level with the soil surface.

If bulbs are planted at the wrong depth, they may fail to flower (a condition referred to as "blindness"). Blindness can also occur when the bulbs become crowded; lifting and replanting bulbs every three to four years should prevent this problem.

The second point to bear in mind is to make sure that the bulb is the right way up. This is easily done with true bulbs, like narcissi, but on corms and tubers (*see p.164*) the buds are not always very distinct.

The most natural way to grow bulbs is in large drifts in grass. There are two ways to do this – but first, cut the grass as short as possible, leaving it uncut until the bulb

Using a bulb planter This tool takes out a neat plug of soil just big enough for one bulb. Push it vertically into the ground, giving it a firm twist before lifting out the plug of soil. If the planter doesn't have depth markings on its side, use a ruler to measure. If it is too deep, top up the level with soil, compost, or grit.

foliage dies down in early summer. With large bulbs, such as daffodils, scatter them over the chosen area. Check they are all at least 4in (10cm) apart, then plant each bulb where it fell. Use a bulb planter (*see above*) or trowel to dig a hole, insert the bulb, and replace the soil.

To plant many small bulbs, such as crocuses, make an "H"-shaped cut in the lawn using a half-moon edger or spade. Turn back the sod. Take out the soil to the correct depth; plant the bulbs about 1in (2.5cm) apart; then fold back and firm the turf.

Planting depths The correct planting depth for each type of bulb depends on its size. As a rough guide, plant each bulb at a depth three to five times the bulb's height. In sandy soils, bulbs should be planted slightly deeper.

Bulb is planted at three times its height

Wet conditions In soil with poor drainage, it is a good idea to fork grit into the surrounding soil and then place each bulb on a thick bed of grit. This will help prevent the bulb from rotting.

Dry conditions Light soils dry out very quickly, especially in hot conditions. To prevent the roots of bulbs from drying out, place each one on a layer of well-rotted organic matter.

Preparing containers

Most plants grow happily in containers but they will demand more attention than if they had been planted in the garden.

Terracotta pots are very attractive but, once planted up, they can be heavy to move around. They are also porous and dry out more quickly than metal or plastic ones. You will need to line the base with screen or gravel to stop the drainage hole from becoming blocked with potting mix. Plastic containers may not look as elegant, but they are inexpensive, light, and good at retaining moisture. They generally have several drainage holes at the base.

Choose a soil-based potting mix, which holds water better than a soilless one, for containers. Mix water-retaining granules and slow-release fertilizer into it to cut down on watering and feeding later.

Break polystyrene plant trays into pieces and use to line pot

Large containers can be heavy. If they are to be planted with shallow-rooted plants, fill the excess depth with polystyrene pieces, then top up with potting medium. See that the pot does not become top-heavy and unstable. Pots planted with deep-rooted plants are easily and safely moved using a specially designed trolley.

Planting a hanging basket

A hanging basket packed full with colorful plants is a spectacular sight, and it is not that difficult to achieve.

There are many types of baskets but the most popular ones are made of wire mesh. These need lining to hold the potting medium in place. Sphagnum moss is no longer recommended, but there are now plenty of modern alternatives, including liners made from coconut fiber, plastic, or wool.

The number of plants you will need to plant up a basket depends on its size, but you can pack them in quite tightly. The plants and potting mix will be very heavy, especially when watered, so it is best to use a lighter, soilless medium. Don't forget to add a slow-release fertilizer to

Planting a basket
❶ *Steady the basket by standing it on an upturned pot. Insert the liner and place a saucer or piece of plastic in the base. Cover with medium. Cut slits in the sides and push through trailing plants from the outside, holding them by their roots. Fill with medium.*
❷ *Plant tall plants in the center and more trailing plants around the edge. Fill any gaps with medium. Firm and water.*

avoid having to fertilize later. Improve moisture retention by mixing in water-retaining granules.

The baskets should be planted thickly so that the plants will grow to conceal the sides. Work from the base of the basket upward, cutting slit holes in the liner and feeding

the plant roots through. Protect the foliage of the plants by rolling them in a tube of paper first.

Plant baskets of summer bedding in midspring, and keep under cover until after the last frost. Baskets of hardier perennials, planted in spring or autumn, can go straight outdoors.

Planting aquatic and water-garden plants

Late spring or early summer are the best planting times. The majority of aquatic plants benefit from being planted in a basket. There are many different planting baskets to choose from – the most common ones are made of plastic mesh and require lining with a piece of burlap to

contain the soil. The mesh allows water to penetrate to the roots, while helping contain the growth of more rampant plants.

Aquatic plants are generally easy to grow. There is available special low-nitrogen aquatic medium (too much nitrogen in water causes green

algae to grow), but ordinary garden soil works just as well if no fertilizer has been added to it.

Correct planting depth is vital: marginal plants need shallow water, while deep-water aquatics, such as water lilies, need deep water to thrive. Always check the care label.

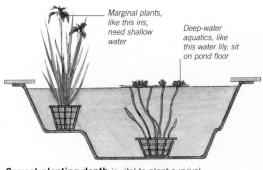

Marginal plants, like this iris, need shallow water

Deep-water aquatics, like this water lily, sit on pond floor

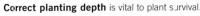

Correct planting depth is vital to plant survival.

Planting in an aquatic basket
Line the basket with burlap so the soil does not escape. Partly fill the basket with soil. Sit the plant (here a water lily) so its crown is level with the top of the basket. Fill in soil around the roots and firm. Top-dress with a thin layer of gravel, so the growing points are exposed, to hold the soil in place. Soak the medium well before setting the basket in shallow water. Move into deeper water as the stems grow.

pruning

If you grow woody plants, sooner or later you will have to prune them to keep them looking good. Pruning is often regarded with dread by gardeners, but it really is just a matter of common sense and learning a few fundamental rules. Also, good-quality tools make the job easier.

Pruning encourages new, strong growth and increases the number of flowers, maintains a well-balanced shape, and keeps a plant to the desired size. The methods vary depending on the type of plant. It is most important in a plant's early years because early pruning affects the shape of the established plant. However, renovation pruning (*see p.384*) can also breathe new life into an old plant. By pruning out dead and diseased growth, you can also improve the health of an ailing plant.

It may seem contrary, but by cutting back a plant you encourage it to grow bigger and stronger, because it reacts by sending out new shoots from below the cuts. You can also persuade a plant

to grow in a particular direction and regulate the quantity and vigor of that growth. Conifers do not need much pruning, except when grown as hedging (*see p.384*) or topiary.

When pruning, make a clean cut just above a bud or leaf joint (*see below*). The cut should not be too close or you may cause the bud to die, but if you cut too wide, the stub will die back and may become diseased.

Before you start pruning, take a good look at the plant. Give some thought to the cuts you are about to make. If you rush in with the pruners, you could end up with a badly shaped plant or lose a season of flowering because you have cut out the wrong stems.

Basic tools for pruning

If you invest in a few good-quality pruning tools, it will make your job much easier. Using good cutting tools will also guarantee that the pruning cuts are clean and heal quickly without becoming vulnerable to disease. For most pruning tasks, you need only a pair of pruners, a pruning

saw, and perhaps some loppers. Use a tool suited to the stem size – if you try to cut a large stem with pruners, you will damage it and make a blunt cut. Keep blades clean and sharp: blunt blades tear rather than cut, allowing disease to take hold.

Loppers, like long-handled pruners, give extra leverage and cut branches up to 1in (2.5cm) in diameter. They also enable you to reach high-up branches.

Folding pruning saws are single-toothed. They cut large branches, are easy to use in awkward spaces, and fold up for safe storage.

Pruners are the most commonly used pruning tool. They will cut all shoots up to ½in (1cm) in diameter. Always cut with the thin blade toward the bud or joint to enable you to cut closer: the cut will be cleaner and will heal more quickly.

Basic principles of pruning

Single bud Make your cut at a 45° angle, ¼in (5mm) above the bud so any moisture runs off.

Prune above outward-facing bud for new growth away from heart of plant

Remove dead wood to stop disease spreading. Cut back to a strong bud or healthy, new shoot.

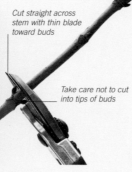

Cut straight across stem with thin blade toward buds

Take care not to cut into tips of buds

Opposite buds Cut straight across the stem as close as possible to the tips of the buds.

No matter what type of plant you are pruning, certain basic principles apply. Fast-growing plants that put on more than 12in (30cm) growth in a year respond well to hard pruning. Slow-growing plants usually do not respond well to being pruned back hard, so avoid it unless absolutely necessary.

When pruning dead or diseased wood, wipe the blades between cuts with a commercial disinfectant to avoid spreading spores or infection to the next plant that you prune.

Crossing stems rub together causing chafing damage to bark, creating a wound where disease can enter. Overcrowded stems are weak, block out light, and trap damp air, which encourages disease. Thinning out such stems restores a plant's vigor.

After hard pruning, always apply a fertilizer and extra mulch, and water if necessary. Inspect your plants regularly and take out any broken or damaged stems without delay to minimize the risk of disease.

Pruning a spring-flowering plant

Spring- or early flowering plants are best pruned after they flower and before they put on new growth. This is because their flowers develop from buds growing on the previous year's stems. If pruning is left too late in the season, you might remove next year's flowering shoots.

Start by thinning out any dead, damaged, and diseased wood. Then cut some older stems back to the ground. Next, cut shoots with buds back to 5 or 6 buds, even if they have started to put on new growth at the tips. The following year's flowering shoots will develop from these buds.

Many spring-flowering shrubs can be trained flat against a wall. On planting, tie in all the main stems and sideshoots into a support. Cut back any shoots that cannot be tied in to one or two buds and pinch out the tips of forward-facing shoots so that they branch sideways. Shorten the longest sideshoots, especially where growth is sparse. After flowering, tie in new growth and cut back badly placed or overly long

shoots. Take out any diseased or dead wood; make sure that the ties are not too tight. Cut back the flowered shoots to 5 or 6 buds; some shrubs, such as flowering quinces (*Chaenomeles, see p.38*) and pyracanthas (*see p.102*), are pruned to 2 or 3 buds for prolific flowering.

Unpruned sideshoots flower sparsely

Sideshoots pruned to 2–3 buds produce more flowers

Results of pruning Unpruned stems (*see left*) of flowering quince produce few flowers; pruning stimulates profuse flowering (*see right*).

Pruning a late-summer flowering plant

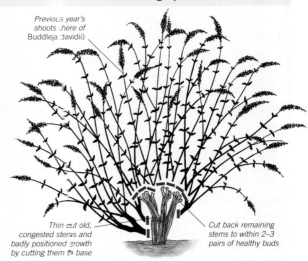

Previous year's shoots here of Buddleja davidii)

Thin out old, congested stems and badly positioned growth by cutting them to base

Cut back remaining stems to within 2–3 pairs of healthy buds

In the first spring, aim to form a base of strong, woody stems from which spring-flowering shoots will grow each year. Cut out any weak or diseased stems and shorten the remainder to 6–18in (15–45cm), or if a large plant is required to 4ft (1.2m). Prune in subsequent early springs before growth starts. Restore the original framework by pruning all the old flowering stems to leave two or three pairs of fat, healthy buds from the previous year's growth. At the same time, if it is necessary, thin out dense congested stems.

Late-summer flowering plants produce flowers on growth made in the current growing season. Early spring is the best time to prune them, because it diverts each plant's energy to existing buds rather than to developing more, and gives it sufficient time to produce new flowering shoots from the buds.

Hard annual pruning suits many deciduous shrubs and climbers, such as caryopteris, ceanothus, *Hydrangea*

paniculata, and phygelius – as well as many gray-leaved evergreens, for example lavenders. It produces the best-quality flowers and prevents the plant from becoming too big. Old or neglected late-summer flowering shrubs respond well to hard pruning.

On windy sites, shorten tall growth by about one half in autumn to prevent the winds from rocking the plant and loosening the roots.

Pruning an early summer-flowering plant

Early summer-flowering shrubs, for example philadelphus (*see p.93*) and weigelas (*see p.128*), and climbing plants are generally pruned in late summer, immediately after flowering has finished. You should aim to open up the plant to allow light and air to reach the center while retaining an uncluttered, balanced shape.

In the first year after planting, remove all weak and crossing shoots by cutting each out just above an

outward-facing bud or at the base. Trim back any overlong shoots to within the overall outline, again cutting each to an outward-facing bud.

In subsequent years, thin out the plant by removing about one in four of the oldest stems, cutting them back to the ground. This makes room for new stems to grow from the base. Shorten younger stems to encourage flowering sideshoots. Wayward stems should be pruned back to maintain a good shape.

Pruning a mature shrub after flowering
Using loppers, cut out one in four of the old stems (here of philadelphus) just above the base. Take care to leave a few strong buds on each. Shorten any younger shoots by a quarter to one-third. This will open up the shrub and encourage new, vigorous growth to flower next year. Any dead, damaged, diseased, or crossing shoots on the remaining stems should be pruned out at the same time.

Renovation pruning

When trees, shrubs, and climbers become overgrown or neglected, their growth weakens and flowering declines. Provided that the plants are basically healthy, renovation pruning can give them a new lease on life, spurring strong growth and flower production. Many deciduous plants, like willows (*Salix*), lilacs (*Syringa*) and buddlejas, respond well to renovation pruning.

The best time is in late winter or spring because the plants have a chance to put on new growth before the next winter. Many plants, though, tolerate drastic pruning at their usual pruning time, for example early summer-flowering philadelphus can be tackled in late summer after flowering.

The stems of some shrubs, like berberis, become so tangled that they need cutting back to ground level.

Less vigorous woody plants, particularly evergreens such as rhododendrons, must be cut back in stages over 2–3 years, to give them a chance to recover.

Unfortunately, not all old shrubs survive such drastic pruning, so be prepared for some losses.

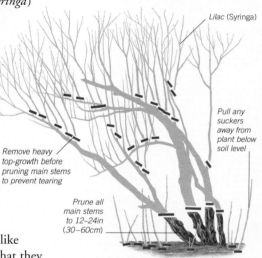

Lilac (Syringa)

Pull any suckers away from plant below soil level

Remove heavy top-growth before pruning main stems to prevent tearing

Prune all main stems to 12–24in (30–60cm)

Drastic renovation involves pruning all growth.

Rhododendron

Each year, prune half of remaining old stems that have not yet been pruned, cutting them to ground level

Thin out new growth arising from last year's cuts to 2–3 strong stems

Staged renovation is done over three years; this is the second year.

Pruning hedges

Regular trimming not only keeps a hedge looking neat, it also promotes strong, dense growth and longevity. Trim established evergreen hedges, for example privet and fast-growing conifers, in late spring or early summer and again in late summer or early autumn, while they are in growth. Deciduous hedges, such as beech and hawthorn, are best trimmed in summer. A second trim can be given in autumn. Time pruning of flowering hedges to suit their flowering periods (*see p.383*).

It is especially important to prune evergreen and coniferous hedges regularly, because very few will reshoot from old wood. When training an evergreen or conifer hedge, keep the sides trimmed, but allow the main stem to reach the desired height before pruning it.

Aim to create a hedge that is wider at the base than at the top. It is less vulnerable to damage from snow and strong winds, and light can reach the lower branches.

As with shears, keep the blade parallel to the hedge for an even cut. Always wear eye and ear protectors and gloves. Sweep the blade away from your body and the wire.

Keeping a climbing plant within bounds

Many climbers, such as *Clematis montana* and rambling roses, put on a lot of growth in one season. Prune spring-flowering climbers after flowering; summer-flowering plants in spring. Remove overlong shoots and unhealthy growth. However, do not prune them too hard because it will encourage leafy growth rather than flowering shoots. You can thin out congested climbers (*see below*), but only once every three years.

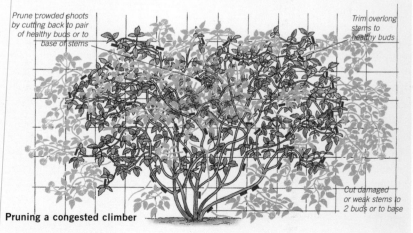

Prune crowded shoots by cutting back to pair of healthy buds or to base of stems

Trim overlong stems to healthy buds

Cut damaged or weak stems to 2 buds or to base

Pruning a congested climber

routine tasks

A little time spent regularly on maintenance, such as fertilizing, watering, weeding, mulching, and deadheading, will keep your plants in top condition so that they perform at their best. Enjoy the chance these simple tasks give you to enjoy your garden, and take in all its scents and colors.

Mulching a raised bed suppresses weeds and keeps the soil moist for the plants (here azaleas).

Any job in the garden is easier if you use the correct tools. Essentials include a spade, a fork, a hand trowel and hand fork, and a hoe and short-tined rake for soil cultivation and weeding. Pruners are needed to deadhead and prune plants and if you have trees, shrubs, or woody climbers, loppers and a pruning saw are useful. If you have a lawn, a good lawnmower and a long-tined lawn rake will help you to keep it looking good. Add to those a watering can and a wheelbarrow, and you can undertake most routine tasks in the garden. Always buy the best-quality tools you can afford since cheap ones may last only one or two seasons.

Routine tasks can be minimized by making sure that plants are growing in a position with a soil and conditions that suit them (*see Climate and location, pp.371–373, and Soils and compost, pp.376–378*). If you grow a plant in an unsuitable site, it is unlikely to flourish and will need much more attention. It is also essential that plants have space to grow to maturity; you may be tempted to cram them in for immediate effect, but this will make them weak and more prone to attack from pests and diseases.

Above all, it is more effective and easier to care for your plants by doing a little quite often, rather than leaving tasks until the garden becomes neglected.

What to do when

Spring
- Cut back any old growth left over winter and clear away insulation
- Begin mowing lawns, with cutting blade set at maximum height, as grass begins to grow; clean up edges
- Fertilize and mulch all woody and herbaceous perennial plants as soon as soil starts to warm up
- Repot or top-dress plants grown in containers
- After they flower, prune spring-flowering deciduous shrubs and climbers; also prune late-flowering shrubs and climbers, all bush roses (*see p.110*), and groups 2 and 3 clematis (*see p.136*)
- Prune or trim evergreens if needed
- Divide clump-forming perennials, bamboos, and grasses
- Plant new plants and autumn-flowering bulbs, and sow seed
- Provide support now for perennials and biennials that will need it when fully grown
- In late spring, start to bring container-grown plants that have been overwintered under cover out into the garden
- Keep young and newly planted varieties watered regularly
- Keep on top of routine tasks such as deadheading, and weeding; start to fertilize plants in containers
- Layer shrubs and climbers
- Plant, thin, and divide oxygenating plants in ponds

Summer
- Mow lawns regularly
- Clip hedges
- After they flower, finish pruning spring-flowering deciduous shrubs and climbers and group 1 clematis (*see p.136*)
- Continue routine tasks such as feeding, deadheading, and weeding
- Prune *Prunus* trees and shrubs in midsummer to avoid infection by silver leaf and other diseases
- Take soft and semiripe cuttings
- In late summer, prune early summer-flowering deciduous shrubs and climbers

Autumn
- Keep up with routine tasks such as weeding and deadheading; stop feeding plants
- Prune flowering hedges and rambling roses after flowering
- Remove stakes from perennials after flowering, but leave dying growth to act as winter insulation
- Lift tender rootstocks, such as dahlias, and store over winter
- Mow lawns at maximum height
- Move tender plants under cover
- Plant hardy trees, shrubs, climbers, perennials, and spring-flowering bulbs; sow seed of hardy plants
- Take hardwood cuttings
- Clear out any leaves and dead material from ponds

Winter
- Throughout the winter, protect plants from winter damage
- Brush snow from conifers
- Plan what seeds and plants you wish to order for next year
- Take root cuttings

fertilizing

Using fertilizers

Plants need nutrients to encourage strong, healthy growth and plentiful flowers. Whether you use organic or nonorganic fertilizers is a personal choice. Organic feeds tend to release nutrients over a longer period; chemicals give a fast but short-lived, boost to growth. Both are available as granules, powders, or liquids. Powdered or granular feeds, such as poultry pellets, can be scattered over the entire planting area or around individual plants. Dry fertilizers, such as bonemeal, have to be watered into the soil, because plants can absorb nutrients only once they are dissolved in water. Liquid fertilizers are quick-acting and easy to apply, using a special hose-end applicator or watering can.

Apply fertilizers from midspring to midsummer, when the plants are growing rapidly and will benefit from extra nutrients. Take care when applying a concentrated fertilizer because it may scorch the stems and foliage. Always read carefully the manufacturer's instructions, and avoid the temptation to overfeed the plants; it is wasteful and results in weak growth and fewer flowers.

Fertilizer pellets
These slow-release pellets are useful for containers.

Forking in fertilizer
Fertilizer granules should be worked into the soil surface around the plant, taking care not to fork too deeply and damage the roots. Unless heavy rain is expected, water the area well to release the nutrients into the soil.

Foliar feeding
Spray liquid fertilizer onto plants as a fast, effective pick-me-up. Most is absorbed through the leaves, and any excess is taken up by the roots. To avoid scorch, apply in the evening or on cloudy days.

Applying a top-dressing

Potting mix in containers becomes less fertile over time as its nutrients are used by the plant and leached out by rain and watering. If the plant has not outgrown the pot and become root-bound, apply an annual top-dressing at the beginning of the growing season to replenish the nutrients. Remove the top layer of old soil and replace it with fresh medium (*see right*).

Alternatively, for shrubs and trees, you could use garden compost or composted bark. A mulch (*see p.388*) of bark chips or gravel will conserve moisture and give a decorative finish.

Rock-garden plants, especially alpine species, like very well-drained soil; a top-dressing of gravel, pebbles, pea gravel, or glass chips avoids water puddling around the plants and causing rot. Top-dressing will mix in with the soil or get washed away, so in spring, scrape it off, fertilize the soil, and top with a fresh layer of grit.

Gently scrape soil away using trowel

Top-dressing a container
Carefully remove the top 2–3in (5–8cm) of old soil, taking care not to go too deep and damage the roots (*see inset*). Then fill the container back up to the original level, using fresh medium of the same type mixed with slow-release fertilizer. Finally, water it in well.

watering

Why water?

Watering is essential for healthy, growing plants. Moisture is taken up from the soil and used by the plant to make and transport vital nutrients for survival. Water keeps every plant cell turgid, so the first visible sign of thirst is the wilting of leaves and stems.

Dry conditions can cause a check in growth and leave plants more vulnerable to attack by diseases or pests. Although you should expect some watering to be necessary after planting and during very hot spells, it can be reduced by choosing plants that tolerate such conditions.

Drought-tolerant plants, such as lavender and stachys, naturally prefer a well-drained or sunny area. Their leaves are often small and silvery or are protected by a hairy or waxy layer. Thirsty plants usually have large, thin leaves, for example trollius or primulas, and thrive in damp, sheltered spots.

To reduce water loss from the soil surface, apply a mulch (*see p.388*); avoid leaving large areas unplanted. Wind draws moisture from leaves, and the plant may suffer. A windbreak is a good deterrent for such water loss.

Waterlogging is also harmful. The soil becomes so saturated that plant roots cannot breathe and thus begin to rot. This occurs after very rainy or snowy periods and on heavy soils with poor drainage. Plant moisture-loving plants in these situations.

When to water

How often you need to water will depend on the local conditions. Frequent rain should supply enough moisture, but in dry spells you may have to water beds and containers daily. Some plants require moist soil and will quickly die if the ground starts to dry out, but others will be able to cope once they become established. New plantings are also at risk from drought until they form a strong root system.

Try basin watering (*see right*) to direct water to the roots. Another option is pot watering: sink a deep pot into the soil next to a plant; fill it with water and allow it to drain into the soil. Seedlings especially need constant attention – too much water and they will rot off, too little and they will quickly die.

In summer, water in the evening or early morning. The heat of the day increases evaporation so your efforts will be wasted; also, water droplets act like lenses to scorch the foliage.

Basin watering Plant slightly lower than the soil surface to create a hollow, or surround the plant with a raised dam of soil. Water into this basin so that all the water is directed straight to the roots, saving time and conserving water.

Watering cans

Every gardener needs a watering can for small areas of the garden and for containers. When buying one, go for the best you can afford because you will find yourself using it often.

Choose a watering can that is well balanced and not too heavy to lift

Watering seedlings Seedlings require only a gentle shower because their tiny roots are easily dislodged. Attach a fine, metal rose to your can so that it points upward. Start watering to the side of the tray to establish an even spray, then pass it smoothly over the seedlings.

when it is full. Other useful features include an opening large enough to make it easy to fill by a faucet or hose, and a strainer at the bottom of the spout so that it does not become clogged by debris. A long spout is useful for reaching to the back of the border.

Most watering cans are fitted with a removable rose. A fine rose is perfect for delicate plants (*see left*). A coarse rose will give a spray that is better for watering larger, more established plantings quickly.

Keep a separate watering can for pesticides or weedkillers to avoid cross-contamination; buy a plastic can because some chemicals will corrode metal.

Hoses and sprinklers

Watering can be a time-consuming task, so consider investing in a hose that will carry water to where it is needed, without having to fill and refill a watering can. Reinforced hoses are less likely to kink than the less expensive, flat ones. Hoses that neatly wind onto their own reels are easy to store. All should be fitted with a nozzle that can adjust the flow of water from a stream to a fine spray, so you can water appropriately (*see right*). Other attachments, such as fertilizer applicators, are available.

Some hoses are laid around the garden as a permanent irrigation system controlled by a tap or a timer. Seep hoses let water ooze out along their entire length; drip hoses deliver water through holes to individual plants in beds or containers. Both types are good for newly planted areas but are unsightly, so it is best to disguise them (*see below*). Sprinklers can be used for large areas. Their fine sprays soak the soil evenly, but they are wasteful and have to be moved often to stop puddles forming.

Using a hose Watering plants with a hose requires some care. A strong stream of water can erode soil from around the plant roots, leaving them exposed and prone to dry out (*see above*). Alternatively, if the ground is hard, it may not penetrate the soil at all and run over the surface away from where it is needed. Always use a spray nozzle on the hose, unless you are watering into a pot placed as a reservoir by the plant.

Installing a seep hose
❶ To lay a seep hose, wind it in loops around the plants in your border, allowing it to moisten the soil for a distance of about 17in (20cm) on each side of the hose. If you find the hose will not lie flat, peg it down at intervals with hoops of strong, galvanized wire.

❷ With the hose in place, rake at least an 3in (8cm) thick layer of mulch, such as bark chips or gravel, between the plants. Cover the bare soil and the hose. The mulch gives a neat, decorative finish, suppresses weeds, and will help prevent moisture from evaporating from the soil. The finished bed is low-maintenance, especially if the seep hose is controlled by a timer.

mulching

Why do you need to mulch?

A mulch is a layer of material applied as a skin over the soil and has many advantages over leaving the surface bare. Loose mulches maintain an even soil temperature; they are warmer in winter and cooler in summer than naked ground. The need for watering is reduced, because moisture cannot readily evaporate

Gravel mulch *provides a good foil for grasses.*

from the soil. Mulches also help to suppress weeds, especially the sheet mulches such as landscape fabric and black plastic. The weeds are prevented from germinating by the lack of light, although some persistent perennial weeds such as dandelions may grow through a loose mulch unless the soil has been thoroughly weeded beforehand (*see p.389*). Any weeds that appear after the mulch is laid will be easier to spot and remove. Mulches can be very ornamental, especially if you use materials such as bark chips, pebbles, or cocoa shells.

These are many types of organic and synthetic mulch available, but to be effective it should be long-lasting

and not easily dislodged by rain or blown away. Organic mulches such as compost will, in time, be carried down into the soil by worms, improving the soil structure and replenishing nutrients, filling the role of mulch and fertilizer in one. If you are using an organic material, make sure it has a loose texture that will allow moisture to pass through easily. If using black plastic, punch some holes in it so air and water can reach the soil.

Well-rotted manure
Cocoa shells
Grass cuttings
Bark chips
Mushroom compost
Gravel

Types of mulch

Organic mulches, such as well-rotted manure, improve soil structure, but do not use mushroom compost with acid-loving plants. Grass cuttings are free, but may turn slimy or spread weed seeds. Bark chips look good and use an otherwise wasted resource, as do sweet-smelling cocoa shells. Sheet mulches are effective but need disguising (*see below*). Gravel is expensive, but makes a handsome mulch.

Applying and using mulches

A mulch will have the effect of stabilizing and maintaining soil conditions, so the best time to apply one is in autumn or spring. At these times of year, the soil should be reasonably warm, not too wet or too dry, and free from weeds – in other words, perfect for plant growth.

A loose mulch, such as gravel, well-rotted manure, and bark chips, can be applied by spreading it liberally around plants with a shovel and raking it level (*see right*).

Sheet mulches of landscape fabric or plastic are easy to use if laid over a bed before planting. Cut the sheet

so that it is at least 6in (15cm) larger on all sides than the area to be covered. Secure the sheet at the edges with pegs, or push the edges into the ground with the edge of a spade, making sure that it is taut. The plants can then be inserted through planting holes (*see below*).

Using a sheet mulch

❶ *Rake the soil level and, if needed, water it well. Lay a sheet mulch (here of landscape fabric) over the bed. To plant, make two cuts, 6–8in (15cm) long and at right angles, in the sheet. Fold the flaps back and dig a planting hole.*

❷ *Insert the plant, firm, water, and replace the flaps. Add a 2in (5cm) layer of organic or mineral mulch to hide as well as hold down the sheet mulch.*

Applying organic mulch Spread loose mulches directly onto the soil to a depth of 2–3in (5–8cm) to control weeds or 4–6in (10–15cm) to provide winter insulation. Tuck the mulch under each plant, but, with organic mulch, leave a 4in (10cm) gap to avoid rot from setting in. Top up the mulch as needed.

weeding

Types of weed

Any plant growing where it is not wanted can be called a weed, although they are often thought of as wild plants. In favorable conditions, some ornamentals can be invasive. Weeds are a nuisance because they grow very fast, taking water, nutrients, and light from less vigorous, cultivated plants.

There are two types of weeds: annual and perennial. Annual weeds, such as annual meadow grass, have thin, shallow roots and complete their life cycle within one year. Left to grow they will self-seed prolifically and grow rapidly, producing up to three generations in a season. If you don't allow them to seed, they are fairly easy to control.

Perennial weeds usually have deep, fleshy, or spreading roots, such as the common dandelion, or creeping underground stems, for example ground elder.

They are difficult to remove completely and return year after year even if only a small piece of root is left in the soil after weeding.

Annual weeds

Common chickweed

Lamb's quarters

Groundsel

Perennial weeds

Underground stems

Couch grass

Stinging nettle

Oxalis

Controlling weeds

The method of control you choose for your garden will depend on the type of weed, the scale of the invasion, and whether you are prepared to use chemicals.

If you want to avoid weedkillers, then mulching (*see facing page*) as well as using groundcover plants will prevent weeds from taking hold. If a few annual weeds appear, they are simple to deal with. Cut them out with a hoe, or pull them up by hand, before they set seed.

Small patches of perennial weeds can be dug out with a fork but may reappear unless you remove every bit of root. If there is a very bad infestation, then a drastic solution may be needed. A sheet mulch (*see facing page*) will kill most weeds if it is left in place over two seasons.

Inevitably, chemical weedkillers save a lot of time and effort. Many are effective only in early summer and should be used on a cloudy, dry day. Some weedkillers are selective and will kill only certain types of plants, so first identify the problem weed. Several applications may be necessary to clear persistent perennial weeds. Always follow carefully the manufacturer's instructions when using chemicals.

Individual weeds can be targeted, but if an area has more weeds than desirable plants, consider digging up the ornamental plants and treating the entire area. Before replanting the ornamentals, wash the soil off the root balls, check, and remove any perennial weed fragments.

Using a hoe Walk backwards, pushing and pulling the blade along the surface as you go, aiming to slice off the tops of annual weeds without digging into the soil. Either leave the hoed weeds to wither if it is hot, or if it is damp remove them and add them to the compost pile, but only if they have not set seed.

Chemical weedkiller Many Canadian municipalities have restricted the use of herbicides, so check if there is a ban. A small hand-sprayer like this is the safest method of application, but it is wise to shield nearby ornamental plants with plastic.

Weeding rows by hand Sowing seed in rows makes it easier to distinguish weed seedlings from the ornamental seedlings. Anything out of line can be pulled out by hand. Hand weeding is easiest to do when the soil is slightly moist.

supporting plants

Providing temporary supports

Many herbaceous plants need some support as they grow to prevent them from being snapped by wind or being flattened by heavy rain, so they look their best throughout the season. Push supports into the soil when the plant is

Slot stakes together

Link stakes These come in varying heights and slot together easily (*see* inset). You can position them around any shape of clump. Insert to a depth of 4in (10cm) to keep them steady.

no more than 12in (30cm) tall, so that it has time to grow through and disguise the support. If you delay staking the plant until it begins to flop, the supports will look obvious and unnatural.

Traditionally, bamboo canes are used – either singly, for tall plants such as gladioli, or in a circle with twine for clumping plants. A more natural alternative is to use twiggy branches usually discarded from coppiced shrubs. You could also use large plastic or wire mesh stretched between stakes; the plant stems grow through the mesh and obscure it. There are also many metal and plastic staking systems available, which are reusable and versatile. Small climbers, like sweet peas (*Lathyrus, see p.145*), can be grown over a wigwam of stakes, tied at the top with raffia, or over a wooden or metal obelisk.

Using trellis

Train climbers and wall shrubs on a trellis used as a freestanding screen, attached to slats on a wall, or to extend the height of a fence. Make sure that the wood has been treated with preservative before it is covered by the plant. Most plants grown on trellises need to be tied regularly into the support; a loose figure-eight loop of twine will allow stems to grow. Once plants are established, check the ties at least once a year and loosen any that are too tight.

Attaching a trellis kit to a drainpipe This is a good way to conceal an unsightly feature. Use two or three narrow, 6ft (2m) trellis panels and place them around the drainpipe. Secure at 18in (45cm) intervals with plastic ties or wire.

keeping plants neat

Deadheading and pinch pruning

Deadheading woody plants
Using pruners, regularly remove withered flowers, cutting back to a strong, outward-facing bud to encourage open growth.

Deadheading by hand
Grasp each fading flower of a herbaceous plant between thumb and forefinger, and bend it over so it snaps off.

Pinching out leafy shoots
The tips of soft shoots (here of purple sage) are nipped out just above healthy buds or sideshoots to encourage denser growth.

During the growing season, you can prolong each plant's flowering period by deadheading. This directs energy that would have gone into producing seed into forming more flowers. Try to get into the habit of deadheading whenever you go into the garden, and you will be rewarded with a constant and neat display of flowers.

Removing the spent flowers of most herbaceous plants can be done by hand. Some perennials, for example delphiniums, lupines, and oriental poppies, can be cut down to the base once the first flush of flower has ended to induce fresh foliage and a second display later in the season. Other plants, such as catmint, cranesbills, and pulmonarias can simply be sheared over.

To deadhead shrubs and woody climbers, use pruners and cut back the flowered shoot to a healthy, outward-facing bud. The new shoot should grow in a direction that will

enhance the shape of the plant. Remember that many plants, including some roses, achilleas, and grasses, should not be deadheaded if you wish to enjoy their decorative seedheads in late autumn and winter.

If you want to save the seed of any annuals or biennials, you can still remove most of the spent flowers because each seedhead produces a large quantity of seeds.

You can also keep the foliage of plants, for example herbs, looking neat by pinch pruning. This is a similar process to deadheading, but involves removing the growing tips of shoots before flowering to encourage lots of new sideshoots and a dense, bushy habit. It is a technique often used with fuchsias and summer bedding plants early in the season; if you stop pinch pruning in midsummer, the plants will burst into bloom, producing a continuous mass of flowers.

raising your own

One of the great joys of gardening is propagating your own plants by taking cuttings, dividing, layering, and sowing seed. Not only are these techniques fun to learn, they will also save you a great deal of money – when compared with nursery plants the price of a packet of seed is negligible.

A potting tray stops potting mix from spilling when sowing seed or potting up cuttings.

It is not necessary to purchase much equipment to raise your own plants, nor do you need a great deal of space – a sunny windowsill will do – but you do need clean containers, good-quality, fresh potting mix (not salvaged from other pots) and, if taking cuttings, a clean, sharp knife. Poor hygiene is the prime enemy of young seedlings and cuttings, because it allows diseases such as rot to attack the young plants.

New seedlings and cuttings need the correct balance of nutrients, a good supply of oxygen and moisture, and appropriate light and temperature levels. All you have to do is provide suitable growing conditions and nature will do the rest for you. Seed and all cuttings, except hardwood ones, succeed in the protected environment of a propagator. Create similar conditions by covering a pot with a clear plastic bag. Warming the potting mix gently will also help.

Division and layering are even easier ways of raising new plants, because they are undertaken outdoors, but these methods produce only one or a few new plants at a time.

growing plants from seed

Sowing seed in containers

Most plants are easy to raise from seed, including annuals, perennials, and even trees. If you have never sown seed before, it is best to buy packaged seed because it is quality controlled and comes with full instructions for each type of seed.

The most natural way to grow seed is, of course, outdoors; by sowing indoors you have more control over the environment, and each seed has a better chance of survival. Indoor sowings can also be made earlier than outdoor ones, getting the plants off to a good start.

Sow seed thinly to avoid problems with overcrowding. Fine seed will be easier to sow if mixed with sand.

Whether you use a full- or half-sized seed tray will depend on the amount of seed that you are sowing. Many gardeners use modular trays or coir or peat seed blocks – if sown one per module or block, each seedling can grow to a good size before being disturbed. Biodegradable pots also avoid root disturbance because each seedling is planted out together with its pot. Seedlings that develop long roots, such as sweet peas, are best grown in tall tube pots.

You can use recycled containers: yogurt pots and foil trays work well (just make drainage holes), while cardboard egg boxes and toilet roll tubes make biodegradable modules.

How to sow seed in a tray

❶ *Fill the tray with good-quality, fresh seed medium. Tap the tray firmly on the bench two or three times to settle the medium and scrape off the excess with a ruler. Press another tray on the surface to firm the medium to ½in (1cm) below the rim. Stand the tray in a reservoir of water until the surface is just moist.*

❷ *Sprinkle seed thinly on the surface of the medium, then cover with a fine layer of sieved potting mix. Press large seeds into the medium, at a depth of twice their diameter; fill in the holes.*

❸ *Water the surface with a fine spray. Cover the tray to prevent moisture loss and maintain an even temperature – use a sheet of glass, clear plastic wrap, or a plastic lid. If in a sunny place, shade the tray with paper to prevent it from overheating.*

Germinating seed successfully

A seed contains a plant in embryo and to kickstart it into life, it needs the correct balance of warmth, air, and moisture. In most cases, you can achieve these conditions by placing pots or trays of seed in a propagator (*see right*). Electric propagators and heated trays provide what is called "bottom heat," gently warming the soil to encourage germination. Alternatively, cover the container with kitchen film or a sheet of glass.

Some seed needs special treatment to trigger it into germination, for example, low light levels. A period of

cold, to mimic winter, can be created by placing the seed container in the refrigerator for a time. Some thick seed coatings need to be soaked before sowing. These details will be listed on the seed packet.

As soon as the seedlings emerge, increase ventilation or remove any film, but keep them out of the sun. If left covered, they may fall prey to damping off, a fungal disease that spreads fast in damp, still air. Seeing the affected seedlings blacken and die is disheartening, but you can protect them by observing good hygiene.

Propagator The cover of the propagator allows light through, while keeping the air moist. Open the vent to get rid of heavy condensation, but don't let the air dry out completely.

Caring for seedlings

Seedlings should never be allowed to dry out, nor should they sit in wet potting mix, which is a breeding ground for diseases such as damping off (*see above*). Watering from overhead can wash seedlings out of the mix. Instead, stand pots and trays in clean tap water and lift them out as soon as the surface of the mix starts to moisten. Allow any excess water to drain away.

Seedlings sown indoors tend to be taller and weaker than those sown outside. Gently stroking their tops 10–20 times a day with your fingers, or a piece of thin card, encourages shorter, sturdier growth.

Overcrowded seedlings compete for light, water, and space. They may grow leggy and more vulnerable to disease. They should therefore be transplanted, or pricked out, as soon as they have formed two true leaves above the first pair of seed leaves, to give them space.

Select the healthiest, strongest seedlings to grow on, and discard the rest. You can thin them out, by pulling out unwanted seedlings with tweezers, or transplant them into new containers of fresh medium (*see below*). Insert them about 5cm (2in) apart with the seed leaves just above the medium. Pop them back in a ventilated propagator and shade from bright sun until they get established.

Etiolated seedlings are weak and spindly as a result of growing in poor light and may never thrive. Bright, diffuse light is best for seedlings – strong sun can burn tender shoots.

Pricking out Use a dibber to ease the seedlings out of the old potting mix. Try not to damage any seedling. Make a hole for each seedling, lower its roots into the hole, and firm gently by pushing in the medium from the sides.

Hold seedlings by the leaves.

Chopstick makes good dibber

Hardening off

Hardening off acclimatizes young plants that have been indoors to the drier and cooler conditions of the open garden. If this is not done, the young plants will be knocked back and suffer a check to their growth. It is best not to rush this final stage, so allow a week or two for the process.

Wait until all danger of frost has passed before moving young plants outdoors. Choose a warm, dry, but dull day to commence hardening off. In the early stages, cover the plants with a layer of horticultural fleece to protect them from windchill, and keep them out of heavy rain or strong sun. Bring them back under cover at night for the first few days.

If the weather stays mild, leave them out overnight under a double, and then a single, layer of fleece. If the plants look healthy, finally remove it altogether. Your plants will be fully hardened off and ready for planting out.

A cold frame is the ideal halfway house for hardening off. For the first few days, open the lid for 2–3 hours, but keep it shut at night. Increase the time the lid is left open during the day, and eventually, leave it open at night.

Making use of plug plants

Raising plants from seed is very satisfying, and it is still the only way you can obtain some of the more unusual plant cultivars. There is no denying, however, that it can be time- and space-consuming.

Plug plants are a speedy alternative. These are young plants that have been grown in modules so that they have a well-developed root system that forms an easy-to-handle plug. You can still enjoy potting up the plants, growing them on to maturity, and hardening them off.

Plug plants and pots of seedlings are widely available, especially of bedding annuals and perennials. They can be bought from nurseries and garden centers, and are also sent out by mail-order companies from early spring. Nurseries sell them in trays or strips, whereas mail-order plug plants are usually supplied in snap-shut plastic containers, which keep plants moist during transit. Pot up or plant out plug plants (see p.380) as soon as possible and water them well.

Hippo plugs are more expensive than standard plugs; however, because they are larger plants, they should establish and flower more quickly.

Plug plant in potting mix

Plug plant in rockwool

Plugs may be joined at tops of root balls but are easily parted

Plug plants are usually grown in potting mix but may also be supplied in rockwool plugs. Rockwool is made from spun molten rock, is sterile, and has good air- and water-holding capacity.

Plugs in strips Never pull plug plants out of their strips or module trays. Push them out of the container from the base – polystyrene strips have specially weakened drainage points for this purpose.

Sowing an annual border

You can create a colorful border full of hardy annuals by sowing seed directly outdoors. The sheer volume of seed sown will more than compensate for any seedlings you lose to pests and harsh conditions. Also, you do not have to worry about pricking out, growing on, and hardening off the seedlings. Start sowing outdoors as soon as the soil has started to warm up in early spring.

Give plants a good start in life by preparing the area thoroughly. Remove any weeds (which could compete for water, light, and nutrients) and large stones, then roughly level the surface. Do this in autumn, or several weeks prior to sowing, so the soil has time to settle, and any germinating weeds can be removed. Before sowing, rake the soil until it resembles fine breadcrumbs (known as a "fine tilth") and the

surface is level. Water the area well if it is dry; otherwise the freshly sown seed might dry out and die.

Fill a bottle with sand and use it to trickle out a line delineating the shape of each sowing area; make these patches irregularly shaped so that the different plants will form drifts.

You can either sow seed in rows, or drills, within each area (see below) or broadcast sow. The latter is done simply by scattering seed as evenly as

possible to fill each sowing area, then lightly raking over the patch to mix the seed into the soil. Rake the soil in two directions to be sure that the seed is evenly distributed. Broadcast sowing is quicker, but it is more difficult to spot weeds among the seedlings later.

Once they have appeared, cover the seedlings with horticultural fleece to protect them from frost or heavy rain and from pests such as mice, birds, and cats.

Sowing seed in drifts

❶ *Mark out the sowing areas for each plant. Within each area, use a stick or a hoe to draw out drills (shallow trenches) for sowing the seed. Check the seed packets for the correct spacings of drills for each plant.*

❷ *Water the drills if the soil is dry, then sprinkle fine seed thinly along each row. Sow large seed in twos and threes. Pull a thin layer of soil gently over the seed with a rake.*

❸ *When seedlings appear, thin them to leave the strongest ones at the correct spacings. Place your fingers around the base of each chosen seedling's stem to keep its roots firm as you pull out unwanted seedlings around it.*

①

②

③

cuttings

Softwood, semiripe, and heel cuttings

Stem-tip cuttings are the quickest and most successful way of propagating many perennials, shrubs, biennials, and alpines. It may be of soft or semi-ripe wood. A softwood, or slightly more mature greenwood, cutting is taken from the actively growing tip of a shoot in spring to early summer.

Look for strong, young growth. It will be a lighter green than older growth or wood. Later in the summer when the shoots begin to ripen or become woody and stiff, semiripe cuttings can be taken. Test stems by bending them – if they split they are still soft, if they spring back they are semiripe.

When taking a stem-tip cutting (*see below*), cut off a shoot about 4in (10cm) long. Handle it carefully: the tissues are soft and easily damaged. Cuttings wilt swiftly – keep them moist and prepare them as soon as possible so they have the best chance of rooting. You can dip the cuttings in

fungicide to protect against rot and the ends in a hormone rooting compound to encourage rooting. You can also take cuttings of woody plants with a heel (*see below, right*).

Cover a pot of cuttings with a plastic bag to retain moisture, or in a propagator, in a warm, light place.

Taking stem-tip cuttings
❶ *Cut just above a leaf joint using a clean, sharp knife. Place cuttings in water or a plastic bag to stop them from wilting.*
❷ *Trim all but the top 2–4 leaves off each cutting and cut the end just below a leaf joint. Insert the cuttings in pots of moist, gritty rooting medium, so that their leaves are not touching.*

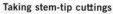

Cuttings inserted so that leaves are just above surface

Heel cuttings Select a new sideshoot that is about 4in (10cm) long and semiripe. Gently pull it from the main stem (*see inset*) so that it retains a small sliver of bark. Trim the bark, using a clean, sharp knife, to leave a small "heel" on the cutting. The heel contains high levels of growth hormone that promotes rooting. Useful for rooting evergreens.

Heel

Hardwood cuttings

Hardwood cuttings are normally taken from the mature wood of deciduous and evergreen trees and shrubs at the end of the growing season (from late autumn until winter). Hardwood in this context does not mean woody and old, but refers to shoots of the current season that have started to toughen up.

Look for stems that are the same thickness as a pencil. Cut them off just above a bud or leaf joint on the parent plant. Trim the cuttings to length and insert in a trench (*see below*) in a cool, sheltered spot in the garden. Hardwood cuttings tend not to dry out as quickly as other types of cuttings, but you should still keep

them watered in dry spells. Instead of planting the cuttings in a trench, you could root them in deep pots of rooting medium in a cold frame.

Leave the cuttings undisturbed for a year, watering and weeding them during the growing season. By the following autumn, they should have rooted and are ready to transplant.

Taking hardwood cuttings
❶ *Trim the cuttings to 8–9in (20–23cm) long. Use a clean, sharp knife to cut the bottom off just below a leaf joint. Trim off any soft wood at the top to just above a leaf joint.*
❷ *Use a spade to sink a shallow (slit) trench about 6in (15cm) deep. Line it with coarse sand. Dip the bases of the cuttings in hormone-rooting medium (see inset). Stand them in the trench, 4in (10cm) apart, firm and water.*

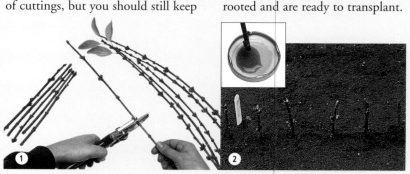

Root cuttings

Fleshy-rooted perennials, such as eryngiums, can be grown from root cuttings. Dig round a plant during dormancy to expose some roots. Cut off a few healthy, medium-thickness roots close to the crown. Wash off the soil and cut the roots in 2–4in (5–10cm) pieces. Dust with fungicide. Lay the pieces flat in a tray of rooting medium and cover.

Root cuttings root faster with bottom heat.

division

Methods of dividing plants

This is the easiest and quickest way of propagating herbaceous (but not woody) perennials, grasses, ferns, and many alpine and aquatic plants. Most of these plants form mats or clumps, and as they grow the center of the plant becomes congested and begins to die. Lifting and dividing a plant every three or four years, in autumn or early spring when it is dormant, restores its vigor and gives the plant a new lease on life. Plants that are marginally hardy or that have large rhizomes are best divided in early spring or after flowering has finished.

When dividing a clump, always look for the natural divisions between the shoots; some plants will have distinct crowns or offsets. Replant only the young, fresh growth from the outside of a clump, or in the case of fleshy crowns, sections with healthy buds or roots. The old, exhausted center will never regain its vigor.

There are various ways to divide a plant and which one you follow depends on the plant and the type of root system it has (see below). First shake or wash off as much soil as possible so that you can see the roots. Pull apart large clumps using forks; small plants with your hands. Cut fleshy crowns into sections.

Dividing with forks Large clumps are best divided with two forks. Push the forks back to back into the root mass and pull the handles apart to split the clump. Alternatively, cut the roots with a sharp kitchen knife or pruning saw.

Dividing by hand Small fibrous-rooted plants are easy to pull apart by hand; cut tough or tangled roots with a knife or pruners.

Dividing rhizomes Use a clean, sharp knife to cut off young pieces with healthy buds, shoots, and roots from old, woody rhizomes. Replant the divided pieces (here of bearded iris), making sure that they sit on the surface so the sun can ripen them. To avoid wind rock, trim the leaves to 6in (15cm). Discard the old rhizomes.

Dividing bulbous plants

Many bulbs, corms, and tubers, of plants such as alliums, crocosmias, crocuses, daffodils (*Narcissus*), and gladioli, increase by producing offsets around the parent bulb or corm. These types of bulbous plants can quickly form congested clumps. Unless they are lifted every three or four years and divided, the plants will lose vigor and stop flowering.

After lifting, remove the offsets by pulling them away from the parent bulb. Many offsets will be small and may take three or four years to mature and reach flowering size, so grow them on in pots of sandy mix in a sheltered spot – a cold frame is ideal.

Replant large bulbs immediately, or if still in leaf plant them temporarily in a corner of a border until they are needed. Insert a label so you don't forget where they are. Alternatively, clean off any soil and store the bulbs in a cool, dark place for replanting at the appropriate time.

Pull offsets from the main parent bulb.

layering

Rooted stems

Some climbers, such as ivies, and woody plants, like heathers, spread by rooting from their stems wherever they touch the soil. Layering takes advantage of this natural tendency. It is a useful technique particularly for evergreens – their cuttings tend to dehydrate before they root.

Select a low-growing stem, and wound it, preferably near a bud, by scratching or twisting it. Bury the wounded part of the stem in soil leavened with sand and rooting medium. Support the exposed shoot, which will receive nourishment from the parent plant while it develops roots.

After six months to two years, once there are signs of new growth, dig up the layered shoot, detach it and plant it out.

Layering a stem Strip the middle stem (here of rosemary) of leaves. Dig a hole beneath the stem, bend and wound it, then peg it to hold in place. Fill in with soil and sand and keep watered. After 4–6 weeks, dig up the rooted shoot, cut off, and plant out.

avoiding problems

If plants are given the best possible growing conditions so that they are healthy and strong, they will be able to survive most pests and diseases. Some problems in the garden are almost inevitable, but the majority are easily kept under control, or cured and prevented from returning.

Raking up leaves makes the garden neat and deprives pests and diseases of a place to overwinter.

If you notice symptoms such as discolored or distorted growth, or holes in leaves and flowers, they are usually caused by pests, diseases, or nutrient deficiencies. The best way to deal with these problems is to use an integrated approach, where cultural and organic methods are used to keep plants healthy, and chemicals are used only as a last line of defense.

Prevention is generally better than cure; given good growing conditions, plants will be strong enough to survive attacks without any lasting damage. Check plants thoroughly before you buy them for any sign of damage or disease to avoid bringing problems into the garden. Keep cutting tools clean so

they do not spread infection. Promptly remove yellowing leaves and faded flowers, and clear plant debris that could harbor insects and spores.

Be vigilant, squashing pests and cutting out diseased parts as soon as you notice them. Some pests and diseases are persistent on certain plants, such as blackspot on roses. If you find the same problem returns year after year, it is worth obtaining a resistant cultivar. For example, *Rosa* 'The Fairy' withstands many common rose problems. If you have to resort to chemicals, use a specific remedy if possible and spray the entire plant thoroughly. If all else fails, remove the plant before the problem spreads.

Keeping a healthy garden

Thriving plants are better able to resist problems, so it is important to maintain a healthy garden. There are several ways in which you can be sure your plants remain in top condition.

Plants that are growing in sites or conditions that do not meet their needs become stressed and more prone to problems. Be especially careful to choose plants that are suited to each aspect in your garden and to the local conditions (*see Climate and location, pp.371–373*). It is rare to find perfect soil; before planting, prepare it well (*see Soils and compost, pp.376–378*).

Pay attention also to watering and feeding your plants appropriately so they do not suffer from insufficient or excessive water or nutrients (*see pp.386–387*). It is essential to weed regularly so that your plants do not have to compete with fast-growing

invaders for vital light, water, and nutrients (*see p.389*).

Diseases such as bacteria, fungi, and viruses are opportunists, and some infect a weak plant through an existing wound. Avoid giving them easy access by cutting cleanly when pruning (*see p.382*) and removing crossing branches that might chafe as they rub together.

Plants that are overgrown or are planted too closely often become weak and sickly, with elongated shoots as they fight for light. Fresh air cannot circulate freely around the stems and leaves, and the still, stagnant air encourages rot, molds, and mildews. To avoid this, prune out congested growth (*see p.382*), divide herbaceous perennials (*see p.395*), and allow room for growth when planting any type of plant (*see p.379*).

Nutrient deficiency symptoms are usually first seen on leaves. A lack of magnesium, shown here, can be identified by yellowing between leaf veins because magnesium is used by the plant to make green chlorophyll. Boron, iron, nitrogen, and phosphates are also commonly deficient.

Waterlogged soils often develop blue mottling on the surface and a bad smell. Plant roots will "drown" through lack of air, rot, and die. The solution is to improve the soil drainage, or to grow bog plants that are adapted to cope in such wet conditions.

Encouraging beneficial wildlife

The only good aspect of insect pests is that they attract lots of wildlife in search of a meal. If you encourage a range of beneficial wildlife into the garden, the pests will be kept down to acceptable levels. Do not be alarmed if you see a few pests about, but allow their natural predators to take action before you think about resorting to chemical means.

Water attracts lots of animals, including frogs and toads, which eat many pests that crawl on the ground. Skunks and raccoons are also valuable friends. They, like frogs and toads, feed on many ground-dwelling plant pests. Spiders and some wasps are also beneficial. Ladybird larvae and adults feed eagerly on the scourge of almost every garden: aphids (*see p.398*).

Birds can damage some seedlings or edible crops, but this is more than made up for by the number of insect pests they eat. Attract birds by planting trees and shrubs that give cover or bear berries, like mountain ash and cotoneasters.

Toad

Smashed snail shells by a stone are a sure sign that a thrush has lent you a helping hand.

A song thrush is a useful ally because it will eat snails, which are a problem for many gardeners, especially on alkaline soils. Encourage a thrush to visit your garden by providing a large, flat stone that it can use as an anvil to smash the snail shells.

Ladybird larvae have voracious appetites for aphids. The adults hibernate in odd corners over winter to emerge in spring as aphid numbers rise.

How to control problems

By keeping a close watch on plants you can stop problems getting out of hand. If you see any pests, pick them off immediately. If you do spot symptoms of disease, remove the affected parts and burn or throw them in the trash can.

Some plants are irresistible to aphids – if you notice that a plant is particularly affected, consider planting French marigolds (*Tagetes, see p.329*) nearby; they will attract hoverflies, the larvae of which feed on aphids. Aromatic plants such as catmint (*Nepeta, see p.290*), and garlic may repel or confuse pests.

Predators or parasites of some pests can be introduced into the garden as a biological control. Nematodes (microscopic worms) can be watered onto the soil or lawn to kill slugs or black vine weevil larvae, but they often need high temperatures and may be more effective in a greenhouse or conservatory than in the open garden.

If you use chemicals, follow the manufacturer's instructions. Fertilizers cure deficiency diseases – if you can identify the missing nutrient, it is better to use a specific cure than an all-purpose fertilizer. Organic pesticides, such as pyrethrum, made from plant extracts, and insecticidal soap, are available. **Usage must be consistent with labeling**. Bear in mind that some inorganic pesticides are toxic to ornamental plants. Spray pesticides in still weather so the wind does not carry spray where it is not wanted. Note that some products are not approved for use in Canada and that a growing number of municipalities have pesticide bans or restrictions.

Earwig traps can be constructed by placing upside-down flower pots on top of stakes among susceptible plants. Loosely fill the pots with hay or dried grass, and the earwigs will crawl in overnight. In the morning, empty the pots and burn the grass. These pests affect many plants including chrysanthemums, clematis, and dahlias, appearing after dark to feed and leaving large holes in petals or young leaves.

Small mites (Amblyseius) *are sold mixed in bran. Hang pack up in your greenhouse to control thrips, at minimum of 64°F (18°C)*

Encarsia *parasites in tube ready for release into greenhouse*

Biological control for thrips

Biological control for greenhouse whiteflies

Number one pests

The most common garden pests crop up regularly from year to year. Slugs and snails attack a wide range of plants. They prefer seedlings and young or fleshy plants, and will eat large holes in leaves or stems or the entire plant. Black vine weevil larvae cause considerable damage to container-grown plants by eating all the roots. The adults graze on foliage, leaving large holes.

Aphids attack the soft shoots and buds of most plants, and introduce viruses through their piercing mouthparts. Red lily beetles eat entire flowers and leaves. Deal with these pests by either picking them off or using a specific biological or chemical control.

Slugs can be very destructive, grazing through stems at soil level and returning to the same plant night after night. They will even strip the soft bark off shrubs. Cultivate to expose eggs, make traps, avoid organic mulches and fertilizers, or lay barriers (see p. 260).

Black vine weevil larvae are up to ½in (10mm) long, creamy white, and attack leaves and roots. The first symptom of these pests is sudden wilting. Biological control is effective.

Whole-plant problems

You may notice that a plant is looking sick. The usual causes are incorrect watering, pests, disease, or nutrient deficiencies.

Newly planted and container-grown plants often wilt because of drought or overwatering (see p.386). Check the soil or the medium and water it or allow it to dry out, as appropriate. Wilting can also be caused by disease, like clematis wilt (see p.136), or pests such as black vine weevils (see left). Lack of nutrients can make a plant sickly and yellow, but it should perk up after applying a liquid fertilizer (see p.386). Clumping plants lose vigor (see below) unless they are divided regularly.

Wilted leaves due to poor watering

Old, woody, congested growth

Neglected plants are vulnerable to a wide range of problems. This heuchera has produced ugly, woody growth at its base and sparse foliage because it has not been regularly divided.

Stem problems

The stems of a plant support the leaves and flowers and contain veins that transport water and food to and from the deepest roots and the tallest shoots. Because they are so important, damage to them may result in the loss of an affected plant. Pests that attack plant stems may eat the skin or bark, suck sap by piercing the veins, or in some cases tunnel through, or live in, the stem. The wounds that they leave then provide doorways for diseases that can spread through the plant and quickly kill it. Bad pruning and extremely cold, hot, or windy weather can also damage stems. Look out for dead, diseased, or damaged parts and quickly cut out and dispose of them so problems cannot spread to other plants.

Foamy, protective coating containing a small insect is made by spittlebugs (froghoppers) and does little harm other than looking unsightly

Frost damage can kill, but if only new shoots are affected they often grow back. If frost is forecast, move tender plants under cover and drape early blossoms and new shoots of hardy plants with horticultural fleece

Mildew is a white, powdery, fungal infection; it attacks if plants are already weak or congested so air cannot move around stems freely

Dieback can occur if pruning cuts are made too far from buds

Aphids, including plant lice, greenfly, and blackfly, are very common; they suck sap from veins, leaving sticky honeydew behind on which sooty mold can develop

Canker first appears as zone of flattened, discolored bark, which later splits, forming ring of flaky bark that kills shoot. Canker affects many plants at any time of the year and should be cut out

Possible stem problems These pests, disorders, and diseases are very common and you will probably see them at some point. Although they can be severe enough to kill, most will cause little long-term damage – especially if they are dealt with quickly – and some can be easily prevented.

Leaf problems

Leaf problems can take the form of discolored, distorted, or damaged growth, or premature leaf fall. This spoils the plant's appearance and reduces its ability to thrive.

Fungi can cause molds, mildews, rusts, or spots. They attack weak plants and are unsightly, but rarely deadly, although some, for example silver leaf on ornamental cherries, are fatal. Bacteria can cause black spots on leaves; they are not raised or patchy like fungal spots but appear more like dark shadows. Foliage with pale flecks, streaks, or mottling often has a viral infection.

Some pests, such as caterpillars, eat leaves and others, like leaf miners, burrow into them. Most plants can withstand an attack but may become weak, providing an easy target for disease. Nutrient deficiencies – the usual cause of yellowing, or chlorosis – also compromise plant defenses. With all leaf problems, the first thing

to do is to try and identify the cause, then take appropriate action. Pest control or removal of affected foliage is often required. Never put diseased material on the compost heap because that will often spread infection.

Lack of water, nutrients, light, and space all favor disease; sometimes pampering a plant by thinning stems, watering, and fertilizing will make it strong enough to fight off infection. If all else fails, chemical controls are often effective. Use one specific to the problem, and follow the instructions carefully. **Usage must be consistent with labeling.**

Possible leaf problems

Some common disorders are shown here. Many of them occur on the undersides of the leaves. Be vigilant and occasionally check under leaves to make sure that there is no problem developing. If you use a contact fungicide or pesticide, spray the whole plant and make sure you include the undersides of the leaves where disease or infestation is usually concentrated.

Adult black vine weevils are slow-moving and eat irregular holes or notches in leaves near ground; they should be destroyed before they lay eggs

Rose blackspot causes dark blotches and early leaf fall

Fuchsia rust forms tiny, orange spots underneath leaves and is encouraged by damp air

Peach leaf curl results in distorted leaves, which may be flushed red

Fungal leaf spot appears as rounded, brown or gray patches containing raised, dark spots

Rusts develop as brown or orange blisters (spores), often arranged in rings, on lower leaf surfaces

Downy mildew shows as pale patches with white fungus on undersides

Flower problems

Discolored flower heads may be a sign of thrips – tiny insects that suck sap from flower buds in hot, dry conditions. White flecks appear on petals and leaves discolor.

Most plants in the garden are grown for their flowers, but a few problems, including pests, diseases, and the weather, can affect them and spoil the show. If the first blooms are ruined, all is not lost; if you can cure the problem you may be able to encourage another, second flush of healthy flowers by regular deadheading and fertilizing.

Sap-sucking insects, such as aphids and thrips can distort or discolor petals (*see left*); watch for them and squash or spray them off. Other insects, for example earwigs, and birds may eat petals or buds before they

open. Diseases can also be a problem, and those affecting flowers are particularly bad if the weather is cool and damp. Symptoms to look out for include white spots, often edged with a darker ring, on the petals; these indicate the presence of gray mold (botrytis). Streaks or flecks, or deformed flowers, usually indicate a viral infection.

Weather damage is also a common problem for delicate blooms. The flowers of roses and other plants often fail to open if wet spells are followed by hot sun because of a condition

known as balling. The damp bud is scorched by the sun and cannot open, causing the inner petals to rot. Flowers that open in early spring are often prone to frost damage, made worse by strong morning sun. Cold, drying winds can scorch petals, turning them brown, so position early-flowering plants with care.

Remain observant so any problems can be overcome before they get a firm hold. If you fail to cure a disease, then it is best to admit defeat and throw away the affected plant before it contaminates others.

plant selections

Every garden presents you with a different challenge. Some have heavy, seemingly unworkable soil; others excessive amounts of shade. The lists in this section are intended to help you identify plants for particular uses, such as herb and bog gardens, and for some of the most common problem areas, such as shaded and dry sites.

Exposed sites

Gardens on hillsides or in flat, open areas regularly experience high winds. Create a windbreak using hedges and trees to filter the worst of the wind, and choose hardy plants that are able to withstand a battering.

Acer pseudoplatanus and cultivars
Achillea
Ajuga reptans and cultivars
Alnus glutinosa 'Imperialis'
Anaphalis triplinervis
Anchusa azurea 'Loddon Royalist'
Anemone × hybrida and cultivars
Antirrhinum majus and cultivars
Arbutus unedo
Arctostaphylos
Artemisia abrotanum
Artemisia 'Powis Castle'
Berberis
Bergenia
Bupleurum fruticosum
Calendula officinalis and cultivars
Calluna vulgaris and cultivars
Caragana arborescens
Carpinus betulus 'Fastigiata'
Chaenomeles
Chamaecyparis obtusa 'Nana Aurea'
Chamaecyparis pisifera 'Filifera Aurea'
Clethra arborea
Colutea arborescens
Coreopsis auriculata 'Schnittgold'
Coreopsis 'Sunray'
Cornus
Corylus avellana 'Contorta'
Cotoneaster horizontalis

Crataegus laevigata 'Paul's Scarlet'
Cryptomeria japonica 'Elegans Compacta'
× Cupressocyparis leylandii
Cupressus macrocarpa 'Goldcrest'
Deutzia
Dryas octopetala
Echinacea purpurea 'Kim's Knee High'
Echinops ritro 'Veitch's Blue'
Elaeagnus
Erica carnea and cultivars
Erigeron aureus 'Canary Bird'
Erigeron 'Dunkelste Aller'
Erigeron karvinskianus
Eryngium alpinum
Eryngium × oliverianum
Eryngium × tripartitum
Escallonia 'Apple Blossom'
Eschscholzia caespitosa
Eschscholzia californica
Eucalyptus
Euonymus alatus
Euonymus fortunei and cultivars
Euphorbia characias 'John Tomlinson'
Fagus sylvatica 'Dawyck Purple'
Felicia amelloides 'Santa Anita'
Ficus carica
Forsythia × intermedia and cultivars
Fraxinus excelsior
Fuchsia magellanica
Gaultheria
Genista aetnensis
Ginkgo biloba
Gleditsia triacanthos 'Sunburst'
Griselinia littoralis
Hamamelis

Helleborus niger and cultivars
Hippophae rhamnoides
Hydrangea paniculata 'Grandiflora'
Hypericum calycinum
Ilex aquifolium
Iris sibirica and cultivars
Jasminum nudiflorum
Juniperus
Kalmia angustifolia
Kerria japonica and cultivars
Kerria japonica 'Picta'
Laburnum
Laurus nobilis
Lavatera
Leucothoe fontanesiana 'Rainbow'
Limnanthes douglasii
Miscanthus
Nepeta sintenisii
Nepeta 'Six Hills Giant'
Osmunda regalis
Phalaris arundinacea var. picta
Phlox subulata 'Lilacina'
Picea abies
Pieris
Pinus nigra
Populus × canadensis and cultivars
Potentilla
Primula
Prunus spinosa
Pulmonaria saccharata
Pyracantha
Quercus
Rubus cockburnianus
Salix alba
Sempervivum arachnoideum
Sempervivum tectorum
Senecio cineraria 'Silver Dust'

Senecio cineraria 'White Diamond'
Sorbus aria
Sorbus aucuparia and cultivars
Spiraea
Symphoricarpos × doorenbosii 'White Hedge'
Tamarix
Tanacetum parthenium and cultivars
Taxus
Thuja plicata
Tiarella cordifolia
Tilia
Tsuga canadensis and cultivars
Ulex
Viburnum × bodnantense 'Dawn'
Viburnum × burkwoodii
Viburnum opulus 'Compactum'
Viburnum rhytidophyllum
Viburnum tinus 'Eve Price'

Coastal gardens

Coastal areas suffer from winter gales and the scorching salt spray that they bring. Create windbreaks by planting trees around the perimeter, and go for tough plants that conserve moisture.

Achillea
Allium
Alstroemeria
Anaphalis triplinervis
Anchusa azurea 'Loddon Royalist'
Anthemis
Anthericum liliago
Antirrhinum majus and cultivars
Arbutus unedo
Armeria

Artemisia abrotanum
Artemisia 'Powis Castle'
Aster
Aucuba
Bergenia
Buddleja davidii and cultivars
Bupleurum fruticosum
Campanula
Centaurea hypoleuca 'John Coutts'
Choisya ternata 'Sundance' ('Lich')
Cistus
Cordyline australis 'Torbay Red'
Cotoneaster
Crataegus
Crocosmia
Cupressus macrocarpa
Cytisus
Dahlia
Dianthus
Dierama pulcherrimum
Echinacea purpurea 'White Lustre'
Echinops ritro 'Veitch's Blue'
Elaeagnus × *ebbingei* 'Gilt Edge'
Erica arborea var. *alpina*
Erica carnea and cultivars
Erigeron karvinskianus
Erigeron 'Quakeress'
Erodium glandulosum
Erodium manescaui
Eryngium alpinum
Escallonia 'Apple Blossom'
Eschscholzia caespitosa
Eucalyptus
Euonymous fortunei and cultivars
Euphorbia
Felicia amelloides 'Santa Anita'
Ficus carica
Filipendula rubra 'Venusta'
Forsythia × *intermedia* and cultivars
Fuchsia magellanica
Garrya elliptica
Gaultheria
Genista aetnensis
Geranium
Gleditsia triacanthos 'Sunburst'
Griselinia littoralis
Gypsophila 'Rosenschleier'
Halimium 'Susan'

Hebe
Hemerocallis
Heuchera
Hibiscus syriacus 'Oiseau Bleu'
Hippophae rhamnoides
Hydrangea macrophylla and cultivars
Ilex × *altaclerensis* and cultivars
Impatiens
Iris
Juniperus
Laburnum
Laurus nobilis
Lavandula
Lavatera
Leycesteria formosa
Lonicera nitida
Lonicera × *purpusii* 'Winter Beauty'
Lychnis coronaria
Melissa officinalis 'Aurea'
Monarda
Oenothera
Olearia
Origanum
Osmanthus delavayi
Pachysandra terminalis
Penstemon
Phormium tenax
Phygelius
Pinus nigra
Pittosporum
Populus tremula
Potentilla
Prunus spinosa
Pulsatilla
Pyracantha
Quercus ilex
Rosa (some)
Rosmarinus officinalis
Rubus cockburnianus
Salvia
Sambucus racemosa 'Plumosa Aurea'
Santolina
Sisyrinchium
Spartium junceum
Stachys
Tamarix
Ulex
Viburnum

Dry sun

Situations prone to drought include steeply sloping sunny banks with rapid drainage; the base of a warm south- or west-facing wall; and shallow, sandy, or stony soils in full sun.

Abelia
Acacia baileyana
Acaena saccaticupula 'Blue Haze'
Achillea
Agapanthus
Allium
Alstroemeria
Anaphalis triplinervis
Anchusa azurea 'Loddon Royalist'
Anthemis
Arabis
Arctotis
Armeria pseudarmeria
Artemisia
Asphodeline lutea
Betula
Brachyglottis 'Sunshine'
Brachyscome iberidifolia
Buddleja
Bupleurum fruticosum
Buxus
Caryopteris × *clandonensis* 'Kew Blue'
Catananche caerulea 'Bicolor'
Ceanothus 'Blue Mound'
Centaurea
Cerastium tomentosum
Ceratostigma willmottianum
Chamaemelum nobile 'Flore Pleno'
Chrysanthemum segetum
Cirsium rivulare 'Atropurpureum'
Cistus
Cleome hassleriana
Clerodendrum trichotomum var. *fargesii*
Cotoneaster
Crambe cordifolia
Crocosmia
× *Cupressocyparis leylandii*
Cynara cardunculus
Cytisus
Dianthus

Diascia
Dictamnus albus
Draba mollissima
Echinops ritro 'Veitch's Blue'
Epilobium
Erica arborea var. *alpina*
Erica cinerea and cultivars
Erodium glandulosum
Erodium manescaui
Eryngium alpinum
Erysimum
Escallonia
Eucalyptus
Euonymus
Euphorbia
Foeniculum vulgare 'Purpureum'
Fuchsia magellanica
Gaillardia 'Dazzler'
Gaultheria mucronata 'Mulberry Wine'
Gaura lindheimeri
Gazania Mini Star Series
Genista aetnensis
Genista lydia
Geranium
Gleditsia triacanthos
Gypsophila 'Rosenschleier'
Hebe
Helianthemum
Hippophae rhamnoides
Hypericum
Impatiens
Ipheion uniflorum 'Wisley Blue'
Iris foetidissima
Iris pallida 'Variegata'
Juniperus
Kniphofia
Kolkwitzia amabilis 'Pink Cloud'
Lavandula
Liatris spicata 'Kobold'
Limnanthes douglasii
Linaria alpina
Linum flavum 'Compactum'
Linum perenne
Lobularia 'Royal Carpet'
Lychnis coronaria
Melissa officinalis 'Aurea'
Nepeta

Nerine bowdenii
Oenothera
Olearia
Origanum laevigatum
Osteospermum
Papaver orientale and cultivars
Pelargonium
Penstemon
Perovskia 'Blue Spire'
Phlomis fruticosa
Phlox subulata 'Lilacina'
Phormium
Phygelius aequalis 'Yellow Trumpet'
Pinus mugo 'Mops'
Potentilla
Pulsatilla vulgaris
Quercus ilex
Ribes
Rosmarinus officinalis and cultivars
Salvia patens 'Cambridge Blue'
Sambucus racemosa 'Plumosa Aurea'
Santolina
Saponaria ocymoides
Schizanthus × wisetonensis 'Hit Parade'
Sedum
Sempervivum arachnoideum
Sempervivum tectorum
Solanum crispum 'Glasnevin'
Spartium junceum
Spiraea
Stachys byzantina
Stachys candida
Stachys macrantha 'Superba'
Stipa
Symphoricarpos × doorenbosii 'White
   Hedge'
Tagetes
Tamarix
Teucrium polium
Thymus
Tulipa
Ulex europaeus 'Flore Pleno'
Verbascum
Verbena bonariensis
Yucca gloriosa

Damp shade

A cool, humid woodland environment where the soil is reliably moist all year.
Acer cappadocicum
Acer griseum
Acer negundo 'Variegatum'
Acer palmatum f. atropurpureum
Acer saccharinum
Alchemilla mollis
Alnus
Aruncus dioicus
Asplenium scolopendrium
Astilbe
Athyrium filix-femina 'Frizelliae'
Aucuba japonica
Betula pendula 'Youngii'
Buxus sempervirens
Caltha palustris
Caltha palustris 'Flore Pleno'
Camellia japonica and cultivars
Cercidiphyllum japonicum
Clethra arborea
Convallaria majalis
Cornus canadensis
Crataegus
Daphne
Darmera peltata
Dicentra
Dryopteris wallichiana
Elaeagnus
Erythronium
Euonymus fortunei
Fatsia japonica
Fothergilla major
Gaultheria
Haberlea rhodopensis 'Virginalis'
Hamamelis
Helleborus
Hosta
Hydrangea
Hypericum calycinum
Ilex aquifolium
Iris sibirica and cultivars
Ligularia 'The Rocket'
Lilium martagon
Lythrum virgatum 'The Rocket'
Mahonia aquifolium

Matteuccia struthiopteris
Metasequoia glyptostroboides
Monarda
Osmanthus × burkwoodii
Osmanthus delavayi
Pachysandra terminalis
Picea
Pieris
Polystichum setiferum
Populus
Primula (candelabra types)
Prunus laurocerasus
Prunus padus 'Watereri'
Quercus
Rhododendron
Rodgersia pinnata 'Superba'
Rubus
Salix
Sambucus racemosa 'Plumosa Aurea'
Sarcococca
Sasa veitchii
Saxifraga fortunei
Skimmia
Smilacina racemosa
Sorbus
Spiraea
Stachyurus praecox
Symphoricarpos
Symphytum
Taxus baccata and cultivars
Viburnum davidii
Viburnum opulus
Viburnum rhytidophyllum

Dry shade

The combined problems of shade and drought are often found by walls and beneath thirsty, shallow-rooting trees.
Acanthus spinosus
Ajuga reptans and cultivars
Alchemilla mollis
Amelanchier lamarckii
Aquilegia
Arum italicum 'Marmoratum'
Astrantia
Aucuba
Berberis

Bergenia
Betula
Buxus sempervirens
Cornus canadensis
Cortaderia
Cotoneaster
Daphne
Dicentra formosa
Digitalis
Epimedium
Euonymus fortunei
Fatsia japonica
Garrya elliptica
Geranium himalayense
Geranium macrorrhizum
Geranium nodosum
Hedera
Heuchera
Hippophae rhamnoides
Ilex aquifolium
Iris foetidissima
Juniperus × pfitzeriana
Lamium
Lunaria annua and cultivars
Mahonia
Meconopsis cambrica
Melissa officinalis 'Aurea'
Milium effusum 'Aureum'
Pachysandra terminalis
Pittosporum tenuifolium
Polygonatum
Polypodium vulgare
Prunus laurocerasus
Pulmonaria
Santolina
Skimmia
Symphoricarpos
Taxus baccata and cultivars
Teucrium polium
Thalictrum
Tiarella
Tolmiea menziesii 'Taff's Gold'
Waldsteinia ternata

umbellata 202
Calceolaria 203
  sowing 203
  arachnoidea 203
  'Bright Bikini' 203
  tenella 203
  'Walter Shrimpton' 203
Calendula officinalis 204, 401, 405
  'Fiesta Gitana' 204
California lilac 36
California poppy 241
Californian fuchsia 129
Calla palustris 204
Callicarpa 30
  bodinieri var. *giraldii* 30
Callistemon 30
  'Firebrand' 30
  linearis 30
  pallidus 30
  speciosus 30
Calluna 405
  vulgaris 31, 401, 404
    'Anthony Davis' 31
    'Beoley Gold' 31
    'Firefly' 31
    'Gold Haze' 31
    'Robert Chapman' 31
    'Silver Knight' 31
Calochortus 205
  amabilis 205
  umpquaensis 205
Caltha palustris 205, 403, 405
  'Flore Pleno' 205, 403
Camassia 205
  leichtlinii 205
Camellia 32–3, 404
  pruning young plants 32
  'Inspiration' 32
  japonica 403
    'Adolphe Audusson' 32
    'Alexander Hunter' 32
    'Apollo' 32
    'Ave Maria' 32
    'Berenice Boddy' 32
    'Betty Sheffield Supreme' 32
    'Elegans' 32
    'Giulio Nuccio' 33
    'Gloire de Nantes' 32–3
    'Hagoromo' 33
    'Julia Drayton' 33
    'Jupiter' 33
    'Mrs D.W. Davis' 33
    'R.L. Wheeler' 33
    'Rubescens Major' 33
  reticulata 'Arch of Triumph' 33
    'William Hertrich' 33
  tsaii 33
  × *williamsii*
    'Anticipation' 33
    'Bow Bells' 33
    'Donation' 33
    'J.C. Williams' 33
    'Saint Ewe' 33

Campanula 206–7, 402, 404
  sowing seed 206
  alliariifolia 206
  carpatica 'Weisse Clips' 207, 405
  carpatica 'White Clips' 207
  'G.F. Wilson' 207
  glomerata 'Superba' 206
  lactiflora 'Loddon Anna' 206
  persicifolia 'Telham Beauty' 206
campion 282, 326
  rose 282
Campsis 135
  grandiflora 135
  radicans 135
  × *tagliabuana* 'Madame Galen' 135, 135
Canadian poplar 98
Canary creeper 154
candelabra primula 312
candytuft 262
canes
  staking asters 192
  supporting plants 390
canker 398
Canna 207
  'Assaut' 207
  'Durban' 207
  'Rosemond Coles' 207
canoe birch 28
Cantabrican heath 48
Cape leadwort 149
Caragana 34
  arborescens 34, 401
    'Nana' 34
    'Pendula' 34
Cardamine 208
  pratensis 'Flore Pleno' 208, 405
Cardiocrinum 165, 208
  giganteum 208
cardoon 221
Carex 343, 345
  mulching 345
  elata 'Aurea' 345
  flagellifera 345
  grayi 345
  oshimensis 'Evergold' 345
  pendula 345
  'Silver Sceptre' 342
  testacea 345
carnation 226–7
  layering 226
Carolina jasmine 141
Carpinus 34, 165
  betulus 34, 405
    'Fastigiata' 34, 401, 404
Caryopteris 34, 383
  × *clandonensis*
    'Kew Blue' 34, 402
    'Worcester Gold' 34
Cassiope 35
  'Edinburgh' 35, 404, 405
Catalpa 35
  bignonioides 35, 405

'Aurea' 35
  speciosa 35
Catananche 208
  caerulea 'Bicolor' 208, 402
  caespitosa 208
catchfly 282, 326
caterpillars 399
cathedral bells 140
catmint 164, 290, 390, 397
cat's ears 205
Caucasian peony 298
Ceanothus 36, 383
  ties 36
  'Blue Cushion' 36
  'Blue Mound' 36, 402, 405
  'Cascade' 36
  × *pallidus* 'Perle Rose' 36
cedar 37
  Japanese 46
  western red 123
  white 123
Cedrus 37
  deodara 'Aurea' 37
celandine, lesser 315
Celastrus 135
  orbiculatus 135
  scandens 135
Celmisia 209
  spectabilis 209
Celosia 'New Look' 162
Centaurea 209, 402
  supporting 209
  cyanus 209
  dealbata 'Steenbergii' 209
  hypoleuca 'John Coutts' 209, 402
Centranthus ruber 159
Cephalaria gigantea 160
Cerastium 210
  tomentosum 210, 402
Ceratostigma 37
  plumbaginoides 37
  willmottianum 37, 402
Cercidiphyllum 37
  japonicum 37, 403, 404
  magnificum 37
Cercis 38
  canadensis 38
    'Forest Pansy' 38
  chinensis 38
  siliquastrum 38
Cerinthe 210
  'Golden Bouquet' 210
  major 'Purpurascens' 210
Chaenomeles 38, 401, 404
  × *californica* 'Enchantress' 38
  speciosa 'Moerloosei' 38
  × *superba* 'Crimson and Gold' 38
chain fern 365
  European 365
chalk soil 376
  plants for 404–5
Chamaecyparis 39
  lawsoniana 'Pembury Blue' 39

nootkatensis 'Pendula' 39
  obtusa 'Nana Aurea' 39, 401
  pisifera 'Filifera Aurea' 39, 401
Chamaemelum 211
  nobile 211
    'Flore Pleno' 211, 402, 405
    'Treneague' 211
chamomile 211
  Roman 211
Cheilanthes 359
  argentea 359
Chelone 211
  obliqua 211
chenille plant 17
cherry
  Fuji 13
  ornamental 100–1, 165
    using in the garden 100
cherry pie 70
chervil 183
chicken manure, conditioning soil 377
chickweed 389
Chilean bellflower 144
Chilean fire bush 51
Chilean glory flower 141
Chimonanthus 39
  praecox 39
    'Grandiflorus' 39, 405
Chinese gooseberry 134
Chinese lantern 308
Chionanthus 39
  retusus 39
  virginicus 39
Chionodoxa 211
  luciliae 211
    'Pink Giant' 211
chlorosis 399
chocolate cosmos 218
chocolate vine 134
Choisya 40
  'Aztec Pearl' 40
  ternata 40
    SUNDANCE ('Lich') 40, 402, 404, 405
Christmas box 116
Chrysanthemum 212–13
  pinch pruning 212
  'Alison Kirk' 212
  'Autumn Days' 212
  'Brietner's Supreme' 212
  'Bronze Fairie' 212
  'Bronze Hedgerow' 212
  'Bronze Yvonne Arnaud' 212
  'Buff Margaret' 212
  carinatum 212
    'Court Jesters' 212
  'Clara Curtis' 212
  'George Griffiths' 213
  'Madeleine' 213
  'Maria' 213
  'Marion' 213
  'Marlene Jones' 213

'Pavilion' 213
  'Pennine' 212
  'Pennine Alfie' 213
  'Pennine Flute' 213
  'Pennine Oriel' 213
  'Purple Pennine Wine' 213
  'Roy Coopland' 213
  Rubellum Group 212
  'Salmon Fairie' 213
  'Satin Pink Gin' 213
  segetum 212, 402
  'Wendy' 213
  'Yvonne Arnaud' 213
Chusan palm 124
Chusquea 346
  culeou 346
cider gum 55
Cimicifuga simplex 169
  'Brunette' 169
cineraria 116
cinnamon fern 364
cinquefoil 99, 311
Cirsium 214
  rivulare 'Atropurpureum' 214, 402
Cistus 40, 402, 405
  × *argenteus* 'Peggy Sammons' 40
  × *dansereaui* 'Decumbens' 40
  × *hybridus* 40
  × *skanbergii* 40
Clarkia 214
  'Sundowner' 214
clay soil 376, 377
Clematis 132, 133, 133, 136–9, 214–15, 405
  pruning 136
  twining leaf stalks 133
  'Abundance' 136
  'Alba Luxurians' 136
  alpina 136
    'Frances Rivis' 136
  armandii 136, 405
  'Ascotiensis' 136
  'Beauty of Worcester' 136
  'Bees' Jubilee' 136
  'Bill MacKenzie' 137
  cirrhosa 132, 137
  'Comtesse de Bouchaud' 137
  'Doctor Ruppel' 137
  'Duchess of Albany' 137
  'Elsa Späth' 137
  'Etoile Rose' 137
  'Etoile Violette' 137
  flammula 137, 405
  florida var. *sieboldiana* 137
  'Gravetye Beauty' 137
  'Hagley Hybrid' 137
  'Henryi' 137
  heracleifolia 'Wyevale' 215, 405
  'H.F. Young' 137
  'Huldine' 137
  'Hybrida Sieboldii' 138
  integrifolia 214

'Jackmanii' 138
  'John Warren' 138
  'Kathleen Dunford' 138
  'Lasurstern' 138
  'Lincoln Star' 138
  macropetala 138
    'Markham's Pink' 138
  'Madame Edouard André' 138
  'Madame Julia Correvon' 138
  'Minuet' 138
  'Mrs. George Jackman' 138
  montana 138, 384
    f. *grandiflora* 138
    var. *rubens* 138
    'Tetrarose' 138
  'Nelly Moser' 138
  'Niobe' 138
  'Paul Farges' 139
  'Perle d'Azur' 139
  'The President' 139
  'Proteus' 139
  'Pruinina' 139
  recta 215
  rehderiana 139, 405
  'Richard Pennell' 139
  'Rouge Cardinal' 139
  tangutica 139
  tibetana 139
  'Venosa Violacea' 139
  'Ville de Lyon' 139
  viticella 132
    'Purpurea Plena Elegans' 139
  'Vyvyan Pennell' 139
Cleome 215
  hassleriana 402
    'Colour Fountain' 215
Clerodendrum 40
  bungei 40
  trichotomum 40
    var. *fargesii* 40, 402
Clethra 41
  arborea 41, 401, 403
Clianthus 140
  formosus 140
  puniceus 140
climate 371–3
climbing plants 132–55
  in containers 133
  deadheading 390
  definition 133
  layering 395
  planting 133, 380
  pruning 384
  roses 150–1
  supports 132, 133, 390
  training 380
  on trees 133
  ways of using 132
cloches, winter protection 372
club-rush 354
clustered bellflower 206
coastal gardens 371
Cobaea 140

scandens 140
cobweb houseleek 325
Colchicum 164, 215
   'Autumn Queen' *215*
   autumnale 'Album' 215
   byzantinum 215
   'The Giant' *215*
   kesselringii 215
   speciosum 'Album' 215
   'Waterlily' 215
cold frames, hardening off plants 392
colour
   annuals and biennials *162*
   planning gardens *159*, 370
columbine 164, 185
   alpine 185
column, fuchsia 60
columnar tree 13
Colutea 41
   arborescens 41, *401*, *404*
comfrey 328
compost 377, 378
composts, for containers 381
conditioning soil 377
coneflower 232–3, 317
Confederate jasmine 154
conifers
   hedges *384*
   pruning *382*
Consolida 216
   'Frosted Skies' 216
container-grown plants 374, 379
containers 369
   annuals and biennials 163
   bulbs 165, 369
   climbers *133*
   grasses in 343
   maples 18
   planting 381
   sowing seed in 391
   top-dressing 386
   trees and shrubs in 12
Convallaria 164
   majalis 216, *403*, *405*
Convolvulus 216–17
   sabatius 216, 217
   tricolor 'Royal Ensign' 216
Cootamundra wattle 17
copperleaf 17
coppicing
   dogwood 42
   eucalyptus 55
   willows 115
coral flower 259
coral plant 135
cord grass 354
   prairie *354*
Cordyline 41
   australis 'Torbay Red' 41, *402*
Coreopsis 217
   auriculata 'Schnittgold' 217, *401*
   'Sunray' 217, *401*

corkscrew hazel 44
corms 164
   buying 375
   division 395
   planting 380
corn cockle 172
corn marigold 212
cornflower 209
   supporting 209
Cornus 42–3, *401*, *404*
   coppicing 42
   staggered pruning 42
   alba 42, *405*
      'Elegantissima' 42
      'Kesselringii' 42
      'Sibirica' 42
      'Spaethii' 42
   alternifolia 42
      'Argentea' 42
   canadensis 42, *405*
   capitata 42
   controversa 'Variegata' 42
      'Eddie's White Wonder' 42
   florida 42
      'Cherokee Chief' 42
      'Spring Song' 43
      'Welchii' 43
   kousa 42
      'China Girl' 43
      var. *chinensis* 43
      'Satomi' 43
   macrophylla 43
   mas 43
      'Norman Hadden' 43
   nuttallii 42, 43
      'Colrigo Giant' 43
      'Porlock' 43
   sanguinea 42
      'Winter Beauty' 43
   sericea 42
      'Flaviramea' 43
      'Kelseyi' 43
Corsican hellebore 257
Corsican sandwort 187
Cortaderia 343, 346, *403*
   cutting down 346
   selloana 346
      'Pumila' 346
      'Sunningdale Silver' 346
Corydalis 217
   flexuosa 217
   lutea 217
   ochroleuca 217
   solida 'George Baker' 217
Corylopsis 44
   glabrescens 44, *404*, *405*
Corylus 44
   avellana 44
      'Contorta' 44, *401*, *404*, *405*
   maxima 44
cosmos, chocolate 218
Cosmos 218
   atrosanguineus 218, *405*

bipinnatus 'Sea Shells' 218
Cotinus 44
   coggygria 'Royal Purple' 44
      'Grace' 44, *404*
Cotoneaster 45, *402*, *403*, *404*
   atropurpureus 'Variegatus' 45
   divaricatus 45
   horizontalis 45, *401*, *405*
   × *watereri* 'John Waterer' 45
cottage-style planting 161, 369
cotton lavender 116
   pruning 116
cottonwood 98
couch grass 389
cow parsley 183
cowslip, American 231
crab apple 88
Crambe 218
   emerging shoots 218
   cordifolia 218, *402*
cranesbill 250–1, *390*
Crataegus 46, *402*, *403*, *404*
   laevigata 46
      'Paul's Scarlet' 46, *401*
   monogyna 46
creeping Jenny 283
creeping thistle 214
Crinum 218
   division 218
   × *powellii* 'Album' 218
Crocosmia 159, 164, 219, *402*, *404*
   division 219, *395*
   × *crocosmiiflora*
      'Gerbe d'Or' 219
      'Star of the East' 219
   'Lucifer' 219
   masoniorum 219
crocus, autumn 215
Crocus 165, 220, *380*
   division *395*
   chrysanthus
      'Gipsy Girl' 220
      'Snow Bunting' 220
   sieberi
      'Albus' 220
      'Hubert Edelsten' 220
   speciosus 220
crowfoot 315
crown imperial 246
Cryptogramma 359
   crispa 362, *404*
Cryptomeria japonica 46
   'Elegans Compacta' 46, *401*, *404*
cuckoo spit 398
cup and saucer vine 140
cupidone, blue 208
Cupid's dart 208
× *Cupressocyparis leylandii* 46, *401*, *402*
Cupressus 13, 47
   arizonica var. *glabra* 47
   macrocarpa 47, *402*
      'Goldcrest' 13, 47, *401*

sempervirens 47
currant, flowering 109
cut flowers 163
cuttings 394
Cyclamen 164, 221
   planting 221
   cilicium 221
   coum 221
   hederifolium 221, *373*
Cynara 221
   cardunculus 221, *402*
   scolymus 221
cypress 47
   false 39
   Italian 13, 47
   Leyland 46
   Monterey 13, *47*
   smooth 47
Cyrtomium falcatum 359
Cystopteris 362
   fragilis 362
Cytisus 47, *402*, *404*
   battandieri 47, *405*
   × *praecox* 'Warminster' 47
   scoparius 47

d

Daboecia cantabrica 48
   'William Buchanan' 48
daffodils 164, 165, 288–9, *380*
Dahlia 222–3, *402*
   storage 222
   'Bishop of Llandaff' 222
   'Candy Cane' 222
   'Clair de Lune' 222
   'Conway' 222
   'Corton Olympic' 222
   'Davenport Sunlight' 222
   'David Howard' 222
   'Fascination' 222
   'Hamari Accord' 223
   'Hamari Gold' 223
   'Hillcrest Royal' 223
   'Nina Chester' 223
   'Noreen' 223
   'Pontiac' 223
   'Preston Park' 223
   'Rhonda' 223
   'Rokesly Mini' 223
   'Small World' 223
   'So Dainty' 223
   'White Alva's' 223
   'Wootton Cupid' 223
   'Wootton Impact' 223
   'Zorro' 223
daisy
   African 186
   blue 244
   double 197
   New Zealand 209

ox-eye *271*
shasta 271
Swan River 200
daisy bush 91
dame's violet 259
damp shade, plants for *403*
damping off, seedlings 392
dandelion 389
Daphne 48–9, *403*, *404*, *405*
   bholua 'Jacqueline Postill' 48
   cneorum 48, *405*
      subsp. *philippi* 49
   mezereum 49, *405*
      'Bowles' Variety' 48
dark mullein 336
Darmera peltata 224, *403*, *404*, *405*
Davidia involucrata 49
dawn redwood 89
daylily 161, 258
dead nettle 269
deadheading 390
   allium 174
   lavender 80
   viola 338
deficiency diseases 396, 397, 399
Delphinium 224–5, *390*
   supports 225
   Blue Fountains Group 225, 370
   'Blue Nile' 225
   'Bruce' 224
   'Emily Hawkins' 225
   'Fanfare' 224
   'Mighty Atom' 225
   nudicaule 225
   'Sungleam' 224
Deschampsia 347
   cespitosa 347
      'Goldtau' 347
   flexuosa 347
desert candle 236
designing a planting scheme *159*
Deutzia 49, *401*
   gracilis 49
   × *hybrida* 'Mont Rose' 49
   ningpoensis 49
   scabra 49
devil-in-a-bush 291
Devil's fig 187
Dianthus 160, 226–7, *402*, *405*
   layering border carnations 226
   taking pipings of pinks 226
   alpinus
      'Becky Robinson' 226
      'Bovey Belle' 226
      'Brympton Red' 226
      'Christine Hough' 226
      'Dad's Favourite' 226
      'Dainty Dame' 226
      'Joan's Blood' 226
   barbatus 226
   deltoides 'Leuchtfunk' 227
   'Doris' 227

'Forest Treasure' 227
'Golden Cross' 227
'Gran's Favourite' 227
'Haytor White' 227
'Houndspool Ruby' 227
'La Bourboule' 227
'Little Jock' *226*, 227
'London Brocade' 227
'Mrs Sinkins' 227
'Musgrave's Pink' 227
PIERROT ('Kobusa') 227
'Valda Wyatt' 227
'Warden Hybrid' 227
Diascia 163, 228, *402*
   barberae
      'Blackthorn Apricot' 228
      'Fisher's Flora' 228
   fetcaniensis 228
   rigescens 228
Dicentra 140, 228–9, *403*, *404*
   cucullaria 228
   formosa 228, *403*
   macrocapnos 140
   scandens 140
   spectabilis 228
      'Alba' 229
Dicksonia 362
   antarctica 362, *404*
Dictamnus albus 229, *402*
dieback 398
Dierama 229
   pulcherrimum 229, *402*
Digitalis 162, 230, *403*, *404*
   self-sown seedlings 230
   davisiana 230
   grandiflora 230
   × *mertonensis* 230
   purpurea Excelsior Group 230
dill 181
Dipelta 50
   floribunda 50
Disanthus cercidifolius 50
diseases 396
dittany 229
division 395
   agapanthus 170
   crinum 218
   crocosmia 219
   erythronium 240
   heuchera 259
   irises 264
   miscanthus 350
   sedum 324
   snowdrops 247
   water lilies 292
Dodecatheon 231
   dentatum 231
   pulchellum 'Red Wings' 231
dog's-tooth violet 240
   European 240
dogwood 42–3
Doronicum 231
   'Miss Mason' 231

Smith/DK (bl, bcl); **307**: Roger Smith/DK (bl); **309**: C. Andrew Henley (br), Roger Smith/DK (ɔc); **310**: John Fielding (tr), Roger Smith/DK (bl); **311**: Roger Smith/DK (ɪr); **312**: Country Park Nurseries, Hornchurch (crb); Eric Crichton (cbɪ), Juliette Wade (bcr), Roger Smith/DK (tcr); **313**: Barnsley House, Nr Cirencester (clb), Juliette Wade (bcl), Roger Smith/DK (cal, tcr); **314**: Roger Smith/DK (cra, br); **315**: Roger Smith/DK (bc, br); **316**: Roger Smith/DK (bl, br); **317**: Roger Smith/DK (tr, bl, bc, br ; **318**: Roger Smith/DK (tr); **319**: Roger Smith/DK (tl, bl); **320**: Roger Smith/DK (tr, br, cbr, tcr); **321**: John Fielding (tcr), Roger Smith/DK (clb, bcr, cbr); **322**: C. Andrew Henley (bl), Garden World Images (br); **323**: Garden World Images (bcr), Roger Smith/DK (bc); **324**: Roger Smith/DK (tr, br); **325**: Roger Smith/DK (bl); **327**: Roger Smith/DK (br, bcl); **328**: Photos Horticultural (br), Roger Smith/DK (tc); **329**: Mr Fothergill's Seeds (bc), Roger Smith/DK

(crb, br); **330**: John Fielding (tc), Roger Smith/DK (bc); **331**: Photos Horticultural (bcr), Roger Smith/DK (bl); **332**: Juliette Wade (tc), Roger Smith/DK (tr, bc); **333**: Roger Smith/DK (br, l); **334**: Roger Smith/DK (car, cbr); **335**: Photos Horticultural (car), Roger Smith/DK (tl, tr, cla, cal, tcl); **336**: Roger Smith/DK (br); **337**: Juliette Wade (br), Roger Smith/DK (bcr); **338**: Roger Smith/DK (tr, bc); **339**: Roger Smith/DK (r); **341**: Roger Smith/DK (tr, br); **343**: Roger Smith/DK (cr); **344**: John Fielding (c), Roger Smith/DK (bl); **345**: Roger Smith/DK (bc); **346**: Roger Smith/DK (tr, bl, bc, br); **347**: Roger Smith/DK (bc); **349**: Roger Smith/DK (c); **350**: Roger Smith/DK (tr, bl, bc, br); **351**: Roger Smith/DK (c); **352**: Roger Smith/DK (bl, bc, bcr, r); **353**: Roger Smith/DK (r); **354**: Roger Smith/DK (bc, br); **356-357**: Roger Smith/DK; **358**: Clive Nichols/Preen Manor, Shropshire (c); **359**: Christine M. Douglas (cl, c), Roger Smith/DK (cr, b);

360: Roger Smith/DK (tr); **361**: Peter Anderson (tr); John Fielding (br); **363**: Roger Smith/DK (bl, bc, br); **364**: Christine M. Douglas (r), Roger Smith/DK (c, bl); **365**: Christine M. Douglas (br), Roger Smith/DK (bl); **368**: Steve Wooster (br); **369**: Trish Gant (cl), Roger Smith/DK (bc); **370**: Roger Smith/DK (tc, tr, bl, bc, bc, br, bfr); **376**: Roger Smith/DK (cl); **377**: Gary Ombler (cr); **385**: Trish Gant; **398**: Peter Anderson (tc); **400**: Photographer: Steven Wooster; "Flow Glow" garden for Chelsea Flower Show 2002 by Rebecca Phillips, Maria Ornberg and Rebecca Heard; **Endpapers**: Roger Smith/DK.

All other images © Dorling Kindersley.
For further information, see: www.dkimages.com

PACIFIC OCEAN

U.S.A. (ALASKA)

YUKON

Whitehorse

NORTHWEST TERRITORIES

Great Bear Lake

Coppermine

Yellowknife

Great Slave Lake

0a

NUNAVUT

Foxe Basin

BRITISH COLUMBIA

Williston Lake

Liard

Slave

Mackenzie

Dubawnt

Kazan

Nueltin Lake

Hudson Bay

C

Fort St.John

Dawson Creek

Peace

Lake Athabasca

0b

Wollaston Lake

A

Prince Rupert

Terrace
Kitimat

Grande Prairie

Prince George

A

ALBERTA

Fort McMurray

N

Reindeer Lake

Churchill

Nelson

0a

A

D

7a
6b
6a
Campbell River
Courtenay
Powell River
Port Alberni
7a 6b
Nanaimo
Richmond
Esquimalt
8a

Williams Lake

Athabasca

Fraser

St.Albert
Leduc
Wetaskiwin
Camrose
Red Deer

Fort Saskatchewan
Edmonton

1a

1b

SASKATCHEWAN

Saskatchewan

Thompson

MANITOBA 0b

Cedar Lake

1a

Severn

James Bay

Kamloops
Squamish
Vernon
Vancouver
Kelowna
Chilliwack
Penticton

7b

Airdrie

Calgary

2a

2b

North Battleford

Prince Albert

Saskatoon

Lake Winnipegosis

Lake Manitoba

Lake Winnipeg

1b

ONTARIO

Victoria

5a/5b

Cranbrook

3a

3b

Lethbridge

Medicine Hat

4a

Swift Current

Moose Jaw

Yorkton

Regina

Albany

2a

2b

Weyburn

Estevan

Brandon

Portage la Prairie

Selkirk

Winnipeg

Lake Nipigon

3a

Thunder Bay

UNITED STATES OF AMERICA

Lake Superior

Sault Ste Marie

Lake Michigan

Windsor

6

Based on the Plant Hardiness Zones of Canada 2000 map developed by Natural Resources Canada and Agriculture and Agri-Food Canada, this map indicates the different zones in Canada where various types of trees, shrubs, and flowers will most likely survive. Ranging from 0 (the harshest) to 8 (the mildest), there are 9 major zones split into 17 subzones.